With Good Intentions

*Edited by Celia Haig-Brown
and David A. Nock*

With Good Intentions:
Euro-Canadian and Aboriginal
Relations in Colonial Canada

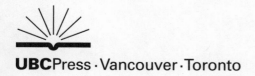
UBCPress · Vancouver · Toronto

15 14 13 12 11 10 09 08 07 06   5 4 3 2 1

Printed in Canada on ancient-forest-free paper (100% post-consumer recycled) that is processed chlorine- and acid-free, with vegetable-based inks.

Library and Archives Canada Cataloguing in Publication

With good intentions: Euro-Canadian and aboriginal relations in colonial Canada / edited by Celia Haig-Brown and David A. Nock.

Includes bibliographical references and index.
ISBN-13: 978-0-7748-1137-8 (bound); 978-0-7748-1138-5 (pbk.)
ISBN-10: 0-7748-1137-4 (bound); 0-7748-1138-2 (pbk.)

1. Native peoples – Cultural assimilation – Canada – History. 2. Canada – Race relations – History. 3. Whites – Canada – Relations with Indians – History. 4. Native peoples – Canada – Government relations. 5. Colonization – History. 6. Racism – Canada – History. 7. Europeans – Canada – History. I. Haig-Brown, Celia, 1947- II. Nock, David, 1949-

E78.C2W583 2005   305.897'071   C2005-905936-2

Canada

UBC Press gratefully acknowledges the financial support for our publishing program of the Government of Canada through the Book Publishing Industry Development Program (BPIDP), and of the Canada Council for the Arts, and the British Columbia Arts Council.

This book has been published with the help of the K.D. Srivastava Fund. UBC Press also acknowledges the support of the Office of the Vice-President, Research, York University, Toronto, Ontario, in the publication of this book.

Printed and bound in Canada by Friesens
Set in Stone by Last Impression Publishing Service
Copy editor: Robert Lewis
Proofreader: Jillian Shoichet

UBC Press
The University of British Columbia
2029 West Mall
Vancouver, BC V6T 1Z2
604-822-5959 / Fax: 604-822-6083
www.ubcpress.ca

Contents

Illustrations

This book is dedicated to my children, Sophie Ruth, Josie Valerie, and Roderick Edwin Vayro, and to my partner, Didi Khayatt.
– Celia Haig-Brown

I dedicate this volume to the memory of Horatio Hale, whose important contribution in portraying Aboriginal giftedness had largely been forgotten in the twentieth century.
– David Nock

Acknowledgments

I want to begin by thanking my parents for giving me the desire to see beyond the master narratives. I want also to thank all those First Nations teachers, students, and friends who have continued the education that my parents and siblings began and for bringing me back to history. And I want to thank David Nock for inspiring this work in the first place and then for working in strength and patience with me as we negotiated the treacherous path of writing, collecting, and publishing. Throughout the process, many have contributed to the work of making a book: each of the authors had faith enough to contribute, respond, and then wait; Lisa D'Aiuto of York University typed, re-typed, and prepared a first draft; Angela Durante of York University and my daughter Sophie Vayro, in turn, put the next sets of pieces together; Jean Wilson of UBC Press guided us along, singing hallelujah choruses when merited; Stan Shapson, Vice-President Research, York University, provided a much-needed small grant to assist with publishing; Jan Hare and Jean Barman worried with us about the title; Matt Haytor and Naomi Nichols worked on the index; Ann Macklem, Robert Lewis, and others focused on final edits; and Didi Khayatt listened to my woes. Finally, two anonymous readers for UBC Press strengthened the manuscript with their critique, supportive comments, and useful suggestions. To all of you, this book stands as a tribute to collegial and collaborative work.

Celia Haig-Brown

I want to acknowledge Celia Haig-Brown for reading segments of my work and for inviting me into this project in the first place; J. Donald Wilson and Michael C. Coleman for also reading my chapters on Hale and Wilson in addition to my part of the Introduction; Mary Nock for technical computing assistance; and the Ven. Harry Huskins of the Diocese of Algoma for help with sources. I expended considerable labour on this project during my sabbatical of 2002-3. I am grateful to Lakehead University for granting me that sabbatical year.

David Nock

Introduction

David A. Nock and Celia Haig-Brown

> Next I observed all the oppression and sadness throughout the
> earth – the tears of the oppressed, and no one helping them,
> while on the side of their oppressors were powerful allies.
>> – Attributed to the Preacher, Ecclesiastes 4:1

> I hate your show and pretence – your hypocrisy of "honouring"
> me with your religious feasts and solemn assemblies ... I want to
> see [instead] a mighty flood of justice [on behalf of the poor and
> oppressed] – a torrent of doing good.
>> – Attributed to God by the prophet Amos, 5:21, 24,
>>> *The Living Bible*

> The "complicity" of individuals with ideological and social
> systems is not entirely a matter of their intentions.
>> – Ania Loomba, *Colonialism/Postcolonialism*

> The road to hell is paved with good intentions.
>> – Traditional

> "I am almost one hundred years old, and I have seen everything
> change, even the position of the stars in the universe, but I have
> not seen anything change yet in this country," he would say.
> "Here they make new constitutions, new laws ... but we are still
> in colonial times."
>> – Gabriel Garcia Márquez, *Love in the Time of Cholera*

Complicating Colonization

Let us begin by saying what this book is not. It is not an apologist text. It is not primarily an effort to argue that some colonizers of the nation that we now call Canada were really "good-hearted" people, although most of the people represented here were that. It is not an effort to vindicate wrongs done to First Nations people and cultures as colonization proceeded.[1] And it is not a book that allows "the voices of once colonized peoples and their descendants to be heard,"[2] although the strength of their actions resonates throughout the chapters. In its focus on some people of Euro-Canadian ancestry who worked to temper the impact of their more corrupt siblings on the peoples and lands of Canada, it might be said to be a book on white studies rather than Native studies. It tries never to lose sight of the fact that those acknowledged herein are fully implicated in the process of colonization despite their sensitivities. While the book concentrates on non-Aboriginal people working with First Nations peoples of this land, often in their resistance to injustices, it also gestures to our current situation of continued participation in a vast web of colonial relations. In the text, then as now, Aboriginal people are active agents negotiating complex sets of relations with the Euro-Canadians engaged in many layers of colonization and its accompanying reciprocal cultural change. From one perspective, we claim that the book is "a repository of bad memories and good intentions, of unworkable ideas and uncomfortable truths."[3] Ultimately, our hope is that this book might contribute to the project that J. Edward Chamberlin calls for in his recent book, *If This Is Your Land, Where Are Your Stories: Finding Common Ground* – it is time to reimagine "them" and "us."[4]

From a range of perspectives, then, this edited collection examines aspects of the lives of individuals of European ancestry and organizations working with Aboriginal people against injustice in colonial Canada.[5] Between the mid-nineteenth century and the first two decades of the twentieth, across the developing provinces of Canada and the Dominion of Canada, colonization of Aboriginal lands proceeded apace. The people in these chapters recognized injustices in this relentless movement, allied themselves with Aboriginal people who also saw the injustices and were actively resisting them, and worked in a variety of ways to address them.

Ultimately, all this book can do is add fragments to our ever-shifting understandings of the history of the relations between immigrants, settlers, and indigenous peoples during the times of overt colonization.[6] Drawing on existing documents, it lays out the views of individuals within each group that, at the time, ran counter to prevailing "wisdom" about appropriate ways and means of colonizing a land. The non-Aboriginal views, furthermore, ran counter to an increasing commitment to biological racism and what came to be called social Darwinism on the part of many people of European ancestry. Sometimes, despite initial expectations about "the Indians," based on beliefs of cultural hierarchy and stereotypes acquired in formal European and Euro-Canadian schooling, the people in the chapters that follow took the time to listen to, observe, and learn from First Nations and Aboriginal peoples. Assumptions interrupted, they saw Aboriginal cultures, languages, and ways of life as deserving of respect. Most came to know First Nations peoples more intimately as time went on. Because Native people worked closely and respectfully with them, people of European ancestry developed an appreciation for the intricacies of their languages and their superior knowledge of the land, a knowledge inextricably linked to intimacy with and long traditions of being in good relation to it.[7] Most also came to a deeper understanding of the concomitant complexities of First Nations cultures. Some brought a sense of justice based on English law and Judeo-Christian precepts that allowed them to see and name injustice. In particular, they often exemplified the religiously based concern for social justice and righteousness toward the oppressed voiced by the prophets of the Hebrew Bible.[8] Many struggled with making sense of Christian morality in the face of opportunities for material gain for themselves or their countrymen and women.[9] They articulated their concerns in a range of fora. For the most part, they were ignored or dismissed by those who continued more aggressive agendas of land and resource appropriation and labour exploitation.[10] Their work is usually invisible in the mainstream presentation of Canadian history.[11]

At the same time, it is important to state that the people represented here rarely deviated from the overall goal of "Christianizing and civilizing" the people that they encountered as they lived and travelled in Canada. Too few vacillated from seeing European values and ways of being as the ultimate goal of interactions with First Nations people. In many cases, their developing respect for Aboriginal people was based on the latter's skill in taking up what they deemed to be appropriate and/or useful aspects of Christianity, European dress, and settlement into farming villages or business ventures.

An Idea in the Making

The idea for this collection began some years ago when Celia Haig-Brown was a doctoral student at the University of British Columbia. Asked to write a review of Professor David Nock's 1988 work, *A Victorian Missionary and Canadian Indian Policy,* she was taken with the sentiments expressed in a series of anonymous pieces included in the text called the "Fair Play Papers," appearing in this book as an appendix. These papers exemplify the thoughts of those well-intentioned and thoughtful people of European ancestry who were working with Aboriginal people during the time of active colonization of the nation now called Canada. They recognized the injustices being perpetrated and worked to temper the process of colonizing while never escaping being its agents. The focus of Nock's work is a compelling argument that the papers are the work of one E.F. Wilson, a missionary sent by the English Church Missionary Society (CMS) in 1868 to work with the Anishnaabek[12] of Ontario. Wilson left the CMS in 1873 and spent the next twenty years as principal of Shingwauk and Wawanosh Residential Schools. Increasingly disillusioned with the lack of success of the schools, he took steps to hand over day-to-day operation of the schools to a manager and travelled with his wife to the Cherokee Republic in Oklahoma and to a number of other "Indian" nations within the United States. He also read the works of Horatio Hale and Helen Hunt Jackson and found his views of Aboriginal people changing dramatically. (His work is discussed more fully in Chapter 7.) The "Fair Play Papers" were written after this trip. In his consideration of the papers, Nock acknowledges that they "retain the Victorian notions of civilization and progress ... But to the modern eye and no doubt to readers of the day, what is striking is the extent to which Fair Play [the pseudonymous author] takes exception with current Anglo-Canadian Indian policy."[13] It was this questioning of policy that captured Haig-Brown's attention. At about the same time as Nock's book, she had published a retrospective ethnography of the Kamloops Indian Residential School.[14] She had been hearing fairly strong criticism of her work, with some claiming that the views represented in the text were a perspective out of the present and that, *at the time,* the people who were involved believed that the schools were the best approach to civilizing the original people of Canada. Wilson, for one, came to appreciate the shortcomings of residential schools and as early as 1891, the year after the first Kamloops school was built, presented those views to the world in *The Canadian Indian,* a journal that would have been available to educators across the country. Nock's text was an indication that some of the concerns expressed implicitly and explicitly in Haig-Brown's book were not simply views from a distanced, contemporary standpoint.

This discovery planted the seed for the book now in your hands. If E.F. Wilson learned from his time and travels with First Nations people and from his reading of existing texts, what other people were working in Canada at the time who may have contributed a more critical view to the ways that so-called Christianizing and civilizing were serving colonization? As Loomba points out, "dominant ideologies are never total or monolithic, never totally successful in incorporating all individuals or subjects into their structures. So, to uncover the rootedness of 'modern' knowledge systems in colonial practices is to begin what Raymond Williams called the process of 'unlearning' whereby we begin to question received truths."[15]

If a number of such people could be identified, they would serve to contradict the presentist claim that, *at the time,* "we" Canadians thought that we were doing the right thing. Gathering historical pieces that documented their work could contribute to a fuller version of Canadian history, one that lays out challenges to the dominant ideology expressed *at the time* and that reveals concerns with the ways that colonization was proceeding.

A deeper historical question also guides this work. It is even more a question from a time beyond memory, what Euro-Canadians might call a question from pre- (written) history. This question has the potential to haunt us all in good ways if we, particularly non-Aboriginal people in this place, ever take the time to ask it: Whose traditional land are you on? And what does that question mean? If one recognizes oral tradition – and the Supreme Court of Canada has taken a step in that direction in its statement on the *Delgamuukw* case[16] – then every place that we set foot in Canada, every city, every farm, every metre of space (admittedly, a limited way to think of the spiritual entity that First Nations people consider land to be) is part of one or more First Nations' traditional territory. If we take this claim seriously – and only those in deep denial of British law and our own historical relation to it might argue otherwise – then the educated Canadian may begin to get a stronger sense of what it means to be Canadian. In a recent study, the Coalition for the Advancement of Aboriginal Studies demonstrated the high levels of dissatisfaction of first-year university students with their knowledge of Aboriginal history and current issues in Canada.[17] While the study did not ask questions about people like those represented in this text, one might find similar levels of concern with presentation in schools of a monolithic, mythic history that not only leaves out Aboriginal people, but also leaves out those of European ancestry who spoke out against the implementation of particular aspects of Indian policy in the process of colonization.

Perhaps we might start our understandings of what it means to be Canadian by acknowledging all our historical relations to the land and First Nations peoples. We might work to create a history with as much complexity as our imaginations can grasp. We might teach our children and ourselves, as lifelong learners, that facing even the partial truths that we are capable of constructing is one way to imagine a strong nation. It is also a way to move out of a state of national denial and studied amnesia that can only weaken us. If we still believe in the importance of becoming and being educated people, we might ask what role history plays in that construction. We might take seriously the place of historical fragments that we conjure up in relation to our country both autobiographically and in larger social and historical contexts. Then we may decide that all citizens should have such education and that it can begin with children in schools. The naive assumption about what children must *not* be taught in order to become good citizens might be overcome.[18] Rather than following in the footsteps of E.F. Wilson, who let acquiescence to received wisdom guide his life until serious travel and reading finally allowed him to make sense of what he had been seeing, hearing, and generally experiencing, we might make an effort to educate ourselves, our children, and new citizens about our history as early and in the most straightforward and honest way that we can. Does it weaken or strengthen citizens to learn that their country has been the site of mistakes and deliberate dishonesty even as it struggled/ struggles to be and become a decent and respectful democracy and to recognize human rights and common humanity of all its – even the reluctant[19] – citizens? Contradiction is a part of most human organizations: nations appear to be no exception. Should disillusion be the wages of maturation? Is there a magic time of life when it is okay to come to know of our folly as a developing country? Or might we see an examination of our scruples, by which we expose our weaknesses and make an effort to acknowledge them, as a move in the direction of strength or at least resiliency for citizens and the nation?

If Canada wants to justly claim to be a country committed to human rights, then perhaps the irony of acknowledging the shortcomings and calculated transgressions that have been made in our history related to land policies and legislation is the place to begin. From there the possibilities are endless. What if we became a country, like few others, that admitted its failures and frailties and built from there to address them? The continued dismissal of the violations of treaties with Aboriginal peoples and the outright land thefts are beginning to be addressed in the courts and in treaty negotiations and renegotiations across the land. Children in schools should come to know the names of people like those in this text, their work, and the injustice that prevailed as well as what is already taught. New citizens should know these names and the names of the peoples of the traditional lands that they are on as the starting place for their coming to know and love a country with a past as flawed and racist as most others. Teaching citizens this history could provide an opportunity for all of us to work seriously to create a country not afraid to see the past for what it has been in order to build a strong present and a stronger future based on respect for future generations, for the ancestors, and for all the human beings who now live together on this land.

A Decolonizing Project

One way to address disillusionment with the current situation and other forms of modern angst is to seek knowledge of the past. Certain aspects of this knowledge may challenge existing understandings of our colonial history as a nation. We want to think of this collection as serving not a postcolonial project but a decolonizing one. First of all, drawing on the work of Linda Tuhiwai Smith[20] and Ania Loomba,[21] we recognize colonialism as an ongoing process in these times in Canada and other "former" colonies across the globe. Even though the Statute of Westminster in 1931 granted the former colonies "full legal freedom except in those areas where they chose to remain subordinate" and, more significant, even though Canada "brought home" the Constitution in 1982 and finally ceased choosing to remain subordinate, the persistence of Euro-Canadian dominance in social structures and the exclusion of perspectives of the original peoples and immigrant groups other than the Europeans indicate that we are still in colonial mode. As Tuhiwai Smith says, "by the nineteenth century colonialism not only meant the imposition of Western authority over indigenous lands, indigenous modes of production and indigenous law and government, but the imposition of Western authority over all aspects of indigenous knowledges, languages and cultures."[22] Too little has changed for us to claim that Canada is now in postcolonial times. In keeping with Loomba's notion of the term postcolonial, we concur that "if the inequities of colonial rule have not been erased, it is perhaps premature to proclaim the demise of colonialism." She goes on to say that "we cannot dismiss the importance of formal decolonisation."[23]

Decolonizing is a process with relevance to those nations formed out of lands traditionally and from time immemorial occupied by indigenous peoples who felt the full impact of being colonized at the time of rapid capitalist development in Europe. According to the *Oxford English Dictionary*, the origin of the word "colonialism comes from the Roman 'colonia' and referred to Romans who settled lands but still retained their citizenship."[24] A colony is: "4. a settlement in a new country; a body of people who settle in a new locality, forming a community subject to or connected with their parent state; the community so formed, consisting of the original settlers and their descendants, as long as the connexion with the parent state is kept up."[25] Citing this definition, Loomba points out that it "quite remarkably avoids any reference to people other than the colonisers."[26] *Terra nullis* (unoccupied land) was one of the drawing cards used to encourage immigration for people hungry to be landowners. The subsequent invasion of the lands of the existing occupants and the ensuing exploitation of the resources and their labour served the project of developing industrialism and the capitalist project of many European countries. England and France, of course, took the lead role in this regard in what we now call Canada. While colonization on the part of other countries may now be less direct and overt, the descendants of the original colonizers and more recent immigrants still live inseparable from this history with past and current indigenous peoples and communities.

While this collection cannot claim postcolonialism as its project – that is, to take Canada or First Nations to a place beyond colonization – it is an effort to acknowledge additional complexities of colonization and, in that work, to serve a decolonizing project. It is an effort to interrupt less complex narratives concerning the ways that colonization in Canada proceeded. Decolonization is a term with increasing usefulness as indigenous peoples around the globe insist on history taking seriously their claims to inherent rights based on their relationship with the land from a time before memory. Nonindigenous allies, following in the footsteps of some of those represented in this collection, hope to contribute to this work, often drawing on principles of social justice that echo the sentiments expressed by these Euro-Canadians. Perhaps ultimately, this book is self-serving. Loomba claims that colonialism degrades the colonizers themselves.[27] Only through the work of decolonizing can this degradation be addressed.

Forms of Racism and Racialism in the Premodern Era

One way to approach our efforts to create deeper understanding of aspects of the complexity of colonization is to place it within a context of a history of related ideas. Racism and racialism have a significant history in this regard. Today "everyone knows" that Aboriginal peoples of what we now call Canada were badly treated by the government and church, as in the notorious case of residential schools. Some things have changed: in 2003 Aboriginal students are more common in universities; many First Nations organizations have become powerful and effective in the last several decades; the churches that operated residential schools are only a shadow of their former strength. In selected spaces, a kind of Canadian political correctness has taken over and is meant to replace once negative stereotypes with new positive stereotypes about Aboriginal people as imbued with extraordinary spirituality, ecological knowledge, and philosophical insight. As remarkable as the content of this change has been its rapidity.[28] This abrupt change in outlook tends to underscore the analyses of regimes of knowledge by scholars such as Thomas Kuhn and Michel Foucault, who point out that what is accepted as solid knowledge can change quite quickly in a generation or less when what Kuhn refers to as normal science is overturned by periods of revolutionary science and when older paradigms are toppled quickly by newer ones. Foucault added to these insights by pointing out the special precariousness and openness to revision of the human and social sciences.[29]

What all this means is that modern readers of *With Good Intentions* may have little background to comprehend attitudes that predate the current regime of knowledge now predominant in Canada and elsewhere. For example, university students will argue with great vigour about the evil of the residential schools and even of its teachers and missionaries without knowing that many in that day and age wished to deny education to Aboriginal people altogether because they believed it was self-evident that First Nations people were too low on the evolutionary ladder to "benefit" from Western-style education. So, although the biological racists and extreme social-Darwinist supporters of previous generations are "innocent," in historical retrospect, of imposing residential schools, one would not expect that they should be given credit vis-à-vis missionary teachers for their biologically rooted racism. Missionary teachers, now often reviled, generally held that Aboriginal cultures were less advanced than those of the white settlers (as did the biological racists mentioned above) but stressed the capacity of Aboriginal students (as the biological racists did not) to ascend the ladder of civilization and held out the prospect of equality of the races. This ascension usually involved the Aboriginal peoples abandoning their traditional ways of life and adopting the cultures and industrial work-world of the whites. There are some individuals who differed yet again in going beyond the attitudes of the day. The individuals discussed in this book all rejected biological racism; many of them also came to reject assumptions of cultural rankings of their day. One of the clearest examples here is Horatio Hale, the subject of Chapter 1. Hale is particularly important because he felt that Aboriginal peoples and cultures were at least equal to, and in many cases superior to, the European-derived white civilization of North America (what he referred to in customary usage of the day, before Hitler and the Nazis hijacked the term, as the Aryan peoples, meaning essentially those Indo-European peoples who are ancestors of most Europeans and many South Asians). All of the people discussed in this book challenged prevailing attitudes and practices visited upon Aboriginal peoples. In some cases, their challenge depended on a theoretical regime of knowledge at odds with the prevailing one, as witnessed in the work of Horatio Hale. In other cases, it had something to do with prophetic notions of justice and equity that may have been connected to Judeo-Christian roots. For example, one should not forget that the campaign to end the slave trade and then slavery in the British Empire was led by religiously motivated Evangelicals such as William Wilberforce and Thomas Fowell Buxton.

Roots of Biological Racism

Modern readers may need grounding in the extent of biological racism in eighteenth- and nineteenth-century attitudes. It was hegemonic, as Gramsci would say, until sometime around the Second World War. It is really only the fairly slow retreat of biological racism after 1945 and its more rapid retreat after the Canadian government's declaration of multiculturalism in 1971 that has made biological racism seem so remote and politically incorrect to modern-day, educated Canadians. However, "scratch one of our ancestors" and we are apt to find a biological racist. Luckily for us, most of these ancestors did not leave written records on the subject. For those who did, however, latter-day reputations have been shattered. Biological racism only retreated with the defeat of Hitler's Nazi regime with its glorification of the "Aryan" redefined as those solely of German (Nordic) blood and with the withdrawal of overtly colonizing nations from Africa, Asia, and elsewhere in the postwar period. In Canada the adoption of multiculturalism in 1971 as government policy, with its legislated rejection of a Nordic identity based on white supremacy, Anglo conformity, and race-based exclusionary migration policies, serves as another marker of the unacceptability of biological racism.

Concerning racial attitudes in the United States with relevance to Canada, noted scientist Stephen Jay Gould provides useful background. He points out that the 1700s and 1800s provided "the cultural milieu of a society whose leaders and intellectuals did not doubt the propriety of racial ranking – with Indians below whites, and blacks below everybody else."[30]

Although he may have overlooked Horatio Hale, he points out how foreign the modern attitude that all cultures are to be equally valued would have been to that era: "I cannot identify any popular position remotely like the 'cultural relativism' that prevails (at least by lip service) in liberal circles today."[31] Gould notes that the nearest approach to such cultural relativism (and by our modern standards it seems quite deficient) was the argument that such "inferiority is purely cultural and that it can be completely eradicated by education to a Caucasian standard."[32]

Gould then goes on to quote racist statements made by eminent scientists and presidents such as Benjamin Franklin, Thomas Jefferson, and Abraham Lincoln that would make most educated moderns blush or fume with anger. Gould explains, "I do not cite these statements in order to release skeletons from ancient closets. Rather I quote the men who have justly earned our highest respect in order to show that white leaders of Western nations did not question the propriety of racial ranking during the eighteenth and nineteenth centuries."[33] Lest Canadians feel smug, we may be reassured that many such statements are available from our early prime ministers, such as Sir John A. Macdonald and William Lyon Mackenzie King. Racially based exclusionary statements continued to be made as late as the 1950s by Liberal Minister of Citizenship and Immigration Walter Harris during the debate about revisions to the Immigration Act in 1952.[34]

A disturbing example of the biologically rooted racism of the day is provided by the endeavours of the Philadelphia physician and university teacher Samuel George Morton and his extensive collection of skulls from peoples around the world (1,000 of them by his death in 1851). Essentially, he measured brain or skull size and estimated that intelligence followed from the size of measurement. His conclusion, as discussed in Gould's *The Mismeasure of Man,* was that Caucasians had the largest cranial capacity, followed by Asians (Mongolians and Malays), then by North American Aboriginal people, then by "Ethiopians" (i.e., blacks).

Morton was not shy about drawing conclusions from his studies, which at the time were considered to be the epitome of empirical research. Morton noted a "deficiency of 'higher' mental powers among Indians."[35] He pointed out that "the benevolent mind may regret the inaptitude of the Indian race for civilization but sentimentality must yield to fact. The structure of his mind appears to be different from that of the white man, nor can the two harmonize in the social relations except on the most limited scale. Indians are not only averse to the restraints of education, but for the most part are incapable of a continued process of reasoning on abstract subjects."[36] This particularly interesting passage shows how biological racists were likely to resist trying to extend the "benefits" of Westernizing educational systems to Aboriginal people on the basis of their inability to benefit therefrom. In a public lecture at Boston entirely devoted to Aboriginal peoples of America, Morton told his audience that the "intellectual faculties" of the Indians were not high and that "as a race they are decidedly inferior to the Mongolian stock." He deplored as a "'cheerless picture' the possibility of Indian intellectual progress."[37] Opposed to this attitude were the so-called humanitarians with benevolent minds who felt that the effort should be made on the basis that while Aboriginals' cultures were inferior, their potential as individuals was not. As we have suggested earlier, the humanitarians of benevolent mind tend to get castigated today for supporting residential schools, while biological racists and social Darwinists tend to be forgotten since they tended to stand aloof from such philanthropic endeavours as being entirely wasted on their subjects. In fact, some biological racists advocated policies that superficially seemed to promise some form of cultural continuity. Thus Francis Bond Head, lieutenant governor of Upper Canada in the mid-1830s, was eager to move all of the province's Aboriginal peoples onto Manitoulin Island, where as far as he was concerned they could continue a traditional lifestyle. In his mind, trying to introduce them to Western civilization and industrial pursuits was a waste of time and money due to their incapacity.[38]

Morton, it may be said, was no fringe or marginal scholar, as he might be today (one thinks of J. Philippe Rushton, a Canadian university professor still employed and still upholding the correlation of biological roots of race with intelligence quotients, who has faced a barrage of criticism and repeated calls for his dismissal).[39] In contrast to this, Gould points out that when Morton died in 1851, he was described as having probably the highest reputation among American scientists in the rest of the scholarly world.[40] The great Harvard scientist Louis Agassiz also shared Morton's paradigmatic idea of "polygeny" and its notion that the races were not linked from one common source (monogenism) but developed separately. Polygeny was especially conducive to a doctrine that the races were inherently unequal in capacity and should therefore be kept separate. Stephen Jay Gould has pointed out the conjuncture between polygenesis and American social structure: "It is obviously not accidental that a nation still practicing slavery and expelling its Aboriginal inhabitants from their homelands should have provided a base for theories that blacks and Indians are separate species, inferior to whites."[41]

Monogenism was not rooted in biological racism to the same degree as polygenesis since it often "upheld the scriptural unity of all peoples in the single creation of Adam and Eve."[42] Many missionaries came to adopt the idea that North American Aboriginal people were related to the ten lost tribes of Israel. (Certainly E.F. Wilson did so in his *Manual of the Ojebway Language*.)[43] To the extent that monogenism was accepted as true, it provided a rationale for the habitual optimism that missionaries felt about the suitability and capability of Aboriginal people for policies of "amalgamation" and "civilization" (or assimilation, cultural replacement, or cultural genocide to use current terminology). However, most monogenists did not uphold ideas about any equality in actual achievement among the races, nor did they entertain the cultural relativist's idea that the practices of any existing society were equally valid. Such ideas were too foreign for the era. Many explained the apparently unequal differences as processes of degeneration that had occurred because of the negative effects of tropical climates on persons of colour. (Such tropical climates were still being cited by Walter Harris in 1952 as a reason for the unsuitability of persons of colour for immigration to Canada.)[44] Monogenists differed among themselves about whether or how quickly racial differences and inequalities initially caused by climate could be reversed. Samuel Stanhope Smith in the colonial period, president of what later became Princeton University, "hoped that American blacks, in a climate more suited to Caucasian temperaments, would soon turn white"![45]

Enter Social Darwinism

These two theories of monogenism and polygenism had both revolved around notions of divine creationism. Darwin's evolutionary theory "swept away the creationist rug that had supported the intense debate between monogenists and polygenists" and resolved the debate by supporting monogenism. At the same time, says Gould, evolutionary theory, especially in its social-Darwinist guise, "present[ed] an even better rationale for their shared racism."[46] Social Darwinism took from Darwin's theory of evolution the grim story of unending competition, with the disappearance of species as the penalty for lack of adaptation and the flourishing of species in number and range of habitat as the reward, characterized as "the survival of the fittest." Social Darwinism took intelligence and signs of cultural advancement as widely differing among the races, and its normal conclusion did not differ from the earlier discussions of racial inequality within monogenism and polygenism. The ability of the Caucasians to spread into Europe and India from their original habitat in Asia and then into the Americas, Australasia, Africa, and elsewhere was seen as evidence of their intelligence, superior culture, and adaptability – in short, the survival and proliferation of the fittest.

One example of this new, social-Darwinist racism is presented by Franklin H. Giddings, professor and head of sociology at Columbia University from 1893 to 1928. Alongside the University of Chicago, Columbia quickly became home to one of the two most important departments of sociology. Giddings was responsible for training an importantly large number of doctoral candidates who later attained distinction in the discipline, among them six future presidents of the American Sociological Society. He is best remembered for his efforts to quantify sociology. Although no great statistician himself, he preached the virtues of such an approach to others.[47] There is no complete biography of Giddings, although Bannister does provide two provocative chapters.[48]

Giddings addressed some concerns related to race in *The Principles of Sociology,* originally published in 1896, the year of Horatio Hale's death. In it, he makes the then customary designation of higher and lower races. After a comment about the extinct Tasmanian people showing little ability, resistance, or adaptability, Giddings commented, "Another race with little capacity for improvement is the surviving North American Indian. Though intellectually superior to the negro, the Indian has shown less ability than the negro to adapt himself to new conditions."[49] Giddings further affirmed his belief in the evolutionary basis of racial inequality in his statement, "It is sometimes said that we ought not to assert that the lower races have not the capacity for social evolution, because we do not know what they could do if they had opportunity. They have been in existence, however, much longer than the European races, and have accomplished immeasurably less. We are, therefore, warranted in saying that they have not the same inherent abilities."[50]

It is not without significance that Giddings was at Columbia, where one of his colleagues was Franz Boas, the German-Jewish founder of university-based anthropology. It is reported that Giddings was anti-Semitic and had poor relations with Boas and Seligman (in economics) because of this. Giddings "was proud of his dolichocephalic skull and believed that all genius and culture were carried by blond Aryans."[51] Oberschall notes that Giddings' only methodological innovation had to do with an early version of measuring the prestige of racial and ethnic groups. This allowed him to rank groups, placing the American born of white American parents at the summit, followed by other whites in a pecking order from northern to southern European, by Latin American whites and eastern Europeans, by the civilized yellow, by the civilized dark, and finally by the uncivilized.[52] A similar ranking of religions gave seven or eight points to Protestants and one to Jews. Given the prejudice and discrimination he faced as a Jew, it is perhaps not surprising that Boas is often considered the founder or at least the apostle of American cultural relativism.[53] The extent to which Boas' cultural relativism as a founder of American anthropology is due to his personal response to Giddings (known as a founder of American sociology) remains open to further research.

After some experimentation with race integration immediately after the defeat of the Confederacy, racial apartheid and the theories justifying it were used to reinvigorate social Darwinism toward the end of the nineteenth century. An example of this, published by the German-born statistician Frederick L. Hoffman in 1896, was *Race Traits and Tendencies of the American Negro.* As with Morton sixty years earlier, Hoffman targeted the humanitarians of his day who wished to benefit the "lower races" with philanthropy and education. He wrote, "The lower races, even under the same conditions of life must necessarily fail because the vast number of incapables which a hard struggle for life has eliminated from the ranks of the white races, are still forming the large body of the lower races. Easy conditions of life and a liberal charity are among the most destructive influences affecting the lower races; since by such methods the weak and incapable are permitted to increase and multiply, while the struggle of the more able is increased in severity."[54] Hoffman worked for an insurance company, and several such companies accepted his work to the extent that they refused to accept policies for blacks.[55] Although one sociologist, the African-American W.E.B. Dubois, wrote a critique of Hoffman's work, William Graham Sumner, known as a founder of American sociology, wrote Hoffman a personal letter congratulating him on "a fine and useful piece of work."[56]

The School Textbook: Inculcating Racism

So far we have been discussing the privileged classes and intellectuals of the eighteenth and nineteenth centuries. However, we might also ask about the working and labouring classes. These included the rapidly expanding blue-collar factory workers as well as those many still working on family farms. Until well into the twentieth century, education for such labouring classes was quite rudimentary. One might ask whether the outlook of the subordinate classes was any less prejudicial toward Aboriginal people than that of the educated classes. The answer is probably not. When agricultural settlement replaced fur trapping and alliances in war as the primary goal of colonial policy, the presence of Amerindians pursuing a traditional hunting, gathering, and fishing lifestyle directly obstructed the way of white settlers wishing to start and expand their farms. They justified their objections not by acknowledging blatant self-interest but by branding the Aboriginal way of life a waste of resources: too much land was required to sustain too few people. "As the settler moved into the wilderness," states historian Robert J. Surtees, "he did not look upon the Indians as a potential ally, nor did he require Indian support. More often he considered the Indians as a retarding influence and a nuisance for they seldom used their land – often good arable land – for agriculture, but continued to live by hunting and fishing."[57] One sees this sentiment in an editorial printed in 1868 in the *Sarnia Observer* protesting the holding of blocks of land by the local Ojibway (Anishnaabe). Representing the white settler attitude described by Surtees, the editorial sermonized, "The enterprise and progress of the country have so far advanced that public opinion now says to the Indian, 'you cannot hold so large a block of land to the detriment of others, obstructing the progress of the country. You must either fall into the ranks of progress, or sell your lands at the high value which our labour and enterprise has given them; and stand aside so that others can perform the work for the public good.'"[58] The missionary E.F. Wilson wrote in 1878 to such a white settler in Algoma, "I am not surprised that people at the Landing should speak hard of the Indians – I am used to that – but I believe that with patience and persistent effort much may be made of them."[59] We do not have the incoming letter that prompted this response, but it is clear from the context that the letters represent the familiar distinction between missionary optimism for the potential of Aboriginal people as individuals and the self-aggrandizing, low estimation of their potential by white settlers.

Aside from the self-interest of farming settlers, it is to Canadian school textbooks that one may look to account for negative attitudes to Aboriginal people among the broad range of the citizenry. Free and mandatory public schooling came about only in the last quarter of the nineteenth century. However, as textbooks became an important aspect of such public schooling, it became one avenue by which the labouring classes were influenced by the outlook of the more educated middle class. Patricia V. Ofner wrote an intriguing MA thesis at Lakehead University that looked at the image of the Indian in sixty-five history and social studies books used in Ontario in Grades 5 to 10 between 1857 and 1980. Her method involved designating all references to Aboriginal people as negative or positive.

Overall, Ofner surveyed six books up to 1900 and found the negative designations at 82.5%, and from 1911 to 1930 the negative terminology actually rose to over 90%. From 1930 to 1970 the negative designations declined slightly to the 80-84% range. In the 1970s there was some noticeable change, although even then 69.4% of designations continued to be negative. Examples of racist statements included that Aboriginal people were "more like hogs than men" (1921); that they were "brute beasts without faith, law, religion, without God" (1912); that they were "childlike" (1902, 1905); and that Indian religion "was purest superstition" (1897) with "strange ideas about nature" (1905). Other references pointed to Indians' belief in magic, their wild orgies, their warlike nature, an emphasis on the use of torture, and their attraction to liquor. As a general conclusion, one might quote a textbook of 1930 stating that "the civilization of America today owes very little to the Aboriginal inhabitants."[60]

Of course, it had always been possible to present a very different and more positive picture, and in the 1970s some textbooks started to do just that. There are examples of Aboriginal people helping whites other than as military allies (for example sharing or teaching about food resources), of whites learning from Aboriginal people, of a positive religious life, of Aboriginal people "develop[ing] a technology suited to a land of long winters and heavy snows" (1978), and of positive estimation of art. In addition, more words were devoted to whites as sometimes treacherous and warlike.

An irony is that the writers arguably could have written more positive textbooks if they had depended on the writings of people like Horatio Hale and E.F. Wilson. Hale wrote, in 1883, *The Iroquois Book of Rites,* truly remarkable for its wonderfully affirmative descriptions and evaluation of Aboriginal life. Although Hale was in fact quite influential at the time in scientific and proto-anthropological circles, his positive views of Aboriginal cultures do not seem to have had much influence on his contemporary public school textbook writers. Clearly, the use of such books and their attitudes must have had important consequences for attitudes at a time when most children ceased their studies by Grade 8, if not before. Thus the self-interest of white settlers and their negative attitudes toward Aboriginal people, based on direct conflict between farming and hunting lifestyles, were further reinforced by the only formal learning that they were likely to acquire. Too little has changed in this regard, as is evident in the recent pulling of a textbook from Grade 2 curricula in which Inuit people are characterized as unemployable.[61]

During the extended historical period under review, it is important to understand that both educated and uneducated citizens of colonial Canada depended on an assumption of clear evolutionary stages leading upward, ladderlike, toward ever-increasing progress. At the bottom was what was termed "savagery," followed by "barbarism," and then finally "civilization." This idea had originally been developed in the eighteenth century by the French and Scottish philosophers and social analysts of the Enlightenment, although the idea itself had been known by the Spaniards and even by the ancient writers of classical civilization. As Robert Berkhofer Jr., describes it, the evolutionary paradigm worked "by analogy between the life cycle of a human being and the history of the species" and thus produced "a history of the sequences of stages of society that the race had passed through to reach the height of progress exemplified by Europe at the time. Just as a single person advanced from infancy through youth to reach adulthood, so all humankind had passed through savagery and barbarism before gaining civilization."[62] Although not new, "the intellectual context that gave real meaning to such a sequence did not develop until the latter half of the eighteenth century."[63] Berkhofer points out the important difference between the French and Scottish advocates of the typology: the French based the stages on "the ability of the human intelligence," while the Scots emphasized "the modes of subsistence and the division of labor."[64] An early writer employing this typology was William Robertson in his 1777 tome *History of America,* which stated that "in America, man appears under the rudest form in which we can conceive him to subsist" and that except for the Aztec and Inca empires, all the Aboriginal societies of America "should be designated 'savage.'"[65]

Virtually all writers of the eighteenth and nineteenth centuries shared in this evolutionary-stage analysis. However, differences in emphasis did exist. The first difference has been noted: whether the stage reached depended more upon innate abilities and intelligence or upon the environment. The second related to placing Amerindians on the steps of the evolutionary ladder. We have seen Robertson place them at the lowest level, savagery. On the other hand, Lewis Henry Morgan, writing a century later in his *Ancient Society, or Researches in the Lines of Human Progress from Savagery through Barbarism to Civilization* (1877), avowed that "the body of them [Amerindians] had emerged from savagery and attained the lower status of barbarism; whilst a portion of them, the Village Indians of North and South America, had risen to the Middle Status."[66] Morgan added to the complexity of the model by specifying three substages for each of the three broader stages. A point to emphasize is how important and influential a popularized form of racial evolutionism proved to be. One can see its influence on the school textbooks analyzed by Ofner, with their implicit or explicit depiction of Amerindians as at the stages of savagery and barbarism, and also on a writer such as McGill economist Stephen Leacock, who wrote "popular" books on academic topics outside his own field for the lay reader interested in self-improvement.

Stephen Leacock's Demeaning Depictions

This kind of dependence on the evolutionary ladder model is employed by Leacock's *The Dawn of Canadian History: A Chronicle of Aboriginal Canada* (1920). This was the first in a thirty-two-volume series described as "thirty-two freshly-written narratives for popular reading, designed to set forth, in historic continuity, the principal events and movements in Canada, from the Norse Voyages to the Railway Builders."[67] The series was edited by George M. Wrong and H.H. Langton of the University of Toronto. Wrong taught history from 1892 to his retirement in 1927 and was the head of his department and founder of what became the *Canadian Historical Review.*[68] Leacock himself is better remembered as a humorist and remains one of Canada's best-known writers. However, he was a professor of political economy at McGill and department head there until his retirement in 1936. Gerald Lynch points to his prolific output and its wide range across many subjects. He quotes Leacock's own boast that "I can write up anything now at a hundred yards."[69]

Perhaps it was this distance that made Leacock still dependent on the evolutionary-stage paradigm developed in the eighteenth and nineteenth centuries. His chapter on Amerindians is more akin to Robertson than to Morgan in placing them at the stage of savagery rather than barbarism. Leacock was willing to grant to Amerindians one great invention – the canoe. Given that Leacock spent his summers every year at a cottage at Old Brewery Bay near Orillia, Ontario, one can understand his own appreciation of the canoe. "In nearly all other respects," he claimed magnanimously, "the Indians of Canada had not emerged from savagery to that stage half way to civilization which is called barbarism."[70]

For the most part, he stands in sharp contrast to the people in this book who had actually spent time with Aboriginal people. Leacock acknowledged the political and cultural distinctiveness and pluralism of Aboriginal people in Canada. He felt qualified to claim that the Iroquois of the Six Nations "were in some respects superior to most of the Indians of the continent" and that they "had advanced further ... than most savages,"[71] but whether describing the somewhat advanced Iroquois or what he portrayed as their less advanced neighbours, the emphasis in Leacock's narrative is always on the deficiencies of Aboriginal cultures. Readers of this text may wish to contrast Leacock's analysis with that of Horatio Hale, Silas Rand, or E.F. Wilson, with their many favourable descriptions and judgments.

In general, Leacock emphasized that Aboriginal people lacked knowledge of the use of metals, lacked "settled abodes or fixed dwelling places," possessed only "the most elementary form of agriculture," had no art of writing, and had only "a rude nature worship." A typical general statement reads that "when the first white men first came these rude peoples were so backward and so little trained in using their faculties that any advance towards art and industry was inevitably slow and difficult."[72] At this point, Leacock points out that this had once been true of Europeans and that they thus "had begun the intricate tasks which a growth towards civilization involved."[73] Leacock then quotes William Robertson in what Leacock called "a vivid passage" that described "the backward state of the savage tribes of America."[74] It seems likely that the entire chapter is indebted to Robertson in placing the Amerindians at the lowest stage of savagery rather than, with Lewis Henry Morgan, at the higher stage of barbarism. At least in theory, Aboriginal people could make the same advance to civilization as had Europeans before them, especially since Robertson emphasized environment rather than innate intelligence. However, given the primitive stage achieved by Aboriginal people in the eyes of Robertson and Leacock, no doubt advance to civilization would be tediously slow. Leacock explicitly states in reference to Aboriginal societies that "they spent a primitive existence."[75]

William Robertson lived from 1721 to 1793 and in his time was an eminent Scottish historian and proto-anthropologist. He wrote celebrated histories of Scotland and of the emperor Charles V. He became principal of the University of Edinburgh and was also moderator of the General Assembly of the Church of Scotland. In 1777 Robertson authored his *History of America*, which was a key source for Leacock. This work, "in common with the thought of the Enlightenment ... accepted the evolution of human *society* as the essential fact of primary importance" and used "three stages of evolutionary typology: savagery, barbarism, and civilization in ascendant order."[76] As mentioned previously, Robertson ascribed all North American Aboriginal people to the stage of savagery. His anthropological chronicler, E. Adamson Hoebel, points to his generalized description of Amerindians as "in the main, dreary ... loosely portrayed as feeble, indolent, improvident, lacking in the virtues engendered by developed property interests, intellectually unimaginative, devoid of love between the sexes, and near anarchists in civil affairs."[77]

Faint comfort that it may be, Robertson actually challenged biological racism. He believed in the common Enlightenment proposition that humans are the same in inherent gifts and intellect. If human societies varied so drastically in the stage of evolution that they had reached, it had not to do with inherent gifts and intelligence but with the nature of the climate. Hoebel shows that other Enlightenment thinkers such as Voltaire, Montesquieu, and Bodin pointed to the influence of climate and that in this regard Robertson was "a child of his times in laying great emphasis upon climate."[78] At the same time, Robertson attributed difference to other causes than climate and specified that "moral and political causes ... affect the disposition and character of individuals, as well as nations, still more powerfully than the influence of climate."[79] The point here in concentrating on Robertson is his extensive influence on Leacock. It is probable that Leacock was no great scholar of the fine points of Robertson's analysis. Rather, what he received was the evolutionary-stage analysis, the specific attribution of North American Aboriginal people to the "savage" stage and a rather pronounced denigration of the social institutions and values of such "savages" as deficient and inferior.

Much more could be written to describe Leacock's work. Many of the adjectives and phrases are deeply disturbing to the modern reader. Aside from the picture of backward technology, the moral life of Aboriginal people is also depicted as inferior, whether it be their religion, male treatment of women, or their exultation in war and torture. Leacock blithely differentiated between Aboriginal people based on their supposed standing on the evolutionary ladder. Thus he writes that "the Athapascans stood low in the scale of civilization."[80] By comparison, the Iroquois stood higher on that ladder in terms of technical and institutional organization. However, what he called their "diabolical cruelty" rather vitiated these more admirable aspects of their society in his eyes.[81]

Horatio Hale's principal ethnographic writing was on the Iroquois, and it is interesting to contrast Hale and Leacock. Hale praised not only their advanced technology and institutions, but also the morality of their society. Even when it came to warfare and the practices of warfare, Hale was able and prepared to provide a defence of the Iroquois based on their situation of having to defend their territories against hostile intruders over a period of centuries.

Unfortunately, Leacock's book of 1920 does not represent the last depiction of the Aboriginal as deplorably primitive in Canada. Daniel Francis describes Leacock's "dismissive, even vicious attitude toward Native people" and points out that he published as late as 1941 a book sponsored by the House of Seagram entitled *Canada: The Foundation of Its Future*, which "took as its theme 'the struggle of civilization against savagery.'" This book included the statements that "the Indians were too few to count" (a theme in the earlier book) and that "their use of resources of the continent was scarcely more than that by crows and wolves, their development of it nothing."[82]

Our point is not that Leacock's was the only opinion on Aboriginal people in Canada in the nineteenth and twentieth centuries, or we would scarcely be memorializing Horatio Hale, E.F. Wilson, and the others. However, it is clear that biological racism and forms of cultural racism based on exaggerated understandings of the evolutionary paradigm were all too common in Canada, as in the United States, even in academic circles such as Leacock's.[83] Many attitudes of Euro-Canadian settlers were influenced by an actual biological racist belief that Aboriginal peoples' intellect was by nature less advanced. Even if their views were not actually rooted in biological racism, other Canadians demeaned Aboriginal people by ignoring or downplaying positive features of their societies and by exaggerating deficiencies. This can be seen by comparing Leacock's comments with those of Horatio Hale and E.F. Wilson. In any society, on important matters there will be a range of opinion. At the same time, any period of society incorporates a kind of shared understanding of social issues due to what may be called the "discursive hegemony" prevalent. One stands in awe of a Horatio Hale, writing in the 1880s and 1890s, overturning much of the social-Darwinist discursive hegemony of his day. All this is not to say that the Euro-Canadians with good intentions whom we are surveying can be measured entirely by the expansive cultural relativism of today. Take E.F. Wilson, for example. For all his efforts to find and highlight positive aspects of Aboriginal cultures, there can be no doubt that Wilson used his own version of evolutionary theory, which led in his case to praising the Cherokee and Pueblo peoples as templates for other Aboriginal peoples. Wilson still positively evaluated many features taken for granted in the evolutionary schema, such as permanent settlements, permanent homes, and lack of a nomadic lifestyle. No doubt modern observers, deeply influenced by cultural relativism, will see and reject this residual evolutionism and will insist on the integrity of each Aboriginal culture and society. In response to this, one can only agree with Stephen J. Gould that complete cultural relativism was almost unknown at this time, even among those with the best of intentions and good hearts. Horatio Hale may have come closest. It is a shame that for a number of reasons, the memory of Hale has been fading, probably because cultural relativism came to be identified with Franz Boas. Since Boas was fortunate to train several generations of graduate students at Columbia, they credited this doctrine solely to their "doktor-vater" (a German phrase meaning literally doctor, as in PhD, and father) without realizing the influence of Hale on Boas in this regard.

However, while evaluating the other figures in this book, let us not engage in what has been called "presentism" or "whig history" – that is, the temptation to judge the past solely in terms of the present. While we will not find much complete modern-day cultural relativism, we will find many of the attitudes and behaviours of the Euro-Canadians examined in this book considerably at odds with those of the majority of their contemporaries. We will find a general tendency on the part of the subjects of this book to look for the positive in Aboriginal cultures; we will find a tendency to see rationality and reverence rather than primitiveness and superstition; we will find a tendency to seek guidance from the prophets of the Judeo-Christian tradition, to seek justice and mercy and right-dealing, to do unto others as we would have done unto us. Although such scriptural injunctions have never been easy to follow (it is always easier to find the mote in another's eye), there is no doubt that the subjects under review in the book were moved in these directions in ways that seemed to escape their non-Aboriginal contemporary fellow citizens.

Euro-Canadians Working for Justice in Colonial Canada

Contributors to this collection have taken up the notion of good intentions in a variety of ways: some argue that good intentions prevailed for the person under study; others show the irony of good intentions gone awry; still others struggle to reconcile their Christian morality with their own desires to get ahead. None escapes the irony of good intentions never being enough – in this case, to allow the respectful coming together of people holding distinct worldviews. Following something of a chronological order, the collection begins with David Nock's representation of Horatio Hale, the world-class scholar who is best known for *The Iroquois Book of Rites,* published in 1883 and still available in bookstores in a 1989 reprint. Initially drawn to Aboriginal people in an accessible winter camp, he published a pamphlet on their language at the age of seventeen that earned him an appointment as a philologist of the United States Exploring Expedition to the Pacific. When he was not appointed to a university following this expedition, he left academic work, married a Canadian, and moved to Canada, where he practised law for over twenty years. He also continued his connections with and interest in Aboriginal people and language. For Hale, the mental facility of a people is reflected in their languages. Based on the respect he developed for a range of Aboriginal peoples with whom he came in contact over the years, Hale diverged greatly from the tenor of the day in his carefully argued expression of admiration of the people of the Six Nations evident throughout his most famous work. Notably, in comparing their cultures to those of Europe, he arrives at the same conclusion held by many "Iroquois" people themselves: their culture is superior in many ways.

Michael Blackstock examines the origins of the Aborigines Protection Society (APS) and several examples of their work in Canada in Chapter 2. Drawing on existing documents, he traces their humanitarian beginnings in an 1837 report to the British House of Commons. His focus on four of their interventions in Canada – and they were active throughout the British Empire – provides important insights into attitudes that ran contrary to the dominant racist thought of the day. At the same time, Blackstock takes the opportunity to argue that, despite their good intentions, ultimately the APS could not counteract their own Christianizing intentions, the impact of the Indian Act, and the disruption of any possibility of reciprocal social relations between Euro-Canadians, the English, and First Nations peoples. Bringing the reader to the present day, Blackstock worries that the Royal Commission on Aboriginal Peoples may meet the same fate as the APS reports as the juggernaut of profit-driven capitalism continues to overshadow humanitarian agendas.

In Chapter 3, Thomas Abler considers the contradictory dimensions of missionary Silas Rand and his shifting attitudes to the Mi'kmaq, with whom he worked for more than forty years. As with Hale, his knowledge of the language and spirituality of the Mi'kmaq people gave him strong respect for their intellectual capabilities, counter to the attitudes of many other people of European ancestry. At the same time, his frustration with his inability to persuade them to abandon their traditional, mobile way of life and become settled farmers like good Christians should is telling. Upon visiting the Mohawks in 1858, he was delighted to find them settled, farming, and attending schools on their reserves, developments that affirmed for him the potential of all Aboriginal people, counter to the beliefs of the biological racists documented above. For readers, it also affirms his persisting ethnocentrism.

In Chapters 4 and 5, Janet Chute and Alan Knight bring us west to the Upper Great Lakes to consider the work of two distant relatives, lawyer and speculator Allan Macdonell and government surveyor and Member of Parliament Simon Dawson. With careful and thorough contextualization, they show Macdonell first as a man of integrity and commitment to justice for the Aboriginal people, with whom he had established good relations and workable business arrangements. Attracted to a Native land-claims movement established long before his time, he became the confidant of

Ojibway chief Shingwaukonse. By 1849, with his legal training serving them well, both worked with others to help create what Chute and Knight claim was, to that time, "the most articulate and forceful campaign for Native resource rights ever raised in the Canadas." Focusing on the Mica Bay incident, the authors show Macdonell as a person of foresight and decency, committed to creating a nation where indigenous peoples would play an integral role economically and politically.

Simon Dawson, Macdonell's distant relative, is the subject of Chapter 5. Here, Chute and Knight show how Dawson, a civil engineer, surveyor, and road supervisor, valued Native prerogatives over the perceived rights of miners, loggers, and settlers. A significant figure in the negotiation of Treaty 3 and the Robinson Treaties, Dawson came to appreciate the intricacies of Ojibway protocol through his respectful attention to detail as he travelled their lands. Negotiating thoughtfully and gently allowed him considerable success in his agenda of road building while maintaining some respect for the needs and wishes of the peoples whose lands and lives were being affected. With increasing knowledge of the people, his admiration and commitment increased. Lobbying for their right to vote and for the payment of annuities long in arrears and generally seeking "fair play" for the Ojibway guided much of Dawson's life work. While both Dawson and Macdonell indubitably contributed to the progress of colonization, they also lobbied strenuously for more respectful ways of proceeding that would include Ojibway concerns in treaty negotiations and Ojibway people in the fabric of the developing nation.

In Chapter 6, Celia Haig-Brown takes us into the life of Nahnebahwequa, also known as Catherine Sutton, an Anishnaabe woman who travelled to see Queen Victoria in 1860 in a fruitless quest to have land rights recognized. Despite the outcome, along the way, Nahne's contacts with supporters of European ancestry, particularly a fortuitous connection with the Quakers, first in New York and then in London, provide insights into the level of humanitarian commitment that some of them had developed for Aboriginal claims. Ultimately, their good intentions and accompanying support were not enough to secure Nahne's land for her before her death in 1865.

David Nock's chapter on E.F. Wilson documents an epiphany that created the impetus for this book. After years as the principal of two residential schools, Wilson travelled to several First Nations in the US and on the Canadian Prairies starting in 1885, an experience that, together with extensive reading, prompted a sea change in his attitudes to and understandings of Aboriginal people in Canada. He was influenced heavily by Horatio Hale, the subject of Chapter 1, as his interest in anthropology and ethnology increased. Hale's positive assessment of Aboriginal peoples' intellectual capacity and cultural achievements affected Wilson's own work. The latter's "Fair Play Papers," while consistent with his ethnocentric view of what constituted civilization, called for an independent nation for Ontario's Indians. This recommendation, foretelling sentiments of many First Nations people in Canada today, was never realized. His best intentions came to naught.

In Chapter 8, Jan Hare and Jean Barman take us to the West Coast of the expanding nation of Canada to see Emma Crosby's work first in supporting her missionary husband and concurrently in providing a model of gender-appropriate Christian behaviour for young Tsimshian women of the north Pacific Coast. Notably, the Crosbys had been invited to come to Tsimshian territory to do their work. Mrs. Crosby's first efforts served her well, as she invited the girls to live in her house where they learned by doing, providing her with much-needed help along the way. Her good intentions manifested themselves not only in the preparation of women to be good wives, but also in their protection from more disreputable settlers (men) who were ready to take advantage of young, unmarried women. Good Christian marriage was the goal that she had for her charges. In 1879, finding the numbers of women needing her attention growing too rapidly, as well as wanting to lessen the Tsimshian influences on her own children, Crosby created a separate "home" for the girls, which was to carry on her work. Over time, the school became a government-funded residential school with all of the accompanying institutional effects. What started as good, albeit ethnocentric, intentions to protect and educate the girls in Christian ways became the confinement of an alien and hostile context.

In Chapter 9, Sarah Carter takes us to the Prairies to introduce a very different woman of colonial times, Amelia McLean Paget, the author of the classic work *The People of the Plains*. Unlike the Tsimshian girls of Emma Crosby's household, the Saulteaux servants in the McLean household had a strong influence on the children. As well as learning to ride and shoot, Amelia became fluent in both Saulteaux and Cree. The focus of the chapter is the development of Paget's book, which was certainly influenced by the time in 1885 that the McLean family spent with the Cree chiefs Big Bear and Wandering Spirit and their group as the First Nations people tried to avoid the North West Mounted Police. Years later, in 1906, she was commissioned by the governor general of Canada to prepare a report on the Plains Cree. As she conducted her fieldwork, many welcomed her as an old friend. Through her knowledge of the language, she listened carefully to the elders' knowledge and wisdom, which served as the basis for her book. Although it was edited by Duncan Campbell Scott, the superintendent of Indian Affairs at the time (known today for his low regard for Aboriginal peoples), Carter argues that much of the text remains true to Paget's sentiments. She challenged dominant stereotypes, including those related to

Cree women, and made efforts to explain particular practices in ways that would bring understanding and respect for the Cree and Saulteaux peoples. Although she wrote the work imagining a dying and disappearing people, her intentions have proven more important than expected, as her work remains a valuable record of aspects of Cree and Saulteaux life of the late nineteenth century.

Another character reaching adulthood in the difficult times of the transfer of Rupert's Land to the Dominion of Canada and Riel's resistance to that move is the subject of Donald Smith's chapter. As a young man, William Henry Jackson, later known as Honoré Joseph Jaxon,[84] was drawn through the logic of Riel's arguments to strong support of the Métis cause. This did not keep him from being imprisoned first by the Métis and then by the Canadians, tried as "Riel's secretary," and from there sent to the insane asylum at Lower Fort Garry. Fleeing to Chicago, Jaxon spent most of the rest of his life in the US. He began by changing his name, claimed to be Métis, and continued his lifetime commitment to fighting injustice wherever he saw it. Jaxon, something of a pack rat, kept records of and collected books related to the various causes to which he was drawn. He always planned that his collection would serve as the basis for a library for the Indians of Saskatchewan. Heartbreakingly, his good intentions went awry when, at close to ninety years of age, along with all his books and endless boxes of papers, he was evicted from his basement apartment in New York. Within a month, he was dead, all his books sold and his papers dumped into the garbage bins of New York City.

The final two chapters of the book take us back to British Columbia, where the turn of the century saw increasing activity for First Nations people working to protect land from encroaching settlement and resources from exploitation. The two men in these chapters dedicated much of their lives to working with First Nations peple on land rights and other aspects of cultural maintenance and survival. Ironically, their presence was used in efforts to dismiss the work of the First Nations leaders and reduce it to that of "white agitators."

A.E. O'Meara was one of those people. The subject of Chapter 11, by Mary Haig-Brown, he was definitely a well-intentioned man, often the centre of considerable controversy, and annoying to his superiors. He was a lawyer turned missionary whose direct political involvement with British Columbia's Aboriginal people began in earnest when he was invited by the Cowichan Nation on Vancouver Island to carry their 1909 petition to England. Following this initial work, he served as consultant for and advisor first to the Nisga'a and then to the Allied Indian Tribes of British Columbia. One of the first to cite the Royal Proclamation of 1763 as the legal reason that Aboriginal people in most of British Columbia still "owned" the land, his foresight receives passing comment, if any, in most histories of the province. Until his death in 1928, O'Meara continued his work to have Aboriginal rights recognized by the Canadian government.

James Teit is another renowned figure in work with Aboriginal people for Aboriginal rights at this time in British Columbia, one who sometimes worked alongside O'Meara. In her chapter on the social activist, Wendy Wickwire nuances Teit's work for the recognition of land title as political rather than salvage ethnography. An immigrant "Scotsman" who married Lucy Antko, a woman of the Nlaka'pamux Nation, and worked in the area, he was originally recruited as an ethnographer by Franz Boas to contribute to the work of the British Association for the Advancement of Science (BAAS). Continuing collaboration with Boas over a number of years, Teit became increasingly committed to learning about and documenting the intricacies of the cultures of the interior of British Columbia. Ultimately fluent in four First Nations languages, his intelligence and sensitivity inevitably drew him into First Nations' land claims, where he served as a tremendous resource for the organizations engaged in the struggles.

All of the people and organizations represented in the ensuing chapters were exceptional people who had good intentions in their work with First Nations people. Wickwire reports that in a memorial that the interior chiefs of British Columbia sent to the Canadian government in 1910, they divided the whites into two groups. Some were "good" people who could be trusted; others were "greedy, ill-mannered people who came in search of gold and land." It could be argued that the subjects of these chapters belonged to the former group. They were "good" people and well intentioned. Their work contributes to deepening and complicating our understandings of relations between Aboriginal and non-Aboriginal people during these times. That being said, their work was not enough. In Canada we find ourselves still in the position of being a colonial country in need of some strong decolonizing work. We hope that this text contributes even in a small way to this work.

Notes

Although we wrote this introduction in stages, with David taking primary responsibility for the longer middle sections on racism and Celia responsibility for the beginning section on decolonizing historiography and the concluding section introducing each chapter, we both read and edited each other's work. Thus the final product is truly a joint construction.

1 Throughout the chapters, the variety of terms used to refer to indigenous peoples are indicative of changing understandings of their histories and current relation to Canada. We have decided not to standardize their use as an indication of the continuing shiftiness of the terms; rather, we have left them as each author has chosen to use them. "First Nations" is a politicized term that assumes three things: primacy of place, a form of nationhood, and a plurality of ethnicities. It is called into question by those who see it as too political and associated with a particular organization to the exclusion of peoples such as the Métis. Olive Dickason uses the term "Amerindian" in her extensive work,

Canada's First Nations: A History of Founding Peoples from Earliest Times (Toronto: Oxford University Press, 1992), as does Georges Sioui in his work, *For an Amerindian Autohistory* (Montreal: McGill-Queen's University Press, 1992). "Indian" is a term still used in federal legislation to legitimate specific descendants of the original peoples. Because of its historical and long-term use, it maintains a currency with the people themselves. "Aboriginal" literally means "out of" the original people. And all of this fussing could be seen as justification for Marie Battiste and James Youngblood Henderson's call for "decolonizing the Eurocentric need for definitions." *Protecting Indigenous Knowledge and Heritage* (Saskatoon: Purich Publishing, 2000), 36. It may be best to think of these terms in the context of Ania Loomba's discussion of "imperialism" and "colonialism" – that is, to acknowledge that each is a concept "best understood not by trying to pin it down to a single semantic meaning but by relating its shifting meaning to historical processes." *Colonialism/Postcolonialism* (New York: Routledge, 1999), 4. Another source of insight into the discussion is Michael Yellow Bird's piece, "What We Want to Be Called: Indigenous Peoples' Perspectives on Racial and Ethnic Identity Labels," *American Indian Quarterly* 23, 2 (Spring 1999): 1-21. He interviewed a panel of indigenous professors and graduate students and reported on terms they prefer and reject, relative to themselves. Increasingly, the names of specific groups such as Haida, Dene, and Mi'kmaq are used; they too are often in flux as people move away from anglicizations to spellings that more closely represent the sounds of the original languages.

2 Loomba, *Colonialism/Postcolonialism,* xi.

3 Adrian Searle, "Bad Memories Are Made of This," *Guardian Weekly,* 18-24 February 2005, 23.

4 J. Edward Chamberlin, *If This Is Your Land, Where Are Your Stories: Finding Common Ground* (Toronto: Alfred A. Knopf, 2003).

5 For the purposes of this book, we see "colonial Canada" officially ending with the Statute of Westminster, 11 December 1931. At that time, a British law granted "the former colonies full legal freedom except in those areas where they chose to remain subordinate." The *Constitution Act* of 1982 finally ended Canada's chosen subordination to Britain in relation to amendments to the Canadian Constitution. *The Canadian Encyclopedia* (Toronto: McClelland and Stewart, 1999), 2249. That being said, we also see the persisting effects of colonialism informing all our relations today.

6 While we were very tempted to include some chapters on negotiations between supportive people of European ancestry and the First Nations peoples of the United States, we decided to stay focused on Canada. For a view of "cultural intermediaries" or "cultural brokers" primarily in the US (of non-Native, Native, and mixed heritage), see Margaret Szasz, ed., *Between Indian and White Worlds: The Cultural Broker* (Norman: University of Oklahoma Press, 1994).

7 Kathy L. Hodgson-Smith, "Seeking Good and Right Relations: Student Perspectives on the Pedagogy of Joe Duquette High School" (MA thesis, University of Saskatchewan, 1997).

8 Marcus J. Borg, "Reading the Prophets Again," in *Reading the Bible Again for the First Time* (San Francisco: Harper Collins, 2001), 111-44.

9 We are grateful to Jan Hare, who, in reading an earlier version of this introduction, pointed out this tension.

10 Interestingly, a number of the people represented were accused at some time in their careers of being insane. The contemporary reader is left to ponder whether this labelling was at least in part a strategic move designed to lessen the effectiveness of the supporter's opposition to the injustices being perpetrated.

11 By mainstream, we refer to the presentation of history in school textbooks, the popular press, and other contemporary media.

12 There are a variety of spellings for the specific nations included throughout the book. The editors have maintained the spellings that the original authors employed and have not attempted to standardize them. "Anishnaabek" refers to the Anishnaabe people.

13 David A. Nock, *A Victorian Missionary and Canadian Indian Policy: Cultural Synthesis vs Cultural Replacement* (Waterloo: Wilfred Laurier University Press, 1988).

14 Celia Haig-Brown, *Resistance and Renewal: Surviving the Indian Residential School* (Vancouver: Tillacum Press, 1988).
15 Loomba, *Colonialism/Postcolonialism*, 66.
16 *Delgamuukw: The Supreme Court of Canada Decision on Aboriginal Title* (Vancouver: Douglas and McIntyre, 1998). See also John Borrows, "Listening for a Change," *Osgoode Hall Law Journal* 39, 1 (2001): 1-38.
17 Coalition for the Advancement of Aboriginal Studies, *Learning About Walking in Beauty: Placing Aboriginal Perspectives in Canadian Classrooms,* http://www.crr.ca. Go to Publications 2002.
18 Susan Dion, "Braiding Histories: Responding to the Problematics of Canadians Hearing First Nations Post-Contact Experiences" (PhD dissertation, University of Toronto, 2002).
19 There are Aboriginal people of many nations who do not want to be considered Canadian citizens. See Celia Haig-Brown, "Democratic Research to Inform Citizenship," in *Citizenship in Transformation in Canada,* ed. Yvonne Hébert (Toronto: University of Toronto Press, 2002), 162-74. A recent CBC radio production (spring 2004) also featured a number of First Nations people on the topic of "Why I am not a Canadian."
20 Linda Tuhiwai Smith is a Maori scholar whose research has focused on both the conceptual and practical applications of the term "decolonizing" in the context of Maori struggles for self-determination. See her work, *Decolonizing Methodologies: Research and Indigenous Peoples* (London: Zed Books, 1999).
21 Loomba, *Colonialism/Postcolonialism*.
22 Tuhiwai Smith, *Decolonizing,* 64.
23 Loomba, *Colonialism/Postcolonialism*, 7.
24 Ibid., 1.
25 *The Compact Edition of the Oxford English Dictionary* (Toronto: Oxford University Press, 1971), 469.
26 Loomba, *Colonialism/Postcolonialism*, 1.
27 Ibid., 22.
28 For a discussion of the change in content in expected narratives about Aboriginal people and the rapidity of the change, see James A. Clifton, *Being and Becoming Indian* (Chicago: Dorsey Press, 1989), 2-5.
29 Thomas S. Kuhn, *The Structure of Scientific Revolutions* (Chicago: University of Chicago Press, 1962). Perhaps appropriately, given his own early background in psychiatry and the Communist Party in France and Russia, Foucault's later understanding was influenced by seeing how regimes of knowledge, including the natural sciences, were politically sustained in Stalin's Soviet Union. Michel Foucault, *Power/Knowledge: Selected Interviews and Other Writings, 1972-1977,* ed. Colin Gordon (New York: Pantheon Books), 109-10.
30 Stephen Jay Gould, *The Mismeasure of Man* (1981; reprint, New York: W.W. Norton, 1996), 63.
31 Ibid., 64.
32 Ibid.
33 Ibid., 66.
34 On Harris, see G.A. Rawlyk, "Canada's Immigration Policy, 1945-1962," *The Dalhousie Review* 42 (Autumn 1962): 287-300 at 292, 294. In reference to King, as late as 1947 he warned the House of Commons that "any considerable Oriental immigration would ... be certain to give rise to social and economic problems of a character that might lead to serious difficulties in the field of international relations." Rawlyk, "Canada's Immigration Policy," 289. On Macdonald, an example would be a statement he made in 1890 regretting the mass influx of Slavic and southern European immigrants into the United States. He warned that as a result the United States "will have its vicissitudes and revolutions. Look at that mass of foreign ignorance and vice which has flooded that country with socialism, atheism and all other isms." Donald H. Avery, *Reluctant Host: Canada's Response to Immigrant Workers, 1896-1994* (Toronto: McClelland and Stewart, 1995), 61.
35 Gould, *The Mismeasure,* 88. On Morton, see also Robert E. Bieder, "Samuel G. Morton and the Calculations of Inferiority," in *Science Encounters the Indian, 1820-1880: The Early Years of American Ethnology* (Norman: University of Oklahoma Press, 1986), 55-103.

36 Bieder, *Science Encounters,* 88-89.

37 Ibid., 85.

38 On Head, see T. Binnema and K. Hutchings, "The Emigrant and the Noble Savage," *Journal of Canadian Studies* 39: 115-38. Head defended his proposals using "Romantic notions that exalted primitivism and the 'noble savage' to justify this plan. A careful analysis of Head's Indian Policy reveals that many Romantic perceptions of Aboriginal peoples, while seemingly benevolent, were consistent with colonial policies that sought to alienate Aboriginal peoples from their lands and to segregate them from contact with European settler societies" (115). See also J.R. Miller, *Skyscrapers Hide the Heavens: A History of Indian-White Relations in Canada,* revised edition (Toronto: University of Toronto Press, 1991), 103-4. It is interesting to see that even in the 1830s, opposition to this plan came from "religious and humanitarian groups" in Canada and the home country, as these persons with good intentions supported a policy of "reserves-education-assimilation" on the basis that while Amerindian cultures were inferior, the individual Amerindians had equal intelligence and potential. Another point that came out in this debate was Amerindian fears that Head's policy meant a "threat to their lands." Thus it is possible that Euro-Canadians and British humanitarians and Amerindians opposed the Head policy for somewhat different reasons. However, the point here is to underline that biological racists such as Head tend to be forgotten, or even absolved, in the rush to blame those such as missionaries and humanitarians who believed that Amerindians were not inferior by nature but equal to Euro-Canadians.

39 See J. Philippe Rushton, *Race, Evolution, and Behavior: A Life History Perspective,* 2nd special abridged edition, distributed compliments of the author to university faculty in Ontario (Port Huron: Charles Darwin Research Institute, 2000). Some of the controversy that currently surrounds the position of the author is discussed in this Introduction. The special abridged edition was first published by Transaction Publishers, a mainstream social-science publishing house that also produces *Society,* a semipopular periodical of the social sciences (not to be confused with *Society-Societé,* a bulletin produced by the Canadian Sociology and Anthropology Association). In response to "self-styled 'anti-racists,'" as designated by Rushton, Transaction withdrew from its involvement in publishing the book and apologized in the January-February 2000 issue of *Society,* 9.

40 Gould, *The Mismeasure,* 83.

41 Ibid., 74.

42 Ibid., 71.

43 E.F. Wilson, *Manual of the Ojebway Language* (Toronto: The Venerable Society for Promoting Christian Knowledge [SPCK], 1874), iv.

44 Rawlyk, "Canada's Immigration," 294. Harris warned that "it would be unrealistic to say that immigrants who have spent the greater part of their life in tropical or subtropical countries become readily adapted to the Canadian mode of life which, to no small extent, is determined by climatic conditions."

45 Gould, *The Mismeasure,* 71.

46 Ibid., 105.

47 Giddings was heavily influenced by the early British statistician, philosopher of science, and eugenicist Karl Pearson. (At this time the development of statistics was closely linked to eugenics.) Eugenics was a social-Darwinist science, at the time quite respectable, that suggested breeding among the less fit should be discouraged, while it should be encouraged among those considered the intellectually most fit (so-called negative and positive eugenics).

48 Robert C. Bannister, *Sociology and Scientism: The American Quest for Objectivity, 1880-1940* (Chapel Hill and London: University of North Carolina Press, 1987), "First Principles," 64-74; "Pluralistic Behaviorism," 75-87.

49 Franklin Henry Giddings, *The Principles of Sociology* (1896; reprint, New York: Macmillan, 1904), 328.

50 Ibid.

51 Anthony Oberschall, "The Institutionalization of American Sociology," in *The Establishment of Empirical Sociology*, ed. A. Obershall (New York: Harper and Row, 1972), 187-251 at 226.
52 Ibid., 228.
53 Citing Michael Rogin's 1996 book, *Blackface: White Noise*, Roseanne Hoefel relates, "Not surprisingly, thus, respected racists like Lothrop Stoddard publicly and professionally belittled Boas as a pathetic Jew pitifully trying to pass as white." See her "'Different by Degree': Ella Cara Deloria, Zora Neale Hurston, and Franz Boas Contend with Race and Ethnicity," *American Indian Quarterly* 25, 2 (Spring 2001): 181-202 at 182.
54 Hoffman as quoted in Robert C. Bannister, *Social Darwinism: Science and Myth in Anglo-American Social Thought* (Philadelphia: Temple University Press, 1979), 191.
55 Ibid., 192.
56 Ibid., 193. On Dubois' criticisms of Hoffman, see page 192. For two chapters on the life of Sumner, see Bannister, *Sociology and Scientism*, "Up From Metaphysics," 89-97; "The Authority of Fact," 98-110.
57 Robert J. Surtees, "The Development of an Indian Reserve Policy in Canada," in *Historical Essays on Upper Canada*, ed. J.K. Johnson (Toronto: McClelland and Stewart, 1975), 262-77 at 263. This article originally appeared in *Ontario History* 61, 2 (1969): 87-98.
58 *The Sarnia Observer* 17, 8 (18 February 1870), as quoted in Nock, *A Victorian*, 68-69.
59 Wilson to McMorine, 19 March 1878, as quoted in Nock, *A Victorian*, 75.
60 Patricia V. Ofner, *The Indian in Textbooks: A Content Analysis of History Books Authorized for Use in Ontario Schools* (MA thesis, Lakehead University, 1983). See also Garnet McDiarmid and David Pratt, *Teaching Prejudice: A Content Analysis of Social Studies Textbooks Authorized for Use in Ontario* (Toronto: Ontario Institute for Studies in Education [OISE], 1971).
61 Sadly, in 2003 the problem with some school textbooks persisted. A recent article from Canada's national newspaper tells of a textbook used for students in Grades 2 to 4 across Canada that contains some very negative stereotypes of Inuit people. The book was taken out of circulation in at least some schools when community members in Iqaluit complained. The publisher, whose mother wrote the book in 1996, has apologized. Paul Waldie, "Grade 2 Text Assailed over Jobless Inuit," *Globe and Mail*, 29 April 2003.
62 Robert F. Berkhofer, Jr., *The White Man's Indian: Images of the American Indian from Columbus to the Present* (New York: Alfred A. Knopf, 1978), 47.
63 Ibid.
64 Ibid., 48.
65 Ibid.
66 Ibid., 53.
67 Stephen Leacock, *The Dawn of Canadian History: A Chronicle of Aboriginal Canada* (1915; reprint, Toronto: Glasgow, Brook, 1920), "Prospectus."
68 M. Brook Taylor, "George MacKinnon Wrong," in *The Canadian Encyclopedia* (Toronto: McClelland and Stewart, 1999), 2556.
69 Gerald Lynch, "Stephen Leacock," in *The Canadian Encyclopedia* (Toronto: McClelland and Stewart, 1999), 1312.
70 Leacock, *The Dawn of Canadian History*, 27.
71 Ibid., 38.
72 Ibid., 33.
73 Ibid., 34.
74 Ibid.
75 Ibid., 26.
76 E. Adamson Hoebel, "William Robertson: An 18th Century Anthropologist-Historian," *American Anthropologist* 62 (1960): 648-55 at 649, emphasis in the original. Details on Robertson's life come from page 648.
77 Ibid., 652.
78 Ibid., 650.
79 Ibid., quoted from the 1812 American edition of Robertson's *History of America*.
80 Leacock, *The Dawn of Canadian History*, 41.
81 Ibid., 37.

82 Daniel Francis, *The Imaginary Indian: The Image of the Indian in Canadian Culture* (Vancouver: Arsenal Pulp Press, 1992), 55.

83 Michael Coleman quotes commissioners of the US Department of the Interior, who had responsibility for "Indians," using the evolutionary-ladder concepts of savagery and barbarism in reference to their charges. These references occurred post-1900 and as late as the 1920s, which would be contemporaneous with Leacock. Michael C. Coleman, "Representation of American Indians and the Irish in Education Reports, 1850s-1920s," *Irish Historical Studies* 23 (May 2002): 33-51 at 38.

84 Songwriter James Keelaghan memorializes Jaxon in his "Honoré," a lament for the passing of Honoré Jaxon, on his fourth CD, *A Recent Future*.

1
Horatio Hale: Forgotten Victorian Author of Positive Aboriginal Representation

David A. Nock

Recovering the Memory of Horatio Hale

Scholars generally acknowledge that biological racism, social Darwinism, and evolutionary theories based on developmental stages bearing such evocative labels as "savagery" and "barbarism" were on the increase in the seventy-five years from 1850 onward. This period was characterized by colonial expansion by European powers around the world and by the development of theories of racial superiority underpinned by notions gleaned indirectly from Charles Darwin about the "survival of the fittest" of animal species. Such biological theories were applied or misapplied to presumed differences in intelligence within the human race. Although such notions came under a cloud as a result of the First World War (seeing the Caucasian race destroying itself in a savage slaughter did little to advance the idea of racial superiority in intelligence), they survived until the Nazi regime of 1933-45 brought racialist ideas into further disrepute. In addition, anticolonialist movements immediately following the Second World War showed that Third World peoples could and would be self-governing.

Seen in this context, it is important to acknowledge the avant-garde thinking of and to retrieve memories of the career of Horatio Emmons Hale (born in the United States in 1817 but resident in Canada from 1856 until his death on 28 December 1896). In his lifetime he fought ideas such as biological racism and the evolutionary perspective. These were rejected later in the twentieth century both as unscientific and as theoretical reflections by colonizing powers to delegitimize Aboriginal peoples under and outside their control. Hale's fight in his century was connected to the struggle in the twentieth century to overthrow such notions because he had an important influence on Franz Boas, one of the key founders of modern anthropology, whose struggle against the same ideas did eventually bear fruit.

Hale was a world-class scholar: member of the Royal Society of Canada; member of the American Philosophical Society; vice-president of the

Horatio Hale in photograph published in *American Anthropologist,* January 1897

anthropological section of the American Association for the Advancement of Science; member, secretary, and research director of the committee established to investigate the Indians of the Canadian Northwest by the British Association for the Advancement of Science; and ultimately president of the American Folk-Lore Society. He had a long connection with Canada, living for forty years in the small southwestern Ontario town of Clinton.

Hale provided very positive images and perspectives on Aboriginal nations and cultures and pictured the intelligence of Aboriginals as being on a par with, if not superior to, that of "Aryans," or white Caucasian settlers of North America. In common and scientific language of the day, most whites were referred to as "Aryans." In the twentieth century the Nazi movement took up this term for its own purposes and turned it into a racist term with a more narrow and specialized meaning. During Hale's lifetime, the term referred to a related group of peoples who migrated westward and south into Europe and the Indian subcontinent from further east in Asia and who all spoke related languages from the common Indo-European family. In Europe all but one handful or so of the peoples of that continent were descended from this Aryan population. When Hale uses this term, then, it is simply his scientific way of referring to the European peoples and their offshoots abroad and should not be confused in any way with the later Nazi usage.

Hale received considerable scholarly recognition during his own lifetime. In addition, the *Encyclopedia Britannica* has played an important role in keeping alive his reputation by including an entry in every edition in the twentieth century from 1910 through 2005.[1] On the other hand, his reputation seems to have diminished over the years relative to that of Franz Boas. Boas is known today as the founder of North American anthropology, rather akin to other disciplinary founders such as Freud for psychoanalysis and Durkheim for sociology. Like such thinkers, Boas had a group of graduate students trained by him at Columbia University who were able to take the name and influence of their founder and perpetuate it over the decades. Jacob W. Gruber suggests that "it is a fact of the history of anthropology that Boas is yet its central figure, a firm point of reference which provides the measure and the perspective for that which went before and for that which followed."[2] Hale never held a university appointment and thus lacked a circle of graduate students to carry on his name. As a result, despite his own personal influence on Boas (the careers of the two men intertwined in the 1880s and early 1890s when Hale acted as research director to Boas in the context of anthropological investigations of the Indians of northwestern Canada) and despite some limited scholarly recognition that Hale influenced Boas' adoption of cultural relativism, Hale's recognition has waned (for example, that important Canadian milestone *The Canadian Encyclopedia* contains no entry for Hale).[3]

The importance of our current discussion is less to rectify the rights and wrongs of anthropological history than to recognize that Hale is an important thinker among whites who had good intentions toward the First Nations and who desired more favourable recognition of Aboriginals by the Euro-Canadian colonizers of Canada and the United States. Although without graduate students, he was not without influence: Hale mentored the amateur anthropologist and activist Rev. E.F. Wilson, and another Canadian missionary scholar, Rev. Dr. John Maclean, dedicated one of his two books to Hale.[4] It is also clear that the career of Franz Boas in the United States did not take off until Hale helped to finance Boas' early fieldwork in the Pacific Northwest from funds provided by the British Association for the Advancement of Science.[5] Hale's own observations of Aboriginal societies, especially the Six Nations in southwestern Ontario, continue to impress readers in the various editions of his most important text, *The Iroquois Book of Rites.*[6] When it is remembered that these observations were made at a time of increasing biological racism, with its assumption of innate racial intelligence, then this appreciation must be even greater.

Hale's Development as a Pioneer Anthropologist

Hale was born on 3 May 1817 in Newport, New Hampshire. His father died suddenly in 1822. His mother, Sarah Josepha Buell Hale, became, as Fenton suggests, "a distinguished journalist and editor, as well as an advocate of women's rights."[7] She edited the leading magazine for women in the United States for forty years (*Godey's Magazine and Lady's Book,* 1837-77), wrote an important encyclopedia of biographies about distinguished women (*Woman's Record, or Sketches of All Distinguished Woman from "the Beginning" till A.D. 1850*) and fought for more access for women to advanced education.[8] Her feminist endeavours influenced Hale in a similar vein, and he fought to ensure the entry of "female pupils into the high schools, on the same terms and with the same advantages which were allowed to male pupils – a privilege which had previously been denied to them."[9] Discussion of the status of women and their esteemed place in Iroquoian society is, in fact, a notable feature of *The Iroquois Book of Rites.* Hale was also influenced by his mother to esteem literary pursuits. His first important academic study was published when he was seventeen, an age at which most students are just completing high school or entering first-year university.[10] This monograph addressed the vocabulary of a group of wintering Aboriginals who made their camp "within a stone's throw of Harvard Yard."[11] Hale was to retain his interest in language during his entire career in anthropology.

As a result of this pamphlet, he was appointed in 1837 as philologist of the United States Exploring Expedition to the Pacific under the leadership of Captain Charles Wilkes. Funded by the United States government, this expedition went around most areas of the Pacific Ocean as well as making a stop in the Oregon Territory. Hale studied the ethnology of all the peoples and languages encountered. This research led to the publication in 1846 of his massive *Ethnography and Philology,* almost 700 pages in length; a second edition was published in 1968.[12] Fenton laments that this study, "immediately acclaimed by scholars here and abroad as indispensable," did not lead to a university appointment and refers to it as "a tragic footnote to the history of American science that a mind of this calibre" could not devote itself to further studies in these subjects.[13]

Instead, Hale took his leave of such interests for twenty-three years (and thirty-five between publications) and devoted himself to law and business. He had moved to Chicago and was admitted to the Illinois bar in

1855. His marriage in 1854 to Margaret Pugh turned out to be of central importance to his public as well as private life. She inherited lands in Canada West (Ontario) in and near the town of Clinton, and Hale became the administrator of the estate. Hale expected the job to end quickly. Instead, as Clinton developed (incorporated 1858), his activities expanded. He became involved as a conveyancer, estate executor, insurance agent, and generally as a lawyer for the town.[14]

Fenton suggests that, unlike his fellow Iroquoianist Lewis Henry Morgan, Hale was unlucky at law in that his "practice kept him too busy to leave but did not make him rich like his friend Morgan in the booming flour town of Rochester."[15] On the other hand, "if Clinton proved an unlucky choice for a law practice, it was a strategic location for ethnology," close as it was to Brantford and the Six Nations of the Grand River and also adjacent to further Aboriginal settlements.[16] In the late 1860s, Hale started to work with various chiefs of the Six Nations, leading to his own fascination with the League of the Six Nations and specifically to the condoling (i.e., mourning) rituals associated with deceased leaders. Given his interest in languages, he was also lucky that the Grand River Reserve, with a population of 3,000, had speakers of all six of the Iroquoian languages as well as speakers of Algonquin, Delaware, and the language of the far-flung and vanishing Tutelos. Fenton refers to this field as "a linguistic laboratory that awaited discoveries."[17]

To estimate the importance of Hale in early Canadian anthropology, it is worth reviewing the late Douglas Cole's "The Origins of Canadian Anthropology, 1850-1910," which appeared in 1973. This article is noteworthy, as it discusses most (but not all) founding figures of preprofessional anthropology in Canada. It establishes that at least by the 1880s these figures were involved in a rather integrated circle with many mutual linkages. Although Hale is only one of the figures featured, Cole does refer to him as "the most significant figure in Canadian anthropology in the pre-Sapir period."[18] (A student of Boas, Edward Sapir was in Canada from 1910-25 and effectively started fully professional anthropology.)

Cole emphasizes the degree to which Hale had departed from biological racism, social Darwinism, and deterministic evolutionism. Cole recognizes the primary importance of *language* to Hale and even calls him a "fanatic in his insistence upon the primacy of language in ethnological study."[19] Cole adds that Hale "was virtually unconcerned with the physical characteristics of races" as being "too easily modified by environment to be at all conclusive as indications of racial character."[20] For Hale, the mental facility of peoples was reflected in their languages. The Iroquoian languages he found to be highly inflected, rich, sonorous, and superior structurally to Aryan and Semitic. His conclusion, based on his measurement of intelligence according to profundity of language, was that the Iroquois were "a people whose achievements, institutions, and language show them to have been in mental capacity and the higher elements of character, not inferior to any race of men of whom history preserves a record."[21] Hale proposed similar positive judgments about a variety of other Aboriginal peoples. He praised the various Algonquin languages for their subtle distinctions, facility of composition, and power of abstraction, referring to the Algonquins as "the native-American Greek race." He referred to the language of the Athapascans as "one of the most remarkable emanations of the human intellect" and commented favourably on the capabilities of its speakers, the Navajos and Apaches.[22] Hale realized that he was swimming against the tide and criticized "the 'Aryocentric' theory of linguistics and ethnology, which, during the past seventy years, has perverted and hampered those sciences."[23] Dramatically (and no doubt conscious of its shock value), he referred to "the Aryo-Semitic superstition" as an ill-founded prejudice similar to the geocentric theory that had been replaced by the Copernican Revolution.[24]

Cole points out that Hale was "harking back" to an earlier tradition of "enlightenment ethnology" influenced by francophone immigrants to America P.E. Duponceau (French) and his friend in scholarship Albert Gallatin (Swiss), which had been well established in the earlier part of the nineteenth century. In explaining differential degrees of "progress" between societies, this tradition emphasized the effects of environment and ecological adaptation rather than innate racial or biological factors.[25] However, by mid-century "anthropology ... had been taken over by the racial assumption," and Hale was attacking the orthodoxy of his day in his "issuing an affirmation of cultural relativism."[26] Cole concluded that "Hale came as close, perhaps, as any of his generation to the position of cultural relativism in anthropology."[27] Hale warned his fellow researchers that they must disabuse their minds of the "delusions of self-esteem which would persuade us that ... the particular race and language which we happen to claim as our own are the best of all races and languages."[28] In the following section, I would like to examine more fully Hale's comments on Aboriginal and specifically the Iroquoian Six Nations' cultures and societies.

Hale and *The Iroquois Book of Rites*

In 1883 Hale published *The Iroquois Book of Rites* as a contribution to D.G. Brinton's Library of Aboriginal American Literature. Along with a series of articles, this book established Hale's reputation as an Iroquoianist second only to Lewis Henry Morgan in the concluding half of the nineteenth century.[29] Hale was listed as an editor because he reduced the condoling rituals of the Iroquois Confederacy to writing with the cooperation of Six Nations' chiefs.[30] However, two-thirds of the book consists of Hale's own observations on the Six Nations.

A predominant tone of admiration begins in the Preface. Here he suggests that "the love of peace, the sentiment of human brotherhood, the strong social and domestic affections, the respect for law, and the reverence for ancestral greatness, which are apparent in this Indian record and in the historical events which illustrate it, will strike most readers as new and unexpected developments."[31] Such general and overwhelmingly positive endorsements occur several places in the text and are clearly designed to counter another more prevalent negative image of the Iroquois as warlike, cruel, and torturing savages. A further example of Hale's representation of Aboriginals against the one he is seeking to displace underscores his differences from the common perception:

> Instead of a race of rude and ferocious warriors, we find in this book a kindly and affectionate people, full of sympathy for their friends in distress, considerate to their women, tender to their children, anxious for peace, and imbued with a profound reverence for their constitution and its authors. We become conscious of the fact that the aspect in which these Indians have presented themselves to the outside world has been in large measure deceptive and factitious. The ferocity, craft and cruelty, which have been deemed their leading traits, have been merely the natural accompaniments of wars of self-preservation, and [do not] indicate their genuine character.[32]

Hale was well aware of the widespread negative reputation of the Iroquois, and he used a number of rhetorical devices to advance the point of his own narrative. One was to diminish or reduce the numbers of such cruelties. He realized that this image of the Iroquois largely came from their custom of burning prisoners and subjecting them to forms of ritual torture. He suggested that "out of the multitude of their captives, the number subjected to this torture was really very small."[33] Another rhetorical device was to point out the custom of incorporating captives into their own nations: "No other Indian community, so far as we know, has ever pursued the policy of incorporation to anything near the same extent, or carried it out with anything like the same humanity."[34] Hale suggests that the Iroquoian peoples used such practices of incorporation "even towards the most determined and the most savage of their foes" and when "finally victorious, showed themselves ever magnanimous and placable."[35]

Another rhetorical device used with relish by Hale was to condemn the condemners – that is, the white European "Aryan" commentators. The number of Iroquois victims, Hale concluded, was no match to "the number of criminals and political prisoners who, in some countries of Europe, at about the same time, were subjected to the equally cruel torments of the rack and the wheel."[36] Later on Hale enumerated "the crucifixions, the impalements, the dreadful mutilations" and many other such details used in "the most enlightened nations of Europe and Asia" and came to his ironically expressed conclusion that the Iroquois were really "far inferior to their civilized contemporaries in the temper and arts of inhumanity."[37] Hale finished with a recognition of the burning of men and women for matters of religious faith in Europe (he carefully distinguished that women were not burned at the stake by the Iroquois) and noted that "to put either men or women to death for a difference in creed had not occurred to them."[38]

This final rhetorical device hinged on the idea that Iroquoian tortures were reserved only for those who had engaged in stealthy, sneaky, and sudden attacks on their villages in the absence of the male warriors, leaving "a heap of embers smouldering over the mangled remains of [their] wi[ves] and children."[39] Indeed, Hale emphasized that a number of such attacks were undertaken by the French or their French-sponsored Aboriginal allies.[40] Seen in this perspective, Hale suggested that it was understandable that torture might be utilized as a response when applied to some (a small number) of the male warriors who perpetrated such outrages.

This is a difficult and contentious topic then as now. My aim here is not to provide a final objective representation of this controversial topic but simply to point out that Hale wished to present an overwhelmingly positive view of the Iroquoian peoples. He felt this necessary to counter the prevalent negative stereotype of the Six Nations (for example, as expressed by Stephen Leacock and discussed in the Introduction to this book).

However, Hale's reimaging of the Iroquois went much further than downplaying their use of warfare or torture. He pictured them as producing the greatest lawgivers, political thinkers, and religious idealists of history. Hale based this portrayal on his understanding of the League, or Confederacy, of the Iroquoian Nations and on his knowledge of its charismatic prophet Hiawatha. Hale was convinced that the aim of the League, as envisioned by its originator, was universal peace. As Hale put it, "We can now see that the plan of universal federation and general peace which Hiawatha devised had nothing in itself so surprising as to excite our incredulity. It was, indeed, entirely in accordance with the genius of his people. Its essence was the extension to all nations of the methods of social and civil life which prevailed in his own nation. If the people of a town of four hundred families could live in constant 'peace and friendship,' why should not all the tribes of men dwell together in the same manner?"[41]

In another passage, Hale described the various ways of the Six Nations in dealing with other peoples, "all tending to the establishment of universal peace."[42] The aim of the League, said Hale, was to extend peace to all nations by incorporating them within the League (the League was devised before contact with Europeans and thus did not anticipate non-Aboriginal nations). Although "experience ... quickly showed them that this project, admirable in idea, was impossible of execution," allowing or even encouraging new members of the League, either as full-fledged nations or as groups of individuals or bands, was nevertheless a "plan ... kept in view as one of the cardinal principles of their policy."[43] Hale's view of the League was certainly elevated and idealistic. He saw it in part as a modern-day United Nations as well as a spiritual and sacred association.

It follows from Hale's fascination with the Iroquoian Confederacy that he paid a great deal of attention to its principal founder, Hiawatha (Hayonwatha, Ayonhwahtha, or Taoungwatha in alternate Iroquoian orthography). As Hale recognized, Iroquoian storytellers had conflated this historical person to a supernaturalistic being akin to a god. Other leading figures of the origins of the League had been portrayed in comparable legends as godlike or demonic: the latter is seen in Atotarho, who was depicted as a vicious would-be tyrant assassinating his rivals and trying to confound Hiawatha.

In addition, some Euro-American scholars and popularizers had taken the figure of Hiawatha and woven their own legends about him. The ethnologist Henry Rowe Schoolcraft and the poet Henry Wadsworth Longfellow are examples cited by Hale: "and thus by an extraordinary fortune, a grave Iroquois lawgiver of the fifteenth century has become, in modern literature, an Ojibway demigod."[44] Hale went on to suggest that if a Chinese traveller from the Middle Ages had mixed up King Arthur (a semimythical figure) with King Alfred (historic) and both with Odin (a god of the Nordic pantheon), then the result would not have been more preposterous than what had happened to the memory of Hiawatha.[45]

For Hale, then, Hiawatha was a real person with a real story that he wished to reconstruct. Despite his success at demythologizing Hiawatha's life, Hale's regard for him remained undiminished. For Hale, Hiawatha remains a personage of religious significance although not supernatural. At one point, he compares Hiawatha to the Prophet Mohammed in reference to his flight from one nation to another before the League became established.[46] There is a comparison to the Protestant Reformation in Europe in Hale's comment that the League "was really a Great Reformation, not merely political, but also social and religious."[47] Hale's most eloquent statement lauds "the persistent desire for peace, pursued for centuries" and "the sentiment of universal brotherhood" among the Iroquois as seen by few other peoples "unless it may be found incorporated in the religious quietism of Buddha and his followers."[48] Further religious undertones were added by Hale in his reference to the rites of the condoling council as forming "an Iroquois Veda" (referring to the Hindu sacred writings). In terms of the Judeo-Christian tradition, Hale went so far as to regard Hiawatha as a "remarkable lawgiver ... [comparable] to Moses."[49]

While Hale's own religious awe for the League is clear, he also uses comparisons to European political institutions and their settler offshoots to enhance his admiration of the Six Nations. He praises the League by pointing out that "the regard of Englishmen for their Magna Charta and Bill of Rights, and that of Americans for their national Constitution, seem weak in comparison with the intense gratitude and reverence of the Five Nations for the 'Great Peace,' which Hiawatha and his colleagues established for them."[50] A further example of the esteem Hale accorded to various institutions of the Aboriginal peoples is gleaned from the appendix "Note F" in *The Iroquois Book of Rites*. This note also establishes two other points. The first is Hale's own style of inverting contemporaneous understandings and stereotypes. The second is his own denigration of the Aryan peoples who settled in Europe and in much of the Indian subcontinent (with the aim of deflating the high ranking attributed by biological racists to supposed Aryan genetic superiority).

His note starts with the observation that the Basque language of northern Spain and southern France is one of the few non-Aryan European languages. He then discusses scholarship, which pointed to parallels between the Basque language and Aboriginal languages in North America. These parallels are indirect, lying in the structure and form of these languages rather than in exact vocabulary. They were salient enough to suggest to Hale that the Basques may have been part of an earlier and larger Aboriginal race that was overwhelmed and incorporated by the Aryan invaders. Hale then attributes different attitudes toward government to the Aboriginal as contrasted with those of the Aryan peoples. The ancient Aboriginal Europeans, including the Basques, were (and are) "a people imbued with the strongest possible sense of personal independence, and resulting from that, a passion for political freedom."[51] The Aryans, especially in Asia, he depicts as "utterly devoid of the sentiment of political rights. The love of freedom is a feeling of which they seem incapable. To humble themselves before some superior power – deity, king or brahman – seems to be with them a natural and overpowering inclination."[52]

The upshot of this analysis is that the Aryans of Asia and those in parts of Europe where the ancient Aboriginal Europeans were few (e.g., eastern Europe) continued to exhibit their love of tyranny and lack of freedom. Where the Aryans confronted and intermixed with the local liberty-loving Aboriginal population, the resulting hybrid race exhibited the best of both political sentiments. The irony and paradox of this analysis to Hale's contemporaneous readers were that Europe's "traits of character and ... institutions which have given them their present headship of power and civilization among the peoples of the globe" sprung "not from their Aryan forefathers"[53] but from the Aboriginal Europeans who had been absorbed but who had carried into the dominant Aryan bloodlines their taste for freedom.[54]

All this may be extremely foreign to modern readers. However, it is important to realize that such an analysis was also foreign, in a different way, to the evolutionary scientific racism of the day. (See the Introduction and below in this chapter for details on biological racism.) Instead, according to Hale, Aboriginal peoples have traits of the most progressive kind, and their values, norms, and institutions show evidence of this. Hale pointed out that Aboriginal communities "have had political systems embodying some of the most valuable principles of popular government."[55] He agreed with various commentators that the Spanish in their conquests of Central and South America "destroyed a better form of society than that which they established in its place."[56] Hale's analysis concludes with the following statement: "The intellectual but servile Aryans will cease to attract the undue admiration which they have received for qualities not their own; and we shall look with a new interest on the remnant of the Indian race, as possibly representing this nobler type of man, whose inextinguishable love of freedom has evoked the idea of political rights, and has created those institutions of regulated self-government by which genuine civilization and progress are assured to the world."[57]

This must have sounded bizarre to readers of his day. Here were the Aryan populations of Europe and Asia, founding ethnicities of the vast majority of the European population, being devalued by Hale just at the time their descendants were colonizing the world and dominating the world economy. At the same time, Hale regarded various Aboriginal peoples of the world as equal or superior in abilities and character because he appreciated their greater love of liberty and democracy.

Hale's analysis was far removed from the modes of thought of his contemporaries. Hale confronted biological racism with his aim to glorify Aboriginal societies and diminish, at least in part, the glories of European civilization and specifically the Aryan bloodlines that had dominated its population.

Hale not only glorified the League of the Six Nations, venerated its founder, and pointed to its ideals in diminishing conflict and war and its quest to establish the Great Peace both within and without. Hale also underscored many other virtues of the Iroquois. One of these takes us back to Hale's mother, who is often identified in current American encyclopedias as a feminist. As noted earlier, Hale himself took measures to bring equality of access for females to high schools. His mother had fought earlier in the United States for expanded postsecondary education for women. The status of women is a major topic in *The Iroquois Book of Rites,* and reading between the lines, one can suggest that Hale thought that the Iroquois had something more to teach the sexist Aryans and their offshoots in

Europe and the Americas about "genuine civilization and progress." Hale points out the "regard" for women among the Iroquois, hotly denies the frequently made charge that Aboriginal men always treated women as beasts of burden, and claims for the Iroquois "the complete equality of the sexes in social estimation and influence."[58] He describes the status and roles of women in some detail and draws upon the early missionaries as providing the best evidence. Hale then warns Europeans and Euro-Americans that the Iroquois do not engage in "artificial expressions of courtesy" toward women, and he brands these as "merely signs of condescension and protection from the strong to the weak."[59] Instead, the status of Iroquois women is grounded in more important and substantial rights, such as rights over property, in choosing future rulers, and over children.[60]

In an earlier passage, Hale details the importance of women in the political system, "in which female suffrage had an important place," a feature that he later refers to as "this remarkable fact."[61] He suggests that female suffrage "remains in full vigor among the Canadian Iroquois to this day."[62]

Contemporaneous readers scarcely had to be reminded that in 1883 female suffrage (i.e., voting and political rights) in the colonizing nations of Canada and the United States was still the stuff of hopes and dreams for "first-wave" feminism. Hale's feminist upbringing and his subsequent positive evaluation of women's rights helped pry him loose from evolutionary-stage sequences that pointed to European or European-derived nations as inevitably being more progressive and advanced in traits and institutions than Aboriginal cultures.

This equality of women was only one more marker of the positive nature of Iroquoian culture as sketched by Hale. He expounded this topic in his chapter on "The Iroquois Character." Hale pointed out that one could hardly have expected something as admirable as Hiawatha's dream of universal federation to spring from a people lacking in intelligence. Instead, he insists that the Confederacy and its ideals were "entirely in accordance with the genius of his people."[63] Hale paints an almost utopian portrait of the Six Nations as possessing a multitude of positive traits. These included their sharing disposition, their sociability, their amiability, their good humour, their relative equality, and their peacefulness.[64] Hale's evidence here is drawn extensively from French missionary accounts from the seventeenth century, and one of these observers (characterized by Hale as fair-minded and cultivated) found in the Iroquois "virtues which might well put to blush the majority of Christians"[65] (a significant admission given its missionary author). Another noted their "perfect goodwill" and doubted "if there was another nation under heaven more commendable in this respect."[66]

Hale knew that he was still fighting the hegemonic negative image of the Iroquois, a stereotype that he credits in part to the celebrated American historian Francis Parkman. Once again he spent considerable ink suggesting that these features came about only when the Iroquois were put "on the defensive" and forced to fight "not merely for their land, but for their lives."[67] Hale felt that it was hardly fair to judge a people fighting wars of self-preservation rather than "by their ordinary demeanor in time of peace, and especially by the character of their social and domestic life."[68]

Hale and the Evolutionary-Stage Paradigm

Hale's relationship to the evolutionary-stage sequence so dominant in his day is worth examining. As discussed in the Introduction, this form of social analysis had become commonplace in the eighteenth century. The French and the Scots were early advocates of it. Such an evolutionary perspective is clearly present, for example, in Adam Smith's economic classic *The Wealth of Nations* (1776), which posits four evolutionary stages: starting with hunters, "the lowest and rudest state of society, such as we find it among the native tribes of North America"; then moving upward to shepherds, "a more advanced state of society"; then "in a yet more advanced state of society" to strictly agrarian societies with little in commerce and manufactures; and finally to a commercially oriented society, again designated as in "a more advanced state of society."[69] The typology proceeded from "low and rude" societies (hunting) and contrasted them to "the civilized nations," such as existed in modern Europe.[70] In the Introduction, Smith's contemporary William Robertson was quoted as using a similar typology in his 1777 *History of America*.[71] The most elaborated evolutionary typology was published in 1877 by Lewis Henry Morgan in his *Ancient Society, or Researches in the Lines of Human Progress from Savagery Through Barbarism to Civilization* (1877).[72]

This lengthy title may help indicate why much of the evolutionary perspective has failed to survive as a dominant paradigm in modern scholarship. Words such as "savagery" and "barbarism" were used by scientists such as Morgan as purely descriptive terms. They might point out that the ancestors of the civilized European peoples had been barbarians or savages at one point in the evolutionary cycle. In other words, scholars did not necessarily assume that a given people was fated by biology or race to stay in one of these lower stages of development. Many scholars suggested that a particular nation could evolve to a higher direction over time, just as the barbarian Anglo-Saxons had evolved into the civilized English. However, much popular usage of terms such as "savage" and "barbarism" was thoroughly negative in its connotations. In common speech, "civilization" and "civilized" were used to denote superiority. In addition, the conflation of race and intelligence complicated the belief in possible progress from one stage to another. It is true that evolutionary analysis still survives, although generally such key terms as "savagery," "barbarian," and sometimes "civilized" and "civilization" have been replaced by more descriptively neutral terms related to economic commodity and food production such as hunting and gathering, horticulture, agriculture, and industrial production.[73] Victorian notions that ideological and cultural systems can be judged along evolutionary lines as superior or inferior have been abandoned.

Because of their common interest in the Iroquoian peoples and Six Nations, Morgan and Hale became scholarly friends in the late 1860s until Morgan's death. However, Hale was uncomfortable with evolutionary-stage analysis because he was unconvinced that the economic means of subsistence of a people implied a lower ranking for their social, political, cultural, religious, and linguistic institutions on the scale of human progress (a staple of Victorian cultural evolutionism). Thus he believed that the Six Nations were more advanced in institutions of political liberty and in the equality of women than the so-called "civilized" peoples of Europe.

Cole points out the cultural relativism of many of Hale's assumptions and his fight within anthropology against "the racial assumption." Hale, as previously mentioned, consistently praised many Aboriginal languages for their complexity and sophistication. Cole suggests that "this conclusion led naturally to an attack on the developmental stage theory of evolutionary progress. Complex and inflected languages, Hale maintained in contradiction to the conventional wisdom, did not grow out of simpler agglutinative or monosyllabic forms: they existed among peoples at all levels of civilization. Similarly, every form of government and social institutions, be it patriarchy or matriarchy, endogamy or exogamy, clans or the absence of clans, could be found among primitive societies."[74] Later Cole refers again to Hale's "hostility to developmental stage theory" and to the fact that this made his framework "strikingly Boasian."[75] Of course, as Gruber has pointed out, Boas actually started out in the late 1880s doing research under the direction of Hale. Hale gave Boas much direction whether wanted or not. Hale was, in fact, a major influence on the development of Boas' thought, despite Boas' erasure of all memory of Hale after 1897 following several initial laudatory obituaries.[76]

Gruber, in addition to Cole, recognizes that Hale's "individuality lies in his rejection of a progressionist [evolutionary-stage] point of view which would substitute a natural hierarchy of cultural systems for that so often raised by those who stressed the importance and permanence of biological differences in the classification of the variety of mankind."[77] Hale's work stressed "a view of a common humanity, an essential human condition, which lay imbedded within the constantly differentiating ways of man's behavior."[78] Focusing on Hale's response to evolutionary theory, Gruber writes: "In a world, however, in which the 'rude' races were assumed to have given rise to the advanced where man was affirmed to have progressed through still apparent stages of savagery and barbarism to a highly selected civilization, and where social policies and political programs were justified on the assumption of innate differences in the cultural capabilities of different races, Hale's was, for a generation, a lonely voice without effect."[79]

Conclusion

The general conclusion of this chapter, then, is to signal the importance of Horatio Hale as one of those Euro-Canadians with serious good intentions toward Aboriginal peoples. He consistently tried to present a positive image of them at a time when a negative image was predominant. This negative image was often based on biological assumptions about innate intelligence. Or such negative images were based on the notion that specific social and political institutions of Aboriginal peoples were inferior and less advanced than those of others, thus tying in with the general assumption of evolutionary stages and their emotive designations, such as "savage" and "barbarian." Hale disagreed with both views and consistently held that intelligence was indicated by language; that Iroquoian and most Aboriginal languages were sophisticated and indicated a highly developed intelligence; that Iroquoian and many Aboriginal social, political, and religious institutions and cultural practices showed just as much or more progress as those of the so-called "Aryan" (i.e., Indo-European) nations. And finally, if Aboriginals had not developed the economic and technological features of European civilization that enabled Europeans to dominate militarily, then it was because of the environmental and geographical advantages of Europe as compared to the lack of such in the Americas.

Hale's true heritage seems to have been the influence of these ideas on Franz Boas and his American school of anthropology.[80] One wonders if Boas' failure in later years to acknowledge this influence on the development of his thought had something to do with the fact that Hale "got on Boas's nerves"[81] during the latter's spell doing research with funding from the British Association for the Advancement of Science under the research direction of Hale. Unfortunately, Hale, as the older man with a name in the field, acted a bit like Polonius in Shakespeare's *Hamlet,* tendering advice to an impatient younger man when it was unsought.[82] As a young but already experienced German academic "Doktor," Boas was not seeking advice. He regarded himself as beyond the apprentice stage and as a fully mature scholar. Some of Hale's other research protégés were amateur anthropologists who were career missionaries (Rev. E.F. Wilson, for example), and Hale's advice probably was better received in such circumstances. Of course, Boas may simply resemble any number of scholars who wish to take sole credit for their perspective without acknowledging the shoulders of the giants they actually stand on.

Going back to the Introduction, it is also clear that Hale did not have an extensive influence on his contemporaries or near contemporaries in Canada. The portrayal of Aboriginals in school textbooks as analyzed by Patricia Ofner and by Garnet McDiarmid and David Pratt (see the Introduction) was consistently negative during this entire period in a way that would have dismayed Hale. His influence on Leacock's image of Aboriginals amounted to exactly zero, although William Robertson's much earlier evolutionary tome of 1777 still resonated with Leacock in a way that Hale's 1883 study did not.

What influence Hale did have seems to have been on the missionary and amateur scholar Rev. E.F. Wilson and on a fellow missionary and scholar, Rev. Dr. John Maclean. (When Wilson turned to serious ethnological interests after 1885, Hale was his main mentor, and the two developed a sustained correspondence that led to Wilson's employment by the British Association for the Advancement of Science in the same research project on the Indians of the Canadian Northwest in which Boas had been engaged.) It is likely that Hale developed this interest in missionaries during his earlier work with the United States Exploring Expedition to the Pacific (1837-42). For Hale, missionaries had been a key available source of knowledge about Aboriginal languages and vocabularies. Boas, in contrast, had little interest in using missionaries, and they were quickly displaced by his graduate students as fieldworkers.[83] With Wilson's retirement from work with Aboriginals in 1893, with Hale's death in 1896, and with Boas' "amnesia" in reference to Hale's formative influence on him, a situation was established that tended to overshadow and erase Hale as one of the prominent Euro-Canadians with good intentions toward Aboriginal Canadians.

Acknowledgments

I would like to thank Celia Haig-Brown, J. Donald Wilson, and Michael C. Coleman for substantive comments on the draft, and Mary Nock for technical advice relating to computers.

Notes

News of William Fenton's death on 17 June 2005 came as this paper on Horatio Hale was being corrected at the proof stage. William Fenton was one of the few scholars who had devoted several projects to reviving Hale's memory. As such, we, the editors, acknowledge his importance in keeping Hale's memory alive after its neglect in much of the twentieth century.

1 See *Encyclopedia Britannica*, 11th ed., vol. 12 (New York: Cambridge University Press, 1910), 34, and *The New Encyclopedia Britannica: Micropaedia*, 15th ed., vol. 5 (Chicago: Encyclopedia Britannica, 1998). Note also that Hale's entry remains in the 2005 *Encyclopedia Britannica* online edition at http://www.britannica.com.

2 Jacob W. Gruber, "Horatio Hale and the Development of American Anthropology," *Proceedings of the American Philosophical Society* 111, 1 (1967): 5-37 at 5.

3 *The Canadian Encyclopedia* (Toronto: McClelland and Stewart, 1999).

4   The dedication reads: "To Horatio Hale, Whose Eminent Labors as a Philologist and Ethnologist Have Been Admired by the Scientific World, The Following Pages are Dedicated By Permission With Sincere Affection and Respect." See John Maclean, *The Indians of Canada: Their Manners and Customs* (London: Charles H. Kelly, 1892). On Maclean, see Sarah Carter, "The Missionaries' Indian: The Publications of John McDougall, John Maclean and Egerton Ryerson Young," *Prairie Forum* 9 (1984): 27-44.

5   On this, see Gruber, "Horatio Hale," 23-24.

6   Horatio Hale, *The Iroquois Book of Rites* (Philadelphia: D.G. Brinton, 1883; reprint, ed. William N. Fenton, Toronto: University of Toronto Press, 1963). A facsimile edition was printed in 1972 by the Coles Publishing Company, Toronto. The original edition appeared as Number II of Brinton's Library of Aboriginal American Literature.

7   William N. Fenton, "Hale, Horatio Emmons," *Dictionary of Canadian Biography, 1891-1900*, vol. 12 (Toronto: University of Toronto, 1990), 400-2 at 400.

8   See the entries on Sarah Josepha Hale, née Buell, in *The New Encyclopedia Britannica*, vol. 5 (Chicago: EB, 1998), and in *Collier's Encyclopedia*, vol. 7 (New York: Collier's, 1996), 593.

9   See entry on Horatio Hale in *A Cyclopaedia of Canadian Biography*, ed. George Maclean Rose (Toronto: Rose Publishing, 1886), 375.

10   Indeed, when cutbacks threatened Hale's place on the United States Exploring Expedition of 1837-42, Sarah Hale lobbied for the inclusion of her son. One of her key points about the young man was that he had "always sustained the reputation of extraordinary talents in all his literary pursuits." See as quoted from William Stanton, *The Great United States Exploring Expedition of 1838-1842* (Berkeley: University of California Press, 1975), 65.

11   Fenton, "Hale, Horatio Emmons," 401.

12   The classic study of the expedition is by William Stanton, *The Great United States*. There is considerable discussion in Stanton's volume of Hale's contributions and their importance; see especially pages 372-77. Horatio Hale, *Ethnology and Philology* (Philadelphia: Lea and Blanchard, 1846; reprint, ed. Fred C. Sawyer, Ridgewood, NJ: Gregg Press, 1968). See also Barry Alan Joyce, *The Shaping of American Ethnography: The Wilkes Exploring Expedition, 1838-1842* (Lincoln: University of Nebraska Press, 2001).

13   Fenton, "Introduction," in Horatio Hale, *The Iroquois Book of Rites,* ed. William N. Fenton (Toronto: University of Toronto Press, 1963), vii-xxvii at ix.

14   There are fascinating extracts from Hale's correspondence to Morgan in Gruber, "Horatio Hale." On the point at hand, see pages 11-12, in which Hale avows that "I came to Canada fourteen years ago on some business, that of looking after some land which had descended to my wife, which I supposed would only occupy a short time. A flourishing village, however, – that from which I write – had just sprung up beside the land and presently spread over it, giving me so much to do though every year proposing to return I have not yet been able to get away. Most of my books still remain in Philadelphia ... Thus I must admit that I have become somewhat rusted in philological studies, though still devoting to them some spare time here and in occasional visits to the libraries of New York and Philadelphia."

15   Fenton, "Introduction," x.

16   Ibid., xi.

17   Ibid., xii.

18   Douglas Cole, "The Origins of Canadian Anthropology, 1850-1910," *Journal of Canadian Studies* 8, 1 (1973): 33-45 at 38.

19   Ibid.

20   Ibid.

21   Ibid.

22   Ibid. for both Algonquins and Athapascans.

23   Ibid.

24   Ibid.

25   Ibid., 38, 39. On Gallatin and Duponceau and their "enlightenment ethnology," see Robert E. Bieder, "Albert Gallatin and Enlightenment Ethnology," in *Science Encounters the Indian, 1820-1880: The Early Years of American Ethnology* (Norman: University of Oklahoma Press, 1986), 16-54 at 35 especially.

26 Cole, "The Origins," 39.
27 Ibid.
28 Ibid.
29 This is suggested by the note on "Decease of Members," in the Royal Society of Canada's *Proceedings for 1897*, vii. Please also note that in Martin J. Cannon's caveat "the word 'Iroquois' is one that is seen as unfavourable to many members of the Six Nations," and that the term "Haudenosaunee" is preferred ("Not Simply Social Darwinism: Exploring the Practical and Pedagogical Utility of Social Evolutionism in Contemporary Sociological Theory," unpublished paper, 2005, n.p.).
30 Hale specified the Iroquoian and English names of these leaders in *Iroquois Book of Rites*, 39-47. They included Chief J.S. ("Smoke") Johnson, Chief George H.M. Johnson (his son), and Rev. Isaac Bearfoot, an Onondaga. A group photograph was taken of his informants examining wampum belts, and the result was distributed by Hale to several prominent ethnologists and came to be placed in the Six Nations Court House at Ohsweken. Fenton comments, "Hale tells us exactly how he worked and who helped. There was never a better set-up for Iroquois ethnology." Fenton, "Introduction," xiv.
31 Hale, "Preface," in *Iroquois Book of Rites*.
32 Hale, *Iroquois Book of Rites*, 37.
33 Ibid., 97.
34 Ibid., 96.
35 Ibid.
36 Ibid., 97.
37 Ibid.
38 Ibid., 97-98.
39 Ibid., 94.
40 Ibid., 94-95.
41 Ibid., 85.
42 Ibid., 88.
43 Ibid.
44 Ibid., 36. On Schoolcraft, see Bieder, "Henry Rowe Schoolcraft and the Ethnologist as Historian and Moralist," in *Science Encounters*, 146-93.
45 Hale, *Iroquois Book of Rites*, 36.
46 Ibid., 23.
47 Ibid., 73.
48 Ibid., 37-38.
49 Cole, "The Origins," 38.
50 Hale, *Iroquois Book of Rites*, 33-34.
51 Ibid., 189.
52 Ibid.
53 The prominence of the "Aryan superiority" theory can be detected in Italian scholars contemporary to Hale who attempted to attribute causes of regional underdevelopment in Italy's south to a deficiency of Aryan bloodlines, which could be found further north in the country. See Peter D'Agostino, "Craniums, Criminals, and the 'Cursed Race': Italian Anthropology in American Racial Thought, 1861-1924," *Comparative Studies in Society and History* 44, 2 (April 2002), 319-43. This view in turn had some influence on the United States' adoption of a restrictive immigration policy in 1924. D'Agostino, "Craniums," 339.
54 Hale, *Iroquois Book of Rites*, 189-90.
55 Ibid., 190.
56 Ibid.
57 Ibid.
58 Ibid., 64-65.
59 Ibid., 65-66.
60 Ibid., 66.
61 Ibid., 29.
62 Ibid., 30.

63 Ibid., 85.
64 Ibid., 84-85.
65 Ibid., 85.
66 Ibid., 84.
67 Ibid., 83, including the reference to Parkman.
68 Ibid., 84.
69 Adam Smith, *An Inquiry into the Nature and Causes of the Wealth of Nations* (1776; reprint, ed. Kathryn Sutherland, Oxford: Oxford University Press, 1998), 393.
70 Ibid., 393, 398.
71 On Robertson, see E. Adamson Hoebel, "William Robertson: An 18th Century Anthropologist-Historian," *American Anthropologist* 62 (1960): 648-55.
72 For a modern edition, see Lewis Henry Morgan, *Ancient Society, or Researches in the Lines of Human Progress from Savagery through Barbarism to Civilization* (1877; reprint, ed. Eleanor Burke Leacock, Cleveland: Meridian Books, 1963). On Morgan, see Bieder, "Louis Henry Morgan and the Evolution of an Iroquois Scholar," in *Science Encounters*, 194-246.
73 See Gerhard E. Lenski, *Power and Privilege* (New York: McGraw-Hill, 1966) and its related introductory textbook, Gerhard E. Lenski, *Human Societies: A Macrolevel Introduction to Sociology* (New York: McGraw-Hill, 1970). See also Stephen K. Sanderson, *Macrosociology: An Introduction to Human Societies* (New York: Harper and Row, 1988). Eleanor Burke Leacock pointed out that "due to the negative connotations of the words 'savagery' and 'barbarism,' other terms for these levels are generally employed." See her "Introduction," in Lewis Henry Morgan, *Ancient Society, or Researches in the Lines of Human Progress from Savagery through Barbarism to Civilization,* ed. Eleanor Burke Leacock (Cleveland: Meridian Books, 1963), i-xx at xi. However, in England archaeologists V. Gordon Childe (1892-1957) and Grahame Clark (1907-95) "buil[t] directly upon Morgan's work and use[d] his terminology." Leacock, "Introduction," xi.
74 Cole, "The Origins," 39.
75 Ibid.
76 For the neglect of Hale by Boas and his students after Boas' obituary of Hale in 1896, see Gruber, "Horatio Hale," 32n91.
77 Ibid., 18.
78 Ibid.
79 Ibid.
80 See ibid. for the classic statement on this topic, particularly its specific section on "Hale's Influence on Boas' Anthropology" (31-34).
81 See, for example, the letter from Boas to his wife complaining of Hale's "most saucy letters" and of Hale's "vanity, pedantry, and sensitivity" (quoted in ibid., 31). It is worth quoting Gruber's point that Hale was a "man of seventy-two, with some fair distinction in the field, addressing a Boas of thirty whose work had not yet found him a position in the establishment" (ibid., 31).
82 Ironically but not unnaturally, Boas quickly developed into the same sort of paternal figure to his graduate students that Boas rejected in Hale. Boas' first doctoral student, Alfred Kroeber, writing in 1956 (fifty-five years after receiving his doctorate), saw Boas "'as a powerful father figure, cherishing and supporting those with whom he identified in the degree that he felt they genuinely were identifying with him, but, as regards others, aloof and probably fundamentally indifferent, coldly hostile if the occasion demanded. A true patriarch, in short, with patriarchal strength and outlook.'" Quoted in Ira Jacknis, "The First Boasian: Alfred Kroeber and Franz Boas, 1898-1905," *American Anthropologist* 104, 2 (June 2002): 520-32 at 528.
83 On this issue of the influence of missionaries in nineteenth-century anthropology, see C.L. Higham, "Saviors and Scientists: North American Protestant Missionaries and the Development of Anthropology," *Pacific Historical Review* 72 (2003): 531-59. E.F. Wilson is mentioned as an example.

2
Trust Us: A Case Study in Colonial Social Relations Based on Documents Prepared by the Aborigines Protection Society, 1836-1912
Michael D. Blackstock

Britain was a leader in the nineteenth-century Industrial Revolution; its political and economic relations were expanding. Hundreds of thousands of "our best and thriftiest sons of toil" poured off the mother country's shores for Canada, the United States, New Zealand, and Australia.[1] Approximately six million people emigrated from Britain during the period 1831-71.[2] The movement of manufactures, people, and money overseas was occurring on an unprecedented scale: "The economic impulse was to find markets and outlets for the new manufacturing potential."[3] Eric Wolf, in *Europe and the People without History* (1982), characterizes the early nineteenth century as a shift away from the use of slaves in the "British orbit" toward the use of free labour "under the rising hegemony of industrial capitalism."[4]

Colonial expansion accelerated in the early nineteenth century, as did accounts of British colonists mistreating Aborigines, angering humanitarians at home and missionaries abroad. A pattern was emerging: unregulated frontier expansion was creating a "calamity" for Native peoples throughout the British Empire – the lawless frontier.[5] Consequently, on 9 February 1836 the British House of Commons ordered that a Select Committee be appointed to review the state of affairs with respect to the treatment of Aboriginal peoples by British subjects throughout the empire. The committee was instructed to propose measures that would: (1) secure to Aborigines the due observance of justice and the protection of their rights, (2) promote the spread of civilization among them, and (3) lead them to the peaceful and voluntary reception of Christianity.[6] The Select Committee published an interim report in 1836, and the final *Aborigines Report* was presented to the British House of Commons in 1837 – a defining document for the Aborigines Protection Society (APS).[7]

The purpose of this chapter is to describe and analyze humanitarian efforts by the Aborigines Protection Society to seek social justice early in the colonization of Canada. The contradictory and paternalistic position held by the society is probed to understand its endeavours to intervene in the brutal and demoralizing colonization of Aboriginal peoples.[8] A chronological discussion of the APS's work in Canada is set against a contextual backdrop, so the chapter begins with an overview of the Select Committee's investigation as described in *The Aborigines Report*. Next, there is an analysis of the colonial actors' interests, as expressed in the report, which informs succeeding sections, including a discussion on the society's advocacy role in Canada and an in-depth analysis of church and state interests. The chapter's concluding argument – trust between the colonizer and First Nations eroded in the absence of reciprocal social relations – is informed by Trudy Govier's (1997 and 1998) treatment of the concept of trust.

The thesis for this chapter is that ultimately economic motives overshadowed the well-intentioned efforts by the APS to influence colonial policy. A complex web of colonial actors' interests and social relations, most notably those of church and state, manifested as Christian and capitalist motives for the colonization process. Even the well-intentioned helping hand of the APS was fatally flawed because of its paternal and impractical imposition of humanitarianism. The members of the APS were motivated by an interest in converting the "heathen" Aboriginal to Christianity, which was promoted as a panacea in the context of the unruly frontiers of capitalist expansion.[9] In a profane sense, Christianized settlements became reserves of "Native geography" dotted on the colonial landscape.[10] A key assumption in this chapter is that the colonial actors' interests defined their social relations.[11]

Setting the Stage: "The Lawless Frontier" in Canada

The *Aborigines Report* clearly demonstrated that the negative effects of colonization on Aboriginal people were already well known by the early nineteenth century. Colonies such as those in what are now called the nations of Canada, Australia, and New Zealand had yet to receive the millions of emigrants from Britain and other European countries. Aboriginal peoples of these newly colonized lands had yet to feel the full impact of the British Empire's moves toward colonial hegemony. However, humanitarians, such as those who became members of the APS, were vigilant because a number of tragedies involving Aboriginal people had already transpired at the hands of the initial wave of British colonists. For instance, the *Aborigines Report* included the following testimony given in a letter addressed to Dandison Coates from Rev. S. Marsden regarding the *Elizabeth* outrage, which occurred in New Zealand in 1831:

> The Captain then took hold of the chief's hand in a friendly manner, and conducted him and his two daughters into the cabin; showed him the muskets, how they were arranged around the sides of the cabin. When all

was prepared for securing the chief, the cabin door was locked, and the chief was laid hold on, and his feet were tied fast; at the same time, a hook with a cord to it was struck through the skin of his throat under the side of his jaw, and the line fastened to some part of the cabin; in this state of torture he was kept for some days.[12]

The Captain of the *Elizabeth* was aiding the Maori chief Koroporo to kill the rival chief Moweeterranne, as a result of a deal he had made for "a quantity of flax."[13]

The Aborigines Report's survey of the empire "examines the actual state of our relations with uncivilized nations," concentrating on the "lawless frontiers" of the empire.[14] The report's review of relations across the world begins with Upper and Lower Canada; some brief excerpts appear here, in the order presented in the report, as examples of the perceived calamity. For instance, the report's authors surmised that the Beothuk must "have been recently very numerous" but concluded, "Under our treatment they continued rapidly to diminish; and it appears probable that the last of the tribe left at large, a man and woman, were shot by two Englishmen in 1823. Three women had been taken prisoners shortly before, and they died in captivity. In the colony of New Foundland it may therefore be stated that we have exterminated the natives."[15] A footnote in the *Aborigines Report* suggests that at least some white settlers thought it a "meritorious" or "religious" act to kill an Indian.[16]

A Chippeway chief gave evidence that "we were once very numerous, and owned all Upper Canada, and lived by hunting and fishing; but the white men, who came to trade with us taught our fathers to drink firewaters, which has made our people poor and sick, and has killed many tribes, till we have become very small."[17] A historical irony is related in the report: "some years ago the Indians practiced agriculture, and were able to bring corn to our settlements, then suffering from famine; but we, by driving them back and introducing the fur trade, have rendered them so completely a wandering people."[18] The report goes on to describe the "wretched condition" of other tribes in New Brunswick and Nova Scotia and then turns to General Darling's observations of the alarming impact of white settlement on the Algonquins and Nipissings. The general worries about how rapid settlement along the Ottawa River may force the Indians to look elsewhere for sustenance: "for, driven from their own resources, they will naturally trespass on those of other tribes ... invading the rights of his brethrens along the river in future," possibly resulting in "bloodshed and murder." The report continues, noting that the Cree population shrank from approximately 8,000 or 10,000 to 200 to 300 people in thirty to forty years.[19] A shortage of game, the injurious effects of alcohol, and the smallpox epidemic are all cited as some of the reasons for the "waste of Indian" life.[20] The only hope for the Indians of Upper Canada, the report's authors believed, was the introduction of Christianity, for, they said, where it had not been introduced, the Indians "were melting away before the advance of the white population."[21]

There is no mention in the report of the Indians in western Canada, probably because explorers such as Alexander Mackenzie had only recently – relative to eastern Canada – reached British Columbia (in 1793). The Select Committee probably did not have access to information on much of British Columbia, and Britain did not officially include this area as part of its survey of the empire in 1837.[22]

"Fair Dealings": Church, State, and Aboriginal People

After this discussion of the lawless frontier, the authors of the *Aborigines Report* reviewed accounts from the colonies about "Fair Dealings" undertaken by church and state representatives with Aborigines, as opposed to the "desolating effects of the association of unprincipled Europeans with nations in a ruder state."[23] Essentially, the committee set out to show that the introduction of Christianity to the "savage heathen" was necessary to counterbalance the injustices inflicted upon the Aborigines by nonmissionaries. An analysis of the "Fair Dealings" sections of the report is presented here in a discussion of the key actors' social relations, with a particular focus on church-state relations.[24] The actors, who were responsible for creating the interwoven pattern of connections between the colonies and Britain, include, among others, missionaries, the Colonial Office, humanitarians, settlers, traders, Aboriginal people, and the Select Committee.

Missionary societies clearly provided the bulk of evidence to the Select Committee, although the Victorian government came to suspect that this focus created a bias in the committee's perspective.[25] The committee agreed with the missionaries' view that nonmissionary Europeans were responsible for immoral conduct in the colonies.[26] The testimony of Quaker Mr. Thomas Hodgkin, MD, was relied upon heavily, and when the committee asked for his source of information, he answered as follows: "The members of the Society of Friends have corresponded with their brethren in America on this very important subject, and their documents in especial manner have been interesting to me. I have had a few opportunities to correspond with North American Indians myself."[27] The Select Committee saw the missionaries as "successful mediators between the natives and those who have injured them" and as teachers of useful trades.[28] They educated and trained new labourers. Missionaries in the colonies often wrote letters and reports to their missionary societies in Britain. The connections established between colonial missionaries and the mother country's government, through humanitarians such as Thomas Fowell Buxton, had a significant "effect on English public opinion at home."[29]

The Colonial Office, based in England, gave policy direction to the colonial governors. Peter Adams, in *Fatal Necessity* (1977), outlines two key attitudes of the Colonial Office toward New Zealand, which have implications for most of the colonies, including the Canadas.[30] First, Britain had a duty to protect subjects settled in New Zealand. Second, Britain was also beginning to recognize its duty to protect Maoris from crimes and exploitation because of the increasing humanitarian concern for the fate of Aboriginal peoples.[31] Ged Martin, in *Britain and the Origins of Canadian Confederation, 1837-67* (1995), casts a critical eye on the role of the mid-Victorian-era Colonial Office. He suggests that those imperial historians' view of the Colonial Office as a "ruthlessly long-sighted policy machine" may be an oversimplification of how British colonial policy unfolded.[32] The impression Martin leaves is that the Colonial Office was a figurehead and that real policy making occurred in more quasi-official environs. However, this was not necessarily so in relation to humanitarian issues during the decade after 1831.[33] Martin may be correct in his view of the office's influence in shaping policy relating to confederation.[34] However, it is more likely that the influence of the Colonial Office waxed and waned depending on the actors in play and the issues at hand. Certainly, the office played a role in matters relating to humanitarian issues in the colony during the 1830s.

Two well-known humanitarians ran the Colonial Office: Lord Glenelg as colonial secretary from 1835 to 1839 and James Stephen as permanent undersecretary from 1836. Public interest was indicated by the foundation of the British and Foreign APS. The report of Fowell Buxton's Select Committee on Aborigines (1837) seemed to provide a possible policy document.[35]

Humanitarian Thomas Fowell Buxton praised Lord Glenelg for his "anxiety to do justice to the Negroes, Caffres, Hottentots, and Indians."[36] Glenelg's undersecretary, Sir James Stephen, was a member of the Evangelically inclined Church Missionary Society. Woodward quotes Stephen as saying that he could feel "thankful for the many opportunities [offered to him of] mitigating the cruel wrongs inflicted [by his countrymen] on so great a portion of the human race."[37] Thus there were, at least at the leadership level, some strong humanitarian connections in the Colonial Office, which had the potential to impact imperial policy for that particular period.

Other humanitarians (most were either Evangelicals or Quakers, properly known as Friends) such as William Wilberforce, Thomas Fowell Buxton, Elizabeth Fry, and the Friends of the Suffering were active in Britain during the early nineteenth century, calling for abolition of the slave trade and then of slavery itself, prison reform, factory laws to protect child workers, and protection of the Aborigines. Thomas Fowell Buxton was a key actor in the humanitarian movement in England, a member of Parliament, and a driving force behind the report of the Aborigines Select Committee and later on in the formation of the APS.[38] He chaired the Select Committee and with four others founded the APS. The Friends of the Suffering, or the Religious Society of Friends, was one of the smaller Protestant denominations, referred to as Quakers, Friends, or Friends Church. Fowell Buxton, a former Quaker, wrote a book entitled *The African Slave Trade and its Remedy* in 1839 after completing his work as chair of the Select Committee. Elizabeth Fry, Fowell Buxton's sister-in-law, was a Quaker who believed in and worked on reforming prisons as well as influencing prisoners by means of personal instruction in Christian religion.[39] Relevant to this book, the Friends were particularly interested in the humane treatment of the North American Indian. The *Aborigines Report* makes special mention of the social-activist Quaker William Penn and his commendable efforts in America.

While missionaries were often in a position to supply information from the colonies, traders commonly made initial contact with Native peoples in Canada. The Select Committee started from the understanding that the Hudson's Bay and Northwest Companies "induced" the Indians to take bloody part in the companies' territorial quarrels, with ruinous effect.[40] The chairman of the Hudson's Bay Company, Mr. Pelly, assured the Select Committee that the rivalry had been resolved and that the company "was well disposed to promote the welfare of the Indians."[41] The committee, not comfortable with Mr. Pelly's reassurance, asked an expert witness, Mr. Richard King, if he could describe the effects of trade on North American Indians. His information appears to be based on his personal observations of the causes of the negative effects suffered by the Cree Indians. He replied to their questions as follows: "The introduction of spirits might be ascribed as one cause, and trading or bartering of vast quantities of provisions might be considered another cause, and also the introduction of a contagious disease, which has, perhaps, done more injury, next to the use of ardent spirits, than anything else; I mean that of the venereal disease."[42] King's testimony highlights a number of important effects, including the drain of winter supplies and the introduction of disease. That being said, it is important to note that experience with traders was highly varied. For example, Robin Fisher, in *Contact and Conflict* (1986), believes that some fur traders were acculturative agents who had a relatively minor impact, until smallpox epidemics, on cultures such as the Tsimshian.[43]

With few exceptions, Aboriginal people themselves provided little direct evidence to the Select Committee. There were accounts from converted Indians "embracing the gospel," such as the Chippeway's Chief Kahkewquonaby, who said: "To the question whether the Christian Chippeways have not made considerable advancement in Civilization? – The improvement the Christian Indians have made, has been the astonishment of all who knew them in their pagan state."[44] Unsuccessful attempts at "preparing them for the truths of the Gospel" were also discussed in the report. The governor general of Canada asked a chief why several attempts were unsuccessful, and the chief replied that "they could see nothing in civilized life sufficiently attractive to induce them to give up their former mode of living."[45] Aboriginal peoples throughout the colonies could be said to be at different stages of development, as defined by Bodley (1988), as they were exposed to different types of traders and to missionaries from various missionary societies. However, they all faced a consistent colonial policy designed to convert them "from heathen ignorance and immoral habits to Christian faith and practice." Significantly, the report does recognize that "the native inhabitants of any land have an incontrovertible right to their own soil: a plain and sacred right, however, which seems not to have been understood. Europeans have entered their borders uninvited."[46] Rights and title issues were still unresolved in Canada, most notably in much of British Columbia. Settlers and humanitarians diverged here in perspectives – many settlers believed that the land was there for the taking, whereas the humanitarians recognized an obligation, to be discussed in detail in a later section, to resolve Indian land claims.

The Select Committee commented that the extermination or banishment of Natives resulted in the loss of "profitable workmen, good customers, and good neighbors."[47] In other words, even at the height of humanitarianism in the nineteenth century, Britain's policy toward Aboriginal peoples was firmly based on the considerations of capitalism and access to a labour force; "virtue would be its own reward."[48] The committee also recognized a "desire to give encouragement to emigration, and to find a soil to which our surplus population may retreat." It proposed regulations "which shall apply to our own subjects and to independent tribes, to those emerging from barbarism, and to those in the rudest state of nature."[49] The committee cited a number of motives for the civilizing process: (1) ideology – there was "a moral obligation to impart [Christian] blessings we enjoy"; (2) colonial security – "savages were dangerous neighbours"; and (3) economics – savages and/or barbarians, as they were called, were "unprofitable customers, and if they remained as degraded denizens of our colonies, they become a burden upon the State."[50] Although the economic and ideological motivations of the key actors were at least partly incompatible, they did share a common goal – to expand into new markets. At the close of the report, the Select Committee asks the question "Can we suppose otherwise than that it is our office to carry civilization and humanity, peace and good government, and above all, the knowledge of the true God, to the uttermost ends of the earth?"[51] This question offers a poignant insight into a motivating humanitarian interest – to conscientiously serve God well, in fear of retribution, among those blessed by providence: "He who has made Great Britain what she is, will inquire at our

hands how we have employed the influence He has lent to us in our dealings with the untutored and defenseless savage."[52] A more detailed analysis of church-state relations and interests follows.

The Aborigines Protection Society's Advocacy Role

The Select Committee's vision of social justice and religious instruction for
Aboriginal peoples became the founding purpose of the Aborigines Protection Society; five people from the fifteen-member Select Committee formed
the society in 1837.[53]

The Aborigines Protection Society was founded "to promote the interests of native races, especially those under British control, by providing
correct information, by appealing to the Government and to Parliament
when appeal is needed, and by bringing public opinion to exert its proper
influence in advancing the cause of justice."[54]

The society's founding members acted as the watchdogs of government
rather than as mere servants of its bureaucracy: by its design, they had the
freedom and even responsibility to criticize. Some prominent members of
the Church Missionary Society were also leaders in the Aborigines Protection Society.[55] The society was active in Great Britain and throughout her
colonies. Four of the society's advocacy efforts to promote social justice
and Christianity specifically for the Aboriginal peoples of Canada are discussed below: (1) opposing Sir Francis Bond Head's removal policy, (2) assisting the Mi'qmaq on Lennox Island, (3) promoting fair treatment in British
Columbia, and (4) assisting William Duncan, missionary to Metlakahtla.

Soon after the APS's founding, it reported on the state of the Indians of
Upper Canada in 1838, with Lord Durham (governor general of the British
colonies in North America) as the primary audience.[56] The Select Committee abstained from making any suggestions regarding the regulation of the
treatment of North American Indians in the *Aborigines Report* because it
did not want to "embarrass" the government. Britain was engaged in sensitive negotiations at the time with the lieutenant governor of Upper Canada.[57] However, the House of Commons' sensitivities did not restrain the
APS's authors of the *Report of the Indians of Upper Canada* (hereafter, *Upper
Canada Report*).

They recognized that Lord Durham was toiling with the turbulent task
of "softening the asperities of opposing factions at Canada," but they also
wanted him to rescue North American Aborigines from annihilation and
to elevate them into the civilized world.[58] The scope of the report included
an assessment of the condition of Indians in the Canadas, New Brunswick,
Nova Scotia, Cape Breton, Newfoundland, Prince Edward Island, Anticosti,
Labrador, and the territories of the Hudson's Bay and Northwest Companies.[59] The report's philosophical and ethical foundation is based "on
the laws of nature and nations; upon the injunctions of Christianity and

upon treaties; and those rights are especially to be collected from *two* documents of high authority, which contain clear declarations of the duty of the Government respecting them."[60] The first document is an instruction issued by the Colonial Office of His Majesty Charles II in 1670. Colonial governors were instructed to "receive" any Indians who ask for the protection of the Crown against adversaries who offer violence to them or their possessions. A closing instruction to the governors was to invite the Indians, no matter how remote within the territory, to share in the knowledge of God and the mysteries of salvation.

His Majesty George III's Royal Proclamation of 1763 is the second document cited, one that offers guidance on the protection of the rights of Indians in colonies such as Upper Canada. The APS placed special emphasis on the sections of the proclamation that cautioned governors not to grant warrants of survey or to pass any patents for lands beyond their scope of authority. Lands that had not been ceded or purchased by the Crown were therefore reserved for the Indians and lay outside the governor's authority. The society also noted the proclamation's guidance on fraudulent purchases of Indian land.[61]

The society asserted that "neither the Home Government, nor the Colonial authorities have enacted upon the injunctions of those two documents of 1670, and 1763, which are unquestionably binding to this day; and the extent to which those injunctions have been neglected, fully accounts to us for the ruin of the Indians."[62] These documents also inform contemporary legal arguments in Canadian courts over Aboriginal rights and title. Numerous appeals by agents of the Crown and church on behalf of the Indians are cited in the report, such as Brant and Kerr's mission to London on behalf of the Six Nations.[63] The *Upper Canada Report* is an appeal to the home government, delivered in London on 3 April 1838, to call for "the immediate cessation of proceedings for the purpose of alienating from the Indians the whole or any part of their reservations in cases of removal stipulated in Sir Francis Bond Head's treaties."[64]

Opposing Sir Francis Bond Head's Removal Policy

A case in point, arguably of competing good intentions, was the society's critique of Sir Francis Bond Head's policy (while he was lieutenant governor of Upper Canada) to banish the Indians to "23,000 rocks of granite, dignified with the name of Manitoulin Islands."[65] The society, on the other hand, advocated the preservation of Indian reserves, which would be recognized as distinct countries or townships and form integral parts of the province, noting that "on such spots, the Indians might be perpetuated in Canada," like the Welsh in Great Britain or the Basques in Spain and France.[66] The society's authors used Sir Francis Bond Head's own words, recognizing the injustice to Indians and noting their good-hearted nature, to argue against "that very policy which Sir Francis has laboured to advocate, and which it is a principal object of this memorial [report] to oppose and counteract."[67] They quoted a letter from Sir Francis Bond Head to Lord Glenelg:

> The fate of the red inhabitants of America, the real proprietors of the soil, is without any exception the most sinful story recorded in the history of the human race, and when once reflected upon, the anguish they have suffered from our hand, and the cruelty and injustice they have endured, the mind accustomed to its own vices, is lost in the utter astonishment at finding that in the red man's heart there exists no sentiment of animosity against us – no feeling of revenge. On the contrary, that our appearance at the humble portal of his wigwam is to this hour a subject of unusual joy.[68]

Sir Francis Bond Head predicted that the Indians would "wither, droop, and vanish before us, like the grass of the forest in flames."[69] The Quakers' Society of Friends interpreted his policy to be similar to the United States approach of inducing the Indians to abandon "almost for nothing, their richest and most valuable tracts of land" in exchange for lands that are "incapable of supporting them for any long time."[70] Sir Francis Bond Head did advocate removing the Indians from their lands to Manitoulin Island "to please the white settlers ... who complain that the Indians have all the best land."[71] Not to distract from this colonial motivation, there does seem to be a measure of good intention in his misguided action – he indicated that he feared the Indian race would otherwise become extinct. Decades later, the Royal Commission on Aboriginal Peoples' (1990s) reflection on Sir Francis Bond Head's policy acknowledges the competing intentions of his directive: "He proposed to relocate Indians to Manitoulin Island, where they could be protected in a traditional lifestyle until their inevitable disappearance as separate peoples. To this end he persuaded some bands to surrender their Aboriginal title to large areas of reserved lands in southern Ontario in exchange for lands on Manitoulin Island. Church groups working to convert and civilize Indians at that time were angered by his approach, since it ran counter to the liberal and philanthropic ideas then coming into vogue in Great Britain and the colonies."[72]

The APS and, to a lesser extent, Sir Francis Bond Head thought that the Indian race was at risk of extinction; they differed on how to enact their "good intentions" while not losing sight of their desires to protect and civilize the Indian. A few months after the *Aborigines Report* was presented, the Society of Friends began lobbying against Bond Head's policy; their members in the Friends of Canada were reporting on the Indian removals, and two members of the Society of Friends in Britain met with the secretary of state for the Colonial Department.[73] As an alternative to the removal policy, the APS advocated the protection of Indian lands and promoted conversion to Christianity as, ultimately, the best protection for the non-Christian Indians. Here lie the subtleties of colonization: although different interests manifested different means, they still moved inevitably toward achieving colonization. For instance, the society took affront at Sir Francis Bond Head's observation that Christianity "has more than decimated its followers!"[74] The society, to further its case for Christianity, responded by comparing the number of Indian deaths in a particular tribe during the four years prior to embracing Christianity (forty-seven deaths) to the number of deaths since embracing Christianity (three deaths). The society dedicated a good deal of the report's text to exhibiting the advancement of Indians due to Christianity; they provided witnesses' testimony, such as the English writer Mrs. Jameson's observations of a Chippeway family, to support their assertion that Indians wished, and had the capacity, to be "civilized."[75]

Authors of the *Upper Canada Report* also suggested that the colonists of the day were divided in opinion. The APS referred to a Toronto newspaper, *The Palladium,* that called Sir Francis Bond Head's removal treaty "perfidious trickery."[76] By 1839 Upper Canada supported the policy of protection advocated by the APS and passed legislation expressly declaring Indian reserves to be Crown lands and therefore off-limits to settlers.[77] The APS's appeal to Lord Durham and the Society of Friends' lobbying of the Colonial Office had significant impact on the move away from Sir Francis Bond Head's removal policy.

Lennox Island

A second example of the APS interventions for good is the purchase of Lennox Island. Fourteen hundred acres in size, it is located at the head of Richmond Bay, on the north side of Prince Edward Island. It was purchased on 2 June 1870 for the sum of £400, in trust, for the Mi'qmaq (Mic-Mac) people residing on the island by the Aborigines Protection Society.[78] Theophilus Stewart, barrister-at-law, who represented the property owners Robert Bruce Stewart and Helen Stewart, approached the society.[79] The purpose of holding Lennox Island as a "special reserve" was for the "use and benefit of the Mic-Mac Indians who then inhabited the said Island" and subject to "such regulations and restrictions and upon such terms and conditions as shall be from time to time declared by any Minute to be passed at any meeting of the said Trustees."[80] As George Dawson, in *Sketches of the Past and Present Condition of Indians in Canada* (1877), points out, this reserve was unique because in all other provinces the Crown held the reserves.[81] The deputy superintendent general of Indian Affairs, L. Van-Koughnet, visited Lennox Island during August of 1877 and left with the following impression: "These Indians present a creditable appearance, and are very intelligent. Some of them have a good house, with fields of grain, potatoes and gardens surrounding them ... There is a substantially built school-house neatly painted; also a neat frame chapel and mission house on the Island. The school teacher is a Mic-Mac."[82] His hope was that the poorer members of the band would build suitable houses, using government assistance, and abandon their "wigwam." A permanent homestead, he felt, would "induce domesticity."[83] At the request of the Department of Indian Affairs, the APS finally transferred Lennox Island, on 30 May 1912, to His Majesty the King in trust "for the purpose of a Reserve within the meaning of the *Indian Act*."[84] Only three of the original eleven trustees of the society were alive at the time; as these remaining trustees were aged, they wished to discharge their responsibilities.[85] Purchasing Lennox Island was clearly a benevolent gesture, although the society showed limited interest, during the forty-year trusteeship, in the Mi'qmaq's affairs.[86] Their influence was perhaps restricted in any case after Britain transferred the administration of Indian affairs to Canada in the 1860s.

Promoting Fair Treatment in British Columbia

Another of the APS's major humanitarian efforts in Canada was an appeal to the secretary of state for the colonies, Henry LaBouchere, for "the preservation of the natural rights of the Indians when the license of trade of the Hudson's Bay Company and the Charter of Vancouver Island come before Her Majesty's Government for renewal; and, lastly, for the establishment of schools for their mental instruction and industrial training, and the appointment of teachers and ministers of religion."[87] The society feared that the miners flocking to the gold rush would treat the Indians harshly.[88] In 1858 Sir E.B. Lytton, the succeeding secretary of state for the colonies, asked the governor of Vancouver Island, Sir James Douglas, to consider the "best and most humane means of dealing with the Native Indians" because the APS was pressuring Her Majesty's government.[89]

George Dawson mocked the society's proposal to employ "in the various departments of government a large proportion of well selected men more or less of Indian blood (many of whom could be found in Red River)! Who might not only exert a greater moral influence over their race than we could." He commented that the "Red River in actual distance and in manners is as remote from Victoria as is St. Petersberg from London."[90] The society's advocacy in this instance was heard, but their well-intentioned solution of hiring Red River Indians as civil servants in British Columbia was imprudent.

Metlakahtla

On 5 March 1886 the Church of England missionary William Duncan, while in London, wrote a letter to the secretary of the APS asking for the society's assistance in "vindicating" Tsimshian people's rights to land.[91]

Duncan's immediate concern was over the Church Missionary Society's (CMS) "overbearing effrontery." They threatened his control, as the CMS was claiming ownership, apparently with Sir John A. Macdonald's sanction, to two acres known as Mission Point at the village of Metlakahtla along the northwest coast of British Columbia. The APS, in a letter of response dated 25 March 1886, committed to meeting with Sir Charles Tupper, high commissioner of Canada, to "discuss the Indian difficulty in British Columbia."[92] The society followed through, but Duncan became frustrated with its lack of impact on the government: "It has been eight months since these assurances were received, and, these hopes indulged, but I regret to say the Indians are now complaining even more bitterly."[93] Duncan's missionary enterprise was considered, from a Victorian perspective, to be "one of the most remarkable of all": he taught the Tsimshian to "talk on paper" and "hear paper talk."[94] However, one twentieth-century perspective is that "Duncan was quite consciously trying to replace the Indian past with a future based on precepts of Victorian England."[95]

The Civilizing Process and the Church-State Alliance

Privileged Quaker men dominated the APS.[96] The Quakers' emigrant infrastructure throughout the colonies assisted the APS in monitoring the treatment of Aborigines and tactfully pressuring the British Government. Quakers emigrated to the United States in the seventeenth century to escape religious persecution; they eventually established a large settlement centred in Philadelphia. (See also Chapter 6.) The Society of Friends, and later the APS, concentrated much of their efforts on the humane treatment of North American Indians.

The missionary societies, the Quakers, and the APS acted as pressure groups and as government watchdogs, as illustrated in the aforementioned advocacy case studies.[97] They also acted as mediators between settlers and Aboriginal peoples. It was expensive for the British Government to protect the settlers from the Aborigines and the Aborigines from the settlers. Thomas Briggs, a nineteenth-century British economist, commented that "we are taxing ourselves to the tune of millions for their [the colonies] protection."[98] The *Aborigines Report* describes a strategy used by the governors of Canada, who "seem to have been brought to the conviction that religious instruction and the influence of the missionaries would be the most likely means of improving their condition, and, eventually, of relieving the Government from the expense of the Indian department."[99] Clearly, a primary ideological motive for colonial expansion in the Victorian era was religious, but economic motives were codominant and eventually dominant.[100] There was even an economic undertone to the Aborigines Protection Society's agenda; they promoted free labour over slave labour and denounced monopolies.[101] Generally, however, the state and church structured, to their mutual benefit, a social relation that served government economics and passed much responsibility for Indian affairs to the churches.

An implicit effect of *The Aborigines Report,* and the ensuing efforts of the APS, may have been to reaffirm and strengthen the social relations between the British Colonial Office, colonial governments, and the missionary societies with respect to administering Aboriginal affairs in the colonies. In a series of lectures at Oxford University between 1837 and 1842, Herman Merivale, permanent undersecretary of the Colonial Office, described such a policy toward Aborigines: "And, lastly, there should be no hesitation in acting on the broad principle that the natives must, for their own protection, be placed in a situation of acknowledged inferiority, and consequently of tutelage ... There we may entrust them to the good offices of the missionary, and the 'protector.'"[102] In other words, Merivale felt that the Natives should best be left in God's hands as the empire got on with its "important" business.

Simply put, while the state and the church both had an interest in civilizing the Aborigines, they chose different means to achieve the same end. The state embraced farming, capitalism, and force as its means, while the church saw Christianity as the gentler way. For example, Rev. William Ellis' testimony, in *The Aborigines Report,* clearly linked the civilized man to Christianity: "No man can become a Christian, in the true sense of the term, however savage he may have been before, without becoming a civilized man. Christianity produces civilization of the best and most durable kind."[103] Humanitarians and missionaries were pressuring the government to legislate standards that protected Aborigines' rights and established a process to educate and civilize the degraded Natives. For example, Standish Motte, Esq., a representative of the APS, proposed a system of legislation in 1840 "for securing protection of the aboriginal inhabitants of all countries colonized by Great Britain; extending to them political and social rights, ameliorating their condition, and promoting their civilization."[104] Their legislation included measures that addressed the "protection" of political and civil rights and "instruction and amelioration." The proposed legislation included an allotment system for establishing and expanding reserves, training Aborigines as a constabulary force, apprenticeship programs, the administration of a justice system, the establishment of labour schools to teach agriculture and ship building along with religious instruction, and the establishment of medical agents.

The government chose not to implement the system of legislation proposed by the APS. Instead, the British government chose a more politically favourable strategy that was intended to appease the APS and other agents of the humanitarian movement by adopting a policy that formally recognized and empowered missionaries as the "protectors" of Aborigines. This policy satisfied a number of the British government's interests and maintained some important social relations. First, this policy did not impede the progress of development and capitalist expansion that was of prime interest to colonial governments, imperial capitalists, traders, and new labourers. Second, it dealt with the APS's negative criticism of the government by empowering the missionaries and therefore improving the relation between the church and the state. Third, it enabled the missionaries to act as mediators, pacifying the Aborigines and at the same time protecting them from settlers and traders. Fourth, the missionaries could train the Aborigines as labourers for the capitalist modes of production, such as agriculture. And finally, adopting the missionary protection policy would help restore Great Britain's honour as a great and just nation. Its reputation had been tarnished by the accounts of immorality and murder described in *The Aborigines Report*. This scenario seems plausible because the interests of the state and church were met and because social relations important to production were maintained.

Slow Change: A Twentieth-Century Perspective

Trudy Govier, a Canadian philosopher, defines trust as "an attitude of positive expectation about other people, a sense that they are basically well intentioned and unlikely to harm us."[105] It is typically based on past experiences, beliefs, and feelings, which imply expectations and dispositions.[106] Trust can also be defined as "the trustor's expectation of being the recipient of the trustee's continuing goodwill."[107] Pragmatically, trust is necessary in social relations because "in most cases we do not – and in some cases we could not – spell out everything a trusted person is supposed to do and not to do."[108] Govier cautions that trust is open-ended in character; keeping commitments is an important kind of trust but not the only one.

The level of trust between parties varies depending on the context and their past experiences with each other. Levels of trust can be determined through heuristics: for instance, if a party followed through with commitments in the past, they are likely to in the future. The APS, acting as protector of the Indians, could be said to analyze this aspect of trust in the *Upper Canada Report*. Again, they juxtaposed Sir Francis Bond Head's benevolent assessment of Indians' verbal commitments alongside his contradictory actions. He is quoted to say, "An Indian's word when it is formally pledged, is one of the strongest moral securities on earth."[109] Yet the APS interprets his intention of removing the Indians from their treaty reservations, which was described as some of the richest land in Canada, as incongruent with his aforementioned benevolence. Additionally, he recommended the discontinuance of payments due by treaty because the Indians were warring against the United States. The society also believed that "modern writers of the laws of nations seem inclined to exclude them [Indians] from its [the treaty of Utrecht] benefits."[110] The original promises to the Indians in Canada, which were outlined in the documents of 1670 (i.e., His Majesty Charles II's instruction) and 1763 (i.e., His Majesty George III's Royal Proclamation), were not kept, according to the society. As time passed after 1837, there was an accumulation of broken promises and cases of mistreatment.

The APS added another layer of complexity to a history of mistrust because their attitude was "trust us; we have your best interests in mind." They clearly recognized the broken promises of the colonial governments and the mistreatment of Indians on the frontier, but their solution, to promote civilization through Christianity or by specific misguided means, such as the Red River civil-servant idea, which George Dawson mocked, was no less harmful to the trust relationship. Govier gives insight, below, to the effects of such a history on social relations.[111]

Many feelings and attitudes, including the attitude of trust and distrust, characterize whole groups or nations of people and affect their relations with each other. When groups or nations distrust each other, they tend to interpret each other's actions, words, and policies in a negative way – just as individuals do when they distrust each other. They are fearful and suspicious, ready to take offence, and hesitant or unwilling to cooperate.[112]

The fundamental problem for the official mind and Aboriginal peoples has been in defining social relations; Standish Motte of the APS proposed that they be "reciprocal and lasting."[113] A reciprocal relationship is defined here as *a mutual relationship with a two-way exchange of ideas and information that is founded on a desire to build and maintain trust in order to facilitate the fair negotiation of interests.* The classic and repeated "mistake" of the official mind has been to develop policy for First Nations without First Nations.

The APS failed to fully heed the internal advice from Standish Motte. The society, however, did capture invaluable snapshots of colonization and raise just concerns over Aboriginal mistreatment, although their approach to resolving the injustice eventually furthered the colonization effect. Zygmunt Bauman, in *Modernity and the Holocaust* (1991), cautions modern society against "the self-healing of historical memory" because as a passive undertaking it is a neglect that is offensive to the victims of genocide and dangerous to the society at large.[114] The *Aborigines Report* and the *Upper Canada Report* provide an opportunity for modern Canada to refresh its collective memory, which in turn establishes a benchmark with which to evaluate the progress of social justice in the twentieth century.

Missionaries and the APS asserted their power of divine providence, derived from their knowledge of and connection to God – it was a power to "protect."[115] Keith Thomas, in *Religion and the Decline of Magic: Studies in Popular Beliefs in Sixteenth and Seventeenth-Century England* (1991), analyzed how the medieval church succeeded in converting pagans as a means of turning them away from magic and how the Protestant interpretation of divine providence provided roots for conversion in sixteenth- and seventeenth-century England: "Conversions to the new religion, whether in the time of the primitive Church or under the auspices of the missionaries of more recent times, have frequently been assisted by the view of converts that they are acquiring not just a means of other-worldly salvation, but a new and more powerful magic."[116] When missionaries and the APS arrived in Canada, they brought a tested conversion approach.

History is littered with unilateral attempts by the official mind to form social relations with Aboriginal peoples. Two common themes have persisted in these social relations since their original expression in the *Aborigines Report* and the *Upper Canada Report*. First, the state's baseline assumption is that capitalist expansion will continue regardless of its effects on Aboriginal peoples. The *Aborigines Report* was largely ignored, as economic expansionist motivations overshadowed the humanitarian ideology.[117] Will a similar fate bestow the Royal Commission on Aboriginal Peoples' (RCAP) *Final Report*? With this lesson in hand, RCAP commissioners might reflect critically on their public justification of the "low" financial costs that they proposed to establish social justice in Canada, which seemed overwhelmingly high in the public's eye.[118] Second, the white iconoclastic consensus was that civilizing and assimilating Indians was the best means of imposing social relations. Using its secular and religious power, the official mind, sometimes with good intentions, unilaterally defines its role as "protector" of Aboriginal peoples. The official mind prescribed social relations primarily based on its own interests, some of which included securing settlement land for emigrants, reducing the cost of Indian affairs, creating a labour force for agriculture and new consumers for capitalism, and converting the heathens to Christianity. The conjugate effect of these themes has been the erosion of trust between contemporary First Nations and the official mind. Cole Harris, in *Making Native Space* (2002), provides a poignant observation: "For all its fervour, the humanitarian discourse confronted the contradictions inherent in colonialism and was longer on good intentions than on practical solutions."[119] Good intentions too often were a means of rationalizing or tempering colonial powers' interests behind the veil of humanitarianism while failing to empower Aboriginal people in their struggle with the official mind for social justice.[120]

Notes

1 Thomas Briggs, *Paper on the Relations of the Colonies to the Mother Country, Considered from an Agricultural, Economical and Commercial Point of View* (Adelphi: National Association for the Promotion of Social Science, 1869), 4; Denis Judd, *The Victorian Empire: A Pictorial History* (London: Wiedenfield and Nicholson, 1970), 22; Standish Motte, Esq., *System of Legislation, for Securing Protection to the Aboriginal Inhabitants of All Countries Colonized by*

Great Britain (London: John Murray, 1840), 2. The Royal Commission on Aboriginal Peoples gave a population estimate: "Lower Canada, with its long-established reserve land policy, was not drastically affected by in-migration. It was different in Upper Canada, however, where reserves were fewer and population pressures proportionately greater. It is estimated that by 1812 the non-Aboriginal population of that colony outnumbered the Aboriginal population by as much as 10 to 1, with the ratio increasing further in the ensuing decades." Royal Commission on Aboriginal Peoples, *Final Report,* vol. 1 (Minister of Supply and Services Canada, 1996), Ch. 6, Sec. 1.

2   Judd, *The Victorian Empire,* 9.

3   Ronald Hyam, *Britain's Imperial Century, 1815-1914: A Study of Empire and Expansion* (Lanham: Barnes and Noble Books, 1993), 21, 86.

4   Eric R. Wolf, *Europe and the People without History* (Berkeley and Los Angeles: University of California Press, 1982), 316. Eric Wolf's political-economy approach provides an analytical framework. Wolf views history as "a manifold of social and cultural purposes at work in their own time and place" (5). Wolf warns against representations of nations, societies, or cultures as internally homogenous and externally distinctive. Forces characterized by the mode of production, or as Wolf says, "the key relationships through which social labour is brought to bear upon nature" (9), guide the social alignments of groups within a society. The capitalist mode of production was predominant in the early nineteenth century.

5   John H. Bodley, *Tribal Peoples and Development Issues: A Global Overview* (Mountain View: Mayfield, 1988), 63.

6   Select Committee, *Report from the Select Committee on the Aborigines (British Settlements), Together with the Evidence, Appendix and Index* (Cape Town: C. Struik, 1836; facsimile reprint, 1966), ii. "Aborigines" was a term used in the nineteenth century to describe indigenous or Aboriginal peoples.

7   Meetings for the Sufferings, *Information Respecting the Aborigines in the British Colonies, Being Principally Extracts from the Report Presented to the House of Commons, by the Select Committee Principally Appointed on That Subject* (London: Darton and Harvey, 1838). The author could not locate the original 1837 report; however, the version, cited above, was a reprint. To avoid confusion, the shortened note for this citation will be: *The Aborigines Report,* as reprinted by the Meetings for the Sufferings (1838).

8   Reader 2 for UBC Press' anonymous initial review of this chapter is credited with inspiring this clarifying purpose statement.

9   Cole Harris, *Making Native Space: Colonialism, Resistance and Reserves in British Columbia* (Vancouver: UBC Press, 2002).

10   Harris briefly discusses the concept of the "missionary solution" in *Making Native Space,* 7, which I interpret as the missionary's idea of protecting Indians, by placing them on Indian reserves, from the heathenous actions of the advancing colonizers. Harris seems to describe a cause-and-effect geography whereby as the colonial geography expands, the Native one shrinks (ibid., xv-xviii). Michael Blackstock, however, describes a coexistence of sacred and profane landscapes, where the profane landscape is a colonial one overlaid upon the original First Nations landscape. The two are not mutually exclusive. Michael D. Blackstock, *Faces in the Forest: First Nations Art Created on Living Trees* (Montreal and Kingston: McGill-Queen's University Press, 2001), 149-54.

11   Wolf, *Europe and the People,* 385-86.

12   Anon., 1836, quoted in *The Aborigines Report,* as reprinted by the Meetings for the Sufferings (1838), 483. Dandison Coates was the secretary for the New Zealand Church Missionary Society.

13   Ibid.

14   *The Aborigines Report,* as reprinted by the Meetings for the Sufferings (1838), 2. This chapter focuses on Canada. However, *The Aborigines Report* surveys the state of affairs in the entire empire, including those affecting New Foundland, North American Indians, South America, Caribs, New Holland, Van Diemen's Land, and Islands in the Pacific, and provides an extensive review of South Africa. For a review of the state of affairs in Australia and New Zealand, see Michael D. Blackstock, "The Aborigines Report (1837): A Case Study in

the Slow Change of Colonial Social Relations," *The Canadian Journal of Native Studies* 20, 1 (2000): 67-94.

15 *The Aborigines Report,* as reprinted by the Meetings for the Sufferings (1838), 4.

16 Ibid., 3.

17 Ibid., 4.

18 Ibid.

19 Ibid., 4-6.

20 Ibid.

21 Ibid., 5.

22 Judd, *The Victorian Empire,* 10.

23 *The Aborigines Report,* as reprinted by the Meetings for the Sufferings (1838), 33.

24 After the "Fair Dealings" section, *The Aborigines Report* examines responses of the secretaries of the missionary societies (i.e., the Church Missionary Society, the Wesleyan Missionary Society, and the London Missionary Society), makes suggestions for future regulation, and finally offers special comments regarding the limited discussion of North America in the report.

25 Hyam, *Britain's Imperial Century,* 86.

26 *The Aborigines Report,* as reprinted by the Meetings for the Sufferings (1838), 55-56.

27 Ibid., 454.

28 Ibid., 45.

29 Sir Llewellyn Woodward, *The Age of Reform, 1815-1870* (London: Oxford University Press, 1962), 369.

30 Peter Adams, *Fatal Necessity: British Intervention in New Zealand, 1830-1847* (Auckland: University of Auckland Press, 1977), 13.

31 Ibid.

32 Ged Martin, *Britain and the Origins of Canadian Confederation, 1837-67* (Vancouver: UBC Press, 1995), 117.

33 Martin quotes Stephen as saying of Colonial Office policies: "they are as good as Parliament will sanction, and the Colonists will accept." *Britain and the Origins,* 120. They were not the ends of a colonial masterplan.

34 Martin, *Britain and the Origins,* 120. As an aside, this dichotomy of interpretation illustrates Wolf's warning to avoid viewing entities, such as the Colonial Office, as homogenous in nature through time.

35 Hyam, *Britain's Imperial Century,* 83.

36 Adams, *Fatal Necessity,* 131.

37 Woodward, *The Age of Reform,* 369.

38 Adams, *Fatal Necessity,* 92.

39 Woodward, *The Age of Reform,* 468.

40 *The Aborigines Report,* as reprinted by the Meetings for the Sufferings (1838), 6.

41 Ibid.

42 Ibid., 640.

43 Robin Fisher, *Contact and Conflict: Indian-European Relations in British Columbia, 1774-1890* (Vancouver: UBC Press, 1986), 42, 146.

44 *The Aborigines Report,* as reprinted by the Meetings for the Sufferings (1838), 36.

45 Ibid., 34.

46 Ibid., 3.

47 Ibid., 57.

48 Hyam, *Britain's Imperial Century,* 83.

49 *The Aborigines Report,* as reprinted by the Meetings for the Sufferings (1838), 57.

50 Ibid., 33.

51 Ibid., 58.

52 Ibid.

53 The Aborigines Protection Society published tracts, pamphlets, and the journal the *Colonial Intelligencer, or Aborigines' Friend.*

54 William Nicolle Oats, *A Question of Survival: Quakers in Australia in the Nineteenth Century* (New York: University of Queensland Press, 1985), 11.

55   Harris, *Making Native Space,* 9.
56   Aborigines Protection Society, *Report of the Indians of Upper Canada* (London: William Ball, Arnold, and Company, 1838).
57   Ibid., 60.
58   Ibid., 27.
59   A few paragraphs at the beginning of the report are dedicated to the story of Natives in Lower Canada.
60   Ibid., 2, emphasis added.
61   Ibid., 3.
62   Ibid., 4.
63   Ibid., 5.
64   Ibid., 27.
65   Ibid., 26. The United States' Indian policy was similar to that advocated by Sir Francis Bond Head: "removal of entire tribes to more isolated locations west of the Mississippi River where they could pursue their own cultures and develop their own political institutions according to their aspirations and capacities." Royal Commission on Aboriginal Peoples, *Final Report,* vol. 1, Ch. 9, Sec. 6.
66   Aborigines Protection Society, *Report of the Indians of Upper Canada,* 28.
67   Ibid., 24.
68   Ibid.
69   Ibid., 35.
70   *The Aborigines Report,* as reprinted by the Meetings for the Sufferings (1838), ix.
71   Ibid.
72   Royal Commission on Aboriginal Peoples, *Final Report,* vol. 1, Ch. 9, Secs. 3-6.
73   *The Aborigines Report,* as reprinted by the Meetings for the Sufferings (1838), viii.
74   Aborigines Protection Society, *Report of the Indians of Upper Canada,* 34.
75   Ibid., 42-47.
76   Ibid., 47.
77   Royal Commission on Aboriginal Peoples, *Final Report,* vol. 1, Ch. 9, Secs. 3-6.
78   The author would like to thank Celia Haig-Brown for her assistance in researching the Lennox Island case.
79   Nancy McMahon, *Description of Negative No. PA-024868 (Native Family on Prince Edward Island),* Industry Canada, Government Archives Division, Digital Collections, http://collections.ic.gc.ca/portraits/index.htm.
80   Aborigines Protection Society, *Indenture Application, May 30th, 1912,* Indian Affairs, RG 10, vol. 1907, file 2307, 4.
81   George M. Dawson, *Sketches of the Past and Present Condition of Indians in Canada* (Canadian Institute for Historical Microreproductions [CIHM] 02365, 1877), 9.
82   L. VanKoughnet, *Report of the Deputy Superintendent General Indian Affairs,* Sessional Papers No. 10, Victoria 41, A, 1878, 13.
83   Ibid.
84   J.D. Mclean, Letter: J.D. Mclean (Asst. Deputy and Secretary, Dept. of Indian Affairs) to the Trustees of the Aborigines Protection Society, 2 January 1911, Indian Affairs, RG 10, vol. 1907, file 2307.
85   Gil Gaudet, Letter: Gil Gaudet to Secretary Department of Indian Affairs, Ottawa, 30 May 1912 (Gaudet and Hazard, Charlotte Town, Prince Edward Island).
86   McMahon, *Description of Negative No. PA-024868 (Native Family on Prince Edward Island),* Industry Canada, Government Archives Division, Digital Collections, http://collections.ic.gc.ca/portraits/index.htm.
87   Aborigines Protection Society, *Canada West and the Hudson's Bay Company: A Political and Humane Question of Vital Importance to the Honor of Great Britain, to the Prosperity of Canada, and to the Existence of the Native Tribes* (London: William Tweedie, 1856), 7.
88   Dawson, *Sketches of the Past,* 25.
89   *Papers Connected with the Indian Land Question, 1850-1875* (Victoria: Richard Wolfenden, 1875), 12.
90   Dawson, *Sketches of the Past,* 25.

91   Henry S. Wellcome, *The Story of Metlakahtla* (London: Saxon, 1887), 302.
92   Ibid., 303.
93   Ibid., 304.
94   Ibid., 135.
95   Fisher, *Contact and Conflict,* 133.
96   See the occupations cited for the society's trustees in the Lennox Island indenture (1912).
97   Adams, *Fatal Necessity,* 90.
98   Briggs, *Paper on the Relations,* 6.
99   *The Aborigines Report,* as reprinted by the Meetings for the Sufferings (1838), 35.
100 Hyam, *Britain's Imperial Century,* 90.
101 Harris, *Making Native Space,* 9.
102 Herman Merivale, "Policy of Colonial Governments towards Native Tribes, as Regards Their Protection and Their Civilization" (1861), reprinted in *Tribal Peoples and Development Issues: A Global Overview,* ed. John H. Bodley (Mountain View: Mayfield Publishing, 1988), 95-104 at 103-4.
103 *The Aborigines Report,* as reprinted by the Meetings for the Sufferings (1838), 540.
104 Motte, *System of Legislation,* 1.
105 Trudy Govier, *Dilemmas of Trust* (Montreal and Kingston: McGill-Queen's University Press, 1998), 3.
106 Trudy Govier, *Social Trust and Human Communities* (Montreal and Kingston: McGill-Queen's University Press, 1997), 4-6.
107 Daryl Koehn, "Should We Trust in Trust?" *American Business Law Journal* 34, 2 (Winter 1996): 183-204 at 183-84. Satish Kumar tells a story relating to trust while on his peace march from Delhi to America. He was about to cross the border between India and Pakistan, which were at war. As Satish Kumar had grown up in rural India, the people in the border town were concerned for his safety and offered him parcels of food. They urged him to carry some food in case he was not offered anything to eat in Pakistan. This is his reply: "We said that taking food with us would mean that we distrusted the Pakistani people. 'These parcels of food are parcels of mistrust. You are very kind, but we cannot take food with us.'" Satish was greeted with hospitality in Pakistan. Satish Kumar, *Path without Destination: The Long Walk of a Gentle Hero* (New York: Eagle Brook, 1999), 74.
108 Govier, *Social Trust,* 13.
109 Aborigines Protection Society, *Report of the Indians of Upper Canada,* 25.
110 Ibid., 4.
111 Michael Blackstock introduces a dispute resolution model that recognizes the importance of repairing trust. Michael D. Blackstock, "Where Is the Trust?: Using Trust Based Mediation for First Nations Dispute Resolution," *Conflict Resolution Quarterly* 19, 1 (2001): 9-30.
112 Govier, *Social Trust,* 200-1.
113 Motte, *System of Legislation,* 6.
114 Zygmunt Bauman, *Modernity and the Holocaust* (New York: Cornell University Press, 1991), x.
115 Harris, *Making Native Space,* 118, provides a good discussion on the "consummate assertion" by George Hills, the Anglican bishop of British Columbia in 1860, of the power and knowledge to understand and predict divine providence.
116 Keith Thomas, *Religion and the Decline of Magic: Studies in Popular Beliefs in Sixteenth and Seventeenth-Century England* (Toronto: Penguin Books, 1991), 27.
117 Hyam, *Britain's Imperial Century,* 85. However, the Aborigines Protection Society's lobbying of the Colonial Office did have some impact, prior to the decline of the humanitarian period, as exampled here in regards to Sir Francis Bond Head's removal policy.
118 "Accordingly, we recommend strongly that governments increase their annual spending, so that five years after the start of the strategy, spending is $1.5 and $2 billion higher than it is today, and that this level be sustained for some 15 years." "People to People, Nation to Nation: Highlights from the Report of the Royal Commission on Aboriginal Peoples," Minister of Supply and Services Canada, 140.
119 Harris, *Making Native Space,* 10.
120 Thank you to UBC Press' two anonymous readers for inspiring this closing sentence.

3

A Mi'kmaq Missionary among the Mohawks: Silas T. Rand and His Attitudes toward Race and "Progress"

Thomas S. Abler

Silas T. Rand (1810-89) spent more than forty years attempting to convert the Mi'kmaq of Canada's maritime provinces to his brand of Protestantism. He was notably unsuccessful as a missionary, having baptized just one convert in those four decades of mission activity. At the same time, his fascination with their language and attempt to master it led him to translate and bring to publication several books of the Bible. It was this fascination with the Mi'kmaq's language and their oral literature that led him to document in text and print these areas of their culture as it existed in the nineteenth century. The posthumous publication of his volume *Legends of the Micmacs* has assured him a permanent and important position in any bibliography dealing with the Mi'kmaq or the Algonquian speakers of northeastern North America.[1] His life has attracted biographies focusing either on the role of his faith in his performance as a missionary or on his intellectual contribution as an amateur anthropologist, linguist, and folklorist. Most do discuss at least in passing both aspects of his multifarious life and personality.[2]

While some attention will be paid to Rand's career both as missionary and as amateur scholar, the focus of this chapter is on Rand's attitudes toward the capabilities and prospects of the Native peoples of North America. Rand had some remarkable views: he expressed support in the mid-nineteenth century for racial tolerance and even called for language that today would be termed "politically correct." As will be seen, Rand's attitudes are complex, for while he was convinced of the intellectual capabilities of the Mi'kmaq population with whom he dealt, he also despaired at their mobile adaptation as peddlers,[3] which did not fit with his concepts of an advanced or "civilized" style of living. Rand in his heart felt that skin colour was irrelevant to basic humanity. Intellectually, he maintained that the qualities of Mi'kmaq language and mythology proved that the Mi'kmaq were the equals of any non-Indian resident of the Maritimes. However, Rand did share with most other nineteenth-century North Americans a view of human social progress that placed Native North Americans in "the hunter state," a social category in their eyes inferior to that of agricultural-ists. He shared with other nineteenth-century reformers of Indian policy in North America a belief in a "progressive cultural evolutionary theory [which] held that the Red race would advance in time" and that "progress" would be marked by complete assimilation within Euro-North American culture.[4] This aspect of Rand's attitudes toward Native Peoples is revealed in the joy he expressed in finding on visits to Upper Canada that there, on the Six Nations Reserve and elsewhere, persons of Native ancestry had been able to make the economic achievements he saw as necessary to demon-strate their equality with their neighbours of European ancestry.

Rand was a largely self-educated Baptist minister, having been ordained in 1834.[5] In the 1840s he was posted in Charlottetown, Prince Edward Island. His self-education had fostered within him an interest in languages and had revealed his talent for learning them. While he was contemplat-ing applying for a mission post in Burma, personal interest and curiosity led him to take up the study of the language of the Mi'kmaq. In 1846 two lucky coincidences led to his acquisition of an understanding of the Mi'kmaq language. He discovered in 1830 issues of the colony's *Register* and its successor, the *Royal Gazette,* extracts of a Mi'kmaq grammar pub-lished by Thomas Irwin.[6] Having found this grammar, Rand then encoun-tered a man who called himself Jo Brooks in the Charlottetown market. Brooks, who was of French ancestry, was married to a Mi'kmaq and spoke Mi'kmaq, English, and French. At this time and place there was considera-ble conflict and hostility between Protestants and Catholics, and since Jo Brooks was anti-Roman Catholic, he was willing to provide linguistic data to Rand, a Protestant clergyman. He also provided the initial contacts be-tween Rand and those Mi'kmaq who were willing to transmit examples of their oral literature to him. With the help of these tutors, Rand's aptitude for language allowed him to make rapid progress in mastering Mi'kmaq.

Rand's Christian zeal was enormous, and he longed to fill a missionary post. Rand had considered replacing the Reverend R.E. Burpee as repre-sentative of the Baptist Board of Missions in Burma, but his wife refused to agree to their moving to Asia. Isaac Chipman, a geologist on the faculty of Acadia College, a Baptist institution in Wolfville, Nova Scotia, suggested to Rand that he fulfill his missionary ambitions and use his language skills to "look after the heathen at home."[7] Rand decided to initiate a mission to the Mi'kmaq but without direct funding from the Baptist Church. Instead, support was obtained from Anglican officers of *HMS Gulnare,* a Royal Navy survey vessel mapping the coast, and from a variety of Protestant congre-gations. A nondenominational (but Protestant) Micmac Missionary Socie-ty was formed to support Rand in his task of Bible translation and mission work among the Mi'kmaq. The Micmac Missionary Society enjoyed considerable local support in Halifax, even though the entire Mi'kmaq population had been Christian for perhaps more than a century. They were, of course, misguided Christians in Protestant eyes, being under the thumb of the Roman Catholic Church.[8]

Rand brought to his mission the conviction, unusual for his day and still unfortunately not universal, that skin colour was irrelevant to intellectual ability and that persons of all races deserved to be treated equally. He expressed "shame that I am a white man" in a Halifax-published Baptist newspaper "since our colored brethren have been so unjustly and unmercifully treated by us, because, forsooth, like ourselves, they have the audacity to wear the skin which the great Creator gave them!"[9] On another occasion, when aboard a ship, he successfully argued that a clergyman of African ancestry should dine with the other passengers rather than being forced to take his meal separately.[10]

Rand was also convinced of the equality of Indians. He wrote that "they have, as a general rule, intellects of a superior kind" and "that they are as capable of improvement in their social condition as any other race."[11] Rand's conviction about the equality of the Mi'kmaq to those of European ancestry was reinforced by his study of the Mi'kmaq language and, concurrent to this study, by his collection of Mi'kmaq oral traditions and myths. Rand repeatedly waxed enthusiastically about the glories of Mi'kmaq, his "favorite language," which he felt was "one of the most marvelous of all languages, ancient or modern." He praised *"real living Micmac,* so comprehensive, so expressive, so musical, so sweet."[12] He was also impressed by the beauties of Mi'kmaq stories. His linguistic and folkloric studies probably reinforced his already-held convictions of the intellectual capacity of Native Maritimers. Indeed, he argued that myth and folklore revealed "the intellectual powers of this wonderful people."[13] He argued that the legends he recorded provided proof of the Mi'kmaq "mental caliber" and asked, "Are people possessed of such mental powers to be despised?"[14]

Rand attempted to communicate to non-Indian Nova Scotians his conviction of the common humanity of Mi'kmaq and other Maritimers. He lectured a Halifax audience that they should not talk of encountering "squaws" and "papooses" in local markets but instead should recognize that they were dealing with "women" and "babies."[15] He countered the misconception that the Mi'kmaq were a "dying race" by pointing out that their numbers were actually increasing. He also called for a recognition of Aboriginal title to lands in Nova Scotia and argued that Mi'kmaq should be compensated for lands lost. As early as 1847, he observed that the Mi'kmaq were forced to obtain permission to camp "on the very land which, by every principle of justice and religion, is their own."[16] Especially notable was the aid that Rand provided for the writing of a Mi'kmaq petition on land rights, which was sent to Queen Victoria in 1853.[17] Hence the

Mi'kmaq were not, in Rand's view, simply another wilderness species that must inevitably make way for the progressive advance of civilization.

Historian L.F.S. Upton has observed that "there was in every generation a handful of whites who undertook to champion the Indian cause as they saw it," and Rand was one of the handful from his generation. Ralston has judged Rand to be "among the few ... who expressed respect for the dignity and culture of the Micmac people, and their voices were drowned out by the cries of the majority who firmly and unshakeably believed that white culture was better."[18]

The views and good intentions of Rand contrasted with those of many of his contemporaries. Sadly, the prevailing racist viewpoint was expressed in the Preface to the posthumously published portion of Rand's Mi'kmaq dictionary by the volume's editor, Jeremiah S. Clark: "Someone has said that the most difficult problem now facing civilizations is the proper treatment of the lower races. Let us assume, as we all do, without argument, that our forefathers were superior to the races they found in America a few hundred years ago, and that acknowledgment forces us, if we be true men, to obey the stentorian command of Kipling when he orders us to take up the White Man's Burden."[19]

In the nineteenth century the Mi'kmaq were seen by many non-Aboriginal people as a degraded and dying race whose way of life reflected a past no longer of relevance to Nova Scotia and its neighbours. It was felt that their language and culture were doomed to extinction, and many believed that the Mi'kmaq themselves were biologically inferior to Europeans and hence would physically share the same fate. In an address to the Nova Scotia Institute of Science, J. Bernard Gilpin spoke of "their old worn-out life and language, now sadly disjointed from the present times" and proclaimed that "the fewness of children amongst them too surely proves a doomed race."[20]

Rand himself observed what he described as "the prejudices of *Caste* among the white people." The president of Acadia College (the Baptist institution in Wolfville, Nova Scotia) refused to allow him to work with a Mi'kmaq collaborator in a room at the college while Rand was engaged in Bible translation. The president "concluded ... that such an unheard-of transaction would operate to the prejudice of the Institution upon whose prosperity his heart was set."[21]

Elsewhere, Rand commented on relations between the Mi'kmaq and their neighbours. He noted that while Mi'kmaq "prejudices against the whites were great" when he began his mission work, these prejudices "were reciprocated with compound interest."[22]

Upton has done much to document the attitudes of settlers toward the Mi'kmaq. He quotes one who described Indians as a "useless, idle, filthy race" that "never can be cured of the wandering habit." The solution was for the Indians to leave Nova Scotia. Upton summarizes the view of Charlottetown's Thomas Irwin about the attitudes he observed: "Whites regarded the very existence of the Indian as a reproach, and seemed to desire his extinction." Upton notes that another observer concluded that "the Indians had descended from powerful lords to beggarly chiefs" and that "they were cursed with lack of foresight and aversion to work, living in seclusion, inoffensive, 'without arts, science, and laws – without the temples of religion.'"[23]

Rand's unusual tolerance in matters of race did not extend to tolerance for religion. He was as biased as any other Protestant of his time against Roman Catholicism. He reported that the Mi'kmaq he encountered were "filled with a multiplicity of erroneous fancies and dogmas, by the Missionaries of the Church of Rome." He was horrified by "the superstition which gives a fulcrum for the use of priestly terrors." He decried "what they call worshipping God" in which "the Pater Nosters and Hail Marys were repeated again and again, as rapidly as they could all go over them."[24] At the chapel on Indian Island, near St. Peter's, Cape Breton, he observed "the prostrations, the kissing the floor, and the toe of the image of Ste. Anne [patron saint of the Mi'kmaq], and the offering of a halfpenny."[25] Rand complained that the Mi'kmaq Catholic book of prayer, written in a system of "hieroglyphs" devised by Abbé Mailard in the eighteenth century, "states things that are false in fact, and ruinous in tendency."[26]

Rand reported that Catholic priests responded to his mission activity by warning Mi'kmaq not to interact with him, even suggesting that he was the devil. He recalls that upon seeing him, children would run, exclaiming in Mi'kmaq that the devil was coming. On occasion he was met by "a woman ... in the doorway brandishing her axe, or holding back the growling dogs, and threatening to let them loose upon me if I dared come any nearer."[27] In Halifax, Rand's mission was characterized in the Catholic press as "The Micmac-Mission Humbug,"[28] and a letter was published alleging that "he is called by some the Rev. Mr. Ranny, by others he is styled Mr. Granny, and he himself strives to fasten on himself the dignity of Mic Mac Missionary."[29]

As liberal and modern as some of Rand's views appear, he still reflected his time in his patronizing view of his Mi'kmaq neighbours. He was never able to accept their embrace of Catholicism as a meaningful and important religious element in their lives.[30] He almost invariably uses the adjective "poor" when discussing the Aboriginal population of the Maritimes – "the poor Indian" seems almost to be a single lexeme in Rand's vocabulary. To Rand, the Mi'kmaq were poor in several respects – they were impoverished economically and also politically. Rand was very conscious of their ill-treatment in their own homeland. But Rand also was unable and unwilling to accept the mobile existence of the Mi'kmaq he encountered in his own frequent and extensive travels through the Maritimes. Part of being the "poor Indian" was that one led a nomadic existence sleeping in temporary shelters rather than living in a substantial and permanent house tied to a productive farm. In the nineteenth century the Mi'kmaq were pursuing an economic adaptation in many ways parallel to that of the Gypsies and other peripatetic minorities in the Old World. Among other things, the bark tepee, or "wigwam" as Rand and the Mi'kmaq themselves referred to it, served as a dwelling to a mobile population that devoted considerable energy travelling to market to sell goods and services to the sedentary, non-Indian population. Gypsies and other peripatetic minorities have engaged in such an adaptation in the Old World for centuries, and the Mi'kmaq tradition of mobility and skills in woodworking predisposed them to play a similar role in the maritime provinces given the destruction of their hunting and gathering economic base. In the Old World, however, Gypsies also have for centuries endured the prejudices of the same sedentist populations that buy their wares and use their services.[31] Like Romany and other Old World peripatetic nomads, the Mi'kmaq found their mobile existence attacked by their sedentary neighbours. Rand shared with his non-Indian neighbours the view that the house was superior to the wigwam and that year-round residence in a single locale was preferable to the freedom to travel the length and breadth of what were to become Canada's Maritime provinces. This was the case despite the considerable mobility Rand himself exhibited during his forty years as a missionary.

As part of their peripatetic adaptation, the Mi'kmaq engaged in a large variety of occupational or economic pursuits. There is a tendency to emphasize those that had an "Aboriginal" or "traditional" base such as the manufacture and sale of basketry or quillwork,[32] but making barrels or axe-handles and other such recently learned activities were important in bringing non-Indian cash into Mi'kmaq hands. Gonzales has pointed to Mi'kmaq activities in such areas as the porpoise fishery, lumbering, and fishing.[33] She summarizes: "Micmac economic activities for this period were multiple and complex. They were a combination of traditional subsistence activities, government subsidized work projects ... wage labor and activities which combined indigenous knowledge and skills with market demands ... These activities were periodically supplemented by begging and government rations. Not every Micmac performed all these activities ... Yet, no Micmac family was committed solely to one economic endeavor."[34] The Mi'kmaq were selling a wide variety of goods and services to their non-Indian neighbours. They were nomadic both to obtain and exploit resources necessary for the goods they manufactured and to market effectively their labour and its products.

Rand faced an intellectual dilemma with respect to his view of Native people. His intellectual conviction in their equality with the rest of humanity clashed with his bias against their nomadic existence. This no-madic existence continued despite three centuries of contact with Europe-ans and despite a program (admittedly flawed and plagued by the tendency of whites, particularly Scots, to squat on Indian lands) of reserving lands for Mi'kmaq use, ideally as farms.[35]

Rand and the Micmac Missionary Society made one valiant attempt to sedentize the mobile Indians of the Maritimes. A scheme was set up to market in Halifax the products of Mi'kmaq labour. This freed those pro-ducing them from the necessity of going house to house to sell their pro-duction. Rand had moved from Charlottetown to Hantsport, Nova Scotia, in November 1853. The Micmac Missionary Society purchased a tract of land, which was dubbed "Mt. Micmac," near Rand's new home. A dozen Mi'kmaq families settled there for the winter of 1854-55 and produced wares for sale in Halifax, suggesting the potential for success of the plan. However, the Micmac Missionary Society was unable to sell through its agents a sufficient volume to meet the expenses of the experiment. It was not tried again, and the dozen families dispersed, returning to their no-madic adaptation.[36]

Rand, then, found his liberal racial ideology at loggerheads with his per-ception of the "poor Indian" in Nova Scotia. While convinced of the Mi'kmaq's intellectual powers, his ethnocentric values led to his percep-tion of their nomadic adaptation as indicative of "uncivilized" behaviour. He desperately wanted evidence to demonstrate the potential of Indians to achieve a style of life that, in his eyes and those of his neighbours, would prove their equality with Maritimers of European descent. Their ability to attain a sedentary residence pattern coupled with formal educa-tion was a key in his evaluation. Unfortunately, from Rand's perspective, the Mi'kmaq of the mid-nineteenth century were unable or unwilling to adopt such an existence.

Rand did find an Indian population that conformed to his expectations of "progress." His delight in finding this was considerable. This Indian population was the Iroquois, principally the Mohawk, in Upper Canada, although Rand was also pleased to observe the style of life on Ojibwa re-serves in the southern portion of Upper Canada.

Rand made his first trip to Canada in the autumn of 1858. In those pre-Confederation times, Nova Scotia, New Brunswick, and Prince Edward Is-land, all of which Rand had traversed continuously, were separate colonies. On this journey Rand was accompanied by his first Mi'kmaq convert, Ben Christmas. The purpose of their trip was threefold: they hoped to raise money to support the Micmac Mission, planned to observe the Protestant missionary efforts among the French Canadians of Lower Canada, and intended to observe mission work among the Indians of the Canadas. It was with considerable pleasure that he reported to the Micmac Missionary

Society upon his return: "There are those in Nova Scotia who affect to think that an Indian cannot be induced to live in a house. And it *does* require some effort and perseverance to enable them to change from the wigwam, and get accustomed to a house. But we saw plenty of Indian houses in Canada, and we did not see a single wigwam. We only heard of *one,* and that was located near the Niagara Falls, connected with a museum, to be seen as a curiosity in connection with two living buffaloes, and the cooking stove Blondin is said to have carried over the river on his shoulder, upon the 'slack rope.'"[37]

Among the communities that Rand visited was "Caughnawaga" (Kahnawake – Rand noted that the name of the community was "pronounced Cog-nay-wah-gay") outside Montreal, and there he found the Mohawk residing in 300 houses. He reported that "some of them are substantial stone buildings." Only the dress of females enabled Rand to distinguish the Kahnawake Mohawks from their francophone neighbours. He found "some very intelligent fellows of the tribe." He was impressed that some engaged in agriculture, that the Mohawks had a school, and that "an Indian pilot generally guides the steamers down the Lachine rapids." Some Kahnawake residents were fluent in three languages. Although like the Mi'kmaq they were Catholic, Rand found the Kahnawake population "very far in advance, to all appearance, of the Micmacs."[38]

In Upper Canada, Rand spent some time at the Ojibwa reserve of Alnwick near Rice Lake but regretted being unable to visit the Mohawk reserve of Tyendinaga since the Indian superintendent in Toronto, William Bartlett, considered the members of the Mohawk community "still in advance of those at Alnwick." Even so, Rand was impressed and pleased by what he observed at Alnwick: "Indian farming, the test of civilization, had come up before us in the ratio of *good* [presumably Kahnawake], *better* [the Ojibwa reserve of Mud Lake, which he had also visited], *best* [Alnwick]. The fields were here large, well laid out, and – what pleased us much, giving the settlement quite an *un*-Indian look – well fenced. Some of them, we were told, grew this year as much as two hundred bushels of wheat. Some of our Cornwallis and Annapolis farmers would be pleased to count so many."[39]

It was not just the farms that impressed Rand in Upper Canada. In the school at Alnwick, Rand encountered "a novel and affecting sight, and what we sincerely hope and pray may yet be seen in Nova Scotia – to see a class of Indian boys and girls stand up to be examined in their Reading, Spelling, Geography, Arithmetic, &c." The "head of the class" was a fourteen-year-old boy who was part Mohawk, of whom Rand observed: "Never was humanity moulded into finer form and features. I could not but think of the lofty and dignified bearing of 'Osceola' the 'Seminole Chief,' or some of those 'Thunderers of the Forest,' painted by Catlin, as he drew himself up to a posture more than erect, his head up, his dark flashing eye looking as though it would pierce the teacher thro' and thro,' as he stood there with a smile playing over his face, ready to catch the question and give the answer, the moment it was uttered."[40]

Other discoveries on this journey to Canada pleased Rand. At the office of the Indian superintendent in Toronto, he found that the head clerk was an Odahwah (Rand's spelling) who had been to college and who had published on Odahwah in the *Canadian Journal*.[41] Rand's pleasure in finding an Indian "capable of being a clerk in a government office" led him to wonder "that we should not see the same thing some day in Halifax?"[42]

He also found aspects of the laws of Canada to his liking. He approved of the Canadian law preventing the sale of alcohol to Indians. He also approved of the law preventing the extension of credit to Indians. One might consider such views to have been generated by paternalistic racism, but then Rand also suggested that both laws be extended to cover the entire population.[43]

In Nova Scotia Rand had been active in supporting Mi'kmaq claims to land. He had aided the Mi'kmaq in preparation of an 1853 petition to Queen Victoria. It is certain that Rand provided the transcription of the version of the petition written in Mi'kmaq, and he is credited with helping with the English text. Upton has described this particular petition, one of a series directed to colonial officials, as "the most ambitious petition of them all"; it outlined past wrongs and complained of discrimination based on skin colour that was "somewhat different" from that of the colonists.[44] As was the case with earlier petitions, this one had no impact. Thus Rand saw hope for the Mi'kmaq cause when he found on his trip that "the claims of the Indians to their own lands have very properly been allowed in Canada, as they should be here [in Nova Scotia] and in all places."[45]

Rand did not again visit an Iroquois community until 1876. In the meantime, Ben Christmas parted company with Rand and the Micmac Mission, and Rand himself withdrew from the Baptist Church to join the Plymouth Brethren. Because the Micmac Missionary Society had a broad Protestant base, Rand continued his work of translation and proselytizing. The British and Foreign Bible Society published a large portion of his Mi'kmaq Biblical translations; these included Matthew, Luke, John, Acts, Genesis, Exodus, and Psalms. After two decades of mission activities among the Mi'kmaq, Rand noticed some change in Mi'kmaq activities. Writing of the Mi'kmaq in 1873, Rand noted that "many of them still retain their roving habits; but a wonderful improvement has taken place in this respect within the last ten years."[46] He refers to the fact that an increasing, yet still small, portion of the Mi'kmaq population had acquired permanent housing.

Agrarian achievement continued to be the measure of "progress toward civilization" of Rand and many of his contemporaries, and on the Six Nations Reserve on the Grand River, Rand found impressive evidence of what he considered the potential for agricultural achievement among Native North Americans when he visited that community in 1876. He reports "several thousands" residing in Tuscarora township, which "belongs to the Indians."[47] Tuscarora township includes most of the Six Nations Reserve. The band list numbered 2,975 in 1875.[48] Rand seems to have spent most of his time interacting with the prosperous Christians on the reserve, but he observed that although "there are a few excellent Christians, and many professors, and many Pagans, it was freely admitted by the former that the latter are the best people taken as a whole."[49] Nonetheless, the economic success of Rand's Mohawk hosts made a great impression on the visiting missionary.

Iroquois settlement on the Six Nations Reserve divided along religious and national lines. "Down below," residing to the south down the Grand River, were the Cayuga, Seneca, and Onondaga, many of whom adhered to the traditional religion. The "upper tribes" – Mohawk, Tuscarora, and Oneida – were upriver and constituted "the more acculturated Christian element of the community."[50] Weaver has noted that Indian Agent Jasper T. Gilkison had encouraged agriculture and that on the reserve "the Upper Tribes" were particularly active.[51] The Six Nations Agricultural Society was founded in 1868 by two chiefs, William Smith and Joseph Powless, "both prominent Mohawk farmers."[52] The Six Nations Council, at Gilkison's urging, supported agricultural activities with a $200 annual grant to the Agricultural Society and through donations of prizes for both the ploughing match and the Fall Fair.[53] Rand's fellow Nova Scotian, Joseph Howe, the superintendent general of Indian Affairs in the federal government, attended the Agricultural Society's Fall Fair in 1870. By 1875 there were nearly one hundred members in the Agricultural Society.[54] Rand visited the reserve at a time when agricultural activity was vital and growing. The agricultural census reveals that both the number of farms and the acreage used as farmland increased steadily from 1851 to a peak in 1891.[55] It was with the successful farmers of the Six Nations that Rand took up residence in order to explore the Mohawk language but also to admire the scope of agricultural advancement on the reserve:

> Some of them are farmers on a scale that exceeds anything I ever saw any where – with one exception. "Mine Host" is a Mohawk, who employs at this season about a half-a-dozen men – owns three spans of horses, has just threshed out his barley, a monstrous pile, about 200 barrels, and his winter wheat ... and I don't know how many acres of summer wheat yet to ripen, & oats &c. His threshing machine has been making music for several days in succession, driven by *ten* horses – and today his brother has gone off with it to aid the neighbours. Another man (an Indian) at whose house I make my home at Onondaga, has already cut about 15 acres of

wheat and as much barley, a large field of oats has also succumbed, and 20 acres of Indian corn are waving their green leaves to the breeze. He owns *five* horses – one – a stallion – valued at 500 dollars.[56]

Rand had observed that his contemporaries held the opinion "that the Indian 'like the partridge' cannot be tamed, cannot be kept from 'running back into the woods' – cannot be induced to live in a house." On the Iroquois and Ojibwa reserves of Quebec and southern Ontario, he found ample evidence to refute such racist judgments. To Rand, it was a thrilling experience: "To us to contrast between what those Indians had been, and what ours are still in Nova Scotia, and what they now are, was wonderful."[57] Rand may have shared with his neighbours an ethnocentric view that denigrated a nomadic, hunter-gatherer existence (and an equally nomadic peddler existence), but he did not share with his neighbours the racist view that such was the only adaptation that Indians were capable of achieving. His faith in the intellectual potential of Indians, which to Rand required the adoption of an agrarian pattern of life, was, in his eyes, proven by the achievements of the Mohawk farmers of nineteenth-century Ontario and Quebec.

Rand, like many others with good intentions, possessed fundamental faith in the inherent abilities of the indigenous peoples of North America. His knowledge of Mi'kmaq language and oral traditions initially provided him with sufficient evidence to confirm this faith. This led to his active stance supporting Mi'kmaq land claims and his vocal campaign advocating better treatment of the Mi'kmaq by his fellow Maritimers. However, he shared with his racist contemporaries a disparaging view of the peripatetic economic adaptive strategy adopted by the nineteenth-century Mi'kmaq. Their unwillingness to adopt a sedentary existence troubled Rand, for it provided his racist opponents with what they saw as evidence of Mi'kmaq inferiority, evidence that Rand felt he was unable to counter. His observations of Native communities, especially those of the Mohawks and other Iroquois, in Ontario and Quebec allowed Rand, despite his bias against a nomadic lifestyle, to continue his advocacy of the fundamental equality of races. Ultimately, however, Rand's good intentions in advocating Mi'kmaq rights and racial equality were doomed, and he would not see a Mi'kmaq population achieving what he and many of his contemporaries saw as desirable, an idealized agrarian existence. Too powerful were the social and economic forces both within maritime society and within the Mi'kmaq community itself that reinforced the continuing Mi'kmaq exploitation of the peripatetic niche.

Acknowledgments

A version of this chapter was presented to the Conference on Iroquois Research in Rensselaerville, New York. Research on the Micmac Mission has been supported by the Social Sciences and Humanities Research Council of Canada (Grants 410-87-0244 and 410-89-1075). I have received excellent assistance from librarians and archivists, particularly at the library of Acadia University, the Public Archives of Nova Scotia, and the library of Wellesley College. As I moved from a focus in Iroquois studies to an examination of the nineteenth-century Mi'kmaq, I benefited greatly from conversations with three established students of Mi'kmaq society and culture: Harold McGee, Virginia Miller, and Ruth Holmes Whitehead.

Notes

1 Silas T. Rand, *Legends of the Micmacs,* ed. Helen L. Webster (New York: Longmans, Green, 1894). "Mi'kmaq" is the current spelling for the First Nation known in Rand's time as "Micmac." In this chapter, I use the current spelling, except in direct quotations and in the names of institutions or places where the older spelling was or is still used.

2 The most lengthy biographical treatment of Rand is Dorothy May Lovesey, *To Be a Pilgrim: A Biography of Silas Tertius Rand, 1810-1889: Nineteenth Century Protestant Missionary to the Micmac* (Hantsport, NS: Lancelot Press, 1992). Other works that deal with Rand's life and contributions include: Jeremiah S. Clark, *Rand and the Micmacs* (Charlottetown, PEI: Examiner, 1889); M.V. Marshall, "Silas Tertius Rand and His Micmac Dictionary," *Nova Scotia Historical Quarterly* 5 (1975): 391-410; Virginia P. Miller, "Silas T. Rand: Nineteenth Century Anthropologist among the Micmac," *Anthropologica* 22 (1980): 235-49; Allison Mitcham, *Three Remarkable Maritimers* (Hantsport, NS: Lancelot Press, 1985), 66-97; Judith Fingard, "Rand, Silas Tertius," *Dictionary of Canadian Biography,* vol. 11 (Toronto: University of Toronto Press, 1988), 722-23; Thomas S. Abler, "Protestant Missionaries and Native Culture: Parallel Careers of Asher Wright and Silas T. Rand," *American Indian Quarterly* 16 (1992): 25-37; and Thomas S. Abler, "Glooscap Encounters Silas T. Rand: A Baptist Missionary on the Folkloric Fringe," in *Earth, Water, Air and Fire: Studies in Canadian Ethnohistory,* ed. David T. McNab (Waterloo: Wilfrid Laurier University Press, 1998), 127-41.

3 On the nineteenth-century economic adaptation of the Mi'kmaq, see Ellice B. Gonzales, "Changing Economic Roles for Micmac Men and Women: An Ethnohistorical Analysis," National Museum of Man, Mercury Series, Canadian Ethnology Service, Paper 72 (1981); Thomas S. Abler, "Micmacs and Gypsies: Occupation of the Peripatetic Niche," in *Papers of the Twenty-First Algonquian Conference,* ed. William Cowan (Ottawa: Carleton University, 1989), 1-11; Nicholas N. Smith, "The Economics of the Wabanaki Basket Industry," in *Actes du Vingtième Congrès des Algonquinistes,* ed. William Cowan (Ottawa: Carleton University, 1989), 306-16; Janet E. Chute, "Mi'kmaq Fishing in the Maritimes: A Historical Overview," in *Earth, Water, Air and Fire: Studies in Canadian Ethnohistory,* ed. David T. McNab (Waterloo: Wilfrid Laurier University Press, 1998), 95-113; Theresa Redmond, "'We Cannot Work Without Food': Nova Scotia Indian Policy and Mi'kmaq Agriculture, 1783-1867," in *Earth, Water, Air and Fire: Studies in Canadian Ethnohistory,* ed. David T. McNab (Waterloo: Wilfrid Laurier University Press 1998), 115-25.

4 On the pervasiveness of the belief in the "hunter state," see Anthony F.C. Wallace, *The Long, Bitter Trail: Andrew Jackson and the Indians* (New York: Hill and Wang, 1993). While Wallace is writing about the nineteenth-century United States, the attitudes he describes were also widely held in British North America. On the attitudes of reformers and others toward American Indian policy, see Robert W. Mardock, "Indian Rights Movement until 1887," in *Handbook of North American Indians,* vol. 4, *History of Indian-White Relations,* vol. ed. Wilcomb E. Washburn (Washington: Smithsonian, 1988), 301-4; Robert F. Berkhofer, Jr., "White Conceptions of Indians," in *Handbook of North American Indians,* vol. 4, *History of Indian-White Relations,* vol. ed. Wilcomb E. Washburn (Washington: Smithsonian, 1988), 522-47; and Robert F. Berkhofer Jr., *The White Man's Indian: Images of the American Indian from Columbus to the Present* (New York: Alfred A. Knopf, 1978).

5   Miller, "Silas T. Rand," 238.
6   Thomas Irwin, "Sketches of the Manners, Customs, Language, &c. of the Mickmac Indians," *Prince Edward Island Register* 7, 332 (8 June 1830): 4; 7, 335 (29 June 1830): 4; 7, 337 (13 July 1830): 4; 7, 339 (27 July 1830): 4; 7, 341 (10 August 1830): 4; Thomas Irwin, "Sketches of the Manners, Customs, Language, &c. of the Mickmac Indians," *Royal Gazette* [Charlottetown] 1, 2 (31 August 1830): 4; 1, 6 (28 September 1830): 4; 1, 16 (7 December 1830): 4. See Silas T. Rand, *A Short Statement of Facts Relating to the History, Manners, Customs, Language, and Literature of the Micmac Tribe of Indians, in Nova-Scotia and P.E. Island* (Halifax: James Bowes and Son, 1850), 36; L.F.S Upton, "Indians and Islanders: The Micmacs in Colonial Prince Edward Island," *Acadiensis* 6, 1 (Autumn 1976): 26-29.
7   Lovesey, *To Be a Pilgrim,* 45-46; Miller, "Silas T. Rand," 239; Rand, *Legends,* xvii.
8   Two public meetings, attended by clergy from a number of Protestant congregations, were held in Halifax on 12 November 1849 and 19 November 1849. Those present agreed to support the work of Rand and to formally constitute the Micmac Missionary Society. See Lovesey, *To Be a Pilgrim,* 50-52.
9   Silas T. Rand, "The Micmac Mission," *Christian Messenger* n.s. 10 (1850): 326.
10 Lovesey, *To Be a Pilgrim,* 34.
11 Silas T. Rand, *A Short Account of the Lord's Work among the Micmac Indians with Some Reasons for His Seceding from the Baptist Denomination* (Halifax: William MacNab, 1878), 4.
12 Rand, *Legends,* xvii; Silas T. Rand, *The Micmac Mission* (Hantsport, NS: s.n., 1882), 14, emphasis in original.
13 S.T. Rand to W. Chipman, v-1848, Silas Tertius Rand Papers, Atlantic Baptist Historical Collection, Acadia University, Wolfville, Nova Scotia.
14 Silas T. Rand, "Reply to the Rev. Mr. Sommerville," *Christian Messenger* 35 (1871): 115-16.
15 Silas T. Rand, "The Claims and Prospects of the Micmacs," *Christian Messenger* 15 (1855): 145.
16 Tertius [Silas T. Rand], "No. 5. For the Royal Gazette: The Indians," *Royal Gazette* [Charlottetown] 17, 894 (7 September 1847): 1.
17 L.F.S. Upton, *Micmacs and Colonists: Indian-White Relations in the Maritimes, 1713-1867* (Vancouver: UBC Press, 1979) 135; Miller, "Silas T. Rand," 242.
18 Upton, *Micmacs and Colonists,* 139; Helen Ralston, "Religion, Public Policy, and the Education of Micmac Indians of Nova Scotia, 1605-1872," *Canadian Review of Sociology and Anthropology* 18 (1981): 470-98 at 491.
19 Jeremiah S. Clark, "Editor's Preface," in *Micmac Dictionary from Phonographic Word-Lists,* ed. Jeremiah S. Clark (Charlottetown, PEI: Patriot, 1902), v-viii at v.
20 J. Bernard Gilpin, "Indians of Nova Scotia," in *The Native Peoples of Atlantic Canada: A History of Ethnic Interaction,* ed. Harold F. McGee (Toronto: McClelland and Stewart, 1974), 102-19 at 114-15.
21 Rand, *The Micmac Mission,* 10.
22 Rand, *A Short Account,* 6.
23 Upton, *Micmacs and Colonists,* 127-41.
24 Micmac Missionary Society, *The Third Annual Report of the Committee of the Micmac Missionary Society from Sept. 30, 1851, to Sept. 29, 1852* (Halifax: James Bowes and Son, 1852), 7-8.
25 Micmac Missionary Society, *The First* [sic – really *Second*] *Annual Report of the Committee of the Micmac Missionary Society, from Oct. 23, 1850, to Sept. 30, 1851* (Halifax: Micmac Missionary Society, 1851), 9-10.
26 Rand, *Legends,* xi. On the prayer book in Mi'kmaq, see John Lenhard, *History Relating to Manual of Prayers, Instruction, Psalms and Hymns in Micmac Ideograms Used by Micmac Indians of Eastern Canada and Newfoundland* (Sydney, NS: Cameron Print, 1932); Marie Ann Battiste, "An Historical Investigation of the Social and Cultural Consequences of Micmac Literacy" (Ed.D. thesis, Stanford University, 1983); Carlo J. Krieger, "Ethnogenesis or Cultural Interference? Catholic Missionaries and the Micmac," in *Actes du Vingtième Congrès des Algonquianistes,* ed. William Cowan (Ottawa: Carleton University, 1989), 193-200.
27 Rand, *The Micmac Mission,* 14-15.

28 "The Micmac-Mission Humbug," *The Halifax Catholic* 1, 16 (1 July 1854): 2.
29 Tim Carthy, "To the Editors of the *Halifax Catholic*," *The Halifax Catholic* 1, 40 (16 December 1854): 3.
30 On the historical role of the Catholic faith in Mi'kmaq communities, see Mildred Milliea, "Micmac Catholicism in My Community," in *Actes du Vingtième Congrès des Algonquianistes*, ed. William Cowan (Ottawa: Carleton University, 1989), 262-66; Harald E.L. Prins, *The Mi'kmaq: Resistance, Accommodation, and Cultural Survival* (Fort Worth: Harcourt Brace, 1996), especially 170-74.
31 On Mi'kmaq mobility, see Peggy Martin, "Micmac Indians as Witches in the Newfoundland Tradition," in *Papers of the Tenth Algonquian Conference*, ed. William Cowan (Ottawa: Carleton University, 1979): 173-80; Abler, "Micmacs and Gypsies." The literature on Old World peripatetic minorities is extensive. See Sharon Bohn Gmelch, "Groups That Don't Want In: Gypsies and Other Artisan, Trader, and Entertainer Minorities," *Annual Review of Anthropology* 15 (1986): 307-30; Aparna Rao, ed., *The Other Nomads: Peripatetic Minorities in Cross-Cultural Perspective* (Köln: Bohlau, 1987).
32 On baskets, see Smith, "Economics"; on quillwork, see Ruth Holmes Whitehead, *Micmac Quillwork: Micmac Indian Techniques of Porcupine Quill Decoration, 1600-1950* (Halifax: Nova Scotia Museum, 1982).
33 Gonzales, "Changing Economic Roles," 62-64.
34 Ibid., 65.
35 See Harold F. McGee, "Ethnic Boundaries and Strategies of Ethnic Interaction: A History of Micmac-White Relations in Nova Scotia" (PhD dissertation, Southern Illinois University, 1973); Harold F. McGee, "White Encroachment on Micmac Reserve Lands in Nova Scotia, 1830-1867," *Man in the Northeast* 8 (1974): 57-64. It is argued (by Redmond, "'We Cannot Work'") that the Mi'kmaq did attempt to farm in the first decades of the nineteenth century but that crop failures in the 1840s and other negative circumstances doomed these efforts to failure. Both Scots squatters and failed attempts to induce the Mi'kmaq to farm are documented in Upton, *Micmacs and Colonists*, 127-41.
36 Micmac Missionary Society, *The Fifth Annual Report of the Committee of the Micmac Missionary Society: From Sept. 29, 1853, to Sept. 30, 1854* (Halifax: James Bowes and Son, 1854); Micmac Missionary Society, *The Sixth Annual Report of the Committee of the Micmac Missionary Society: From Sept. 30, 1854, to Sept. 30, 1855* (Halifax: James Bowes and Son, 1855); Micmac Missionary Society, *The Seventh Annual Report of the Committee of the Micmac Missionary Society: From Sept. 30, 1855, to Sept. 30, 1856* (Halifax: James Bowes and Son, 1856).
37 Micmac Missionary Society, *The Tenth Annual Report of the Committee of the Micmac Missionary Society: From Sept. 30, 1858, to Sept. 30, 1859* (Halifax: Wesleyan Conference Steam Press, 1859), 20, emphasis in original. On the early-nineteenth-century development of tourism and Niagara Falls bad taste, see Ralph Greenhill and Thomas D. Mahoney, *Niagara* (Toronto: University of Toronto Press, 1969), 6. For a brief outline of wire-walker Blondin's feats, see ibid., 82-84.
38 Micmac Missionary Society, *Tenth Annual Report*, 20-21.
39 Ibid., 28, 30, emphasis in original.
40 Ibid., 29.
41 See F. Assikinack, "The Odahwah Language," *Canadian Journal* n.s. 3, 18 (1858): 481-85.
42 Micmac Missionary Society, *Tenth Annual Report*, 28-29.
43 Ibid., 33. For problems on the Six Nations Reserve caused by the *Indian Protection Act* of 1850, see Sally M. Weaver, "The Iroquois: The Consolidation of the Grand River Reserve in the Mid-Nineteenth Century, 1847-1875," in *Aboriginal Ontario: Historical Perspectives on the First Nations*, ed. Edward S. Rogers and Donald B. Smith (Toronto: Dundurn Press for the Government of Ontario, 1994), 182-212 at 186-88.
44 Upton, *Micmacs and Colonists*, 135.
45 Micmac Missionary Society, *Tenth Annual Report*, 28.
46 Rand, *A Short Account*, 6, 8.
47 Silas T. Rand to Rev. George Patterson, 7 August 1876, Public Archives of Nova Scotia, MG 100, vol. 212, #25.

48 Sally M. Weaver, "Six Nations of the Grand River, Ontario," in *Handbook of North American Indians,* vol. 15, *Northeast,* ed. Bruce G. Trigger (Washington: Smithsonian, 1978), 525-36 at 527.

49 Rand, *The Micmac Mission,* 5.

50 Weaver, "The Iroquois: The Consolidation," 185.

51 Weaver, "Six Nations," 529.

52 Sally M. Weaver, "The Iroquois: The Grand River Reserve in the Late Nineteenth and Early Twentieth Centuries, 1875-1945," in *Aboriginal Ontario: Historical Perspectives on the First Nations,* ed. Edward S. Rogers and Donald B. Smith (Toronto: Dundurn Press for the Government of Ontario, 1994), 213-57 at 220.

53 Virginia J. Cooper, "A Political History of the Grand River Iroquois, 1784-1880" (MA thesis, Carleton University, 1975), 93.

54 Weaver, "The Iroquois: The Grand River," 221.

55 Katherine Ann Sample, "Changes in Agriculture on the Six Nations Reserve" (MA thesis, McMaster University, 1968).

56 Rand to Patterson, 7 August 1876, Public Archives of Nova Scotia, MG 100, vol. 212, #25, emphasis in original.

57 Micmac Missionary Society, *Tenth Annual Report,* 25.

4

A Visionary on the Edge: Allan Macdonell and the Championing of Native Resource Rights

Alan Knight and Janet E. Chute

An Attentive Ear

Non-Native entrepreneurs have been characterized as self-interested agents if they mined, logged, or constructed colonization roads on Aboriginal lands. Allan Macdonell (1808-88), while he engaged in mining and lumbering, nevertheless can be said to have been sympathetic to aspects of Native resource claims. Macdonell was a member of the militarily, politically, and professionally auspicious Macdonell clan of eastern Upper Canada – Roman Catholic Scots to whom the call of lineal kith and kin ultimately predominated over personal considerations like marriage. Macdonell himself remained a bachelor, which allowed him to pursue a mobile, independent lifestyle. He had trained as a lawyer in Hamilton, which gave his input in the treaty negotiating forum special clout. By the early 1850s Macdonell had become a propagandist for a small group of expansionists who endeavoured to reshape the image of the Canadian West as a distant, inhospitable wilderness by promoting it as a land of agricultural and entrepreneurial opportunity.[1]

Macdonell never exercised any significant influence over either the content or purpose of any Native claim but simply responded to appeals for assistance from Aboriginal leaders whom he had come to know well and admire. Unlike his fellow expansionists, who saw the West's prime value as a resource hinterland to feed Canadian markets, he felt that western settlement should progress only under conditions ensuring that indigenous rights to land and resources would be respected by the state. In some respects he remained an unsung Canadian hero who helped Native leaders launch their claims into the public forum by holding that non-Native entrepreneurial interests and national goals, such as the building of westward transportation systems, were not necessarily an anathema to Aboriginal claims and aspirations. He viewed Native peoples as sovereign over unceded lands and resources and on this basis developed visions of the future that involved the Aboriginal population as integral to the development of the Canadian nation-state.

Macdonell and the Upper Great Lakes Ojibwa

The Founding of an Agreement

The Native-claims campaign that attracted Allan Macdonell's attention had been fostered by the Native community long before the middle-aged mining prospector ever came to lend his assistance. By the mid-1840s, moreover, the Ojibwa of the Upper Great Lakes were facing a crisis. Bands on the American side of the border, from Sault Ste Marie to Leech Lake in northern Minnesota, feared removal by the American government west of the Missouri. Southwestern Ojibwa leaders, among them a well-known Leech Lake civil chief, Eshekebugekoshe, prosaically known as "Flat Mouth" in the English language, had approached other head men north and west of Lake Superior for help. In response, Ojibwa chiefs from the British Sault to Fort William, the site of an old Northwest Company fort at the far western end of Lake Superior, offered to give the southwestern Ojibwa refuge by inviting them to swell the ranks of the British Ojibwa. Since the British side was perceived to offer potential respite from the cutting edge of American resource development, great consternation arose when, suddenly in the mid-1840s, miners appeared north of Lakes Huron and Superior. A frontier confrontation between encroaching metropolitan interests and local Native interests seemed imminent.

This ominous outcome was averted because of a daring scheme devised by Shingwaukonse, or "The Little Pine," head chief of a band living at Garden River, near Sault Ste Marie, Canada West. In his seventies at the time, Shingwaukonse was a métis[2] steeped in Ojibwa culture, a veteran not only of the War of 1812, for which he had accumulated medals for bravery in aid of the British cause, but also of numerous Roman Catholic, Anglican, Methodist, and Baptist missionizing enterprises in and around the Sault. From each experience he derived novel ideological information to add to his already auspicious store of traditional knowledge and wisdom.[3] At various times Shingwaukonse claimed to have kin ties to John Askin, a Scottish fur trader located first at Mackinac and later at Detroit, although any relationship that may have existed may have been mainly symbolic, not directly consanguineous.[4]

Macdonell, by contrast, was the scion of the Collachie branch of the Scottish Highland Macdonell family. Like Shingwaukonse, he would be cast in a unique role on the frontier that time would eventually erase. Macdonell's Scottish ancestry weighed heavily in his choice of career options. His grandfather, Allan Macdonell of Collachie, had joined with two of his brothers, Alexander Macdonell of Leek and John Macdonell of

Aberchalder, in bringing 600 of their kinfolk to the Mohawk Valley in 1773. All three men were heads of *cadet* families, which meant that they were linked closely to the chief of their clan. With these brothers was their cousin, Spanish John Macdonell of Scothouse, well known in the annals of Highland history as an extraordinarily brave soldier in the continental wars. All four men had responded to Sir William Johnson's invitation to establish a Scottish border settlement in what is now upper New York State.

With the onset of the American Revolution, the Macdonell brothers, Loyalists all, removed to eastern Upper Canada, settling principally in Stormont and Glengarry counties.[5] Allan Macdonell's son, Alexander Macdonell of Collachie, the father of the younger Allan Macdonell, who would assist in the Native cause, fought with Butler's Rangers during the American Revolutionary War, acted for several years after as the Earl of Selkirk's agent for the Baldoon settlement on Lake St. Clair, and later assisted in settling Scots Highlanders at Perth.[6] He represented Glengarry and Prescott in the Legislative Assembly of Upper Canada,[7] was Speaker of the assembly from 1805 to 1807, and, fluent in several Native languages as well as English, Gaelic, and French, in 1816 became assistant secretary of the British Indian Department. He assumed other offices, including that of sheriff of the Home District from 1792 to 1805, and became a legislative councillor in 1831. On his auspicious marriage to Anne Smith, daughter of a prominent Loyalist family, he was accepted into Tory compact circles, with increased opportunities for public recognition.[8] His social and political status became further entrenched through his close friendship with the Reverend Alexander Macdonell, a canny Scot who arrived in North America in 1803 and, by ingratiating himself not only with the Tory elite but also with Bishop Plessis of Quebec, became the first Roman Catholic bishop of Kingston in 1826. Meanwhile, other close relatives of Alexander Macdonell were making a mark on Canadian history. One cousin, John Macdonell of Greenfield, became attorney general of the fledgling colony of Upper Canada at a young age and died a heroic death along with Isaac Brock at Queenston Heights. This man may have known Shingwaukonse, who also had been at Queenston Heights. Two other relatives, Miles Macdonell[9] and John Macdonell of Scothouse,[10] sons of Spanish John, were to become, respectively, first governor of Assiniboia and a leading partner in the Northwest Company. Undoubtedly, his father's connections with Lord Selkirk and his knowledge of Miles and John Macdonell's careers on the frontier whetted the young Allan Macdonell's interest in lands and peoples residing on Lake Superior and beyond.

By the time of the birth of his eldest son, Allan, in 1808, Alexander Macdonell had ensconced his family in a comfortable house at York, now Toronto. He had proven equally at ease in frontier conditions or in the urbane company of York's upper class. As he matured into a young man, Allan came to long for his father's aptitude for community leadership, as well as his resilience and resourcefulness in dealing with challenges posed by the frontier milieu. His father, however, had more established plans for his eldest son, and, after completing grammar school, Allan was sent to study law in the office of Henry John Boulton, after which he entered a law partnership with Alan Napier McNab of Hamilton.[11] But since Allan's primary career aspirations did not lie with law, by 1837 he had given it up to become sheriff of the Gore District, a position likely obtained through the good graces of the Tory establishment and Bishop Macdonell. In the tradition of the more warlike of his ancestors, Macdonell held a commission as a major in the Queen's Rangers and, along with McNab, raised a battalion of cavalry to fight in the 1837 Rebellions in the Canadas. Then, after Bishop Macdonell's death in 1840 and his father's death the following year, Allan felt himself somewhat freer of the obligations of clan and immediate family. With sufficient means to branch out on his own, he began prospecting for copper north of Lake Superior in 1845. Though his younger brother Angus Duncan Macdonell dutifully stuck to paternal injunctions to carve out a niche in Toronto's legal elite for himself and his heirs,[12] he too was not above joining Allan in his speculative mining ventures, along with a mutual friend, an artist named Wharton Metcalfe.

On the traprock cliffs and the islands north of Sault Ste Marie, the three men found fields for adventure as well as potential earnings. Allan Macdonell in particular rapidly grew attached to the Ojibwa and métis settlement at the British Sault. While retrenchment in the wake of the Northwest Company's union with the Hudson's Bay Company in 1821 had left many former métis fur-trade employees eking out a living fishing, trapping, and engaging in marginal agriculture, the Sault community still evinced a form of community life that appealed to Macdonell, as it remained close to the land and was bound by intimate ties of kinship and friendship.[13] Signs of economic hardship loomed everywhere, for the Hudson's Bay Company had relegated its Sault post to a mere storage depot ever since 1827.[14] Overfishing by rival companies, furthermore, had depleted local fish stocks.[15] Yet Macdonell noted that Ojibwa from nearby Garden River were encouraging the métis to act in concert with them on a plan to rectify their mutual economic problems.[16] Chief Shingwaukonse attested that he had received a vision from the Great Spirit informing him that mineral revenues would replace income from the declining fur trade, in which both the métis and the Ojibwa once had played integral roles.

The southeastern Lake Superior coastline had exhibited a major mining boom ever since the discovery in the 1830s of a famous copper boulder along the Ontonagon River of Upper Michigan. Instilled with the hope that British territory might evince similar prospects, both the government and several mining companies despatched geologists to assess the northern region's mining potential.[17] Amid this frenzied race exhibited by southern interests to stake claims to hidden wealth, Shingwaukonse's vision constituted a brave plan, for traditional Ojibwa beliefs held that any unregulated taking of copper would offend spiritual guardians and bring cosmological disruption. A noted orator, Shingwaukonse won over Chief Eshekebugekoshe of Leech Lake and many other southwestern Ojibwa leaders, as well as Chiefs Joseph Peau de Chat of Fort William, Nebenagoching of Sault Ste Marie, and Keokonse of Thessalon.[18]

The British Ojibwa initially welcomed the coming of the mining prospectors to the Sault area.[19] When Allan Macdonell elicited Shingwaukonse's help in locating promising mineral outcroppings, the chief, likely because of Macdonell's father's reputation on the frontier and his close kin ties to John Macdonell of Scothouse and to Colonel John Macdonell of Queenston Heights' fame, even made the mining prospector his confidante. If Macdonell would help the chief's people realize their scheme, the chief promised, he would grant Macdonell, his associates, and other whites sympathetic to the Native cause leases to specific mining locations. These leases were for 999 years,[20] but the mineral deposits had to be worked within five years, or they would be forfeited.[21] Macdonell also received a strip of land along the old rapids portage at Sault Ste Marie in order to construct a short railway for exporting ore from Lake Superior to southern markets.

The chief's offers had special meaning for Macdonell since, by this time, his independent mining activities had encountered a serious impediment. Along with several other businessmen – Arthur Rankin of Sandwich, John Douglas of Fort Erie, James Hamilton of London, Charles Jones of Toronto, and Alexander Douglas McLean of Chatham – Allan and Angus Macdonell formed the Quebec and Lake Superior Mining Association in 1845. Acting under the auspices of the Association, Macdonell's brother Angus and Wharton Metcalfe staked two sites on eastern Michipocoten Island in 1847, while Allan Macdonell took out a patent in 1848 for a 6,400 acre mining location at Maimanse on Mica Bay, eastern Lake Superior.[22] Despite their initial optimism and energy, however, the association's original partners soon ran short of capital and had to take associates into their organization. As early as 1846 they had been compelled to turn their company over to a board of Quebec-based directors. This second group, manifesting a penchant for speculative enterprise, sought rapid returns by focusing on the promising location Allan had staked at Maimanse.[23] In consequence, on 23 July 1848, the association's trustees announced that all the company's Michipicoten holdings would be going up for sale. Clearly, there was copper on the island, and the Macdonells were prepared to mine it, but the Montreal trustees were not interested in any long-term involvements. The Macdonells and Wharton Metcalfe knew that they had to act quickly.

They were infuriated when they realized they had sunk monies into ventures over which they now had so little control. By contrast, the Ojibwas' stance promised to restore some measure of their former influence. Their scheme was intended to be legal and orderly in keeping with relational precedents that had characterized ethnic interactions in the upper Mohawk and Ohio Valleys prior to 1812.[24] Yet while the Native leaders, with Allan Macdonell's assistance, readied themselves to introduce their new scheme to the government, their deliberations were disrupted as early as 1846 by the appearance of a young government official named Alexander Vidal conducting surveys within the métis settlement and laying out mining locations without the Ojibwas' consent.[25] Both the Ojibwa and métis were enraged, and while the métis vociferously defended their rights to their lots at the rapids, Shingwaukonse confronted the surveyor directly and asked him to leave the Sault. The chief then requested that Alexander Murray, a government geologist also working in the area, report to his superiors that nineteen mining locations in the vicinity would be leased as revenue sources for the Aboriginal community. If Canada West wished to extend its jurisdiction westward peacefully, it was going to have to come to terms with sophisticated Native demands.[26] At last, here was the opportunity Macdonell had been looking for. Like his father before him, he could act as a facilitator in the birth of a new frontier order while at the same time promoting his own personal career aspirations in the mining field. In the end he decided that he would wholeheartedly support the Native campaign for land and resources.

When Shingwaukonse received no response from the government to his demands, he, his son Ogista, his interpreter Louis Cadotte, Nebenagoching, and several others from the Sault Native community visited the lieutenant governor, Lord Elgin, at Montreal early in the spring of 1848. The Native delegation informed Elgin that the miners' activities caused them economic hardship. The incomers restricted Ojibwa access to saleable timber, building materials, and firewood on mineral locations, and the fires that they set in the forest and the noise of their blasting drove away game. Since they received no response to their grievances, the bands sent a second, similar delegation to Montreal in May of 1849. This time Macdonell went with them, partly for his own private purposes and partly to secure media coverage in the *Montreal Gazette* for the Ojibwas' appeal. Consequently, the public could read, first hand, Shingwaukonse's lyrical and stirring appeal to the governor general, which proclaimed: "The Great Spirit in his beneficence, foreseeing that this time would come when the subsistence which the forest and lakes afforded would fail, placed these mines in our lands, so that the coming generation of His Red Men might find thereby the means of subsistence. Assist us, then, to reap that benefit intended for us ... Enable us to do this, and our hearts will be great within, for we will feel that we are again a nation."[27]

Despite his assistance in this respect, Macdonell's personal business pre-dilections temporarily threatened to overwhelm his loyalty to his new Native allies. While in the city, he became caught up in debates surround-ing Britain's repeal of her imperial trade preferences, and he even briefly supported the annexationist movement calling for union with the United States.[28] His return to the Sault community seems to have cooled his an-nexationist fervour, although it does point to a degree of unsteadiness that may have characterized Macdonell's business orientations in 1849. In the end, however, he remained steadfast to his commitment to the Ojibwa. Shingwaukonse's determination in pursuit of his goals seems to have ex-erted a steadying influence on him. By the summer of 1849, Macdonell's legal training, coupled with the old chief's creativity and strength of mind, gave birth to what, to date, stood as the most articulate and forceful cam-paign for Native resource rights ever raised in the Canadas. Like the legen-dary Scots chieftains of old, Macdonell would establish reciprocal ties of interest with his new allies and fight unwaveringly for their cause. The Ojibwa, he proclaimed, were free and independent.[29] They had the right to hire whom they pleased to forward their interests, for they were the sover-eign proprietors of the land and its resources.[30] Ironically, at the very time that the Montreal poet Charles Sangster was expounding on the doleful theme of the "disappearing Indian" in penning his "The Lament of Shing-waukonse,"[31] Macdonell was proclaiming that, owing to its new plan, the Sault Native community would grow and prosper.

Macdonell meanwhile continued to oppose the directorship policies of the Quebec and Lake Superior Mining Company.[32] There can be little doubt that by legally establishing Ojibwa proprietorship of land and minerals, he, at least initially, may have thought that he could recover personal los-ses incurred by the implementation of company policies contrary to his interest. Yet, by the summer of 1849, disquieting things were happening around the Sault not easily explainable by any individual's self-interested scheme. Powder and other ammunition began disappearing mysteriously from mine workings, while rumours spread of a possible Ojibwa attack on Bruce Mines on Lake Huron.[33] It was these ominous rumblings on the fron-tier that finally stirred the government into directing two commissioners to visit the bands on the Upper Great Lakes. One of these men, Thomas Gummersall Anderson, was an elderly gentleman who had joined the In-dian Department at the close of the War of 1812. The other, an unfortu-nate choice for the Ojibwa, was Alexander Vidal.[34]

With a surprising disregard for Anderson's long-term career within the Indian Department, the government made the inexperienced Vidal the lead-er of the expedition and relegated the elderly Anderson, fluent in the Ojibwa language and aware of Shingwaukonse's loyalty to the British cause during the War of 1812, to a secondary position. The government estimated that approximately fourteen Ojibwa bands resided on the north shores of the Upper Great Lakes. Since cholera had broken out at the Sault by the spring of 1849, it was impossible to summon the sixteen or more chiefs to meet in formal council in any one place. Instead, the commissioners decided to confer with band leaders individually or in small groups. These meetings were meant to convey the purpose of the government's mission and to elicit additional information about the nature of the Native claim. Anderson, in particular, held that the Ojibwa should receive compensation through the cession and sale of the mineral locations and "an application of the annual interest of the sum [from the sales] to the general benefit of all the Indians" occupying the north shores of Lakes Huron and Superior.[35] Vidal soon aroused their ire, however, by asking them on what authority they claimed their lands.[36]

After the numerous petitions that they had made to the government, the Sault Ojibwa in particular felt justified in cutting off all further communication except through their lawyer and agent, Allan Macdonell. "We thought of our ignorance and employed Macdonell," Shingwaukonse retorted, "we wish you to hear him and do not think right in you to put him aside." The chief continued that he viewed his land grants to Macdonell as private and independent agreements and succinctly enumerated the terms that he and his people had struck with their agent. "I have lent the island of Michipocoten [sic] to the white man for some time and I intend to reserve it in the treaty with the Government; a lease for 5 years only has been given; at the expiration of that time if we are satisfied a new one will be made – I have also lent to the same person a piece of land near Pointe aux Mines, [Maimanse] worked by the Quebec [and Lake Superior] Mining Company: The white man to whom they are leased is Mr. Macdonell." The chief also stated that he had "lent" Macdonell a strip of land at the Sault rapids on which to build a railroad. The Ojibwa were to "receive a toll upon all that passes over."[37]

At the final meeting between the Sault Ojibwa and the commissioners on 15 October 1849, Macdonell gave full vent to his oratorical and campaigning fervour on the Ojibwa leader's behalf. Did the Indian Department realize that the Native people were not minors in law? If they remained unaware of the fact, he had good information on the subject, he stormed. Vidal surveyed Macdonell with a disdain that he reserved for unscrupulous manipulators. Determined to prove that the Ojibwa were mere occupants and not proprietors of land and resources, he soon walked out of the meeting, while Anderson remained, listening with ever-growing agitation.[38]

Vidal was not alone in questioning the sincerity of Macdonell's motives. Several Sault residents weighed to what degree Macdonell's actions were guided by personal self-interest and to what degree by the altruism he so avidly espoused. Shingwaukonse's own son, Ogista (Augustin), along with several others of the chief's band, secretly confided to Vidal that they disapproved of their leader's close associations with the prospector.[39] As a bachelor with a flamboyant streak, Macdonell's activities also became a favourite subject of local gossip. William Mactavish, the Hudson's Bay Company factor at the rapids,[40] thought it incongruous that a miner would consider his mineral locations less important than his obligations to the Ojibwa and métis, whom he had come to address as "his people."[41] Macdonell said that "if the Indians can obtain better terms from others, he will have great pleasure in giving them up," the factor wrote George Simpson, governor of the Hudson's Bay Company.[42] Mactavish added that Macdonell spoke of two thousand Ojibwa who would be coming down to take part in a treaty. "Doubtless they will have an auxiliary corps of Eskimaux," he concluded dryly.[43]

The "Mica Bay Incident"

As things happened, what came to be known later as the "Mica Bay Incident" turned out to be a well-planned pressure tactic devised by a small, ethnically diverse group of people. Early in November of 1849 factor Mactavish reported that Macdonell and his Ojibwa allies intended to take over the Quebec and Lake Superior Association's holdings at Mica Bay, Maimanse, including a mining settlement of about one hundred miners and their families.[44] Their idea was to put the "Indians in possession, but to carry on mining operations under the superintendence of the present acting captain [Joseph Rodd], [by] removing the manager Mr. Bonner, [one of the company's trustees] altogether from the mines."[45] Mactavish, it turned out, proved well informed.[46] On 11 November 1849 two vessels, one a schooner named the *Falcon,* owned by Allan Macdonell,[47] set out for the Quebec and Lake Superior Mining Association's holdings on Mica Bay. Aboard were Allan and Angus Macdonell, Wharton Metcalfe, Shingwaukonse, Nebenagoching, about twenty-five other Ojibwa, including the American head chief Cassaquadung, and four prominent métis leaders. Ojibwa oral traditions further maintain that a smaller Ojibwa and métis party travelled to Mica Bay overland. These persons were reputed to have built huge bonfires at several points on Lake Superior's northeastern coastline to mislead the authorities into thinking that there were hundreds of people involved in the affair.[48] The Native contingent was not heavily armed, and the fact that it had absconded with two small cannons originally belonging to the Hudson's Bay Company[49] gave the expedition a theatrical flair.[50]

On the group's arrival at Mica Bay, Allan Macdonell confronted the mine's manager, John Bonner, one of the Quebec and Lake Superior Mining Association's directors. Macdonell announced that he had accompanied the Ojibwa and métis to prevent bloodshed and that the mine personnel must leave immediately.[51] Press accounts appearing soon after this event portrayed Macdonell as a colourful figure dressed in buckskins, and wielding a Bowie knife. Most emphasized the latent threat of violence,[52] while at least one grossly distorted events to the point of reporting deaths of company personnel.[53] Macdonell claimed that he calmly asked Bonner to arrange for the workmen and their families to leave Maimanse since the Ojibwa intended to dispossess the mine. The manager, after presiding over his employees' departure by schooner for points east, particularly for Bruce Mines, where most found immediate employment, sued the government for damages. A contingent of fencibles of the Second Rifle Brigade subsequently arrived from Toronto under the leadership of Captain Ashley Cooper but failed to reach Mica Bay owing to inclement weather[54] and so spent a dispiriting winter at the Sault.[55] Allan and Angus Macdonell, Wharton Metcalfe, and Chiefs Shingwaukonse and Nebenagoching, as well as the métis kin leaders Pierre Boissoneau, Pierre LeSage, and his brother Eustace, all peacefully turned themselves in on 4 December. They were brought in the steamer *Gore* to Penetanguishene and then taken to Toronto, where they were briefly imprisoned and released.[56] Wharton Metcalfe fled to the American side and, after being apprehended and escaping, left for England.[57]

Allan Macdonell meanwhile refused to elaborate on his own role in the Mica Bay Incident until a trial date was set.[58] "I have lived among the Indians some little time and am received among them as one of their own people," he wrote to Robert Bruce, the superintendent of Indian Affairs. "The chiefs of the different bands upon the Lake [Superior] have reposed a trust and confidence in me which I deem worthy of attention."[59] To divulge information carelessly might harm their case, he continued, a theme he repeated in an open letter to the *Toronto Patriot*.[60] Macdonell also used press channels to refute Bonner's allegations that he had feigned a semi-barbaric persona in the fall of 1849. Bonner had charged that "I carried a Bowie knife ... which is an instrument that I never carry and Mr. Metcalfe would scorn it as well as I."[61] He next denied that he had offered Ojibwa leaders liquor in order to bend them to his will. His role had been merely that of an auxiliary; the chiefs had been the real strategists behind the mine dispossession. To support this assertion he explained that in July, while he was away in Montreal, Chief Peau de Chat of Thunder Bay had arrived at Mica Bay with a large Native following and had declared that unless a treaty was made with his people, the miners "must leave the country."[62] He concluded by castigating Bonner, not the chiefs, for the mining company's sad predicament.[63]

Macdonell's statements in the press kept officials guessing as to the reasons behind his actions in the fall of 1849. Captain Cooper of the Rifle Brigade expressed astonishment at Macdonell's energy and zeal but found him a complete enigma as far as motivations were concerned. "Macdonell has returned with his Indian allies and has succeeded, I hear, in persuading 'his people,' as he affects to call them, in that he has been completely victorious over government and forced it to agree with the basis of a treaty with the Indians, all of which statements are, I observe, contradicted by reports in the newspapers," he noted confusedly.[64] Meanwhile, the *Montreal Gazette* heralded Macdonell as no less than the champion of Native rights while attributing most of the blame for the mine dispossession to Lord Elgin, who was charged with duplicity in his treatment of the Native claim.[65] Yet the only rationale Lord Elgin could discern for the recent events at Mica Bay lay in Bonner's bid for damages and the Montreal merchants' seeming stranglehold on the Upper Great Lakes economy.[66]

The source for the best insights into Allan Macdonell's motives in November of 1849, however, is a letter he directed several years after the Mica Bay Incident to George Brown, the proprietor of the *Toronto Globe*.[67] In this missive, dated 30 April 1853, he confided that he had promoted the Ojibwas' plan because he had wanted to reestablish a fertile middle ground on the frontier for diverse ideas, where Native prerogatives could be recognized equally along with settler rights. Without his assistance at the time of the Mica Bay Incident, violence might very well have broken out.[68] This letter ensued after two treaties had been signed in 1850 with the Upper Great Lakes Ojibwa, both of which ignored Native proprietary rights to minerals and other natural resources. These documents, known as the Robinson Treaties, nevertheless included an escalation clause that allowed for the Ojibwas' annuities to be raised to four dollars, provided resource revenues enabled the province to shoulder such payments without loss. Shingwaukonse's dream of bringing the southwestern Ojibwa, including chiefs such as Eshekebugekoshe, onto British soil died a sudden death with the government's refusal to countenance his scheme. Shingwaukonse and his allies had been pardoned, although Macdonell knew perfectly well that these pardons ensued only because of government reluctance to pursue matters further.[69] He himself was too well socially connected to be penalized harshly, for he had even stayed at the residence of the chief justice, John Beverley Robinson, while fruitlessly awaiting trial. It particularly riled him that on being summoned to the assize courts, five times he had appeared and five times the trial had been postponed. Worse, George Brown apprised him that the attorney general, Robert Baldwin, had introduced a bill for the administration of justice in the unorganized parts of the province that would halt his efforts on behalf of the Sault Native community. Brown enclosed a copy of the new bill in his missive to Macdonell.

Clause 9 of this bill, which passed into law on 14 June 1853 under the name *An Act to Make Better Provision for the Administration of Justice in the Unorganized Tracts of Country in Upper Canada* (16 Vict. Cap. 176), warned that "any person inciting Indian or half-breeds frequenting or residing in such tracts of country ... to the disturbance of the public peace ... shall be guilty of a felony, and upon conviction thereof shall be sentenced to not more than five years nor less than two years in the Provincial Penitentiary." "It appears to me that it would have been appropriately entitled an Act to procure the conviction of Allan Macdonell," its recipient lamented.[70] By this time Macdonell was deeply involved in the Toronto-based campaign for opening up the Hudson's Bay Company's territory to Canadian enterprise.[71] Neither his three well-publicized pamphlets on western expansion[72] nor the series of public lectures that he gave in Toronto on the same topic between 1851 and 1853 ever raised the issue of Aboriginal rights.[73] When shots were fired in November of 1854 at workmen connected with the Quebec and Lake Superior Mining Association's operations on Michipicoten Island, the *Lake Superior Journal* reported the event as a strictly Native-directed incident.[74] There was no mention of unscrupulous white agitators stirring up the frontier population to create a disturbance. And in an 1857 report addressed to a legislative committee examining the Hudson's Bay Company's rights in the Northwest, Macdonell referred to the Ojibwa solely when he wanted to impress upon his audience the potential benefits that might be conferred on the indigenous people by opening up the vast tract lying west of Lake Superior to Canadian enterprise.[75] Yet the fact that the Sault Ojibwas' case never went to trial continued to pique Macdonell, as his candid words to Brown indicate, although owing to Baldwin's silencing legislation, he could no longer express his thoughts on the subject publicly. He nonetheless retained contact with the Garden River Ojibwa as director of the Victoria Silver Mine, located just north of the Garden River Reserve.[76] And he certainly would not be the last nineteenth-century non-Native entrepreneur to act as a fosterer of mutual interests among diverse ethnicities on the western frontier. After 1858 this role would be assumed by his distant cousin Simon J. Dawson.[77] Macdonell in his later years retreated from public life to live quietly in Toronto. Little is known of his final years. He remains one of Canada's unsung heroes, who courageously upheld a vision of a country in which indigenous peoples would play an economically and politically integral role in the development of a new nation.

Notes

1 Doug Owram, *Promise of Eden: The Canadian Expansionist Movement and the Idea of the West, 1856-1900* (Toronto: University of Toronto Press, 1980), 4.
2 The authors' use of lower-case "m" distinguishes the Great Lakes métis from the western community Métis. It is not an attempt to minimize their presence, only to signal important distinctions.

3 Shingwaukonse and Eshekebugekoshe, although from opposite ends of the Lake Superior region, likely first encountered each other through the auspices of the Upper Great Lakes Ojibwa Midewiwin, or Grand Medicine Society.

4 Shingwaukonse may have been the son of Lavoine Barthe, who in turn may have been a brother of Jean Baptiste Barthe, who did have kin ties with John Askin, as Askin married Archange Barthe, Jean Baptiste's sister. This would have made Shingwaukonse, by marriage, Askin's nephew, or *nitawis*.

5 John Prebble, *Mutiny: Highland Regiments in Revolt, 1743-1804* (1975; reprint, London: Pimlico, 2001), provides historical background on the Glengarry Regiment.

6 Macdonell worked hard for the Perth settlers regardless of a lack of surveyors to lay out the land and other difficulties. Most of these Perth immigrants were disbanded Scottish soldiers. Archives of Ontario (henceforth AO), Brother Alfred, *Honorable Alexander McDonell (Collachie)*, pamphlet, Toronto, n.d., 14.

7 He served in this capacity from 1800 to 1812 and from 1820 to 1823.

8 Macdonell married Anne Smith, daughter of James Smith and Anne Valentine of Hendricks, Long Island. Anne's half brother, the Honourable Samuel Smith, a United Empire Loyalist colonel in the Queen's Rangers, had served under Simcoe during the American Revolution and later was appointed administrator of Upper Canada from June 1817 to August 1818 and from March to June of 1820.

9 Miles Macdonell preferred to marry within his own clan. His first marriage was to his cousin, Isabella Macdonell of Morar, while his second was to Alexander Macdonell's sister, Catherine. This would have made him the younger Allan Macdonell's uncle by marriage.

10 For a discussion of the importance of such family ties, see J.M.S. Careless, *Frontier and Metropolis: Regions, Cities and Identities in Canada before 1914* (Toronto: University of Toronto Press, 1989), 66-67.

11 Donald Swainson, "Macdonell, Allan," in *Dictionary of Canadian Biography*, vol. 11, *1881-1890* (Toronto: University of Toronto Press, 1982), 552-53. Macdonell's paternal grandmother, Nancy McNab Macdonell, was the daughter of the McNab clan chief who was known as "The McNab."

12 This is evident from an obituary of Claude Macdonell, son of Angus Duncan Macdonell and Pauline Macdonell. *Toronto Globe*, 19 April 1929.

13 Janet E. Chute, "Preservation of Ethnic Diversity at Garden River: The Key to Ojibwa Strength," in *Papers of the Twenty-Eighth Algonquian Conference*, ed. David H. Pentland (Winnipeg: University of Manitoba, 1997), 44-70 at 54-55; Janet E. Chute, "A Unifying Vision: Shingwaukonse's Plan for the Future of the Great Lakes Ojibwa," in *Journal of the Canadian Historical Association* n.s. 7 (1997): 55-80.

14 Hudson's Bay Company Archives, Winnipeg (henceforth HBCA), D 4/91, folio 17d, "Governor George Simpson to Hudson's Bay Company Headquarters, London, England," 5 September 1827.

15 HBCA, 4/104, folio 5-5d, "Simpson's Report to London Headquarters," 1835-36; G.P. de T. Glazebrook, ed., *The Hargrave Correspondence* (Toronto: Champlain Society, 1938), 312-13.

16 *Toronto British Colonist*, letter from Allan Macdonell, 18 December 1849.

17 In the 1830s Dr. Douglas Houghton found iron ore and copper deposits in Upper Michigan. Houghton's publication of his findings touched off the first American mining boom. During the following decade, the Ojibwa showed a Canadian prospector, John William Keating, and George Ironside, who was connected with the Indian Department, copper deposits at Bruce Mines and on Manitoulin Island, on the north shore of Lake Huron. AO, Ontario Land Surveyors, *Report*, 1887. The Montreal Mining Company despatched a geologist, Forrest Sheppard, and a well-equipped party to explore the tract that they intended to buy on Lake Superior. The government had decided to grant a single mining location to each person holding a licence of exploration. Each location was to be purchased as a block, the limits of which were not to be less than two miles in front by five miles in depth, for a total of 6,400 acres. The purchaser would be charged eighty cents per acre. It soon became evident that the government's regulations would ensure that locations fell to speculators who were already wealthy. These speculators formed companies with

interlocking directorates. These included the Montreal Mining Company, the Huron Copper Bay Company, the Quebec and Lake Superior Mining Association, the Upper Canada Mining Company, the British North America Mining Company, and the Canada Mining Company. Montreal capitalists dominated the scene, among them George Desbarats, Lewis Thomas Drummond, Stewart Derbishire, Peter McGill, William Collis Meredith, George Moffat, George Pemberton, and George Simpson. A smaller number came from the towns of Chatham and Sandwich in the Western District. For instance, James Cuthbertson, Arthur Rankin, and Robert Stuart Woods, all from the Western District, temporarily formed the Huron and Sault Ste Marie Mining Company and sank shafts at present-day Bruce Mines. Once the sites became productive, they were sold to the Montreal Mining Company. At the same time, a provincial geologist, William Logan, his assistant, Alexander Murray, another government geologist by the name of James Richardson, and surveyor John McNaughton visited the Upper Great Lakes region. William E. Logan, *Journal of a Survey of Lake Superior* (Montreal: Geographical Survey of Canada, 1846).

18 Janet E. Chute, in *The Legacy of Shingwaukonse: A Century of Native Leadership* (Toronto: University of Toronto Press, 1998).

19 The Ojibwa knew many local mining deposits, and early finds by whites may have been made with their help. Louis Jolliet is credited as the first white person to discover copper during his exploration west of Lake Superior in 1665. Following the discovery of silver, lead, and copper by Sieur de la Ronde at Point Maimanse and Michipicoten on Lake Superior's eastern shore in 1767, Alexander Henry formed a company with his fellow fur traders from Michilimackinac – Henry Boswick, Alexander Baxter, John Chinn, and Jean Baptiste Cadotte. In 1770 these mining partners constructed a shipyard at Pointe aux Pins, to the west of Sault Ste Marie, and built a forty-ton sloop to transport the ore. After penetrating to a depth of thirty feet, however, shaft collapses and other problems forced them to discontinue their work in 1773. Then, in the late 1830s, Dr. Douglas Houghton discovered iron ore at Marquette and scattered copper deposits through Michigan's Upper Peninsula. His most impressive find was the famous Ontonagon copper boulder. See, for instance, Public Affairs of Ontario (PAO), *Report of the Trustees of the Montreal Mining Company to the Shareholders,* 30 November 1846, no. 4, 41.

20 Not all these mineral leases were for Allan Macdonell and his associates. For instance, Captain William Ermatinger, the son of an independent trader who had retired to Montreal in 1828, also received a lease on the same terms.

21 A concise description of these leases is given in HBCA, MG 20, B/194/b/15/1849-50, Sault Ste Marie Post, Correspondence Books, "Mactavish to Simpson," 17 October 1849. These leases followed the format of many earlier leases granted by Native groups to non-Natives in the late eighteenth century. One such lease covered extensive territory on Point Pelee in Upper Canada. Another lease, granted by the Sault Ojibwa to the Northwest Company in 1798, may have constituted the model for the leases prepared in 1849. AO, Russell Papers, "Treaty with the Northwest Company," Sault Ste Marie, 10 August 1798.

22 Crown Lands Department, *Report, Sessional Papers,* 1860.

23 AO, Pamphlet #15, 5, *Articles of the Quebec and Lake Superior Mining Association, 20th October 1846.* Under the terms of the amalgamation, the property and funds of the association would be vested in the five new trustees – Peter Patterson, John Bonner, Henry LeMesurier, Thomas William Lloyd, and William Petry. Of the 40,000 shares owned by the association, the original shareholders each retained 2,641, while each of the new associates would be entitled to 1,975 shares.

24 Richard White has called this workable forum for the exchange of cultural ideas in the Great Lakes region the "middle ground." Richard White, *The Middle Ground: Indians, Empires and Republics in the Great Lakes Region, 1650-1815* (Cambridge: Cambridge University Press, 1991).

25 Chute, *The Legacy of Shingwaukonse,* 104.

26 For a more intensive look at this major Native campaign for land and resources, including the copious references associated with it, see Chute, *The Legacy of Shingwaukonse,* and Rhonda Telford, "The Sound of the Rustling of the Gold Is Under My Feet Where I Stand, We Have a Rich Country: A History of Aboriginal Mineral Resources in Ontario" (PhD dissertation, University of Toronto, 1995), 124-80.

27   *Montreal Gazette,* 7 July 1849.
28   Macdonell's name appears on the annexation manifesto, published as "The Montreal Annexation Manifesto: To the People of Canada," in *The Elgin-Grey Papers, 1846-1852,* vol. 4, ed. A.G. Doughty (Ottawa: Patenaude, 1937), 1487-94, Appendix 17. See also Gilbert N. Tucker, "Montreal in 1849, and the Annexation Movement," in *The Canadian Commercial Revolution, 1845-1851* (Toronto: McClelland and Stewart, 1964), 129-47. This action also might stem from Macdonell's connections with an American Sault merchant, Peter B. Barbeau, and his hope to attract New York capital to challenge the Montreal interests.
29   AO, Aemelius Irving Papers, "Extract from Notes Taken at the Conference with the Indians at Sault Ste. Marie – October 15th and 16th, 1849," in *Report of Commissioners A. Vidal and Thomas G. Anderson on a visit to Indians on North Shore Lakes Huron & Superior for purpose of investigating their claims to territory bordering on these Lakes.*
30   He realized as well that they were not dependent on the Hudson's Bay Company, for there were far too many free traders in their midst. Most of their dealings in timber, furs, fish, cordwood, vegetables, and preserves were with a local merchant, Philetus Swift Church, who maintained a trading establishment on Sugar Island, just across the North Channel on American territory.
31   See Leslie Monkman, *A Native Heritage: Images of the Indian in English-Canadian Literature* (Toronto: University of Toronto Press, 1981), 79.
32   Alan Knight, "Allan Macdonell and the Pointe aux Mines-Mica Bay Affair," research paper for York University, 1982.
33   Library and Archives Canada (henceforth LAC), RG 10 1-360-0-61.1, Montreal Mining Company papers, 1846-51, "W.D. Cockburn, Secretary of the Montreal Mining Company, to the Commissioner of Crown Lands," 31 December 1849.
34   Productive mineral workings at Bruce Mines on Lake Huron and at Mica Bay not far north of the Sault, as well as at Princess Bay near Fort William, had increased the worth of mining locations to such an extent that any dispute with the Ojibwa would prove embarrassing to the government.
35   AO, Aemelius Irving Papers, MU 1464, Pkg. 31, Box 26, Item 4, "Report of Commissioners A. Vidal and Thomas G. Anderson," 1849.
36   The *Toronto Globe,* 5 January 1850, reported that Vidal "used the most intemperate and irritating language, and told them in plain terms that they [the Ojibwa] should never be paid for their lands."
37   AO, Aemelius Irving Papers, "Extract from Notes."
38   Ibid. Anderson had good cause to feel upset, for Peau de Chat and a retinue had approached the Sault in July to determine if any form of a treaty were imminent. If Peau de Chat had joined Shingwaukonse after the commissioners had left the Sault, the outcome of what did happen in November of that year might have been far more severe. But Peau de Chat, on hearing rumours of cholera at the Sault, returned home to Fort William, where he stayed until the fall, fruitlessly awaiting word that treaty negotiations were about to begin.
39   On 18 October Anderson and Vidal met privately with Ogista (Augustin) Shingwauk (1800-90) and several others from Garden River. They impressed on these younger men the dangers of their chief refusing to speak and employing Macdonell as an agent. Ogista then stated that some portions of his father's address, as interpreted by Macdonell, contained "ideas and words for which there are no corresponding expression in their language." Ogista promised not to associate with Shingwaukonse as long as the chief remained with Macdonell. According to Vidal, Ogista even went on to say that Macdonell had written the address. AO, Aemelius Irving Papers, "Extract from Notes."
40   Like Alexander Macdonell, Allan's father, Mactavish was a protégé of a declining clan system. Mactavish's kin ties to the Mactavish clan chief had gained him his initial position with the old Northwest Company many years before. N. Jaye Goosen, "Mactavish, William," in *Dictionary of Canadian Biography,* vol. 9, *1861-1870* (Toronto: University of Toronto Press, 1976), 529-32 at 529.
41   While he might have received confirmation of his possession of the mining leases from Shingwaukonse, it remained that neither Macdonell nor his brother had the means to

work the locations or to pay the royalties demanded by the Ojibwa on the output of the mine.

42 HBCA, MG 20, B/194/b/15/1849-50, Sault Ste Marie Post, Correspondence Books, "Mactavish to Simpson," 17 October 1849.

43 Ibid. See also Macdonell's article in the *Toronto Patriot,* 19 December 1849, stating that there would be "1500 or perhaps 2000 determined to maintain their rights." Meanwhile the Reverend James D. Cameron, a Baptist missionary labouring among the Ojibwa on the American side of the rapids, sent a letter to the commissioner of Crown lands, the contents of which supported the validity of Mactavish's statements to Simpson. AO, RG 1, Crown Lands Records, A-1-7, vol. 7, (12), "Cameron to James Price, Commissioner of Crown Lands," 19 June 1849.

44 This operation was held to show great promise. Of five lots claimed by the original partners of the Quebec and Lake Superior Mining Company, Lot 26 was held in Allan Macdonell's name. John Bonner meanwhile held a private location on the western half of Michipicoten Island, which would have brought him into mining competition with Wharton Metcalfe and Angus Macdonell, who held lots on the eastern half of the island.

45 HBCA, MG 20, D 5/26, folio 479, 12 November 1849.

46 The local Anglican missionary, the Reverend Frederick O'Meara, was also aware of this plan.

47 In the fall of 1849 Allan Macdonell had purchased a schooner named *Florence* from Joseph Wilson, the collector of customs at the Sault, and renamed it *Falcon.* The schooner had previously been seized by Wilson from a Mr. Herrick and authorized for public sale. Supplies for the Mica Bay expedition had been bought from the American merchant Peter B. Barbeau. Barbeau, also a judge of Chippewa County and president of the newly incorporated village of Sault Ste Marie, Michigan, would remain a friend of the Macdonells for many years. Bayliss Library, Sault Ste Marie, Michigan, Peter B. Barbeau Papers, B6, Box 2.

48 Oral testimonies of John Boissoneau and Joseph LeSage of Garden River, Ontario.

49 In 1849 these cannons stood in front of the house of the collector of customs, Joseph Wilson.

50 HBCA, B.194 6/15, folio 15; D 5/26, folio 547-8, "Archibald Hamilton Campbell, Montreal Mining Company, Bruce Mines, to Chief Factor William Mactavish, Sault Ste. Marie," November 1849. Immediately upon learning of the expedition, Joseph Wilson, the collector of customs, in his additional capacities as a justice of the peace, a captain of a newly formed Volunteer Rifle Company at the British Sault, and the only governmental authority in the region, set off in pursuit of the *Falcon* in a birch bark canoe. Accompanied by six men, Wilson arrived at the mine early in the evening of 12 November. He alleged to have passed a Native group at Pointe aux Goulais. His intention had been to warn of the possible onset of hostilities, although he found that the mine's personnel already intended to surrender since they had neither weapons nor ammunition. Ojibwa oral traditions maintain that the Ojibwa arrived at Mica Bay before Wilson and that the militia captain was frightened away.

51 *Toronto British Colonist,* 8 February 1850.

52 *New York Commercial Advertiser,* 5 December 1849. This article was reprinted from the *Detroit Free Press and Tribune; Toronto Globe,* 5 January 1850.

53 *Montreal Gazette,* 27 November 1849.

54 The eighty-seven troops sent from Toronto, at considerable expense, had a long and arduous trip to the Sault in winter weather. The *Toronto Globe,* 5 January 1850, noted, "Having sailed with a detachment of the Rifle Brigade ... [the steamer *Gore*] was compelled through stress of weather to return to Pentanguishene. We understand she left that place again on Tuesday week but again encountered a storm, and on Thursday was driven back to Christian Island." There were also rumours that Captain Herbert of *HMS Mohawk* had found the missing steamer embedded in ice and that four soldiers had died due to the cold. After finally reaching the Sault, the main body of the troops tried to proceed northward in the propeller *Independence* but were driven back to the rapids by a heavy storm.

55 The troops were barracked for the winter in the Hudson's Bay Company fort at the Sault. They arrived after Archibald Hamilton Campbell of the Montreal Mining Company notified his company's president, George Moffat, of the Mica Bay Incident. Moffat (1787-1865) had been a fur trader and later an executive councillor, merchant, and insurance agent, civic magistrate, and leader of Montreal's British Party. On 22 November 1849 Moffat requested that the provincial secretary despatch one hundred men with arms and ammunition to Bruce Mines to provide his own company with protection against the Ojibwa. Civic disorder at Montreal and Beauharnois during the 1840s had compelled Moffat to propose that police forces in the Upper Great Lakes area be augmented by placing them under the direct control of the Executive Council. The Provincial Secretary's Office assured Moffat that troops were on their way. At the same time, the attorney general increased the number of justices of the peace. Added alongside Joseph Wilson were Sir George Simpson, Archibald Campbell, John Bonner, George Ironside, Dr. Paul Darling, William Mactavish, and Thomas Anderson. AO, Miscellaneous Collections, 1849, #8, MU 2110. See also Gerald Tulchinsky, "Moffatt, George," in *Dictionary of Canadian Biography*, vol. 9, *1861-1870* (Toronto: University of Toronto Press, 1976), 553-56.

56 A Baptist minister, James Douglas Cameron, the métis son of a Hudson's Bay Company fur-trade factor, had also been arrested because he had notified authorities concerning the Native unrest and so aroused suspicions concerning the nature of his own involvement in the affair. In Toronto, Henry Sherwood had been retained to defend the parties. The parties were charged as guilty of a misdemeanour and entitled to a preliminary examination before a magistrate, an affair that was postponed. The parties instead were brought by the sheriff of the Home District to the home residence of the chief justice, John Beverley Robinson. Also present were Attorney General Robert Baldwin, Dr. Connor, the public prosecutor, and George Philpotts of the Indian Department. There was a degree of disagreement between the chief justice and the attorney general. Beverley Robinson held Bonner's affidavit to be "wholly illegal and invalid, and refused to hold the parties to bail on the same," a stance that obliged the attorney general to file a new deposition. Meanwhile, concern was expressed for the welfare of Shingwaukonse and his party, so far away from their families during the winter season, and a subscription list was opened to raise funds to enable the chiefs to return to their people. *Toronto British Colonist*, 14 December 1849; 8 January 1850.

57 Wharton Metcalfe, an artist, fled to the American Sault and was apprehended early in the spring at Macdonell's house on the British side. He must have jumped bail when he turned up in Sault Ste Marie, Michigan, where he spent the winter sketching the local village scenery. His sketches are contained in Otto Fowle, *Sault Ste. Marie and Its Great Waterway* (New York: G.P. Putnam's Sons, 1925). He repeatedly crossed the St. Mary's River to the Canadian side, was captured, escaped, and was captured again. This time, in mid-March of 1850, he was turned over to Joseph Wilson. Wilson, however, could not retain him indefinitely, and when he asked Captain Cooper to take him in charge, the captain replied that he could not unless Wilson made a requisition as a justice of the peace. Wilson could only reply that he could not act as constable and justice of the peace and had to let Metcalfe go once again. Bayliss Library, Sault Ste Marie, Michigan, Peter B. Barbeau Ledger, July 1850. Metcalfe, who held a share in the *Falcon*, then was made responsible for empowering Barbeau to sell the schooner in the spring of 1851. Metcalfe further recorded Macdonell's dissatisfaction with Orkneyman Alexander Clark of Pointe aux Pins, whom Macdonell had hired to pilot the schooner to Maimanse. Clark reputedly declared the vessel unseaworthy and proved reluctant to follow Macdonell's orders with regard both to the vessel's movements and to its later sale. Bayliss Library, Peter B. Barbeau Letters 1848-52, B6 28, Box 2, Folder 5. Clark formerly had been master of the Hudson's Bay Company's supply ship *Whitefish*. Little is known of what became of Metcalfe following the Mica Bay Incident other than that he returned to London and, by the 1870s, had attained minor prominence as a British watercolourist.

58 *Toronto Patriot*, 8 December 1849.

59 LAC, RG 10, vol. 179, 103884, "Macdonell to Bruce," 10 January 1850.

60 See, for instance, *Toronto Patriot*, 29 December 1849.

61   Macdonell's article, written for the *Toronto Patriot,* was reprinted in the *Montreal Gazette,* 28 December 1849. Macdonell continued, "I was at that time in Montreal awaiting the result of the address carried down by the Indian chiefs [Shingwaukonse and Nebenagoching]; when I arrived at Sault Ste. Marie, I found a message from Peau de Chat, stating that he would wait until he heard from me; I sent him word that a treaty would be speedily entered into by the government. He and his people then returned to their homes. Subsequently to this a like notice was given by three other chiefs, that if no settlement was come to, they would put the miners off the land."

62   Ibid.

63   Ibid. This article includes a notice to Quebec and Lake Superior Mining Association shareholders. "I call upon you as a stockholder," Macdonell stated, "for Mr. Bonner's assertion to the contrary notwithstanding, I am still considerably interested in the Company's property – to take some other mode of placing the Association in its proper position, than through him who has thus recklessly placed it in its present unprofitable predicament, knowing as you all well do, from sad experience, that of all others, he is not a person to be relied upon, or capable of getting you out of your present difficulties."

64   Toronto, Metropolitan Public Library, Thomas G. Anderson Papers, S29, Folder D: 114. Macdonell's invectives against local officials in support of the Native claim did hit some magistrates and military men close to the quick. The Hudson's Bay Company tenure to land at the rapids stemmed from a 1798 lease from the local Ojibwa signed by Nebenagoching's grandfather, Maidsosagee. This lease closely paralleled the documents drawn up for Macdonell and Ermatinger as well as for the Roman Catholic and Anglican missions at Garden River.

65   *Montreal Gazette,* 23 November 1849.

66   "Lord Elgin to Lord Grey (Private), CO 4," 24 December 1849, in *Elgin-Grey Papers,* vol. 2, ed. A.G. Doughty (Ottawa: Patenaude, 1937) 563-64; "Lord Elgin to Lord Grey," 27 November 1849, in ibid., 551.

67   J.M.S. Careless, *Brown of the Globe,* vol. 1, *The Voice of Upper Canada, 1818-1859* (Toronto: Macmillan, 1959), 230.

68   AO, MS 91, Pkg. 11, George Brown Papers, Correspondence, "Macdonell to Brown," 30 April 1853.

69   Macdonell disliked the attorney general, Robert Baldwin, and repeatedly made him the target of his invective. For instance, he wrote to Brown comparing the talents of "his people" with those of the attorney general. There were many, he stressed, who proudly sent their sons to Montreal or to Europe for their education, among all of whom "may be found men superior to Mr. Atty. Genl. in education as well as intellect." AO, MS 91, Pkg. 11, George Brown Papers, Correspondence, "Macdonell to Brown," 30 April 1853.

70   Ibid.

71   Owram, *Promise of Eden,* 39-40.

72   These, published by the North-West Transportation and Land Company, respectively proposed a mail service to Red River, emphasized the employment benefits of western expansion, and promulgated the eventual opening of a rail line across the Prairies.

73   In 1851 Macdonell appeared before the Legislative Committee to propose a plan for the construction of both a railway and a canal at the British Sault. His vision, however, soon expanded to embrace a railway to the Pacific Ocean, a dream he shared with his brother Angus. Bayliss Library, Sault Ste Marie, Michigan, Peter B. Barbeau Letters 1848-52, Box 2, Folder 6, "Angus Macdonell to Peter Barbeau," 29 May 1851.

74   *Lake Superior Journal,* 4 November 1854. See also Chute, *The Legacy of Shingwaukonse,* 161.

75   AO, Allan Macdonell, *Report to the Legislative Committee,* 1857.

76   After 1860 Macdonell seems to have retreated from public life, although he did permit his name to stand as an independent in the election of 1867 as MP for Algoma. It is unknown, however, whether or not he actively campaigned in the region. He came fifth on the ballot and was defeated by Wemyss Simpson, cousin of Sir George Simpson, the governor of the Hudson's Bay Company. Following this, he continued to live in relative obscurity until his death in 1888. He was buried in the family mausoleum in St. Michael's Roman Catholic Cemetery, Toronto. His brothers Angus and Alexander continued to practise law in Toronto.

77 Because Allan and his brother Angus Macdonell and Simon James Dawson and his brother William all, by their own admissions, belonged to *cadet* families of the Macdonell clan – Allan and Angus through their father, Simon and William through their mother – the two Macdonells and the two Dawsons would have considered themselves distant cousins. The Dawsons also may have been related to Bishop Alexander Macdonell. One writer has argued that the bishop had one sister by his mother as well as a half brother, Allan Macdonell, who had come to Glengarry. Allan, furthermore, was supposed to have had a sister married to a Dawson, and this sister may have been Simon J. Dawson and William Macdonell Dawson's mother. AO, MU 828, Dawson Family Papers, "Ewan McDonald of Alexandria to J.P. Bertrand, Convenor Centennial Committee, Port Arthur," 10 April 1956.

5

Taking up the Torch: Simon J. Dawson and the Upper Great Lakes' Native Resource Campaign of the 1860s and 1870s

Janet E. Chute and Alan Knight

Rise of a Voice from the Corridors of Power

Simon J. Dawson (1818-1902), a distant relative of Allan Macdonell, has been remembered chiefly for his role as government surveyor, expedition leader, and eventually, supervisor of what became known as the "Dawson Route." This route, which opened up the territory lying between Lake Superior and Red River, proved crucial to the colonization and development of the Canadian West. For this reason it may seem surprising that the man most instrumental in this road's construction and maintenance was known on occasion to value Native prerogatives above the rights of miners, loggers, and even incoming settlers.

Like Macdonell, Dawson was proud of his kin connections to the Macdonell clan and harkened more to his occupational duties, quest for political position, and entrepreneurial activities than to personal concerns like marriage. He, too, remained a bachelor. Not only was Dawson's ancestral Scottish background similar to Macdonell's, but the two men also knew each other well and exchanged stories about the Native people with whom they interacted. Ten years Macdonell's junior, Dawson may even have been privately party to Macdonell's reasons for participating in the Mica Bay Incident.[1] Macdonell, however, was closest to Simon's elder brother, William McDonell Dawson, who during the late 1840s worked for the Department of Crown Lands.[2] Upon his promotion to head of his branch in 1852, William undoubtedly helped secure important government appointments in the Northwest for his younger brother Simon. Dawson received a government appointment in 1857 to explore west of Lake Superior and in 1859 wrote a report promoting the possibility of settlement in the Northwest. In 1870, following two years of survey work on what became known as the "Dawson Route" running west of Lake Superior, he supervised the transportation to Red River of Colonel Garnet Wolseley's troops, responding to Riel's first resistance campaign. From 1878 to 1891 he sat as the member of Parliament for Algoma, a vast constituency extending westward to the Manitoba border and so could keep Native issues alive in the House of Commons. In 1858 William Dawson was elected to the provincial legislature for Trois-Rivières and then, two years later, for the riding of Ottawa County. Yet his expansionist leanings linked him most closely to Toronto, where he and Macdonell persuaded several prominent financiers, including Thomas Clarkson, William McMaster, and George Munro, to form the North-West Transportation, Navigation and Railway Company, incorporated in 1858 with William as its first president. Both men looked forward to the opening up of the Hudson's Bay Company's territories as fruitful fields for Canadian enterprise. In anticipation of this, Dawson's company obtained a government contract to carry mail by steamer from the Sault to what is now Port Arthur and then overland to Red River along a route surveyed by Simon in 1857.

William and Simon Dawson were proud of their Macdonell clan ancestry, which they traced through their mother, Anne Macdonell. Simon Dawson even claimed, a year after his election as member of Parliament for Algoma, that his maternal grandfather had been "heir presumptive to the estate and honors of the ancient house of Glengarry," the Macdonell clan seat.[3] His knowledge of clan connections and history nevertheless would have been learned from immediate family members and from books, for Simon had been born in 1818 at Redhaven, Banffshire, well outside of the Macdonell and Davidson clan territories traditionally flanking opposite sides of Loch Ness. According to his biographer, Elizabeth Arthur, Simon Dawson remained in Scotland before emigrating around 1841 to join his parents near Bytown, now Ottawa.[4]

Simon Dawson arrived in Canada West to observe the waning of Macdonell ties to the declining fortunes of the old Family Compact. The upcoming generation of Macdonells had been compelled by the resulting dearth of clan ties and patronage appointments to turn their attention to business, the scientific professions, or politics – or, in lieu of this, to making it on their own as much as possible. He also witnessed his elderly kinsman, John Macdonell of Scothouse, settling into retirement with his métis family at Point Fortune on the Ottawa River. This made the retired Nor'wester conveniently accessible when Dawson needed information on the Ojibwa and other groups living toward Red River, where John had once been stationed.[5] Both William and Simon Dawson viewed the interplay of ethnic diversity as a creative process, whose catalytic qualities along the frontier would be necessary for the rise of the strong new nation of their dreams. It would form a theme that William addressed in the early 1840s in letters to his brother Father Aeneas Macdonell, one of Bishop Macdonell's last protégés.[6] To encourage Aeneas to move permanently to Canada, William had stressed, "[Here] we have men of all creeds and countries, jumbled together, this, in the first place does away with prejudice, and, in the end, order and religion will be more likely to spring from this map of confusion, than from the settled bigotry of the Scotch peasantry."[7]

In the same vein, Simon Dawson's close examinations of frontier culture exhibited a flair for ethnographic accuracy unsurpassed by most of his contemporaries. While surveyor with the 1857 Gladwin-Hind expedition, he noted that Ojibwa leaders restricted access to vast tracts of their domain. Not only did they keep wayfarers to strictly designated routes, but they also demanded tolls for passage over stretches of waterway that they considered under their aegis.[8] Native protocols took time to learn. When Dawson offered presents to one band near Lake of the Woods, he was haughtily refused.[9] So until August of 1857, when typhus relegated him to the care of an Anglican missionary at Islington on the Winnipeg River, he continuously jotted down interesting observations about the Boundary Waters Ojibwa.

Although his early writings evinced certain Victorian prejudices,[10] he was aware of the broad diversity of talents among groups whom the press stereotypically branded as "Indians." He bolstered his insights with appreciation for the valuable aid that the Ojibwa rendered his survey crews. They proved indispensable, he declared, since their "occupations of hunting pursued from a youthful age, within particular areas, rendered their local knowledge of greatest value."[11] Without guides such as Shainbians and Akoosayins, his work would have been far harder. Such individuals acted in a dual role, however, not only as guides but also as monitors for their bands as to Dawson's whereabouts on the landscape. As Dawson progressed across the glacially scarred landscape, strewn with lakes and rivers and only here and there exhibiting pockets of fertile alluvial fill, he found principal chiefs waiting for him at various places. Evidently, his movements were being closely watched. He, in turn, kept a close eye on the chiefs. He observed that they eschewed missionary overtures, a fact that he lamented when he thought of the kindnesses shown him by the Reverend Macdonald during his sickness.[12] They also remained defiantly independent of the Hudson's Bay Company. In 1849 explorer John Richardson had observed that chiefs could be "saucy" to company officials since they had bargaining power. Not only did they have access to copious resources – rich sturgeon fisheries, "great quantities of wild rice," and hunting territories that were "tolerably rich in furs"[13] – but they also had opportunities to play off the Hudson's Bay Company against its American trading rivals located across the border in Minnesota.

When George Gladman was dismissed the following year on charges of corruption and incompetence, Dawson shouldered the leadership of the expedition with Henry Youle Hind, a geologist. During the summer of 1858, Dawson participated in an important meeting, encompassing two days, with the Ojibwa Grand Council at Fort Frances, on Rainy Lake. The chiefs questioned Dawson as to why his party had come onto their lands. Then, after hearing Dawson's explanations and accepting a presentation of gifts, they informally struck a bargain with him to allow a right-of-way though their territories, provided that no non-Native travellers interfered with their traditional prerogatives.[14] This outcome enhanced Dawson's reputation as a negotiator, and soon afterward Peter M. VanKoughnet, the commissioner of Crown lands, requested that he obtain surrender of a portion of the Fort William Reserve for white settlement.[15] The way that Dawson handled this assignment would remain characteristic of his negotiating style with the Ojibwa for the rest of his life. He travelled between Fort William and the Height of Land canvassing head men's views on the projected cession. To his surprise he even found that he liked this work since the Ojibwa manifested a high "degree of thought and foresight."[16] Their acts of kindness also touched him, such as when a Lac des Milles Lacs chief, unbidden, guarded Dawson's cache of supplies for several months.[17] He found that the Fort William Ojibwa were concerned about their rights over their traditional fisheries, and he would not consent to any surveys that prejudiced their interests in this regard.[18] Then, when he determined that the majority of the Ojibwa denounced the idea of a surrender, Dawson considered the matter closed. If "I have not met in full success," he related to the commissioner of Crown lands, "I have at least done what I could."[19] His reluctance to use pressure tactics contrasted sharply with the strategies employed by S.Y. Chesley, a senior Indian Affairs official who on 4 July 1859 pushed through a surrender, heedless of Dawson's disinclination to pursue such a course.[20] In later years Dawson's penchant to weigh Native opinions in the balance would be interpreted as indicative of a streak of weakness and vacillation in his character.[21] Yet Dawson's attitude toward the Native people in 1858 and 1859 issued from strength rather than from weakness. It arose from a blend of admiration and protectiveness, in the same way that an Ojibwa chief customarily regarded those for whom he was responsible.

Meanwhile, work on the Dawson Route had come to a temporary standstill. The line that Dawson had surveyed in 1857 meandered west from present-day Port Arthur to the Height of Land and then followed the Rainy River trade route. Rendering it passable for colonization purposes would involve erecting dams and locks on major waterways.[22] When Dawson tendered his estimate of the expense of doing this, the provincial assembly blanched with trepidation at the potential drain on its coffers.[23] Heedless of such projected high costs, William Dawson and Allan Macdonell sanguinely set out with the intention of having the North-West Transportation, Navigation and Railway Company establish the first link in this magnificent dream. It was a challenge that the province relinquished to the company with evident relief. Yet when Simon Dawson looked into it in 1860, he found the company, now revamped as the North-West Transit Company with its headquarters in England,[24] floundering in a welter of mismanagement and debt.[25] Following two major court cases involving angry creditors, the company expired in 1861, having laid less than six miles of road between Lake Superior and the Height of Land. This was a series of events that would place a pall over both William Dawson's and Allan Macdonell's political futures.[26] By contrast, Simon's political career had not yet even begun.

Following Confederation in 1867, government interest in the Dawson Route revived, and in June 1867 Simon Dawson became superintendent of road construction. In a report written at this time, Dawson provided further insights into what he had come to term the "Indian Element."[27] While an occasional slighting remark on Ojibwa culture still crept into his observations, Dawson's views were being purged of their earlier prejudicial undertones as he came to know more about the bands. Most important, his report provides such detailed data on the Ojibwa's traditional political system, religious rituals, and economic activities that his information is frequently used today as evidence by the Boundary Waters Ojibwa in support of their land and resource claims. In his report Dawson also included a cautionary note that unruly contract labourers might offend Native sensibilities. The 3,000 Boundary Waters Ojibwa could muster 600 warriors, and whites who disregarded boundaries set by the chiefs might cause widespread disruption. Committed to adhering to the promises that he had made to the Grand Council in 1858, he warned against unruly elements entering the territory and stressed that any talk of surrender should pertain, at least initially, wholly to the right-of-way.[28] The chiefs probably would agree to such a cession, provided their sturgeon fisheries and their gardens were reserved for them.[29] Yet good relations would only be preserved by a "cautious and delicate approach."[30] "I would have the fullest reliance as to the Indians observing a treaty and adhering most strictly to all its provisions," he emphasized, "if, in the first place, it were concluded after discussion, and after all its provisions were thoroughly understood by the Indians, and if, in the next, it were never infringed upon by the whites, who are generally the first to break through Indian treaties."[31]

Dawson's sympathy for the Native people manifested itself particularly poignantly in a vitriolic report that he wrote regarding Colonel Garnet Wolseley's treatment of the Aboriginal workmen hired for the military expedition sent to Red River in 1870 to quell the Riel uprising. In hindsight Wolseley might be forgiven for his chagrin at having most of the Great Lakes métis and all of the Nipigon Ojibwa desert his enterprise, especially when his own troops ended up contributing over 5,000 man hours of labour making passable what he considered a somewhat tortuous route through complete wilderness.[32] Dawson nevertheless railed against

Wolseley's lack of consideration for the sensibilities of the Ojibwa and métis, who were unused to being "worked like beasts of burden – at labour which their experience told them was worse than useless."[33] The Ojibwa naturally feared that white incomers would drive away their game and ruin their fisheries.[34] Once again, Dawson stressed that all intercourse with the bands should be governed by circumspection and respect.[35] Haughty or bellicose behaviour toward the Ojibwa would only mark the Boundary Waters region with bloodshed.

Dawson was beginning to weave a creative tapestry of what he conceived Canada might become in the future. The only way that Canada could evolve peacefully from a mix of ethnicities suddenly thrown into uneasy juxtaposition, he ventured tentatively, was to establish an independent northern province, spanning the middle reaches of the developing nation, with centres of population at the Sault, in the Thunder Bay region, and at Fort Frances. Since immigration was central to his scheme, he urged the Department of Public Works to prepare the Red River route for public transport as quickly as possible.[36] Yet, as the welfare of the local Ojibwa especially concerned him, he recommended the appointment of special agents to prevent any "tampering" in band activities by discontents from Red River. His advice was heeded, and soon two men associated with the Hudson's Bay Company, Robert John Nicholson Pinther and Nicholas Chatelain, acquired a new slate of responsibilities toward the Fort Frances and Rainy River Native power holders.[37] At the same time, Dawson acquired a degree of discretionary spending power to acquire presents for prominent chiefs.

In 1869 Dawson had built a residence at Prince Arthur's Landing, which now became a magnet for Ojibwa leaders curious to learn more about Canadian policies regarding the future of their lands and resources. For instance, despite an outbreak of scarlatina along the frontier,[38] Dawson met with a large Native assemblage at Shebandowan Lake in 1870 and was then confronted the following year at Prince Arthur's Landing by a delegation headed by a Shebandowan chief named Muckudayassin, or "Blackstone." Dawson held a lengthy audience with his Native guests, distributed some gifts to them, and sent them home in a four-horse carriage. This cemented a close relationship between Dawson and the Shebandowan Ojibwa that soon brought him into competition with miners prospecting in the Shebandowan Lake region. The most vocal of these rivals was an American, Captain William Frue, superintendent of Shebandowan's Jackfish Lake Gold Mine. Frue and his associates had staked their mining location in 1870, although they realized that their right to do so was tenuous given the absence of a Native treaty west of the Height of Land.[39]

When Blackstone and his band suddenly dispossessed the Jackfish Mine on 29 March 1872,[40] Frue sent letters to Queen's Park indirectly accusing Dawson of prompting Blackstone's actions. The mine takeover, he fumed in a missive to Frederick W. Cumberland, the member of the provincial assembly for Algoma, constituted "good grounds to appoint a committee to investigate, and should such an investigation prove the reports to be correct, I should think that the law of the land would mete out to him the punishment due to those who tamper with the Indians."[41] He further confided to Adam Crooks, the attorney general, that if a committee was appointed "to investigate the disbursement of money supposed to be expended upon the Red River Road sufficient evidence might be obtained around Prince Arthur's Landing and Fort William to establish the fact that a considerable amount of the public funds was expended for the survey and explorations of lands for private interests."[42] Ed Trowbridge and Major Sibley of Detroit, Frue's American backers, received similar letters.[43]

Frue's allegations that questionable practices had guided disbursements on the Red River Road implied only that Dawson had taken part in nefarious activities;[44] they neither proved that a crime had been committed as charged nor named Dawson directly.[45] Yet the recipients of Frue's letters knew exactly who was being pinpointed and why, and, although unfounded, the tenor of Frue's words would continue to cast a negative light on Dawson's reputation for years to come. As late as 1893, for instance, an elderly stipendiary magistrate, E.B. Borron, would reminisce on the events that he had heard about twenty years before and still blame Dawson for self-interestedly thwarting both Ontario's and the Americans' interests in the Shebandowan Lake region. "Dawson and others," he declared, "finding themselves shut out, got the Dominion to set up claims."[46]

Dawson hotly denied that he had tampered with the Ojibwa in any way. "Surely common intelligence – to speak of no higher influence – would alone prevent a man of my years from adopting a course which would at once mar his usefulness and render him ridiculous," he countered.[47] Fortunately, Frue's criticisms could not undermine the conviction espoused by William Spragge, the deputy superintendent of Indian Affairs, that Dawson had little, if anything, to do with the Ojibwa's resistance to the miners.[48] "The attitude assumed by these Indians (who it seems threaten to expel the miners) it is well to remark here is not without a Precedent," Spragge maintained, after reflecting on the many events that had occurred during his long career with the Indian Department. After all, Shingwaukonse and Nebenagoching had adopted a similar stance to Blackstone's back in 1849.[49] The Boundary Waters Ojibwa had resurrected an ongoing campaign for Native land and resources. Events after 1850 simply had driven the movement westward.

Despite criticisms against him, Dawson's knowledge of Ojibwa culture, and of the geography and geology of their terrain, led to his appointment in 1872, along with Wemyss Simpson and W.J. Pither, a Hudson's Bay Company employee, as a commissioner to intercede with the Boundary Waters Ojibwa.

This time the government stressed that the goal was not to secure merely a right-of-way but the whole of the Ojibwa's lands. This new government mandate did not particularly trouble Dawson. He had always considered a major land surrender necessary once the Hudson's Bay Company's territory was opened up. Furthermore, he did not think that the Ojibwa would object strenuously to such a course, provided they retained their hunting rights, fisheries, and gardens. Mining and logging interests formerly operating in the area had been stalled by an Order-in-Council until such a treaty was secured,[50] and these anxiously lobbied for a speedy agreement.[51]

Wemyss Simpson nevertheless already had a reputation for ruthless dealings with the Ojibwa on Lakes Huron and Superior, which tarnished his integrity in the Ojibwa's eyes.[52] Owing to this, and the small sum offered by the government for the Ojibwa's lands, talks bogged down almost as soon as they started. Simpson did not help matters by declaring that Dawson had already paid for the right-of-way through the whole tract by giving presents to Chief Blackstone at Prince Arthur's Landing.[53] This placed Dawson in an awkward predicament since the Grand Council immediately retorted that whatever had happened earlier at Shebandowan had not affected them.[54] Clearly, Simpson was willing to use Dawson as a scapegoat whenever a crisis arose in his own dealings with the Ojibwa. After seventeen days of fruitless negotiation in July of 1872, all further meetings were broken off for the rest of the season.

His relationship with Blackstone meanwhile threatened to continue to be a thorny problem for Dawson. A series of *Toronto Globe* articles by F. Burton Marshall, the government storekeeper at Fort Frances, which appeared soon after the breakdown of the talks, castigated Dawson for befriending the "dishonest ruffian" Blackstone. Marshall, it turned out, hoped to be rewarded for his revelations by being made a special agent at Shebandowan.[55] Blackstone's loyalty to the British Crown was repeatedly questioned. It was alleged that he had obstructed Wolseley's expedition in 1870 and threatened to prove fractious if proper remuneration were not forthcoming for minerals taken from his lands. It was feared that his views might influence the Grand Council chiefs.[56] Wemyss Simpson, federal member of Parliament for Algoma since 1869, further charged that Dawson should have rebuffed the chief, not treated him hospitably, since, he held, leaders like Blackstone were "incapable of understanding generosity" and would only up their demands after receiving largesse.[57]

Dawson proved no more shaken by the forceful tenor of the Ojibwa's demands for remuneration for their lands and resources than he was by the assaults on his credibility in government circles and the press. The Ojibwa had been setting a high price on their lands for several years. In 1869 the Grand Council requested $50 for every head chief, $20 for every *anikeogima,* or councillor, and $15 annually for every man, woman, and child. They also wanted agricultural implements, annual suits of clothing, tool kits, guns and ammunition, fishing gear, and net twine. Chiefs were to receive a horse and buggy every four years – the last a ploy to outbid the Dakota Sioux chiefs, who each received a one-time payment of a horse and buggy in a recent American treaty settlement.[58] They complained that $5 had been paid per head the first year that the Red River Road had been in use but that nothing had been offered them since.[59] At the negotiations in July of 1872, the Grand Council's spokesperson, Mowedepenais, proclaimed that "the sound of the rustling of the gold is under my feet where I stand; we have a rich country." Using wording highly reminiscent of Shingwau-konse's appeals twenty years before, he further charged that "it is the Great Sprit who gave us this; where we stand upon is the Indians' property, and belongs to them."[60] These Ojibwa, Dawson mused in listening to Mowede-penais' appeals, exercise "not only territorial but sovereign rights."[61] But Ottawa, which previously had capped the amount of money to be used for treaty-making purposes at $50,000 per annum, deemed the Ojibwa's de-mands, which would cost in excess of $123,112 yearly, to be exorbitant and cut off any further negotiations.[62]

Dawson immediately called for the government to reconsider. He stressed that the reservation of lands and resources for future economic develop-ment was extremely important to the Native people and that every effort should be made to grant them exclusive use of their traditional fishing grounds should an agreement be signed. The outcome of any treaty natu-rally would be of utmost importance to them since it could not but radi-cally change their way of life. For this reason a representative of the Queen should be present at the deliberations, including a ceremonial military presence, as a gesture of respect. The amount offered for annuities, $3 per head per annum, he continued, was far too small. No less than $5, he attested, would be acceptable.

Dawson's quick thinking and acting broke what first had looked like an intractable deadlock. Historians have failed to grant him the credit that he deserves for preserving peace at this time between the Ojibwa and the encroaching Canadian interests. Without his respectful intervention, there might well have been outbreaks of violence along the frontier.[63] Fortunate-ly, the government heeded his appeal. When the Grand Council sent a petition to the governor general early in October the same year manifest-ing their distress at the low amount offered for their lands, the govern-ment agreed to reconsider its former hardline position.[64] Later the same month, a federal Order-in-Council approved modifications to Ottawa's trea-ty proposals, several based on Dawson's recommendations. Meanwhile, Dawson, acting as a barometer of Native attitudes throughout the fall, fi-nally apprised the government that negotiations might profitably be re-sumed in September of 1873.[65]

There was still one hurdle for Dawson to face as 1872 drew to a close. A communication, purportedly written under Blackstone's direction on 12 December, reached the governor general's office maintaining that Dawson had threatened the Ojibwa by claiming that they would all "be murdered" if they refused to accept the $3 annuity offered by the treaty commissioners the preceding summer.[66] But this final stir died down rapidly. Blackstone denied having anything to do with the letter to the governor general, while Dawson found that he could explain the incident away as a fabrication of American smugglers from Saginaw, Michigan, vengeful at the commissioner's attempts to curtail their illicit whiskey trade.[67] Yet, possibly because Dawson was seen as vulnerable to attacks of this sort, he was not at first appointed to the slate of commissioners delegated to negotiate with the Ojibwa in 1873. Only when one of the appointees, Lindsay Russell,[68] resigned early in the proceedings was Dawson called upon to serve. The lieutenant governor of Manitoba, the Honourable Alexander Morris, determined to meet the chiefs at the Northwest Angle, a more neutral ground than the politically charged heartland of the Grand Council at Fort Frances. A military escort would accompany Morris to this site. The three commissioners, the third being a youthful Albert Norbert Provencher, were directed to offer annuities, if necessary as high as $7 per head. The commission was to sit no longer than a week.[69]

The Ojibwa negotiators strove to drive a hard bargain by first demanding that Dawson pay them for timber cut on their lands between 1868 to 1871. In the face of their importunity, the commissioner replied by stating that all timber cut in the unceded district was the property of the commons.[70] This, to Dawson, was likely an unpalatable compromise, for he could hardly have failed to note that Shingwaukonse and his allies had extended their prerogatives to include timber in 1849. His remarks on this issue, while effective in silencing further accusations against his past handling of Native affairs from either the Native or non-Native side, simply may have been the last recourse of a man driven into a very uncomfortable position. Dawson undoubtedly remembered the harsh threats levelled against Allan Macdonell in 1853 for "tampering" with Native peoples in an unorganized district. Such censures would cost him his official career, so doubtless such considerations guided his tongue, although not necessarily his heart, when it came to denying the Ojibwa certain resource rights in 1873. Mowedepenais must have discerned a degree of contradiction in the commissioner's stance since he claimed, "When he [Dawson] understood rightly what was my meaning yesterday [about the timber], he threw himself on your help. I think I have a right to follow him to where he flew."[71] It was a position Dawson took pains not to be placed in again.

For the remainder of the day, he played only a minor role, while the Honourable Alexander Morris, the chief negotiator, swung the weight of the Canadian state apparatus against the interests of the shrewd Ojibwa power holders, whom even Morris had to admit were difficult to best in close argument. So resolute was the Grand Council to stick to its original demands that had it not been for the intervention of Dawson's Sheband-owan contacts, Blackstone and Rat McKay, as well as the Lac Seul chief,[72] who persuaded the Native assembly to continue sitting, discussions could have been postponed indefinitely, with Native violence born out of anger and frustration possibly erupting along the frontier.

Soon afterward, on 3 October 1873, Treaty 3, or the "North-West Angle Treaty" as it came to be known, was signed. Under it, the Ojibwa ceded fifty-five thousand square miles of territory, with each individual receiving a one-time present of $12 and an annuity of $5. Bands reserved the right to hunt and fish across the ceded territory. They would receive agricultural implements, seed, livestock, tool chests, and $1,500 worth of net twine yearly. Chiefs and other head men would be singled out for annual salaries commensurate with their rank, along with suits of clothing and honorifics such as flags and medals.[73] Minerals and timber on reserves would be administered for the bands' "benefit," and Native persons could also acquire money from mineral exploring rights if they could find purchasers for their information.[74] Yet, despite Dawson's insistence on the importance of fishing to Ojibwa culture, there were no provisions for the Ojibwa's exclusive use of their traditional fishing grounds.

Dawson recognized the inequitable position in which the Ojibwa had been placed by the new treaty terms but hoped to rectify it somewhat by personally assisting the Ojibwa to choose reserves that, he stated enthusiastically to Indian Affairs, would have minerals and timber capable of providing revenues to swell Native coffers. In keeping with governmental mandates, there were to be two classes of reserved lands: wild lands, to be administered by the government on behalf of the bands, and farm lots, equal to 160 acres for each family of five. Under Dawson's supervision, three Shebandowan chiefs – Paybamachas, Kebaquin, and Metassoque-neskang – and their people,[75] who had failed to be present on 3 October, signed an adhesion to the recent treaty. In his report on these proceedings, Dawson reflected that the Shebandowan people with whom he had dealt would be particularly benefited by his approach toward Native land allocation since Paybamachas' tract had valuable timber, while Kebaquin's lands contained gold deposits.[76] He further revealed that the Grand Council had its own immigration scheme, similar to the one devised by Shingwaukonse and his allies in the late 1840s, whereby it would sponsor a movement of métis as well as American Ojibwa onto a fertile tract lying along the Rainy River between Fort Frances and an outpost known as Hungry Hall.[77] He began gathering information on this and other Native land issues for use when it came to deciding where best to locate the wild-lands reserves.

These good intentions were thwarted, however, by new directives from Ottawa stating that no wild lands could contain mineral deposits.[78] Dawson was instructed to put his stamp of disapproval on the Grand Council's removal scheme as well by carving out a separate tract for each band. In response, he vacillated on the chiefs' claims until the Ojibwa themselves began to question the utility of having him assist them in making their selections.[79] Frustrated, Dawson soon vacated the scene,[80] leaving John Stoughton Dennis – who had already overseen the manipulation of reserve boundaries in the Robinson Treaties area[81] – to impose an alien order over the Native landscape completely at odds with the Ojibwa's own understandings of their traditional homelands.

After 1875 Dawson raised Native issues in a new forum, as the member of the provincial assembly for Algoma.[82] He served in this office for three years, during which time he introduced his earlier dream of having Algoma become a separate province. This vision involved the economic enhancement of small centres established during the fur-trade era, to which Dawson believed people would continue to be drawn.[83] Fort Frances, Prince Arthur's Landing, and the Sault would all be central to his purpose. But it was not a stance calculated to win him many plaudits in Toronto, with that metropolis' business community beginning to covet Algoma's rich mineral and timber lands.[84]

A second proposition, equally gauged to be unpopular with Queen's Park, involved annuity payments under the Robinson Treaties. In April of 1873 the Upper Great Lakes Ojibwa had presented Dawson with a petition stating that annuities in the Robinson Treaties area should be raised to $4 per head, in keeping with the treaties' escalation clause.[85] Dawson was not long in bringing this grievance to public attention. It also appeared that there were arrears owing since for many years Ontario had been reaping resource revenues far in excess of the monetary reserves needed for the increase in payments.[86] While Ontario's premier, Oliver Mowat, maintained that Ottawa, under section 109 of the British North America Act, was liable, Dawson countered by stating that annuities stemmed from a lien on the land, and so Ontario remained wholly responsible.[87] Native title was not one of mere occupancy or courtesy, he charged, "but of right – conferred by the Imperial Government – long before Ontario had any existence."[88] Dawson and Mowat would be at loggerheads over this particular issue for many years to come.

Yet Dawson introduced his most controversial proposal to the federal House of Commons a year after winning the Algoma seat in 1878 on an Independent platform. He proclaimed that Native individuals who owned property valued at $150 or more and who had a degree of education and a steady occupation should be allowed to vote in federal elections, even though they may retain their Indian status and connections to their reserve communities.[89] He further contended that educated Native persons willingly would embark more rapidly on the path toward enfranchisement if having the vote did not mean their being divorced from kinship ties and cherished traditions. Indian status, with its emphasis on common ties to the land, also offered Native people protection from the rapacity of their white neighbours. And since receipt of accrued annuities ensued from land surrenders, he concluded, it should not constitute a liability to anyone's right to vote.[90]

When apprised of Dawson's stance on 31 March 1879, the prime minister, John A. Macdonald, approached the news cautiously. Since the law already allowed for gradual enfranchisement provided persons were willing to relinquish their legal status as "Indians," Macdonell ventured, he "did see the hardships the hon. gentleman [Dawson] complained of."[91] Yet he soon swung round to support the idea. While this endorsement likely evinced a political character, as the Liberal Opposition were quick to point out, there can be no doubt that Dawson's position was genuine. When Dawson raised the issue a second time in the House in 1880, in conjunction with the government's revision of the Indian Act, he claimed that the vote would assist Native individuals to rise from the state of powerlessness into which they were being thrust by legal strictures that denied them rights to resources even on their own reserves.[92]

The Liberal Opposition lashed out at Dawson's proposals by branding them as part of an elaborate Conservative gerrymander and highlighted examples of corrupt practices that had occurred when the Native vote had been counted in provincial elections. Since the federal constituency of Algoma formed an anomaly, in that Native persons whose names, for whatever reason, appeared on voters' lists could cast votes in national elections, Dawson was less vulnerable to such attacks than Conservative members in the House. He nevertheless spared no pains in pointing out that individuals of Native ancestry who voted in his constituency were outstanding citizens and in the future should fear penalization because in many instances they still lived on reserves and drew annuities. He regaled the House with examples of such individuals. "I know some wealthy Indians who draw this annuity from the government because it marks their connection with their race," he declared. "There is one of the island of Manitoulin, who has a shop in which there are $10,000 worth of goods. It is a mistake to suppose that these Indians are without the affection common to other men; they are not the barbarians which many people imagine and I say that this law [the Indian Act] is antiquated. I know of another case of an Indian in Algoma who sends his children to Paris to be educated, who has white people in his employ as servants, and yet, because he draws his annuity, he is not allowed by the Ontario law to vote [in provincial elections]."[93] In an era when the majority believed that annuitants were mere government mendicants, Dawson's arguments in the House of Commons that Aboriginal persons characterized an intelligent, high-spirited people[94] and that annuities were no more than payments for lands broke new ground. They came to form seminal planks in later campaigns for the Native franchise in Canada.[95]

Dawson's views on the Native franchise went hand in hand with his cherished dream of a separate northern province. Yet Dawson's hopes in this respect were threatened, owing to the comprehensiveness of Ontario's submissions in support of its claim to the disputed tract. Dawson chaired a House of Commons Select Committee on the boundary issue during March and April of 1880, and although he asked for time to strengthen the federal position, Ontario ultimately proved victorious.[96] In addition, news that the transcontinental railway would run well to the north of Fort Frances ended Dawson's vision of that community becoming a sizable northern centre, composed of long-time Native residents as well as newcomers.[97] One silver lining for all these clouds, however, was that Dawson's political agenda now had more time for further Native issues.

It was not long before he was wrestling with Native grievances issuing from a timber dispute at Fort William. A timber lease had been drafted for twenty square miles of the Fort William Reserve in 1870, when the community's leaders were still participating in the Red River expedition. In 1883 a Fort William spokesperson, John Binessi, held that these chiefs, on their return the following year, flatly rejected the idea of alienating any timber land, even though the signature of one of these men had materialized mysteriously on the document. In 1875 there had been further complaints of timber being stripped from the reserve without any revenue accruing to band funds.[98] Binessi and others had presented petitions in 1881 both to Jean François Jamot, the Roman Catholic bishop of Peterborough, and to Lord Lorne, the governor general, asking that the lease be repealed.[99] Although approached by Lorne, John A. Macdonald nevertheless held off acting on the grievance since Thomas Marks,[100] the lease's holder at the time, was a staunch supporter of the Conservative Party. So initiated in dubious circumstances, the lease continued to have a chequered history. For a nominal sum Thomas Marks transferred the lease to other parties once construction on a local section of railway raised timber prices. When the Ojibwa contested this conveyance,[101] the prime minister, knowing that the issue was still politically sensitive, asked Dawson to intervene.[102] At first, Dawson was reluctant to take up the challenge, although he began his characteristic questionings among the chiefs. In the end, however, he chose to appoint a disinterested investigator, a local civil engineer by the name of J.H. Caddy, who had previously drawn Dawson's admiration for his competent work on the Red River route.

Caddy found that the local Roman Catholic missionary, Father Hebert, clandestinely had been encouraging the Ojibwa to cut timber on their lands and sell it to a local merchant, W.H. Carpenter. On finding this out, the leaseholders, Josephine Farijana and H.B. Valliere, had complained to Ottawa.[103] Their major source of income threatened, the Fort William Ojibwa petitioned Parliament in 1884, with their document ending up in the hands of the Liberal Opposition.[104] Caddy meanwhile submitted a detailed report sympathetic to the Ojibwa viewpoint.[105] In the end the Conservatives were shamed into exacting $12,000 from Farijana's and Valliere's operations to deposit into the Fort William Band fund. Dawson's and Caddy's work had borne fruit, but it remained obvious that for many years political considerations had overridden any government stewardship of resources.[106]

Around this time Dawson's reputation as a sincere advocate of Native causes was again brought into question, this time on a very serious charge that still proves difficult, owing to lack of evidence, either to sustain or deny. George Burden, Ontario's commissioner responsible for monitoring illicit timber cutting activities west of the Height of Land, alleged that in 1883 Dawson was a director of the Rainy River Lumber Company, owned by Hugh Sutherland, estimated to have harvested over $30,000 worth of wood from the Eagle Lake Reserve.[107] Although Burden's statement has been touted as proof that Dawson at times compromised his relationship with the Boundary Waters Ojibwa for his own self-interested purposes,[108] Dawson himself admitted that, while he sent requests for timber licences to Ottawa for his political friends, who included men such as Marks and Sutherland, he also had little influence over the ultimate fate of such petitions.[109] And more than once he attested in the House of Commons that systems governing timber harvesting on reserves should be more flexible than on Crown lands in order to privilege local reserve residents over large timber companies.[110]

At the same time, he observed that there were Upper Great Lakes groups, including The Pic Band on Lake Superior and the Temagami group north of Lake Huron, that, although they resided within the Robinson Treaties area, did not receive any annuities at all. Leaders of these bands joined the chiefs of annuitant groups in venting their anger and frustration as the arrears issue dragged on, unresolved, for decades. In the intervening years, Dawson continued to stress the potential value of the arrears in particular to Native education and local community development.[111] Seeing that they had a sympathetic listening ear in Parliament, Ojibwa leaders, among them Chief John Pinessi of Fort William and Chief Buhkwujjennene of Garden River, urged him to place pressures on the government to pay up as well as to attend to their grievances regarding their fisheries, timber rights, and local education.[112] "The poor Indians," he announced to the House in 1886, "are too often accused of being in a chronic state of grumbling, because in addresses and petitions, which are sometimes but little heeded, they tell of their grievances, but let an equal number of poor white men have a wrong like this to complain of, and it is needless to say that they would grumble in a much more audible manner than the Indians have done."[113] This would be a position that he adhered to unwaveringly until, finally, Ontario paid the arrears in 1896.[114]

Dawson persisted in offering such aid even when there were political liabilities.[115] While he still won elections until 1887, his strengthening support for Native issues cut deeply into his election returns, to the concern of his Conservative allies.[116] His occasional favouring of Ojibwa over settler interests was viewed as political ineffectiveness by some, by others as sheer naiveté. One historian has even stated that "perhaps he was not cynical enough to reflect that few Indians could vote."[117] He may not have manifested the shrewd political insight of John A. Macdonald, who as superintendent of Indian Affairs was always keenly aware of political gains or losses in supporting certain Native campaigns. Yet Dawson's actions usually benefited his Native constituents. For instance, heedless of the ire of his political rival William McDougall,[118] he branded the Manitoulin Island Treaty of 1862, whose terms had been set out by McDougall, as the "worst treaty ever made" since the annuities offered were so low.[119] Not long afterward the Manitoulin Island Treaty annuitants became placed on the same footing as those who had signed the Robinson Treaties. As Ojibwa leaders grasped the fact that their peoples' grievances received quicker and fuller attention from Dawson than from Indian Affairs, Dawson's desk became strewn with letters and petitions relating to Native fisheries, schools, actions of Indian Agents, and concerns arising from various treaties.[120] Dawson tried to respond as effectively to these grievances as he could. The fact that he might suffer some degree of political backlash from his many interventions did not deter him.

That Dawson was usually not self-interested may be gleaned best from his strenuous efforts on behalf of Native fishing rights. As early as 1860 he had advocated that the rights of the Fort William Ojibwa prevailed over all other classes of fishing prerogatives in the western sector of Lake Superior. The reserve community, he stated, should have "full rein to reserving fishing rights, as this regulation would help the Indians and not harm the fisheries at all."[121] The same year, he relayed appeals to Ottawa from the Pic leaders, who also wanted fishing grounds reserved solely for their own use. By contrast, the Honourable James Cockburn, the solicitor general of Canada West, had argued in 1866 that even under their treaties, "Indians had no larger right over public waters than those which belonged at common law to Her Majesty's subjects in general."[122] Dawson repeatedly clashed with expounders of this view.

Twenty years later he demonstrated ever more tenacity in pursuit of his Native-fisheries campaigns by decrying the use of pound nets near the mouths of the Garden, Thessalon, and Mississauga Rivers. Such fishery locales, he held, should be reserved exclusively for the local Native residents.[123] What is the point of having fishing rights included in any treaty, he queried, if "the whiteman is about to ... sweep the waters of every living thing down to a minnow?"[124] With more than a hint of the old fervour that he had shown prior to the downfall of his campaign for an independent province, he contended that northern resources henceforth should be kept for northerners, which naturally included the Native people. Otherwise, he continued, vulnerable fishing stocks would simply become the prey of speculators who drained off both fish and profits to southern markets.[125] In the same vein, he seconded a proposal by the federal member of Parliament for Muskoka that new regulations should exempt the Native population of Lakes Huron and Nipissing from fishery closing dates.[126]

Even as an elderly man, Dawson remained an easy target for ambitious individuals who believed that their entrepreneurial aspirations had been frustrated in order to give Native rights some due. Doubtless, persons intent on obtaining lucrative fishing licences in the Treaty 3 area in 1889 were responsible for articles in the *Rat Portage News* that derided Dawson, then seventy years old, as an "old fossil" intent only on raising yet "another Indian cry to the detriment of white settlers."[127] Such comments failed to stir him from his course. By the late 1880s Dawson had begun advocating the privileging of Aboriginal fisheries in the Lake of the Woods to preserve Ojibwa economic self-sufficiency.[128] These appeals eventually struck a responsive chord in Ottawa, for in August of 1890 the Canadian government passed an Order-in-Council banning gill and pound nets in the lake's Canadian waters.[129] The moratorium only worked to a point since fish moved around and American fishers were not curtailed. Dawson nevertheless kept up his endeavours in this respect even after he had left the political forum in 1891.[130] Following his retirement in Ottawa, he continued to direct letters to both levels of government against the leasing of Ojibwa sturgeon fishing grounds.[131] But he knew that for many formerly highly productive Aboriginal fisheries, it was already too late. When his opinion was solicited in 1895 regarding what remained of the Native fishery in the Treaty 3 region, he reflected sadly that he, as well as the other treaty commissioners, had not made the point of pressing for Aboriginal fishing rights more strongly in 1873.[132]

Time and time again Dawson's sympathy for the Ojibwa and métis would be held up as evidence of his inability to respond effectively to the needs of his constituents. Few of those who dogged him in his later years saw him as a former peacekeeper on the western frontier, yet preservation of peace was one of his greatest achievements. If disaffected, the Boundary Waters Ojibwa could have proved warlike enough to halt Canada's westward expansion for a time, yet they, albeit reluctantly, came to the negotiating table without once ever raising a gun. Even those who preferred to see Dawson as a man who "did what he could," could not deny that he had the ability to intercede with the Ojibwa on sensitive issues without ever affronting them and prompting them to take up arms. Dawson himself must have experienced a sense of accomplishment in this regard since by the late 1890s he felt entitled to ask Ottawa to furnish his only living relative, an elderly niece, with a small pension "in view of his great service to the Indian Department."[133]

Conclusion

Dawson did not act principally from self-interested motives in regard to the Ojibwa, as some have suggested. As soon as Canada West extended its jurisdiction over the Sault region in 1845, the Ojibwa became cast as inexorably pitted against the public good. Both Dawson and his distant relative Allan Macdonell knew this but refused to follow the grain, and in the end they emerged as two of the most significant voices in support of Native resource rights. Dawson also believed that his ethnographic treatises might serve some future purpose for the Native people. To this end, he endeavoured over time to purge his writings of prejudicial attitudes and present an accurate picture of important aspects of Native society and life.

When Macdonell encountered Shingwaukonse in 1845 and Dawson met with the Grand Council chiefs at Fort Frances in 1858, both Scotsmen dealt with Native leaders who were still politically autonomous. Yet within the short space of twenty years, a Native chief residing north or west of the Upper Great Lakes could become liable to imprisonment if he removed one "stick" of timber from a reserve for sale without the permission of the Indian Department. Even in the mid-1840s, however, Macdonell had many more choices open to him than did Dawson in the ways that he could support Native rights. In 1849 Macdonell could protest vehemently that the Ojibwa were not minors in law, that they were proprietors of land and resources, and that these rights should be respected. Dawson, coming at a later date, was in a much different position. The best he could do was to try to reclaim as many rights for the Native people as possible from the restricting legislation encapsulated in the Indian Act once it had been unilaterally imposed on bands west of Lake Superior. Many missionaries and local-government agents simply turned a blind eye to Native resource-harvesting activities considered illegal under this act. They did not try to force changes in the law, even when illicit harvesting proved crucial for Native survival. Dawson at least spoke out, a difficult thing to do once he became elected to Parliament and so was expected to give the interests of his non-Native constituents, the voting majority, the most weight in any contested issue. Given the hardships of hanging on to political power and still retaining one's integrity when it came to upholding Native rights,

Dawson showed tremendous resilience. Rarely, if ever, did he stoop, as did so many of his rivals, to making Aboriginal individuals or groups scapegoats for any of his personal political losses. Instead, Dawson forced government officials to heed Native resource claims at a time when the province of Ontario, in particular, would have preferred having people forget that any such rights existed.

Despite the different circumstances under which they acted, Dawson and Macdonell were similar in many respects. Both had visions of Canada's future that included the Native population as integral participants. Macdonell manifested his attachment to his national dream by supporting resource royalty payments for the Ojibwa. Dawson argued for the Aboriginal vote, recognition of Native fishery rights, and the elevation of the reserve community as a viable hub for economic enterprise and growth. While Dawson, like Macdonell, cannot be seen as a *creator* of Aboriginal campaigns for land and resources,[134] he observed that the Native movements not only failed to obstruct the national good, but also potentially served to integrate the developing social fabric. For this reason his words and actions have received acclaim in Native circles, a circumstance that testifies to his integrity, a quality that both he and his kinsman Macdonell valued strongly. There was little that was insincere in Simon J. Dawson's campaigns to engender harmonious and equitable ethnic relationships along the western frontier; such relationships were the stuff of which he hoped the new nation would be made.

Notes

1 Even though no documented proof can be found, it is likely that information about the Mica Bay Incident (treated in Chapter 4), including the motives of its Native perpetrators and of its participants in general, passed between Allan Macdonell and the two Dawson brothers. Various Macdonells and members of the Dawson family corresponded frequently in the 1840s. See, for instance, Archives of Ontario (henceforth AO), MU 828, "Simon Dawson to William Dawson," 18 March 1847. One of Dawson's biographers, Elizabeth Arthur, noted that Dawson maintained family contacts and business associations that encouraged him to be aware "of old fur trade history and transportation routes crossing over the roof of Ontario." Elizabeth Arthur, *Simon J. Dawson, C.E.* (Thunder Bay: Thunder Bay Historical Society, 1987), 4.

2 William Dawson had been dismissed from the Crown Lands Department in 1845 but returned to the Woods and Forests Branch of the same department in 1849. His office was in Trois-Rivières. Promotion to supervisor of his branch, however, compelled him to move to Toronto in 1852.

3 John Alexander Gemmill, *The Canadian Parliamentary Companion* (Ottawa: John Duirie, 1879), 111-12.

4 Elizabeth Arthur, "Dawson, Simon James," in *Dictionary of Canadian Biography,* vol. 13, *1901-1910* (Toronto: University of Toronto Press, 1994), 261-62. Dawson was trained in civil engineering in Canada.

5 W. Stewart Wallace, ed., *Documents Relating to the North West Company* (Toronto: Champlain Society, 1934), 465.

6   This is mentioned in the introduction to the Dawson Family Papers, housed in the Archives of Ontario, Toronto. Father Aeneas, however, did not arrive in Canada West until after the bishop's death in 1840.

7   AO, MU 828, "Wm McD. Dawson to Rev. Aeneas MacDonald (McDonell) Dawson," 24 March 1842.

8   AO, MU 831, "A.W. Wells, Deputy Provincial Surveyor to S.J. Dawson," 29 July 1859. In 1859 Simon Dawson was informed that Wabinogigok, chief of the Seine River area, claimed ownership of the river and its tributaries by rights handed down through his father and grandfather. The chief then asked for compensation from the surveying party who would use the route.

9   AO, RG 1-369-0-1, Box 1, "Red River Settlement," 17 December 1857.

10 For instance, he referred to Ojibwa raids on the Dakota Sioux as "savage acts." The tenor of these remarks nevertheless seems to have been tempered by his realization that, prior to Culloden, members of the Macdonell clan itself on occasion were called "savage" by British officialdom, even though the clan had in its ranks many educated gentlemen, priests, and scholars, as well as noted warriors.

11 Simon J. Dawson and Alexander Jamieson Russell, *The Red River Country, Hudson's Bay and the North-west Territories Considered in Relation to Canada, with the Last Two Reports of S.J. Dawson, Esquire, C.E., on the Line of Route between Lake Superior and the Red River Settlement by Alexander Jamieson Russell, C.E., Inspector of Crown Timber Agencies, Canada East and West* (Ottawa: George Desbarats, Queen's Printer, 1868), 165.

12 Simon J. Dawson, "Response to an Address from the Legislative Assembly to His Excellency the Governor General, dated 23rd April, to be laid before the House 4th July 1858. Copies of Reports and Plans regarding the explorations of the previous two years," in *Report of the Exploration of the Country between Lake Superior and the Red River Settlement and the Latter Place and the Assiniboine and Saskatchewan* (Printed by order of the Legislative Assembly by John Lovell, Toronto, 1859), 12.

13 Ibid., 26.

14 Dawson, *Report of the Exploration*, 8-12.

15 When miners and settlers lobbied for the alienation of large tracts of Indian land reserved under the Robinson Treaties, many reserves were subdivided and portions ceded in 1858 and 1859. Proceeds from land sales were to be placed in band funds to assist local economic development and provide for schools, so chiefs sometimes willingly acquiesced to the demand. In a few years, however, it became apparent that much of the sale monies and other revenue were used to create colonization roads and to pay for surveys.

16 AO, MU 831, Dawson Family Papers, "Dawson to P.M. Vankoughnet," 11 June 1859. Arthur, *Simon J. Dawson, C.E.*, 11.

17 AO, MU 829, "J.F. Gaudet to Dawson," 17 February 1859.

18 AO, MU 830, "Dawson to the Reverend C.P. Chonem," 10 June 1859.

19 AO, MU 830, "Dawson to Vankoughnet," 10 June 1859.

20 The following year, John McIntyre asked Dawson to go about acquiring yet more land from these Ojibwa, although Dawson seems to have done little in response to McIntyre's request. AO, MU 831, Dawson Family Papers, "John McIntyre to Simon Dawson," 9 February 1860.

21 On Simon J. Dawson's death on 30 October 1902, the *Hamilton News* printed an account of his life, reprinted in the *Fort William Times-Journal*, 6 December 1902, noting that "he deserves a high place upon the honor role of Canadians who have done what they could." Reprinted in Arthur, *Simon J. Dawson, C.E.*, 31.

22 Dawson agreed with his brother and Allan Macdonell that an eventual rail connection across the Canadian Northwest would be an ideal goal but warned that any such undertaking would be premature in the late 1850s.

23 The total was £50,475. Arthur, *Simon J. Dawson, C.E.*, 10.

24 Donald Swainson, "Macdonell, Allan," in *Dictionary of Canadian Biography*, vol. 11, *1881-1890* (Toronto: University of Toronto Press, 1982), 552-54 at 554.

25 Ibid.

26 For instance, it likely underlay Macdonell's difficulties in 1869 when he unsuccessfully ran as a Reform candidate for Algoma in a national election. The winning candidate was the Conservative campaigner, Wemyss Simpson. For a commentary on William McDonell Dawson's declining political fortunes by this time, see Arthur, *Simon J. Dawson, C.E.*, 9-10. Like his brother William, Simon Dawson stressed the need for westward expansion in order to aid the cause of nation building, but unlike his sibling, he chafed against any American financial involvement in the process. His brother William's penchant for encouraging American investment both in the now defunct North-West Transit Company and in mining north of the Height of Land had riled him. Nevertheless, in 1860 he and William briefly had considered trying to form a rival fur-trade organization to the Hudson's Bay Company, hiring disenchanted free traders and métis youth, but neither man had sufficient financial resources to get such an ambitious enterprise launched. AO, MU 831, Dawson Family Papers, "S.J. Dawson to J.A. Nicholay," 19 April 1860.

27 Dawson, "The Indian Element," in Dawson and Russell, *The Red River Country*, 194-97.

28 Ibid., 197.

29 Many of these gardens, in which they grew corn, potatoes, and even melons, lay on islands. Tim E. Holzkamm and Leo Waisberg, "Agriculture and One 19th Century Ojibwa Band: 'They Hardly Ever Loose [sic] Sight of Their Field,'" in *Papers of the Twenty-Fourth Algonquian Conference*, ed. William Cowan (Ottawa: Carleton University, 1993), 407-29.

30 AO, Aemelius Irving Papers, MU 1514, "Dawson to Langevin" (1870/1908), 75/16, 137.

31 Dawson and Russell, *The Red River Country*, 196.

32 Sir Garnet Wolseley, *Narrative of the Red River Expedition* (reprinted from *Blackwood's Magazine*, London, December 1870-December 1871), 41-42.

33 Simon J. Dawson, *Report on the Red River Expedition of 1870, by Simon J. Dawson, Civil Engineer, with Remarks on Certain Strictures published in England by an Officer of the Expeditionary Force* (Ottawa: I.B. Taylor, 1871), 40. Dawson may have modified his views somewhat with time since a decade later it was Dawson who transmitted Wolseley's request to the Upper Great Lakes Native community to participate in the Nile expedition. It must be noted that few of the community went, however.

34 Library and Archives Canada (henceforth LAC), RG 10, vol. 448, 184286-184287, "Dawson to Howe," June 1870.

35 LAC, RG 10, vol. 448, 184275, "Memorandum to the Honorable H.P. Langevin, Minister of Public Works," 31 March 1871.

36 *Canadian Sessional Papers* 1869, 16, "Report to William McDougall, Minister of Public Works," 1 May 1869.

37 AO, MS 775, R. 31, vol. 448, Indian Affairs, Ministerial Administration Records, Superintendent General's Office, Secretary of State for the Province's Correspondence, Indians during the Red River Rebellion, 1869-70, "Office of the Secretary of State for the Provinces, 1870," 184200; "Recommendations of S.J. Dawson as noted by Adamsey Archibald," 7 February 1871, 184230; "Memorandum in reference to the Indians on the Red River Route, by S. J. Dawson," 17 December 1869, 184248-184250.

38 LAC, RG 10, vol. 1864, file 375, "Dawson to Joseph Howe, Superintendent General of Indian Affairs," 11 January 1871.

39 LAC, MG 28 III-19, "Frue to A.H. Sibley," 4 April 1872. For a discussion of this, see Elizabeth Arthur, "Introduction," in *Thunder Bay District, 1821-1892: A Collection of Documents*, ed. Elizabeth Arthur (Toronto: The Champlain Society, 1973), lxx-cv at lxxii. Although Dawson did not mention it in his letter, these finds may have resulted from two Fort William Ojibwa, Jean Baptist and Michael Puchot, releasing information to Peter McKellar, an American entrepreneur who became Frue's employee. Marian Henderson, *The McKellar Story* (Thunder Bay: Thunder Bay Historical Society, 1981), 38. Although dimly aware that Native rights were an issue and although he had been warned that Blackstone had refused to participate as long as Simpson remained a treaty commissioner, Frue simply expected a treaty to be made in the near future.

40 This occurred just before the opening of the navigation so that the miners could not muster outside assistance.

41 LAC, Algoma Mining Company Papers, MG 28, 111-19 (7-2394), copies of William Bell Frue's correspondence when superintendent of the Silver Islet Mining Company from 1871-75. This correspondence was typed from a letterbook of the Silver Islet Mining Company, now the property of W.C. Frue, grandson of W.B. Frue. "Frue to F.W. Cumberland," 4 April 1872.

42 LAC, MG 28, 111-19 (7-2394), "Frue to Adam Crooks," 4 April 1872.

43 LAC, MG 28, 111-19 (7-2394), "Frue to Sibley," 4 April 1872; "Frue to Trowbridge," 4 April 1872.

44 Under Dawson's direction, $6,169.65 was spent on provisions in 1871, quite a hefty sum.

45 Elizabeth Arthur certainly made this connection in Arthur, "Introduction," lxxiii.

46 AO, MU 1468 30/36/06 (1), "Borron's Memorandum on events at the Jackfish Mine in 1872," 1872; AO, Irving Papers, MU 1465 27/32/10, "Report by E.B. Borron relative to annuities payable to Indians as terms of the Robinson Treaties," 31 December 1892.

47 LAC, RG 10, vol. 1872, file 747, "Dawson to the Secretary of State," 12 December 1872.

48 LAC, RG 10, vol. 724, 43, "Memorandum from William Spragge," 27 July 1872.

49 Ibid. Spragge, furthermore, was probably not unaware that Dawson was a relative of the man who had acted as Shingwaukonse's legal counsel.

50 AO, RG 3, Executive Council Office, Ontario, Department of the Prime Minister, Orders-in-Council, "Staying issues of Patents and Mining Licenses in the neighbourhood of Lake Shebandowan and Head of Lake Superior," Order-in-Council, 28 December 1871.

51 LAC, RG 10, vol. 1884, file 1264, "Simpson to Howe," 30 July 1870.

52 A nephew of Sir George Simpson, the long-time governor of the Hudson's Bay Company, Wemyss Simpson had already shown ruthlessness toward Native interests by forcing a Manitoulin Island Native storekeeper named George Abatossaway out of business by appropriating, under the auspices of the Hudson's Bay Company at LaCloche, all the land on which Abatossaway kept a store and wharf. LAC, RG 10, vol. 614, 227; "Regarding Abatossaway's enterprise at Little Current," 19 January 1858.

53 AO, MU 1468, 30/36/07, "Notes on first Indian meeting at Fort Frances," 20 June 1870.

54 Provincial Archives of Manitoba, MG 12, A1, "Wemyss Simpson to Secretary of State Joseph Howe," 19 August 1870.

55 LAC, RG 10, vol. 1869, file 582, Reel C-11104, Fort Frances, "F. Burton Marshall relating the status of treaty with the Indians at Fort Frances, along with newspaper clippings, April-October, 1872."

56 Religious ties centred on the Midewiwin, or Grand Medicine Society, which brought Midewiwin practitioners together from as far away as the Sault and as far south as interior Wisconsin and Minnesota. A thorough discussion of the importance of the Midewiwin in this area may be found in J.A. Lovisek, "The Political Evolution of the Boundary Waters Ojibwa," in *Papers of the Twenty-Fourth Algonquian Conference,* ed. William Cowan (Ottawa: Carleton University, 1993), 280-305.

57 AO, MS 775, R. 31, vol. 44, 184324-184330, "Wemyss Simpson, MP for Algoma, to Joseph Howe, Secretary of State," 19 August 1870.

58 LAC, RG 10, vol. 1918, file 2790B, "Demands made by the Indians as their terms for treaty," 22 January 1869.

59 LAC, RG 10, vol. 2790A, "Report of Alexander Morris," 10 September 1873. At the time, Morris stated that he was glad to have Dawson as a commissioner.

60 The Hon. Alexander Morris, *The Treaties of Canada with the Indians of Manitoba and the North West Territories* (Toronto: Bedfords, Clarke, 1880), 70-71.

61 *Canadian Sessional Papers,* 1873, 6; "Appendix No. 19 – Red River Route," *Annual Report of the Department of Public Works for 1872* (Ottawa: House of Commons, 1873), 133-35.

62 LAC, RG 10, vol. 1918, file 27903, "Demands of the Fort Frances Indians," 22 January 1869. The amount was written in the margin of the document.

63 Dawson had also acted at times of economic crisis for the bands. When the Ojibwa of Lake of the Woods asked for employment cutting wood on the road since there had been a scarcity of fish for subsistence the previous fall, he acquiesced to their demands, gave them work, and found that they proved to be good workers.

64 LAC, RG 10, vol. 1872, file 747, "Petition to His Excellency the Governor General," 3 October 1872.

65 LAC, RG 10, vol. 1902, file 2122, part 0, "Dawson stating that negotiations with the Saulteaux could be resumed in Sept. of 1873," 1873.

66 LAC, RG 10, vol. 1872, file 747, part 0, "Regarding the letter against Dawson," 1872.

67 LAC, RG 10, vol. 1872, file 747, "Statement by Chief Blackstone, at Prince Arthur's Landing, 4th Feb. AD 1873"; "Extract of T.A.P. Towers' letter, 5th Feb. 1873 addressed to S.J. Dawson"; "S.J. Dawson to J. Howe, Secretary of State," 4 April 1873; "Dawson to the Secretary of State regarding Letter of 12 December 1872 addressed to the Governor General in Council," 30 August 1872.

68 Lindsay Russell would become surveyor general. In 1858 he had been Dawson's surveying assistant on the Dawson Route.

69 LAC, RG 10, vol. 1889, file 1264, "Telegram from Alexander Morris," 1 August 1873.

70 Morris, *The Treaties of Canada*, 56-57. According to Barry Cottam, Dawson invoked the rights of the common, a stance where labour entitles proprietorship, because he stressed that "wood on which Indians had bestowed labour was always paid for; and wood on which we had spent our own labour was ours." Barry Cottam, "Federal/Provincial Disputes, Natural Resources and the Treaty #3 Ojibwa, 1867-1924" (PhD dissertation, University of Ottawa, 1994), 252.

71 Morris, *The Treaties of Canada*, 59.

72 Ibid., 63-64.

73 Ibid., 320-27.

74 This information is presented by Alexander Morris in his published report (Morris, *The Treaties of Canada*, 70). Interpretations on this point differ. In the notes that he kept of the proceedings, Dawson penned that "if minerals were found on the Reserve the mine would be administered for their benefit, otherwise, the Indians could not claim it." LAC, MG 29 C76, "Notes taken at Indian Treaty, North West Angle, Lake of the Woods, from 30th Sept. 1873 to close of Treaty on 30th Sept." Even more interesting is what has been called the "Paypom Treaty," actually a set of original notes made by Joseph Nolin for Chief Powason at the treaty negotiations in 1873, which claimed that if the Ojibwa found minerals off the reserve, they could surely have them. Grand Council #3, "The Paypom Treaty," printed copy. Nolin's words have been interpreted to mean that the government bore a responsibility to remunerate successful Native exploring activities off the reserve. Dawson, however, for whatever reason, restricted his discussions of Native mineral rights in 1873 wholly to the reserve context. But for a fuller discussion of the controversy, see Rhonda Telford, "The Sound of the Rustling of the Gold Is Under My Feet Where I Stand, We Have a Rich Country: A History of Aboriginal Mineral Resources in Ontario" (PhD dissertation, University of Toronto, 1995), 211-12; Cottam, "Federal/ Provincial Disputes," 48-49.

75 "Adhesion to Treaty #3, made at the north-west angle of Lake of the Woods," 13 October 1873. Morris, *The Treaties of Canada*, 326-27. The erroneous spelling of the three chiefs' names in the above work shows that Morris had no idea how these names were pronounced and knew nothing of the Ojibwa language.

76 "Dawson to the Honorable Minister of the Interior," 26 December 1873. Morris, *The Treaties of Canada*, 327-29.

77 LAC, RG 10, vol. 1914, "Dawson to the Minister of the Interior," 29 January 1875.

78 An Order-in-Council, passed 8 July 1874, stated that reserves "should not include any lands known to the Commissioners to be mineral lands or any lands for which mineral lands bona fide applications have been filed with either the Dominion or Ontario Governments." For Dawson's report, see LAC, RG 10, vol. 1918, file 2790D, "Dawson to the Minister of the Interior," 29 January 1875.

79 Some of their lands had already been damaged by rising water levels associated with the construction of dams along the Dawson Route. Valuable ricing beds, shoreline gardens, and encampment grounds had all been flooded. For a discussion of what happened in this respect at Lac des Milles Lacs, see J.A. Lovisek, "Lac des Mille Lacs 'Dammed and Diverted': An Ethnohistorical Study," in *Papers of the Twenty-Fifth Algonquian Conference*, ed. William Cowan (Ottawa: Carleton University, 1994), 285-314 at 296-97.

80 Morris, *The Treaties of Canada,* ft. 328.

81 Janet E. Chute, *The Legacy of Shingwaukonse: A Century of Native Leadership* (Toronto: University of Toronto Press, 1998), 149-50.

82 Dawson obtained 227 votes out of the small number, 783, cast for three candidates. His victory was based mainly on Prince Arthur's Landing's opposition to the Mackenzie railway scheme, which would have bypassed Prince Arthur's Landing. Elizabeth Arthur, "The Frontier Politician," in *Aspects of Nineteenth-Century Ontario: Essays Presented to James J. Talman,* ed. F.H. Armstrong, H.A. Stevenson, and J.D. Wilson (Toronto: University of Toronto Press, 1974), 278-96 at 279-81.

83 Dawson, *Report of the Exploration,* 25-26.

84 Donald Swainson, "Introduction," in *Oliver Mowat's Ontario,* ed. Donald Swainson (Toronto: Macmillan, 1970), 1-11.

85 AO, Aemelius Irving Papers, MU 1465, 27/31/1 (1), "Simon J. Dawson to the Secretary of H.E. the Governor General," 7 April 1973, included with "Petition to His Excellency the Right Honourable Earl of Dufferin, K.C.B., Governor General of Canada in Council, 1873."

86 AO, MU 1465, 27/31/1 (1), "S.J. Dawson to the Secretary of H.E. the Governor General," 7 April 1873, included with "Petition to His Excellency the Right Honorable Earl of Dufferin, K.C.B., Governor General of Canada in Council, 1873"; AO, Aemelius Irving Papers, MU 1465, 27/31/1 (1), "S.J. Dawson to Colonel C. Stuart," 7 October 1881.

87 Canada, *House of Commons Debates,* 1885, 3243.

88 AO, MU 1465, 27/31/1 (1), "Simon J. Dawson to the Secretary of H.E. the Governor General," 7 April 1873.

89 Canada, *House of Commons Debates,* 31 March 1879, "Enfranchisement for Indians, Motion for Return," 844-45.

90 Canada, *House of Commons Debates,* 1 May 1879, 1689.

91 Canada, *House of Commons Debates,* 31 March 1879, 845.

92 Canada, *House of Commons Debates,* 5 May 1880, "An Act to Amend the Indian Act," 1995-96.

93 Canada, *House of Commons Debates,* 30 April 1885, 1487. Ontario's Mowat government gave some persons holding Indian status the vote and then retracted it, on charges of corruption, in 1883.

94 Canada, *House of Commons Debates,* 20 May 1885, 2007.

95 While the vote for Native people still retaining their Indian status would not be won in Canada until 1960, Dawson's efforts in this direction in the House between 1879 and 1886 should be noted as a crucial part of the history of the campaign for the Native franchise.

96 Canada, *House of Commons Debates,* 1880, vol. 1, 61-62. Dawson's speech to the House of Commons on the boundary question for 18 February 1880 is reprinted in Arthur, ed., *Thunder Bay District,* 25-26.

97 Arthur, "Dawson, Simon James," 262.

98 LAC, RG 10, vol. 1955, file 4492, part 0, "Fort William Indians claim reserve being stripped of timber," 1875.

99 LAC, RG 10, vol. 2115, file 21,900, "Petition of the Fort William Ojibwa to Lord Lorne," 1881.

100 Thomas Marks, born in Ireland, was a merchant and Prince Arthur's Landing's leading commercial figure. He served nine years as the reeve of Shuniah township and was elected Port Arthur's first mayor. He had been active in the Prince Arthur's Landing and Kaministiquia Railway. Marks' niece, Maria Wiley, married William Henry Plummer of Sault Ste Marie. Plummer had worked for the Marks family in Bruce Mines and, when he moved to the Sault in 1867, went into partnership with Thomas Marks to form Plummer and Marks General Merchants and Grocers. This partnership lasted until 1875 when Marks departed to Thunder Bay. Plummer's father, William Plummer, Sr., was the same person who had forced the Native land cession at Fort William in 1855, despite Simon Dawson's reluctance to engage in such a proceeding. William Plummer, Sr., had been mine manager in Bruce Mines but in 1868 was appointed superintendent of the Northern Superintendency in the Department of Indian Affairs. In 1873 he was promoted to central superintendent in the same department.

101 The Ojibwa also contended against the low price that they had received for a parcel of land that they had been pressured to cede by their agent, Amos Wright. LAC, RG 10, vol. 1080, 42, "L. Vankoughnet to J.A. Macdonald," 18 April 1882, "Indian Affairs' Deputy Superintendent's Letterbook, 28 April 1881-30 March 1882."

102 LAC, RG 10, vol. 2115, file 21,900, part 1, "John A. Macdonald to S.J. Dawson," 4 November 1882.

103 LAC, RG 10, vol. 2115, file 21,900, part 1, "Fort William Reserve, Surrender of Timber Land and Granting of Timber Licenses in Neebing Township," 1872-96.

104 Canada, *House of Common Debates*, 46 Vict., 1st Session, 5th Parl., 1883, 50-51. Edward Blake read a petition from the Ojibwa on the issue to the House.

105 LAC, RG 10, vol. 2115, file 21,900, part 1, "J. Caddy to L. Vankoughnet," 25 November 1882.

106 Canada, *House of Commons Debates,* 25 January 1884, 51-52. Although the government would not retract the hated lease, Indian Affairs blandly replied that as Farijana had a lawyer, she could take legal proceedings if she wished, but it would do nothing to intervene. LAC, RG 10, vol. 1085, 706, "L. Vankoughnet to J.A. Macdonald," 22 April 1884. And, when Josephine Farijana further threatened in 1886 to impose 5 percent interest on wood taken for building bridges and other local construction projects, the government's reply remained the same. "Father Jones' Inquiry into Difficulties on the Fort William Reserve" [*A.S.J. C.F., D-8, Memoir of Father Jones*], cited in Arthur, ed., *Thunder Bay District,* 200-4.

107 AO, Aemelius Irving Papers, MU 1476, 38/37F/4, G, "Letter from George Burden, Ontario Commissioner, to T.B. Pardee, Commissioner of Crown Lands for Ontario," 15 August 1883; "Letter from George Burden to T.B. Pardee," 17 August 1883.

108 Two historians have taken this stance, and one has even suggested that Dawson's presence in the House of Commons could have facilitated the company's acquisition of the lease. Cottam, "Federal/Provincial Disputes," 110; Telford, "The Sound of the Rustling of the Gold," 198.

109 Canada, *House of Commons Debates,* 4 May 1886, 1072.

110 Dawson even maintained that the system governing proprietorship of wood on reserves should be flexible enough so that voyageurs, presumably with the permission of the local band, could cut enough wood to make a shanty and collect firewood for an overnight stay. Canada, *House of Commons Debates,* 1890, 4903-4.

111 Canada, *House of Commons Debates,* 1886, 62-63; Canada, *House of Commons Debates,* 1886, "Fishing Rights of Indians on Lakes Huron and Nipissing," 693.

112 Dawson was not necessarily for or against Indian residential schools, for it was the economic health of the reserve community, not the state's assimilation policies, that engrossed his attention.

113 Canada, *House of Commons Debates,* 1886, 63.

114 Attorney-General's Office, 1252, "Correspondence in connection with arbitration re. Settlement of accts. between Dominion and the Provinces of Ontario and Quebec. Indian annuity claims from E.B. Borron to Aemelius Irving, 1891-1896."

115 When the Fort William Ojibwa objected to Wright renewing the timber licence covering their reserve, Dawson recommended a new man, J.P. Donnelly, for their agent. In making this decision, he sought the advice of Bishop Jamot, who upheld Dawson's contention that Donnelly would appeal to the Roman Catholic mission settlement. But when the local missionary, Father F. Hebert, received letters from Hector Langevin and Sir William Van Horne instructing him to support Dawson's electoral campaign during the 1887 election – evidently to capture what Native votes existed – Hebert became chagrined and instead encouraged those of his flock who exercised the franchise to vote for Dawson's political rival. LAC, Macdonald Papers, "Dawson to Lawrence Vankoughnet," 10 January 1883. See also LAC, RG 10, vol. 1080, 8 August 1882, "Father Jones' Inquiry into Difficulties on the Fort William Reserve" [*A.S.J. C.F., D-8, Memoir of Father Jones*], cited in Arthur, ed., *Thunder Bay District,* 200-4.

116 Until 1887 he still nominally ran under the Independent banner.

117 Arthur, *Simon J. Dawson, C.E.,* 27.

118 McDougall had been minister of public works in Mackenzie's Liberal government from 1867 to 1869, when work first began on the Dawson Route. He helped arrange the transfer of the Hudson's Bay Company's territories to Canada.

119 McDougall briefly acted as the first lieutenant governor of Manitoba.

120 LAC, RG10, vol. 1091, "Indian Affairs' Deputy Superintendent's Letterbook, 1 June-29 October 1886." From the evidence in this volume, it is obvious that, while upholding Native fishing rights, Dawson refused to get embroiled in charges and counter charges by competing parties.

121 AO, MU 831, Box 4, Dawson Family Papers, "Memorandum of S.J.D., Three Rivers, for Mr. Pennyfather. A report on the Indians at the head of Lake Superior, their habits, methods of subsistence etc.," 1860.

122 LAC, RG 10, vol. 3908, file 107,297, part 1, "Correspondence relating to fishing rights on Indian reserves throughout Canada, 1897-1898"; "Memoranda on the same."

123 Canada, *House of Commons Debates,* 11 May 1887, 382.

124 Dawson urged all relevant departments not to abide by the letter of the treaty on the matter of Native fisheries but to respect its "evident *spirit and meaning."* LAC, R. 10, vol. 3800, file 48,542, "Dawson to Deputy Minister of Indian Affairs," 28 May 1888, emphasis in original.

125 Canada, *House of Commons Debates,* 13 February 1889. See also LAC, RG 10, vol. 3800, file 48, 542.

126 Canada, *House of Commons Debates,* February-April 1886, 693-96, "Fishing Rights of Indians on Lakes Huron and Nipissing."

127 *Rat Portage News,* 1 March 1889, cited in Arthur, *Simon J. Dawson, C.E.,* 27.

128 Tim E. Holzkamm and Victor P. Lytwyn, "Rainy River Sturgeon: An Ojibwa Resource in the Fur Trade Economy," *The Canadian Geographer,* 32, 3 (Fall 1988): 194-205 at 202.

129 LAC, RG 20, vol. 3800, file 48,542.

130 In 1891 Dawson, departing from his former Independent stance on the encouragement of John A. Macdonald, lost the Conservative leadership nomination for Algoma to George Macdonell.

131 These appeals contain ethnographic evidence that in later years would appear in the context of Native fishing campaigns in the same region. See, for instance, Grand Council Treaty #3, *The Fishing Rights of Treaty #3 Indians* (Kenora: Grand Council Treaty #3, 1986), 16-25, 34-43.

132 LAC, RG 10, vol. 3908, file 107,297, part 1, "Simon J. Dawson, Commissioner, to Hayter Reed, Deputy Superintendent General of Indian Affairs, Ottawa," 26 April 1895, quoted in Hayter Reed, "Memo for the Information of the Minister," 18 November 1895.

133 LAC, RG 10, vol. 1921, file 2914, part 0, "Documents and correspondence relating to Simon J. Dawson's pension, 1874-1922." Simon's niece Mary Fuller (née Dawson) was the daughter of his brother Cosmo, who died when Mary was just a girl. She had been brought up by Father Aeneas Dawson, another of Simon's brothers. Simon's petition was later taken up by the Fort William City Council and the Thunder Bay Historical Society at a time when Mary was elderly and destitute. Arthur, *Simon J. Dawson, C.E.,* 31.

134 This status must be reserved exclusively for certain prominent Native chiefs.

6

The "Friends" of Nahnebahwequa

Celia Haig-Brown

But is it not a very unreasonable thing, that whilst persons from all parts of the world can settle in Canada, and have no questions put to them respecting their literary attainments – persons of the lowest grade, can settle there without question if they are willing to pay the price of the land – that these people who are the natural and original owners of the soil, are not permitted even to purchase the land on which they have been living for many years, but are liable to be dispossessed of it by their white neighbours.

– Robert Alsop, 1860[1]

I shall be going to a land of strangers, but I hope that I shall meet with honest justice and this hope keeps up my sagging spirits. I cannot bear to see my children deprived of their lawful home and inheritance.

– Nahnebahwequa, 1860[2]

One of the purposes of this chapter is to highlight concerns expressed by a number of non-Aboriginal people in nineteenth-century North America and England regarding injustices being perpetrated on Aboriginal peoples *as colonization of their territories proceeded*. An examination of the history of the struggle of one remarkable Aboriginal woman, Nahnebahwequa, to obtain title to her land, demonstrates how various non-Aboriginal friends and her husband recognized the worthiness of her quest and worked to support her in it. It also shows her and her supporters deserving of a place in the histories that we teach the citizens of Canada. A close look at documentary evidence related to Nahnebahwequa's life complicates dichotomous separations between missionaries and Aboriginal people: it shows Christians of Aboriginal and of European ancestry working together to try to redress the injustices of colonization during the second half of the nineteenth century. It shows that some Christians and faith communities wanted to move beyond talk and proselytizing to acts of social justice and equitable treatment as part of their expressions of faith. Tangentially, it reveals the extent to which some people of Aboriginal ancestry were doing the missionary work of Christianizing their own people even as they were seeking the justice that conversion to the faith had promised them.[3]

In this investigation lies a productive possibility of engaging in "imaginative understandings"[4] of the well-intentioned although often misinformed colonizers and settlers who came into contact with Aboriginal people of nineteenth-century Canada. At least some of the missionaries who saw their work of conversion as serving God did not miss seeing the corruption of the land speculators who followed on their heels. As the latter pushed the newly Christianized Indians from their traditional lands and hard-wrought farms, thoughtful missionaries and others questioned the role that they played in facilitating the displacement. Aboriginal people themselves were often the clearest spokespeople in bringing this injustice to their consciousness. The recognition that, in promoting the acceptance of Christianity in the lives of Aboriginal people, they were also contributing to making them easy targets for dishonest government officials and land speculators with whom they were connected had a significant impact on some Euro-Canadians at the time. These people, including a number represented in this chapter, added work with Aboriginal people seeking justice, particularly around land and other rights as citizens, to their labour as missionaries, lawyers, and developers. Not only did their understanding of Aboriginal people shift over time as they came to know and were influenced by them, but their understanding of their co-colonizers in government and real estate also deepened. Questions about European missionaries' responses to the greed for land and resources that was facilitated through their proselytizing and about the ways that Christians in London, specifically the Quakers, or members of the Society of Friends, responded to and supported trips that Aboriginal people made there to plead the case for their lands have provided some of the impetus for this chapter.

Indeed, the chapter's primary impetus was a reading of Penny Petrone's fascinating collection *First People, First Voices*,[5] in which a reference to a trip that Catherine Sonego Sutton made in 1860 to see Queen Victoria about her property stands out. Nahnebahwequa, as Sutton was more commonly known – an Anishnaabe[6] name meaning "Upright Woman" – wrote to her uncle and grandfather on the 19 June[7]: "So you see I have been to see the Queen. The Duke [of Newcastle] went before us, and he made two bows, and then I was left in the presence of the Queen; she came forward to meet me, and held out her hand for me to kiss, but I forgot to kiss it, and only shook hands with her ... Then the Queen bowed to me and said, 'I am happy to promise you my aid and protection.'" What followed from this reading was a desire to know about the sincerity and efficacy of this promise. Did the queen take the actions necessary to permit Nahne, as she is still called by those close to her history,[8] to regain her land? This initial question led to additional ones regarding the details of Nahne's trip and the support that she received during and after her travels.

Setting the Scene

The narrative that follows provides insight into those non-Aboriginal people on both sides of the Atlantic who worked for some form of justice for the Aboriginal people being exploited and cheated as Canada's nation building progressed. It presents the story of a strong woman who stood up for her rights and those of her family at a time when too many women are constructed in history books as silent and apparently dependent on the men in their immediate context. Her story interrupts any simple understandings of the role of all women, but particularly Aboriginal women, in Canada's development as a nation. While the focus of the chapter is her 1860 trip to London and the people who found ways to support her in her venture, aspects of her biography and her band's situation provide relevant context for the trip. Most important, from the early 1800s onward, settlers were increasingly encroaching on Anishnaabe lands in southern Ontario.[9] Deliberately shady land deals and treaties presented to desperate people augmented the effects of a fundamental lack of understanding between the parties based on incongruous worldviews in relation to land ownership, among many other things.

Nahnebahwequa was born on the Credit River flats, near what is now Port Credit, Ontario, in 1824.[10] Also known as Catherine Brown Sunegoo,[11] she was the niece and adopted daughter of the Anishnaabe Methodist minister, Peter Jones (Kahkewaquonaby).[12] Her family, along with several other Anishnaabe families, became Methodists while she was still a toddler and settled at the Credit Mission located on Lake Ontario southwest of Toronto.[13] At the age of thirteen, she made her first trip to England, travelling with her English-born aunt, Eliza, and uncle during the year 1837-38. Peter Jones was there for an earlier meeting with Queen Victoria to discuss land title for his band at Credit River.[14] Certainly, this trip and her aunt and uncle's influence must have had an impact on Nahnebahwequa, placing her in a more knowledgeable position from which to make the later trip when subsequent land concerns emerged. While her uncle was assured of Queen Victoria's support of the recommendation to grant land titles to his people, over the years that followed, ownership was never achieved.[15] In 1839, at the age of fourteen, Nahne married William Sutton, an English shoemaker[16] who had immigrated to Canada in 1830,[17] later becoming a Methodist missionary. A number of years later, one of her friends recorded these words about William, based on her conversations with Nahne: he "was an Englishman, rather older than herself, who, she used to say, 'had gone over to Canada when in his teens, from a sense of duty towards the Indians, and had become an Indian that he might be useful to them.'"[18] Clearly, his later expression of commitment to her cause came out of a deep and personal understanding of the situation that his wife and other members of her community faced.

When pressures to give up the last of their land at the mouth of the Credit River finally drove Chief Joseph Sawyer (Kawahjegezhegwabe) to conciliate, most of the band moved to what came to be called New Credit on the Grand River – ironically, to land that the British had earlier secured by "purchase"[19] from the Mississauga for the Iroquois refugees of the war between the British and the United States.[20] Although some band members considered moving north to Owen Sound, the soil quality was so poor that most changed their minds and returned to or stayed in the south.[21] By 1846 Catherine and William, along with two other families, had already commenced clearing land and decided to follow through on the original plans to stay in Owen Sound.[22] There the Nawash Band allocated Catherine Sutton two hundred acres, giving her written title to it based on her Anishnaabe ancestry.[23] They also welcomed her and her children into the band, expecting that they would be entitled to the same claims and annuities as other band members.[24] Shortly thereafter, Nahnebahwequa ceased to be a member of the New Credit Mississauga, receiving a cash settlement in relation to her entitlement from that band.[25]

The move from a community of like-minded Mississauga Methodists to a remote and undeveloped wilderness appears to have been most difficult. In a letter written back to the Credit people, among whom she had been the "Leader of a Class" of young women,[26] Nahnebahwequa talks of the trials and hardships of the world and looking forward to "the glorious day when I shall meet you and all good Missionaries in the kingdom of our Saviour."[27] Homesickness overwhelming her, she writes of the "happy hours we used to spend together, while I was with you at Credit. But the happy hours are gone."[28] Work must have occupied most of her days given that she had a growing family and was developing a farm in the wilderness. The couple cultivated forty or fifty acres, "erected thereon a commodious house, barn and stables; involving an outlay of 1,000 dollars," and generally proved to be the ideal Christian farmers and citizens that the missionaries and government of the time were purportedly looking for.[29]

Indeed, they were so successful that in 1852, William was asked by the Missionary Board to go to Garden River near Sault Ste Marie to be the superintendent of a model farm. In light of later developments, it is interesting to speculate about possible meetings between William, Nahne, and

Shingwaukonse and his son Ogista, leaders in Garden River during and after this time. In addition to making a trip to London in the early 1830s, Shingwaukonse had also, before his death in 1854, "just finished forcing the colonial crown to negotiate the Robinson Treaties (1850) by resisting forcefully an invasion of his territory by mining companies."[30] About the time that he was to leave Owen Sound, William, based on his English heritage, submitted a petition to the earl of Elgin, the governor general of British North America, asking to purchase the two hundred acres of land encompassing the lots where they had made improvements for protection "should the Indians ever surrender the said land to the Government, of which there is indeed too great a probability."[31] William and Nahnebahwequa were probably concerned that the deed that the band had issued her would not be recognized by the government under such circumstances. Nahnebahwequa and the children joined William in Garden River the following year; he had expressed concerns that the family was too far from a place of worship and from schools. Presumably Garden River promised some sense of community that they had missed in their move to Owen Sound. From Garden River, they moved again when William "was engaged by the Rev. W. Shaw to asist [sic] him in making improvements on a new mission in the State of Michigan."[32] Returning to Owen Sound in the spring of 1857,[33] they discovered that the land surrender they had feared had occurred.

In their absence, a few members of the band had met with government people and surrendered a huge portion of the band's land,[34] which had subsequently been divided into farm lots and was being offered for sale by the Indian Department. At this time, Chief David Sawyer, another Credit River Mississauga who had moved to Owen Sound and become chief at the band's request, had also been away doing missionary work. The lots for sale included the Suttons' two hundred acres. David Sawyer lost his forty-three-acre farm as well as a three-acre site that he had been preparing for a wharf. Nahnebahwequa and others decided to go to the sale, where she informed the land purchaser of her claims on her house and requested that the land be removed from the sale because she would purchase it as well as additional acreage being farmed by her sister and mother at the "upset price"[35] – in total, 491 acres.[36] As it turned out, she, David Sawyer, and school teacher Abner Elliott were not permitted to make the first payment, which would have allowed them to exchange certificates of sale for the deeds, being told that the lots could not be sold to Indians. Conrad Van Dusen, the Methodist missionary in the area, wrote, "They placed in my hands the certificates they had obtained from Mr. Bartlett, the agent, certifying that they had purchased the lots at a certain price, and also the money to make the payments required; and on my way to Mr. Jackson's office in another part of town, Mr. Bartlett[37] asked me to see those certificates, and retained them, informing me at the same time he had just

Wearing what she called "simple Christian dress," Nahnebahwequa appealed to her many friends and supporters on two continents in her struggle for justice in land ownership

received instructions from the Department not to sell any of those farms to Indians."[38]

Compounding the injustice, Nahnebahwequa was told that she was no longer eligible for the annuity that was to be distributed to band members in partial payment for the surrendered lands because she was married to a white man.[39]

At a meeting of the General Indian Council held at Rama in July of 1858, where the land grievances were discussed, Nahnebahwequa was appointed as the representative of the chiefs to travel to England to let the British authorities know what had happened and to seek their support to address the disagreement over the land.[40] It appears that the chiefs recognized what was continually noted as she travelled: Nahne was an accomplished orator. In addition, they would have been aware of her earlier trip, which they may have seen as giving her an advantage in negotiating with the English authorities. Perhaps she was also seen to have some of the characteristics of a traditional Anishnaabe leader described in detail in Janet Chute's study of Shingwaukonse, the chief of the Garden River Nation at the time that Nahne and her family lived there. Chute argues that great Anishnaabe leaders were those who listened carefully to what the people wanted and then worked with them to get there. In addition, they rarely put themselves forward as leaders; rather, they worked quietly and effectively to accomplish results when the time was right.[41] Although her initial leave taking was interrupted when it appeared that at least one of the petitions submitted to the authorities would yield results,[42] it again became clear that such was not the case. Having exhausted all channels of appeal, including the Legislative Assembly of Canada, the Anishnaabe saw the trip to England as the only remaining hope that justice would be done. Indeed, a number of members of Parliament encouraged them in this line of action.[43] On the other hand, not all felt that an Aboriginal woman in this role was fitting: "Some laughed and others, through the public journals, reproached her as an 'arrant impostor,'" claiming that "Indians could purchase land without impediment."[44]

The Trip to London

It was on her trip to London that Nahne first encountered the friends who were to remain connected to her and her family's cause throughout her life. Nahne began her trip with little more than a strong faith in her project, her community's belief in her, at least one contact name in New York, and the ability to persuade people of the justice of the cause. Along the way, through her cultural and personal strengths, she gained the support of a variety of non-Aboriginal people with whom she came in contact, people to whom she communicated clearly the injustice of the loss of her land. On the first leg of her journey, Nahnebahwequa travelled to New York, where she was to embark on the boat to England; she had a letter of introduction but on approaching that person "was disappointed"[45] by a cold reception.[46] By a stroke of good fortune or fate, "entire strangers" noticed her despondency as she returned to her hotel.[47] Feeling at least temporarily hopeless, she had gone to her room to pray when a knocking at the door interrupted her. "I arose from my knees and opened it, when there stood a little girl, with a smiling countenance. She said her mother wished to see me. She said she was a little Friend. I could not think what she meant by the term 'friend.' I thought I understood what was included in the word, but now it seemed to have another application."[48] In the dining room, Nahnebahwequa met the girl's mother and a Captain Nab, who, upon hearing her mission, indicated great interest in supporting her. This was the first of many contacts with Quakers in New York and England. The two explained to her that "they were frequently called Quakers, but that 'Friends' was their right name."[49] The following day, "another aged gentleman, Mr. H. Meriam,[50] of Brooklyn Heights, came on purpose to see me, and questioned me closely, and examined all my papers, and then entered into the spirit of my mission with all his heart and told me that he was a Friend."[51]

Relations between the Quakers whom Nahne encountered that day and those she met in the weeks and months that followed exemplify some of the commitments of the Society of Friends in England and the United States. Building on George Fox's own experience of inner light – or the experience of Christ within – in mid-seventeenth-century England, many Quakers have continued to see as central to their spirituality "'a first hand knowledge of God,' a knowledge *ultimately* grounded on his [sic] own personal conviction and not on outward authority."[52] This light is present in all human beings, and therefore all have the potential to achieve salvation through their own connection to this inner spirit. William Penn and 1,400 English settlers established the first major presence of Friends in New England in 1681. Although a few others had come to the United States, notably to Massachusetts starting about twenty-five years earlier, they were sent out of the country, jailed, and persecuted in many other ways. Upon arriving in the "new world," Penn almost immediately recognized the injustices being dealt "Indians" and advocated good relations with the "red man" as one way to approach redress. Unlike the dealings of non-Aboriginal peoples in so many other areas of the United States and Canada, "Under [his] rule no Indians were made drunk that they might sign away valuable claims, no false maps were shown them, no false weights deceived them in their trading intercourse."[53] Starting in Carolina and New Jersey, Penn eventually drew up the Constitution for the state of Pennsylvania and there began a very progressive and consistently free colony. In the years that followed, however, the Aboriginal peoples' relations with Penn's sons and other successors deteriorated; only toward the end of the century did the Friends once again work to make amends for the wrongdoings.[54]

Quietism is the term most often used to characterize Quaker spirituality, particularly in its early days. At monthly meetings, men and women bowed their heads in silence with spoken prayers or messages arising "out of this silence." In direct contrast to the biological racists and hierarchical social Darwinists who controlled many other Christian sects, the ministry came from all those attending no matter their station in life, age, gender, or education. While not an entirely unique approach to religion, this paradoxical fusing of individualized experience of "inner light" into a loose organization provided a space where the committed could relate to one another. "By the early nineteenth century, the Society of Friends [in the United States] had created a system of religious doctrine and moral regulation of considerable complexity."[55] Notably absent from this set of regulations was any mention of rebirth, revival, consistent interpretation of the Bible, conversion, or even church aspects central to other denominations of America's evangelical churches.

As the century unfolded, by 1860, when Nahne made her first acquaintance with the Friends in New York, major splits had rent the Society of Friends. Some remained focused on quiet spirituality, while others aligned more closely with the evangelical churches, their doctrinaire Biblical interpretation, and a more hierarchical form of meeting, including the appointment of a minister rather than seeing each member as equally able to minister. One of these latter factions, strongly influenced by Englishman John Joseph Gurney, particularly during his visit to the United States in 1837-40, was known for the active pursuit of social reform.[56] Central to the Renewal in the late 1850s, following Gurney's influence, was the understanding that Quakers were "a people apart from the world yet actively involved in it."[57] It is this sentiment that arguably placed the New York Friends in a position to work closely with Nahne in her project. Significantly, Quakers have always given strong credence to women as equal in ministry to men. It was natural for those she encountered to invite Nahne to accompany them to a meeting to make a plea for help.

Indeed, one of the first things that the Friends whom she met at the hotel did was to give her the opportunity to address the Friends of New York at their public worship. The assembly listened intently as she told them of the reasons for her travels, introducing herself as the Christian daughter of a chief of the Ojibwa tribe and focusing on the denial of land title to Indians. Caught up by the passion of her speech, and consistent with their commitment to working with Indians for justice in the face of colonization, the group assigned a committee to work with her. Ever vigilant, they in turn reviewed the papers that she carried with her, which included: a letter from the Indian Department; some letters from ministers of various congregations; copies of newspaper articles on the topic;[58] and most important, the memorial addressed to the Duke of Newcastle, principal secretary of state for the colonies, and the petition of David Sawyer, Catherine Sutton, and Abner Elliott, which made the request that they be allowed to retain the farm lots that they had purchased in the sale.[59] On 29 March the committee called a public meeting on her behalf at the Friends' meeting house on 20th Street. They presented her to a packed house, outlining their informed support of her venture. She then spoke for nearly an hour[60] and "was listened to with great interest, and many Friends shed tears,"[61] agreeing to support her in her venture.[62] The New Yorkers gave her letters of introduction to a number of Quakers in England and Scotland, raised approximately $500 for the passage and trip – "two young ladies, members of two opulent New York families, opened their purses to this gifted daughter of the forest"[63] – and secured a first-class cabin for her on the steamship *Persia,* which incidentally did not keep her from severe seasickness. She left New York on 25 April with enough additional money for her expenses while in England.[64]

The connections maintained between English and American Friends as committed pacifists, during and after the War of Independence, served Nahne well. On her arrival in Liverpool, Friends who had been informed of her mission came on board to meet her.[65] Mr. and Mrs. J. Hadwin took her to their house, from where, after a few days of recovery in Liverpool, Nahnebahwequa continued on to London and the beginning of an enduring alliance and friendship with Christine and Robert Alsop. This couple, two English Friends with whom she stayed for most of the next four months, welcomed her into residence at 36 Park Road, Stoke Newington. They received her "with warm and open hearts ... To their devoted and persevering labor, on her behalf, is largely to be ascribed the prosperity which attended her mission."[66] They began by providing important connections with other members of a very powerful group of British humanitarians, many of whom were also Friends, the ever well-intentioned Aborigines Protection Society (APS). (See Michael Blackstock's chapter in this volume for more detail on their work.) In the introduction to his history of the society, Bourne writes, "In attempting to befriend the native races in the ever growing British dominions and 'spheres of influence,' and as far as possible those in other parts of the world who are bound to us by the ties of our common humanity, the Aborigines Protection Society has inevitably been principally occupied in calling attention to what appeared to it errors in policy, administrative abuses, instances of wrong-doing by irresponsible adventurers, and other faults and crimes, in hopes of procuring such correction and reparation as were possible."[67] Clearly, this progressive group had a commitment to supporting people like Nahne in their efforts to achieve justice in the face of colonial government. In addition to their recognition of Nahne's cause, they seemed particularly taken with her strong connections to Christianity, which she never hesitated to declare.

Nahne made an immediate impact on the Quaker community generally. A description of her in an article in the *Intelligencer* describes her being of "'tawny skin,' of pleasing aspect and most gentle manners, refined by Christianity, and gifted with the simple eloquence of nature."[68] She caught the imaginations of her host, Robert Alsop, and of Thomas Hodgkin, honorary secretary of the Society of Friends, who wrote evocatively of her: "Alone and unfriended, this heroic woman left her husband and five children, her forest home still bound up in ice and snow, resigning herself to encounter unknown difficulties and perils, to prevent, if possible, the extinction of the few scattered remnants of a noble race of people."[69] At a well-attended gathering at the Friends' meeting house on Gracechurch Street shortly after her arrival in London, Nahnebahwequa worked her oratorical magic once more with another gathering of sympathetic listeners. She addressed "the audience with such true pathos, as deeply to interest them in the story of the wrongs of the poor Indian. It was a touching appeal to those who loved and valued their homes with all their pleasing and tender associations and struck a chord that vibrated near the heart."[70] She was careful to outline the injustices and contradictions inherent in her situation: "When I wanted to buy my home, they took me for an Indian, and said I was an Indian: I could not buy. And when I applied as an Indian for my payment, they said I was a white woman, because I was married to a white man: and so you see they can turn the thing whichever way they have a mind to just suit their cause."[71] Ever focused on her assignment, she also made clear her need to meet with the queen. A number there, including John Bright, an influential member of Parliament, took up her case. With an introductory memorial signed by many members of the Friends, she met with the Duke of Newcastle. The court circular of the *London Times* for 16 June 1860 indicates that at this meeting "on the subject of the Canadian Indians' lands,"[72] she was accompanied by the Alsops and John Bright. It goes on to say that "private influence that had near approach to the royal family was employed and ere long she received a message through the Duke that there was an open door, and an invitation to call and see the Queen on the following day."[73]

On 19 June 1860, Nahnebahwequa wrote excitedly to Canada in the letter also quoted above:

My Dear Uncle and Grandfather – I have just returned from the palace ... The Duke [of Newcastle] went before us and he made two bows, and then I was in the presence of the Queen. She came forward to meet me, and held out her hand for me to kiss, but I forgot to kiss it and only shook hands with her. The Queen asked me many questions, and was very kind in her manners, and very friendly to me. Then my Quaker friend spoke to the Duke, and said, "I suppose the Queen knows for what purpose my friend has come?" The Duke said, "All my papers have been explained and laid before Her Majesty, and I have Her Majesty's commands to investigate the Indian affairs when I go to Canada with the Prince of Wales." Then the Queen bowed to me, and said, "I am happy to promise you my aid and protection" and asked me my name. The Queen then looked at her husband, who stood at her left side, and smiled.[74]

The queen herself also noted the visit in her journal;

19 June 1860 (Buckingham Palace)
After luncheon, the Duke of Newcastle introduced ... an Indian Chieftainess of the Ojibeways, called Nahnee-bah-wee-quay, or Mrs. C. Sutton, as she is a Christian and is married to an English sailor. She is of the yellow colour of the American Indians, with black hair, and was dressed in a strange European dress with a coloured shawl and straw hat with feathers. She speaks English quite well, and is come on behalf of her Tribe to petition against some grievance as regards their land.[75]

The entry in the court circular for Wednesday, 20 June, records, "Her Majesty the Queen gave audience yesterday at Buckingham Palace, to Nah-ne-bah-wee-quay, Mrs. Catherine B. Sutton, of Owen Sound, Canada West accompanied by Mrs. Christine R. Alsop. Mrs. Sutton was presented by the Duke of Newcastle, Secretary of State for the Colonies."[76] Nahnebahwequa brought with her "some pretty articles of Indian manufacture for the Queen's children, which were presented. They were accepted and doubtless appreciated."[77]

In a letter to E. Meriam in New York written on 7 July, Robert Alsop further described the visit, confirming the queen's promise of support, to which his wife, Christine, was witness. In particular, at Her Majesty's command, the Duke of Newcastle and the Prince of Wales, who were about to leave on an official visit to Canada, were to investigate the case.[78] All felt very hopeful for a speedy resolution to the concerns. In another letter written by Nahnebahwequa herself to a friend in New York, she acknowledged having "dined with Mr. Rothschild in the company of thirty or forty others, and spoke of the splendour and riches of the table."[79] But the Alsops remained her primary connection, and they wrote fondly of her in a letter to a friend: "Nah-nee-bahwe-qua has been our guest for seven weeks. We are much edified by her Christian character, and feel it is a privilege to have her under our roof."[80] This comment, of course, articulates the inescapable, contradictory tension that Friends and members of the APS especially respected Aboriginal people who shed their traditional spirituality and took up a good Christian life. Even as they worked against injustice, they implicitly honoured Nahne for her Christian faith.

While engaged in the serious business of seeking justice for her people, Nahnebahwequa was also engaged in another serious activity. In July she gave birth to her sixth child, a son, whom she named Alsop Albert Edward in honour of her host and the Crown Prince. In the memoirs of both Christine and Robert Alsop, the birth is mentioned, as is the significance of the time that they spent with Nahnebahwequa. Christine's includes the comment that both she and Robert "entered warmly into the case,"[81] while

Robert's states, "An occurrence which took place in the year 1860 was of such an interesting character, and it engaged so much of his time and attention that we cannot pass it by. It may be remembered that an Indian lady came to this country."[82] Robert wrote to his sister in August, apologizing for not writing sooner: "Our time has been so fully occupied that there has been no opportunity for writing. We now seem to have come to a little pause. As for our Indian guest, she is now so far recovered as not to be an object of anxiety, and her little man doing well. They call me Grandpapa, and nothing will do but he should bear the name of 'Alsop,' a perpetuation of the name very unlooked for."[83] He went on to write about how busy he had been making sure that the Friends "in the country" were getting Nahnebahwequa's case into the press and also communicating to Canada to arrange a deputation to meet the Duke of Newcastle when he arrived there with the Prince of Wales.[84]

Following the birth of her son, as August moved into the beginnings of fall, Nahnebahwequa made plans to return to Canada. The Alsops accompanied her and her son to Liverpool, where, on 14 September, she made a final, stirring speech to a public meeting held under the auspices of the Aborigines Protection Society of London. The reporter for the *Liverpool Courier* chose to include the text of her speech *"verbatim et literatim,"* recognizing her oratorical prowess with an acknowledgment that "her strong emphasis gave additional point to the words."[85] Her speech again captures the complex location she occupied and her clear sense that her support depended on her alignment with Christianity. She began by expressing her happiness that the audience was considerably larger than she had been led to expect and went on to talk about her choice of "simple Christian dress" as opposed to "dress in an Indian style."[86] Her intent, she said, was to impress upon them her Christianity and civilization; throughout her speech, she strategically separated herself from paganism or what we might refer to as Native spirituality today.[87] "I have been asked by different people, why didn't I fetch my Indian dress. I tell them I had none; this was my dress; this is the way we dress. I tell them we are not pagans, that we try to be like white people – to be clean and decent, and do what we can to be like the civilized people." She moved from an elaboration of this point to a focus on the real concern: "But how can the poor Indian be civilized? As soon as he makes his land valuable then he is driven further back, and the poor Indian has to begin over again. It is said that the Indian is lazy; but he is lazy because he has alway [sic] to go further back; he is only clearing the land for the white man and making it valuable for the Indian department; and so he has to go further back. And they know that the work they put on their land, that their children won't get the benefit of it."[88] She encouraged members of the audience not to lose sight of the struggle in which her people were engaged: to be able to purchase their land and ensure that this cycle would stop. "We want people to help the poor Indian because they have been driven from one place to another, but now we are getting to the end of the peninsula, and where to go next, we dont [sic] know." Having received a letter from her husband, saying that Indians were to be able to purchase land, she saw that this flawed proposal established a double standard:

> We can purchase land – but on what conditions? Why, the Indian must be civilized: he must talk English, talk French, read and write, and be well qualified for everything before he can purchase land. Why, the poor Indians, none of them can go there. Poor things, how are they to get their education? And is that the way they do with your own people? Why, I can tell you something. I have seen people in our own county that came from your country that could neither read nor write; and they came to buy Indian land! But the poor Indian must be so well qualified before he can have a house of his own.[89]

Demonstrating the way that her Christianity allowed her to maintain her connections with and commitment to all the "poor Indians" of her community, she clearly impressed her audience one more time. She closed this final talk to the people of England to great applause; indeed, as the reporter comments, "she had also been frequently interrupted in the course of her address, which she delivered with considerable force."[90]

The next day, the Alsops saw her and their tiny namesake off as Nahne boarded the vessel *Persia* once more to return to New York. Christine's memorials record the final parting: "The morning on which they left Liverpool, on their return to America, it was touching to see Christine Majolier Alsop carrying the little one in her arms on board the large steamer; evidently feeling the parting from him as from a loved and cherished object of her affection."[91] Back in New York, Nahnebahwequa was welcomed and stayed with friends for a couple of weeks, recovered from her fatigue, and took the train on 8 October, by way of Suspension Bridge and Toronto.[92] From there, she took the train to Collingwood, where William met her "with a small boat" to bring her home.[93] No doubt, she arrived with considerable hope in her heart and some sense of satisfaction with her mission.

Home Again

It soon became clear that there was only disappointing news.[94] Although the Duke of Newcastle and his associates had met a deputation of ten or eleven white men and three Indians on 11 September, the "five minute" meeting was most unsatisfactory. In a memorandum presented on behalf of the Walpole Island chief, Petway Gishick, another non-Aboriginal supporter, J.W. Keating, outlined a summary of the major concerns. The first was land tenure: the memorandum proposed that an allotment be made for each family according to size, which "should be made in fee ... without the power of alienation except to transfer to the children;"[95] that reserves be secure from further dispossession; and that if land surrenders were made, the people who have farms should be allowed to purchase those lands. Some specific requests regarding the situation of the Walpole Indians were included as well as a reference to government mismanagement of funds that had come directly from Indian lands and the outright dishonesty of some officials of the Indian Department. The solution to these problems (ironically, it turns out) was seen to lie in the transfer of Indian administration from Britain to Canada. Finally, Keating raised and commented on the issue of a woman being deprived of her annuity because she married a white man: "that a woman and her offspring should be punished, mulcted of their dues, for indulging her legitimate inclinations, seems to me, and to them, a crying injustice."[96]

William Sutton recorded in his journal that "the Duke remarked that he did not see how he could do anything in regard to redressing the Indians' wrongs as the Power was allmost [sic] entirely in the hands of the Provincial Authorities."[97] Mr. Pennefeather then "talked very rapidly for a few seconds to show that the subject of redressing Indians wrongs was beyond the Dukes [sic] jurisdiction."[98] Indeed, the transfer of the Indian Department from England to Canada had occurred in February of that year.[99] The meeting ended abruptly, although the Duke did indicate that he would take the time to go over the papers that he had been given and that he expected there would be another opportunity to meet before he left the country. The original petitioners waited in vain for a response to their submission.

The next year saw continuing disappointment with efforts to secure land title. On 3 March 1861 Nahnebahwequa continued to appeal to her non-Aboriginal supporters, writing to a friend in New York, "We ourselves do not know what to do till we hear from the Duke of Newcastle, or maybe we will not hear from him. He said he could not give an answer until he got to Portland."[100] Another letter written on 26 March was described as one "written after all hope of redress was given up."[101] She refers to accusations made by the Duke that she had been engaged in land speculation when she bought more than her own farm at the sale and that she was a white woman because she had married an Englishman, pointing out that if the Duke had listened to the Indians at the meeting instead of to the government officials who surrounded him during his trip, he could have heard the truth.[102] In a letter to the Friends of New York dated 30 March, Nahnebahwequa wrote in unequivocal terms:

We were sure, that if we could only have an investigation, the dark deeds of the department would be brought to light; and so we have been doomed to disappointment of a most vexatious kind. It would not be so vexing, if the Duke had been manly enough to acknowledge that he had failed in making satisfactory examination ... I argue that the Duke is guilty of a great wrong towards the Indians. As he has made his investigation based entirely through the parties complained of to her majesty; for he did not allow a solitary friend of the Indians to be present to plead our case.[103]

In addition, the Duke had sullied Nahnebahwequa's name by suggesting that she was "a bearer of false accusations."[104] In her growing frustration, she writes, "I have always heard that Canada was a free country; but it is only for some, but not for the Aborigines of America."[105]

Similarly, in the Aborigines Protection Society's annual report of 1861, an entry indicates that their memorial, given to the Duke as he left for Canada, had not been addressed, nor had any satisfaction been secured by the supporters and complainants with whom the Duke had met in Canada. As the Aborigines Protection Society sought reasons for this lack of response, the Suttons were more focused on serious questioning about the intents of those in power. Their communications with each other proved invaluable in their continuing pressure for a just resolution to the situation. In June, William Sutton again wrote to Robert Alsop about the progress to date on the land, "We are trying to purchase our home, and expect to succeed"[106] – an indication that they were still living on it and planting crops. Sutton disagreed with Alsop's account of the Duke's inaccessibility during the visit and the subsequent lack of response, pointing out that the Duke had had ample time to prepare and could have arranged more time to be with the deputation about which he had been forewarned. Rather, Sutton posited that the Canadian officials had deliberately limited the time in order to conceal "their system of wholesale Robbery and corruption."[107] In her account of the whole situation, Nahnebahwequa railed against the Indian Department:

The Indian Department have tried every Dodge and Quirk they could think of no matter how flimsy – at one time they have told me that I had no connection with the Owen Sound or Cape Crocker Indians – but that I allways [sic] belonged to the Credit Tribe. At another time, they have told me that I had no connection with any Band or Tribe of Indians because I had sold all right title and Claim to all Indian Benefits – and then again that I had Forfeited all my Claims because I had been living in the United States – and lastly because I was married to a White Man I could not any longer be considered as an Indian.[108]

She went on to say: "I am charged with the unpardonable sin of marrying a White Man, I should like to know if you have a law in England, that would deprive a woman of Property left her, by her Fathers will or if you please inherited property – I ask have you a Law that would deprive that woman of her property because she got married to a Frenchman?"[109]

In 1862 there was still no result. The Aborigines Protection Society reported: "We regret to say that thus far these efforts have not resulted in the removal of the anomalies of which we complained; and we fear that the present state of things will continue until the friends of the Red Man in Canada itself endeavour, by local organization and influence, to obtain for their oppressed fellow-subjects those rights which it is practically within the power of the Canadian Executive and Parliament to bestow."[110] Even as her health failed, Nahnebahwequa continued to write to the Alsops, keeping them apprised of some of her news. A travelling Friend, John Ray, wrote of his visit to her and her family in the fall of 1863 in their two-storey log house "standing upon the bluff shore of the Georgian Bay." The two elder daughters played the harmonium, "performing several pieces accompanied by voice." By this time there were eight children, "the youngest a few days old."[111] Ray was warmly received, spending the evening listening to Nahnebahwequa reminisce about her travels and the many friends she had made.[112]

Within two years, at the age of forty-one, Nahnebahwequa was gone. She struggled with asthma the last two years of her life but on the day of her death had seemed much better. She accompanied William in the boat to visit a neighbour and on the return home said that she felt very sick; within minutes, she was dead. Catherine Sutton never saw the deed for her land. Her mission, which had shown much promise, turned out to be only one piece in the continuing unsatisfactory efforts to secure justice for the Anishnaabe people. Significantly, the deed was eventually granted to her white husband, William Sutton. David Sawyer and Elliott Abner, the other two Aboriginal people whom she had represented, received no land and no recompense for the loss of their land. In 1867, two years after Nahnebahwequa's death, Conrad Van Dusen wrote about David Sawyer, "The chief was therefore dispossessed of his house and land, for which he had obtained an Indian Deed; and that part also for which he had paid the Indians in cash down the full amount agreed on before the surrender of the land; and being dispossessed of all, he was left with a large family as a pauper, without any means of support."[113]

Reflections on Implications for Teaching History and Canadian National Identity

Catherine Sutton (Nahnebahwequa) is a fascinating and provocative figure in Canadian history. She and the people who worked with her are only some of those in this text who should be a focus of studies in Canadian history in that they complicate several assumptions that conventional school texts perpetuate. Nahne exists as a tension in the developing country. On the one hand, she complies with the stated agenda of the colonizers: she is a "civilized," Christian Indian. On the other hand, her Anishnaabe abilities and knowledge, as well as her sense of justice reinforced through her Christianity, position her in a border world moving with facility, but ultimate frustration, between clashing worldviews and several ideologies. She faced no simple opposition between European and Aboriginal perspectives: it is apparent that at least some of the missionaries and devoted Christians tried, albeit unsuccessfully, to fight the agenda of the profit-driven speculators, who then, as now, had access to the lawmakers. As the Aborigines Protection Society reported in England: "Land sharks and speculators abound in Canada as they do in all countries where land is plentiful, and fortunes may be made by trading in the ignorance or weakness of its aboriginal owners."[114] Nahnebahwequa knew the laws and desires of the white colonizers but saw no reason to deny her Indianness because of this knowledge; existing in and negotiating two worldviews became her. She steadfastly refused the choice decreed by the legislation pertaining to Indians between being a landowner and being an Indian. Racism based in an assumption of the superiority of European ways of life undergirds this exclusionary choice. A question that we as Canadians are left with is how Nahnebahwequa got as far as she did. Her upbringing in the powerful Methodist family of the Reverend Peter Jones (Kahkewaquonaby) and his English wife, Elizabeth, gave her knowledge of two cultures, and her two names, one Anishnaabe and one European, exemplified her continuing commitment to both worlds. Nahnebahwequa persisted with this practice and presumably this commitment with her own children.[115] She and her family were fluent in English and "Indian."[116] She was a strong orator who at home and in her travels swayed audiences to her cause. She and her family apparently never left their farm unattended once the difficulties began. Her marriage to a white man gave her added legitimacy in the eyes of non-Aboriginal people from whom she sought support. In the end, her white husband received the title to her land, which allowed the government to maintain its position with respect to Indians owning land.

Also significant in this chapter is the strength of commitment to social activism and justice demonstrated by the members of the Society of Friends, particularly those with ties to the Aborigines Protection Society. They enacted a belief in the presence of "God in every man [sic]," "even in the heathen who knew not the Scriptures nor Christ in the flesh,"[117] and demonstrated a prescient recognition of the fundamental equality of men and women. Interrupting notions of European male superiority, they became strong supports for the work that Nahne set out to do. At the same time, we cannot lose sight of the fact that, despite her own claims to the contrary, Nahne's Christianity and her European-inspired dress were frequently commented on as positive indications of her abandonment of her Indianness. Part of the members' acceptance of and support for her was based on their commitment to good and right ways to proceed with settlement in the Americas. Their intentions never moved beyond seeking justice as colonization inevitably proceeded across the landscape and into the lives of Nahne and the other Anishnaabe people. Yet in this complexity, they challenge simple understandings of European-Indian relations while failing to shift the power relations between the two in any really significant way.

What does Nahne's struggle for justice mean? Nahnebahwequa (Catherine Sutton) is one of a number of heroic figures who should be recognized for their roles in the early foundations of this country, ones who trouble our notions of what it means to be Canadian. Her story is at least as deserving of a place in every child's mind as the endless stories of men of European ancestry whose contributions fill most textbook pages. On several levels, her story helps us understand the complexity of a nation built through colonization and the people who dwell therein. She embraced European ways to a significant degree, referring to her contemporaries – and herself – as "poor Indians" and to others as pagans on occasion. In this she exemplifies the contradiction of being and becoming when cultures meet and clash.[118] Although she complied with a Christian agenda and, with her family, took up farming, she refused to deny her "Indianness." In this steadfastness, she serves as a model for those who would hold to two strong cultures – both recent and longer-term immigrants and settlers – not feeling the need to foster one at the expense of the other. Not least, her story exemplifies some of the complexities of the racist history of this land, one that some people at the time recognized as unjust and one that we can continue to think through in order to understand more completely who we are in relation to one another and how we have come to the current state of affairs.

Postscript[119]

Nahnebahwequa's story is not over. The foundations of her house and barn still stand near her simple grave site, the latter most likely located on Lot 34, Concession 3, Sarawak Township, Grey County, Ontario. The land has been purchased by a developer from Toronto who is planning a 2,000-home project, golf course, hotel, village, and marina on the land that Nahne was not allowed to own because she was Anishnaabe. As of 2002, the Chippewas of the Nawash and Saugeen were still in negotiation to protect the grave and the land around it, considered to be of "great historical importance."

Acknowledgment

I am grateful to research assistant Kate Eichhorn for her great sleuthing skills. I also want to thank the librarians for all their help in locating information. And Don Smith remains one of the most generous researchers ever, having left copies of his findings in opportune places and having provided words of guidance and advice to those of us who follow. This chapter draws significantly on an earlier publication: Celia Haig-Brown, "Seeking Honest Justice in a Land of Strangers," *Journal of Canadian Studies* 36, 4 (Winter 2002): 143-70.

Notes

1 British Library (henceforth BL), Robert Alsop, "The Twenty-Third Annual Report of the Aborigines' Protection Society, May 1860," in *The Colonial Intelligencer and Aborigines' Friend, 1859-1866*, n.s. vol. 2 (London: W. Tweedie, n.d.), at 29.

2 Library and Archives Canada (henceforth LAC), RG 10, vol. 2877, file 177, 181, Catherine Sutton, c. 1858, "For a Reference," summary of her claim to land at Owen Sound attached to a letter from chiefs supporting her claim, 9. This document is included with materials submitted to the Department of Indian Affairs by Catherine Sutton's daughter, also Catherine Sutton, who was petitioning to be reinstated to the Cape Crocker Band. In LAC, RG 10, vol. 2877, file 177, 181, an attached "Letter from Solicitor F.B. Geddes to the Honourable Clifford Sifton, Superintendent General of Indian Affairs," includes the comment, "Mrs. Sutton's statement of facts enclosed, which though unsigned by her, is stated by her daughter to have been written in her presence, throws a good deal of light on the case."

3 There are many people of Aboriginal ancestry who combined their cultures of origin with their developing Christianity. Nahne's uncle Peter Jones is an obvious example. For details of his life and work, see Donald B. Smith's *Sacred Feathers: The Reverend Peter Jones (Kahkewaquonaby) and the Mississauga Indians* (Toronto: University of Toronto Press, 1987). Another example is Charles Pratt, a Cree catechist in Saskatchewan who lived from 1816 to 1888. His work is the subject of a moving article written by his granddaughter, historian Winona Stevenson, "The Journals and Voices of a Church of England Native Catechist: Askenootow (Charles Pratt), 1851-1884," in *Reading Beyond Words: Contexts for Native History*, ed. Jennifer S. Brown and Elizabeth Vibert (Peterborough, ON: Broadview Press, 1996), 304-29.

4 E.H. Carr, *What Is History?* (London: Penguin Books, 1961), 24. He writes: "The second point is the more familiar one of the historian's need of imaginative understanding for the minds of the people with whom he is dealing, for the thought behind their acts: I say 'imaginative understanding,' not 'sympathy,' lest sympathy should be supposed to imply agreement ... History cannot be written unless the historian can achieve some kind of contact with the mind of those about whom he is writing."

5 Penny Petrone, ed., *First People, First Voices* (Toronto: University of Toronto Press, 1983), 110.

6 "Anishnaabe" is closer to the name that this group of Aboriginal people use to refer to themselves. This name was given several forms by the early colonizers: Chippewa, Ojibwa (with a variety of spellings), and for the group living around the north shore of Lake Ontario, the Mississauga. All of these names are used today dependent on context.

7 Based on the Court Circular published in the *London Times*, the date of this meeting was 19 June 1860. The confusion recorded in some places probably arises from a copy of the letter written by Catherine Sutton that appears in the *Aborigines' Friend and the Colonial Intelligencer* (January-December 1860): 154. The letter is headed 20 June 1859 and incorporates a request from the Duke of Newcastle dated "Monday Night, 28 June 1860," indicating that she is to be received by the queen "tomorrow, (Tuesday)." These dates are changed to 29 June 1860 and 28 June 1860 respectively in the version of this article attributed to E. Merriam [sic], in Owen Sound Museum (henceforth OSM), "Nah-nee-Bahwe-qua presented to Queen Victoria," *Friends' Intelligencer* 17 (1861): 372-73, photocopy.

8 Darlene Johnston, land-claims coordinator for the Chippewas of Nawash and Saugeen, telephone conversation with author, 28 September 1998.

9 See notes 14-16 for more details.

10 Donald B. Smith, "Nahnebahwequay," in *Dictionary of Canadian Biography,* vol. 9, *1861-1870* (Toronto: University of Toronto Press, 1976), 590-91 at 590.

11 "Catherine Sunego" has a variety of spellings, and there is also contradictory presentation of her second name. Smith writes in the *Dictionary of Canadian Biography* that her birth name is Catherine Bunch Sonego, presumably a derivation formed by adding her father's name to a Christian first name. Smith, "Nahnebahwequay." However, in a later one of Smith's works, he writes her name as Catherine Brown Sunegoo, pointing out that she was named after "an exemplary Cherokee Christian." Smith, *Sacred Feathers,* 115. Giving traditional Anishnaabe names, in this case Nahnebahwequa, as well as English names was one of the symbols of the melding of the two ways of life rather than an indication of an abandonment of Native ways. Again this name has many spellings but in some form or another was the name by which she was known.

12 There are a variety of spellings for the Anishnaabe names of the Mississauga in this chapter. This spelling for the original name of Peter Jones is taken from the memorial submitted by Nah-ne-bah-wee-quay [sic] to the Duke of Newcastle and reproduced in "Aborigines' Friend and the Colonial Intelligencer, Jan. to Dec. 1860," in BL, *The Colonial Intelligencer and Aborigines' Friend, 1859-1866,* n.s. vol. 2 (London: W. Tweedie, n.d.), 149.

13 "The Mississauga" is the name that British settlers used for the Anishnaabe living on the north shore of Lake Ontario. "Around 1700, they [the Mississauga] had expelled the Iroquois from their hunting territories so recently acquired from the Huron, Petun, and Neutral half a century earlier." Robert J. Surtees, "Land Cessions, 1763-1800," in *Aboriginal Ontario: Historical Perspectives on the First Nations,* ed. Edward S. Rogers and Donald B. Smith (Toronto: Dundurn Press, 1994), 92-121 at 94. In 1805 William Claus, deputy superintendent of Indian Affairs, negotiated the first land purchase from the Mississauga, part of which allowed the Credit River Mississauga to keep their fishing sites at the mouths of the Credit River (twenty kilometres west of York, now Toronto), Sixteen Mile (Oakville) Creek, and Twelve Mile (Bronte) Creek. Surtees, "Land Cessions," 110. Surtees emphasizes that it is unlikely that the Indians of Ontario understood the full implications of the land deals as "their communal approach to land use varied so much from the Europeans' attitudes" (ibid., 112). In 1818, with increasing encroachment on lands and fisheries by settlers and weakened by diseases such as smallpox, the Credit people agreed to a further surrender in exchange for much needed cash annuities. This time they maintained only the Credit River site, with the other two river reserves to be sold in 1820 (ibid., 116-17). By 1826, working with Methodist missionaries who now included Mississauga Peter Jones and using monies from their land surrender, the people had constructed a model farming village there. Edward S. Rogers, "The Algonquian Farmers of Southern Ontario, 1830-1945," in *Aboriginal Ontario: Historical Perspectives on the First Nations,* ed. Edward S. Rogers and Donald B. Smith (Toronto: Dundurn Press, 1994), 122-66 at 126. They had the use of nearly four thousand acres adjacent to the reserve. Smith, *Sacred Feathers,* 121.

14 In the United States when Andrew Jackson forcibly removed the Cherokee from their lands, Peter Jones feared for the Mississaugas' claim to their lands. Jackson's tactic had been to deal with 300 to 500 of the Cherokee to seal the fate of over 17,000. When Sir Francis Bond Head attempted relocation of the Mississauga to Manitoulin Island, the Credit people were determined not to comply and sought the assistance of Britain to secure written title to their lands. Smith, *Sacred Feathers,* 114, 165-66.

15 In 1847, despite strong efforts to resist, the Credit River Anishnaabe finally gave up their land on the river. "The government refused to grant the band secure title to its reserve, so instead of letting the settlers take their land for nothing, the Credit River band accepted the government's offer for it and relocated to the Grand River valley." Arthur J. Ray, *I Have Lived Here since the World Began: An Illustrated History of Canada's Native People* (Toronto: Key Porter Books, 1996), 159.

16 William Sutton, "Obituary," *Christian Guardian,* 13 June 1894, 379. Copy in United Church Archives, Toronto (henceforth UCA), vertical file, "William Sutton."

17 Smith, "Nahnebahwequay," 590.

18 Friends House Library (London, UK) (henceforth FHL), Martha Braithwaite, comp., *Memorials of Christine Majolier Alsop* (London: Samuel Harris, 1881), 152.

19 Surtees claims that by the 1820s, in the face of increasing encroachment of settlers on their traditional land, the surrender by "the Indians of the Southern region" of Upper Canada was "an indication that Native peoples had lost confidence in survival. In such circumstances, the presentation of an alternative lifestyle, it was felt, would be gratefully, even eagerly embraced." Robert Surtees, "Indian Land Cession in Upper Canada, 1815-1830," in *As Long as the Sun Shines and the Water Flows: A Reader in Canadian Native Studies,* ed. Ian Getty and Antoine Lussier (Vancouver; UBC Press, 1983), 65-84 at 81.

20 "For the 5,000 Iroquois refugees who congregated between the Genesee River and the Niagara, the British negotiated with the Mississauga, as they called the Ojibwa on the north shore of Lake Ontario, and purchased land along the Grand River in Upper Canada." Olive Dickason, *Canada's First Nations: A History of the Founding Peoples from the Earliest Times* (Toronto: Oxford University Press, 1992), 186-87. See also Deed No. 8 for the purchase on behalf of the Mohawk and Deed No. 9 for Joseph Brant's taking possession of the land for his people, in Canada, *Indian Treaties and Surrenders from 1680-1890,* vol. 1 (Ottawa: Brown, Chamberlin, 1891), 22-25.

21 Sutton, "For a Reference," 1.

22 LAC, RG 10, vol. 2877, file 177, 181, "Letter from W.R. Bartlett, Indian Agent to R.T. Pennefeather, Supt. General of Indian Affairs," 16 August 1859.

23 LAC, RG 10, vol. 2877, file 177, 181, "Deed indicating gift of two hundred acres to Catherine Sutton and her heirs," 7 November 1845.

24 LAC, RG 10 vol. 2877, file 177, 181, "Letter signed by three chiefs Peter I. Kegedonce, George A. Tabeguon and James Newash," 29 June 1859. Also "Letter from T.G. Anderson, former Indian Agent, to W.R. Bartlett, the current Indian Agent, in which the former recounts from memory the admittance to the band of Catherine Sutton and her family," 4 July 1859.

25 LAC, RG 10, vol. 2877, file 177, 181, "R. Bartlett to R.T. Pennefeather, Superintendent of Indian Affairs," 16 August 1859.

26 Don Smith recounts that her work included leading a class of ten or more female Methodists in a weekly review of "their spiritual progress," after which Nahne was responsible for giving appropriate advice to each member. Donald B. Smith, "Nahnebahwequay (1824-1865): 'Upright Woman,'" in *Canadian Methodist Historical Society Papers,* vol. 13 (Toronto: Canadian Methodist Historical Society, 2001), 74-105 at 88.

27 UCA, "Letter from Mrs. Sutton," quoted by S. Belton, in the "Report of the Credit Mission," in *21st Annual Report of the Missionary Society of the Wesleyan Methodist Church in Canada, 1845-1846,* xiii.

28 Ibid.

29 OSM, "Nah-ne-bah-wee-quay," *Friends' Review* 14, 1 (8 September 1860): 9.

30 I am grateful to Jim Miller for pointing this out in his unpublished notes "Commentary on Missions and Education Seminar: 'Missions and Canadian National Identities,'" York University, 27 February 1999.

31 LAC, RG 10, vol. 2877, file 177, 181, William Sutton, "Petition to the Governor-General, the Earl of Elgin," 30 June 1852. As far as I am aware, this is the only request regarding the land that is signed by William rather than by Nahnebahwequa.

32 Sutton, "For a Reference," 2.

33 Ibid., 1.

34 UCA, Conrad Van Dusen (Enemikeese), *The Indian Chief: An Account of the Labours, Losses, Sufferings, and Oppression of Ke-zig-ko-e-ne-ne (David Sawyer), a Chief of the Ojibbeway Indians in Canada West* (London: William Nichols, 1867; reprint, Toronto: Canadiana House, 1969). Van Dusen writes: "Up till 1854, this tribe owned the whole of the peninsula between Lake Huron and the Georgian Bay, from eight to eighteen miles wide and about seventy miles long" (128).

35 Ibid.

36 Sutton, "For a Reference," 5.

37   LAC, RG 10, vol. 2877, file 177, 181. In a letter written by Bartlett dated 16 August 1859, he raises another issue pertaining to Van Dusen's connection to the land purchase. He writes, "The Rev. Vandusen acted as agent for the whole of the Indians who purchased, and could probably have advanced the money to pay their installments, with the view no doubt of ultimately getting possession of the whole of the lots, which were worth much more than the upset prices."

38   OSM, "Nah-ne-bah-wee-quay," *Friends' Review* 14, 1 (8 September 1860): 131.

39   Sutton, "For a Reference," 2. See also LAC, RG 10, vol. 2877, file 177, 181, "Letter from R. Bartlett to R.T. Pennefeather, Superintendent of Indian Affairs," 16 August 1859, which states, "The rule of the Department is, that an Indian woman who marries a white man, follows the fortunes of her husband, becomes literally a white woman, and is deprived of her individual interest in the funds of her tribe."

40   LAC, RG 10, vol. 2877, file 177, 181, "Authorization signed by Cape Crocker Chief, Peter Kegedonce, Retain and Rama Chief, William Yellowhead," 1860. See also Van Dusen, *The Indian Chief*, 138.

41   See Janet E. Chute, *The Legacy of Shingwaukonse: A Century of Native Leadership* (Toronto: University of Toronto Press, 1998).

42   The various petitions and documents are outlined in Van Dusen, "Deeds Withheld," in *The Indian Chief*, 119-32. They include a petition to the Legislative Assembly addressed to Mr. Hogan, MPP, and dated 1 April 1858, and a follow-up letter written by Van Dusen, dated 15 April 1858.

43   Sutton, "For a Reference," 3.

44   Van Dusen, *The Indian Chief*, 138. See also Smith, "Nahnebahwequay," 91. He points out that "the *Globe* called her an impostor and claimed that Indians could purchase land in Upper Canada where they were well-treated."

45   J.G., "Mrs. Catherine Sutton, Sarawak," biographical column, *Christian Guardian*, 8 November 1865. In her own account, Nahnebahwequa does not refer to this disappointment. OSM, Nahnebahwequa, "Is There Hope for the Indians?" published in the *Christian Guardian*, 28 May 1862, photocopy.

46   OSM, "The Mission of Nah-nee-bah-wee-quay, or the Upright Woman," *Friends' Review* 14, 9 (3 November 1860): 140, photocopy.

47   Nahnebahwequa, "Is There Hope for the Indians?"

48   Ibid.

49   Ibid.

50   In other places, there is reference to an E. Meriam. The "H" may be a typographical error.

51   Nahnebahwequa, "Is There Hope for the Indians?"

52   Alfred Neave Brayshaw, *The Quakers: Their Story and Message* (York, England: William Sessions Book Trust, 1982), 34, emphasis in the original.

53   Ibid., 95.

54   Ibid., 99. This new wave began with the formation of "The Friendly Association for gaining and preserving Peace with the Indians by Pacific Measures" (ibid., 97).

55   Thomas D. Hamm, *The Transformation of American Quakerism: Orthodox Friends, 1800-1907* (Bloomington: Indiana University Press, 1988), 1.

56   His close relatives included prison reformer Elizabeth Fry, and Sir Thomas Fowell Buxton, who was one of the leaders of the British antislavery movement. Hamm, *Transformation*, 20.

57   Ibid., 50.

58   OSM, "Nah-nee-bah-wee-qua (the 'Upright Woman')," *Friends' Review* 13, 37 (26 May 1860): 587, photocopy.

59   Robert Alsop and Thomas Hodgkin, "Nah-ne-bah-wee-quay," *Aborigines' Friend and the Colonial Intelligencer* (January-December 1860): 149-50.

60   OSM, "Nah-nee-bah-wee-qua (the 'Upright Woman'), *Friends' Review* 13, 37 (26 May 1860): 587-88, photocopy. Most of the preceding account is based on this article, which does not indicate an author but which is dated 30 April 1860, New York.

61   OSM, Anonymous, with line added New York, 5th mo., 14, 1860, "Nah-nee-bah-we-qua," *Friends' Intelligencer* (2 June 1860): 182, photocopy.

62   See Smith, "Nahnebahwequay," 103, for more details of her fundraising in New York. He cites a letter by Robert Lindley reprinted in a biography written by his wife, Ruth Murray, *Under His Wings: A Sketch of the Life of Robert Lindley Murray* (New York: Anson, D.F. Randolph, 1876), 75-76.

63   Meriam, "Nah-nee-Bahwe-qua presented to Queen Victoria," 311.

64   OSM, "The Mission of Nah-nee-bah-wee-quay, or the Upright Woman," *Friends' Review* 14, 9 (3 November 1860): 140, photocopy.

65   Although the Friends are pacifists and officially did not participate in the War of Independence, some did align with one side or the other. Some of those who associated with the British migrated to Canada around this time and established settlements there. For more detail, see Arthur Garratt Dorland, *The Quakers in Canada: A History* (Toronto: Ryerson, 1968).

66   Ibid.

67   For a history of the Aborigines Protection Society, see BL, H.R. Fox Bourne, "Introduction," in *The Aborigines' Protection Society: Chapters in Its History* (London: P.S. King and Son, 1899), 1-2 at 2.

68   Alsop and Hodgkin, "Nah-ne-bah-wee-quay," *Aborigines' Friend and the Colonial Intelligencer* (January-December 1860): 148.

69   Ibid. Note the oblique challenge to the notion that Aboriginal people were disappearing. Even this minutia is an indication of the unconventional views of the APS.

70   OSM, "The Mission of Nah-nee-bah-wee-quay, or the Upright Woman," *Friends' Review* 14, 9 (3 November 1860): 140, photocopy.

71   BL, Nah-ne-bah-wee-quay's speech, "The Twenty-third Annual Report of the Aborigines' Protection Society, May 1860," in *The Colonial Intelligencer and Aborigines' Friend, 1859-1866*, n.s. vol. 2 (London: W. Tweedie, n.d.), 31. James Miller points out in his discussion of the presentation version of this paper that the Indian Department was at that time moving away from their promised annuities, which may have influenced this move.

72   Newspaper Library, British Library (henceforth NLBL), court circular, *The Times,* Saturday, 16 June 1860, 2nd ed., 12, column E.

73   Ibid.

74   Alsop and Hodgkin, "Nah-ne-bah-wee-quay," in *Aborigines' Friend and the Colonial Intelligencer* (January-December 1860): 148-49.

75   Queen Victoria, journal entry for 19 June 1860, typescript at County of Grey: OSM. The note includes comments that there is no indication elsewhere that Mr. Sutton was a sailor. His obituary in the *Christian Guardian,* 13 June 1894 (typescript copy in UCA, vertical file, "William Sutton") indicates that he worked as a shoemaker when first in Canada.

76   NLBL, court circular, *The Times,* Wednesday, 20 June 1860, 9, column F.

77   Meriam, "Nah-nee-Bahwe-qua presented to Queen Victoria," 311.

78   OSM, E. Meriam, "Nah-nee-bahwe-qua," *Friends' Review* (28 August 1860): 789-90 at 789, photocopy.

79   Meriam, "Nah-nee-Bahwe-qua," *Friends' Intelligencer* 17 (1861): 343-44 at 343.

80   Meriam, "Nah-nee-bahwe-qua," 789.

81   Braithwaite, comp., *Memorials,* 151.

82   FHL, author unknown, *A Tribute to the Memory of Robert Alsop* (London: West, Newman, 1879), 30, for private circulation.

83   Ibid., 31.

84   Ibid., 32.

85   NLBL, "Aborigines' Protection Society," *Liverpool Courier,* 15 September 1860, 3.

86   Talk about dress occurs in a number of places in reference to the degree of "civilization" of the Aboriginal peoples being scrutinized – whether by themselves or others. For example, in a piece in the *Intelligencer* entitled "The Prince of Wales in Canada," it is pointed out that while the prince may have expected to find half-naked savages, in at least one village, "the chief was dressed like an ordinary country farmer." Further research on the trappings or signs of Christianity and/or civilization could prove revealing. "Aborigines' Friend and the Colonial Intelligencer, Jan. to Dec. 1860," in BL, *The Colonial Intelligencer and Aborigines' Friend, 1859-1866*, n.s. vol. 2 (London: W. Tweedie, n.d.), 57.

87 Even today, there are Aboriginal people who state that they combine their traditional spirituality with Christianity without hesitation. See for example, a former residential-school student who says, "I'm a Catholic today, a practicing Catholic. And whatever I believe from my ancestry is real and I believe in that." Quoted in Celia Haig-Brown, *Resistance and Renewal: Surviving the Indian Residential School* (Vancouver: Tillacum Press, 1988), 122.

88 Ibid.

89 Ibid.

90 Ibid.

91 Braithwaite, comp., *Memorials,* 152.

92 "Lo! the Poor Indian," *Friends' Review* 14, 34 (27 April 1861): 538.

93 Ibid.

94 This situation affirms Blackstock's claim in Chapter 2 of this text that, despite all good intentions and in this case strong support, the Aborigines Protection Society proved to be no match for the will of the Canadian government.

95 "The Indians of Canada," in "Aborigines' Friend and the Colonial Intelligencer, Jan. to Dec. 1860," in BL, *The Colonial Intelligencer and Aborigines' Friend, 1859-1866,* n.s. vol. 2 (London: W. Tweedie, n.d.), 145.

96 Ibid., 147.

97 William Sutton, *Farm Journal,* 112-18, taken from typescript in Owen Sound Museum.

98 Ibid.

99 An excerpt from one of William Sutton's letters to Robert Alsop indicates that An Act Respecting Indian Lands and Property was passed on 28 February 1860 at Quebec. OSM, Robert Alsop, "Nahnebahweequay and the Indians of the Manitoolin Islands," *The Friend* n.s. 2 (1862): 4-5, photocopy. See also Dickason, *Canada's First Nations,* 251-52. The Management of Indian Lands and Properties Act of 1860 transferred Indian administration from the Colonial Office to Canada.

100 "Lo! the Poor Indian," *Friends' Review* 14, 34 (27 April 1861): 538.

101 Ibid.

102 Ibid., 539.

103 OSM, "Letter to the Friends of New York from Nah-nee-bah-wee-quay," 30 March 1861, in J.C., "Nah-nee-bah-wee-quay," *Friends' Intelligencer* (22 April 1861): 119, photocopy.

104 Ibid.

105 Ibid.

106 "Extracts from a Letter from W. Sutton, of Owen Sound, Upper Canada, husband of Nahnebahweequay, to Robert Alsop, of Stoke Newington," in "Aborigines' Friend and the Colonial Intelligencer, Jan. to Dec. 1861," in BL, *The Colonial Intelligencer and Aborigines' Friend, 1859-1866,* n.s. vol. 2 (London: W. Tweedie, n.d.), 219.

107 OSM, copy of "Letter from William Sutton to Mr. R. Alsop," 17 March 1861, typescript.

108 Sutton, "For a Reference," 9.

109 Ibid., 10.

110 Canada, "Twenty-Fourth Annual Report of the Aborigines' Protection Society, 1862," in *The Colonial Intelligencer and Aborigines' Friend, 1859-1866,* n.s. vol. 2 (London: W. Tweedie, n.d.), 17.

111 John Ray, "A Visit to the Ojibway Indians," *The Friend* (April 1864): 79.

112 Ibid.

113 Van Dusen, *The Indian Chief,* 156. It is important to note that Van Dusen also refers to the fact that, although Sawyer had used his influence to have Nahnebahwequa become their representative to the queen, only the Suttons had benefited from the trip. He carefully states, "In regard to this, we have no information, only that we know that the chief, nor any other Indian that we know of, ever received a cent through her agency" (ibid.). This note is disturbing for two reasons. First, it may be an indication of the divide-and-conquer mentality that seems to have characterized many colonial efforts. Paulo Freire, *Pedagogy of the Oppressed* (1970; reprint, New York: Continuum, 1982), 137. Second, Catherine Sutton wrote several times to Friends in England looking for help for the poor Indians. There are also several places where she accounts for the monies received. While it may be

that she chose a select group to whom to distribute the funds, she does appear to have distributed it. This certainly raises some questions about the relationship between Van Dusen and Nahnebahwequa. A draft letter apparently written by Nahnebahwequa indicates her concerns about what she sees as an opportunist relationship Van Dusen is developing with David Sawyer. Nahnebahwequa also expressed annoyance at a visit that Sawyer made to her mother, commenting, "why does he not come to me?" OSM, William Sutton, Ledger 1961.27.23, reference could be Donald Smith's notation, 58-62, typescript. She goes on to write a long account of Van Dusen's dishonest claim to an invention for addressing newspapers as part of the printing process.

114   "The Canadian Indians and the Manitoulin Islands," in "Aborigines' Friend and Colonial Intelligencer, Jan. to Dec. 1862," in BL, *The Colonial Intelligencer and Aborigines' Friend, 1859-1866*, n.s. vol. 2 (London: W. Tweedie, n.d.), 253.

115   At least with the first five children, Nahnebahwequa gave Anishnaabe names as well as English ones. Her children included: "Sah-gar-se-ga (rising sun) Joseph, 18, Nah-we-ke-gee-go-quay (blue sky) Catherine, 17, Nah-koo-quay (top buds of a tree) Sophia, 14, Sun-e-goo-nec (little squirrel) Wesley, 5, Sah-sa-kah-noo-quay (little hail) Mary Margaret, 3, [and] Little man from over the great waters, Alsop Albert Edward." "Lo! the Poor Indian," *Friends' Review* 14, 34 (27 April 1861): 539. She apparently had two more children after these ones, as Ray mentions eight children during his visit in 1863. Ray, "A Visit to the Ojibway Indians," 79.

116   Ray, "A Visit to the Ojibway Indians," 79.

117   Brayshaw, *The Quakers*, 53, 45.

118   For a fuller discussion of the dialectical contradiction, see Celia Haig-Brown, "Contradiction, Power and Control," in *Taking Control: Contradiction and Power in First Nations Adult Education* (Vancouver: UBC Press, 1995), 233-54 at especially 233-36.

119   Research assistant Kate Eichhorn first drew my attention to this development in a news article about the negotiations. Later a conversation with Darlene Johnston, land-claims coordinator for the Chippewas of Nawash and Saugeen, added details, and a CBC interview with Stephanie McMullen on 13 January 1999 provided further elaboration. See also Roberta Avery, "Woman Seeks Indian Status Lost by Relative," *Toronto Star*, 21 March 2002, A4, and Scott Dunn, "Native Woman's Burial Site Still a Mystery," *Sun Times* (Owen Sound), 23 July 2003, A3.

7
Aboriginals and Their Influence on E.F. Wilson's Paradigm Revolution

David A. Nock

We are inclined to think of nineteenth-century missionaries as bringing their notions of education and religion to Aboriginal peoples in a one-way direction. Prominent Canadian church historian John Webster Grant writes that the missionaries' "major mistake, understandable in the circumstances, was in relying too much on one-way communication."[1] The North Atlantic Missiology Project itself has written that "much current writing on missions posits the essentially closed nature of the missionary mind."[2] Perhaps most of us do not conceive of the possibility of influences moving in the other direction. But it is simplistic to think that missionaries could work for decades among Aboriginal peoples and not themselves be influenced by what they experienced and saw. Such a scenario may have existed in some cases, but when such factors as major social upheaval *and* personal mid-life issues are intertwined, then it becomes easier to understand major conceptual shifts in the thinking of a missionary. The Reverend E.F. Wilson (1844-1915) experienced such a shift.

In his case, the conversion involved an abandonment of one-way communication based on a closed mind as he became influenced by his own visits with and direct perceptions of Aboriginal peoples in their communities and nations. Increasingly, this missionary's good intentions derived not only from his religious motivations as an earnest Evangelical, but also from his developing understanding that Aboriginal societies were valuable and competent in and of themselves and, therefore, worthy of self-government. Ever since Louis Althusser's study of Karl Marx emphasizing the divide between the earlier and later Marx, it has been easier to understand that intellectual trajectories may not trace simple processes of incremental change but deep-seated transformations.[3]

Such a revolutionary change did occur in the life and thought of the Reverend Edward Francis Wilson. In his own lifetime he was best known for his Shingwauk and Wawanosh Residential Schools in Sault Ste Marie and for another at Elkhorn, Manitoba. He built them starting in 1873 and

E.F. Wilson with children from Shingwauk School on their way to Montreal and Ottawa in celebration of Queen Victoria's Jubilee

ran them himself until 1893, when he retired from this work and moved to Salt Spring Island in British Columbia for quite a different life as an agriculturalist and pastor to white settlers in an isolated and sparsely settled part of the province. However, from 1885 until 1893, he became intensely interested in ethnology, anthropology, and philology, and started to write about these subjects and to travel widely in support of them. This led to a major revisioning of how the dominant colonial society ought to deal with Native peoples.

Before 1885, Wilson had accepted contemporary programs of cultural replacement and political incorporation without much reflection. In the words of the blunt and influential Captain (later General) Richard Henry Pratt (founder of the important Carlisle Indian School in the United States in 1879), such a program would be necessary "to kill the Indian and save the man."[4] Pratt felt that it was necessary for Aboriginal cultures and cultural practices to disappear, insisting that Aboriginal individuals would benefit from incorporation into the dominant society.

Wilson came to doubt the wisdom of such a root-and-branch assimilationist program and instead supported an important degree of cultural continuity and synthesis as well as self-government by Aboriginal peoples. In his eighteenth annual report for his schools, published in 1892 just before he announced his retirement, Wilson stated, "In my own brain I have had plans of Indian self-government and the Native Indian church supported by themselves." Nevertheless, consistent with the disillusionment that led to his retirement, he also noted, "I fear that there is little chance of these schemes ever being realized at any rate in my own day."[5] On this matter, Wilson may be seen as a prophet in that Canada, unlike the United States and the American regime of John Collier in the New Deal era (1933-45), did not see such ideas proposed again on a wide scale until the 1970s.

However, it is unlikely that such ideas could have developed in Wilson's mind had it not been for the influence of Aboriginal people and their cultures. This influence came about both indirectly, as filtered through the writings of Horatio Hale on the Iroquois League of Six Nations, and directly, as when Wilson took an extended journey of over 7,000 miles into the United States and other lengthy journeys onto the Prairies of Canada. Wilson was heavily influenced by his own direct perceptions of the Cherokee Nation and of the Pueblo and Zuni settlements in the American Southwest. Wilson came to see these as templates for other North American First Nations.

Wilson's Direct Perception of Aboriginal Cultures

Wilson had first come to work among Canadian Indians in 1868, ministering among the Ojibway (Anishnaabek) of southwestern Ontario. In 1871 he had moved to Garden River near Sault Ste Marie and several years later had opened there the Shingwauk Home. His motives at this time had essentially been religious and evangelical, and certainly ethnological and anthropological motivations were far from his mind. This may be said despite the early publication of his *Manual of the Ojebway Language* (1874), which was intended as a primer for other prospective Evangelical missionaries. Real interest in the history and ethnology of the Aboriginal nations came about quite abruptly in 1885.

A good example of Wilson's dramatic turnabout in motivations from that of missionary to scholar and social activist was his response to a letter from Major J.W. Powell, one of the most famous of pre-Boasian American anthropologists. In 1881 Powell had sent Wilson a copy of his *Introduction to the Study of Indian Languages* and asked for information about the languages known to him. Wilson had enquired briefly and curtly what he would be paid for such efforts.[6] In the spring of 1885, Wilson "fell all over himself" to redeem this missed opportunity now that he realized and cared whom he had dismissed so abruptly. Wilson pleaded that four years earlier he had been "so over-pressed with routine work" at the school that he had no time "to pay much attention to their history, language, etc., or afford to give you the information which I think you desired." Wilson now proposed to hire a superintendent to relieve him of such routine work so that he could "pay more attention than I have hitherto been able to do to the history, tribal relations, language, etc. of these interesting people."[7]

After reading about these matters for several years, Wilson prepared to make an extensive journey to study Aboriginals in their own communities and nations, although this trip also included visits to residential and boarding schools and to other American institutions dealing with Aboriginals. This trip allowed him to mix his serious interest in ethnology and anthropology with a kind of picaresque journey undertaken with his wife after many years in the isolated Sault Ste Marie location. He published a lengthy account of this trip in the periodicals *Our Forest Children* and *The Canadian Indian* entitled "My Wife and I: A Little Journey among the Indians," and he recycled the material, most noticeably in another series entitled "The Indian Tribes," published in the same journals, which he had hoped would be published as a book. He explained that his own motive or "object" "would be to see as much as possible of the Indians – and perhaps – ... to enlighten the public by-and-bye as to the present condition and chances for improvement of that interesting, but little known and little understood people." In connection with this object, Wilson avowed that he was "greatly interested in Indian history, and Indian languages, and expect to spend what time I can during the next few years of my life, if God will, in collecting from all possible sources all the material that I can, bearing on this two-fold interesting subject." He then outlined the trip, which included stops in Ottawa at the Indian Affairs Department to obtain documents that would help in the United States, a visit to the Lincoln Institute in Philadelphia (a residential school), a visit to the Carlisle Indian School and its founder Captain Richard Henry Pratt, a stop in Washington to visit the Smithsonian Institution and the Bureau of Ethnology, and a sojourn in Ohio to examine the Aboriginal mounds before continuing south through St. Louis and on to the Indian Territory of Oklahoma. Here his aim was to visit "the Cherokees and other civilized tribes who were said to have their own Legislative Assembly, their own judges, lawyers, and other public officials, and to support their schools and public institutions entirely out of their own funds, without any help from the U.S. Government." He then went west to visit the "wilder tribes who still wear blankets and paint their faces," continued into New Mexico and Arizona to visit the Moki (now Hopi), Zuni, and Pueblo peoples, proceeded north to Denver, next visited the Genoa Indian School in Nebraska, and finally via Omaha and St. Paul returned to Sault Ste Marie. A little journey indeed![8]

I wish to concentrate specifically on some of his travels to Aboriginal tribes and nations in their own communities. In particular, the Cherokee demand special attention because they influenced Wilson to move away from considering only programs of cultural replacement and assimilation to ones of cultural synthesis and self-government. Complete cultural continuity in traditional precontact form Wilson never thought practical or desirable. However, cultural synthesis (including selected aspects of cultural continuity) and a considerable degree of political autonomy were ideas which Wilson came to consider favourably. The reason for this stemmed from his own observations on this trip.[9]

Since the story of the Cherokee is well known, I will summarize just a few essentials. They originally resided in the American Southeast, were distantly related to the Iroquois,[10] found their ancestral lands being squeezed by American settlers and states in the early nineteenth century, and were perhaps the only Aboriginal people to invent their own system of writing through an inspired inventor (Sequoyah). As a consequence, they developed literacy in both their own language and in English. They experienced extensive intermarriage with whites, were forcibly removed in the infamous "Trail of Tears" from the Southeast to Oklahoma in the 1830s, rebuilt their institutions (increasingly "formal," constitutional, and bureaucratic in nature), were conflicted by the Civil War (partly because of their own practice of slavery), rebuilt their society yet again in the aftermath of the Civil War, conducted a government that was acknowledged to be sovereign in its own territory, but finally were subjected to the same pressures of individualization and Americanization as other American Aboriginals. Ultimately, their communal lands were parcelled out in severalty (i.e., individual title) and their autonomous government destroyed. Wilson observed the autonomous Cherokee state and its culture and institutions in what was perhaps its final period of glory before its enforced dissolution in the decade of the 1890s and the first decade of the twentieth century.

The Cherokee Nation
In his account of his visit, Wilson described the constitutional political system, which included a governor, or principal chief, two elective houses composed of senators and councillors, nine electoral districts, laws read three times in each house, an executive council, a Parliament House, and two major parties: the Downings and the Nationalists. He actually was present at a political gathering involving the newly elected governor, or chief, Joel Bryan Mayes – the election took place in August 1887, and he was installed in January 1888. Wilson commented, "The Chief read his message in English and the interpreter translated it sentence by sentence into Indian. The subjects dealt with were 'our financial affairs,' the leasing of the Cherokee strip to American cattle-men, the judiciary, education, orphan asylum, etc."[11]

It is unclear whether Wilson knew it, but the Cherokee political system had just weathered great turbulence. The election was held in August 1887.

The National Council failed to make the required canvass of election returns. As a consequence, the retiring chief, Dennis W. Bushyhead (undefeated as he could not run for a third term; the defeated National Party candidate was Rabbit Bunch), continued to serve. The situation, says Stanley W. Hoig, grew "more and more tense with supporters of Mayes arming themselves for potential action ... Finally, in January 1888, an appointed committee invaded the council building, broke into the locked executive office, counted the votes, and installed Mayes."[12] The retiring chief, Bushyhead, presided over the more culturally conservative National Party, while Mayes was the candidate of the Downing Party, which was more accommodating to the American presence. In fact, Champagne recounts that "there is a conservative tradition that says that Rabbit Bunch won the election but that the American government supported Mayes and the Downing party."[13]

Later at tea with a new acquaintance, Wilson met two Cherokee judges and commented that "the Cherokee authorities have full power over their own people. A Cherokee judge can condemn a Cherokee, or other Indian offender, to any term of imprisonment in the Cherokee penitentiary, or he may condemn him to be hung [sic]. The Cherokee penitentiary, at Tahlequah [in present-day Oklahoma], has at present 34 inmates, serving terms of from three months to ten years."[14] Later Wilson got to visit the penitentiary (built in 1873 and 1874 with an appropriation of six thousand dollars).[15] He provided a rather positive report on it: "The Cherokees do not believe in treating their prisoners with unnecessary severity ... the Cherokee prison was much better than a U.S. Prison ... Indian prisoners are easily kept. It is said that even if the door is left open they will not run away."[16] Contributing to the upbeat nature of the account was Wilson's observation that inmates were allowed "to enliven the dull hours of captivity by playing the fiddle and dancing," and he provided a sketch in one of his accounts.[17]

Wilson also visited the new female seminary (i.e., high school), which was actually under construction. He commented: "This latter is a fine imposing structure, such as any city in the country would feel proud of ... it will cost $100,000. It is all paid for with Cherokee money."[18] The previous female seminary had been destroyed by fire on 10 April 1887. The construction of a new building started on 3 November 1887 and was completed on 18 April 1889.[19] Wilson did not visit but caught just a glimpse of the male seminary. Nevertheless, he recounted various details about it: the number of students; the number of windows, chimneys, and pillars; and the nature of their studies, "as high as geometry." As far as the costs were concerned, he explained how the funding of the schools was tied to the Cherokee Strip, a large block of grazing land rented out to American ranchers at a cost that brought in, so Wilson said, $100,000 each year. In the

1890s, using technical arguments, the US government forced the Cherokee to forego this arrangement of renting out the Cherokee Strip, and it
was one of the final nails in the Cherokee coffin.[20]

One particular highlight in this trip had to be his interview with the new
governor, Joel Bryan Mayes. He was introduced to him by the sheriff, Jesse
Bushyhead Mayes,[21] a kinsman according to Wilson.[22] Wilson met Mayes
in a private interview. Joel Bryan Mayes had graduated from the male seminary in 1856 and had risen to become associate justice of the Supreme
Court of the Cherokee Nation. He also had experience as clerk of the Citizenship Court from 1879 to 1881 and as clerk of the National Council from
1881 to 1883.[23] Hoig says that Mayes farmed and taught school prior to the
Civil War, served with the Confederacy as a quartermaster, and then entered Cherokee politics and the legal system as a circuit judge. Aside from
his other accomplishments, he was described as a "splendid cider maker."[24]

In the course of their meeting, Mayes told Wilson that "the Cherokee
people were quite satisfied with their present condition, and desired no
change; they did not desire to hold their land in severalty; they had adopted
white man's methods up to a point, but beyond that point they did not
wish to go."[25] Wilson reused this interview several times, but its recounting
is not always exactly the same. In his account in the "Indian Tribes Series,"
actually published earlier, Mayes was disguised as simply "a well-educated
Cherokee lawyer," and he again opposed the allotment of land in severalty:
"(1) By holding it in common, they are better able to resist the aggression
of the whites; (2) Their present social system has never yet developed a
mendicant or tramp; (3) Although poor, yet they have no paupers, none
suffering from the oppression of the rich. With the whites, every one is
scrambling to live, the strong trampling down the weak, but not so with
them; (4) They do not believe that the whites have any better condition to
offer them, therefore they prefer to remain as they are."[26] The same interview was quoted virtually verbatim by "Fair Play" (April 1891) in the latter's series on "The Future of Our Indians," published in *The Canadian Indian*
(a journal coedited by Wilson).[27] It has long been my hypothesis that Fair
Play was, in fact, a pseudonym for E.F. Wilson.[28] These papers are included
as an appendix in this text because of their clear portrayal of a person of
European ancestry coming to some understanding of the injustices being
perpetrated on Aboriginal peoples as colonization proceeded. Fair Play attempts to redress these wrongs, albeit partially.

As indicated above, the "Indian Tribes Series" actually predated Wilson's
account of his extended American trip, as did his account of the Cherokee
in this series; however, his analysis included both his own perceptions of
the Cherokee Nation as well as printed sources acknowledged at the end of
the article. Influenced by Horatio Hale's interest in philology as he was, he
included a vocabulary of the relevant Aboriginal language collected either

personally or for him. Also very Halian in tone is his comment that the Indian "languages are not rude barbarous tongues, as those who have never studied the subject might suppose, but are capable of giving expression to the most abstruse ideas. The grammar is very full and the inflections of the various parts of speech most extensive."[29]

After a brief description of the original Cherokee lands in the Southeast, the article went on to describe the sorry story of the dispossession of the Cherokee as recounted in another prominent influence on Wilson, Helen Hunt Jackson's *A Century of Dishonor* (1881). Then there was a quick history emphasizing their interaction with and adoption of white institutions (e.g., the adoption of a formalized constitutional system of government in 1827) and their removal west to Oklahoma with its considerable loss of life, known as the "Trail of Tears." Recent estimates place the loss of life at one-quarter, although Wilson in his account speculated the loss at 10 percent.[30] This article covered some of the same ground as the later article taken from Wilson's observations on their political, legal, and penitentiary system and on their schools, based on his interview with the principal chief. He provided details on the economic and school systems. He mentioned that formal steps had been taken in 1791 to "induce" the Cherokee to take up farming – actually this brief statement is misleading, as the Cherokee had always been agriculturalists, with the women taking the lead in hoe-based horticulture[31] – and that this effort was successful from reports thirty years later. The article mentioned the farms, the orchards, the farm houses and log cabins (actually 5,000 brick, frame, and log houses), the keeping of hogs and cattle, the towns with their "broad streets and business houses built of stone, brick, and wood," the churches (64 of them), and the schools (75 schools and 2,300 scholars); Starr confirms that there were 75 public schools in 1877, about ten years before Wilson's arrival. By the time of the dissolution of the Cherokee Nation, there were more than 120.[32] Wilson estimated the progress of literacy, noting that there were publications in both English and Cherokee and that out of 22,000 inhabitants, 13,000 had the ability to read. A recent historian mentions that in 1880 the Cherokee Nation was "almost purely an agrarian society, with 4,224 families and 4,054 farms, the principal crops being corn, wheat, oats, and cotton," with 107,721 hogs, 66,746 cattle, 13,512 horses, and 1,239 mules.[33] Wilson also mentioned the invention of the Cherokee alphabet in 1820 by the mixed-blood Sequoyah, also known as George Guess. Wilson noted that Sequoyah had been given a silver medal in 1823 by the General Council of the Nation, and he stated that "it is said that a clever boy [sic] can learn to read in a single day with the Cherokee alphabet."[34]

In this article, Wilson's admiration for the Cherokee and their success at self-government was unbounded. The descriptive words that he used were positive. He referred to their "determination and perseverance that could not fail to win success" and to "the wonderful progress that these people have made." He also referred to the Cherokee as "this great and remarkably intelligent people." His overall conclusion was that "and now, to-day [1889], the country of these Cherokee Indians is fair and prosperous, and long may they be allowed to enjoy it. Few people on the face of the earth have made so great progress in so short a time, and in the face of so great difficulties and discouragement as have these Cherokees."[35]

Wilson raised the issues of whether complete cultural replacement could be expected of the Cherokee and whether they would adopt "the white man's views in regard to the desirability of each individual having his own holding" – that is, ownership of land in severalty. Wilson pointed here to the concept of cultural synthesis without, of course, using the term when he answered this query: "But not so. They still hold their lands in common, and they are utterly averse to any change being made in this respect. The land, they say, belongs to the Cherokee nation, and not to the individuals thereof; land is as air and water, the property of all, it cannot be given away to the few."[36] When one adds to this the use of the Cherokee language and alphabet, the use of Cherokee as a printed language, the self-governing nature of the Cherokee Nation, the existence of conservative cultural forces in the Nation, such as the Keetowah Society, and the traditional and continued prominent role given to women (however diminished as a result of the "civilizers"),[37] the extent of this cultural synthesis must be appreciated. Despite the extent of borrowing and adoption from American society and culture, the Cherokee system was based on cultural synthesis.

Perhaps this can be better appreciated by considering the opposition to the Cherokee system found in the wider American society. Senator Henry L. Dawes was the initiator of the Dawes Severalty Act of 1887, which pointed to the "denationalization," Americanization, and distribution of Aboriginal lands to individual ownership as the answer to the Indian "question." In 1880 a Quaker philanthropist, Albert Smiley, had written the secretary of the interior that "'the greatest good for the Indian' would be 'the speedy enactment of the pending bills in Congress providing for lands in severalty ... and ultimate [American] citizenship.'" Another such Quaker philanthropist, Philip Garret, wrote in 1886 that the Indian should "lay aside his picturesque blankets and moccasins, and clad in the panoply of American citizenship, seek his chances of fortune or loss in the stern battle of life with the Aryan races." In 1893 the Dawes Commission was authorized by Congress to negotiate with the Cherokee and affiliated so-called "civilized" tribes of Oklahoma for allotment of their land in severalty. In 1894 this committee reported that these five tribes were "'non-American' because they held their lands in common."[38] Captain Richard Henry Pratt of the Carlisle School was not charmed by the Cherokee and did not see them as any exception to his goal to eradicate a separate sense of Aboriginal identity or citizenship. He acknowledged that they had been praised by whites for their "tribal schools until it was asserted that they are civilized," but he lamented that "yet they have no notion of joining us and becoming part of the United States. Their whole disposition is to prey upon and hatch up claims against the government ... to meet the recurring wants growing out of their neglect and inability to make use of their large and rich estate ... What else but demoralization and destruction of principle and manhood could follow in the train of such a course of action towards any people?"[39] In a more general vein, Pratt had written to Senator Henry L. Dawes about his famous or infamous Severalty Bill congratulating him, as it would lead "to the divorcement of the Indian from the worse than slavery of his old Communistic system."[40]

The Cherokee responded to this insistence on denationalization and land in severalty. In 1887, for example, in a memorial to Congress against the Dawes Bill, the Cherokees, Creeks, and Chickasaws stated that the act unilaterally contravened treaties made with them and "went on to explain the religious significance of communal landowning. 'Ownership of lands in common ... is with them a religion as well as a law of property. It is based upon peculiarities and necessities of the race.'"[41] After the twin policy of denationalization and allotment in severalty was set in motion, further resistance was manifested. The culturally conservative Keetowah Society engaged in passive resistance by failing to enrol for their individual tracts. McLoughlin comments that this "did little more that reveal the iron fist within the velvet glove of the civilizers. Hundreds of them were sent to jail" for this act of resistance, "which would then make them citizens of the United States."[42] As late as 1898 the Cherokee were foot-dragging on allotment, but Congress passed the Curtis Act of 1898, which abolished all tribal law and tribal courts and prohibited tribal councils from instituting any new legislation. In 1902 the Dawes Commission reached agreement for each Cherokee citizen to be awarded 110 acres individually. The Keetowahs finally capitulated in 1910. McLoughlin calls them "the last resisters in the lost cause of Cherokee sovereignty."[43] Coleman reports that the schools of the Cherokee and the other Aboriginal nations of Oklahoma were taken over by the federal government in 1906.[44] A last-ditch effort in 1905 to keep some semblance of self-government by establishing a separate Indian state out of the eastern part of Oklahoma also failed. Within twenty years, McLoughlin tells us, "two-thirds of the Indians had lost the small allotments given to them – partly through their inability to pay their taxes, partly through agreeing to sell it to whites, and partly through outright fraud."[45] Given the extent of cultural replacement accepted by the Cherokees, some might be tempted to ask if the term cultural synthesis is applicable to them. Some of these reactions from the dominant colonial American side, both philanthropic and governmental, show the keen desire to crush any remnant of Cherokee cultural continuity, whether related to systems of landownership, citizenship, self-government, or schools.

One concern that Wilson did have about the Cherokee, presumably because of its bearing on whether the Cherokee system could serve as a template for other Amerindians, was the degree of intermixture with whites. This had already proceeded to a considerable extent. A recent historian has referred to "the Cherokees' more open policy regarding blood," which "has helped define it as the second largest tribe in the United States," noting that "unlike many other tribes in the United States, the Cherokee Nation has no blood quantum limitation, and the blood quantum of tribal members ranges from 'full blood' to 1/2048. Indeed, out of a total tribal enrollment of 175,326 in February 1996, only 37,420, or 21 percent, had one-quarter Cherokee blood or more."[46] Degrees of blood quantum became heavily related to social stratification. Sturm points out that "only one percent of all full-bloods owned slaves" but that 78 percent of the slave-owning class claimed white descent.[47] Back in the 1890s when a census was undertaken for allotment of land by the Dawes Commission, it was found that 8,698 of the total Cherokee population were full-bloods,[48] although one should take note of Sturm's comment that "the calculation of Indian blood quantum during the Dawes enrollment process was a purely subjective process based in part on earlier tribal rolls and on oral testimony from enrollees and their supporting witness."[49]

Given these considerations, it is perhaps not surprising that Wilson paid a great deal of attention to the issue in his writings on the Cherokee. When he and his wife had arrived at Vinita (in present-day Oklahoma), he stated that he had heard that it was "a civilized Indian town" with a variety of formal institutions and businesses run by "an Indian proprietor," an "Indian editor," and by "all Cherokees."[50] When he got to inspect Vinita more fully, Wilson became more and more struck by the American stamp of the people and their character. He spoke with the principal of the Worcester Academy and saw his school. Surveying the learners, Wilson estimated that they had "all of them, far more white blood in their veins than Indian blood. A large proportion of them seemed to be entirely white, and shewed [sic] their white character by their behavior; some few were partly Cherokee; of full blood Cherokees there were none."[51] He learned that the local newspaper was owned by a man with a Cherokee blood quantum of one-quarter and that there did exist a full-blood Cherokee dentist, although Wilson did not meet him. Asked about this issue, Professor Jones of Worcester Academy explained the Cherokee "open policy" about intermixture: "All these grey-eyed, brown bearded, red-bearded men; and all these blue-eyed, golden-haired children, which you see about are, in fact, Cherokees, members of the great Cherokee Nation; entitled to hold Cherokee property, and to have a vote in the Cherokee elections, – not because they have Cherokee blood, but because they have been united in marriage with some one having a slight taint of Cherokee, or the offspring of such marriage."[52]

This explanation had cleared up what Wilson termed "the mystery," but, as he avowed, "it did not seem a very satisfactory clearing up. It would have been more satisfactory to have found a veritable Indian community, unmixed with white blood."[53] Professor Jones suggested that Wilson pay a visit to the Cherokee capital, Tahlequah, especially as its Parliament was due to open during Wilson's visit. And so Wilson pressed on, still consumed by the same issue. He ventured to ask the question of blood quantum of his fellow passengers on a stage coach, specifically how many of the Cherokee Nation might be full-bloods. "The opinions expressed by the passengers and driver were a little varied. One-sixth of the whole population is full-blood, said one; about thirty per cent, said another."[54] Wilson could not help but raise the issue when he saw the new principal chief, Joel Bryan Mayes, who, he said, "was not very much Cherokee. I was told that his mother was half Cherokee and his father was a full-blooded Irishman."[55] In fact, a recent historian confirms that Mayes "was born in Georgia in 1833, his mother being a mixed-blood Cherokee and his father a white man."[56] While Mayes addressed the crowd, Wilson "took a good look at the motley throng assembled under the trees. I was glad to see so many dark faces, and so much of the pure Indian element among them. True, there were a good many American-looking beards and American-looking eyes and noses, but the great bulk of the assembled throng was Indian, or at least half-breed; a goodly proportion might even have passed for full-bloods."[57] This was underscored in that Mayes' address, although delivered in English, was translated into Cherokee, and it is worthwhile noting that the Cherokee preferred a definition of full-blood as based on language rather than biology – that is, "as one who speaks only Cherokee."[58] The final note that Wilson made on the matter was in reference to the male seminary. He was told that "about one-third of the students ... were full-bloods, the rest half-breeds, and no whites."[59]

Although Wilson's "Indian Tribes" paper on the Cherokee was actually published earlier than the travel account, it was in part based on that experience in addition to printed sources. It is worth pointing out that there is very little of this discussion of blood quantum and intermarriage and intermixture in this article, except for a statement about Vinita: "It should be added, however, that there are very few full-blooded Cherokees in the town – the population consisting mostly of half-breeds and whites adopted into the nation."[60] I have already indicated that in this "Indian Tribes" paper, whatever misgivings he may have felt about the blood-quantum factor and what it might imply about the Cherokee system as a model, he already used words and terms indicating how he had been enchanted by the Cherokee, referring to "their wonderful progress" and so on.

Starting in March 1891, a series of papers bearing the title of "The Future of Our Indians" was published by *The Canadian Indian*, edited by E.F. Wilson. As mentioned earlier, it has long been my thesis that their pseudonymous author, Fair Play, was in fact E.F. Wilson. Here I simply wish to indicate the extent to which Fair Play had come to rely on the Cherokee example as a template for Aboriginals in general. In the second paper (April 1891), Fair Play wrote that "the Cherokees, in Indian Territory, who for many years past have been permitted to manage their own affairs, hold their own public purse, and make their own laws, are as a people, very far advanced in education; and have large schools and colleges built out of their own funds, established in their midst." He went on to advocate the same system for "civilized Indians in Canada," one involving "more management of their own affairs."[61] In the same paper, Fair Play summarized the Cherokee governmental and judicial systems and their prison and their seminaries. "And yet, with all this advance in the ways of civilization, these Cherokee Indians do by preference hold their lands in common, and retain several of their other ancient customs."[62] Fair Play also quoted E.F. Wilson's interview with "a well-educated Cherokee lawyer," as quoted above. In the fourth and last of the "Fair Play Papers" (June 1891), Fair Play recalled his description of the Cherokee and suggested that "what the United States has done for one tribe of 22,000 Indians [a figure obviously in accord with the Cherokee census of 1880 at 21,920; the 1890 census showed a population of 28,000][63] I propose our Dominion Government should do for her 17,000 Ontario Indians; hand over to them their funds, which are at present held in trust for them, appoint them a Lieutenant-Governor from among their own people, let them select a spot for their capital, and have their own Parliament and make their own laws. And if this be successful, I think, as time goes on, the whole management of Indian Affairs might be transferred from the Indian Department in Ottawa to the Indian Government at the Indian Capital."[64] The Cherokee had become the pattern, in the mind of E.F. Wilson and Fair Play, for other North American Indians. If the Cherokee could do it, so could other Indian tribes and nations; they had the potential because of other instances of what Fair Play referred to as examples of Aboriginal "excellent laws,"[65] but similar "wonderful progress" was being denied to these other Indian tribes and nations because of the withholding of self-government. In an editorial for *The Canadian Indian* from March 1891, coincidentally the same issue as Fair Play's first paper on "The Future of Our Indians," Wilson concluded, "We see in their [the Cherokees'] history and achievement the key to the Indian problem."[66]

The Zuni and Pueblo Peoples

A second important positive Indian model in Wilson's mind were the Pueblo and Zuni peoples. As with the Cherokee, Wilson was able to see them in person and to have direct perceptions of their settlements and culture. In Fair Play's second paper (April 1891), the Zuni were mentioned after a lengthy passage on the Cherokee and a briefer one on the Delawares. Fair Play spent most of this passage describing their "most elaborate religious system" and although the author avowed that there was "a great deal of what we would call superstition mixed up in all they do ... yet there can be no question but that they are a most religious people; they have the most profound belief in the doctrines handed down to them from their ancestors; nothing is done without prayer; some sort of religious rite or ceremonial seems to be a necessary accompaniment to all their undertakings," and further detail was added about the careful religious education of the children.[67]

When Wilson visited Zuni in 1887, he was invited to attend their religious dances through the good graces of the Hemenway archaeological expedition (financed by the wealthy Bostonian Mary Hemenway), which was excavating in the area. Wilson had already read accounts of the Zuni by proto-anthropologist Frank Cushing in *The Century Magazine*.[68] Eliza McFeely writes about Cushing, "a graceful writer working creatively within the tradition of travel journals, Cushing wrote a marvelous adventure story with himself as hero. The plot involved mystery ... as well as danger, and ... descriptions of wonderful ceremonies."[69] It is hardly surprising that Wilson avowed "How often I had dreamed of Zuni."[70] Despite having "seen a good many Indian dances and witnessed a good many curious Indian performances," he concluded that the Zuni dances were "new and startling."[71] Just as did Fair Play, Wilson pointed out that these were "religious dances, performed for a religious purpose," in fact to consecrate seven new houses.[72] Later on, Wilson was "struck, too, by the reverent way they approached, one by one, a heathen shrine which had been erected at the end of the room, muttered some words of prayer or address to their unseen God, then put out their hands, grasped the air in front of the shrine, raised their hands to their lips and drew in the breath. These people certainly seemed to be in earnest about their religion, worthless though it might be – far more in earnest than are the great majority of professed Christians."[73]

Other aspects of the Zuni and Pueblo peoples called forth praise from Wilson. This included their dress: "You see no rags at Zuni, all the people are well and cleanly dressed, and are adorned with really valuable jewellery – no brass rings or cheap beads, but ornaments of solid silver, real coral, turquoise, rubies, and other precious stones."[74] Another item of material culture coming in for praise was the home manufacture of blankets "hanging up on a horizontal stick suspended from the ceiling, all beautifully made," and Wilson referred to the Pueblo peoples (and Navajos) as "adepts working in silver."[75] He also praised their character as "uncommonly friendly and hospitable. What more beautiful and graceful a way of receiving a stranger could be conceived than to take his hand, shake it kindly and smilingly, then lift the hand that has held the stranger's to the lips and draw in the breath. I noticed my new-found friends of Zuni doing this, so, of course, I did the same."[76] It may have been premature to refer to his new-found friends, but it does bespeak the charm and enchantment that Wilson found at Zuni. Wilson was not the first white to be charmed and impressed by the Zuni and Pueblo peoples – Frank Cushing was such a one; Elsie Clews Parsons was another in the period 1915-40.[77] He comments that "people have said that the Pueblo Indians and Zunis are not Indians at all, that they are a distinct and superior race."[78] According to Margaret D. Jacobs, "during this period [before the 1910s], the U.S. government had not even classified the Pueblos as Indians," and the courts exempted the Pueblos from laws "'made for wandering savages.'"[79] Only in 1913, in the Sandoval case, did "the Pueblos finally become classified as Indians."[80] Long before 1913, Wilson had anticipated this judgment, an important conclusion if he was to hold them, along with the Cherokee, as templates for other North American Indians. Wilson pointed to "their wild music," similar "in its notes and rhythm to that which I have heard repeat-edly among the wild tribes of the North-west [of Canada]. I could have no doubt at all but that the Zuni people are North American Indians, just as much as the Ojibways or the Blackfeet."[81]

Wilson's accounts of the Pueblo peoples in his "Indian Tribes Series" added other positive points as he saw them: they had never been nomadic, they dwelt in towns and villages, and they had always cultivated the soil. They had permanent dwellings and buildings built in adobe mud. They had always had "an organized system of government," with each village having a governor, a council, village meetings, and so on. In reference to their character, Wilson describes them as "remarkably temperate" smokers and drinkers, as personally very clean, as having neat dwellings, and as pleasant and hospitable. He refers to the women as "notably chaste and well behaved"[82] – the sexuality of the Pueblo residents, whether male or female, later became a point of great discourse among interested white observers, especially in the 1920s.[83] And he commends the parents for taking care to bring up children "in the paths of honesty and industry." There were further details on their clothing and manufacturing of pottery, blankets, and silver ornaments. Wilson commented, "It is wonderful what beautiful, closely-woven, vari-colored blankets are turned out on these looms. No less rude in construction are the bellows, anvil, and tools used by the silver smith, and yet very chaste and beautiful articles are produced."[84] In general, Wilson acknowledged that "in their mode of living and their style of dwelling they differ very materially from any other North American Tribe."[85]

Conclusion

It seems indisputable that Wilson's warmest feelings were expressed about Aboriginals who lived an agricultural, nonnomadic lifestyle. His own direct perceptions had corroborated his good knowledge of printed sources on the positive features of these peoples. Admittedly, the number of white Cherokee citizens and their mixed-blood descendants caused him some pause for thought, as observers who were caught up in attributing the successes of such groups to racial and biological roots might have been quick to attribute all aspects of the Cherokee's "wonderful progress" to the extent of white blood. Wilson dutifully raised the issue in his travel notes but suppressed this concern in some accounts. The issue was not raised in his accounts of the Zuni and Pueblo peoples, who charmed and impressed him so greatly. Since they lived in settled and enclosed communities, racial intermixture was probably not as likely as among the more dispersed Cherokee. These examples were both held out by Wilson as templates for the "wilder Indians," even though their economies and social institutions differed rather greatly. This conclusion that the Cherokee and Pueblo peoples could be regarded as templates came to its best expression in the "Fair Play Papers," which I have attributed to Wilson.

However, it should not be thought that Wilson's increasingly positive view of Indians was dependent only on the rather special cases of the Cherokee and the Pueblos. He had positive things to say about a variety of other Aboriginal nations, including those that had been nomadic or seminomadic and whose economies were based on hunting and gathering. In fact, another article might be written about Wilson's positive comments on these other peoples. But the Cherokee, Zuni, and Pueblo peoples were important to him for several reasons – no doubt because he had seen them first-hand in their principal communities, using his own eyes, which had enabled him to use his own participant or nonparticipant observation of them to supplement his reading of secondary sources, and of course, because he had adopted them as templates for the "wilder tribes who still wear blankets."

As a disciple of Horatio Hale, Wilson wrote several positive Indian papers on the various Iroquoian Six Nations, extensively drawing on Hale's writings and generally borrowing Hale's admiring view of them. Wilson was influenced not only by Hale's published writings, but also by an extended correspondence with him that consisted of twenty-four letters sent by Wilson to Hale over a period of three years (autumn 1885 through September 1888).

As for Wilson's good intentions (and those of Hale), the spirit of the times should be understood. The last decades of the nineteenth century and the first several of the twentieth saw a rising tide of scientific and nonscientific racism and racial categorization of peoples, encouraged but not originated by social Darwinism and by the development of eugenics. For example, writing in 1896, Columbia University's Franklin H. Giddings, one of the first prominent American sociologists, wrote in an introductory textbook on sociology about "North American Indians":

> It is sometimes said that we ought not to assert that the lower races have not the capacity for social evolution, because we do not know what they could do if they had the opportunity. They have been in existence, however, much longer than the European races, and have accomplished immeasurably less. We are, therefore, warranted in saying that they have not the same inherent abilities ... Another race [after a discussion of the extinct Tasmanians] with little capacity for improvement is the surviving North American Indian. Though intellectually superior to the negro, the Indian has shown less ability than the negro to adapt himself to new conditions.[86]

It will be recalled that Hale had raised the same issue about comparing North American Indians and Europeans, with a very favourable verdict for North American Aboriginals and one that departed significantly from the habitual favourable judgment accorded to Europeans (often identified as "Aryans").

Nonscientific racism among white settlers had long been rampant. In the context of Algoma, Wilson found himself writing a Mr. McMorine of St. Joseph's Landing, on a small agricultural island adjacent to Sault Ste Marie, "I am not surprised that people at the Landing should speak hard of the Indians – I am used to that – but I believe with patience and persistent effort much may be made of them."[87] It should be noted that Wilson's letter to McMorine was written *before* his eyes were opened by his new ethnological and anthropological interests and by his later estimation of Native self-government. This letter, however, does hint at the unfavourable attitudes held by average white settlers.

Ultimately, Wilson's good intentions along these new lines came to nothing, as he had anticipated in 1892. He had planned for an Indian conference to discuss and debate such ideas as self-government and cultural retention and synthesis, but it was a conference that was never held. The conference was to be sponsored by the Canadian Indian Research and Aid Society, of which Wilson was an officer. Proposals for topics included the holding of land communally or individually, whether Indians should "continue to dwell in separate communities and to retain their own language or ... to become one with the white people and adopt their language," and whether Aboriginals should "have more voice in the management of your own affairs than at present." In the planning for the conference, several forthright statements were received from Aboriginal leaders. One wrote strongly "against the abolishment of their Indian language and claim[ed] the right to maintain their own nationality."[88] In the event, however, the conference had to be cancelled. The reasons included both the organizational weakness of the Canadian Indian Research and Aid Society, which soon collapsed, and doubts expressed by Native spokespersons about the effectiveness of such a conference.

Wilson had planned to publish a book based on his "Indian Tribes Series," utilizing his new positive perceptual filter relating to Aboriginal peoples, but it never came to be. His suggestions of an Aboriginal parliament with its own funds, lawmaking capacity, capital, and lieutenant governor (along with the termination of the Department of Indian Affairs) were ignored. As already quoted, he had realized in 1892 that "there is little chance of these schemes ever being realized at any rate in my own day." It was not until the rejection of the White Paper on Indian policy of 1969 that calls for similar ideas came to be loudly proclaimed – however, see the campaign of Deskaheh to have Six Nations' sovereignty recognized in the 1920s.[89] When this occurred, it was due not to the good intentions of Euro-Canadians but to the insistence of the Aboriginal leadership itself.

The experience of Hale and Wilson shows that ideas too far in advance of their time are likely to lead to the marginalization of prophets. This, in fact, is what several writers who have used the term "prophet" in the more secular pursuit of social-science scholarship have found as a likely outcome of proposing ideas that go against the grain.[90] Sometimes a sharp change in the spirit of the times can reverse how prophets are perceived within their lifetimes – after marginalization in the 1930s and 1940s, the sociologist Pitirim Sorokin lived long enough to become a president of the American Sociological Association in 1963, and as the McCarthyite scare receded in the 1960s and 1970s, the avowed Marxist sociologist Arthur K. Davis found himself the president of the Canadian Sociology and Anthropology Association, albeit suffering exile from the United States. In the case of prophets such as Wilson and Hale, they were dead for a half-century or longer before the tides of opinion started to change in the directions that they had championed in the 1880s and 1890s.

Acknowledgments

An earlier version of this chapter was the basis for an invited presentation prepared for the conference "(Re)Making Anglican Tradition(s) in North America," held at Trinity College, University of Toronto, 23-27 June 2001. I would like to thank the Ven. Harry Huskins, J. Donald Wilson, Michael C. Coleman, Celia Haig-Brown, and Mary Nock for their assistance and advice.

Notes

1   John Webster Grant, *Moon of Wintertime: Missionaries and the Indians of Canada in Encounter since 1534* (Toronto: University of Toronto Press, 1984), 189.

2   North Atlantic Missiology Project, prospectus for "Christian Missions and the 'Enlightenment' of the West Symposium," Boston University, Boston, MA, June 1998, n.p.

3   Thomas S. Kuhn, *The Structure of Scientific Revolutions* (1962; reprint, Chicago: University of Chicago Press, 1970). Louis Althusser, *For Marx* (Chicago: University of Chicago Press, 1964).

4   On Wilson, see David A. Nock, *A Victorian Missionary and Canadian Indian Policy: Cultural Synthesis vs Cultural Replacement* (Waterloo: Wilfrid Laurier University Press, 1988). On Pratt, see F.P. Prucha, ed., *Americanizing the American Indians* (Cambridge, MA: Harvard University Press, 1973), 261.

5   E.F. Wilson, "The Principal's Report," in *Eighteenth Annual Report of the Shingwauk and Wawanosh Homes in the Diocese of Algoma* (Sault Ste Marie: Sault Express Print, 1892), 4-5.

6   Wilson to Powell, 5 January 1881. Correspondence, Wilson Letterbook, Anglican Diocese of Algoma, Provincial Archive of Ontario.

7   Wilson to Powell, 28 April 1885. Correspondence, Wilson Letterbook, Anglican Diocese of Algoma, Provincial Archive of Ontario.

8   E.F. Wilson, "My Wife and I: A Little Journey among the Indians," *Our Forest Children III*, 3 (June 1889): 8-12 at 8-9.

9   I define these terms in Nock, *A Victorian Missionary*. I had taken and slightly reworked these terms from C.W. Hobart and C.S. Brant, "Eskimo Education, Danish and Canadian: A Comparison," *Canadian Review of Sociology and Anthropology* 3 (1966): 47-66. My definition of "cultural synthesis" reads "a policy of cultural adaptation that encourages the synthesis of two cultures, that retains elements of both, and that encourages the *voluntary* borrowing and adaptation by the weaker cultural system" in ways that "make sense to the borrowing society." Nock, *A Victorian Missionary*, 1-2. Hobart and Brant (48) defined cultural replacement as "the attempt, in undeveloped areas, to replace the traditional culture with a modern one in a short period ... through the introduction of modern technological means, organizational forms, and ideological orientations, on a more or less massive basis." Quoted in Nock, *A Victorian Missionary*, 1.

10 Horatio Hale, *The Iroquois Book of Rites* (Philadelphia: D.G. Brinton, 1883; reprint, ed. William N. Fenton, Toronto: University of Toronto Press, 1963). For a good general and popular overview, see Ronald Wright, *Stolen Continents* (Toronto: Penguin, 1993).

11 E.F. Wilson, "My Wife and I: A Little Journey among the Indians," *Our Forest Children III*, 8, n.s. 6 (November 1889): 88-93 at 90.

12 Stanley W. Hoig, *The Cherokees and Their Chiefs* (Fayetteville: University of Arkansas Press, 1998), 251. For another account, see Duane Champagne, *Social Order and Political Change: Constitutional Governments among the Cherokee, the Choctaw, the Chickasaw, and the Creek* (Stanford: Stanford University Press, 1992), 216-17.

13 Champagne, *Social Order*, 217.

14 Wilson, "My Wife and I" (November 1889), 90.

15 Emmet Starr, *History of the Cherokee Indians* (1921; reprint, New York: Kraus, 1969), 298.

16 This and the following quotation come from Wilson, "My Wife and I" (November 1889), 90.

17 E.F. Wilson, "Indian Tribes-Paper No. 2, The Cherokee Indians," *Our Forest Children III*, 4, n.s. 2 (July 1889): 19, 29.

18 Wilson, "My Wife and I" (November 1889), 91.

19 Starr, *History of the Cherokee*, 235.

20 For a modern and somewhat negative or at least mixed assessment of the seminaries, particularly their role in exacerbating class and racial tensions, see William G. McLoughlin, *After the Trail of Tears: The Cherokees' Struggle for Sovereignty, 1839-1880* (Chapel Hill and London: University of North Carolina Press, 1993), 92-96. A more laudatory view is seen in Starr, *History of the Cherokee*, 229. Also commenting favourably on the Cherokee schools

more recently is Roger L. Nichols, *Indians in the United States and Canada* (Lincoln and London: University of Nebraska Press, 1998), 230.
21 See Starr, *History of the Cherokee,* 235.
22 Wilson, "My Wife and I" (November 1889), 91.
23 Starr, *History of the Cherokee,* 233, 284, 293, 298.
24 Hoig, *The Cherokees,* 251.
25 Wilson, "My Wife and I" (November 1889), 91.
26 Wilson, "Indian Tribes-Paper No. 2," 19.
27 See the reprint of this in Nock, *A Victorian Missionary,* 168; and also in this book.
28 Ibid., 135-50.
29 Wilson, "My Wife and I: A Little Journey among the Indians," *Our Forest Children III,* 5, n.s. (August 1889), 41-45 at 43.
30 Wright, *Stolen Continents,* 221. See Wilson, "Indian Tribes-Paper No. 2," 18.
31 For details, see Theda Perdue, *Cherokee Women: Gender and Culture Change, 1700-1835* (Lincoln and London: University of Nebraska Press, 1998).
32 See Starr, *History of the Cherokee,* 229. The other data are from Wilson, "Indian Tribes-Paper No. 2," 18.
33 Hoig, *The Cherokees,* 249.
34 Wilson, "Indian Tribes-Paper No. 2," 20. No doubt the sexism of the statement will strike the modern reader, as no mention is made of a clever girl.
35 Ibid., 17-18.
36 Ibid., 19.
37 See Perdue, *Cherokee Women.*
38 For the references to Dawes, Smiley, and Garret, see McLoughlin, *After the Trail of Tears,* 368-69.
39 Richard Henry Pratt, "The Advantages of Mingling Indians with Whites," from an 1892 address, in *Americanizing the American Indians,* ed. Francis Paul Prucha (Lincoln: University of Nebraska Press, 1978), 260-71 at 265.
40 Quoted from Loring Benson Priest, *Uncle Sam's Stepchildren: The Reformation of United States Indian Policy, 1865-1887* (New York: Octagon Books, 1969), 249.
41 McLoughlin, *After the Trail of Tears,* 370.
42 Ibid., 371.
43 Ibid., 376.
44 Michael C. Coleman, *American Indian Children at School, 1850-1930* (Jackson: University Press of Mississippi, 1993), 56.
45 McLoughlin, *After the Trail of Tears,* 376.
46 Circe Sturm, "Blood Politics, Racial Classification, and Cherokee National Identity: The Trials and Tribulations of the Cherokee Freedmen," *American Indian Quarterly* 22, 1-2 (Winter/Spring 1998): 230-58 at 240.
47 Ibid., 256.
48 McLoughlin, *After the Trail of Tears.*
49 Sturm, "Blood Politics," 256.
50 Wilson, "My Wife and I: A Little Journey among the Indians," *Our Forest Children III,* 7, n.s. (October 1889), 71-74 at 73.
51 Ibid., 74.
52 Ibid.
53 Wilson, "My Wife and I" (November 1889), 88.
54 Ibid., 89.
55 Ibid., 90.
56 Hoig, *The Cherokees,* 251.
57 Wilson, "My Wife and I" (November 1889), 90.
58 McLoughlin, *After the Trail of Tears,* 433.
59 Wilson, "My Wife and I" (November 1889), 90.
60 Wilson, "Indian Tribes-Paper No. 2," 18.
61 As reprinted in Nock, *A Victorian Missionary,* 166-67.
62 Ibid., 168.

63   Starr, *History of the Cherokee,* 261.
64   As reprinted in Nock, *A Victorian Missionary,* 175-76.
65   Ibid., 175.
66   Editorial, *The Canadian Indian,* vol. 1 (March 1891): 161.
67   As reprinted in Nock, *A Victorian Missionary,* 169.
68   Jesse Green, ed., *Zuni: Selected Writings of Frank Hamilton Cushing* (Lincoln: University of Nebraska Press, 1979); Margaret D. Jacobs, *Engendered Encounters: Feminism and Pueblo Cultures, 1879-1934* (Lincoln and London: University of Nebraska Press, 1999); Eliza McFeely, *Zuni and the American Imagination* (New York: Hill and Wang, 2001).
69   McFeely, *Zuni,* 84.
70   Wilson, "My Wife and I: A Little Journey among the Indians," *The Canadian Indian* 1 (October 1890): 7-10 at 7.
71   Ibid., 9.
72   Wilson, "My Wife and I" (October 1890), 47.
73   Ibid., 48.
74   Ibid., 73.
75   Ibid., 50.
76   Ibid., 48.
77   On Parsons and other positive "antimodern feminist" observers of the Pueblo, see Jacobs, *Engendered Encounters.*
78   Wilson, "My Wife and I" (October 1890), 47.
79   Jacobs, *Engendered Encounters,* 109.
80   Ibid., 223-24.
81   Wilson, "My Wife and I" (October 1890), 47.
82   E.F. Wilson, "Indian Tribes-Paper No. 4, The Pueblo Indians," *Our Forest Children III,* 6, n.s. 4 (September 1889): 49-54 at 51.
83   See Jacobs, *Engendered Encounters.*
84   Wilson, "Indian Tribes-Paper No. 4," 52.
85   Ibid., 49.
86   Franklin Henry Giddings, *The Principles of Sociology* (1896; reprint, New York: Macmillan, 1904). On Giddings, see Robert C. Bannister, *Sociology and Scientism: The American Quest for Objectivity, 1880-1940* (Chapel Hill and London: University of North Carolina Press, 1987), 64-86.
87   Wilson to McMorine, 19 March 1878. Correspondence, Wilson Letterbooks.
88   See Nock, *A Victorian Missionary,* 145-46, on this proposed conference and its failure to be held. See also David A. Nock, "The Indian Conference That Never Was," *Ontario Indian* 5, 2 (February 1982): 39-45 at 39-41, 43, 45.
89   Wright, *Stolen Continents,* 322-26.
90   On the employment of the term "prophet" by social scientists, see Robert C. Friedrichs, *A Sociology of Sociology* (New York: The Free Press, 1970). On its application to specific case studies, see Barry V. Johnston, *Pitirim A. Sorokin: An Intellectual Biography* (Lawrence: University Press of Kansas, 1995). On Arthur K. Davis, see David A. Nock, "Lessons from Davis: The Sociology of Arthur Kent Davis," *The Canadian Journal of Sociology* 20, 3 (1995): 387-407, and David A. Nock, "Prophetic versus Priestly Sociology: Arthur K. Davis," *The American Sociologist* 33, 2 (2002): 57-85. For another and influential use of this distinction in the social sciences, see Donald N. Levine, *Visions of the Sociological Tradition* (Chicago: University of Chicago Press, 1995), 76-77.

8

Good Intentions Gone Awry: From Protection to Confinement in Emma Crosby's Home for Aboriginal Girls

Jan Hare and Jean Barman

Along the established routes of the fur trade in western Canada travelled missionaries seeking another kind of trade, a trade of souls. By relinquishing their nomadic lifestyles and spiritual ways, rooted in their land, languages, traditions, and customs, hence their souls, Aboriginal groups would become "civilized" to a world of education, improvement, and Christianity. The zealousness with which missionaries pursued their "trading" relations was sustained by their confidence in the superiority of their culture and faith. Missionaries believed that this spiritual and moral transformation was in the best interest of indigenous peoples and also maintained that it contributed to colonialism's agenda of "civilizing the Indian" and to the Christianizing of frontier settlements. Missionaries came with what might be termed, from their perspective, "good intentions."

Early missionary efforts in Canada began in the 1600s with the Jesuits' arrival in eastern Canada. On the West Coast, a Spanish voyage in the late 1700s brought the first Catholic missionaries, whose presence on Vancouver Island and further up the coast was brief. Catholic priests came again in the 1840s, effecting little change on Indian lifestyles and beliefs but successfully initiating contact in areas of the fur trade. As the province began to sustain more permanent settlements, the stability of missions increased, as did their influence. Anglican missionary William Duncan began work at the trading post of Fort Simpson on British Columbia's north coast in 1857. Several years later he established nearby Metlakatla as the centre of Anglican missions on the north coast until the last decade of the nineteenth century.[1] Only Methodist missions and, in particular, Thomas Crosby's arrival in 1874 would rival Duncan's work.[2]

The trade in Indian souls was accompanied by a trade in the body. Aboriginal peoples' physical appearances, as well as their social organizations and family dwellings, were being constantly renegotiated in order that missionaries might recreate a "civilized" Victorian order. This obligation placed particular kinds of demands on missionaries. It was considered desirable, if not essential, in the enterprise that male missionaries have a wife. Marriage to a single partner provided for a significant and stable institution to which Aboriginal people should aspire. Wives were also essential models of appropriate behaviour for their Aboriginal counterparts while, at the same time, ensuring that their husbands did not, for any reason, become too involved with their female converts. Dana Robert makes the important point that missionary wives counted within the larger setting in which their men folk established priorities: "The activities of missionary wives were not random: they were part of a mission strategy that gave women a particular role in the advancement of God's kingdom."[3]

Until recently, the role of wives in the missionary enterprise has received little attention.[4] As missionary work was men's work, it has most often been examined from a male perspective that downplays the nature and extent of wives' involvement. Women had good intentions that both mirrored those of their husbands and were also their own. Wives who accompanied their husbands to what were often desolate places, enduring hardship and poverty, were fulfilling several aspirations. As well as modelling Victorian ideals of family, which promoted the roles of mother and housewife as central to womanhood, marriage to a missionary gave these women a chance to express their own religious interests, be it in an ever so obsequious manner.

While the women shared with their husbands a sense of duty to improve the lives of indigenous peoples, they were restricted in their roles within the mission. Gender attitudes at the time – indeed, over the next century – prevented a woman from being a full-fledged missionary in her own right. As a missionary wife, she could assist in some helping capacity, but she was not considered capable of, on her own, preaching the word of God and offering the rites of baptism and marriage that marked stages in the life cycle. What she could contribute was clearly defined by this male-dominated institution. Yet women were complicit in the missionary understandings of good intentions. As with others who came with a "conscience," their priorities did not match those of Aboriginal peoples. Aboriginal peoples were never in need of the protection and salvation on which the good intentions of missionary men and women rested.

One such woman who used her marriage to her advantage in the missionary enterprise was Emma Crosby, wife of Methodist missionary Thomas Crosby. Her birth into and upbringing in a missionary tradition shaped her good intentions from an early age. A Methodist minister's daughter who studied and taught at a Methodist women's college in Hamilton, Ontario, Emma accepted without question the obligation within colonialism to civilize indigenous peoples around the world. Thus she sought her parents' permission to marry a virtual stranger so that she could travel to British Columbia and become "not exactly as a missionary on my own responsibility" but as close to one as it was possible for a woman to be at

Emma Crosby just before her marriage

the time.[5] "The conviction grows upon me that I might be both happy &
useful – perhaps more so there than anywhere else," she concluded in a
letter to her parents.[6]

Arrived at Fort Simpson on British Columbia's north coast in the spring of
1874, Emma and her new husband had come with the best of intentions.

They sought the salvation of the local Tsimshian people, who unless they accepted the precepts of Christianity were, in the Crosbys' view, doomed to eternal damnation. "Tsimshian" was, and is, the most commonly used name for the culturally related peoples of northwest British Columbia living between the Nass and Skeena Rivers from the Pacific Coast inland to the two rivers' headwaters. Despite the Crosbys' motivations, their presence was at the invitation of the Tsimshian, who, in response to the threats to their way of life wrought by colonialism, invited them onto their territory.

Emma Crosby took the lead in the feminine work of the mission, teaching school, caring for the sick, and leading in social activities aimed at improving the missionary spirit. Her husband's conversion exploits resulted in lengthy absences from this community, positioning Emma as a maternal authority and requiring her to oversee this mission to the Tsimshian, as "it would never do to leave these people all alone."[7] Her work kept her in close relations with the Tsimshian women and children, so much so that she took the first of what would be numerous local girls into her home shortly after her arrival. Because the maintenance of the home was, everyone agreed during these years, women's work, it was absolutely essential that girls be prepared for marriage and motherhood so that they could eventually maintain their own households fashioned on newcomers' practices. She might not be able to be a missionary in her own right, but she could model within the home patterns of behaviour and a way of life consistent with Christianity, as a Christian home was a civilized home. It was on this precept that Emma's good intentions were directed toward the girls that she took into her care.

Emma accepted without question the need to protect the Aboriginal girls who came to her home, writing to her mother how "one who was in trouble and friendless almost had to be brought in – she is older than the others and not particularly bright but we do not choose."[8] During Emma's second year at Simpson, as it was often called, she explained: "We have taken another young girl into the house – she was without home or friends to care for her. It is a great care & anxiety to have these girls. We cannot trust to their truthfulness or honesty altogether but this seems the only way to help them."[9] As Emma's husband Thomas explained, "they would come, one after another, and ask the Missionary's wife for her protection; and thus one and another and another were taken into the house."[10]

Operating on their own understandings about what the Crosby home could offer their daughters, many Aboriginal parents made conscious choices about placing their children in Emma's care. They may have wanted to relieve their children from the hardships that resulted from the destructive consequences of encroaching settlement, such as loss of a subsistence economy, loss of land, and the erosion of their spiritual base. Others saw the opportunity that care in the Crosby home offered their children. With new skills and knowledge, their children could participate in the newcomers' world, gaining social and intellectual access through Christian means. So they brought their children to Emma, knowing full well the advantages of being part of a Christian home. In other circumstances, the Crosbys' may have been the only choice.

Even as Emma saw her role as the girls' salvation, her charges responded in ways that she never would have anticipated. The girls' companionship to Emma during Thomas' numerous, and sometimes lengthy, absences, their maintenance of the home, and their oversight of the Crosby children formed a mutual exchange in protection, which permitted Emma a greater role in the missionary enterprise than otherwise may have been possible. The Tsimshian were as concerned to care for Emma as she was to care for them. Assuring her mother that she could bear the hardships of the mission, she wrote: "Don't feel anxious about us, we are well, and quite content. I have a young woman to help me in the house. She is clean & tidy & does her best, only she has a great deal to learn."[11] The challenges of keeping up the mission home and caring for her own young children made the girls all the more a necessity in the home. When one of her charges went off fishing with friends, Emma was left to her own devices: "For about a week I was without any one to help me – except, indeed, Thomas – but we got on very well, and now the girl we had is back."[12]

Only when Emma took notice of this escalation of exchange did she set in motion events that would remove the girls from the Crosby home, resulting in their formal institutionalized care. About Emma's good intentions there can be no doubt, but it was also the case that by the time she left the north coast of British Columbia with her husband in 1897, her good intentions had gone dreadfully awry. What she reports to her mother in her personal correspondence and her decision to place the girls in a new "home" separate from her family's suggest Emma's increasing discomfort with the Aboriginal girls' influence on her own home and family. Most telling of the distance that Emma may have wanted to create is a family photo taken by a visiting photographer in 1884 in which Emma, Thomas, and their family are positioned carefully separated from the Aboriginal girls. Eventually, the girls would be placed in institutional care identified far less with protection than with confinement and even incarceration.

Almost as soon as the Crosbys arrived in Fort Simpson, Emma took the first of what would be numerous Aboriginal girls into her home. "We have a young girl now and I know if she stays long she will be able to keep a house clean and tidy," she proudly informed her mother in the late summer of 1874.[13] No question exists that Emma took very seriously the responsibility to mentor her charges in colonial ways. Two months later, she explained to her mother the sense of obligation that she felt: "My little girl does just as well as I could expect in the house, but of course she can take no responsibility – at all – & I have not the time I would like to teach her. Besides I want to make her neater & tidier than she is now and have to take time to show her how to sew all I give her."[14] Shortly after her first child, Jessie, was born at the end of 1874, Emma reiterated her good intentions to assist these girls. "This little girl we have is about fifteen – she is really a very faithful, devoted cheerful little thing and, I believe, will do very well. Indeed now she does very nicely as long as I can direct her a little."[15]

Emma incorporated the girls into her daily routine so that they could understand what it meant to partake of a civilized home. Carrying out cleaning chores, "they did their very best, I believe, the house was swept about half a dozen times a day – that is the broom was flourished about in the middle of the room so as to send all the dust into the corners. With the exception of the woman who comes to wash & do extra work for me I do not know an Indian who seems to have an idea of thorough cleanliness. The first sight I had of the kitchen made my heart go right into my moccasins ... We struggled through, and now the house is quite settled."[16] Emma was doing her duty by letting the girls be household helps.

It was essential that the girls participate in all aspects of running a household: "Our cow proves a very good one ... the girls do all the churning. I merely over-see it, and I will say we have very good butter."[17] Emma went out of her way to teach other skills as well: "We have four girls – we took a new one lately – they had so little to do that two might have done far better than four. I have constantly to study to arrange work for them and keep them all employed when I am well. I have been teaching them lately some kinds of fancy knitting and crochet work and they do very well at it."[18] Many years later, one of the girls recalled for a reporter her experience of living in the Crosby home: "That's where she learned to do things ... They taught her to do things in the house, you know, sweeping, cooking, and things like that."[19]

Convinced that Christian ways of life were the only right ways and that, until indigenous peoples accepted these precepts, their actions were wrongminded, Emma was always concerned that the girls might be led astray by less principled colonizers: "I sometimes think surely this Pacific coast is the wickedest place on earth. White men living unmarried with Indian women is perhaps the chief evil. There are none in the village – but some not many miles away who come to the village & decoy away the young girls. It is dreadful."[20] Increasingly, Emma saw the end result of the protection she afforded the girls to lie in marriage. Women's destiny lay in making a home for their husbands and families, and she believed further, as did others, that men were meant to have ultimate authority within the home. So long as she delivered each of her charges into the arms of a man, she was fulfilling her good intentions that formed the missionary agenda. Emma's perspective comes out graphically in a letter written to her mother in the fall of 1876: "One of our girls is to be married in about a week, to a very promising young man ... This is the girl who came to us first. I am rather sorry to lose her. She is a good nurse though not a very good worker, but of course it is best for girls to be married, Indian girls more especially."[21]

As the girls taken in by Emma reached the age of marriage, she ensured that the transition conformed as far as possible to the practices with which she had been raised, practices that were consistent with Victorian values. One girl recalled many years later how "Mrs. Crosby provided the wedding breakfast and invited all the Indian chiefs of the district to attend," a touch deemed so significant that it even made it into her husband's obituary.[22] By so doing, Emma ensured that the entire community gave witness to this Christian form of union, in her view an eminently superior means of doing things. She was unaware that the presence of the chiefs to bear witness was consistent with Tsimshian tradition marking important events. The finishing touch, accomplished with her husband's help, was even more longlasting. It was absolutely critical, Crosby penned in his memoir, that local families "put up little 'Christian' homes, of three to four rooms each, and thus [be] got out of the old heathen lodges or community houses, where four or five families had often been herded together."[23] Emma took delight, a few years later, in how "very few have left us except to be married."[24]

Having come to live among the Tsimshian at their invitation, the Crosbys were particularly anxious to get their mission underway. "We hoped to learn the language, preach the Gospel and teach them, as well as we knew how, the arts of civilization."[25] In order to carry out their intentions, they required conduits to Tsimshian society. Although Thomas had been in British Columbia previous to his marriage to Emma, he was not familiar with the languages, customs, and traditions of these coastal peoples. The Crosbys' knowledge and understandings of their surroundings came from the Tsimshian and, more particularly, from a prominent couple, Kate and Alfred Dudoward, who had been among those inviting the Crosbys onto their territory: "Most of our services had to be carried on through an interpreter. We felt that every effort must be made to get hold of this new tongue. In this Mr. Dudoward, our interpreter, was a great help. We had many a struggle before we were able to preach and teach the people in their own tongue."[26] Emma's teaching duties required her to seek their help, her husband recalled: "For some time after our arrival, with the assistance of Mr. and Mrs. Dudoward, Mrs. Crosby had taught the school, of about sixty or seventy adults in the afternoon and one hundred children in the morning."[27] Over the course of the Crosbys' nearly quarter of a century at Simpson, the Tsimshian proved invaluable to both Thomas and Emma.

For Emma, this help was extended into the Crosby home, provided by the very girls she sought to protect. Gathering up converts kept Thomas absent from the mission: "It was something of a trial for me to have my husband go, but I saw the importance of it, though it was uncertain when he would get back."[28] In these times, she knew she did not have to be alone. Preparing for Thomas' three-week departure, she rejected the help of a nurse, for "we have so many in the house – with four girls."[29] Thomas' duties kept him busy while at home, but she had the company of the girls: "If Thomas cannot go with me when I go for a walk, I take one of the girls."[30] While Emma modelled for these girls how to become good housewives, they made life endurable for her.

Emma repeatedly wrestled with the consequences of her good intentions aimed at converting the girls in her home. Briefly, it began to appear that she might come to consider, albeit hesitantly, that her actions had sufficiently influenced her charges that she might trust them. Jessie was aged ten months when Emma explained: "The girls are kind to her and often amuse her but we never leave her to their care."[31] Some months later, she wrote: "I do wish you could see our home, and our little daughter – our little 'moonbeam' as she stands now on a chair at the table when I write – one of the girls holding her – and pretending to read from an old envelope she has ... The girls are very fond of her and take charge of her a good [deal] – though seldom away from one of us – however lately I have been leaving her with one or the other of them Sunday afternoons while I went to S.S. [Sunday school] where teachers are so much needed that I could scarcely conscientiously stay away."[32] And a bit later, she noted: "Jessie had to be left almost entirely to their care and though, I believe, they did all they could for her still they cannot manage her properly. However I do not wish to complain – we have so very much to be thankful for I must not do that."[33]

Yet, however much Emma might have tried, she never quite learned to trust. Thus, when her second child came along in September 1876, she eagerly used the event as a reason to quit teaching: "Now that I have two little ones to care for I feel that my work must be almost wholly at home – this little baby will need great care all winter, if it is spared to us, and it is better for Jessie to be with me than with the girls."[34] For all her good intentions to protect these girls, Emma simply could not accept that her charges could be as well intentioned as herself, as evidenced during a trip to Victoria: "A little girl I brought down with me carries baby. This little nurse is of but little use to me but is better than no one."[35]

Two factors coalesced to initiate the formal institutionalization of Aboriginal girls. One was pragmatic. Over time the numbers of girls grew, which increased Emma's sense of responsibility toward them: "I find there is so little for three girls to do that I fear their getting into bad habits on that account. We think of sending one away – though I do not like to do it. If we had a house arranged properly we might have things more on the plan

The Crosby family posed with the girls in their home

of a school and let them take turns in the kitchen – but as things are now that is impossible. Then the expense of keeping up such a family is not a little – perhaps more than we ought to undertake."[36]

The second factor had to do with the escalation of exchange in protection between the Crosbys and the girls, as it now extended to the Crosby children. Perhaps Emma's observances of her children's behaviours revealed the nature and extent to which the Aboriginal girls' presence came to bear upon them. Reporting to her mother in a letter dated 1877, she noted, "Jessie seems every day to grow more interesting. She enters into everything with keen enjoyment and nothing escapes her. If wood is being carried in she must have some sticks tied to her back. When the girls carry in the hay she goes along with a little bundle across her shoulder."[37] Uneasy with the increasing influence of the girls on her young children, Emma reached the limits of her beliefs. She had taken the girls into her home but had never come to accept that they belonged there. The best interests of her own children, as she perceived them, were paramount. Thus, when her good intentions to care for these Aboriginal girls clashed with her concern for her children, her good intentions had to give way: "As our own family increased we felt that our house was not the place for these girls."[38]

Emma's solution was to construct a home within the home: "We could not abandon the work, so, after much prayerful consultation, we decided to build an addition to the Mission-house which should serve as a 'Home' for the girls, and could be under our closer supervision, but entirely separate from our own family."[39] The necessary funds had to be raised in Ontario, and here Emma depended on her own family, prominent in Methodist circles, and on her contemporaries, mostly fellow teachers. Emma wrote excitedly to her mother in the spring of 1879: "I am very glad to hear that this female home of ours is so favorably considered. We hope to have it in operation in some shape next summer."[40] Two months later, she reported: "The 'Home' is not completed yet, and the back part of our house is to be rebuilt, and, if possible, a school house to be put up. We shall be very glad to receive subscriptions towards the 'Home.'"[41]

For a time Emma continued in her role as protector, as she explained in late 1879: "There are now nine girls in the 'Home.' I find it quite impossible to give them the attention they need. I think we shall have to get some elderly Indian woman to superintend them until we can do better."[42] Numbers grew: "We have had twelve girls under our care all winter so our 'Home' may be said to be in fair operation. One was married a few weeks ago, but a little girl from another village, a heathen village, has since come to us to make up the number. Quite a family to look after is it not? We are seventeen souls in all, including the young man who has charge of the [day] school."[43]

Emma's success in reconciling her good intentions with her primary concern for her own family initiated the process by which protection of the girls became a matter of their confinement in a "home" built especially to house them. Her fundraising encouraged the formation of a Woman's Missionary Society within the Methodist Church of Canada. Its first monies raised were "devoted to the use of Mrs. Emma Crosby (wife of the Rev. T. Crosby), of Port Simpson, B.C., for the use of her (Indian Girls') Home."[44] Emma explained the purposes of separating the girls from her family: "Our plan would be to train the girls in general housework, in needlework of various kinds, in spinning, and weaving, if possible, and whatever else they might be able to turn to good account. We aim at making them capable Indian women, fitted for such a life as they are likely to be called to in after life. The most they can do is, as they leave us, to establish Christian homes for themselves where, as wives and mothers, they may show what industrious habits and a Christian spirit can do." Institutionalization was formalized by the decision of the Woman's Missionary Society to fund the salary of a matron, whom Emma termed "a thoroughly practical and competent woman to give her whole attention to the work."[45]

The shift from protection to confinement and increasingly to what might be seen as incarceration also related to growing racism. Around the world indigenous people had their land and resources usurped on the grounds that newcomers knew how to make best use of them. This fundamental shift, which we know as colonialism, was based on circular reasoning. Newcomers justified their intrusion by their paler skin tones, with the success of their actions, sometimes through force, subsequently confirming to them that they were, after all, destined to rule. A divide based on what is usually termed "race" grew over the course of the nineteenth century. People of darker pigments became perceived as inherently inferior. They had to be minded in their own best interests. Missionaries like the Crosbys were essential to indigenous peoples' being made subservient. The comparative ease with which Emma trusted one of her girls to accompany her to Victoria, if acting condescendingly toward her, was replaced by a regime where there was virtually no freedom whatsoever. Whatever the extent to which Emma bought into this thinking, she found it useful as a means of convincing her counterparts in Ontario to provide funds: "The alternative was often coming under our roof or going to ruin, and, alas! to our grief, we found in the case of two or three girls whom we felt we were not prepared to take in at the time they applied to us, ruin speedily followed ... The temptation to this was strong, and we found it one of the most difficult things we had to contend with."[46]

At its extreme, colonial views of race doomed persons of darker skin tones. As to whether the girls possessed the capacity to be converted and civilized, Emma equivocated: "You ask if Indian girls will stay Christianized and civilized ... There are those among our Indians here who for some years have adored the doctrine of Christ, and among our girls there are several who have long given every evidence of being true Christians. Of course, the ignorance and inexperience of such a people as this, and the absence of the restraints thrown round a more refined state of society, leave them an easy prey to many temptations." Like most colonizers, Emma found it difficult to conceive that Aboriginal persons might eventually become good Christians, thereby reinforcing the need for a continued missionary presence:

As to civilization these people are, many of them, very ambitious. Sometimes they try to take it on too fast, they want to play the organ before they know how to make bread, and a necktie is of much more importance often than an apron. Still, we can see considerable improvement throughout the village in the keeping of the houses, while the children are much better cared for than formerly. The people come to Church, almost invariably neatly dressed, and observe the strictest decorum. The girls are, as a rule, quick to learn, both in school and housework, though, of course, we find some who naturally lack all idea of order, and can never be thoroughly neat and clean.[47]

Emma remained ambivalent about the force of race; others did not do even that. A fundamental aspect of confinement cum incarceration had to do with the character of the matrons now in charge of the home. As did Emma, the women who succeeded her came with good intentions to save and protect the Aboriginal girls. Perforce unmarried and without children of their own, they sometimes initially transferred their maternal desires onto their charges. "They often call me mama," the first one reported proudly, stating another time, "My family have all been so well."[48] When two girls were permitted to return home to their mother, this matron could not quite understand why they were so eager to do so: "I believe I had a mother's love for those poor girls & it has been the saddest trial of my life but thank God I have been enabled to lean hard on the strong arm of Jesus."[49] These women's convictions were undoubtedly sincere, perhaps too much so in that they set them up for a fall.

The matrons were at the same time paid employees hired to do a job. Forced to watch over ill children during Christmastime on the north coast, one matron reflected how "a few days ago the enemy tried hard to tempt me by telling me I could be very much better employed than waiting on poor ignorant rude Indian girls."[50] Almost like clockwork, the women each stayed the three years to which they had committed themselves with the Woman's Missionary Society and then got married, an easy task given the sharp gender differential that marked the newcomer population in British Columbia. Most often their marriages were to Methodist missionaries junior to them in age.[51]

However good their intentions, and there were many indications of empathy with the young girls in their charge, the string of women who ran the girls' home from the early 1880s onward found it incredibly difficult to get beyond their racist assumptions. At the home a year, the first matron confided to her family: "They are a very suspicious thankless people no matter what you do they think you should do more."[52] The solution to the matrons' distrust of the girls was to establish a strict routine. Girls went for "some very nice walks" but carefully out of sight of the village where their families lived.[53] As a visitor explained, it was "taking them through the Indian village daily that caused the teachers so much trouble by keeping them in constant touch with the people and informed of all that transpires."[54] Organization was paramount, a matron explained in 1886: "We do everything by rule. We have bedroom, dining-room, kitchen and wash-room rules, also general rules, or a time-table giving the hour for everything, from the rising-bell to bed-time."[55] As to whether the girls could, even so, become Christian and civilized, great doubt existed. One matron

A typical photograph of the Crosby home for girls

reflected in her memoir: "I had some girls who used to 'get converted' regularly every few weeks, would cry and mourn over their bad behaviour and make a great profession of repentance in class meeting and in a day or two be as bad as ever – I never respected such conversions – tho' I might have had quite a list in the course of a year – it wasn't the kind of conversion I waited for."[56]

Surveillance was key to the enterprise. The girls were taken on a summer camping trip to compensate for their being "so used to migrating from place to place" with their families. The report emphasized how "it was not much of a rest for the teachers, as ears and eyes must always be on the alert as well as hands to keep things as they should be."[57] As to surveillance's benefits, the home's matron explained at the beginning of 1886, "On the dining-room wall I have two large sheets of paper containing the names of all, for good and bad marks; I find they have a very good effect upon them. Knowing that if a rule is broken there will be a bad mark for the disobedient one, makes them very careful and often saves them from more severe punishment ... Sometimes there is stubbornness hard to conquer, but when such is the case I let Mr. Crosby undertake for me, and the naughty one is soon penitent."[58]

The girls, for their part, continued to believe, at least at rare moments, that their surrogate mothers in their new "home" were teachable. One matron described how the children "have a wonderful facility for finding something to eat every time they go out; sometimes it is mussels off the rocks, sometimes roots or young shoots, or various plants which they tell me 'the people eat,' so they know they are safe."[59] Come the spring, "they are very anxious to borrow a boat and go for fish eggs."[60] The girls were enormously resourceful at retaining skills: "The children used to delight in gathering large quantities [of berries] which we preserved for winter use – In the late winter they always begged to take our walks on the beach so they could gather clams and mussles [sic]." The girls also maintained the familiar in other ways: "They weren't as fond of romping as white children. ... they seemed to enjoy a quiet walk & talk best – While passing through the village I always had them walk in order but once out in the bush or on the sea-shore the older girls would join me & they would tell me of their earlier life or legends of their people, or I would tell them tales of the white folks of my own childhood – & I used to enjoy it as much as they did, & any treasures in the way of sea-shells, wild flowers or fine berries were always saved for me."[61] Perhaps it was for this reason, but more likely simply because it was more economical and less stressful, that by the end of the century "native food is purchased for the children of the Home – salmon, sea-weed, small fish and game."[62] One of the most difficult aspects for the girls was to maintain communication with their families. Some of them tacitly or deliberately effected a trade-off, so a matron unwittingly revealed: "It has been cheering to have some of the girls who have always refused to pray in public, of late pray with the sick ones, as we visit from house to house together. We usually take two with us when visiting in the village; the children deem it a special privilege to accompany us."[63]

As to how it was that the various women in charge had such absolute certainty in their perspective and also remained largely unaware of girls' strategic responses to their confinement, one of them explained: "My Savior comes & talks with me & sweet communion there have we. He gently leads me with his hand for this is Heaven's border land." It was not that the job was so wonderful. Tempted by the devil to leave, "I soon drove his majesty back by telling him I was quite willing to do my Father's work whatever that work might be & had no desire but to do the whole will of God. Oh it is grand when we have the right weapon of defense & ... I may run with patience the race that is set before me looking onto Jesus."[64] This woman's successor was equally convinced of the rightness of her ways with the Aboriginal girls in her charge: "Their dispositions and habits are so very different from those of white people that we need not expect the same results from our efforts to improve them."[65] Three months later she still held to her assumptions: "They do not appreciate it very much, it is true, but that is nothing to us; our work is for the Master; and I hope it will meet with His approval."[66] Girls' parents were expected to promise in advance that they would refrain from retrieving their daughters for ten years, which in most cases equated to the time until their marriages.[67] The matrons were absolutely convinced that they knew best: "It seems to me a great pity that there is no way to prevent them taking their children out until the time specified in the agreement has expired. This is to me the most trying part of my work, for sometimes, just when we see that the child is being influenced for good, why something occurs that she must go home."[68]

The greatest pleasure came when the girls "married Christian Indians, ... helped to build up Christian homes, ... civilize the people generally and ... aid in developing their own neighborhood."[69] As one matron put it, "No higher work need be desired by any one anxious to help in extending Christ's kingdom, than the opportunity of assisting day after day in the education and development of the young girls who must so early in life take their places as wives and mothers of this people."[70] Confinement was intended to prepare them by example to be subservient to the men who would be their husbands. Women might no longer be sold, as missionaries were convinced occurred up to the time of their arrival on the north coast, but they were no less valuable commodities when it came to marriage. Crosby in his memoir, which was written in close consultation with Emma, explained the shift: "Instead of a young man with his friends going with property and buying a wife, as was done formerly, many of our brightest young men tried to make the acquaintance of the girls in the Home." Missionaries like the Crosbys often attempted to put a romantic gloss on what were very often limited options, if any, for young women from among the handful of men who were considered suitably Christian to become their husbands: "There was no doubt in our minds that real, true love again and again developed between the young people who thus became acquainted. This acquaintance finally resulted in their marriage and the happy life that followed. We taught them to consult their parents, as well as the Missionary, at this time, and also to pray much to the Lord for help." In his memoir, Emma's husband gloried over the Aboriginal women "who married into Indian homes in the different villages and, by their industry and cleanly habits in caring for their homes and children, showed the marvelous civilizing influence such work as ours may exert on whole communities."[71]

Another shift occurred in 1891 when Emma effectively turned over administration of the girls' home to the Woman's Missionary Society, which purchased two acres at Simpson for a new building.[72] The careful design of the two-storey structure by a Victoria architect makes clear that the enterprise was now a professional undertaking.[73] It was no longer the personal initiative of a missionary wife seeking, directly or indirectly, to protect girls by taking them into her home. Two years later the federal government undertook to support the Crosby Home for Aboriginal Girls as an

Indian residential school at their standard annual rate of $60 a year per child.[74] Confinement cum incarceration was complete.

Emma, who still lived nearby and kept up strong informal ties, long struggled with the meaning of the girls' home. She never had any moment of reckoning, where she suddenly took a stand, or, if she did, it went unrecorded. She could not have done so publicly in any case, for she herself was largely responsible for the changes that caused her good intentions to go awry. Emma had incorporated the girls into her daily life, and the girls, too, had included the Crosbys in theirs, whereas her successors in charge sought to bend the girls to their will. The closest Emma ever came to being visibly ambivalent was when she broached the notion of giving the home "more the character of an orphanage" or "a refuge" in contrast to the institution it was fast becoming.[75]

The shift from protection to confinement became so totalizing that the girls took it as their due. The assumption that they had somehow become the home's property, to remain there indefinitely, came to the test when, at the beginning of 1898 just after the Crosbys left the north coast, Nellie Atanasse's father asked for her return on the grounds that she was now "past sixteen." The home refused on the grounds that he was "a Catholic and a worthless man." The father got an injunction, obliging Nellie to testify in court. The home got itself a first-rate lawyer in Emma Crosby's new son-in-law and fought the order. The judge gave Nellie an opportunity to decide her own future, whereupon she, hardly surprising given that she was accompanied to court by the home's matron and that it was the only "home" she had known for half a dozen years, chose to remain there. The matron in charge asserted proudly, "We have reason to believe that the case, ending as it did, will be a great help to the standing of the Home in the future." She added, almost as an afterthought, "Nellie is still with us, and seems happy and contented."[76] Not to chance a change of heart, before the year was out, "Nellie Atanasse, the heroine of the lawsuit, was married," a Methodist missionary publication proudly reported.[77] The Crosby Home for Aboriginal Girls was maintained by the Woman's Missionary Society, with federal support, until 1948.

Once the girls were wholly removed from her care, Emma assumed a new set of social responsibilities. Whereas she was initially the only newcomer woman in Simpson, increasingly there were more and more others like her. The formation of the girls' home brought matrons and assistant matrons. Women whose missionary husbands were stationed in outlying parts of Crosby's domain would make their way to Simpson from time to time. Other women accompanied their husbands in new ventures, among them Nellie Bolton, wife of the first medical doctor at Simpson. Nellie kept a diary in 1890 and 1891. Its entries, if far sketchier than Emma's letters, give glimpses into the increased sociability among what Nellie termed "the white residents" of Simpson.[78] She wrote four months after her arrival, "Began to feel tired of Indian life," a perfectly plausible observation given that the Tsimshian were no longer at the heart of everyday missionary activity, as they had been during Emma's first years at Fort Simpson.[79] New alliances were formed among these women replicating the ways of life in the places whence they came. They would visit back and forth, share a meal, sew together, go for a walk, or just have a chat. Emma was at the centre of this circle. When the women formed a local Woman's Missionary Society Auxiliary, she was elected president.

The new sociability did not lessen Emma's obligations to the Crosby mission. She was still expected to fill in whenever the need arose. The teacher of the village school, which enrolled a good hundred Tsimshian children, left in the spring of 1890 when Emma's youngest child was just over two years of age. Come September, Emma took "the school for an hour and a half" every morning, the matron doing the same in the afternoon.[80] A contemporary recalled how Emma would also take the Sunday school for "all the white children" for two months each summer to relieve the regular teacher: "She was such a dear little thing, I remember her well."[81] Emma filled in at emergencies in the girls' home, as during a bout of whooping cough in 1891: "Mrs. Crosby stayed with the sick ones while I took those who were able out for a short walk." The next day, "Mrs. Crosby came in and stayed quite a time" to give the matron a rest. After one of the girls died, it was Emma who was left to deal with a "room ... full of Indians." She "came in shortly after the mother did," whereupon "we talked to the mother, but of course she feels terribly, and said some very hard things."[82]

For nearly a quarter of a century, Emma Crosby was instrumental in shaping the lives of young Aboriginal girls at Fort Simpson. Her commitment, grounded in Christian belief, to protect them from the dangers that she saw impinging on them provided her with the validation that she needed to act upon her good intentions by taking young Tsimshian girls into her own home. It was when there became too many girls for Emma to protect and their presence began to have some bearing on her own children's lives that Emma modified her position. Seeking to lessen the influence that these girls would have on her offspring, Emma gave priority to her own children, separating them physically from the Aboriginal girls mingling with them in the house. She led the move to secure for the girls a separate home, which continued to go by that name well into the twentieth century, long after protection had become confinement. It is hard not to conclude that, with the passage of time, Emma Crosby's good intentions to protect the young Tsimshian girls who came into her care went dreadfully awry.

Notes

1 Susan Neylan, *The Heavens Are Changing: Nineteenth-Century Protestant Missions and Tsimshian Christianity* (Montreal and Kingston: McGill-Queen's University Press, 2003).

2 On Crosby, see Clarence Bolt, *Thomas Crosby and the Tsimshian: Small Shoes for Feet Too Large* (Vancouver: UBC Press, 1992).

3 Dana L. Robert, *American Women in Mission: A Social History of Their Thought and Practice* (Macon, GA: Mercer University Press, 1996), xvii.

4 Among the growing body of scholarship on missionary women, if not necessarily missionary wives, are Mary Taylor Huber and Nancy C. Lutkehaus, eds., *Gendered Missions: Women and Men in Missionary Discourse and Practice* (Ann Arbor: University of Michigan Press, 1999); Robert, *American Women in Mission*; Fiona Bowie, Deborah Kirkwood, and Shirley Ardener, eds., *Women and Missionaries: Past and Present* (Providence, RI: Berg, 1993); Patricia Grimshaw, *Paths of Duty: American Missionary Wives in Nineteenth-Century Hawaii* (Honolulu: University of Hawaii Press, 1989); Amanda Porterfield, *Mary Lyon and the Mount Holyoke Missionaries* (New York: Oxford University Press, 1997); Hilary M. Carey, "Companions in the Wilderness? Missionary Wives in Colonial Australia, 1788-1900," *Journal of Religious History* 19, 2 (1995): 227-48; Patricia R. Hill, *The World Their Household: The American Woman's Foreign Mission Movement and Cultural Transformation, 1870-1920* (Ann Arbor: University of Michigan Press, 1985); Leslie A. Flemming, *Women's Work for Women: Missionaries and Social Change in Asia* (Boulder: Westview, 1989); Susan M. Yohn, *A Contest of Faiths: Missionary Women and Pluralism in the American Southwest* (Ithaca: Cornell University Press, 1995). For Canada, see Ruth Compton Brouwer, *New Women for God: Canadian Presbyterian Women and India Missions, 1876-1914* (Toronto: University of Toronto Press, 1990); Rosemary R. Gagan, *Canadian Methodist Women Missionaries in Canada and the Orient, 1881-1925* (Montreal and Kingston: McGill-Queen's University Press, 1992); Margaret Prang, *A Heart at Leisure from Itself: Caroline Macdonald of Japan* (Vancouver: UBC Press, 1995). For British Columbia in particular, see Myra Rutherdale, *Women and the White Man's God: Gender and Race in the Canadian Mission Field* (Vancouver: UBC Press, 2002); Margaret Whitehead, "Women Were Made for Such Things: Women Missionaries in British Columbia, 1850s-1940s," *Atlantis* 14, 1 (Autumn 1988), 141-50; Margaret Whitehead, "'Let the Women Keep Silence': Women Missionary Preaching in British Columbia, 1860s-1940s," in *Changing Roles of Women within the Christian Church in Canada*, ed. Elizabeth Gillan Muir and Marilyn Färdig Whiteley (Toronto: University of Toronto Press, 1995), 117-35.

5 Emma Douse to her mother, Hamilton, 18 February 1874, University of British Columbia Library, Special Collections. All references, unless otherwise indicated, come from this collection. The correspondence is reprinted in its entirety in Jan Hare and Jean Barman, *The Woman Behind the Missionary: Emma Crosby's Letters from the British Columbia North Coast* (Vancouver: UBC Press, forthcoming).

6 Emma Crosby (henceforth EC) to mother, Hamilton, 18 February 1874.

7 EC to mother, Fort Simpson (henceforth FS), 29 March 1876.

8 EC to mother, FS, 21 October 1875.

9 EC to mother, FS, 3 June 1875.

10 Thomas Crosby, *Up and Down the North Pacific Coast by Canoe and Mission Ship* (Toronto: Missionary Society of the Methodist Church, 1914), 85.

11 EC to mother, FS, 15 August 1874.

12 EC to mother, FS, 27 March 1875.

13 EC to mother, FS, 3 September 1874.

14 EC to mother, FS, 2 November 1874.

15 EC to mother, FS, 5 January 1875.

16 EC to mother, FS, 26 January 1875.

17 EC to mother, FS, 26 July 1876.

18 EC to mother, FS, 26 September 1876.

19 "Local lady's Great-Aunt is 'Grand Old Lady of Q.C.I.,'" *Omineca Herald*, 25 July 1952.

20 EC to mother, FS, 10 July 1875.

21 EC to mother, FS, 20 October 1876.

22 "Colorful Indian Character Called to His Forefathers," *Western Recorder,* December 1934.
23 Crosby, *Up and Down,* 75-76.
24 EC to Mrs. H.M. Leland, Secretary of Hamilton Woman's Missionary Society (henceforth WMS), Port Simpson (henceforth PS), 28 July 1881.
25 Crosby, *Up and Down,* 39.
26 Ibid., 41.
27 Ibid., 43.
28 EC to mother, FS, 27 March 1875.
29 EC to mother, FS, 3 June 1878.
30 EC to mother, FS, 5 January 1875.
31 EC to mother, FS, 21 October 1875.
32 EC to mother, FS, 8 February 1876.
33 EC to mother, FS, 26 September 1876.
34 Ibid.
35 EC to mother, Victoria, 29 March 1877.
36 EC to mother, FS, 10 July 1875.
37 EC to mother, FS, 30 July 1877.
38 EC to Mrs. H.M. Leland, PS, 28 July 1881.
39 Ibid.
40 EC to mother, FS, 8 April 1879.
41 EC to mother, FS, 3 June 1879.
42 EC to mother, FS, 5 November 1879.
43 EC to mother, FS, 10 March 1880.
44 "Open Letter to the Members of the W.M.S. of the Methodist Church," *Missionary Outlook* 17, 5 (May 1897), 76.
45 EC to Mrs. H.M. Leland, PS, 28 July 1881.
46 Ibid.
47 Ibid.
48 Kate Hendry (henceforth KH) to unnamed, PS, 11 June 1883, and KH to friends, PS, 21 January 1884, British Columbia Archives (henceforth BCA), ECH/38.
49 KH to unnamed, PS, 11 June 1883, BCA.
50 KH to Maggie, PS, 26 December 1882, BCA.
51 See Hare and Barman, *The Woman Behind the Missionary.*
52 KH to family, PS, 11 June 1883.
53 Kate Ross, PS, 23 July 1890, *Missionary Leaflet* 6, 10 (October 1890): 5.
54 Martha Cartmell, Victoria, n.d., *Missionary Leaflet* 6, 11 (November 1890): 3.
55 Agnes Knight, January 1886, cited in H.L. Platt, *The Story of the Years: A History of the Woman's Missionary Society of the Methodist Church, Canada, from 1881 to 1906* (Toronto: Methodist Church, 1908), 34.
56 Agnes Knight Walker, "Reminiscences of Miss Agnes Knight (later Mrs. R.J. Walker), Bella Bella, PS and Cape Mudge," 34, BCA, F7/W15r/A1.
57 WMS, *Annual Report 1895,* 19.
58 Agnes Knight, PS, 27 January 1886, "The Crosby Home," *Missionary Outlook* 6, 5 (May 1886): 74-75.
59 Agnes Knight Walker, "On Board B. Boscowitz, 16 July 1890," *Missionary Leaflet* 6, 9 (September 1890): 6.
60 Sarah Hart, PS, n.d., *Missionary Leaflet* 7, 6 (June 1891): 6.
61 Walker, "Reminiscences," BCA.
62 Platt, *Story,* 38-39.
63 Sarah Hart, FS, 31 March 1892, *Missionary Leaflet* 8, 6 (June 1892): 6.
64 KH to Maggie, PS, 26 December 1882, BCA.
65 Mrs. Redner, PS, 21 June 1893, *Missionary Leaflet* 9, 8 (August 1893): 5-6.
66 Mrs. Redner, PS, n.d., *Missionary Leaflet* 9, 10 (October 1893): 1-2.
67 Sarah Hart, PS, 5 January 1891, *Missionary Leaflet* 7, 3 (March 1891): 3.
68 Mrs. Redner, PS, 3 September 1894, *Monthly Letter* 11, 10 (November 1894): 5.
69 Crosby, *Up and Down,* 89.

70 Mrs. Redner, PS, 3 January 1894, *Monthly Letter* 10, 3 (March 1894): 9.

71 Crosby, *Up and Down*, 92-93.

72 "Executive Committee," *Missionary Outlook* 11, 4 (April 1891): 59; "Indian Work," *Missionary Outlook* 11, 7 (July 1891): 110.

73 Designs and WMS petition to Superintendent General of Indian Affairs, 13 April 1891, *Department of Indian Affairs*, Black Series, RG 10, vol. 3853, file 77, 025.

74 WMS statement, n.d., and Deputy Superintendent General of Indian Affairs to Superintendent General of Indian Affairs, Ottawa, 24 February 1893, *Department of Indian Affairs*, Black Series, RG 10, vol. 3853, file 77, 025; 17 October 1893, 11th annual meeting, minute book, *Woman's Missionary Society,* United Church Archives, Emmanual College, Victoria University, University of Toronto.

75 EC, unpublished letter sent to WMS annual meeting, November 1885, quoted in WMS, *Annual Report,* 1885, 17; and "Woman's Missionary Society: Annual Meeting," *Missionary Outlook* 6, 1 (January 1886): 5.

76 Miss Paul, PS, 8 March 1898, *Monthly Letter* 15, 5 (March 1898): 6; Mrs. Redner, PS, n.d., *Monthly Letter* 15, 7 (July 1898): 7.

77 Miss Clarke, PS, 20 January 1899, *Monthly Letter* 16, 4 (April 1899): 6.

78 12 March 1890 entry, Nellie Bolton diary, BCA, E/C/B631, reel 472A.

79 24 February 1890 entry, Bolton diary, BCA.

80 Martha Cartmell, Sunnyside, North Pacific Cannery, Skeena River, 11 September 1890, *Missionary Leaflet* 6, 11 (November 1890): 3.

81 Katie O'Neill, interview with Imbert Orchard, 9 September 1966, BCA, tape 1231.

82 Sarah Hart, PS, 23 October 1891, *Missionary Leaflet* 8, 1 (January 1892): 3.

9

The "Cordial Advocate": Amelia McLean Paget and *The People of the Plains*

Sarah A. Carter

While in Ottawa in 1911 the British travel writer and fellow of the Royal Anthropological Institute Bessie Pullen-Burry was pleased to secure an introduction to Amelia Paget, the author of "a valuable work entitled *The People of the Plains,* in which she describes sympathetically and graphically the life, customs, with their religious beliefs, of the Crees and Saulteaux, her life-long friends, to whom she is devoted; their gentle and dignified manners are to her their striking characteristic." Pullen-Burry admired Paget not only because of her book, but also because of her intriguing family background, noting that her maternal family had for several generations held positions in the Hudson's Bay Company (HBC), that she had been born at a northern trading post, and that during the Métis Resistance of 1885, she and her family had been captives of "hostile Indians," their eventual release coming about "through the intervention of friendly Indians." When asked of this experience, Paget told her visitor that "I have heard of savage, revengeful cruelties, but I have never seen that side of Indian nature, and speak as I find."[1]

Amelia Paget defied and complicated colonial categories and divides in her book *The People of the Plains,* published in 1909.[2] As a person of part-Aboriginal ancestry, she also complicated boundaries of identity and difference.[3] She was not radically subversive and outspoken, however, and thus never provided a sustained or strident indictment of prevailing assumptions and the effects of colonialism. She was a "cordial advocate" for Aboriginal people, as poet and Department of Indian Affairs bureaucrat Duncan Campbell Scott described Paget in the introduction to her book, rather than a "frigid critic" of colonialism.[4]

The People of the Plains directly challenged negative representations and distortions of Aboriginal people by providing sympathetic and nuanced descriptions of their spirituality, community life, language, humour, music, artistry, and oral culture.[5] The book should be understood in part within the context of the American writers analyzed by Sherry L. Smith in her recent book *Reimagining Indians: Native Americans through Anglo Eyes, 1880-1940*.[6] At the turn of the twentieth century, a number of Anglo men and women, including George Bird Grinnell, Walter McClintock, Frank Bird Linderman, and Mary Roberts Rinehart, became captivated by Native American cultures and were determined to fashion new, positive images. They urged their readers to cast aside the prejudice, ignorance, and hostility that prevailed at that time among non-Aboriginal people. Smith writes that "in encouraging their countrymen to understand and sympathize with Indians, they both championed the distinctions of Indians' cultures while simultaneously insisting on their shared humanity."[7] They produced books for popular audiences that "offered new ways to conceptualize Indian people, alternatives to the images that had transfixed Americans for centuries."[8] In stressing the richness and value of the cultures and communities of Plains people, Amelia Paget encouraged her readers to rethink derogatory attitudes and to have greater compassion, tolerance, and generosity.

Paget's background made her quite distinct from other champions of Aboriginal people, such as Grinnell, McClintock, Linderman, and Rinehart. She was born in the Northwest, unlike the other authors, who travelled west with the intention of discovering "exotics" and becoming immersed in an "alien" culture. She was raised at HBC posts and was fluent in Aboriginal languages. She experienced first-hand times of great upheaval in western Canada. In 1885 Amelia McLean and her teenage sisters Eliza and Kitty were briefly national celebrities during their family's two-month residence with a mobile group of Plains and Woods Cree. The McLean family was involved in three violent confrontations during 1885 at Fort Pitt, Frenchman Butte, and Steele's Narrows.

Also distinguishing Paget from the other authors is that her great-great-grandmother was an Aboriginal woman. This is not mentioned in *The People of the Plains* or in any other McLean family memoirs. Like members of other fur-trade, mixed-ancestry families of the later nineteenth century, the McLeans did not acknowledge, and even took steps to obliterate, this heritage. In the obituary for Paget's grandmother Anne Campbell Murray, for example, it was stated that she was born at Fort Dunvegan in 1822 and that she was "the first white child to claim those distant northwestern regions as a birthplace."[9] Yet in 1876 Anne Campbell Murray applied for and received Métis scrip.[10] Amelia McLean, her mother Helen, and most of her siblings also received Métis scrip.[11] Amelia applied on her own, while her father applied on behalf of his children Kate Flora Yuill, Angus Samuel Archibald McLean, Duncan James McLean, John Rose McLean, Helen Louise Isabella McLean, Ewen Lawrence Bedson McLean, and Frederica Middleton McLean.[12] Many other of Paget's relatives similarly received Métis scrip, including her great-uncle Duncan Campbell, great-aunt Magdaline Bunn (née Campbell), and aunts Flora Murray, Eliza McDonald (née

Murray), and Jemima Bedson (née Murray) and her five children, Paget's cousins.[13] While this Aboriginal ancestry was somewhat distant by the time of Amelia Paget's generation, it was not forgotten or ignored by others who identified her family as "half-breeds." Artist Edmund Morris, who was acquainted with fur-trade families from his childhood in Winnipeg – his father Alexander Morris was lieutenant-governor of Manitoba and the North-West Territories – wrote in his 1909 diary, after receiving a copy of *The People of the Plains*, that it was "By Mrs. Padgett [sic], whose grandmother was one of the Dog Ribb [sic] (Dene) Indians. She is related to the Campbells & Murrays – half breeds."[14] Although Morris had details of Paget's ancestry wrong, this notation indicates how the McLeans and their relatives were perceived. Paget had highly personal reasons then for countering derogatory contemporary representations of Aboriginal people.

It would not be appropriate, however, to view Amelia Paget as a woman "ahead of her time" in her positive portrayal of Plains Aboriginal people, nor does she provide readers with an unproblematic "authentic" insider's perspective by virtue of her ancestry.[15] Her book reveals that she was not able to depart from the influence of ideas and attitudes about vanishing Aboriginal people that were current in her day. While her book celebrated Plains culture, it also conveyed the idea that much had disappeared, been diminished, or been altered forever. The goal of the book was to capture a portrait of this life before it faded. There was also distance between author and subject despite her close acquaintances and knowledge of languages. At HBC posts there was a distinct hierarchy, and the McLean family would have enjoyed elite status and treatment. As the memoirs of her sister Kitty suggest, the McLean children learned most of what they knew about Aboriginal people through their servants and nursemaids. As in a Victorian middle-class home, servants did not enjoy the status of family members. The McLean children would have been protected from and often oblivious to much of the world beyond the stockade of the trading post.

Amelia Anne McLean was born in 1867 at Fort Simpson (present-day Northwest Territories), a fur-trading post situated on an island at the confluence of the Mackenzie (Dehcho) and Liard (Naechagah) Rivers.[16] For hundreds of years this had been an important rendezvous site for the Dene, who called it Liidli Kue, or the place where the rivers come together.[17] Amelia's family had a long association with this and other fur-trading posts of the Mackenzie and Athabaska districts. She was the eldest of twelve children born to HBC employee William J. McLean, who was from the Isle of Lewis, Scotland, and Helen Hunter Murray. Amelia's parents exemplified the marriage pattern of the previous generations: the men came from elsewhere (Scotland and in one case Upper Canada), and the women were born and raised in the North. Amelia's mother, Helen, was born in 1848 at Fort Yukon. She lived there for her first five years, then resided at other posts, including Fort Simpson, and later at Fort Garry (Winnipeg), Pembina, and Fort Georgetown (Minnesota). She was the daughter of the founder of Fort Yukon, HBC chief trader Alexander Hunter Murray, who was from Kilmun, Argyllshire, Scotland, and Anne Campbell, mentioned above, one of many children born to Elizabeth McGillivray and chief trader of the Athabaska district Colin Campbell, who was from Upper Canada.[18]

Elizabeth McGillivray was the daughter of an Aboriginal woman and Scotsman John McGillivray of the North West Company (NWC). The nation to which John McGillivray's Aboriginal wife belonged is not certain, but she was likely Woods Cree. They were married *à la façon du pays* around 1796 when McGillivray was serving in the Lower English (Churchill) River Department, which was Woods Cree territory.[19] They had one son, William, as well as Elizabeth. More is known about William than about his sister. William is identified in HBC governor Sir George Simpson's character book as "a half breed of the Cree nation."[20] He was educated in Montreal for four years and returned to work first for the North West Company and then for the Hudson's Bay Company as a clerk at Fort Chipewyan and later in New Caledonia.[21] William married a daughter of chief trader Alexander Stewart and Susan Spence. He drowned in the Fraser River in January 1832.[22] (When William and Elizabeth's father, John McGillivray, retired from the NWC in 1818, he settled in Upper Canada, married for a second time, and had a family of eight.[23] These children would have been nearly the same age as his grandchildren born to Elizabeth and Colin Campbell.)

While for several generations Amelia's family was located in the Mackenzie and Athabaska districts, there were close ties and associations with the Red River Settlement. In the 1850s Colin and Elizabeth Campbell sent nine daughters, presumably one of which was Amelia's grandmother Anne, to Red River all at the same time to attend school. There was "a boatload of handsome young girls," according to one account.[24] Anne Campbell and Alexander Murray's children also went to school at Red River. The daughters, including Helen, attended Miss Davis' School, and the sons attended St. John's College.[25] The trip from Fort Simpson to Red River, which Amelia and earlier generations of her family would have made, is vividly described in the book *Women of Red River*. Nineteen-year-old Sarah Foulds made the journey in 1868, leaving on 4 June by York boat from Lower Fort Garry and arriving at Fort Simpson on 18 August:

> We went down the Red to Lake Winnipeg, up the Lake to Grand Rapids, where the Saskatchewan River, after seven miles of rapids, empties into the Lake. There we had to make our first portage. The boats were taken over on low cars drawn by horses along a narrow little wooden railway from the Lake to above the rapids. There they were put into the Saskatchewan river and started on the long journey to Portage la Loche, or

the Long Portage, as it used to be called, which was a portage over the height of land dividing the drainage areas of the two great river systems between the Hudson Bay and the Rocky Mountains. That portage was sixteen miles long. The boat brigade which had brought us more than eleven hundred miles from Fort Garry turned back there. When we had crossed Portage la Loche we had entered the basin of the Mackenzie River system, which empties into the Arctic Ocean. There were ponies and oxen and carts to carry the freight across to the end of the portage, where the brigade of boats from the Mackenzie River was waiting for us. And then we had nearly a thousand miles more to travel with the Mackenzie boats before we arrived at Fort Simpson.[26]

Amelia's earliest years to 1873 were spent at Fort Liard, North-West Territories, where her father was clerk-in-charge. W.J. McLean was transferred to Fort Qu'Appelle in 1873, and his family joined him there one year later. The post was situated in the beautiful Qu'Appelle Valley, formed by an ancient meandering river that is framed by deep ravines, gentle hills, and wooded coulees. For generations of Aboriginal people, the Qu'Appelle Valley has been a treasured gathering place, an oasis because of its generally abundant and varied resources. In the late 1850s explorer H.Y. Hind found clear evidence of the antiquity of the Qu'Appelle Valley as a gathering place, as he found numerous remains of encampments that he thought must have been used for centuries.[27] The Qu'Appelle Valley was also a place of great spiritual significance and attachment dating to ancient times. The Moose Bay burial mound, on the crest of a high rim of the Qu'Appelle commanding a majesterial view of the river with Crooked Lake directly below, has been dated to AD 1040.[28]

To the Plains Cree this was the valley of the What Is Calling River, in Cree *ka-tepwewi-sipiy.*[29] The Calling River Cree, or Ka-tepwewi-sipiyiniwak, a branch of the Plains Cree, had a deep and longstanding attachment to this river valley. In Aaron Arrowsmith's 1814 map of North America, the river is clearly identified as the territory of the Calling River Cree.[30] The name is derived from the way that sounds echo and reverberate in the valley, and there are many stories about the spirit that travelled the river, calling with a human voice. Amelia Paget told several of the legends of the spirit of the valley in *The People of the Plains*:

One of the prettiest of the many traditions relating to the valley was that of the young woman who, imagining her lover was calling to her from one of the hills, pushed off in her little bark canoe and was never heard of any more. Her voice was left in the valley and answers back in plaintive tones when anyone calls. Her lover returned a short time after her departure, but, though he followed her, never found even a trace of her canoe. At twilight her canoe would appear for a few minutes upon the surface of one of the many beautiful lakes in the valley, only to disappear again in a soft mist if anyone tried to approach it.[31]

By the 1870s the Qu'Appelle Valley was also home to some Saulteaux (Plains Ojibway), and there were many mixed Plains Cree and Saulteaux bands. One of the largest of the Qu'Appelle bands in the 1870s, led by Chief Piapot, was mixed Cree and Assiniboine. Groups of Dakota and Métis were also occupants of the Qu'Appelle Valley. The reserves surveyed closest to Fort Qu'Appelle in the 1870s were Piapot, Pasquah (Saulteaux and Cree), Mucowpetung (Saulteaux), and Standing Buffalo (Dakota).

The McLeans' arrival at Fort Qu'Appelle coincided with a period of unprecedented, momentous change and turmoil. In 1869-70 the vast expanse of territory known to fur traders as Rupert's Land was transferred to the new Dominion of Canada, and ambitious plans were in the works to build a railway and settle the West with agriculturalists. By the 1870s buffalo had all but vacated the Qu'Appelle Valley, and the staple of the Plains economy collapsed. In September 1874 the Cree, Saulteaux, and Assiniboine Nations of this region negotiated Treaty 4 at Fort Qu'Appelle, ushering in the era of reserves, government administration, and efforts to create a new economy based on agriculture. (Helen McLean was one of the witnesses who signed Treaty 4.) The North West Mounted Police (NWMP) were created in 1873 and were dispatched on their famous "March West" in the summer of 1874, travelling through Treaty 4 territory before the treaty was made that fall. In 1875 a police detachment was located at Swan River, briefly the capital of the Northwest.

W.J. McLean took over from Isaac Cowie as the clerk-in-charge at Fort Qu'Appelle, and in his memoirs Cowie described "the pleasure of meeting his good wife and fine family of little children [four at that time], whose rosy appearance reflected great credit on their place of birth, in McKenzie River."[32] During their Fort Qu'Appelle years, the McLeans had four more children. The HBC first established a trading post in the Qu'Appelle in 1854 (Qu'Appelle Lakes Post), and by the time of the arrival of the McLeans, Fort Qu'Appelle was a substantial establishment of seven houses as well as trading, fur, and provision stores surrounded by a stockade. During Isaac Cowie's residence there in a typical winter (1867-68), he described a lively settlement with over sixteen engaged servants (clerks, interpreters, bowman, watchman, middleman, carpenter, cattlekeeper, woodcutter, voyageurs, and labourers), eleven wives, twenty children, and thirty train dogs.[33] The servants and their families were mostly Métis, Saulteaux, and Cree, while the clerks, traders, and chief factors were from Scotland.

W.J. McLean was promoted to junior chief trader in 1877 and to chief trader in 1880, so by this time he and his family occupied the top rung of

the social ladder of the establishment. HBC posts were not egalitarian set-
tings. There were many ways that ordinary workers were distinguished
from their superiors. W.A. Griesbach, who was born at Fort Qu'Appelle in
1878, described the eating arrangements that reinforced the sense of social
station observed at HBC posts: "At the 'Big House' three tables were set for
each meal. At the first table was the MacLean [sic] family and such officers
as might be about. The second table was for clerks and traders and the
third table there was a sort of free-for-all for people of lesser degree."[34]

Amelia's younger sister Kitty (Kate Flora, born in 1871) wrote a memoir
that featured the Fort Qu'Appelle years, and she described a nearly idyllic
setting for children.[35] In winter they coasted on sleds and on their moc-
casined feet and went cariole driving. In summer they tramped in the woods
and rode after wild horses. Among the highlights of the Fort Qu'Appelle
years were greeting a contingent of newly minted North West Mounted
Police upon their arrival in the West. According to Kitty's account, it was
Helen McLean who trained Aboriginal women of Fort Qu'Appelle to cut
and sew the first buffalo coats for the police. The McLeans also met the
famous Lakota chief Sitting Bull, who visited Fort Qu'Appelle. The children became well acquainted with the people, customs, and languages of
the Plains Cree and Saulteaux, forming friendships and attending special
events and ceremonies in their communities. Some of the children were
"adopted" by Aboriginal people. An old woman named Appearing Over
the Hill adopted Kitty and helped an injury to her knee to heal.[36] Duncan,
born in 1877, was adopted by a couple who had had a son born to them
the same day, but the infant had not survived for long.[37] Every year until
they left the fort, this couple and their relatives brought gifts for Duncan.
According to Kitty, the children learned the languages through their maids.[38]
One of their housemaids was named Eloquent Speaker, and she was a daughter of the prominent Saulteaux chief Pasquah, one of the Treaty 4 signatories. The McLean girls also became proficient riders and learned to shoot.
They were not allowed to go any distance from the fort without their ri-
fles. Kitty described her sister Amelia on one occasion being chased by a
timber wolf when some distance from the fort. "She was the eldest of my
sisters, and though often called 'the brave one' she found her bravery was
not sufficient on this occasion to face a huge timber wolf. So she ran as
hard as she could, reaching the gate of the Fort and slamming it just in
time!"[39]

Kitty's memoirs emphasized the positive side of life at Fort Qu'Appelle;
there is almost no indication that they were living in the midst of Cree
and Saulteaux territory at a time of great destitution and distress for these
nations. Conditions were grim by the late 1870s, as environmental conditions and the government's failure to provide the assistance promised under treaty resulted in little progress in agriculture.[40] There was widespread

suffering, and there were many deaths from disease. In the winter of 1878 seventy-five people were found starving on the plains fifty miles south of Fort Qu'Appelle.[41] They had camped near the fort that winter, which was severe, and toward spring they all contracted a fatal disease and died within three or four days. The first farm instructor to the reserves near Fort Qu'Appelle found in the winter of 1879-80 that the people were suffering greatly, showing clear signs of starvation. The children, he reported, were "*really* crying for food."[42] As the McLean children were housed behind the stockade of the fort, it is possible that they were not aware of the extent of the suffering around them.

The older McLean children spent the winter months of their later Fort Qu'Appelle years at school at Red River, by that time known as Winnipeg. The girls attended the Anglican St. John's College Ladies School in Winnipeg. The register of attendance and conduct for 1881 of this school indicates that Amelia and her sister Eliza (b. 1869) were in the same class and that they took scripture, composition, object lessons, geography, poetry, reading, writing, spelling, French, and English history.[43] Amelia was first in the class and Eliza second. Their classmates were other children of prominent fur-trade families with last names such as Rowand, Begg, Pritchard, Norquay, and Bruce. The McLean girls had many relatives in Winnipeg, and they would have been part of an elite of the old fur-trade set, which was rapidly being displaced by new business and industrial elites. Their grandfather Alexander Hunter Murray, who had been in charge of Lower Fort Garry and had designed the gates of the Upper Fort – which still stand near the Forks of the Red and the Assiniboine Rivers in downtown Winnipeg – died in 1874, but their grandmother Anne lived until 1907 at their home, "Bellevue," a mile below Lower Fort Garry. According to Kitty's memoirs, many distinguished guests were entertained at Bellevue over the years, including General Garnet Wolseley, Lord Minto, and the poet John Greenleaf Whittier.[44]

In 1884 W.J. McLean was appointed chief trader at Fort Pitt, a small HBC post consisting of a few buildings forming a square and situated on the North Saskatchewan River in the parkland region at the intersection of the territory of the Plains Cree and the Woods Cree. The McLean children spent their first and only winter at Fort Pitt riding, snowshoeing, and coasting, and on rifle and revolver practice. They also had music, cards, and occasional dances. Amelia would entertain at times by translating songs into Cree or Saulteaux.[45] In the world just beyond Fort Pitt, it was a winter of hardship and rising tensions. The arrival of the McLeans coincided with that of the Plains Cree chief Big Bear and his approximately 500 followers in the Fort Pitt and Frog Lake district. In 1876, when Treaty 6 was made with the Plains Cree and Assiniboine at Forts Carleton and Pitt, Big Bear, a distinguished leader with a following of approximately 2,000, refused to

Image from the *Montreal Daily Star,* 23 May 1885, shows how the McLean women took turns at sentry duty at Fort Pitt. The original caption read: "Noble Women on the Defensive: The Misses McLean show great courage, each one rifle in hand, stands at a loophole."

adhere. He initially wanted to see if the government would keep its side of the bargain, and he then wanted to negotiate better terms. He only agreed to take the treaty in 1882 following years of meagre subsistence for his followers, many of whom had dispersed, while others questioned and challenged his leadership.

In the fall of 1884, Big Bear was obliged to choose a reserve in the Frog Lake district near the government agency that served the 500 Woods Cree resident there, but arrangements had not been finalized. It was a winter of great want and discontent, as the food resources of the district were strained.[46] On the morning of 2 April 1885, nine men, including government employees and two priests, were killed at Frog Lake by some Plains Cree men of Big Bear's band. This event took place after a 26 March confrontation at Duck Lake between NWMP and Métis of nearby Batoche and St. Laurent that left fifteen dead. A massive mobilization of troops for the Northwest campaign began with word of Duck Lake. Non-Aboriginal people from surrounding settlements sought the safety of Fort Pitt in the light of these events. Many of them were escorted there by Cree friends and associates who feared for their safety in that climate of tension.[47] There were sixty-seven people then housed at Fort Pitt, including a contingent of twenty-three NWMP under the command of Francis Dickens (son of the famous novelist Charles Dickens). Sentries were posted around the buildings, and the three eldest McLean girls, including eighteen-year-old Amelia, took their turns at sentry duty.

On 14 April Fort Pitt was visited by Big Bear and about 250 Cree, and W.J. McLean was requested to meet with them at the Cree camp. Two days of consultation followed, which were interrupted by a violent confrontation that began when it appeared to the Cree that they were under attack. One policeman was killed and another seriously wounded. The wounded man was successfully brought into Fort Pitt while Amelia and others provided covering fire. Three Cree were killed during this confrontation. Concerned about their father after these events, Amelia and Kitty left the fort on foot and walked unescorted into the Cree camp. According to McLean family accounts, some of the Cree were astonished at their nerve and asked if they were afraid. In her perfect Cree, Amelia replied, "Why should we be afraid of you. We have lived together as brothers and sisters for years. We speak the same language. Why should we be afraid of you?"[48] The sisters returned with a message that Cree chief Wandering Spirit had McLean write, requesting that the rest of the McLeans and other occupants join the Cree camp.

Under the leadership of W.J. McLean, the people housed at Fort Pitt – not including the NWMP who were allowed to depart for Fort Battleford – agreed that they would evacuate the fort and join the Cree camp. For the next two months the McLean family travelled with the Cree, and they endured many hardships, including a lack of food, miserable weather, and menacing, threatening behaviour from some of their hosts. Helen McLean was pregnant with her tenth child, Freda, who was born later that year. The group first travelled to Frog Lake to meet up with the remainder of Big Bear's camp, which by this time contained a great number of the Aboriginal and non-Aboriginal residents of the surrounding settlements. These included two widows of Frog Lake, Theresa Delaney and Theresa Gowanlock. Concern for the safety of the two widows and rumours of their ill-treatment reached hysterical proportions that spring. At about the end of April, the camp moved to Frenchman Butte, where on 28 May there was a confrontation with the pursuing Alberta Field Force. From there the Cree camp moved in a northeasterly direction, and it was here that the McLean family endured some of their most trying conditions, including having to cross a mile-wide muskeg at one point that successfully halted the Field Force pursuit. There was a confrontation with the NWMP under the command of Inspector S.B. Steele at the narrows of Makwa Lake, during which five Cree were killed and two NWMP scouts wounded. The shots fired by the police endangered the McLean family, as did the deaths of the Cree, as there were some who began to talk about taking revenge against people in their camp. On 15 June the McLeans were allowed to leave the Cree, and they arrived back at Fort Pitt on 22 June.

During their months with the Cree, rumours had circulated that the older McLean girls were being mistreated, that they had been made "slaves of the lesser chiefs" and had suffered the "final outrage."[49] They were not, however, the objects of the same level of frenzied attention that was directed toward Delaney and Gowanlock, the two white women widows of Frog Lake. As I have argued in the book *Capturing Women*, the resilience and resourcefulness of the McLeans, their shooting skills, courage, and independence, did not conform to prevailing expectations of white women as weak, vulnerable, and passive. There was also the issue of their Aboriginal ancestry, which complicated their perceived need to be "rescued from the Indians" in the same way as the two widows. When the family arrived at Battleford late in June 1885, a policeman described Helen McLean as a "thin woman with Indian blood in her veins."[50]

Rumours of their mistreatment and even demise – Eliza recalled that all of the McLeans' relatives thought that they had perished and had spent many tearful hours making mourning clothes – proved untrue. Once they emerged from their ordeal, correspondents commented at length on the "plucky" McLean girls. They were all reported to be strong and healthy, particularly Amelia, who was descried as "plucky enough for life guardsmen."[51] She was praised for her courage, especially for having shouldered a Winchester and taken her turn at sentry duty. Amelia was quoted as saying that she "would not have believed the endurance they all manifested possible, but now looks back at most of it with enjoyment." One of the McLean girls told a correspondent that although she was glad to have her life among the Indians at an end, she had "rather enjoyed the trip as a whole. She appeared inclined to look upon their experience as a joke."[52] Members of the Alberta Field Force who went to the rescue of the McLeans were apparently disappointed that the young women had not displayed more gratitude. According to one account:

> Instead of the young ladies rushing promiscuously into the arms of the soldiers, calling them their deliverers and rewarding the best looking with heart and hand, they took the matter very coolly [sic] and seemed ... if the scouts are to be believed ... to regret rather than otherwise having been compelled, through vulgar scarcity of grub, to sever their connections with their Indian friends. Apparently the blood-thirsty Indians had not been altogether unsusceptible to the charms of the prisoners, and instead of maltreating them, or hanging their gory scalps on lodge poles, they used them with all possible consideration.[53]

In the American West, women like Amelia and her sisters might have enjoyed greater and more long-lasting fame (as "Amelia-Get-Your-Gun," for example), but little attention was paid to them after the spring of 1885. A book published in London, England, in 1896 called *The Red House by the Rockies: A Tale of Riel's Rebellion,* by Anne Mercier and Violet Watt, was about the events of 1885 in Saskatchewan, despite the title, and it featured the story of the McLeans, although the name was changed to McIntosh. This change of name was explained in the introduction, which praised the "valour and pious courage shown by [W.J. McLean], his wife, and daughters, [which] are matters of history." Any hints of Aboriginal family connections were removed. The dark-haired McLean girls were given a different appearance. There are only two daughters in the story, and the eldest has become Maggie "a typical Scotch lassie, freckled, sandy, with high cheekbones, and no charm but a look of honest sense and good nature."[54]

Aside from *The Red House by the Rockies,* the adventures of Amelia and her sisters during 1885 garnered little attention. Following the events of that year, the family lived quietly at Lower Fort Garry, where W.J. McLean was in charge of the Lake Winnipeg district (1886-93). There were compelling reasons for the McLeans to avoid the limelight after 1885. Sylvia Van Kirk has described the "particular tragedy of the 'British-Indian' people of Rupert's Land [which] was that, in the end they were neither white nor Métis."[55] They tried to disappear into the white world but were never fully accepted or included in that select category; they were seen as "white but not quite."[56] In western Canada they were identified by many as "half-breeds." While at Red River in 1874, British traveller Peter O'Leary noted, for example, that "several white men, including some of the leading citizens, are married to half-breeds." He wrote that "some of those women are very handsome, combining the delicacy and grace of the whites, with the dignity and keen perception of the Indians." But "half-breeds" were typically described as deficient in comparison to non-Aboriginal newcomers. O'Leary described

The McLean family, c. 1895. *Left to right, top:* Helen (Sapomin), Duncan, Kitty, William; *middle:* Freda, John, Eliza, Angus, Amelia; *bottom:* Murray, Lillian, Lawrence

their "social habits" as "very primitive and simple" and noted that "they are fond of excitement, such as hunting, whiskey drinking and going to balls and parties."[57]

The events of 1885 further intensified colonial racial categorization and shattered hopes for a more inclusive and tolerant nation.[58] Aboriginal people were viewed as a threat to the property and safety of the non-Aboriginal newcomers, who took steps to enhance segregation. It increasingly became a social and economic liability to be of mixed ancestry. The Métis had led two resistances and were perceived as a dangerous, sinister influence. As Ann Laura Stoler has written, in colonial contexts Métis people "ambiguously straddled, crossed, and threatened" imperial divides and colonial categories. Métissage was "conceived as a dangerous source of subversion, it was seen as a threat to white prestige, an embodiment of European degeneration and moral decay."[59] Discourses of racial and social purity, which warned of the threats of decline and pollution of the imperial race, characterized English Canadian constructions of national identity in the 1880s.[60] At this time throughout the British Empire, there was a pervasive anxiety about imperial degeneration and concern to enhance racial renewal through purity campaigns. Powerfully negative images of Aboriginal women, which served to symbolize the shortcomings of their societies, were assiduously promoted during and after 1885. They were depicted as abused and overworked drudges in their own communities and as a source of immorality, vice, and corruption in the new white communities. These negative images of Aboriginal women combined with anxieties about the perils of racial mixing and concerns about threats to the purity and sanctity of white women. (Illustrating these dangers, and complicating colonial categories in the West, was that the woman often celebrated as the "first White woman" in the West, Marie-Anne Gaboury Lagimodiere, was Louis Riel's grandmother.)[61]

Negative representations of Aboriginal women, concerns about racial mixing, and intolerant attitudes were extraordinarily resilient, persisting well into the next century. They pervaded "society" at the highest level in Canada and the British Empire. In 1901 Governor General Lord Minto expressed his scorn for Lady Strathcona, the wife of Lord Strathcona (Donald A. Smith). The former Isabelle Hardisty had, like Paget, an Aboriginal foremother. Minto was highly critical of "poor old Strathcona attempting to lead society[,] the ways of which he is ignorant of, with a squaw wife who is absolutely hopeless what could he expect."[62] These attitudes also permeated the work of poet Duncan Campbell Scott. While there is debate about Scott's attitudes toward Aboriginal people as expressed in his poems, there is no doubt that he articulated his concern about the dangers of racial mixing in poems that feature Aboriginal women as remnants of their nations.[63] In "Onondaga Madonna" (1894) and "The Half-Breed Girl" (1906), Scott associated racial mixing with decline and despair.[64] According to one critic, "Onondaga Madonna" is about "the tragic confusion of the *Métis* ... the general tragedy of all blood-mixture."[65] The "half-breed girl" is tormented and haunted by her mixed ancestry. There is "something behind her savage life / [that] shines like a fragile veil." According to Stan Dragland, "That something, 'what she knows and knows not,' is her Scottish heritage. It torments her because she senses it without being able to identify what it is."[66]

Living in Winnipeg after 1885, Amelia McLean worked occasionally for the federal Department of Indian Affairs, as her language skills were highly valued.[67] Duncan Campbell Scott praised her linguistic skills in his introduction to *The People of the Plains*, writing that she was "gifted with a language-sense which made possible a knowledge of the subtlest peculiarities of two languages, the Cree and Ojibway, both highly expressive, but the last eminently flexible and poetic."[68] In 1899 Amelia married Frederick

Paget, who just at that time was appointed chief accountant of the Department of Indian Affairs; he had worked in the Regina office of the department as assistant to Indian commissioners Hayter Reed and Amedee Forget.[69] Although an accountant, Paget was also valued for his advice on western Indians, and in this regard his wife would have been an asset. He was the author in 1908 of a lengthy report on residential schools in the West based on his own inspection, which was highly critical of the condition of many school buildings and of the quality of the staff.[70] The Pagets had one child, a daughter, Helen Charlotte (Holmes).

In 1906 Amelia Paget received a small commission from the Department of Indian Affairs to interview Plains elders concerning their history, customs, and folklore. As Duncan Campbell Scott explained in the introduction to the book, the small commission was for the "purpose of gleaning such memories as remain of the bygone domestic life of the western tribes."[71] The project was initiated by the Governor General of Canada, Earl Grey. As explained in a newspaper report: "His excellency the governor general who has taken a great interest in the Cree Indians, their mode of living and their history, ever since his visit to the northwest a year ago, is most anxious that the annals, lore and traditions of this decreasing but interesting race should be preserved and handed down to posterity, and in order to do this, he has made arrangements with the Dominion government to send out a special emissary to obtain the requisite information." It was further noted that Amelia Paget had been chosen to undertake this task as it was necessary to find someone with "a complete mastery of the Cree language, as well as clear insight into and knowledge of the Indian character." It was not clear at this point that a book would result from this fieldwork, only that "the information and interesting data thus gained will be preserved in the archives of the Indian department and no doubt will be an important factor in histories yet to be written."[72] Earl Grey apparently did not perceive that a book would result from this research, as he only grudgingly allowed *The People of the Plains* to be dedicated to him in 1909, writing that he could not refuse to accept and noting, "I confess, however, to a feeling of surprise that this report of Mrs. Paget's has developed into a publication which justifies such a dedication."[73]

Amelia Paget set off in the late summer of 1906, accompanied by her friend Mabel Ferguson of the post office, who was to act as private secretary. After arriving by railway, they travelled about 1,100 miles, with Paget as the driver.[74] The two women camped out, except when the weather was poor, in which case they stayed at the homes of Indian Agents or farm instructors. In *The People of the Plains*, Paget expressed her admiration for the camping skills of the Plains people, who "took the greatest possible comfort out of the camper's life, and had all its procedure reduced to a science ... Anyone who had 'camped out' and travelled to any extent in the West before railways and stages had appeared would recall this resourcefulness and adaptability."[75] Paget did not require an interpreter, except when speaking to the Assiniboine of Moose Mountain, and she visited there as well as the File Hills, Mucowpetung, and Crooked Lake Agencies. According to a Winnipeg newspaper report, Paget interviewed the oldest inhabitants that she could find and found it necessary to talk to a great many "to get all the facts." It was reported that she was cordially received as an old friend. Her method was to gather together several elders, and when one began to tell his or her narrative, the others would corroborate what was said, making corrections and adding further details. Certain stories were only told during the winter months, and Paget informed this reporter that she would need to return to record these, although she recalled many of them from her own childhood: "The Indians have a series of such stories dating back to the flood; she used to hear them in her childhood and she is able to write many of them from memory: but it would be necessary for her to visit the people in the winter to get them to tell the old tales over again."[76]

Among the notable persons that she interviewed were the distinguished and aged Chief Piapot as well as Qui-witch, of the Sakimay Reserve, who was 102 years old. Paget expressed concern that she had little time, as the old people were rapidly passing and the younger generation was losing the elders' knowledge of earlier life. She believed that a number of visits would be necessary to complete her work, but it is unclear whether there were other visits. There was likely also a visit during the winter months, as the book features two chapters of "Wee-sack-ka-chack" stories, told only during the winter. According to Pullen-Burry, Paget returned in 1910, after the book was published, and travelled over 1,800 miles of prairies "visiting the different reservations, where she is well known and where the Indians hailed her approach with feelings of genuine welcome. Here she read to various chiefs portions of her book, wherein she describes ceremonials, or folklore, asking them if she had given accurate descriptions."[77]

Paget submitted her manuscript to D.C. Scott, who edited and reorganized the material. The extent to which he altered the work is unclear, but he may have rewritten some of it. E.S. Caswell, of Methodist Book and Publishing House and one of the readers of the manuscript, praised the material in a letter addressed to Scott, writing that "I don't think there is anything as good written on our Indians of the West." He cautioned, however, that "Mrs. Paget has *the stuff* here, but fails in putting it into good literary form" and that it "will need to be practically re-written." Caswell was "glad this work is in your [Scott's] hands, for I know it will be carefully done."[78] It was Scott who corresponded with the publisher about the book's title, design, cover, and illustrations. In the entire Department of Indian Affairs file dealing with the book, there is no correspondence to or from Amelia Paget.

Some of Paget's ideas for the book were cast aside, apparently without any consultation with her. The title that she had proposed for the book, in Cree or Saulteaux, was rejected. The publisher wrote, "I shy at that musical but formidable title. It looks like a deliberate attempt to provoke lockjaw." Painting and drawing by one of the McLean sisters was also rejected, as was Paget's idea for the cover – "I am returning under separate cover Mrs. Paget's original design"[79] – and she appears to have had no say over the illustrations that were included or their captions. The illustrations, which were collected by Scott and the publisher, were not always of the people featured in the book, and they contain words that Paget did not use, such as "squaw." (An example is "Mutsinamakan and Squaw, Sarcees," 24.) While it cannot be assumed with complete confidence, then, that *The People of the Plains* is entirely the work of Amelia Paget alone, it seems safe to conclude that the heart of the book, particularly her sympathetic and positive portrait, represents her own work, as Scott found it necessary to explain this approach in his introduction.

In the early days of their existence, Plains people were a "model race," according to Paget.[80] They had all that they desired, including a nourishing diet and no sickness. They were hospitable, courteous, kind, and generous. After describing modes of travel and how camping places were chosen and the tepees constructed, Paget depicted an idyllic scene: "Such an encampment amid beautiful scenery, astir with prosperous and contented Indians, must have been a most striking illustration of the Indians' own idea of the wonderful love and care bestowed upon them by the Great Spirit ... The young children played their games amidst these lovely scenes; the little babes, tied up in the mossbag or Indian cradle, awoke from their slumbers and looked upon the joyous and happy lives of their brothers and sisters, and grew up to appreciate everything which made life so pleasant an existence for their tribe."[81]

Paget argued that it was not "quite" fair to call Plains people pagans or heathens, and she provided extensive evidence of the depth and complexity of their religious beliefs.[82] She stressed especially their belief in the Great Spirit as the one Supreme Being and clearly implied that this had a direct parallel to the Christian God: "So in all their doings they never lost sight of the fact that for everything they must look to His help and love. And when the Indians were first met by intelligent white men, they certainly were examples of the blessings which come from faith in a higher beneficent Power."[83] She wrote at length and in several places in the book about the powerful significance of dreams. Paget described many of their ceremonies and dances in great detail, and she displayed a depth of understanding not found in other published accounts. An entire second chapter was devoted to the central religious ceremony of the Sun Dance, which as she explained is sometimes spoken of as the "Thirst Dance" among the

Cree because in their language it was called "Nee-pah-quah-see-mun, which means 'dancing through a day and night without quenching one's thirst.'"[84] Her description is unique, compared to other published accounts of that time, which stressed the "barbarous" nature of the event with an emphasis only on the self-torture.[85] She described the complexity and deeper meaning of the Sun Dance as "primarily a thank-offering to the Great Sprit, Kichie Manitou, for the re-awakening of all nature after the silence of the winter. It was a time for the making of braves, or, rather, an opportunity for the test of courage and endurance; it was a time for mourning their dead, and a time of petitions through their Pow-wah-kuns [dreams] for future blessings and love."[86]

While a ceremony like the Sun Dance was highly sacred and solemn, Paget also pointed out that other dances were intended for entertainment and to cause great merriment. At the "Giving-away Dance" many would "make up the most ridiculous words in praise of some article they were giving away, and thus cause no end of amusement to the onlookers."[87] The book contains many examples of Cree and Saulteaux humour, including the practical jokes that they delighted in playing on each other, such as the false alarm in the dead of night. No one was permitted to be vain and proud, as there were always "many wags who were ever ready to effect a cure for such cases."[88]

Derogatory representations of Aboriginal people are most directly challenged in Paget's treatment of women. As mentioned above, she did not use the term "squaw" at all in her text. She consulted women elders in her fieldwork, writing that "one sometimes met with a particularly interesting old woman, whose life had been passed in keen observation of all the triumphs and trials of her band, who in a quiet and gentle manner would recount the many events she had lived through."[89] Women were featured throughout the book in a way that has remained rare until recent times. When writing about the Sun Dance, Paget explained that women, too, went through certain forms of torture that required a great deal of courage.[90] She noted that women and men took part in the Mee-tah-win, or Medicine Dance, but that women had their own special dances, such as the Round Dance, in which "they were very picturesque and graceful in their movements."[91] In describing the work of medicine men and women, Paget had particular praise for the women specialists, whose cures of roots and herbs were in many cases wonderful.

In particular, Paget challenged the dominant stereotype of the "squaw drudge." Representation of the Indian woman in a degraded position, particularly as a beast of burden hauling wood behind her "lord and master," was a standard cliché.[92] Paget stressed that while they did carry the fuel and water, this was not a great hardship, as they carried wood of the lightest kind and did not overburden themselves. Heavy logs were drawn by horses, and young men chopped and cut the wood. "The popular idea of the poor Indian woman doing all the hard work has too often been over-drawn."[93] Another of the dominant stereotypes was of the enslavement of Plains women in polygamous marriage and the notion that their lives were characterized by jealous bickering. Paget presented the practice of polyga-my sympathetically, noting that the wives "called each other 'sister' and might, indeed, have been sisters in so far as their fondness for one another was concerned. They divided their labours equally, and tried in every way to cultivate mutual forbearance."[94] In many others ways, Paget addressed misperceptions of Aboriginal women, demonstrating that they were excel-lent housekeepers and industrious workers and that they "displayed much artistic taste in their fancy-work. Their designs were perfect as to detail."[95]

Aboriginal women were described as the most attentive of mothers, chal-lenging the stereotype of their indifferent and neglectful care that sus-tained the residential-school system.[96] Paget wrote that "there surely never were any happier or healthier babies than the little Indian 'Awassisah.'" Paget also stressed the bravery, courage, and endurance of women. In de-scribing warfare, Paget wrote that "many women, indeed, took part in these fights when the men were outnumbered, and by their daring and courage often turned the tide in their favour."[97] They were very modest, however, in speaking about their exploits. The insight that Paget provides into the lives of Plains women is the most vivid example of the unique knowledge that she brought to bear on her project, not just through her fieldwork but through her life experiences. Ethnographer David G. Mandelbaum, who in 1940 published his study, regarded as the more definitive, scholarly work on the Plains Cree, did not have women informants, and his book lacks the rich detail on women found in *The People of the Plains*.[98]

Many of the prevailing representations of Plains people were directly confronted and challenged but in a muted and understated tone. In Paget's section on warfare, she wrote that "the courage and daring of the Indians has often been discussed, and usually very much to their disadvantage."[99] Their methods of warfare had been the subject of much disparagement in 1885, compared to representations of the heroic and dauntless Alberta Field Force.[100] But Paget "furnished evidence of the stuff the Indian was made of," stressing their "wonderful feats of bravery," as small expedi-tions could defeat "overwhelmingly larger numbers of the enemy." In her section "Aboriginal Hospitality," Paget emphasized their kindness to stran-gers; they were not "of the savage nature so many writers have made them out to be."[101] Her knowledge of the languages added great depth to these observations. She noted that the Plains people had many phrases to ex-press their hospitality: "One of their favourite expressions when welcom-ing a stranger or a friend into their midst is 'Ta-ta-wah,' which means, 'There is always room for you.' Another expression when serving a visitor to a meal or any refreshment is 'Kes-poo,' meaning 'May it satisfy you, or may it refresh you.'"

Paget carefully explained how certain practices that appeared cruel or heartless to outsiders, those condemned in the standard descriptions of Plains life, made sense in the Plains Cree and Saulteaux world. This is most obvious in her discussion of the Windigo complex. People who suffered dementia or who were insane were believed to be possessed by evil spirits, and the greatest fear was that they would become cannibals. These people, if they did not recover through the intervention of medical specialists, were put to death. During the McLeans' months with the Cree in 1885, there was one such incident when an elderly woman named She-wins was killed because it was believed that she was dangerous to others. Paget explained that "the Indians, having no asylums or any means of isolating their unfortunate lunatics, were compelled to do away with them. It was utterly impossible for an Indian to go on a hunting expedition and leave his family to the mercy of a lunatic; so that any person showing marked signs of insanity was dispatched by his sorrowing and superstitious friends."[102]

The People of the Plains contains a wealth of information on the people and history of the Qu'Appelle Valley, with an emphasis on stories of deeds of bravery, courage, and endurance. Paget recorded the story of the famous distance runner Acoose from the Sakimay Reserve, who, she wrote, in 1884 "ran after seven jumping deer" from Moose Mountain to the Crooked Lake Agency.[103] As mentioned above, one of Paget's main informants was Qui-witch, Acoose's father. One chapter is full of the histories of the "courageous dead, the great Koo-min-ah-koush, the intrepid Yellow-Head and the cunning Chim-ass-couse."[104] She provided deep understanding of how landscape features in the region of the Qu'Appelle came to have their names, writing that "the most appropriate place names in Canada are Indian names, and to assign to each and all their significance would be an attractive task."[105]

Paget's versions of these stories should not, however, be presumed to provide "authentic," "insider" perspectives, despite her background, knowledge of the languages, and long-standing acquaintance with the people that she consulted. As Saulteaux storyteller Alex Wolfe relates in *Earth Elder Stories*, stories and songs belong to and are passed down through families, and the keepers and conveyors of these learn them over many years, not through brief visits.[106] Paget's understanding of Plains people was also filtered through prevailing ideas about a "vanishing race." Throughout the book there is a clear message that the Plains culture and way of life that Paget praised so highly had been significantly diminished and altered and that she is describing an ever more distant past. This sentiment is expressed, for example, in her regret over the loss of dances, ceremonies, and songs. Paget was passionate about Cree and Saulteaux music and the poetry of their words, writing that "it is a matter of regret that the Indians had no way of writing down or recording words and music. To many of them these are but a memory of happier times when upon every possible occasion they broke out into song. For them these times have gone, like the passing of the buffalo, never to return."[107] There were many other expressions of her belief that praiseworthy attributes were disappearing. Paget wrote, for example, of the "remarkable decline of good manners and polite usages among the Indians; years ago, everyone who studied their ways intimately was impressed with their dignity and fine manners."[108] Overall, Paget appears to share the idea that prevailed in her time that Plains culture would vanish, and she sympathized with her elder informants, "types of a dying race, in their lament for the days gone by when they were the sole inhabitants of the vast prairies in the West, free to roam wherever they felt inclined to go."[109] Paget is also not able to step entirely outside of her status as a detached observer of Euro-Canadian background. She describes certain customs and ceremonies as "peculiar" and some of their beliefs as superstitions.[110] Their faith in prayers she describes "as the faith of a little child."[111]

Yet *The People of the Plains* remains a remarkable and unique book in the social and cultural setting of the turn of the twentieth century. At that point the major published works on the Aboriginal people of Canada's West were produced by missionaries who left the overall impression of a backward people inhabiting a world of ignorance, cruelty, and superstition.[112] Instead, missionaries stressed that a glorious future was in store for them if they cast aside their past and consented to be guided by their stronger and more enlightened guardians. Paget's book provided a sharp critique of these convictions and the shallow observations that characterized these books. She did not directly articulate her thoughts on the reasons for the decline that she lamented, but her book is a call for tolerance and generosity, hinting at a critique of government policy and parsimony. If she did have more to say, it would surely not have been wise to do so, as her husband was employed by Indian Affairs and her project was sponsored by that department. Yet her message came through. She hints at a critique of the poor housing on the reserves, which was a cause of tuberculosis and other diseases, in her passage on the tepees of the past, which were "comfortable and roomy, and could be kept fresh and clean; the opening at the top of the doorway caused a constant current of air, and they were very healthy places of abode."[113] In one of her most compelling passages that shows her understanding of the Cree and Saulteaux, Paget called for a greater sense of generosity:

Perhaps few realize how hard it is for our Indians to have to beg for the common necessities of life. They are naturally very proud and reserved, and among the older ones to beg is most humiliating. Being brought up to look upon everything as for the 'common good,' it is hard for them to have to remind people by begging that they are in want. There is, as a matter of fact, no such word in either the Cree or Saulteaux languages as 'beg.' The only thing approaching such a word in their language is 'Puck-oo-she-twan' (Share with me). A nation whose expressive vocabulary holds no such words as 'beg' or 'beggar' we should be proud to help if ever it happens to be in need.[114]

Paget did her fieldwork and wrote at a time when activities such as the Sun Dance were banned under the Indian Act, when the mothering and housekeeping skills of women were criticized in government publications to justify the residential-school system, and when distinguished chiefs were being deposed because of their beliefs and practices. She threatened powerful conventions and proposed a radical departure from prevailing wisdom.

Paget did not include herself and her experiences in *The People of the Plains,* except in one brief passage at the end of her chapter on the Sun Dance, which notes that it was regarded as an omen of misfortune and loss if a ceremony was disturbed by the approach of enemies and that "the last instance of such an unwelcome visit happened early in June, 1885, during the North-West Rebellion. The Indians had only just begun the ceremonies when they were surprised by General Strange's column."[115] This is a curious addition that may have been inserted by D.C. Scott. Paget would have known from her fieldwork that Sun Dances were regularly being disrupted and broken up and the participants arrested, particularly under the administration of Scott, and she thus knew that 1885 was not the last incident of an unwelcome visit. It was Scott who provided details of Paget's background in his introduction to the book, in which he felt it necessary to explain why Paget's portrait was so positive. He informed readers that the author and her family had been captured at Fort Pitt by Big Bear and his men and for a time had "shared all the hardships of his shifting camp." Scott claimed that it was this experience that accounted for her positive portrait of Plains people: "During this experience Mrs. Paget's knowledge of the Cree language and her intimacy with all the ways of the Indians, even the very fashion of their thoughts, proved a constant defence for the whole party. The following pages must be read by the light of these facts; they account for the tone of championship for all Indians, and for the idealistic tendency which places everything in a high and favourable aspect. If there were hardship, squalor, starvation, inhumanity and superstition in this aboriginal life, judged by European standards, here it is not evident."[116] Scott suggested that both the author and her informants had overlooked the "real felicities of the situation" and that their memory of the events had been "heightened by the glow which might be spread over the reminiscences of some ancient chief whose lines had been cast in pleasant places, and to whom everything in the old days had become transfigured."[117]

The People of the Plains elicited a variety of responses from reviewers.[118] There were positive reviews from those who appreciated the "first-hand information," who were pleased to find that "her testimony tends to upset a number of popular superstitions," and who felt that the book ought to find a place in every library in the land.[119] The reviewer for the *Calgary Herald* wrote that "Mrs. Paget's book should be bought and read by everyone interested in the history and development of the Canadian West."[120] One reviewer appeared bemused that readers were to understand that wives agreed to polygamy or that their language was poetic although they had no poetry.[121] Others were sharply critical, such as the reviewer for the *Montreal Standard,* who felt that the book contained too much "rose-color," that "even when free from contact with the white man they were not exactly the Arcadian shepherds and shepherdesses that Mrs. Paget presents ... the cruelty, the squalor, the dirt are glossed over. It is too late in the day for any Fenimore Cooper romance of the redskin."[122]

While her positive portrait was unpalatable to many readers, her work nonetheless had an important impact. It was read by artist Edmund Morris, quoted earlier, who painted portraits of western Aboriginal people, including many mentioned in Paget's book. Like Paget, Morris was determined to preserve what he regarded as a vanishing Aboriginal past. (Two of his portraits appear in the book: one of Cree chief Poundmaker and another of the Ojibway chief Moonias.) In 1909 Morris was commissioned by the Governments of Saskatchewan and Alberta to do portraits of Indians of those provinces, and he received his copy of Paget's book during that trip.[123] (According to Morris biographer Jean S. McGill, one of his subjects, Blackfoot medicine man Wolf Collar, was a relative of Paget's.)[124] Although not heralded in his own time, Morris' work is regarded today as a vibrant, powerful record of the male leaders of the Plains people.[125]

The People of the Plains was of course read by Duncan Campbell Scott, and he would also have read any material that he edited out. He likely had conversations with Amelia Paget about the project as a whole, including her informants. In his poem about Morris, who drowned in 1913, Scott borrows from Paget's book, according to critic Leon Slonim.[126] In "Lines in Memory of Edmund Morris," set on the Prairies, Scott imaginatively places himself and Morris inside the aged Saulteaux chief Sakimay's tent to hear stories of the past. Scott was often "manipulating fact to serve the truth of the poem" and changed names and other features.[127] In this case, Chief Sakimay could not have been his informant, as he had been dead since the 1880s, although a reserve in the Qu'Appelle Valley was named after him. It is also unlikely that Morris and Scott together had the occasion to be inside any Cree or Saulteaux elder's tent as described.[128] It is likely that Scott based his portrayal of this ancient elder on Paget's description of her meetings with Qui-witch, of the Sakimay Reserve.

Amelia Paget did not continue to pursue a writing career after her book, although she did publish her report on a 1912 visit to Indian reserves for the Canadian Handicraft Guild.[129] She was a member of the Guild's Ottawa branch. Participation in this organization permitted Paget to help preserve and revive Aboriginal traditions in a tangible way, and it also allowed her to pursue her critique, if muted, of government administration. This organization was opposed to the assimilation policies of the Department of Indian Affairs that sought to undermine Aboriginal fine arts and crafts.[130] The guild, by contrast, was organized to "encourage, retain, revive and develop handicrafts and home art industries throughout the Dominion, and to prevent the loss and deterioration of these crafts."[131] In 1912 the Guild sent Amelia Paget to Saskatchewan to explain the organization's goal of reviving and perpetuating Aboriginal arts and crafts. She accompanied her father to James Bay and other northern areas covered by Treaty 9 and then visited the reserves and schools of the people of her book in the Moose Mountain and Qu'Appelle districts. She found many women who excelled in beadwork, dressing leather, and moccasin making. She recommended to the Department of Indian Affairs that Indian handicrafts be taught at the Industrial School at Lebret, and she indicated in her report that an instructor was to be hired for this purpose. This report appears to have been Paget's last publication. She died in Ottawa on 10 July 1922 and is buried in the cemetery of old St. John's Cathedral in Winnipeg along with many others of the old fur-trade elite of the West.[132]

Both the appreciative reviews of Paget's book and the work of the women of the Canadian Handicraft Guild indicate that there were Canadians who were sympathetic to Paget's views and vision. But negative depictions resurfaced and prevailed. In 1910, while marking the twenty-fifth anniversary of the North-West Resistance of 1885, Western Canadian newspapers revived stories of "naked savages" and "horrible atrocities" committed during what were called the "Indian Massacres of 1885."[133] Edmund Morris responded to one such article entitled "Indian Savagery in the West," arguing that they were "in natural qualities ... far ahead of many of the whites with whom they are thrown in contact." Paget's response to such derogatory representations, to which she would have been so keenly sensitive during her lifetime, was eloquently expressed for all time in *The People of the Plains*. Like one of her contemporaries, the writer and performer E. Pauline Johnson, Paget "talked back," challenged demeaning narratives, and championed a more inclusive and tolerant nation that would incorporate dignity and respect for Aboriginal people.[134] She did so, however, in a much more muted way, remaining the "cordial advocate."

Acknowledgment

This chapter is reproduced courtesy of the Canadian Plains Research Center.

Notes

1 B. Pullen-Burry, *From Halifax to Vancouver* (Toronto: Bell and Cockburn, 1912), 122. It was noted on the title page of this book that Pullen-Burry was also the author of *Ethiopia in Exile, Jamaica as It Is,* and *A German Colony.*

2 Amelia McLean Paget, *The People of the Plains* (Toronto: William Briggs, 1909).

3 Ann Laura Stoler, "Sexual Affronts and Racial Frontiers: European Identities and the Cultural Politics of Exclusion in Colonial Southeast Asia," in *Tensions of Empire: Colonial Cultures in a Bourgeois World,* ed. Frederick Cooper and Ann Laura Stoler (Berkeley and Los Angeles: University of California Press, 1997), 198-237 at 198.

4 D.C. Scott, "Introduction," in Paget, *The People of the Plains,* 5-15 at 14.

5 Paget, *People of the Plains.*

6 Sherry L. Smith, *Reimagining Indians: Native Americans through Anglo Eyes, 1880-1940* (New York: Oxford University Press, 2000).

7 Ibid., 45.

8 Ibid., 5.

9 It was noted in the obituary for Amelia McLean's grandmother Anne Campbell Murray that she was born at Fort Dunvegan on Peace River in 1822 and that "she was the first white child to claim those distant northwestern regions as a birthplace. Her father being Colin Campbell, Chief Trader of the Hudson's Bay Company." Manitoba Legislative Library, *Manitoba History Scrapbooks,* P1, 39. In Amelia's sister Kitty's memoirs, a similar statement is made, although with more ambiguous wording. It was noted that Anne Campbell Murray "is said to have been the first white woman to enter the interior of northern Alaska, and her two daughters are said to be the first white children born there." Kitty McLean Yuill and Helen Yuill Perry, "Pioneers and Prisoners in the Canadian North West," unpublished manuscript, n.d., in the possession of Megan Wells, Winnipeg, 8. Some excerpts were published as "Adventures of Kitty," *The Nor'Wester* 100, 1 (15 July 1970): 36-46.

10 Library and Archives Canada (henceforth LAC) Record Group (henceforth RG) 15, Department of the Interior, series D-11-8-a, vol. 1322, reel C-14931, scrip affidavit for Murray, Ann, claim no. 1023, scrip no. 7762-7769, date of issue 30 July 1876, amount $160.00.

11 LAC, RG 15, series D-11-1, vol. 679, reel T-14427, file 315563, "Halfbreed Claim of Ann Amelia McLean," and file 315589, "Halfbreed Claim of Helen Hunter McLean."

12 LAC, RG 15, series D-11-8c, vol. 1359, reel C-14989, 1) McLean, William Alexandre, address Winnipeg, Man, born 11 October 1872 at Fort Simpson, father William James McLean (Whiteman), mother Helen Hunter (Métis), scrip cert. no. 36B, claim no. 265; 2) McLean, William James, for his daughter Kate Flora Yuill, née McLean, born 15 January 1871 at Fort Liard, address Winnipeg, father William James McLean (Whiteman and deponent), mother Helen Hunter Murray (Métis), scrip cert., form E, no. 3384, claim no. 226; 3) McLean, William James, for his living children Angus Samuel Archibald, born 2 March 1875 at Fort Qu'Appelle; Duncan James, born 19 February 1877 at Fort Qu'Appelle; John Rose, born 8 March 1879 at Fort Qu'Appelle; Helen Louise Isabella, born 27 October 1881 at Fort Qu'Appelle, address Winnipeg, father William James McLean (Whiteman and deponent), mother Helen Hunter Murray (Métis); Angus S.A., scrip cert., form E, no. 2810; Duncan J., scrip cert., form E, no. 2811; John R., scrip cert., form E, no. 3092; Helen L.I., scrip cert., form E, no. 3093, claim no. 227; 4) McLean, William James, for his living children Ewen Lawrence Bedson, born 16 August 1883 at Fort Ellice; Frederica Middleton, born 15 December 1885 at Fort Alexander, address Winnipeg, father William James McLean (Whiteman and deponent), mother Helen Hunter Murray (Métis), Ewen Lawrence Bedson, scrip cert., form E, no. 3091; Frederica Middleton, scrip cert., form C, no. 2255, claim no. 228.

13 LAC, RG 15, series D-11-8-a, vol. 1319, reel C-14926, scrip affidavit for Campbell, Duncan, claim no. 2217, scrip no. 11086, date of issue 2 October 1876, amount $160.00;

ibid., scrip affidavit for Bunn, Magdaline, claim no. 2216, scrip no. 11085, date of issue 2 October 1876, amount $160.00; ibid., vol. 1322, reel C-14931, scrip affidavit for Murray, Flora; ibid., scrip affidavit for McDonald, Eliza (née Murray); ibid., vol. 1319, reel C-14925, scrip affidavit for Bedson, Jemima Mrs. (née Murray), concerning the claims of her five children.

14   Mary Fitz-Gibbon, *The Diaries of Edmund Montague Morris: Western Journeys, 1907-1910* (Toronto: Royal Ontario Museum, 1985), 92.

15   For a discussion of the issue of "Native," "indigenous," or "insider" perspectives, see Kirin Narayan, "'How Native Is a 'Native' Anthropologist?'" in *Feminist and Postcolonial Theory: A Reader,* ed. Reina Lewis and Sara Mills (New York: Routledge, 2003), 285-305.

16   In the *Manitoba Free Press,* 11 July 1922, it is noted that Amelia Paget was born at Fort Simpson.

17   http://www.fortsimpson.com/history.html.

18   Manitoba Legislative Library, *Manitoba History Scrapbooks,* P1, 39, obituary notice of Mrs. Alex H. Murray.

19   Marianne McLean, "McGillivray, John," *Dictionary of Canadian Biography,* vol. 8 (Toronto: University of Toronto Press, 1985), 546-47 at 546. See also Jennifer S.H. Brown, *Strangers in Blood: Fur Trade Company Families in Indian Country* (Vancouver: UBC Press, 1980), 98.

20   Simpson wrote: "No. 64 McGillivray, Wm. A half breed of the Cree Nation. About 36 Years of Age 18 Years in the Service. Writes a good hand and rather clever, but of a Sour temper and a great deal of the sullen vindictive disposition of the Indian. Tyrannical and Oppressive in his management of the people by whom he is obeyed more through the fear of his Club than from personal respect. Manages the Trading Post entrusted to his charge very well. Conceited and self-sufficient like the generality of his Countrymen and altogether a disagreeable fellow. Has the vanity to look forward to an interest in the business but his prospects of success I imagine are very Slender. Stationed in New Caledonia District. [I have received information of his death since writing this.]" "The 'Character Book' of Governor George Simpson, 1832," in *Hudson's Bay Miscellany, 1670-1870,* ed. Glyndwr Williams (Winnipeg: Hudson's Bay Record Society, 1975), 151-236 at 222-23. Editor Glyndwr Williams notes that chief factor William Connolly had a much higher opinion of William McGillivray and thought that he should have a much higher salary. Williams, ed., *Hudson's Bay,* 223.

21   Brown, *Strangers in Blood,* 181. See also Williams, ed., *Hudson's Bay,* 222-23.

22   Williams, ed., *Hudson's Bay,* 222-23.

23   McLean, "McGillivray, John," 546. McGillivray and his second wife, Isabella (McLean), lived on a farm near Williamstown, Upper Canada, and they had four sons and four daughters. Before his death in 1855, McGillivray returned briefly to Scotland to claim the estate of Dunmaglass and recognition as chief of the McGillivray clan. This recognition was officially awarded to his son (with Isabella) in 1857.

24   W.J. Healy, *Women of Red River: Being a Book Written from the Recollections of Women Surviving from the Red River Era* (Winnipeg: Women's Canadian Club, 1923), 136.

25   Yuill and Yuill Perry, "Pioneers and Prisoners," 8.

26   Healy, *Women of Red River,* 169.

27   H.Y. Hind, *Narrative of the Canadian Red River Exploring Expedition of 1858,* vol. 1 (1860; reprint, New York: Greenwood Press, 1969), 340.

28   Liz Bryan, *The Buffalo People* (Edmonton: University of Alberta Press, 1991), 163.

29   Dan Ring, ed., *Qu'Appelle: Tale of Two Valleys* (Saskatoon: Mendel Art Gallery, 2002), 36.

30   Quoted in ibid., 36.

31   Paget, *People of the Plains,* 163.

32   Isaac Cowie, *The Company of Adventurers: A Narrative of Seven Years in the Service of the Hudson's Bay Company during 1867-1874 on the Great Buffalo Plains* (Toronto: William Briggs, 1913), 465.

33   Ibid., 214-15.

34   W.A. Griesbach, *I Remember* (Toronto: Ryerson Press, 1946), 31.

35   Yuill and Yuill Perry, "Pioneers and Prisoners."

36   Ibid., 29.

37 Ibid., 19.

38 Ibid., 20.

39 Ibid., 30.

40 Sarah Carter, "The Queen's Bounty," in *Lost Harvests: Prairie Indian Reserve Farmers and Government Policy* (Montreal and Kingston: McGill-Queen's University Press, 1990), 50-78.

41 N.M.W.J. McKenzie, *The Men of the Hudson's Bay Company* (Fort William: Times-Journal Presses, 1921), 62-63.

42 LAC, RG 10, Records relating to Indian Affairs, vol. 3687, file 13,698, F.L. Hunt to Edgar Dewdney, 16 March 1880, emphasis in the original.

43 Provincial Archives of Manitoba, MG 10, B6, St. John's College Ladies School Register of Attendance, Conduct and Marks, 1881.

44 Yuill and Yuill Perry, "Pioneers and Prisoners," 8.

45 Elizabeth M. McLean, "The Siege of Fort Pitt," *The Beaver,* outfit 277 (December 1946): 22-25 at 22.

46 Sarah Carter, *Capturing Women: The Manipulation of Cultural Imagery in Canada's Prairie West* (Montreal and Kingston: McGill-Queen's University Press, 1997), 51-60.

47 Sarah Carter, "Two Months in Big Bear's Camp, 1885: Narratives of 'Indian Captivity' and the Articulation of 'Race' and Gender Hierarchies in Western Canada," in *Readings in Canadian History: Post-Confederation,* ed. R.D. Francis and Donald Smith (Toronto: Nelson Thomson Learning, 2002), 75-93 at 82.

48 Duncan McLean with Eric Wells, published as "The Last Hostage," in *Frog Lake Massacre,* ed. Harold Fryer (Surrey, BC: Frontier Books, 1984), 80-85 at 81-82.

49 Charles R. Daoust, *Cent-vingt jours de service actif: Recit historique tres complet de la Campagne du 65eme au Nord-Ouest* (1886; trans. Roberta Cummings, Wetaskiwin: City of Wetaskiwin, 1982), 58.

50 John G. Donkin, *Trooper in the Far North-West* (1889; reprint, Saskatoon: Western Producer Prairie Books, 1987), 158.

51 *Charlottetown Daily Patriot,* 27 June 1885.

52 *Montreal Daily Star,* 23 June 1885.

53 City of Edmonton Archives, W.J. Carter manuscript, unpublished, 167.

54 Anne Mercier and Violet Watt, *The Red House by the Rockies: A Tale of Riel's Rebellion* (London: Society for Promoting Christian Knowledge, 1896), 62.

55 Sylvia Van Kirk, "'What If Mama Is an Indian?': The Cultural Ambivalence of the Alexander Ross Family," in *The Developing West: Essays on Canadian History in Honour of Lewis H. Thomas,* ed. John E. Foster (Edmonton: University of Alberta Press, 1983), 123-36 at 134.

56 Ann Laura Stoler, "Cultivating Bourgeois Bodies and Racial Selves," in *Cultures of Empire: A Reader,* ed. Catherine Hall (New York: Routledge, 2000), 87-119 at 91.

57 Peter O'Leary, *Travels and Experiences in Canada, the Red River Territory, and the United States* (London: John B. Day, 1877), 145.

58 See Carter, *Capturing Women,* and Carter, "Turning Point: 1885 and After," in *Aboriginal People and Colonizers of Western Canada to 1900* (Toronto: University of Toronto Press, 1999), 150-75.

59 Stoler, "Sexual Affronts and Racial Frontiers," 198.

60 Mariana Valverde, *The Age of Light, Soap and Water: Moral Reform in English Canada, 1885-1925* (Toronto: McClelland and Stewart, 1991). See also Cecily Devereux, "'And Let Them Wash Me from this Clanging World': Hugh and Ion, 'The Last Best West' and Purity Discourse in 1885," *Journal of Canadian Studies* 32, 2 (Summer 1997): 100-15.

61 M. L'Abbe G. Dugast, "The First Canadian Woman in the Northwest," *Transactions of the Historical and Scientific Society of Manitoba,* no. 62 (Winnipeg: Manitoba Free Press, 1902). Read 12 December 1901. See http://www.mhs.mb.ca/docs/transactions/1/first woman.shtml.

62 Quoted in Donna McDonald, *Lord Strathcona: A Biography of Donald Alexander Smith* (Toronto: Dundurn Press, 1996), 448. Minto's remarks here are curious in light of the fact that his own wife claimed to have Aboriginal ancestry. Mary, Countess of Minto, told the Kainai (Blood) of southern Alberta during an 1899 visit that she was descended from an

Indian "princess," Pocahontas. According to a policeman who accompanied the viceregal party, "They were not at all impressed by the circumstances, and as a matter of fact, did not believe the story." See R. Burton Deane, *Mounted Police Life in Canada: A Record of Thirty-One Years' Service* (London: Cassell, 1916), 89.

63 Gerald Lynch, "An Endless Flow: D.C. Scott's Indian Poems," *Studies in Canadian Literature* 7, 1 (1982). See http://www.lib.unb.ca/Texts/SCL/bin/get.cgi?directory=vol17_1/&filename=lynch.h.

64 Veronica Strong-Boag and Carole Gerson, *Paddling Her Own Canoe: The Times and Texts of E. Pauline Johnson (Tekahionwake)* (Toronto: University of Toronto Press, 2000), 26.

65 E.K. Brown, quoted in Stan Dragland, *Floating Voice: Duncan Campbell Scott and the Literature of Treaty 9* (Concord: Anansi, 1994), 191.

66 Ibid., 196.

67 *Ottawa Free Press*, 11 July 1922.

68 Scott, "Introduction," 12.

69 *Regina Leader Post*, 15 June 1944.

70 LAC, RG 10, vol. 4041, file 334503, reel C-10178, "Report of F.H. Paget, who deals with the Western accounts, of his visit to Indian reserves and schools in Saskatchewan and Alberta, 1908."

71 Scott, "Introduction," 14.

72 Manitoba Legislative Library, *Manitoba History Scrapbook*, P1, 53. There is no date on the clipping and no newspaper source.

73 LAC, RG 10, vol. 4018, file 276,916, Earl Grey to Frank Oliver, 8 April 1909.

74 The most extensive coverage of this trip is found in an article in the *Calgary Herald*, 23 October 1906.

75 Paget, *People of the Plains*, 90-91.

76 *Calgary Herald*, 23 October 1906.

77 Pullen-Burry, *From Halifax*, 122.

78 LAC, RG 10, vol. 4018, file 276,916, E.S. Caswell to D.C. Scott, 8 January 1909, emphasis in the original.

79 Ibid., Caswell to Scott, 3 March 1909.

80 Paget, *People of the Plains*, 24.

81 Ibid., 102. For an excellent and very different analysis of Paget's book, see Shelly Hulan, "Amelia Paget's *The People of the Plains:* Imperialist and Ethnocritical Nostalgia," *Journal of Canadian Studies* 37, 2 (Summer 2002): 47-68.

82 Paget, *People of the Plains*, 22.

83 Ibid., 27.

84 Ibid., 28.

85 W.H. Withrow, *The Native Races of North America* (Toronto: Methodist Mission Rooms, 1895), 107-10.

86 Paget, *People of the Plains*, 29.

87 Ibid., 51.

88 Ibid., 134.

89 Ibid., 99-100.

90 Ibid., 39.

91 Ibid., 52.

92 Carter, *Capturing Women*, 109.

93 Paget, *People of the Plains*, 99.

94 Ibid., 123.

95 Ibid., 101.

96 Sarah Carter, "Categories and Terrains of Exclusion: Constructing the 'Indian Woman' in the Early Settlement Era in Western Canada," *Great Plains Quarterly* 13, 3 (Summer 1993): 147-61 at 150.

97 Ibid., 88-89.

98 David G. Mandelbaum, *The Plains Cree: An Ethnographic, Historical and Comparative Study* (1940; reprint, Regina: Canadian Plains Research Centre, 1979).

99 Paget, *People of the Plains*, 82.

100 See for example, the *Qu'Appelle Vidette*, 10 December 1885: "Indian warfare being a war of extermination without mercy to defenceless people, women and children."

101 Paget, *People of the Plains*, 129.

102 Ibid., 57.

103 Ibid., 87. There is much debate about this event. According to HBC employee N.M.W.J. McKenzie, the event took place in November 1886. His article in the *Qu'Appelle Vidette*, 2 December 1886, was written on 17 November 1886, and he is describing an event that had just happened. According to McKenzie, Acoose chased a herd of elk or red deer on horseback from Moose Mountain to the Crooked Lake Agency, but there his horse played out, and Acoose then started after them on foot after obtaining ammunition from the HBC store there. He took off "like a streak of light passing over the snow" and within two hours shot three of the elk within three miles of the agency. McKenzie regarded this as an amazing feat and concluded that "Akoose should get a medal." In his diary Edmund Morris wrote that Paget was wrong in referring to them as deer and that they were elk, yet he called them deer himself in the catalogue to his 1909 exhibition, which included his portrait of Acoose. See Dragland, *Floating Voice*, 212. In his poem "Lines in Memory of Edmund Morris," D.C. Scott writes that Acoose chased antelope (the "jumping deer" that Paget refers to). See Duncan Campbell Scott, *The Poems of Duncan Campbell Scott* (Toronto: McClelland and Stewart, 1926), 141-50 at 148. According to Brenda Zeman, "anybody on Sakimay could have told him [Scott] it wasn't antelope, it was elk." Brenda Zeman, *To Run with Longboat: Twelve Stories of Indian Athletes in Canada* (Edmonton: GMS2 Ventures, 1988), 217.

104 Paget, *People of the Plains*, 88.

105 Ibid., 111. It is interesting to note that Duncan Campbell Scott's poem "Indian Place Names" is about the traces of the past that linger in place names. It begins: "The race has waned and left but tales of ghosts, / That hover in the world like fading smoke." See Scott, *The Poems of Duncan Campbell Scott*, 22.

106 Alexander Wolfe, *Earth Elder Stories: The Pinayzitt Path* (Saskatoon: Fifth House, 1988), xi-xxii.

107 Paget, *People of the Plains*, 164.

108 Ibid., 132.

109 Ibid., 71.

110 Ibid., 25, 48.

111 Ibid., 22.

112 Sarah Carter, "The Missionaries' Indian: The Publications of John McDougall, John Maclean and Egerton Ryerson Young," *Prairie Forum* 9, 1 (Spring 1984): 27-44.

113 Paget, *People of the Plains*, 97.

114 Ibid., 11-12.

115 Ibid., 41.

116 Scott, "Introduction," 13-14.

117 Ibid., 14.

118 Book reviews are included in LAC, RG 10, vol. 4018, file 276,916.

119 *Manitoba Free Press*, 21 September 1909, in ibid.

120 *Calgary Herald*, 21 August 1909, in ibid.

121 *Ottawa Civilian*, 29 August 1909, in ibid.

122 *Montreal Standard*, 9 October 1909, in ibid.

123 Fitz-Gibbon, *Diaries*, 92.

124 Jean S. McGill, *Edmund Morris: Frontier Artist* (Toronto: Dundurn Press, 1984), 116. No reference is given for the statement that "Wolf Collar, a relative of Alexander McLean and Mrs. Paget, came to the camp to be painted." One possibility of a family connection is provided in the *Fort Edmonton Journal* for 1826, which notes that chief factor Rowand sent William McGillivray to live with the Peigan to halt the advance of American traders from the south. This may have been Paget's great-great-uncle William McGillivray. For the information from the *Fort Edmonton Journal*, see http://www.telusplanet.net/public/dgavneau/alberta2a.htm.

125 Geoffrey Simmins and Michael Parke-Taylor, *Edmund Morris "Kyaiyii," 1871-1913* (Regina: Norman Mackenzie Art Gallery, 1984).

126 Leon Slonim, "Notes on Duncan Campbell Scott's 'Lines in Memory of Edmund Morris,'" http://www.uwo.ca/english/canadianpoetry/cpjrn/vol02/slonim.htm.

127 Dragland, *Floating Voice,* 209.

128 Ibid., 210. As Stan Dragland notes, "there is no written evidence that Scott and Morris ever sat together in Sakimay's tent, with the kinnikinnick and the stories." Dragland further notes, drawing on Morris' diary, that Morris did meet Scott and his wife in Regina around 25 July 1910 while Scott was on a tour inspecting the reserves. Scott then left for Duck Lake and File Hills. On 10 August 1910 Morris met Scott again at Lebret, and the next day he accompanied Scott and Indian Agent W.M. Graham to the Standing Buffalo Lakota Reserve.

129 Amelia McLean Paget, "Report on Mrs. Paget's Trip to Indian Reserves in Saskatchewan, 1912," in *Annual Report of the Canadian Handicraft Guild* (Montreal: Canadian Handicraft Guild, 1912), 15-17.

130 Gerald R. McMaster, "Tenuous Lines of Descent: Indian Arts and Crafts of the Reservation Period," *The Canadian Journal of Native Studies* 9, 2 (1989): 205-36. See also Ellen Easton McLeod, *In Good Hands: The Women of the Canadian Handicraft Guild* (Montreal and Kingston: McGill-Queen's University Press, 1999).

131 Quoted in McMaster, "Tenuous Lines," 211.

132 The inscription on her memorial stone reads:

     Paget
     Amelia McLean
     Wife of F.H. Paget

     Born July 16, 1867
     Died July 10, 1922

     To live in the hearts of those
     we leave behind is not to die
     In thy light shall we see light. Ps 36.9

     Thanks to Shirley Collicutt, office manager, St. John's Cathedral, Winnipeg.

133 A series of articles appeared in the *Manitoba Free Press,* beginning April 1910, by John Hooper, who had been with General Middleton's column.

134 Strong-Boag and Gerson, *Paddling Her Own Canoe.*

10
Honoré Joseph Jaxon: A Lifelong Friend of Aboriginal Canada

Donald B. Smith

On 13 December 1951 the New York dailies carried a short human-interest story from the previous day about an extraordinary pack rat named Major Honoré Joseph Jaxon. On page one the *Daily Mirror* ran a photo of the ninety-year-old "Major" firmly clutching his cane, holding his chin high, and sitting amidst a small mountain of crated newspapers, magazines, and books, all removed from his lodgings at 159 East 34th Street. His landlord had just evicted him from his basement apartment.

Since 1946 the elderly man had risen at 5 a.m. to stoke the furnace of the fourteen-suite apartment building,[1] but the owner now claimed that frequent illness prevented his aged custodian from doing his job. And, he added, the huge amount of paper that Jaxon stored in his musty apartment constituted a fire hazard for the paying tenants. A three-man crew took a full six hours to remove his books, manuscripts, and personal belongings onto 34th Street. Once stacked, the paper-stuffed cartons and boxes extended in a pile six feet high, ten feet across, and thirty-five feet long.

Even by august New York standards, Major Honoré Joseph Jaxon was a character. Regally seated on an old orange crate, the white-bearded, fragile-looking man, covered with a blanket, wearing ancient clothes, running shoes, and a broad-brimmed black hat, held court with the representatives of the press. Obviously well educated, he used a full and well-chosen vocabulary, this advocate of the disadvantaged. Although just 5'8" in height,[2] his powerful voice gave the impression that he was very tall.[3] The *Times* reporter learned from one of "the Major's" acquaintances that "he was the son of an Indian maiden and an adventurous Virginian; that he spoke Latin and Greek, and was tried for treason by the Canadian Government."[4]

Shaken by his hasty eviction, Jaxon described the contents of his grocery boxes as "the most valuable library in the U.S. on the history of the American Indians." For forty years he had collected all this material, which he valued at $100,000. All day he sat or stood protectively by his "library." Finally, when darkness fell, he made the hard, agonizing decision. Harry

Honoré Jaxon, evicted

Baronian, the editor of the *Bowery News*,[5] offered refuge at his newspaper's office, but the paper could only temporarily store sixty boxes of his collection. Without any other option, Jaxon sold the remaining two tons of newspapers, books, and magazines on the street as wastepaper.[6]

The major stayed at the *Bowery News* offices for the next two weeks. Later Baronian recalled how his guest acted as a "a real gent and always thanked everybody like a duke for any little favor you did for him."[7] But one obsession ruled Jaxon: he needed to keep all his remaining sixty boxes together. "The Major" explained to his host that he had collected these, the most important books and newspaper and magazine articles, with the intent of building a library for the Indians on the 288 acres of land that he owned in Saskatchewan, Canada.[8]

Two weeks later Jaxon suffered a serious stroke. Admitted to Bellevue Hospital on 27 December, he died there on 10 January.[9] Harry Baronian contacted the papers and supplied them with additional details on Jaxon's life. The *Times* learned that he had been "a major in the cavalry of the Métis tribesmen, who fought the Canadian government." The *Herald-Tribune* reported that he had been "an aide to Louis Riehl [sic], leader of a half-breed rebellion in the Saskatchewan Valley."[10]

Realizing the Canadian interest, the Canadian Press in New York wired the story northward on 4 January, the day of the major's funeral.[11] On the fifteenth he was buried in a Salvation Army plot in the Flushing Cemetery.[12] Shortly after his funeral, his books were sold at a public auction. (They realized just $2,000, one-fiftieth of the value he placed on them.) The remaining boxes, full of correspondence and notes, newspapers and magazines, went immediately to the dump.[13]

On 19 January the Canadian Press wire story from New York appeared on page one of the *Regina Leader-Post*, prominently captioned, "Riel Vet who lived as Derelict owned Property in Saskatchewan." The article repeated the New York papers' findings: "Jaxon, a militant friend of the Indian and the underdog ... born to a Virginian father and a half-breed mother ... became a major – a title he wanted to be called until his death – in Louis Riel's force of Métis Indians."

Bruce Peel, chief cataloguer for the Rutherford Library at the University of Alberta, saw the story. On account of previous research that he had undertaken on the history of Saskatoon, Peel knew that Jaxon was really William Henry Jackson, Riel's secretary in the Rebellion of 1885. Judging Jaxon to be suffering from a mild form of insanity, the Regina court had dispatched him not to the gallows like Riel but to a mental institution in Manitoba. The reluctant inmate, within a few months, escaped to the United States, where he adopted the name of Honoré Joseph Jaxon. In 1909 he returned to Saskatchewan and participated in a labour dispute between the builders of Saskatoon's first sewer system and their employer, the City of Saskatoon. Thanks to surviving letters in various archives, correspondence saved by the Jackson family, as well as scattered newspaper references, the story of this extraordinary friend of the Native peoples can be told.[14]

William Henry Jackson was born in Toronto on 3 May 1861, just three weeks after the beginning of the American Civil War and six years before Confederation. Will's parents had recently emigrated from England. Thomas and Elizabeth Jackson were good church people, both of whose fathers were Wesleyan Methodist ministers. There were three children in the family: Eastwood, the eldest; then Will; and finally his sister, Cicely. After several years as a merchant in the hamlet of Stanley's Mills, just northwest of Toronto, Thomas moved with his family in 1864 to begin a store in Wingham, about 150 kilometres to the north in Huron County. Here young Will grew up in an area with an overwhelmingly Protestant and British population. The family's business prospered until the late 1870s.

Will's father was miscast in his profession. An avid reader, he spent more time studying works like Henry Hallam's two-volume *Constitutional History of England* than he did keeping store. Like Hallam, Thomas Jackson attacked the tyranny of English kings Charles I and James I and glorified the

Eastwood Jackson (left), aged 12, and Will Jackson (right), aged 10

English Revolution of 1688. A great admirer of the Upper Canadian rebel William Lyon McKenzie, Thomas believed, and taught his children, that every citizen had the God-given right to rise up in the face of tyranny. Thomas took Will to his first political meeting at age eleven.

As a young boy Will loved studying, improving himself. While the other boys were out playing, he stayed at home to read. At age nine he completed a history of ancient Greece and Rome. His parents encouraged him in his dream of one day studying Greek and Latin at university. While most of his boyhood contemporaries quit after completing primary school, Will went on to high school and attended university.

Will's parents saved all that they could to send him off to the University of Toronto. Already they had helped to pay for Eastwood's studies at the Ontario College of Pharmacy. A few years later they would also send Cicely to teacher's college.

For three years Will studied classics at University College. One of his fellow students in his first years was Fred Haultain,[15] who later became a premier of the North-West Territories and after 1905 the leader of the provincial Conservative Party in Saskatchewan. During his first two years, Will did well, standing in the top quarter of his class of nearly fifty. But in the late 1870s misfortune struck. A fire in the store and the continuing economic depression ruined Thomas Jackson. In 1879 the family left for the Northwest, where Eastwood planned to open a drug store. Now without money for his tuition and living expenses, Will dropped out of university at the end of his third year. Shortly after his family's arrival in Prince Albert, he moved west to join them.

In Prince Albert Will helped his father with his farm-implement business. Quickly he learned of the western farmers' deep hatred of the Canadian tariff. The high duties forced up the cost of machinery while at the same time leaving the price of wheat unprotected on a world market. The farmers felt that Ottawa paid little attention to their needs. Prime Minister John A. Macdonald and the Conservatives betrayed them by suddenly switching the route of the projected transcontinental railway from near Prince Albert to more than three hundred kilometres southward.

Will's accent and pronunciation, his conversation, and his soft, uncalloused hands marked him as an educated man. The farmers badly needed him. When the local farmers established a union they approached Will to become the first secretary. Full of fire, the intense-looking young man with the big, booming voice accepted.

From his early boyhood on, Will read voraciously: history, biography, and the great classical authors. He saw the struggle in the Northwest in much wider terms than did his farm colleagues. Yes, the Ottawa government impinged upon their rights, but it did so as well as with those of the original inhabitants. In the summer of 1884 Will argued that the settlers must enlarge their movement to include the Métis and First Nations. Louis Riel's return to Canada in July 1884 made possible a coalition of Métis and non-Native settlers.

At first the farmers' union agreed to cooperate with the Métis. Together Riel and Jackson prepared petitions to the federal government outlining western grievances. Gradually, Will came more and more under Riel's influence. The Métis leader won him over by the soundness of his arguments. In their meetings with discontented First Nations leaders, like Big Bear of the Plains Cree, Will discovered additional injustices. Angry First Nations people told Riel: "The Government sent to us those [who] think themselves men. They bring everything crooked. They take our lands, they sell them and they buy themselves fine coats ... They have no honesty."[16] The speeches made a profound impression on Will. Later he wrote of Riel: "The oppression of the aboriginals has been the crying sin of the white race in America and they have at last found a voice."[17]

Riel's attempt to extend the alliance of farmers and Métis to the First Nations proved unpopular with the settlers, who mistrusted the First Nations. Frank Oliver, then a young Fort Edmonton politician, read the popular mood correctly. Many settlers feared a possible Native uprising. While Oliver, a Liberal, kept up his attacks on the Conservatives in Ottawa, he avoided an alliance with Riel, particularly as the Métis leader now reached out to the First Nations.[18] Will responded totally differently – instead of abandoning the Métis, the young idealist bunkered in even deeper. He went to live at Batoche. Moreover, when the farmers' union dropped its ties with Riel, Will, in early March 1885, left the union.

At Batoche Will forged a deeper emotional bond with the Métis. The young romantic saw in them the ancient Greeks, whom he idolized, men and women willing to follow "a just and simple way of life."[19] At the Métis settlement he fell in love with Rose Ouellette, the young sixteen-year-old daughter of Moise Ouellette.[20] To become closer to his adopted people, he became a Roman Catholic. The former Methodist was baptized "Joseph" in mid-March. But he remained a Catholic only temporarily, as a few days later he chose to adhere to Riel's new religion.[21]

On the eve of the outbreak of the uprising, Will remained with the Métis, hoping to bring about a peaceful understanding between them and the settlers. He felt torn within, for "to one side I was allied by blood, to the other by ties of religion, friendship and concurrence in certain political views."[22] Unfortunately, like neutrals in most armed conflicts, he became the enemy of both sides. After the first clash at Duck Lake in late March, the Métis, doubting his loyalty in a fight against his own people, imprisoned him. After the fall of Batoche six weeks later, the Canadians, in turn, seized and held him prisoner.

The trial in Regina of "Riel's Secretary" lasted less than half an hour. Will's Protestant inquisitors (and his own family) felt that his acceptance of Romanism and then Rielism proved his mental instability. Roman Catholics, of course, saw wisdom in his first conversion but madness in the

Will Jackson's bust of Riel, completed while he was held at Lower Fort Garry

second. Once he was judged insane, the authorities whisked William Henry Jackson away to the Lunatic Asylum at Lower Fort Garry in Manitoba.

The new accommodations proved to be a distinct improvement on those at the Prince Albert jail, where for four weeks he had lived in a tiny 8' × 10' lock-up with five Métis. He had slept each night on a vermin-infested floor. In his first letter home from Lower Fort Garry, he stated: "Mother must not trouble herself anymore about my lacking sleep – for I can both sleep soundly and eat heartily – both requirements being exceedingly well catered to in this establishment." Believing that the asylum authorities would hold him until the following spring, Will hoped "to make the most of the interval in improving myself in such directions as may be practicable." He asked his parents to send books and newspapers as well as his guitar. The books that he requested included the Bible, Horace's poems, Plato's *Republic,* and the American economist Henry George's *Progress and Poverty.*[23]

Will's enforced sojourn in the mental hospital allowed him to catch up on both his reading and his hobbies. While in the institution, he carved a bust of Riel. He also practised the guitar. But all this time he desperately wanted to escape, to warn the settlers that they "were sleeping on a volcano ... security can never come back to the Northwest again for if Mr. Riel is hung and the prisoners kept at Stony Mountain a bloody cruel war will result."[24] Two weeks before Louis Riel's announced execution day, Will left the asylum. On 2 November he simply walked away, fleeing southward to the American border. For five increasingly colder late fall days and nights he went without food, living on a few berries and nuts. Upon his arrival in Crookston, Minnesota, he telegraphed Prime Minister John A. Macdonald to warn him that Riel's death would only provoke a more dangerous and atrocious outbreak.[25] Riel was hanged in Regina a few days later on 16 November.

At a protest meeting in Crookston, Will termed the act "the legal murder of a patriot and statesman." He repeated the charge in Fargo, North Dakota; St. Paul, Minneapolis; Chippewa Falls, Wisconsin; and Chicago.[26] Riel, he argued, "made the fight because it had to be made."[27] Was he insane? Absolutely not, Will thundered back. "What was termed 'insanity' with him and Riel was their admiration of the Indian mode of living, that it was free from selfishness, and from the grasping for property and riches as among the whites."[28] To audiences in North Dakota, Minnesota, Wisconsin, and Illinois, wearing a tattered grey tweed suit with patches on the knees of his pants and moccasins on his feet,[29] Will defended Riel and called for the independence of the Northwest. Carried away with emotion, he spoke for over five and a half hours in his final lecture in Chicago's Central Music Hall, the exciting city in which he had already decided to establish himself.[30]

The impoverished twenty-four-year-old faced hard times on his arrival in Chicago. At first he lived on a dollar a week, but gradually his fortunes improved. He met local carpenters, affiliated with the Knights of Labor. The carpenters and other Chicago unions had just begun to organize their campaign for the eight-hour workday and an hourly wage of 30 cents an hour. Will joined a French-Canadian carpenters' local of the Knights of Labor. He later served in the summer of 1886 as secretary of the United Carpenters Committee, the umbrella-grouping of all of the Chicago carpenters' assemblies and unions.[31]

In the 1880s Chicago was America's fastest growing city. Half a century earlier, only 100 people had lived on this spot in the middle of a stinking wild-onion swamp at the foot of Lake Michigan. Subsequently, the population soared to 300,000 in 1871 and to 500,000 in 1881. From 1880 to 1910 it rose by 500,000 every ten years. In 1890 nearly 80 percent of the city's population was of foreign parentage.[32]

The economic inequality was extreme. While the big meat packers like Armour and Swift and merchants like Marshall Field and Montgomery Ward made vast fortunes, working men toiled from dawn to dusk for a dollar a day, and women earned half as much, 5 cents per hour. The upper crust lived in mansions, and the poor in wretched and disease-ridden slums. The air smelled of the industrial stench and the polluted waters of Lake Michigan near Chicago.[33]

Will had been in the city only a few months when labour violence occurred. A small group of anarchists demonstrated on the evening of 4 May 1886 to protest police brutality against the strikers at the McCormick Harvester Plant. About 2,500 people gathered at Haymarket Square. All remained peaceful until the police tried to disperse the meeting. Suddenly a dynamite bomb exploded. During the rioting that followed, seven police and four workers died, most of the deaths occurring when the police opened fire on the crowd, killing in the darkness several police constables as well as workers.[34]

The next day Chicago's ultraconservative press called for revenge. Police raided working-class neighbourhoods. In the panic that followed, the police arrested hundreds of labour and ethnic-community leaders. Without any proof the authorities ruled that the bomb was the work of anarchists, socialists, and communists. Eight anarchists were subsequently tried, and without concrete evidence to prove that they had made or thrown the bomb – only three of the eight had been at the meeting – the court convicted them of inciting violence. Four of them were hanged, and one committed suicide in his cell.

In Chicago Will discovered his true politics, anarchism. He had no time for the violent, distorted form of anarchism, the promotion of senseless violence. The appeal of anarchism for Will came from its idealistic philosophy. The anarchists he met argued that society could exist without the state coercively enforcing rules of conduct. Wherever authority is asserted and self-expression limited, the anarchist reacts.[35] After Haymarket Will Jackson knew where his heart belonged. He became a collector for the anarchist defence fund.[36]

Upon his arrival in Chicago Will made a very important decision. While in the Prince Albert jail, he wore a Métis headband in his cell.[37] Now in Chicago he completed the transformation. He decorated the room he rented as a Métis hunter's shack. At home he began baking his own bannock.[38] When asked his identity, he said Métis. In 1889 he went one step further, changing his name to the French-sounding Honoré Joseph Jaxon.[39]

To support himself Jaxon built sidewalks and curb walls on contract. He initially did well at it, even hiring his own crew.[40] After work he put his university training to use, tutoring in Greek and science as well as in Hebrew, which he apparently learned on his own.[41] From his fellow construction workers he also learned German.[42]

As a Métis spokesperson Jaxon gained considerable public attention. His belief in the wisdom of First Nations ways increased. In the mid-1890s he once wrote his mother back in Saskatchewan: "Study the Indian and his ways if you would find the light which alone can save the whiteman's civilization."[43] He joined the Chicago committee of Credit Foncier, an American colonization company sponsoring a model communal settlement at Topolobampo Bay on the west coast of Mexico. For some time he discussed with A.K. Owen, the colony's leader at Topo, the possibility of his Métis compatriots settling there.[44] Jaxon realized the interest that he could attract as a Native American spokesman. His straight raven-black hair, which he wore quite long, identified him as having some First Nations ancestry.[45]

Jaxon's "identity" as a "Métis" opened doors for him. At the founding convention of the new third party, the populists, in Omaha, Nebraska, in July 1892, he convinced the organizers to allow him to address the 8,000 delegates. Speaking as "a half breed Indian of the Métis tribe," he reviewed for half an hour "the Indian's views upon the land question."[46] In his remarks he stressed the need for public ownership of railways and endorsed all measures needed to bring about the full emancipation of the labouring classes. The next year Jaxon gained admittance to the Chicago Columbian Exposition at the Chicago World's Fair as the representative of the "Métis Indian nation of Canada." The attendants seated him with the foreign diplomats.[47]

Less than ten years after his arrival in America's second largest city, Honoré Joseph Jaxon had become a local celebrity. With his customary surplus of energy, he successfully worked to expose a graft ring at City Hall.[48] He also campaigned vigorously, but unsuccessfully, to defeat the incumbent mayor, Harrison Carter. Chicago's self-declared Métis leader supported the banker Lyman Gage,[49] an anticorruption candidate – who, although he failed to be elected Chicago's mayor in 1893, three years later became President William McKinley's secretary of the treasury.

In Chicago Jaxon made a number of good friends. He became a regular at the whimsical Whitechapel Club, formed by a group of junior reporters and cartoonists together with a few congenial spirits in other occupations. The club was organized for "no other purpose than the promotion of good fellowship, with good liquor on the table and a good song ringing clear."[50] Playfully, the organizers named their club after the London site of the atrocious Jack-the-Ripper crimes. Together the young men talked the radical politics that their own conservative newspapers refused to print.[51]

Jaxon's love of politics seriously hurt his own business. Initially, he had prospered at contracting and even once won a $50,000 contract. But his unpaid political activity caused him to so neglect his major contract that he eventually had to let his employees go. Subsequently, a rival contractor completed the sidewalks.[52]

Immediately after his business failure, Chicago's leading "Indian" activist rented a room in the *Chicago Times* building, suite number sixteen, right next to the office of the paper's owner, one Harrison Carter, the same man who had just won reelection as the mayor of Chicago. During the Chicago World Exposition, Jaxon organized a meeting, a World Conference of Anarchists. It met in Jaxon's office in late September, and in attendance, among others, were Lucy Parsons, the widow of one of the Haymarket Martyrs; the Chicago anarchist Voltarine de Cleyre; and Van Ornum, author of "Why Government at All?"[53]

Not wishing to return to sidewalk contracting, loving the excitement and attention that came from political activism, Jaxon joined Coxey's march of the unemployed in the late spring of 1894. With the well-known Chicago Métis in its vanguard, the group left Massillon, Ohio, for Washington to deliver their demands for relief. The free-spirited Jaxon travelled dressed in a white sombrero, leather breeches, a decorated belt, and a blanket.[54] The *Pittsburgh Post* interviewed him en route. He convinced them of his racial ancestry. The *Post* wrote on 31 March of the "half-breed Indian" that he was "a man of keen wit and is consumed with a love of his people."

In Washington Jaxon found a new audience for his wild, radical talk. On 18 June the *Washington Post* disclosed an anarchists' plot to bomb the White House, the treasury building, and the war and navy building. Papers across the United States picked up the extraordinary story of the plot. Back in Chicago the *Times* roared with laughter at the eastern press, so easily taken in by the harmless Honoré Jaxon:

> The proposition in itself is a mild one for Jaxon to make and to that extent discredits him. His long march with Coxey seems to have impaired his powers. If he had been in his usual cheerful frame of mind his plan would not have halted at dynamiting the treasury building; it would have comprehended burning some hundred federal officeholders at the stake and holding the house, senate, and foreign embassies to ransom. Such a villainous everyday scheme as that imputed to Jaxon is one that a man with a common school education might formulate and get no headache. At home in Chicago Jaxon would reel off while you wait specifications for an uprising which in theory would terminate in the holding of a sun dance in the county building and the lighting of a Métis council fire in the Criminal Court building. It was his practice, when he had his daily plot

for revolution well in hand, to seek some yearling reporter and impart the plan in strict confidence.[55]

After the excitement of the Columbian Exposition, the Coxey march, and his Washington "plot," Jaxon, now thirty-three years old, took a break from political activism. Upon his return to Chicago, he encountered the new world religion, Baha'i, an Eastern faith originating in Persia. The new belief stressed the simplicity of living and service to suffering human beings. It appealed to him, and he joined in 1897.[56]

At the age of forty, Jaxon, who now had greying hair and a receding hairline, married for the first time. His partner was Aimée Montfort, an attractive Chicago schoolteacher, about ten years younger that he was.[57] She liked her husband's intellect but not his love of "roughing it." As a new bride she left to live in Jaxon's two cluttered rooms at the back of a vinegar factory. His lodgings were "full of books, and scientific apparatus, and firewood, and chemicals, and pictures, and old clothes and various other things."[58] Years later she complained about her husband's choice of accommodation: "He has roughed it so many years that he has little idea of what physical comfort means and basic necessities to me are luxuries to him. We just never could meet on these points. For years his ideal of living was the 'igloo' or tent."[59]

Aware of new responsibilities as a married man, Jaxon returned to construction work. In his spare hours he designed a new tunneling machine that he claimed would cut the cost of excavating tunnels.[60] He also drew up plans, which he patented, for building structures complete with a device for preventing or decreasing the effects of earthquakes.[61] But politics, not science or business, was his lifelong interest, and he soon came to it again. Aimée always regretted this. She lamented years later that he should have made his fortune first, then used his money to help others: "If H[onoré] had not got mentally switched for some reason against possessing any property at all, of any nature, he could have made a million long before he was 30 and then could have accomplished so much more, I believe, than with the exhausting struggle against want that has always been his lot."[62]

At the turn of the century, Jaxon worked to convince Chicago's city fathers to build a Grecian peristyle,[63] or a row of columns surrounding an open court, by the lakefront. This could become a speaker's corner, Chicago's equivalent of London's Hyde Park. He also remained active in the Chicago Federation of Labor and worked as an editorial writer on their monthly publication, the *Union Labor Advocate*.[64]

In the early years of the twentieth century, Jaxon also devoted a great deal of his time to the Spirit Fruit Society,[65] a small utopian sect, which relocated from Lisbon, Ohio, to Chicago; and then from Chicago to Ingleside, about seventy-five kilometres northwest of the city. With his

Honoré Jaxon (far right) in his building construction phase, Chicago, c. 1900

knowledge of construction, Jaxon, in fact, helped design the Spirit Fruit Temple, their large communal house in Ingleside.⁶⁶ The Spirit Fruiters sought equality of the sexes, and pursued an anarchist-like lifestyle of unrestricted freedom. Elbert Hubbard, one of America's foremost disciples of John Ruskin, the successful English art critic, and William Morris, the English poet, decorator, and artisan, came to know Jacob Beilhart, the founder of the Spirit Fruit Society, very well. In 1905, he described him in this manner: "Jacob does not want you to do what he does, nor believe what he does. He only asks you to live your own life – express yourself according to the laws of your own nature."⁶⁷

Jaxon's name again appeared in newspapers across the United States in early spring 1907 – thirteen years after his massive coverage in 1894 as a member, and ex-member, of Coxey's march of the unemployed to Washington. President Theodore Roosevelt had recently denounced the leaders of the radical Western Federation of Miners (WFM). The Federation's leaders had been charged with complicity in the assassination in 1905 of the union-bashing former Idaho governor Frank Steunenberg. He called WFM president Charley Moyer, national secretary-treasurer Big Bill Haywood, and the union's long-time adviser and strategist George Pettibone "undesirable citizens." Immediately Jaxon protested against the president's use of language, "designed to influence the course of justice in the case of the trial for murder of Messrs. Moyer and Haywood."[68] From the hundreds of protest notes, Theodore Roosevelt selected just one for his reply – Honoré Joseph Jaxon's, the one written under the heading: "Cook County Moyer-Haywood-Pettibone Conference. *Death* – can not – will not – and shall not claim our brothers!"[69] The publicity-loving champion of the underdog loved the attention. Of the celebrated Métis, the *Saturday Evening Post* wrote: "He looks like an Indian, talks like a graduate of Oxford and writes like a professor of rhetoric."[70]

Others were not impressed. Resentful that Jaxon had written his letter as a member of the Moyer-Haywood-Pettibone Defence Conference, instead of the Chicago Federation of Labor, the federation – jealous of the publicity angle lost – expelled him.[71] This pushed Jaxon in another direction. He had long planned on making an extended visit to Saskatchewan to see his mother, brother, and sister (his father had died in 1899).[72] Free of his commitments to the *Union Labor Advocate,* and with the new Spirit Fruit Temple well underway, he now could visit western Canada. The WFM delegated their champion to take the mining union's fraternal greetings to the annual convention of the Trades and Labor Congress of Canada.

Like a Rip van Winkle awakening after a long sleep, Jaxon found the Northwest transformed. He had left twenty-two years earlier.[73] The open grassland was now fenced in and farmed. A human tide of settlement was sweeping the West, particularly the two new provinces, Alberta and Saskatchewan, formed in 1905. A new set of Liberal politicians ruled, the most prominent westerner in Laurier's Cabinet being his old acquaintance Frank Oliver, the minister of the interior.[74] Once in the West, he discovered that his University of Toronto classmate Fred Haultain, then Conservative Party leader in Saskatchewan, had served as premier of the North-West Territories. Jaxon also learned that Haultain had joined the fight in the early 1890s to eliminate French-language and Roman Catholic school rights in the North-West Territories.[75]

The Trades and Labor Congress of Canada, then holding its annual convention in Winnipeg, welcomed him as a representative of the WFM. From Upton Sinclair's *The Jungle,* a bestseller the year before, the delegates knew of the horrors experienced by workers in Chicago. They also knew of the WFM's heroic efforts to secure the release of their officers. Invited to speak at the convention, the guest, in the *Voice's* words, "made a short but effective speech and left an impression with his earnestness and ability."[76]

While in Manitoba, Jaxon also looked up the sons of two men who had been very important to him in the years 1884-85. In Winnipeg he saw Hugh John Macdonald, who had briefly served as premier of Manitoba in 1900.[77] Hugh John's father, Sir John A. Macdonald, sent Riel to the gallows in 1885. He also visited Jean, the twenty-five-year-old son of Louis Riel,[78] who then lived in the old Riel family home (built in 1880-81). Here his father's body had lain in state for two days after his execution by the Canadian government.[79]

In early December Jaxon travelled to Regina, now a town of 8,000,[80] eight times as large as it had been at the time of the Rebellion trials in 1885. He addressed the local trade unionists as comrades and continually referred to the working-class struggle. Throughout western Canada he urged workers to fight the bosses' attempt to reduce them to "one level mass of broken wretches past salvation."[81] Familiar with Marx's *Capital*, Engel's writings, and works by the anarchist Prince Kropotkin,[82] he cited them repeatedly.

At a Regina branch meeting of the Labour Party on 8 December, the radical social critic went to the heart of the matter. Society, he began, divided into two classes: "the people who ate and those who were eaten." So many injustices cried out for correction. Workers needed living wages. The resource-rich Crown land should belong to all and not be divided up by an eastern government for sale to speculators. Above all, the farmers and labourers should strive for "fair play" for the First Nations and Métis, whose economic state remained inferior to even that of the hard-pressed workers.[83]

Poor Jaxon: again he missed the crest of the wave and instead surfaced in a trough. Had this been a dozen years later in the Winnipeg or Regina of 1919, his words would have found a ready audience. But in 1907 the public, apart from a very small number of adherents, was not ready to establish Producers' Social and Economic Discussion Circles in which farmers and workers could explore the causes of their inferior economic status.[84]

The man still remembered as "Riel's secretary" left Regina to visit his family in the North. He attended an agricultural convention the next week,[85] then departed for the Mistawasis Cree Reserve (just west of Prince Albert), where his brother Eastwood was the acting Indian Agent.[86] He spent the next few months with him and visited with his mother.

In the fall of 1908 the lure of politics attracted Jaxon again. Having never taken out American citizenship, he could run in the federal election. Distrusting established political parties like the Liberals and the Conservatives as the tools of private interest groups, the man from Mistawasis ran as an Independent. Laurier again won the country, and the Liberals took the Prince Albert district. Jaxon suffered a crushing defeat, obtaining only 87 votes to the Liberals' 2,398 and the Conservatives' 2,209.[87]

Jaxon returned to his history of the Rebellion, which he had been planning for over twenty years.[88] In a note dated 8 June 1908, Jean Riel encouraged him to write it "because you were an eye witness and know the truth."[89] With his wife, Aimée, he visited the battle sites "in a prairie schooner, with a teepee of his own design for shelter."[90] Jaxon, at least, was in his element, as Aimée noted: "H[onoré] has always had a passion for igloos and tepees which I have never shared."[91] He took copious notes and shot photos of Riel's surviving acquaintances, such as Louis Schmidt, Riel's boyhood friend, and the old-timers of the Northwest, like Alberta's Father Lacombe.[92] In the fall of 1909 Jaxon made a special trip to Ottawa to obtain government support for the preservation of the historic landmarks of the early West.[93]

The *Edmonton Journal* described Riel's former secretary when he passed through Edmonton as "a rotund little man, with a huge forehead that shone out from beneath a spacious Christie set far back on his head, and with features that radiated good nature." One of the reporter's questions, however, did annoy him. Pounding the palm of his left hand with his right fist, Jaxon thundered back: "Louis Riel died a patriot. He was not a corrupt man. He could not be bought. He had his ideals, and they were high ideals. He believed he was right in attempting to put them into effect. I believe he was right. Fresh from Toronto University, an idealist myself, I joined him and his party, and did my best to back him up in his fight. We did not want the rebellion. It was not our intention to rebel. The rebellion was forced upon us. What we wanted was justice for the half-breeds and justice for the white settlers."[94]

The fact that he had changed his name surprised some of his old acquaintances. W.J. Carter of Prince Albert was one. As a friend of the Jacksons, Carter knew quite well that both his parents were English, but he accepted him on his terms and recognized his ability. Later he wrote of him, "in many ways Jaxon was a very clever man; was widely informed in all classes of literature and philosophy both ancient and modern. His memory of everything he had ever heard or read about was almost uncanny in its thoroughness."[95]

In May 1909 Jaxon travelled to the Rockies and addressed hundreds of striking coal miners at Frank, Alberta. "Riel's Secretary" encouraged them to stand firm in their demands.[96] While in Calgary for several weeks in June, he was elected to a committee of the Calgary Socialist Party.[97] Travelling eastward to Regina, he revealed at a meeting on 18 July the philosophy that motivated him: "It was the duty of all men to live for others."[98] From Regina he went north to Saskatoon, then in the midst of a strike by the labourers building the city's first sewer system.

During the first decade of this century, Saskatoon was the fastest growing town in western Canada. Its population had risen from 113 people in 1901 to nearly 7,000 by 1908.[99] As a contractor himself, Jaxon knew how much the city's sewer workers were being exploited. The city neither paid an adequate wage nor took enough safety precautions. The workers called for an increase of 5 cents per hour (to 25 cents) and requested that all the contractors or corporations conducting public works furnish adequate cribbing, after a depth of six feet, to prevent cave-ins. When a board of conciliation was struck, the workers asked their friend from Chicago to act as one of their three representatives on the six-man board. He gladly accepted. Once the hearings ended a few weeks later, Jaxon left for Ottawa and then went back to the United States.[100]

Upon his return to Chicago, Jaxon remained politically active, as did Aimée, who joined the Women's Civic Club, a statewide organization that fought for the vote for women.[101] As usual the gregarious Jaxon had a large circle of acquaintances. In 1947, Lloyd Lewis, a *Chicago Sun* columnist, quoted what Otto Feeley, labour editor of the *Chicago Evening Post* at the turn of the century,[102] recalled of Jaxon. The veteran journalist spoke of him as "very learned and very cultured." While the police and middle-class Chicagoans dismissed him as a crank, "the intelligentsia, the bankers, the college professors and the labor union men knew he was worth listening to, for he could not only talk classic English with an Indian eloquence but he had an immense amount of learning."[103]

Included among Jaxon's Chicago friends was a young man later recognized as one of the greatest architects of the twentieth century, Frank Lloyd Wright.[104] Jaxon spent the spring of 1913 at Wright's country home of Taliesin, in the Wisconsin Valley, helping him to put in a vineyard and orchard. Apparently Wright wanted him to teach him how to keep a few beehives and offered to set him up in the business "if I should ever get a couple of acres and locate here."[105] But Jaxon preferred to stay in Chicago.

Among Jaxon's many causes, he supported the Mexican Revolution of 1911. As secretary of the "Mexican Liberal Defense conference of Chicago,"[106] he sailed in mid-July 1911 to England as a delegate to the Universal Races Conference in London.[107] In September he attended the 44th Trade Union Congress in Manchester as a "Special Envoy to Europe on behalf of the Insurrectos of Mexico."[108] From England he wrote to "Comrade Joseph Riel," Louis' brother in Manitoba, explaining that in England he "had been presenting the case of the Spanish-Indian Métis of Mexico in their noble struggle for land and liberty."[109]

Aimée thought the world of her husband: "He is not only abreast of most modern thought but in the front rank with the most radical. He is just the most splendid chap & I am very proud of him."[110] Yet he did have what she saw as one very serious personal shortcoming: he refused to try to make money for himself. While Aimée respected Jaxon enormously, his refusal to build up a bank account greatly troubled her. As she wrote to her mother-in-law and brother-in-law Eastwood in late 1911: "To me, monetary reward for legitimate effort, is both interesting & attractive; to him it seems to be the repellant element."[111]

Upon his return to North America from Britain, Jaxon spoke in Montreal to a meeting of the local Trades and Labour Council, where he was warmly received.[112] He also visited Louis Riel's daughter-in-law, Madame Jean Riel (her husband had died in July 1908), in Quebec City.[113] Finally, the wander-

Honoré Joseph Jaxon

ing champion of the Métis of North America returned to Aimée in Chicago, a city in 1911 with a population of two million, greater than the entire population of Canada's four western provinces. Soon after his return, he wrote a short article in the *Star of the West,* in the volume for 1912, describing the visit of Abdul-Bahá, the world leader of the Baha'i community.[114]

It took some tough years in the mid-1910s for Aimée to win Jaxon over to her point of view that they needed to make, and put away, some money for their old age. In the summer of 1919, her beloved crusader for the underdog attended the Atlantic City convention of the American Federation of Labor and then went to New York City for the Pan American Labor Convention.[115] In the New York area he sensed great economic opportunities. With Aimée's approval he decided to stay. For a short time he lived in New Jersey, where he worked briefly as the editor of a small paper,[116] but he soon left for New York itself. He loved the opportunities offered in New York to learn, with its museums and its libraries.[117] To earn his living he worked in real estate, a transformation that he explained to his relatives back in Saskatchewan in this fashion: "It is very funny that I should have drifted into this real estate and insurance game considering my views about land title. Perhaps it will be another case of 'young radical – old conservative.'"[118]

Jaxon bought a number of properties in the Bronx, the area in New York that he considered had the greatest real-estate potential.[119] As Frank Lloyd Wright discovered when he called on him around 1930, Jaxon lived simply. Otto McFeely, a newspaper friend of Wright's from his years in Oak Park, outside of Chicago, later recalled the architect's comments: "Frank Lloyd Wright saw him around 1930 living in New York in a big barn amid vast piles of stacked newspapers, dreaming of world reform while rats raced past him. Since then nobody knows what happened to him."[120]

Aimée held her husband in the highest regard for his devotion to social justice. But her support did have one condition. She refused to join him in New York until he had proper accommodation, with at least running water. Always the dreamer, many times he wrote her about how close he was to securing enough income to have her come and join him and live in proper comfort. He needed only another six months. At long last she refused to believe that he ever would succeed with his finances. In Aimée's last letter to her brother-in-law Eastwood, written on 30 March 1931, she lamented: "Do you know that for 30 years I have lived on that same idea of 'another six months would find us on easy street'? Do you wonder that it has ceased to mean anything beyond a sort of nightmare?"[121]

In time Jaxon put on an addition to his home in the Bronx. The materials were not exactly what Aimée would have approved of, as he used orange crates filled with earth for the walls.[122] But whether or not these improvements would have convinced Aimée to leave Chicago was no longer an issue, as she had died in the mid-1930s.[123] What guilt Jaxon carried for his failure to meet her minimal demand, the installation of plumbing and heating in a proper house, remains unrecorded. Instead, he chose to invest her hard-earned money in his New York property investments.[124] The unrealistic Jaxon always believed that his land investments would result in a pot of gold, but they never did.

Clearly, Jaxon sympathized with Aimée's role in their marriage. Once he described his opinion of marriage to his nieces in Saskatchewan: as far as the woman's interest was concerned, he saw the institution "as a man-made scheme for the annexing of female slaves."[125] Perhaps Jaxon did put the needs of others before himself, but his blind spot remained the wishes of his wife.

In his seventies Jaxon lost none of his enthusiasm for public controversy. In 1933 he appeared before the mayor of New York and the city's Board of Estimate. He protested against the city's expropriation of land for street purposes in the vicinity of McDowell Place, Schurr Avenue, and East

Aimée Montfort Jaxon, wife of Honoré Jaxon, c. 1910

Tremont Avenue in the Bronx. He argued that it was unsurrendered territory and then challenged the Board of Estimate to show that any of the
local First Nations had ever ceded the land.[126] The following year, while
thumping a 200-year-old Bible, Jaxon, in his loud, booming voice, told

Mayor Fiorello La Guardia at a public hearing on a proposed city lottery that no biblical injunction existed against one.[127]

The 1930s, the Depression, proved a terrible decade for Jaxon. He lost Aimée, whom, in his own way, he truly loved; in fact, over the roughly ten-year period of their separation in the 1920s, he sent her, by Aimée's count, 500 letters.[128] Now in his seventies, he became somewhat unstable. Although Jaxon tried to practise his belief that it was one's duty to love "one's neighbor as oneself,"[129] his letters in the 1930s betray an intense mistrust of his Bronx neighbours, who were, he felt, determined to steal his properties. By the early 1940s, he had lost most of his real estate, not on account of his neighbours, but because of his failure to pay his taxes. To a great extent, he now withdrew from the world.

Disaster struck in 1942 when the City of New York evicted him from what he called his "Bronx Castle." At the hearing in the Bronx Magistrate's Court, the Health Department's inspector charged that Jaxon's so-called "palace" was unsafe to live in, a fire hazard, and that it violated the city's sanitation laws. The eighty-one-year-old Jaxon shot back: "That's a misstatement of fact. For 20 years, I have lived there and there was nothing wrong with it. Why this proceeding?"[130] But the city proceeded. They demolished his orange-crate house, which contained almost all the personal papers that he had saved in order to write his memoirs. Yet he bounced back. As he wrote his sister Cicely in Saskatchewan: "In a way I am now free for new and joyous adventures, all my records having been scattered and destroyed. Still I can write a fine book of memoirs on fragments packed up. In one way a great tragedy – but what does it matter if God is coming soon?"[131]

Lacking a place to stay, and not wishing to be dependent on anyone, Jaxon eventually took a job as the janitor of a fourteen-suite apartment building on East 34th Street. He lived in the basement unit, which could be reached only by a sidewalk trapdoor and a twenty-foot ladder.[132] Every morning he rose at 5 a.m. to feed the furnace with coal. At 6 a.m. all year long, he opened a newsstand.[133] To save money he lived on a special cereal that he cooked on a great cauldron once a week.[134] During his afternoons he went to auction sales looking for second-hand books.[135] Regularly in the 1940s he attended meetings of the Caravan, a break-off group from the Baha'i movement, which met on East 65th Street. They knew him there as "a most dignified character," a "scholarly hobo."[136]

In 1947 Jaxon's sister and her eldest daughter, named Cicely after her mother, visited him in New York. His mother and brother Eastwood had died, so his sister and her six daughters were his only blood relatives. After their return, his nieces Cicely and Mary tried to convince their uncle to come back home to Saskatchewan. He would not leave until he could arrange for the safe transport of all his books and papers. His one "great passion" was to educate the Indians "so that they'd get a better deal in this generation than they did in the past."[137] He wanted to get his books back to Saskatchewan for, in his words, "an interesting and instructive and useful library ... [which] constitutes, as Thomas Carlyle has said, the best of all universities."[138]

Just two and a half months away from his ninetieth birthday, he wrote Cicely and Mary, on 22 February 1951, outlining the philosophy that had guided him for the last half-century:

> First, I want to do everything that is humanly possible as my contribution to the peace of mind of the descendants of Cicely senior. Secondly, I want to do everything that I humanly can to promote the happiness and peace of mind of the French-Indian people with whose affairs I was so closely associated in the eighties of the last century – a people whose fine qualities were revealed to me during their struggle against great hardship, and connection with whom was accentuated by evidence brought through Louis Riel which I have never been able to dismiss as irrelevant or incompetent. Thirdly, I want to do all that is humanly possible in the way of contributing to the solving of the difficulties and hardships of the many fine honest hardworking people with whom I have become associated in the United States during the last seventy years of my life, and fourthly, I want to do all this in submission to the will of God, and without foolishly interfering with the designs of God himself to bring about the elevating of the entire human race from its initial attribute of cannibalism – each person and each nation seeking only to grab for oneself – to that ultimate state of Grace in which each person and each nation will seek and find happiness only in promoting the general welfare ... all in accordance with Christ's wonderful definition of pure religion; to "Love God with all one's heart and one's neighbor as oneself."[139]

Jaxon had hoped to live to one hundred.[140] He did not make it. Within a year of sharing his life's philosophy with his nieces, he was dead, his books sold, and his papers buried in a New York City garbage dump. On account of his extraordinary appreciation of the Métis and First Nations, so far ahead of his non-Native contemporaries, this fascinating individual deserves to be remembered today.

What was the inspiration for Jaxon's lifelong association with and work for the Aboriginal peoples at a time of great public neglect of their cause? The pivotal moment of his life appears to have been his incarceration with Métis prisoners after Batoche. In his cell he began to wear a Métis headband. He bonded completely with them. Later in Chicago he reinvented himself as a Métis. No doubt, he relished the role as a Métis spokesperson in exile in Chicago and later New York. Clearly, it enhanced his role as a radical social critic to present himself as a member of an oppressed community. His new identity allowed him to say what he pleased on topics of social justice. Throughout his adult life he worked to improve the well-being of the Aboriginal peoples of North America. In his eighties he devoted all his energy and resources to assembling books and articles for a library for the Aboriginal peoples of Saskatchewan. Until his death Jaxon fought for a proper appreciation of the contribution of Louis Riel. As he wrote of Riel in 1885, "the oppression of the aboriginals has been the crying sin of the white race in America and they have at last found a voice."[141]

Acknowledgment

This chapter is a considerably revised version of an earlier paper, "Honoré Joseph Jaxon: A Man Who Lived for Others," *Saskatchewan History* 34, 3 (Autumn 1981): 81-101. In the original article, published almost a quarter of a century ago, I warmly thanked Lorne Grant, great-nephew of Honoré Jaxon, Professor Cyril Greenland, Dr. John Griffin, Dr. Thomas Flanagan, and the late Cicely Plaxton, niece of Honoré Jaxon, for their invaluable assistance in locating research material. Judy Abel, Audrey Swaffield, and Dr. Tom Flanagan provided useful comments on a preliminary draft. For this revision I am most grateful to Lisa D'Aiuto of the Faculty of Education, York University, for retyping the original text onto a computer disk, making changes possible. In 1991 Lorne Grant allowed me to see numerous letters of Honoré and Aimée Jaxon to their Jackson relatives in Saskatchewan. I have incorporated new information from these sources in this revision. I appreciate the comments and research assistance of my son David with this revision. My thanks as well to the copyeditor, Robert Lewis, who helped enormously in presenting a clear text. Any errors that this new edition of the paper might contain remain my responsibility.

Notes

1 Honoré Jaxon to Mary Plaxton Grant, New York, 21 January 1949, in the documentary collection gathered by Cyril Greenland, Documentary History of Canadian Psychiatry Project, Canadian Mental Health Association, 2160 Yonge Street, Toronto, Ontario (Greenland/Griffin Collection). This valuable collection has been donated to Special Collections, University of Saskatchewan Library, University of Saskatchewan, where it is now known as the Griffin/Greenland Collection.

2 "Warned of a Plot," *Washington Post,* 18 June 1894.

3 An earlier article, "Hut-Dweller, 80, Clashes with Law," *New York Times*, 20 February 1942, 19, c. 7, described "the major, a tall, sombre person with thinning hair and a military bearing."

4 "Major Jaxon, Who's Used to It by Now, Finds Himself, at 90, Thrown Out Again," *New York Times,* 13 December 1957, 50, cc. 4-5.

5 For information on the colourful Baronian, see "Harry Baronian of Bowery News. Editor of Hoboes' Chronicle Is Dead Here at 54," *New York Times,* 4 August 1965, 35, c. 2. He called his twelve-page tabloid "The Voice of Society's Basement." The *Times* described it as "an occasional publication that celebrated the pleasures of unemployment."

6 "Champion of Indians Dispossessed Here," *New York Times,* 14 December 1951, 23, cc. 2-3.

7 Harry Baronian, quoted by Nathaniel A. Benson, in Louis Blake Duff, "Amazing Story of the Winghamite Secretary of Louis Riel," *Western Ontario History Nuggets* 22 (1955): 1-37 at 30. See also Benson's original notes of his interview with Baronian in New York, 14 July 1954, in the documents collected from Mrs. Benson by Cyril Greenland, Greenland/Griffin Collection.

8 Harry Baronian, quoted by Nathaniel A. Benson, in Duff, "Amazing Story," 29.

9 Dr. Joseph Zinkin, City of New York, Dept. of Hospitals, Bellevue Hospital Centre, to Cyril Greenland, 20 May 1970, Greenland/Griffin Collection.

10 "Honoré Jaxon, 91, Friend of Indians, Major with Métis Tribesmen during Fight in Canada, Is Dead – Later Jersey Editor," *New York Times*, 12 January 1952, 13, c. 5; "Honoré Joseph Jaxon, 90, Dies; Long a Fighter for Indian Rights," *New York Herald-Tribune*, 12 January 1952, 12, cc. 4-5.

11 "Indians' Friend, Jaxon was Colorful Figure," *Edmonton Journal*, 14 January 1952.

12 Copy of Salvation Army Letter re: Funeral of our Uncle Honoré J. Jackson, Greenland/Griffin Collection.

13 Photostat copy of letter from Kurt Mertig, New York City, to Cicily [Cicely] Plaxton, Prince Albert, 31 January 1952, Greenland/Griffin Collection; Harry Baronian, quoted by Nathaniel A. Benson, in Duff, "Amazing Story," 31.

14 Was William Henry Jackson mentally unbalanced? In several treatments of his participation in the Rebellion, he is presented as such. Sandra Estlin Bingaman, "The Trials of the 'White Rebels,' 1885," *Saskatchewan History* 25 (Spring 1972): 41-54, contends that Jackson was "suffering from mental illness" at the time of the Rebellion (54). Donatien Frémont, "Henry Jackson et l'insurrection du Nord-Ouest," *Memoires de la Société Royale du Canada*, 3rd series, 46 (1952): first section, 19-48, terms him "déséquilibré ... comme son chef" (first section, 48). Duff's inaccurate article, "Amazing Story," is regularly cited in reference to Jackson. In his essay Duff argues that Will Jackson "wore the banner of mental instability faithfully from the beginning of his life to the end" (4). Louis Blake Duff's failings as a historian need to be underlined, as this essay has been accepted as a reliable secondary source. W.J.C. Cherwinski, for example, refers to it in describing Jackson's youth; see his interesting review of Jackson twenty years after the Rebellion, "Honoré Joseph Jaxon, Agitator, Disturber, Producer of Plans to Make Men Think, and Chronic Objector," *Canadian Historical Review* 46, 2 (June 1965): 122-33 at 123-24. George F.G. Stanley also cites Duff's account of Jackson in *Louis Riel* (Toronto: Ryerson, 1963), 268, 410.

Duff's article, composed when he was in his late seventies, contains a number of inaccuracies. Chronologically, he incorrectly states that Riel returned to Canada in the spring of 1884 (2) instead of in early July. Other errors include his dating of the first meeting at which Riel and Jackson both spoke. Duff mentions 11 May 1884 (5), but the reference should read 11 July 1884. Will also met Big Bear in mid-August 1884, not in May 1884 as the author infers. One very serious error appears in his references. He introduces an article from the *Toronto World* of 22 May 1885 (21-4). Unfortunately, none of the May issues of the *World* for 1885 contain this article.

The evidence that Duff collected from old Wingham residents (as well as his own alleged recollection of once having seen Will Jackson in Wingham, when Louis Blake Duff, born in 1878, would have been three or four years old!) must be used with great caution. Cyril Greenland and John D. Griffin correctly point out that the available evidence on Will's youth is highly selective and insubstantial; see "William Henry Jackson (1861-1952) – Riel's Secretary: Another Case of Involuntary Commitment?" *Canadian Psychiatric Association Journal* 23, 7 (November 1978): 469-78 at 470.

For a review of Jackson's early life to 1885, see Donald B. Smith, "William Henry Jackson: Riel's Disciple," in *Pelletier-Lathlin Memorial Lecture Series, Brandon University, 1979-1980*, ed. A.S. Lussier (Brandon: Department of Native Studies, 1980), 47-81. The information that follows on Will Jackson's life until the end of the Rebellion comes from the above article. An undocumented, illustrated version of this essay appeared as "William Henry Jackson: Riel's Secretary," *The Beaver*, outfit 311, 4 (Spring 1981): 10-19.

15 Grant MacEwan, *Frederick Haultain: Frontier Statesman of the Canadian Northwest* (Saskatoon: Western Producer Prairie Books, 1985), 12; Kathleen Kritzwiser, "K.M.K.'s Column," *Regina Leader-Post*, 24 January 1952.

16 Statement about treaties by an Indian, Louis Riel Papers, Dept. of Justice, R.G. 13 B2, microfilm C-1228, 144-45 (my thanks to Miriam Carey, author of "The Role of W.H. Jackson in the North West Agitation of 1884-1885," honours essay, Department of Political Science, University of Calgary, April 1980, for this reference).

17   William H. Jackson to "my dear Family," Lower Fort Garry, 19 September 1885, Archives of Manitoba, MG3 C20 (henceforth AM).
18   Frank Oliver to William Henry Jackson, 22 October 1884, quoted in George F.G. Stanley, *The Birth of Western Canada* (Toronto: University of Toronto Press, 1961), 308-9.
19   William H. Jackson to "my dear Family," 19 September 1885, AM.
20   See Smith, "William Henry Jackson," 79 n. 80.
21   For more information on Riel's religion, see Thomas Flanagan, *Louis 'David' Riel: 'Prophet of the New World'* (Toronto: University of Toronto Press, 1979).
22   William H. Jackson to "my dear Family," 19 September 1885, AM.
23   Ibid.
24   Ibid.
25   William Henry Jackson to Dr. Young, Crookston, 15 November 1885, in "Jackson's Escape," *Manitoba Free Press,* 24 November 1885; William Henry Jackson to Sir John A. Macdonald, telegram, Crookston, 15 November 1885, John A. Macdonald Papers, M.G. 26, A 1(a), vol. 108, 43-44, Library and Archives Canada.
26   "Louis Riel and the Northwest, Lecture of W.H. Jackson," *Crookston Times,* 28 November 1885, 7, c. 4; "Riel's Secretary," *The Daily Argus* (Fargo, ND), 28 November 1885, 5, c. 3 – the *Argus* termed him a "very fluent speaker"; "Riel's Private Secretary Says the Cause of the Late Chief is Not Yet Dead," *St. Paul Globe,* 2 January 1886, 9, c. 3; "Brief Items," *The Herald* (Chippewa Falls, WI), 8 January 1886, 5, c. 2: "Jackson is an eloquent speaker"; "W.H. Jackson, Riel's Secretary," *Chippewa Times* (Chippewa Falls, WI), 6 January 1886, 5, c. 5: "His entire review of the rebellion was full of striking incidents and very effectively related"; "Minneapolis. A Benefit for Riel's Family," *Manitoba Free Press,* 20 January 1886, 1, c. 4: "The secretary gave a comprehensive and interesting statement of the circumstances which led to the insurrection"; "Riel's Secretary," *Chicago Inter-Ocean,* 17 March 1886, 5, c. 2.
27   William Henry Jackson, quoted in "Riel's Private Secretary," *St. Paul Globe,* 2 January 1886, 9, c. 3.
28   "W.H. Jackson, How He Appeared on Arriving at Fargo," *Toronto Daily Mail,* 3 December 1885 (my thanks to Miriam Carey for pointing out this clipping).
29   Ibid.
30   "Riel's Secretary," *Chicago Inter-Ocean,* 17 March 1886, 5, c. 2; W.H. Jackson to Michel [Dumas], Chicago, 6 September 1886, Archives de l'Archevêché de Saint-Boniface, Manitoba, Correspondence générale T53009-11 (henceforth SB).
31   W.H. Jackson to Michel [Dumas], 6 September 1886, SB; "President Chides Treason Fugitive," *Chicago Daily News,* 24 April 1907, 1; "Father of Labor Sluggers Joins U.S. Army Camp," *Chicago Tribune,* 18 September 1915. On the Carpenters' Union's demands, see *Chicago Inter-Ocean,* 16 April 1886, 2, c. 4; 26 April 1886, 3, c. 6; Richard Schneirov and Thomas J. Suhrbur, *Union Brotherhood, Union Town: The History of the Carpenters' Union of Chicago 1863-1987* (Carbondale and Edwardsville: Southern Illinois University Press, 1988), 32.
     An early reference to William H. Jackson in Chicago newspapers appears in the *Chicago Tribune,* 1 October 1886, 3. The *Tribune* states that shortly after arriving in Chicago, "He joined the Carpenters' Union, was soon elected to an office, and among the ignorant class he gathered about him as he has become little less than a demi-god" (my thanks to Richard Schneirov, then a PhD candidate at Northern Illinois University, De Kalb, Illinois, for this reference). Interesting references to Jackson's first year or so in Chicago also appear in Steven Sapolsky, "The Making of Honore Jaxon," in *Haymarket Scrapbook,* ed. Dave Roediger and Franklin Rosemont (Chicago: Charles H. Kerr Publishing Company, 1986), 103-5.
32   Stewart H. Holbrook, *The Age of the Moguls* (Garden City, NY: Doubleday, 1953), 102; Ray Ginger, *Altgeld's America* (Chicago: Quadrangle Books, 1958), 5; Bessie Louise Pierce, *A History of Chicago,* vol. 3 (New York: Alfred A. Knopf, 1957), 22.
33   William Adelman, *Haymarket Revisited* (Chicago: Illinois Labor History, 1976), 2; Ginger, *Altgeld's America,* 8.

34   Adelman, *Haymarket Revisited*, 15-19; Milton Meltzer, *Bread and Roses: The Struggle of American Labor, 1865-1914* (1967; reprint, New York: New American Library 1977), 110-14.

35   Adelman, *Haymarket Revisited*, 15-19; James D. Forman, *Anarchism: Political Innocence or Social Violence?* (New York: Dell, 1975), 15.

36   *Chicago Tribune*, 22 December 1886 (my thanks to Richard Schneirov for this reference).

37   "Riel's Secretary," *The Daily Argus* (Fargo, ND), 28 November 1885, 5, c. 3.

38   William H. Jackson to A.K. Owen, Chicago, 4 April 1888, William Henry Jackson Papers, University of Saskatchewan Library, Saskatoon, Saskatchewan (henceforth USL).

39   One can date his name change from his letters to A.K. Owen, USL. He signed his name "William H. Jackson" in the letter of 8 December 1888 and "W.H. Joseph Jaxon" on 4 March 1889, and by 30 May 1889 he had dropped the William for "H. Joseph Jaxon."

40   William H. Jackson to A.K. Owen, 4 April 1888, USL; "Jaxon Will Bear Watching," *Washington Post*, 19 June 1894, 1, c. 2.

41   "Does Jaxon Injustice," *Chicago Times*, 19 June 1894, 4, c. 5.

42   Interview with Miss Cicely Plaxton, Prince Albert, 7 June 1979.

43   Honoré J. Jaxon to his mother, 10 January 1895 [1896], Jackson Family Collection, photostats of letters kindly mailed to me by Lorne Grant, great-nephew of Honoré Jaxon (henceforth JFC).

44   William H. Jackson, Secretary for the Métis Council of the North West, to A.K. Owen, Chicago, 8 December 1888, USL. For information about A.K. Owen, see David M. Pletcher, "Utopian Reformer: Albert Kimsey Owen," in *Rails, Mines, and Progress: Seven American Promoters in Mexico, 1867-1911* (Ithaca, NY: Cornell University Press, 1958), 106-48.

45   The American press apparently believed that he was of Indian ancestry. The *New York Times* wrote on 28 November 1885: "he looks as if he has some Indian blood in his veins." Seven years later on 3 July 1892, the *Omaha World Herald* noted: "He is a man below medium in height with straight cut semi-aboriginal features and long black hair which protrudes in massive locks from a massive forehead." On 18 June 1894, the *Washington Post* wrote, he has "the high cheek bones and coppery complexion of the red men. His hair is raven black and very straight."

46   "Have Begun. The People's Party National Convention Makes a Start in Its Work," *Omaha World Herald*, 3 July 1892, 1; "All at Sea Now," *Omaha Bee*, 3 July 1892, 2, c. 5; "Jaxon Has a Record," *Washington Post*, 18 June 1894, 1, c. 4.

47   Carolyn Ashbaugh, *Lucy Parsons: American Revolutionary* (Chicago: Charles H. Kerr, 1976), 192 (my thanks to Professor William J. Adelman of the University of Illinois, Chicago Circle Campus, for this reference).

48   "Jaxon Will Bear Watching," *Washington Post*, 19 June 1894, 1, cc. 1-2.

49   "Does Jaxon an Injustice," *Chicago Times*, 19 June 1894, 4, c. 5. For information on Gage, see Reginald C. McGrane, "Lyman Judson Gage (1836-1927)," *Dictionary of American Biography*, vol. 7 (New York: Charles Scribner's Sons, 1931), 85-86.

50   Elmer Ellis, *Mr. Dooley's America: A Life of Finley Peter Dunne* (New York: Alfred A. Knopf, 1941), 48.

51   Ibid., 50.

52   "Jaxon Will Bear Watching," *Washington Post*, 19 June 1894, 1, cc. 1-2.

53   Ashbaugh, *Lucy Parsons*, 192.

54   Donald L. McMurry, *Coxey's Army: A Study of the Industrial Army Movement of 1894* (Seattle: University of Washington Press, 1929), 43.

55   "Does Jaxon Injustice," *Chicago Times*, 19 June 1894, 4, c. 5.

56   Mrs. Janet Rubenstein, for the Office of the Secretary, National Spiritual Assembly of the Baha'is of the United States, to Donald B. Smith, Wilmette, Illinois, 26 June 1979.

57   Cicely Plaxton, Honoré Jaxon's niece, kindly showed me a photo of her aunt Aimée, Prince Albert, 7 June 1979. A "Miss Aimée Montford, teacher," appears in the *Chicago City Directory*, 1897, 1458. Apparently, she married in 1900, as the directory for that year no longer includes her name. My thanks to Ronald Ramsay, North Dakota State University, Fargo, for sending me the entry for Aimée Jaxon in the 1910 census, Cook County, Illinois, Supervisor's District 1, Enumeration District No. 1455, Sheet No. 3A 935. In 1910 she gave her occupation as newspaper storywriter.

58 "Who's Who – And Why," *The Saturday Evening Post,* 1 June 1907, 17.

59 Aimée Montfort Jaxon to "Cicely [Jaxon's mother] and all," Chicago, 4 February 1931, JFC.

60 Honoré Jaxon to "Mother and Eastwood," Chicago, 22 May 1905, JFC.

61 Honoré Jaxon to "Mother and Eastwood," Chicago, 23 May 1906, JFC.

62 Aimée Montfort Jaxon to Cicely [Jaxon's sister], Chicago, 27 November 1930, JFC.

63 "An Appeal to Chicagoans in Their Own Interest," undated circular, containing the name "Honoré J. Jaxon, Sec'y Fellowcraft Ass'n, Room 614, 108 Dearborn St.," JFC.

64 (Copy of a letter) George Hodge, Publisher, *Union Labor Advocate,* to Frank Oliver, Minister of the Interior for Dominion of Canada, Chicago, 29 June 1906, JFC.

65 James L. Murphy explains the origin of the Society's name in *The Reluctant Radicals: Jacob L. Beilhart and The Spirit Fruit Society* (Lanham, MD: University Press of America, 1989), 2. Apparently Jacob Beilhart, the Society's founder, suggested this name on account of his belief that humans "remained in a spiritual state akin to the bud or blossom, that man's soul had not yet achieved the spiritual perfection analogous to full fruition."

66 H. Roger Grant, *Spirit Fruit: A Gentle Utopia* (DeKalb, IL: Northern Illinois University Press, 1988), 104-5.

67 Elbert Hubbard, in *The Philistine*, February 1905, 86-88; quoted in Grant, *Spirit Fruit*, 114.

68 Jaxon's letter has not survived. The phrase is that of Theodore Roosevelt, who is paraphrasing Jaxon's note. Roosevelt to Honoré Jaxon, 22 April 1907, Theodore Roosevelt Papers, reel 345 (volume 72), 259, Library of Congress. For an account of Jaxon's role in the incident, see J. Anthony Lucas, *Big Trouble* (1997; reprint, New York: Touchstone, 1998), 462-63. The defence of the three by Clarence Darrow led to their eventual acquittal.

69 The letter heading is quoted by Roosevelt in his letter to Honoré Jaxon, 22 April 1907, Theodore Roosevelt Papers, reel 345 (volume 72), 259, Library of Congress.

70 "Who's Who – And Why," *The Saturday Evening Post,* 1 June 1907, 1.

71 "Chicago Federation to Expel Jaxon for Stirring President," *Chicago Inter-Ocean,* 26 April 1907, 1, c. 4.

72 Thomas Gethyn Jackson died on 31 October 1899. Interview with Miss Cicely Plaxton, Prince Albert, 7 June 1979.

73 For a full account of Jaxon's return, see Donald B. Smith, "Rip Van Jaxon: The Return of Riel's Secretary in 1884-1885 to the Canadian West, 1907-1909," in *1885 and After: Native Society in Transition,* ed. F. Laurie Barron and James B. Waldram (Regina: Canadian Plains Research Centre, 1986), 211-23.

74 Oliver became minister of the interior, 8 April 1905. *The Canadian Who's Who* (London, England: The Times Publishing Co., 1910), 176.

75 MacEwan, *Haultain,* 69-70.

76 *Winnipeg Voice,* 20 September 1907, 1.

77 To "Mother and Eastwood," Winnipeg, 17 September 1907, JFC. He met Hugh John Macdonald on 16 September.

78 "Il a vu la veuve du fils Louis Riel," *La Presse* (Montreal), 22 February 1912 (my thanks to Diane Payment, historian, projet de Batoche et Maison Riel, Parks Canada, for this reference).

79 "Riel House, National Historic Site," pamphlet published by Parks Canada, 1980 (Q-5-R103-000-BB-A1).

80 Earl G. Drake, *Regina: The Queen City* (Toronto: McClelland and Stewart, 1955), 131.

81 Honoré J. Jaxon, "The Struggle for Life Under Western Conditions," *Labour's Realm,* 2 August 1909, 6.

82 "The Discussion Circle Movement," *Labour's Realm,* 2 August 1909, 9, c. 3, 10.

83 "The Function of the Labour Party," *Regina Morning Leader,* 9 December 1907, 7, cc. 1-2.

84 Ibid.

85 "Convention Opens at Regina Today," *Regina Morning Leader,* 11 December 1907, 7, c. 3.

86 W.J. Chisholm, Inspector of Indian Agencies, Prince Albert, 20 April 1908, Department of Indian Affairs, Annual Report, 1907-8, 161.

87 "Rutan's Majority 189," *Prince Albert Times,* 2 December 1908, 4. Jaxon was a British subject: "Conciliation Board Opens with a Spat," *Saskatoon Phoenix,* 13 August 1909.

88   William H. Jackson to Michel [Dumas], 6 September 1886, SB; Kathleen Kritzwiser, "K.M.K.'s Column," *Regina Leader-Post,* 24 January 1952.

89   Jean Louis Riel à Honoré Jaxon, Saint Vital, Manitoba, le 8 juin 1908: "je vous prie d'écrire l'histoire de la rébellion de 1885, au Nord Ouest, parce que vous avez été témoin oculaire et que vous pourrez dire la vérité." The translation into English is the author's.

90   "Was Secretary of Louis Riel," *Manitoba Free Press,* 14 October 1909, 12, c. 2 (my thanks to Clarence Kipling of Calgary for this reference.)

91   Aimée Montfort Jaxon to Eastwood Jackson, Chicago, 6 October 1931, JFC.

92   Raymond Huel, "Louis Schmidt: A Forgotten Métis," in *Riel and the Métis,* ed. A.S. Lussier (Winnipeg: Manitoba Métis Federation Press, 1979), 103; Katherine Hughes, *Father Lacombe, the Black-Robe Voyageur* (Toronto: William Briggs, 1911), 294.

93   "Jaxon Would Preserve Historic Landmarks," *Edmonton Journal,* 14 October 1909.

94   "Riel a Martyr Says H. Jaxon," *Edmonton Journal,* 4 October 1901, 1, c. 1.

95   W.J. Carter, "Forty Years in the North-West," Special Collections, University of Saskatchewan Library, Saskatoon, Saskatchewan (MSS C550/1/24.1).

96   "Would Force Lewis' Hand," *Frank Paper* (Alberta), 13 May 1909.

97   "Socialists Discuss Religion in Schools," *The Morning Albertan* (Calgary), 21 June 1909, 1, c. 2.

98   "Economic Circle, Honoré Jaxon Addresses Opening Meeting of New Society," *Regina Morning Leader,* 19 July 1909.

99   James Oliver Curwood, "Saskatoon – The Wonderful," *The Bookkeeper,* reprinted in the *Saskatoon Phoenix,* 11 September 1909.

100 "Witnesses Tell of Conditions of Work," *Saskatoon Phoenix,* 18 August 1909, 1; "Saskatoon Labour Dispute Findings," *Saskatoon Phoenix,* 14 September 1909, 1; "Official Report on the Dispute," *Saskatoon Phoenix,* 18 September 1909, 1; "Was Secretary of Riel," *Manitoba Free Press,* 14 October 1909, 12, c. 2.

101 Aimée Montfort Jaxon to Eastwood Jaxon, Chicago, 5 September 1911, JFC.

102 Robert St. John, *This Was My World* (Garden City, NY: Doubleday, 1953), 111. Robert St. John (1903-2003) was a celebrated American war correspondent and print and broadcast journalist. He worked for Otto Feeley, as a young man, after Feeley had left the *Chicago Evening Post* to edit the *Oak Leaves,* a weekly published in Oak Park, Illinois.

103 Lloyd Lewis, "It Takes All Kinds: Honore Jaxon, Forgotten Crusader," *Chicago Sun,* 3 February 1947.

104 Aimée Montfort Jaxon to Eastwood Jaxon, Chicago, 21 July 1911; also Honoré Jaxon to "Folks," Chicago, 31 May 1913, JFC.

105 Honoré Jaxon to T. Eastwood Jackson, Spring Green, Wisconsin, 31 May 1913, JFC.

106 "Chicago Comrades Display Great Activity," *Los Angeles Regeneracion,* 19 August 1911, 4, c. 7.

107 Aimée Montfort Jaxon to "dear folks" [the Jackson family in Saskatchewan], Chicago, 26 July 1911; Honoré Jaxon to "Mother and Eastwood," Newcastle on Tyne, England, 4 September 1911, JFC.

108 "A Statement from the Working Class of Mexico, to the 44th Annual Congress of the Trades Unions of Great Britain," four-page circular, "By Honoré J. Jaxon, Special Envoy to Europe on Behalf of the Insurrectos of Mexico," Louis Riel Collection, no. 475, Public Archives of Manitoba.

109 Honoré Joseph Jaxon to Joseph Riel, London, England, 11 October 1911, Louis Riel Collection, no. 475, Public Archives of Manitoba.

110 Aimée Montfort Jaxon to "dear folks," Chicago, 26 July 1911, JFC.

111 Aimée Montfort Jaxon to "mother & Eastwood," Chicago, 4 October 1911, JFC.

112 "Dans le monde ouvrier," *Le Devoir* (Montreal), 16 February 1912.

113 "Il a vu la veuve du fils de Louis Riel," *La Presse* (Montreal), 22 February 1912, 1, cc. 8-9.

114 Honoré J. Jaxon. "A Stroll with Abdul-Baha, Culminating in a Typical Bahai Meeting under the Trees of Lincoln Park, Chicago," *Star of the West* 3, 4 (1912): 27-29.

115 Honoré Jaxon to "mother and folks," New York, 12 December 1919, JFC.

116 "Honoré Jaxon," *New York Times,* 12 January 1952, 13, c. 5.

117 Undated manuscript written by Cicely Plaxton, Jaxon's sister, after visiting him in New York, July 1947, JFC. Mrs. Plaxton died two years later in 1949.

118 Fragment of a letter by Jaxon, probably written around 1920, JFC.

119 Aimée Montfort Jaxon to Cicely Plaxton, Chicago, 15 May 1930, JFC.

120 Otto McFeely, paraphrased in Lloyd Lewis, "It Takes All Kinds: Honoré Jaxon, Forgotten Crusader," *Chicago Sun,* 3 February 1947.

121 Aimée Montfort Jaxon to Eastwood Jackson, Chicago, 30 March 1931, JFC.

122 "Soldier of Fortune, 80, Rails at City," *The Home News* (Bronx and Manhattan), 20 February 1942, 3.

123 Honoré Jaxon to Eastwood and Cicely, New York, 14 December 1935, JFC.

124 Honoré Jaxon to Cicely Plaxton, New York, 21 February 1923, JFC.

125 Photostat copy of a letter from Honoré Jaxon to Mary Plaxton, his niece, "Bronx Castle Garden," Bronx, NY, 25 February 1931, Greenland/Griffin Collection.

126 "Honoré Joseph Jaxon," *New York Herald-Tribune,* 12 January 1952, 12, cc. 4-5.

127 "Aldermen to Scan New Taxes Monday," *New York Times,* 28 September 1954, 1, c. 2. Jaxon is not mentioned in the *Times* story, but he appears in a photo of the hearing in the *New York Daily News* photo library.

128 Aimée Montfort Jaxon to "Cicely and all," Chicago, 30 March 1931, JFC.

129 Photostat copy of letter from Jaxon to Cicely Plaxton and Mary Grant, New York, 22 February 1951, Greenland/Griffin Collection.

130 "Soldier of Fortune, 80 Rails at City," *The Home News* (Bronx and Manhattan), 20 February 1942, 3.

131 Honoré Jaxon to Cicely Plaxton, New York, 28 April 1942, JFC.

132 "Fought All His Life for Others. At 91, He's Evicted From Cellar," *New York Herald-Tribune,* 13 December 1951, 29, c. 5.

133 Photostat copy of a letter from Honoré Jaxon to Mary Plaxton Grant, New York, 21 January 1949, Greenland/Griffin Collection.

134 "A Scholarly Hobo," *The Caravan* (New York), April 1952.

135 Photostat copy of a letter from Kurt Mertig to Miss Cicely Plaxton, New York, 31 January 1952, Greenland/Griffin Collection.

136 "A Scholarly Hobo," *The Caravan* (New York), April 1952.

137 Harry Baronian, quoted by Nathaniel A. Benson, in Duff, "Amazing Story," 31.

138 Photostat copy of letter from "Uncle Honoré" to Cicely and Mary, New York, 22 February 1951, Greenland/Griffin Collection.

139 Ibid. Jaxon's sister, "Cicely senior," had died two years earlier in 1949.

140 Photostat copy of letter from Kurt Mertig to Miss Cicely Plaxton, New York, 16 January 1952, Greenland/Griffin Collection.

141 See note 17.

11

Arthur Eugene O'Meara: Servant, Advocate, Seeker of Justice

Mary Haig-Brown

> By a Royal Proclamation put forth in 1763 the whole of the far western and far northern territory was reserved for the use of the Indians, and so far as I can at present ascertain the Proclamation continues in force, and these Indians have never surrendered their rights.
> – Letter from Rev. A.E. O'Meara, to Bishop Stringer, 1 December 1908[1]

Until the time of his death in 1928, Arthur Eugene O'Meara worked to have the Aboriginal rights of the people of the North American West recognized by the government of Canada. In the course of this work, he was supported by many of the First Nations people in British Columbia and reviled by members of Parliament and the civil service. By 1908, while he was in the Yukon, he had already earned a reputation among some in the First Nations community as a knowledgeable and articulate advocate and legal advisor. He also had so thoroughly annoyed some members of the church community that they refused to have him as their priest, and two years later his bishop suggested that he give up the wearing of the cloth. His difficult nature alienated politicians, civil servants, and even his family. O'Meara's persistence in trying to gain legal recognition of Aboriginal rights to the North American Northwest occupied him fully for nearly twenty-five years. This dedication, or obsession, gained him few friends and many enemies. O'Meara was persistent to the point of stubbornness and, in the course of pursuing what he considered just, alienated many who could perhaps have helped secure the results that he desired.

Although the years during which O'Meara worked were times of some hope for addressing land rights, his work ended at a time of repression when even the small gains made over the years of struggle were being clawed back. Following the establishment of the colony of British Columbia in 1849 under the auspices of the Hudson's Bay Company, throughout

James Douglas' tenure first as factor and later as governor of the colony, an unwritten policy of "justice and laissez-faire, leaning heavily on the educating effects of time and White neighbours" had dominated.[2] When British Columbia joined Confederation in 1871, confusion and disagreement between the Dominion and provincial governments regarding Indian land rights and claims rose to the fore.

An early effort to address the land question in British Columbia was the establishment in 1876 of a Joint Commission of the Dominion and provincial governments to allocate reserve lands. It abandoned its work in 1909 before any final resolution could be reached and when the problems of the designated allotments were already becoming evident.[3] Both governments as well as the First Nations peoples were highly frustrated. It was in this year that A.E. O'Meara was asked to carry a petition from the Cowichan people to the king. The next significant government initiative was the establishment of the McKenna-McBride Agreement in 1912. It formed the basis for the Royal Commission whose mandate it was to investigate land matters, although its focus quickly became reducing the current acreages of reserves and substituting valuable land with less valuable land.[4]

In the first two decades of the new century, Indian efforts to address the injustices affecting their lands and other rights seemed destined for some success, although hindsight demonstrates that the counter-efforts of governmental officials undermined them at every turn. Tennant claims that moves to restructure tribal governments in order to deal more effectively with white government mark the earlier decade. Originally consolidating around tribally specific issues, such as those of the Nisga'a Land Committee, this initiative formed the basis for a temporarily more unified provincial political movement, in which O'Meara came to play a significant role. More important, the first Native students of English-language schools and European ways were emerging as "neo-traditional leaders," taking on the ways and even the dress of Europeans as strategies in their efforts to be taken more seriously by the two governments affecting their lives on a daily basis.[5] The efforts of organizations of Indian nations to resist the recommendations of the Royal Commission prevented their implementation for almost ten years following the report. However, a powerful adversary in the person of Duncan Campbell Scott, superintendent of Indian Affairs for the Dominion government, worked to see that Bills 13 and 14 were passed, ensuring that the recommendations could be implemented without the consent of the First Nations peoples themselves. The enforcement of the potlatch laws,[6] which made it increasingly difficult for the tribes to gather to discuss their affairs, was also the work of Superintendent Scott. It seems possible that the growing animosity of the Dominion government toward the claims of the Indians was related to the persistence and clarity with which O'Meara presented the evidence in support of these claims.

Early Life and the Law

O'Meara was born in Ontario in 1861 while his father, Frederick A. O'Meara, was a missionary for the Church of England on Manitoulin Island.[7] Arthur Eugene graduated from the University of Toronto in 1882 with a bachelor of arts degree.[8] Three years later he was called to the bar.[9] O'Meara then embarked upon a law career in Toronto, where he was associated with the firm Fox and Preece. His highest-profile case was one in which he represented The Lord's Day Alliance in an action that in 1903 went to the highest court in the empire, the Judicial Committee of the Privy Council.[10] Five years later, from another area of the country, he began an action to take a different case to this court. The issue of title to the lands of British Columbia had never been settled, and O'Meara devoted the last twenty years of his life to attempting to have this issue brought before the Judicial Committee of the Privy Council.

On 13 July 1887, when he was twenty-six years old, he married Marion Katie Greene, one year his senior, of Burlington, Ontario.[11] The ceremony was performed by the groom's father, the Reverend Frederick O'Meara, and the witnesses were the bride's two sisters and the groom's brother Thomas. The young couple lived in Toronto, where O'Meara continued his law practice and his close association with the church. In the early 1890s a daughter, Kathleen, was born, and about five years later a son, Robert, known in the family as Robin, completed the family.

In March 1906 Bishop Isaac Stringer was staying with Arthur's brother, Thomas O'Meara, in Toronto. He was there to appeal for more missionaries to come to his Diocese of Selkirk, later renamed the Yukon. After several long talks with Stringer, Arthur Eugene O'Meara volunteered to go to Selkirk.[12] On Tuesday, 27 March, Stringer wrote, "Spent evening talking with A.E. and Mrs. O'Meara re going out to Windy Arm work."[13] Two days later he wrote, "A.E. O'Meara to Weston with me. He decided to go to Selkirk and leave family behind for a time." One wonders about the discussions in the O'Meara family at this time. Whose idea was it to leave the family in Toronto? There were further discussions, and then on Sunday, 29 April 1906, Stringer wrote, "Ordination service at Trinity Church, Toronto. Canon Cody preached the sermon ... I ordained the following to Deacon's orders: Arthur Eugene O'Meara for Selkirk ... A.E. O'Meara read Gospel ... Dinner at Mr. O'Meara's." On Thursday, 10 May, Stringer had lunch at Eaton's with his wife and A.E. O'Meara. He left on the 11:30 p.m. train for the Yukon. By 29 May Stringer was on board the *Princess Beatrice* sailing from Vancouver for Skagway, the saltwater access to Selkirk, with, among others, A.E. O'Meara, Mrs. O'Meara, Robin, and Kathleen. The decision to have the family remain in Toronto had obviously been overturned. Thus began O'Meara's important association with western Canada.

Missionary in the Yukon

> On Sundays they hold regular morning and evening services,
> using hymns, chants and prayers in their own language taught
> them some years ago by the Russian Church. These are repeated
> by all the people standing, one person acting as leader. I
> attended these services and shall always retain a very vivid
> recollection of that worship of God in a strange unknown
> tongue, and of the reverent and earnest manner of the people.
> – A.E. O'Meara, in *The New Era,* December 1907[14]

The O'Meara family went to the mining town of Conrad on Windy Arm,
Tagish Lake, a train and boat ride from Whitehorse. The town was new
and rough, a combination of log houses and tents. Church services were
held in the tent reading room. O'Meara wrote of a trip that he made to
Teslin Lake to do missionary work. His positive attitudes, perhaps learned
as a young boy in his father's house, were obvious in his writing. The people whom he met were of the Tlingit Nation, originally from the coast of
Alaska, where they had come into contact with Christianity through the
Russian Church. "During part of the morning service they hold in their
hands lighted candles, symbolical, as I understand, of the light for which
they seek to guide them through the darkness. At the conclusion of each
native service, I spoke to the people through an interpreter."[15] O'Meara
discussed education for young people, and the people "expressed their
willingness to contribute towards the support of such a teacher."[16] He also
had lengthy discussions with a young man who spoke English and who
wished to become a minister. "It also appeared quite possible that he might
ultimately be able to translate the scriptures into the Klinkit [sic] language."[17] O'Meara had indeed learned well from his father, Rev. Frederick,
who "was instrumental in producing the first translation of the Bible and
the Prayer Book in the Ojibway Language."[18] Arthur Eugene was continuing to build on the foundation that would serve him in his later work for
the First Nations of British Columbia.

O'Meara made many trips to isolated miners and trappers and to various
Native villages, during which he spread the word of God and learned about
the needs of the people. Spiritual matters were not O'Meara's only concern. Soon after his arrival in the Yukon, Bishop Stringer appointed O'Meara
financial secretary for the diocese, a position that involved him in discussions concerning the administration of the diocese.

In October and November 1907, O'Meara was in Ontario, where he attended the meeting of the Board of the Missionary Society of the Church
of England in Canada (MSCC) and met with the deputy superintendent

general of Indian Affairs and the minister of the interior. This was a beginning of many years of meetings between O'Meara and members of these government departments. He wrote from Conrad to Bishop Stringer on 17 January 1908, saying that he was including a memo "re Indian matters presented by me to the Minister."[19] The memo itself deals with a variety of issues to do with both the church and the administration of the Yukon.[20]

> Many matters relating to the welfare of the Yukon Indians were the subject of prolonged interviews with the Deputy Superintendent General of Indian Affairs and also an interview with the Minister of the Interior. The Minister approved of setting aside reserves for the residence of the Indians at the various centres. The appointment of a Superintendent for the Yukon was urged and was favourably considered. Our request for the building and equipment of a new central school was also well received, and I hope that a sufficient appropriation for that purpose will be made at the present Session of Parliament. The carrying of this plan to completion may however be delayed until important questions regarding Indian Schools throughout Canada now under consideration have been settled.[21]

The memo concludes with a reference to another matter:

> Regarding law-enforcement and action taken to that end at Ottawa, much nonsense has appeared in the Press. The effort to secure enforcement in the Yukon of these provisions of the criminal law of Canada was initiated by Bishop Stringer and myself in interviews had with Col. White, Head of the R.N.W.M.P. [Royal North West Mounted Police], the Minister of the Interior, and the Deputy Minister of Justice at Ottawa in November 1906.[22] As a result of the effort thus commenced it became necessary in October last, to present the matter to the Prime Minister. In doing so I secured the co-operation not only of the Board of M.S.C.C. but also the Presbyterian, Methodist and Baptist Churches. The Presbyterian and Methodist Moral Reform Boards were already contemplating similar action.
>
> This interview with the Prime Minister was the first occasion upon which the great Protestant Christian forces of Canada were united for such a purpose and from such united action there has already resulted the formation of a Moral Reform Council for Canada.[23]

The law enforcement issue was referred to frequently in memos and letters at least until O'Meara left the Yukon. The need for a police presence to see that the laws of Canada were upheld was a concern of his that was not shared by all residents of the Yukon. The comments perhaps tell more about O'Meara's relationships with other people than they do about the issue itself. His dismissal of concerns expressed in the press as "much non-sense" presages his dismissal of statements by both Dominion and provincial governments during the long struggle in British Columbia. Bishop Stringer often attempted to help O'Meara in this difficult area. On 7 December 1907, Stringer wrote to O'Meara:

> Now this is my proposal – not a command or a request, but a suggestion if you think it wise, you can come on at once. Sometime in the early part of the New Year come down to Dawson and work for a few months at any rate on the Creeks [where the miners were prospecting for gold]. It would be to some extent, an unsettled life, but you would probably like it. I have considered the problem of your family etc. They of course could not come with you. Then it would be for you to decide whether they should remain in Conrad or make an extended visit to the outside. I cannot of course allow any travelling expenses for your family, on account of the precedent, but it is just possible that the difference in the cost of living during say six months stay on the outside might balance the travelling expenses ... If you think favorable of it you could come down on the stage, and of course your own travelling expenses would be paid. It would give you a good idea of this part of the country, and at the same time disarm some of the newspaper critisisms [sic] regarding your personal ignorance of Dawson affairs. I must send you some clippings regarding this.[24]

O'Meara agreed to go to Dawson and planned to be there by the end of January. The letters between the two men flowed regularly, and on 3 January Stringer wrote: "I note what the Whitehorse 'Star' has to say about you in its editorials. It is very unjust. I am not sure if it is worthwhile replying – except perhaps on general principles ... Certainly the morals of Dawson are wonderfully improved according to everyone's opinion – or at least according to the opinion of many here ... There are evils here yet but not so flagrant – partly no doubt because of the smaller population but partly I hope and believe because of better administration of the law."[25] The newspaper articles critical of O'Meara were noticed by others as well. On 17 February 1908, H.A. Cody wrote to Bishop Stringer, "It grieves me much to see the article in the 'Star' re O'Meara. I should have answered them long ago, but I consider it O'Meara's place to do so. He is the one attacked, and not only for his own sake, but for the Cause I feel some strong, clear answer should be made. O'Meara has splendid grounds for defense it seems to me."[26] This difficulty with the press and other people in the Yukon was to continue for some time to come. The animosity that O'Meara seemed to engender in other people was to plague him throughout his life. Despite cautions and warnings from Stringer, he seemed unable to prevent these strong adverse reactions.[27]

O'Meara prepared to leave for Dawson and asked that when he reached there he be ordained a priest. Despite concerns raised by Stringer, he entered into the Holy Order of Priests on 16 February 1908.[28]

First Nations Rights and the Legal Mind

> As an indirect result of my negotiations on behalf of the Yukon
> Indians I have now been requested on behalf of a large number
> of Indians of British Columbia to wait upon the Secretary of
> State for the Colonies and discuss with him the Indian land
> situation in the Province of British Columbia with a view to the
> intervention of the Imperial Government in securing a
> satisfactory adjustment of the claims of the Indians.
> – Letter from A.E. O'Meara to Rev. C.C. Owen
> of Vancouver, 11 March 1909[29]

From this point onward Rev. O'Meara's time was spent more on his interests on behalf of First Nations peoples and less on his ministry. His visits to government officials and senior members of the civil service became more frequent, and the time that he spent doing research in preparation must have been considerable. His dedication to and concern for the rights of First Nations peoples was not a new theme in O'Meara's life. It probably arose naturally from the work that he had seen his father do as a missionary and as a translator of the Bible and Prayer Book into the Ojibway language. On 28 January 1908, as he arrived in Dawson for his ordination and to satisfy the people of Dawson that he knew something of their needs, he wrote a letter to Dr. Alfred Thompson, member of Parliament for the Yukon.

Dear Dr Thompson;-

When I had the pleasure of meeting you in 1906, you expressed the opinion that the Government had not done all that should be done for the Yukon Indians.

It would be of great service if this view were now pressed upon the Minister of the Interior.

I asked Rev. Dr. Tucker to hand you copy of the memo which I recently presented to the Minister and I trust he did so. If not you could see copy of this memo in Mr. Pedley's office.

I enclose copy of a letter which on behalf of the Bishop of Yukon I am addressing to the Minister.

If our position, as stated in the memo and letter, should commend itself to you, will you kindly discuss the subject with the Minister and also give me your advice as to what further steps are desirable for securing the object sought.

Yours very truly.[30]

The memo addressed three issues. These were the setting aside of land for reserves at the various centres of population, the appointment of a superintendent for the Yukon, and the establishment of a new central school.

During 1908 Stringer and O'Meara moved about but kept up a busy correspondence. Although many of the issues discussed had to do with the affairs of running the diocese, there were also frequent exchanges to do with the needs and rights of the First Nations peoples. In May Stringer was in Toronto and wrote to O'Meara in Whitehorse. He had been to see Mr. Blake about funding for the "Indian School" that was needed. He also felt the need to caution O'Meara about leaving the Yukon: "I suppose you are planning to come out to Ottawa. Personally I still feel that it would be better if you could arrange the work to have it done without coming out this fall. I am more convinced of that, I think, since coming here. However, I do not wish to interfere with the arrangement already made unless you can see your way clear to deferring your visit until next year ... I suppose Archdeacon Canham and Mr. Cody will be out, but I have not heard from them since I arrived."[31] Stringer did not say what in Ontario had convinced him that O'Meara should stay in the Yukon. He also suggested, rather than ordered, that O'Meara stay. In another letter, dated 27 May 1908, he elaborated on his discussions with Mr. Oliver of the Department of Indian Affairs. Mr. Pedley had appointed Mr. Vowell, the superintendent of schools and Indian reserve commissioner for British Columbia, and Rev. Mr. Green, a BC Indian Agent, to study and report on Indian schools in the Yukon. He asked them "to visit Carcross as well as look into the situation at Atlin and Teslin Lake and to report." Stringer continued: "Again, Mr. Oliver has no desire to make treaty with the Indians. He thinks it would destroy their independence and perhaps tend to pauperize them if compensation as a regular thing were recognized. He would rather encourage them to make their living by hunting, fishing etc. I pointed out that the advent of the white man had injured their prospects as hunters etc."[32] O'Meara in his characteristic style circumvented Stringer's suggestion that he not come to Ontario and pursed his own course:

Realizing that the last paragraph of your letter of 11 May places upon me a heavy responsibility, I conferred with Mr. Hawksley who once more expressed strongly the opinion that my Eastern work should be carried through as planned, and also agreed with me in thinking desirable that before deciding I should confer with Archdeacon Canham as Commissary and secure his mind. We therefore arranged that I should carry out part of my travelling plans by visiting Little Salmon and Tantalus and should go on to Selkirk.

I went by steamer to Little Salmon, there I found about 40 Indians and secured valuable information. The rest of the journey was accomplished in a skin canoe bought from an Indian. My service at Tantalus was the first ever held there. I also visited Yukon Crossing and Minto, at both of which places useful information regarding Indians was obtained.

In conferring with Archdeacon Canham, we first fully considered the Eastern work which the Archdeacon was clearly and strongly of opinion that such work should be pushed through during the present year. As the most anxious reconsideration had only served to strengthen my own view there was but one conclusion to which we could come [word unclear] of that work. The Archdeacon subsequently informed me of the situation in Dawson, which we considered together from every point of view.

You will have been informed by the Archdeacon of his decision and action.

About several other matters I hope to write by steamer of 28th.[33]

Stringer replied from London, 22 July 1908, again in the gentle way that was lost on O'Meara:

I am sorry to think that the Archdeacon may have to go to Dawson instead of attending the General Synod, but I shall have to leave it to his own judgement. I hope, however, something may turn up to allow him to go ...

With reference to yourself, you say that Mr. Hawksley and the Archdeacon still advise your going to Ottawa. Of course, I value their opinions, though different from my own, and as I left the matter for you to decide after expressing my own opinion, I have nothing more to say. I was very much interested in your visit to Little Salmon and Tantulus.[34]

Stringer closed by sending his regards to Mrs. O'Meara, hoping that she had enjoyed her stay in Whitehorse, where she had been while O'Meara was pursuing his ministry along the gold-bearing creeks near Dawson. He also sent kind remembrances to Kathleen and Robin.

O'Meara now put most of his energy into what he called his eastern work. This work involved establishing the rights of the Native peoples to their lands and all that was in them. He spent a good deal of his time researching and on 1 December 1908 was able to write to Bishop Stringer a letter containing a very important result of that research. The information contained in this letter was the basis of the work that would occupy O'Meara until his death. His identification of the terms of the Royal Proclamation of 1763 and the fact that they were still valid were central to his contention regarding the rights of the Native peoples of the North American Northwest.

My dear Bishop,

The work on behalf of the Yukon Indians, which it is my privilege [sic] to have in hand, has grown to considerable proportions, and I have thought it convenient that in form of a letter I should lay before you the main points of the situations and the plans which I have made. As I think I mentioned to you I have recently secured important information regarding the rights of the Indians of British Columbia, the Yukon and a large part of McKenzie River and Athabasca. By a Royal Proclamation put forth in 1763 the whole of the far western and far northern territory was reserved for the use of the Indians, and so far as I can at present ascertain that Proclamation continues in force, and these Indians have never surrendered their rights. If the position can be thoroughly established, it seems to me to have a double bearing. It should greatly strengthen the claim for financial help, as even a very large expenditure would be only a part of the compensation to which the Indians are entitled. It seems also to form a strong answer to Mr. Blakes'[35] view that we are pauperizing the Indians. For on the contrary it would seem to me that we are giving them not charity, but only a partial measure of justice. It is a fact of much importance that the Dominion Government and that of British Columbia are at present arranging to submit to the Imperial Privy Council the whole question of the Indian title in British Columbia. I think that those in British Columbia who are interested in the Indians, and also the Special Indian Committee and the Advisory Board [of the MSCC] should certainly take up this matter and endeavour to secure that the Indian Department shall provide a Counsel who will specially represent the Indians upon the argument of the case. I am planning to take steps with this end in view.[36]

The significance of this statement cannot be overestimated. If O'Meara was correct in his assumption that the Royal Proclamation of 1763 was still in force, this would establish a basis in law for the land claims of the First Nations peoples. His suggestion that interested people in British Columbia and in the church should urge the Government of Canada to provide a lawyer to represent the interests of the First Nations peoples was a first step in establishing the status of the Proclamation. The work entailed in doing this excited O'Meara. From Victoria, on 6 January 1909, he wrote again to Stringer:

I enclose copy of a letter which I am addressing to the special Indian Committee [of the MSCC], a meeting of which may be held on the 15th inst., at Toronto. This letter which I am writing after conference with Archbishop Matheson, and with his approval, will indicate my view regarding the general Indian situation. As a result of the Synod's action I have been brought into a prominent position which I would certainly prefer not to occupy. Mr. Blake certainly shows a great tenacity in still advocating his 'new policy.' But I do not think he will be able to carry the committee with him. The matter of Indian title which I mentioned to you will also I think soon come to the front, and one of my present efforts is to secure some wise action in the direction of the representation of the interests of the Indians before the Judicial Committee of the Privy Council.[37]

O'Meara was also meeting with members of the Anglican Church who were working to establish a theological college in western Canada, and the Synod had asked him to engage in a fundraising trip to eastern Canada and England. He carried on his work as financial secretary of the Diocese of Yukon, sending stipends to the ministers and paying accounts by mail. In March he was in Toronto, and on 10 March he wrote to Stringer, enclosing a copy of Vowell and Green's report about Indian schools. He also sent copies to Archdeacon Canham and Messers Hawksley and Totty. Vowell and Green favoured, as did O'Meara and Stringer, residential schools where necessary and day schools where possible. On 11 March he wrote again to Stringer saying that he would be sailing to England on the Cunard liner leaving New York on 17 March. He was carrying with him what became known as the Cowichan Petition.

O'Meara also wrote letters to several friends telling them of his imminent trip to England. Typical of these letters is the one to Rev. C.C. Owen of Vancouver, quoted in part at the beginning of this section. The letter continues: "For 40 years these Indians have been in some respects treated most unjustly by the British Columbia Government, and this course of injustice has now reached a sort of crisis, which will require to be most carefully dealt with if serious trouble is to be avoided. In taking this first step towards reaching a settlement of the whole matter I have the advice and help of a leading Toronto Counsel, Mr. J.M. Clark, K.C., who has an expert knowledge of the whole matter of Indian title. All expenses are to be paid by the Indians themselves."[38] The petition that O'Meara was taking to England was a result of the Cowichan people's growing frustration with the injustice with which they were being treated, a frustration that O'Meara understood and hoped to mitigate with action from a higher authority. It seems likely that O'Meara and his fellow clergymen had discussed the affair when they met at the Synod meetings, and as a result O'Meara was asked to take the petition with him on his trip.

On the same day, 11 March 1909, O'Meara also wrote to Rev. H.A. Cody in Whitehorse saying that he was "about to leave for England upon a mission of considerable importance." He would interview the secretary of state for the colonies "with a view to securing some satisfactory adjustments of the claims" of the Indians of British Columbia at the "request and expense of the Indians themselves ... Those Indians have for 40 years been treated in some respects most unjustly by the Government of British Columbia."[39] As his trip had initially been suggested in order to raise funds for the theological college, it seems a bit unfair to travel at the expense of the First Nations peoples. However, it must have made good sense to Financial Secretary O'Meara, who was always looking for ways to cover costs. However, much more important, it establishes the fact that O'Meara was acting for the First Nations peoples. He followed their instructions and was paid by them for his work. It is interesting to note that O'Meara was apparently never called to the bar in British Columbia.[40] Over the years he supplied information and advocated for the First Nations of BC, but he did not represent them in court. Several years later, in answer to a question about the Cowichan Petition,[41] O'Meara answered: "I am in a position to state the main facts relating to the Cowichan Petition. That is the Petition which in the spring of 1909, at the request of the Cowichan Indians, I took to England, and presented to His late Majesty and the then Secretary of State for the Colonies. The request was conveyed to me by means of a telegram from Mr. C.M. Tate, who is the Secretary of the Indian Rights Association."[42] While in Toronto O'Meara had an interview with the Hon. Frank Oliver, superintendent general of Indian Affairs, to protest an application by BC Packers for foreshore rights in front of the reserves and Church Missionary Society property in Alert Bay. Mr. Oliver suggested that O'Meara write a letter stating his concerns, which O'Meara did:

> Upon the occasion of our interview, you suggested the question whether the Indians have any rights in respect of the foreshore in front of a Reserve, and you stated you were inclined to think they had no such rights. With regard to this matter I may be permitted to point out that the Indians of British Columbia have always claimed and continue to claim that they are entitled to a beneficial interest in all the lands of the Province, with the exception of some small portions lying principally at the southerly end of Vancouver Island, their title to which had been surrendered before British Columbia entered Confederation.
>
> You are no doubt aware that from a time long prior to that at which British Columbia became part of the Dominion, no treaty had been made with any of the British Columbia Indians.[43]

On the following day, 13 March 1909, he wrote happily to Stringer from Ottawa: "Have made great progress in Indian title plans. Today had conference with Governor General's Secretary, who assures me Governor General will give letter introducing me to Secretary of State for Colonies. For this purpose he is to arrange interview with Governor General for Tuesday next, and I intend going to New York via Ottawa, having sufficient time there to see Governor General."[44] Stringer himself was not quite so happy. In response to O'Meara's letter of two days earlier, Stringer replied:

I note what you say regarding your proposed trip to England. Though I do not approve of your going I do not wish, since you have decided to go, to put anything in the way of the successful issue of the different questions you have referred to. In the first place, after deciding to go to England it appears to me that you will find it a mistake to make your stay there so short. I do not know how you are going to get through with the work planned in two weeks' time. You had better count on a longer stay. It appears that you are hurrying back to attend the M.S.C.C. Board meeting in April. Had you better not leave those questions that you wish attended to in other hands? In many ways I think it will be to the interest of our work if you are not present at the Board meeting. Two weeks longer in England would mean much more effective work there.[45]

O'Meara apparently took his bishop's advice and stayed longer in England. The suggestion that matters would go more smoothly in O'Meara's absence may have helped influence him. On 23 March O'Meara wrote to the bishop and enclosed a copy of a memo about Indian marriage. In April 1909 he met with the Aborigines Protection Society in London. Their purpose was to "help the Indians when occasion might require. The opinion was then expressed that it would be very desirable to form in Far-Western Canada a committee for co-operation with that Society, the scope of whose work is Imperial."[46] As a result of this suggestion, when O'Meara returned to British Columbia, he spearheaded the formation of the group the Friends of the Indians, largely made up of Anglican clergy. O'Meara also presented the Cowichan Petition to His Majesty and the Colonial Office.[47] As with the petition of 1906 presented to the king by Joe Capilano (Squamish), Charlie Tsilpaymilt (Cowichan), and Basil David (Bonaparte), three chiefs from British Columbia, no direct action was taken. The Imperial government requested that a statement be sent from the Dominion government regarding the petition of the Indians. This appears not to have happened despite repeated attempts by O'Meara and others over the next several years to obtain such a statement.

O'Meara returned to North America aboard the *S.S. Mauretania,* which docked at New York City on 27 April 1909. He was greeted by a letter from Stringer cryptically referring to the issue of the discontent in Dawson, which had apparently not subsided in the year since O'Meara's ordination:

You will see a copy of letter written by Mr. Aylesworth to Mr. Shearer. Canon Inglis has a copy. It is strange that five Dawson ministers should write as they have done. I imagine there is simply a sort of re-action against what they consider extreme statements made by yourself and Dr. Pringle. Of course, this is only my supposition but it seems to indicate that in the opinion of Dawson people, your action is not approved, at any rate so far as the reports that reached Dawson are concerned. I do not wish to tie your hands but I do beg of you to be a little more careful.[48]

O'Meara went directly to Ottawa, where he presented the Cowichan Petition to the governor general.[49] He was quick to get back to Canadian affairs and was able to report to Stringer on 1 May 1909: "Regarding the Alert Bay Reserves, I have just received a letter from the Indian Department indicating an attitude decidedly more favorable than Mr. Oliver's seemed to be at the time of my interview. I mentioned this especially as you may see Mr. Hall or some one else at Alert Bay. You may safely say that the Indian Department seems now to be alive to the necessity of watching this application and protecting the interests of the Indians."[50]

O'Meara returned to the Yukon but remained actively involved in the work for the Native peoples of British Columbia. In early September, while in Skagway en route from the Yukon to Victoria, he made notes for a letter to Stringer. "With the approval of Archdeacon Canham I am continuing for a time my outside work in particular that on behalf of the Indians of B.C. in connection with which there have been very important and encouraging developments."[51] From Victoria, on the 23 September, reunited with his typewriter, he wrote a long report to Stringer concerning many Yukon matters. He introduced the letter by saying, "After the meeting of Indians and their advisers to be held on the 29 instant, when I shall know more definitely what they want me to do, I shall write you fully about these plans."[52] Representatives of the tribes of the coast, including Sechelt, Squamish, and Vancouver Island, met in Vancouver on 29 September 1909. Their final statement endorsed the action taken by the Cowichan in having their petition presented to His Majesty and the secretary of state for the colonies and the request that the matter be brought directly to the Judicial Committee of the Privy Council. They said, "The title which we are asserting was recognized and guaranteed by the proclamation issued by King George the Third in 1763, and was subsequently recognized both by the Parliament of Great Britain and by the legislature of the Colony of Vancouver Island, but has been ignored and denied by the government of the Province of British Columbia."[53] The petition asked that the Dominion government facilitate the request to forward their claims, and they appealed to "every tribe of Indians throughout the province to avoid all resort to force and violence in the assertion of their rights" and to "press forward unitedly and harmoniously." The petition had twenty-nine signatories, including Mrs. S. Cook of Alert Bay, the only woman among them, Peter Kelly of Skidegate, A.N. Calder of Nass River, and W.J. Lincoln of Nass River.

After the meeting O'Meara again wrote to Stringer from Victoria. He continued his account of affairs in the Yukon: "Was able at Dawson to pretty well reach the bottom of situation regarding law enforcement. Remembering your wishes used all possible caution. Letter of five ministers can be proved to have no reasonable foundation. Securing of it was undoubtedly a political device. Secured official evidence showing there had been no real attempt to fully enforce the law. Have reported to Moral Reform Council, and hope that very soon no further special responsibility will rest upon me. My most earnest effort is directed to this end."[54] He enclosed a clipping from the *Colonist,* a Victoria newspaper, about the Vancouver meeting. "In connection with this work I am about to leave on a trip to Toronto and Ottawa." On 6 October 1909, he was on the train near Revelstoke, making notes for a letter to Stringer, "It was unanimously desired by the Indians that I should continue to take an active part in the efforts being made on their behalf ... One object of this trip is to confer with M. Clark regarding plans for future actions."[55] Shortly thereafter, O'Meara decided that his outside work would take all of his time and that he would need to leave the Diocese of Yukon.

On 4 January 1910, a meeting was held in Victoria of Christian missionaries of various denominations to discuss issues "brought to the front by the Indian Movement in British Columbia."[56] This was the first meeting of the group called the Friends of the Indians, formed as the result of a suggestion from the Aborigines Protection Society of London to O'Meara on his visit there the previous March. O'Meara addressed the gathering of six clergy "regarding the Indian land situation in British Columbia and the Yukon, and progress that had been made in dealing with that situation."[57] It was decided that the group would ask the bishop of Yukon to allow O'Meara to continue his work. To this end, on 7 January O'Meara, after drawing up a new will leaving everything to his wife Marion Katie,[58] left on the *Princess May* to return to Carcross and meet with the bishop. The two men worked together to settle the financial affairs of the diocese so that there could be an orderly transfer. Extracts from Stringer's diary give an idea of the work:

> Sat Feb 12, 1910
> Worked most of the day at my accounts – travelling expenses etc. Dinner at school. Mr. Young, Mr. O'Meara and I in woods cutting wood in afternoon ...
> Wed Feb 23. 1910
> Spent most of the day writing letters and consulting with Mr. O'Meara. Decided to go with him to Skagway tomorrow ...
> Thur Feb 24
> Mr. O'Meara and I got ready and left on 10:25 train for Skagway. His side caused him a good deal of pain ... Dr. Leslie [?] found Mr. O'Meara had a rib broken and bandaged his side with adhesive plaster mobilizing [sic] it ... Talk with Mr. O'Meara re his future work. Took a bath.[59]

Mrs. Stringer was about to come to the Yukon with their children, including a new baby. She had hoped that her husband could come to travel with her. He replied that as he and O'Meara had both been much away, he could not do that, but he was sure that people along the way would help her with the children. In Skagway he decided to ride south on the boat with O'Meara so that they could continue their work, he could help O'Meara, who was in considerable pain, and he could perhaps meet his family at the train. O'Meara returned to Victoria, and Stringer happily greeted his wife and children in Vancouver. They sailed north on the *Princess May,* and Stringer found time to write several letters to O'Meara. He writes of business and family matters: "They are all well and we had a busy time shopping and getting ready to leave last night. I enclose my signature for Robin's collection of autographs. Tell him it is not of much account as an autograph and if he wants a real curiosity in the way of autographs he should be sure to get his father's signature."[60] Two days later he wrote again just before the boat reached Skagway. The letter contained more business discussions, hopes that O'Meara's rib was mending, and thoughts about O'Meara's future now that he would no longer be serving the church in the Yukon. Stringer concluded:

I feel strongly on the point we discussed the other day with regard to your taking up secular rather than ministerial work. You can easily return to your legal practice and work of that character is what I think your qualifications fit you to take up. I do not consider that you are fitted for the work of the ministry partly, perhaps, because of your training in other directions but chiefly I think because of personal characteristics. It would be unfair to you and I think it would be unkind of me as a friend if I did not tell you frankly my opinion. In my judgment you would be making a great mistake if you continued in the work of the ministry. I consider that you would be acting wisely if you took up secular work again as soon as convenient, giving up the wearing of clerical dress as I think that you would find it more satisfactory all around. I do not hesitate to say that it was a mistake for me to have ordained you. A certain responsibility rests on me for having done so and on that account if for no other reason, I feel it my duty to tell you plainly my honest opinion. This conclusion is not affected by any complications that may have arisen in connection with your work in Yukon. Judged on the basis simply of your fitness and suitibilaty [sic], I consider that you are not adapted for the work of the ministry and I think it would be a great mistake for you to continue in that work. I hope you will forgive my speaking plainly on this question. I do it simply because I consider it my duty.

Wishing you every blessing and prosperity in your future work I remain yours faithfully Isaac O. Stringer, Bishop of Yukon.[61]

This blunt talk did not seem to damage the friendship between the two men. They continued to write frequently, discussing matters of their families and their work as well as concerns regarding the transfer of accounting for the benefit of a new financial secretary for the diocese. This seemed to take a great deal of time, and by the summer Stringer was sounding politely frustrated. It is not difficult to imagine O'Meara finally taking all the papers that he could lay hands on, including his new will, and turning them over to Mr. Sampson, the accountant who was later to leave his practice to the Genns, father and son. Despite the suggestion that O'Meara not continue in the ministry, he asked for and received a transfer from Stringer to the Diocese of Victoria.[62]

Friends of the Indians

> The subsequent proclamation of His Majesty King George the
> Third issued in 1763, furnished them (the Indians) with a fresh
> guarantee for the possession of their hunting grounds and the
> protection of the Crown. This document the Indians look upon
> as their Charter. They have preserved a copy of it till the present
> time and have referred to it on several occasions in their
> representations to the government.
> – The Indian Commissioners appointed by the
> Government of Canada in 1844[63]

As stated earlier, the Friends of the Indians was formed at the suggestion of members of the Aborigines Protection Society with whom O'Meara had spoken on his trip to England in 1909. The second "Informal Conference of Friends of the Indians" was held in Victoria on 28 March 1910. To a slightly larger audience than had been at the first meeting on 4 January 1910, O'Meara read a letter from lawyer J.M. Clark of Toronto and "reported an interview with Tom James, Indian, of Victoria." Then F.C. Wade, KC, made a concise statement of the condition of affairs regarding the Indian lands of British Columbia.[64] The conference moved that as they knew that the governments of British Columbia and Canada were meeting to draw up a list of questions to be referred to the Supreme Court of Canada concerning Indian title to lands in the province and the duties of the two governments concerning these matters, "the Indian tribes of the Province, as wards of the nation, should be separately represented upon any such reference to the very fullest extent."[65] They also set up a committee to find means of supporting O'Meara in his work. O'Meara then spoke at length about the history of Indian title. He gave a similar talk to a larger audience at Aberdeen School in Vancouver a few weeks later. He referred to the Proclamation of 1763, which stated that unless lands have "been ceded to or purchased by the Sovereign of Great Britain they are to be considered as reserved for the Indians."[66] This Proclamation was cited by the "Indian Commissioners appointed by the Government of Canada in the year 1844, while Indian affairs were still under the direction of the Imperial Government."[67] O'Meara traced the history of the question of Indian title through the Imperial statutes of 1803, 1821, and 1849 and the Douglas Treaties to the 1861 request from the Legislative Assembly of the Colony of Vancouver Island that the Imperial government "provide funds for extinguishing 'the Indian title' to the remaining lands of the Island."[68] The Imperial government refused on the grounds that the money should properly come from the colony, not from the British taxpayer. As the colony had no money, Douglas was unable to make any more treaties. Upon the founding of the United Colony of British Columbia in 1866, the policy of recognizing Indian title to the land was discontinued. According to O'Meara in January 1870 the government of the colony specifically denied title: "But the title of the Indians in the fee of the public lands, or any portion thereof, has never been acknowledged by Government, but, on the contrary, is distinctly denied. In no case has any special agreement been made with any of the tribes of the mainland for the extinction of their claims of possession: but these claims have been held to have been fully satisfied by securing to each tribe, as the progress of the country seemed to require, the use of sufficient tracts of land for their wants for agriculture and pastoral purposes."[69] O'Meara pointed out that under Article 13 of the Terms of Union, charge of the Indians and the trusteeship and management of the lands reserved for their use and benefit were to be assumed by the Dominion government. The province was to transfer such lands as were needed, and in the event of a dispute between the two governments, the issue was to be settled by the secretary of state for the colonies. "As the Indians were not parties to this arrangement, the provisions made by it could not, of course, affect their title."[70] This point was underlined by Lord Dufferin, governor general of Canada, who on 20 September 1876 said, "Most unfortunately as I think there has been an initial error, ever since Sir James Douglas quitted office, in the Government of British Columbia neglecting to recognize what is known as Indian title."[71] O'Meara continued his tracing of events leading to the current time:

> From time to time, efforts have been made by the Indians themselves to obtain what they consider justice. A very notable example of this is that in the year 1906 three Indian chiefs, taking with them an interpreter, made a journey from British Columbia to London, England, and had a short interview with His Majesty the King. They spoke to him and everything was very pleasant; but the interview accomplished nothing. The chiefs did not even present any written document showing what their claims

were.[72] Having spent a large amount of money, they started back again to British Columbia.

The next event of considerable importance is what was done by the British Columbia Government in the fall of the year 1908. At that time the Provincial Government submitted to the Supreme Court of BC eight questions relating to the Indian reserves.[73]

The only rights to be considered in these questions were the rights of the two governments. The rights of the First Nations were not considered at all. Finishing with a report of the petition that he had carried to the king in the spring of 1909 for the Cowichan people, O'Meara emphasized the need for a settlement of the claims if security for all was to be achieved.

The Work for Justice in British Columbia

> Mr. O'Meara will handle Nishga Petition whether in Canadian
> Court or Privy Council. Already he has secured, both in Canada
> and in England, much information and advice bearing upon the
> selecting of one or more additional counsel. When the proper
> time arrives he will advise and we will decide ... W.J. Lincoln.
> – Resolution passed by the Nisga'a at Kincolith
> on 22 January 1913 and read to Mr. D.C. Scott,
> Ottawa, February 1915

The formation of the Friends of the Indians, led by O'Meara and mostly made up of non-Native clergy, did not take place in a vacuum. In 1907 the Nisga'a Land Committee had been formed. As Tennant wrote in 1999, "The formation of the committee was apparently the first instance among British Columbia Indians of a planned political restructuring for the purpose of achieving greater effectiveness in dealing with the white political system."[74] The Nisga'a Land Committee members met with people along the coast and discussed common concerns. By August 1909 a meeting in Vancouver of representatives of coastal and mainland people endorsed the Cowichan Petition, asking permission to present their case directly to the Judicial Committee of the Imperial Privy Council. In December 1909 a large assembly was held in Victoria at which The Indian Rights Association was formed.[75] This organization took a very active role in pressing for recognition of First Nations' rights until it was dissolved at a conference in North Vancouver in June 1916 when the Allied Tribes of British Columbia was formed.

In January 1910 the Indian tribes placed a "Statement of Facts and Claims" in the hands of the Department of Justice in an effort to have the Canadian government facilitate the request of the 1909 petition that the claims be decided by the Imperial Privy Council. The Department of Justice decided that the claims should be tested by the Supreme Court of Canada, but the questions to be asked of the court concerning "Indian title" were objected to by the British Columbia government. In August 1910 the Friends of the Indians presented a memorial to the prime minister stating their concerns about this. On 23 September of that year the Moral and Social Reform Council of Canada, which O'Meara had helped form in 1907, "expressed sympathy with the aims of the Conference of the Friends of the Indians of B.C."[76] in seeking a rapid and advantageous solution to the problems, and in October the two groups met with the prime minister, the superintendent general of Indian Affairs, and the deputy minister of justice, who suggested that they meet with the premier of British Columbia. This they did on 14 December 1910. Letters back and forth acknowledged the meetings. In early March 1911 ninety-six delegates representing a large number of the "tribes of British Columbia" met in Victoria, and on 3 March they all met with McBride's government representatives and presented their "Statement of Claims." On 26 April a delegation representing the Friends of the Indians and the Moral and Social Reform Council of Canada again met with Prime Minister Laurier, the superintendent general of Indian Affairs, and this time the minister of justice. They asked that a report of the meetings be sent to the Imperial government together with supporting documents and a request that the king and the Colonial Office consider the matter and act as they "deemed wise." The delegation also requested that the Government of Canada send a report regarding the Cowichan Petition, as requested by the Imperial government one year before. This support had been promised the First Nations peoples by Laurier himself on his visit to the province in 1910. A summary of this year's work was presented by O'Meara on behalf of the Friends of the Indians to the Special Joint Committee in 1927.[77] Apparently, the Imperial government was equally anxious for a settlement. On 6 July 1911 Mr. Harcourt, secretary of state for the colonies, issued a statement to both the federal and provincial governments referring to Indian land claims as this "troublesome question."[78]

In the general election of 1911 Laurier was defeated, and Robert Borden became prime minister of Canada. His Conservative government brought "with them an outlook on Indian matters welcomed by Richard McBride and his provincial Conservatives."[79] Borden appointed J.A.J. McKenna special commissioner of Indian Affairs. His responsibility, with McBride, was to "'settle all differences between the Governments of the Dominion and the Province respecting Indian lands and Indian Affairs' and to provide 'a final adjustment of all matters relating to Indian Affairs in the Province.'"[80] With this agreement signed in September 1912, what became known as the McKenna-McBride Commission began preparations for holding hearings throughout the province.

These events were watched by all concerned, and on 15 November 1912 O'Meara wrote from Ottawa to Hon. Dr. Roche of the Department of the Interior asking for the terms of the discussion in progress between the Governments of Canada and British Columbia. He wanted to know how soon the Government of Canada "will communicate with us the contents of Mr. McKenna's report and discuss with us such matters arising from that report and our Memorial as it may be found necessary to discuss ... so that I may be enabled to act intelligently under these circumstances, and in view of the general meeting of the Indians of British Columbia which it is proposed to hold at an early date."[81] On 4 December Frank Pedley, deputy superintendent general, sent a copy of the Order-in-Council, report, and agreement of terms.[82]

In January 1913 O'Meara was present[83] when the Nisga'a[84] met at Kincolith and prepared a statement in which they claimed Aboriginal rights to the land that they had occupied "from time immemorial," the fisheries, the hunting, and other natural resources. They stated that these rights had been guaranteed by the Proclamation of 1763: "For more than twenty-five years, being convinced that the recognition of our aboriginal rights would be of very great material advantage to us and would open the ways for the intellectual, social and industrial advance of our people, we have, in common with other Tribes of British Columbia, actively pressed our claims upon the Governments concerned."[85] Copies of this statement were circulated to, among others, Mr. J.M. Clark, KC, counsel for the Indian Rights Association. This statement was followed by a petition to His Majesty's Privy Council, which was lodged on 21 May 1913. The petition made reference to the agreement of September 1912 establishing the McKenna-McBride Commission and stated that the commission's terms did not include Aboriginal title. In stating clearly that the terms of the McKenna-McBride Commission did not overlap with the concerns expressed in the petition, O'Meara was attempting to avoid having the presentation of the petition to the Privy Council delayed until the commission had made its report.

On 11 March 1914 Duncan Campbell Scott, deputy superintendent general of Indian Affairs, replied. He said that there were two problems with the petition: first, the refusal of the British Columbia government to consent to a case that would include any reference to Indian title and, second, the uncertainty as to the extent of compensation that might be demanded if the petition were successful. Scott suggested that the claim be referred to the Exchequer Court, with right of appeal to the Privy Council. In a letter to O'Meara, the Hon. Dr. W.J. Roche, minister of the interior, confirmed that the term "Privy Council" was intended to mean the Imperial Privy Council.[86] The letter from O'Meara asking for this clarification was another of O'Meara's attempts to anticipate delaying actions on the part of the government. The conditions of acceptance of Scott's suggested route to the Imperial Privy Council were included in the subsequent Order-in-Council of 20 June 1914. There were four conditions. The first was that the Indians accept the findings of the court and take what was offered them for extinguishment of their title. The second was recognition that the Government of British Columbia had fulfilled its obligations by giving land for the reserves and that further costs should be borne by the Government of Canada. The third seemed aimed directly at O'Meara: it said, "Indians shall be represented by counsel nominated and paid by the Dominion." The final condition was that if the court decided that the "Indians" had no title, the Dominion would do what was best for them.

Naturally, the Nisga'a wanted to discuss these terms and in February 1915 met in Ottawa with Charles Doherty, minister of justice, and Hon. Dr. W.J. Roche, minister of the interior. Mr. Lincoln, chairman of the deputation, opened the discussion by saying that the Nisga'a were pleased to see a reaction from the government but that they could not accept its terms. The main reasons were that they could not agree in advance to the findings of the Royal Commission of McKenna-McBride; that they did not want their appeal to the Privy Council attached to a document stating that their claims were "fancies," as Scott said in his preamble; and that they wished to choose their own counsel. Two days of frustrating talks followed, during which O'Meara said very little. The Nisga'a were told frequently that issues they wished to discuss were not the mandate of those present: the Department of Fisheries should address concerns about fishing rights, and the Province of British Columbia should address concerns about land preemption.[87] These talks were followed by talks with Mr. Scott, who asked for information regarding the choice of counsel. A resolution passed at the Kincolith meeting in January was produced:

We desired that Mr. O'Meara, who has full authority to handle the case of the Nishga Nation, should consult with Mr. Clark, as counsel for the Indian Rights Association of British Columbia so that we might act in harmony with the plans of the Association. We regret that Mr. C.M. Tate should have taken action interfering with this course.

We authorize Mr. O'Meara to secure on our behalf the advice of Mr. Clark or any other counsel as he may decide to be necessary.

We also authorize Messers. Fox and Preece, of London, England, to act as our agents and on our behalf to present a petition to His Majesty's Privy Council.

That still stands and the people desire it should stand to the end. The two are quite distinct – Nishgas and Indian Rights Association. Mr. O'Meara will handle Nishga Petition whether in Canadian Court or Privy Council. Already he has secured, both in Canada and in England, much information and advice bearing upon the selecting of one or more additional counsel. When the proper time arrives he will advise and we will decide ... W.J. Lincoln.[88]

Two days later, on 17 February 1915, a meeting was held with the Hon. Dr. Roche. Present were Mr. Scott, the Nisga'a delegates, and O'Meara, as well as Rev. Dr. Tucker and Rev. Dr. Moore, who were speaking as members of the Social Services Council of Canada. The meeting began with a memo for Hon. Dr. Roche submitted by Mr. Lincoln. It concerned the expenses incurred by and on behalf of "all the Tribes in the Province": "The 'Friends of the Indians' have expended upwards of $17,500. We ourselves have expended upwards of $5,000. Our counsel, Mr. O'Meara, who for nearly four years has been our chief adviser, and has acted as our Counsel in the matter of our Petition which is before the Privy Council, has given us legal services which, if given in a professional way, would have cost many thousands of dollars, without making any charge whatever, and in addition in order to help us through has advanced out of his own pocket towards expenses, upwards of $2,500."[89] The memo said that the Friends of the Indians did not intend to ask for any money, but the Nisga'a knew that $5,000 was set aside by Parliament for legal and other costs each year. They asked that the money advanced by O'Meara be paid immediately and the balance be made available for future expenses. Dr. Tucker thought that the matter should be settled in a way that satisfied the "Indians" and could "be looked upon as creditable to the people of Canada." He added that "he would like to bear his personal testimony to the vast amount of work that Mr. O'Meara had done in connection with this question, both in England and in Canada and the vast amount of information he had acquired regarding it. For years past his whole time and thought had been given without stint to the subject."[90] A statement from the Indian Affairs Committee of the Social Service Council of Canada concurred and asked that the $2,500 be repaid to O'Meara.[91] As an example of expenses incurred, O'Meara pointed to the current Spences Bridge meeting proposed by James Teit to explain the Nisga'a Petition to the interior tribes. O'Meara continued, "Mr. Teit is one of the best friends of the Indians of British Columbia. Also probably no other man to be found in the province has a better knowledge of their mind, or is better able to advise them well. In common with myself, he has set before him as the object to be aimed at, an equitable solution of the land question."[92] The minister replied that the appropriation of funds was no longer in operation and that if it were reinstated, it would be difficult to pay expenses incurred without its prior approval.

Word came from the Spences Bridge meeting that the interior tribes were in agreement with the Nisga'a Petition. Mr. Woods, the Nisga'a interpreter, added that the Nisga'a were in agreement now but had not always been:

"I want to tell you that it was not always smooth sailing, there are a number of hotheads in that Tribe that have wanted to take drastic action in keeping the whites out of the Naas Valley, but, through the efforts of the Nishga Land Committee, and especially Mr. O'Meara, since he undertook to advise the Nishgas, these hotheads have been persuaded not to cause any trouble."[93]

The ministers recommended that the terms of the Order-in-Council not be modified. The Committee of the Privy Council concurred.

The Cause and The Man

> Sir: It is in my view unnecessary to correct the narrative of your letter of the 26th ultimo, because except for two points it is immaterial to any question under consideration. The government has no power to refer directly to the Judicial Committee of the Privy Council. If there is any way to convince you of this please consider those words to be included in this letter.
>
> – Letter from Minister of Justice Charles Doherty
> to A.E. O'Meara, 14 November 1914[94]

While O'Meara was travelling the province and crossing the continent, his family was living on Cadboro Bay Road in Victoria, where they had been since soon after their arrival in the city in 1909. Once he had given up his position with the Diocese of Yukon, O'Meara's stipend was, of course, gone. The fact that he not only was receiving very little, if any, money for the work that he was doing but also was contributing his own funds to the cause must have meant straitened circumstances for the family. His son reported that "during the summers of 1913 and 1914, he had gone among the Nishga on the Nass River, carrying a portable typewriter, attending meetings, and acquainting himself with people."[95] His frequent letters to government officials, church officials, and other interested parties show that he travelled frequently, staying in hotels and working to press his point that the legal claim to the lands of the province by the First Nations peoples had not been given proper consideration. While he was doubtless propelled by the excitement of being involved in such a fundamental issue in the beginning, this cannot explain his continued insistence that the claim must go forward.

O'Meara was devoting his life to the issue. His belief that the First Nations peoples had been treated "most unjustly by the British Columbia Government" for more than forty years led to his asking to be relieved of his post with the Anglican Church in the Yukon. He did not separate himself from the church but used it, and his new, less structured position within it, to pursue justice for the people. As he had when he left his law practice in Toronto to become a missionary in the Yukon, he now left the Yukon to pursue justice for the First Nations peoples of British Columbia. These apparently sudden changes of direction in his life can be seen as really variations on a theme. In his childhood he saw his father work within the church to help the First Nations peoples, in his Toronto law practice he helped members of the Lord's Day Alliance maintain their point of view, in the Yukon he worked for education for First Nations children, and in British Columbia he expanded this help to include land claims. He spent his life working to help people receive justice. His single-mindedness and determination to follow his course no matter what the consequences made life difficult for his family and made O'Meara unsuited for life under the discipline of the church. Bishop Stringer was aware of this when he confessed that he should not have ordained O'Meara. The single-mindedness also led to his inability to work with elected officials and civil servants in search of any alternative route to his goal. However, this same determination enabled him to stay with the issue of land claims over many years despite a shortage of money, many rebuffs by members of government, and no concrete signs of progress. He had said in 1909 that "those [British Columbia] Indians have for 40 years been treated in some respects most unjustly by the Government of British Columbia."[96] In 1915 he said that the object of discussions with ministry officials in Ottawa was an equitable solution to the land question. He was compelled by a sense of fair play to set right this injustice, this inequity.

O'Meara was probably gaining some of his information from *British Columbia Papers Connected with the Indian Land Question, 1850-1875,* a collection of treaties, letters, and reports published by the government.[97] These papers demonstrate much stalling and lack of goodwill on the part of the provincial government in its dealings with the Dominion government over the setting up and registration of reserves. An example is a request from the superintendent of Indian Affairs to the chief commissioner of lands and works for field notes of surveyors in order to define boundaries of reserves. The reply was that staff were too busy to provide these, but the chief commissioner would "be happy to place a desk in the office at the disposal of any gentleman you may authorize to take copies of the said field notes."[98] O'Meara undoubtedly understood that attitudes had not changed and that the only way to see wrongs righted was to persist. This persistence, combined no doubt with his ability to upset people, as shown by his difficulties with the people of Yukon, and given that there was no Stringer to attempt damage control and urge caution, resulted in O'Meara's words receiving little of the respect that they deserved from people in the government and the civil service. Despite strong letters telling him that he did not have a case, O'Meara persisted. On 14 November 1914 the minister of justice, Charles Doherty, wrote in response to a letter from O'Meara that it was unnecessary to correct his narrative because except for two points it was immaterial to any question under consideration. The point was that the government had no power to refer directly to the Judicial Committee of the Privy Council. Doherty concluded, "If there is any way to convince you of this please consider those words to be included in this letter."[99] In December 1918, Almeric Fitzroy, Clerk of the Privy Council, wrote to the Nisga'a care of Messers Smith, Fox, and Sedgwick of London to tell them what steps were available to them to litigate the matter in a Canadian court and then appeal to the Privy Council. In a letter of 17 March 1920, the governor general's secretary wrote to O'Meara quoting the Fitzroy letter as saying that no action on the part of the Privy Council was required. He continued: "You have already been informed on several occasions of the attitude of the Dominion Government towards this claim and there does not appear to be anything further for me to add except that the Governor General takes no action, nor does he desire to take any action, except upon the advice of his constitutional advisers. Under these circumstances, I must ask you to consider this letter as final."[100] Of course, O'Meara did not consider anything "as final." He persisted because he was hired to by the Nisga'a and because he knew that the cause was just. However, this persistence, or dedication, did little to endear him to the civil servants in Ottawa or to their superiors.

The Allied Tribes and the Special Joint Committee Inquiry

> We do not belong to Mr. O'Meara. We have engaged Mr. O'Meara
> as legal adviser, and, as I said to the Minister of the Interior in
> Vancouver, I think in the year 1922, he agitates just insofar as we
> allow him to agitate, just as any legal adviser.
> – Peter Kelly, speaking at the Special Joint
> Committee hearings[101]

The Allied Tribes, which had been set up at the North Vancouver meeting in June of 1916, continued the work of their predecessors, notably the Indian Rights Association, to press for justice. In September 1916 they received assurances, conveyed through the governor general, the Duke of Connaught, from His Majesty that the Imperial Privy Council would consider the Nisga'a Petition once the McKenna-McBride Commission had made its report. Since the terms of this commission were very clearly limited to a discussion of reserve sizes, the larger question of Indian title would not be addressed. The Allied Tribes were concerned with this larger question. In February 1919 O'Meara and J.A. Teit presented a petition to Premier Oliver on behalf of the Allied Tribes. They asked that the government not take action on the recommendations of the Royal Commission until they had heard from the Privy Council. This meeting was reported in the local newspaper.[102] A few days later the chief inspector of Indian agencies sent a copy of the newspaper report to D.C. Scott and further reported that the provincial government seemed about to take action:

> The Minister of Lands has written letters to the various members of the Legislature asking their opinions as to how their constituencies will be affected in the event of the report being adopted in view of the fact that a number of new reserves have been allotted. Accompanying the letter of the Minister is a map on which it is shown the new reserves, the reserves which have been confirmed and also the cut-offs. It is apparent that the Government is looking at this matter more from its political aspect than that of carrying out a duty laid down by the 13th article of the Terms of Union.[103]

No words of encouragement or support were forthcoming for Teit, O'Meara, or the Allied Tribes.

In 1921 a case did reach the Judicial Committee of the Privy Council that had great bearing on the events in Canada. From Southern Nigeria the case known as *Amodu Tijani v. Secretary, Southern Nigeria*, was brought to London, where Judge Haldane ruled that preexisting title continuously demonstrated continued under British rule. Whether land was held communally or individually did not affect the validity of this title. Haldane ruled further that even if the Aboriginal people were conquered, their claims to the land were not extinguished.[104] Both Peter Kelly and Arthur O'Meara quoted this case in their evidence at the 1927 committee hearings.[105] There can be little doubt that the Canadian government was also aware of the case and recognized its implications. As the Allied Tribes persisted in their demands that their case be taken to the Imperial Privy Council, the government continued with its stalling tactics.

On 7 August 1923, in Victoria, the Allied Indian Tribes of British Columbia held a conference with Duncan Campbell Scott and W.E. Ditchburn, chief inspector of Indian agencies of British Columbia. As well as Peter Kelly and Andrew Paull, with O'Meara as general counsel, there were representatives of the United Tribes of Northern British Columbia, Kamloops, Fountain, Okanagan and Lillooet in the interior, Lower Fraser, Cowichan, and Saanich. Also in attendance was Mrs. Cook of the Kwawkawlth, still the only woman. This was a continuation of a meeting held a few days earlier in Vancouver to discuss the report of the Royal Commission. The provincial government declined to attend, saying that the matter was between the Indians and the Canadian government. Kelly wanted to discuss Aboriginal rights, which were not part of the McKenna-McBride

Commission. Scott said, "You are not expected to accept as final the report of the Royal Commission; or to promise anything beforehand."[106] Kelly noted that he was changing the agreement without the British Columbia government agreeing and asked if that was possible. Dr. Scott replied that he had the authority to discuss and advise the minister of what was said but that he could not commit to anything. Kelly replied that he could not speak finally for any particular band. Kelly then said that he wanted to "define our stand along constitutional lines" and asked O'Meara to make the constitutional position clear. Scott asked, "How long will that take? You have done it before." Kelly replied that they wanted it on record so that what they said could not be held against them later. This pattern of Kelly having to defend O'Meara's right to speak and of O'Meara having to endure blatant rudeness was repeated often in the ensuing years. O'Meara outlined the areas of concern for his clients, which included territorial land rights, foreshore, fishing, hunting, and water rights, lands to be reserved, and compensation for the lands to be cut off. He urged that the Order-in-Council to accept the McKenna-McBride Report not be passed. However, the Order-in-Council was passed in 1924.

Since the work of the commission was finally completed, with no respect for Aboriginal title, the Allied Tribes were more determined than ever to reach the Judicial Committee of the Privy Council. In June 1926 the executive of the Allied Tribes petitioned the Dominion Parliament to set up a committee to facilitate this plan. On 30 March 1927 the first session of the Special Joint Committee of the Senate and the House of Commons Appointed to Inquire into the Claims of the Allied Indian Tribes of British Columbia as Set Forth in Their Petition Submitted to Parliament in June 1926 was held. A very vocal member of this committee was H.H. Stevens, member of Parliament for Vancouver Centre. Although the provincial government declined to send representatives directly, several British Columbia senators joined Stevens in presenting the views of the province. What the executive of the Allied Tribes had hoped would be their chance to reach the ultimate court of appeal turned into another of the many obfuscations of government in connection with Aboriginal rights. In addition, perhaps due in part to the lack of progress on the issue of Aboriginal rights, there was increasing fragmentation among the groups of Aboriginal people in British Columbia. Submitted as evidence to support the request to go to the Privy Council were a number of documents that outlined the attempts to date to reach the Privy Council, including the 1911 "Memorandum for the Government of Canada" and a letter from Scott from 1914 that had led to the Order-in-Council of June 1914. This letter included the odious statement, "In appraising the Indian title we should go back to the time when the lands were a wilderness, when we find a wild people upon an unimproved estate. The Indian title cannot increase in value with civilized development."[107] The "Statement of the Nisga'a Nation," adopted at Kincolith in January 1913, and several letters written to O'Meara telling him that the Judicial Committee of the Privy Council would not hear the claims because the Canadian government would not forward them were followed by a summary of the 1923 Victoria Conference with D.C. Scott. At the start of the second day of hearings, O'Meara was asked to state whom he represented. He asked Mr. Beament, a barrister-at-law in Ottawa, to respond, which he did by filing documents stating that O'Meara represented the Allied Indian Tribes of British Columbia. He was interrupted by lawyer McIntyre, counsel for the interior tribes, who said that they were not members of the Allied Tribes. Andrew Paull was recalled to confirm that indeed they were. O'Meara then attempted to read a prepared statement giving reasons for the claim to all the lands of the province, except for those covered by the Douglas Treaties. Among other things, he referred to the Haldane ruling in the Southern Nigeria case, decided in July 1921. After much heckling, he was asked to sit down, which he did. Andrew Paull spoke again, demonstrating a thorough knowledge of the history of land claims, statistics, fisheries, and other matters as he answered the questions of the committee.

At the start of the next session, 4 April 1927, Paull, over the committee's objections, read from a statement by David Laird, minister of the interior, from the Journals and Sessional Papers of British Columbia of 1876, in which Laird urged the British Columbia government to address the concerns of First Nations peoples if they wanted to avoid an "Indian war." The committee said that this had been superceded by later acts. Paull also quoted from an 11 April 1859 letter from Lord Carnarvon to Governor Douglas: "There is not a shadow of a doubt, that from the earliest times, England has always felt it imperative to meet the Indians in council, and to obtain surrenders of tracts of Canada, as from time to time such were required for the purposes of settlement."[108] Paull went on to say that orders in council and discussions between Dominion and provincial governments went against this. He was then questioned by the Hon. Mr. Stevens:

Q. Is it not true, that up until recently, the Indians have always discussed with the Dominion and Provincial authorities their rights on the basis of the adequacy or otherwise of the area of their reserves; that is, that the reserve was too small or too large, as the case may be? – A. Yes.

Q. That has been the basis until Mr. O'Meara advanced before Parliament and other bodies the claim of the aboriginal title to the whole of British Columbia? – A. No, I think the Indians took steps before that.

Q. Will you point out when, please? – A. In 1906, Chief Joe Capilano and two other chiefs waited on His late Majesty, King Edward VII.

Q. Yes, I remember that. – A. And he was told by some authority in England, that he should go back to Canada, and take this matter up with the Canadian Government, and if you cannot get satisfaction there, come back to us, and we will take it up.

Q. Have you any record of that? Anything you can put in as evidence of that? – A. Only this, that Chief Joe Capilano told me that himself.

Q. I remember the occasion, and I knew Chief Capilano very well, but you could hardly call that evidence upon which to base a claim for aboriginal title, could you? – A. No, no. The reason I say that I got that from Chief Joe Capilano is, because I was groomed in my young days to be his successor, and he would speak to me more confidentially and earnestly than he would to anybody else.[109]

Peter Kelly then spoke. He referred to Haldane's Southern Nigeria land-title decision, to Canada east of the Rocky Mountains, and to New Zealand as support for the claims. This was followed by A.D. McIntyre speaking on behalf of the interior tribes. He was followed by Chief Johnny Chillihitza and Chief Basil David speaking through an interpreter. Then O'Meara said that he would like to ask some questions.

Hon. Mr. Stevens: We do not want to get into a wrangle between Mr. O'Meara's group and these others, if it is some personal fight.

Mr. Kelly: We do not want to get into a wrangle, but I do not like to have our group referred to as Mr. O'Meara's group, and somebody else's group. We do not belong to Mr. O'Meara. We have engaged Mr. O'Meara as legal adviser, and, as I said to the Minister of the Interior in Vancouver, I think in the year 1922, he agitates just insofar as we allow him to agitate, just as any legal adviser. We take exception to that sort of statement very much, that we belong to Mr. O'Meara or are Mr. O'Meara's children. I, for one, do not wish to say anything to the Chief who was the last speaker, or to the other Chief. They have made their statement and that is all there is to it.

Hon. Mr. Stevens: There was no offense meant when I said that. What I mean is this; we have two groups of Indians here and it is quite clear that there is some feeling between the two, and we do not want to listen to a wrangle between two groups of persons. That is my objection, Mr. Chairman, and I think it is pertinent.[110]

On this note the meeting adjourned for lunch. In the afternoon Kelly again spoke to the committee. He asked that he be able to present their case in a "connected way," and again he had to beg that O'Meara be allowed to speak:

I beg of you to be a little more tolerant [of what our legal advisor has to say], and if we are to have a constitutional argument to present, I think it is only fair that this Committee should hear it on record. Now, I know that by saying these things, I may raise several vexatious points, and that some such thing as a shadow of doubt may be cast upon our general counsel. I would like to say this; would you kindly forget any disagreeable features which may have arisen in the past, and give us the same right and the same privilege as would be extended to any other body of people, coming with their grievances, to present our constitutional argument in a connected way, so that it will appear before you in a connected form; because you would have to consider it in any case.[111]

Kelly continued speaking for the rest of the day. There was the occasional clarification from Paull, but O'Meara was not called upon or allowed to present the claims. The following morning the hearings resumed. O'Meara was not there, and Kelly was asked if O'Meara wanted to make a statement. "Yes, Mr. Chairman, he wishes just what I asked for yesterday," replied Kelly. The chairman suggested that this could be done in a written statement, which Kelly said could be done if such was the ruling of the committee. There followed a discussion about how O'Meara rambled on and did not stick to the point and how he read bits of documents but did not submit them. Kelly said that O'Meara would be quicker if he were not interrupted so often and that he was at the moment looking up a document that had been quoted the day before. Kelly said that he had known Mr. O'Meara for a long time and that he and Paull would work with O'Meara to prepare a statement supported by documents.

The contrast between the respect shown O'Meara at this time and the respect that he was shown as he presented the case for the Lord's Day Alliance to the Imperial Privy Council in 1903 was marked. The years of hard work and the intransigence of representatives of the Governments of British Columbia and Canada had obviously taken their toll on this once self-confident man. What did he think of his life's work as he attended the Ottawa hearings in 1927?

The following day, Wednesday, 6 April 1927, O'Meara was cautioned to be brief and to have his supporting documents in place. He listed the documents that he would be quoting. One was a newspaper article giving the text of a memorandum issued by the Department of Indian Affairs in 1924. He was told that he should have an original or a certified copy. There followed a discussion of whether copies of O'Meara's evidence should be included with the final report, as the reprinting of these would take time and money.[112] O'Meara was finally allowed to begin his tracing of the history of the claim for Aboriginal title to the land through many acts issued by governments and legal decisions rendered by courts. Stevens continually interrupted to object to O'Meara's "opinions" and to his quoting of pieces of documents instead of the whole document. Despite his not quoting entire documents, Stevens still insisted that O'Meara was taking too long. It had already been made clear that the report of the Special Committee had to be through Parliament before it prorogued in the middle of the month, about ten days away. Stevens then asked O'Meara what he knew about the Oregon Treaty Lands and the San Juan. O'Meara said that he had no knowledge of these. Stevens did but fortunately did not take time explaining them. After more harassment, there was only a mild protest from O'Meara: "I appreciate the remarks of Mr. Stevens. May I suggest to him that he exercise a judical [sic] mind." Stevens replied, "Oh, I have had twenty years of your nonsense, and I am tired of it." The chairman asked for original documents, not notes of documents, and shortly after ended the hearing of evidence.

The wait for the report was short – three days. It was so predictable that it is difficult not to think that it was written to orders given beforehand. It opened with a history starting with the first contact. "The fact was admitted that it was not until about fifteen years ago that aboriginal title was first put forward as a formal legal claim by those who ever since have made it a bone of contention and by some a source of livelihood as well."[113] The report then continued by condemning O'Meara:

> Counsel representing the Allied Indian Tribes continued to press the aboriginal title claim upon the attention of successive Governments, and although the Government was willing to litigate the claim, Counsel for the Indians sought permission to take the matter direct to the Imperial Privy Council, instead of first submitting it for judicial decision to the Courts of Canada. This the Government very properly declined to do; but at the same time it made a generous offer to the Indians, the details of which are embodied in an Order in Council passed on June 20, 1914 ... Instead of accepting the offer thus made by the Government, it was rejected and Counsel for the Indians kept up a correspondence on irrelevant issues with the then Minister of Justice until the latter gentleman ended the controversy with the following letter.[114]

The letter, dated 14 November 1914 and signed by Doherty, minister of justice, was addressed to O'Meara at the Prince George Hotel in Toronto. It said that the government would not allow the question of rights of Indians to go directly to His Majesty's Privy Council and that the Indians must abide by the terms of the Order-in-Council of June 1914. The verdict followed:

> Having given full and careful consideration to all that was adduced before your Committee, it is the unanimous opinion of the members thereof

that the petitioners have not established any claim to the lands of British Columbia based on aboriginal or other title, and that the position taken by the Government in 1914, as evidenced by the Order in Council and Mr. Doherty's letter above quoted, afforded the Indians full opportunity to put their claim to the test. As they have declined to do so, it is the further opinion of your Committee that the matter should now be regarded as finally closed.[115]

This must have been a bitter blow to the executive of the Allied Tribes and to their advisor, Arthur Eugene O'Meara. The work of many years was counted as worthless. Mindful of the 1921 ruling of the Judicial Committee of the Privy Council in the Southern Nigeria case, the Dominion government could not risk the chance of the Allied Tribes finding some other route to justice. They had one more blow to deliver: "In concluding this Report your Committee would recommend that the decision arrived at should be made known as completely as possible to the Indians of British Columbia by direction of the Superintendent General of Indian Affairs in order that they may become aware of the finality of the findings and advised that no funds should be contributed by them to continue further presentation of a claim which has now been disallowed."[116] To ensure that no funds were contributed by anyone to further the claims, an amendment was added to the Indian Act specifically prohibiting it.

With this double blow there was little left for O'Meara to do publicly. He returned to his family home in Abbotsford, where he had lived for about four years. From there, for the last year of his life, he continued to write to members of the government in Ottawa, attempting to right the wrong that had been done.

O'Meara, the Man

This was a man who as a young lawyer in Toronto had taken a case to the Judicial Committee of the Privy Council. Three years later he had volunteered to leave this promising law practice to go as an Anglican missionary to the Yukon. There he had worked under difficult conditions not only to spread the word of God, but also to better the lot of his parishioners. With accustomed thoroughness he had set about learning the history of the people with whom he worked. Instead of accepting the conditions that he found, he petitioned those in authority on behalf of his parishioners. His attempts to have schools for First Nations students, increased law enforcement, and more religious teaching did not go unnoticed by people in British Columbia.

His invitation by the Cowichan people in 1909 to take their petition to England led to increased involvement in the struggle for recognition of Aboriginal title. He worked for the Cowichan, the Nisga'a, and finally the

Allied Tribes of British Columbia as their counsel to present a coherent, logical, and verifiable case to the government. When this failed he attempted to have the courts state the case. The intransigence of the government in protecting their illegal claim to the land eventually wore O'Meara down. The energy and enthusiasm exhibited in his letters to Stringer of 1908-10 were gone by the 1920s. At this point he suffered such taunts and rudeness from elected and appointed officials that it is difficult to think of them as anything more than schoolyard bullies. However, they were more powerful than that and were able to pass legislation that effectively ended the work that O'Meara's employers had hired him to do. The legal quest for justice for Aboriginal title was stopped by the legislation of 1927. Peter Kelly, Andrew Paull, and the other members of the Allied Tribes were no longer able to solicit funds for the pursuit of their claims to the land. Since it was also illegal for people to give funds for the cause, there were no further avenues of appeal for O'Meara to explore.

On 2 April 1928, at 8:30 in the morning, O'Meara died of cardiac failure.[117] This was just one week short of a year after the devastating report of the Special Joint Committee. It was many years before the ongoing struggle was allowed to resurface. When it did, O'Meara's careful, thorough work was put to good use.

Notes

1 Genn Collection, Box 141, file 7, O'Meara in Toronto, 1 December 1908, to Stringer in Kincardine, Ontario, Provincial Archives of British Columbia. This collection is described in the archives catalogue as a "Large diverse collection of records by Victoria accountants W. Curtis Sampson, Reginald Genn, and K.R. Genn. Includes financial records of many B.C. businesses. Also includes documents pertaining to missionary work in the Yukon (1905-1909)." There is a footnote stating, "But how O'Meara's private correspondence with Bishop Stringer, Archbishop of Rupert's Land [sic], found its way into Curtis Sampson's accountancy files is something of a mystery." A close reading of the correspondence shows that when O'Meara left the Yukon, he was already very involved with the work for First Nations' land claims and that, despite repeated requests from Bishop Stringer, he probably never completed the books he kept as financial secretary for the Diocese of Yukon. One suspects that in the end he took all the papers that he had at hand to the accountant Curtis Sampson. These papers included his sheepskin from the University of Toronto and his will as well as many letters and carbons of replies from a period when O'Meara was in the Yukon.

2 H.B. Hawthorn, C.S. Belshaw, and S.M. Jamieson, eds., *The Indians of British Columbia: A Study of Contemporary Social Adjustment* (Toronto: University of Toronto Press, 1958), 50.

3 Hawthorn et al., *The Indians of British Columbia,* 53.

4 Cut-off lands included 47,058 acres valued at $1,522,704; added lands consisted of 87,291 acres valued at $444,838. Hawthorn et al., *The Indians of British Columbia,* 55; Paul Tennant, *Aboriginal Peoples and Politics: The Indian Land Question in British Columbia, 1849-1989* (Vancouver: UBC Press, 1990), 98.

5 Tennant, *Aboriginal Peoples,* 85-86.

6 An 1884 amendment to the Indian Act made it an offence to engage in the festival known as potlatch. At these festivals First Nations peoples had traditionally gathered to discuss concerns, meet with family and friends, and witness important events. The ban was irregularly enforced until Scott took control.

7   Genn Collection, file 12, contains a handwritten copy of a certified true copy of O'Meara's baptismal certificate. It states that he was born on 10 April 1861 and baptized on 9 June of that year in the Mission of Georgetown, Ontario. His father was the officiating minister. The year given for his birth is 1862, as recorded on his death certificate in the Provincial Archives of British Columbia. This information was given by his daughter. However, doing the arithmetic from his age at time of death suggests that he was born in 1861. His age, 26, as given on his marriage certificate of 13 July 1887 in the Provincial Archives of Ontario, also results in 1861 as the year of his birth. E. Palmer Patterson, "Arthur E. O'Meara: Friend of the Indians," *Pacific Northwest Quarterly* (April 1967): 90-99 at 91, states that he was born in Port Hope, Ontario, in 1859.

8   Genn Collection, file 3, contains the large piece of sheepskin on which his degree is printed.

9   Patterson, "Arthur E. O'Meara," 91.

10 House of Lords, Judicial Committee of the Privy Council and Peerage Cases, *The Law Reports of the Incorporated Council of Law Reporting* (London: William Chowns and Sons, 1903), 524-30. The Government of Ontario had passed the Ontario Act to Prevent Profanation of the Lord's Day, which made it a criminal offence to disobey the act. The Hamilton Street Railway Co. and others, including The Lord's Day Alliance, protested, and the case went through a series of appeals and cross-appeals. On 14 April 1902 the Ontario Court of Appeal ruled against the government. The Ontario government then appealed to the Judicial Committee of the Privy Council in London. On 9, 10, and 14 July 1903 the Judicial Committee heard the case. O'Meara contended that the subject of the act in question was a matter of civil right and not of criminal law. He argued that disobedience to a statute is not always indictable and cited twelve cases in support of his argument. The court ruled that the Ontario government did not have the right to enact criminal law and that the act was thus *ultra varies*.

11 Archives of Ontario, Marriage Certificate, MS 934, reel 6.

12 Stringer Papers, Series 1-B M 74-3, Box 6, Diaries 24-36, the Anglican Church of Canada/ General Synod Archives, Toronto, Isaac O. Stringer Papers. This collection contains the diaries, journals, and correspondence of this remarkable man.

13 This and the following quotations are from Stringer's diary for 1906.

14 Anglican Church of Canada/General Synod Archives, *The New Era* (Toronto: December 1907), 423-24. *The New Era* was the official organ of the Missionary Society of the Church of England in Canada. The people to whom O'Meara was referring were Klinkit, now usually written Tlingit.

15 Ibid., 424.

16 Ibid.

17 Ibid.

18 *The New Era,* May 1906, 154.

19 Genn Collection, file 5, a carbon copy of the outgoing letter from O'Meara in Conrad, 17 January 1908, to Stringer, in Dawson.

20 A copy of the memo is contained in Stringer Papers, Series 1-A-2, A.E. O'M. Memo, Conrad, 15 January 1908.

21 This report was being prepared by Indian Reserve Commissioner for British Columbia A.W. Vowell and by Mr. Greene, a BC Indian Agent. In December 1908 O'Meara was wondering if a full report would ever be available to the missionaries.

22 "Another former editor of this department, Rev. A.E. O'Meara, has unexpectedly returned to Toronto from his post in the far-off Diocese of Selkirk. Mr. O'Meara has been stationed at Conrad, a mining town on the Windy Arm; he accompanies Bishop Stringer on important diocesan business, and will return in about three weeks." *The New Era,* November 1906, 374.

23 Stringer Papers, Series 1-A-2, A.E. O'M. Memo.

24 Genn Collection, file 6, Stringer in Dawson, 7 December 1907, to O'Meara in Conrad.

25 Ibid., Stringer in Dawson, 31 December 1907, 2, dated 3 January 1908, to O'Meara in Conrad.

26 Stringer Papers, Series 1-A-2, H.A. Cody in Whitehorse, 17 February 1907, to Stringer in Dawson.
27 Family relations appear to have been so strained that his granddaughter, Gail O'Meara Gatehouse, reports that her father spoke very little of his father as she was growing up. Personal communication, Victoria, British Columbia, 22 April 2002.
28 Genn Collection, file 7, Stringer in Dawson, 26 January 1908, to O'Meara, which says in part, "I have not heard from you regarding the matter of our last conversation at Carcross i.e. concerning the wisdom of going on for priest's orders but your reference to examinations implies that you have decided to do so and if you have fully determined in your own mind to go on for ordination after considering carefully the views I place before you at Carcross then I suppose there is no need for further delay and you might be ordained with Mr. Comyn-Ching on Feb. 16th." File 2 of the Genn Collection contains the certificate recording O'Meara's entry into the Holy Order of Priests. An announcement in the *Yukon World* (Dawson), 15 February 1908, stated that the ordination would take place the following day and that the Reverend A.E. O'Meara would preach at evensong.
29 Genn Collection, file 5, O'Meara in Toronto, 11 March 1909, to Rev. C.C. Owen, Vancouver.
30 Genn Collection, file 5, O'Meara in Conrad, 28 January 1908, to Thompson in Ottawa.
31 Genn Collection, file 7, Stringer in Toronto, 11 May 1908, to O'Meara in Whitehorse.
32 Ibid., Stringer in Ottawa, 27 May 1908, to O'Meara in Whitehorse.
33 Ibid., O'Meara in Whitehorse, 25 June 1908, to Stringer in London.
34 Ibid., Stringer in London, 22 July 1908, to O'Meara in Whitehorse.
35 It was actually Mr. Oliver who was quoted by Stringer as having said this.
36 Genn Collection, file 7, O'Meara in Toronto, 1 December 1908, to Stringer in Kincardine, Ontario.
37 Genn Collection, file 8, O'Meara in Victoria, 6 January 1909, to Stringer in Kincardine, Ontario.
38 Genn Collection, file 5, O'Meara in Toronto, 11 March 1909, to Rev. Owen in Vancouver.
39 Ibid., O'Meara in Toronto, 11 March 1909, to Rev. Cody in Whitehorse.
40 Hamar Foster, professor of law, Faculty of Law, University of Victoria, e-mail to the author, 13 April 2001.
41 The origins of this petition are an area for further research.
42 Friends of the Indians of British Columbia, *The Nishga Petition to His Majesty's Privy Council: A Record of Interviews with the Government of Canada* (British Columbia: The Conference of Friends of the Indians of British Columbia, July 1915), 107, 61, together with related documents. This document is in the Provincial Archives of British Columbia, call number NWp/970.5/F913n (henceforth *The Nishga Petition*).
43 Genn Collection, file 5, O'Meara in Toronto, 12 March 1909, to Hon. H. Oliver, Ottawa.
44 Genn Collection, file 8, O'Meara in Ottawa, 13 March 1909, to Stringer in Kincardine, Ontario. In the event, it appears that O'Meara did not see the governor general until his return from England.
45 Ibid., Stringer in Kincardine, 13 March 1909, to O'Meara at Wycliffe College, Toronto. Stringer wrote four letters to O'Meara that day. He noted that O'Meara was in Ottawa for the day.
46 *The British Columbia Indian Land Situation: A Great Question to be Settled,* 9 (henceforth *A Great Question to be Settled*). This is a pamphlet printed in 1910 for private circulation containing notes of the first two meetings of the Conference of Friends of the Indians, in Provincial Archives of British Columbia.
47 Canada, Parliament, Special Joint Committee of the Senate and House of Commons appointed to inquire into the Claims of the Allied Indian Tribes of British Columbia, *Report and Evidence* (Ottawa: King's Printer, 1927), 52 (henceforth Special Committee [1927], *Report*).
48 Genn Collection, file 8, Stringer in Ottawa, 27 April 1909, to O'Meara, New York City. Despite reading much discussion regarding this issue in letters in the Genn Collection in the Archives of British Columbia, I have not been able to ascertain the exact nature of the difficulty. Neither could I find an explanation in the Anglican Church of Canada/ General Synod Archives in Toronto.

49   Special Committee (1927), *Report,* 52.

50   Genn Collection, file 8, O'Meara in Ottawa, 1 May 1909, to Stringer in Vancouver.

51   Genn Collection, file 8, O'Meara in Skagway, 2 September 1909. These scrawled notes are in sharp contrast to the tidy carbon copies of most of O'Meara's correspondence.

52   Ibid., O'Meara in Victoria, 23 September 1909, to Stringer in Dawson.

53   *Victoria Daily Colonist,* 2 October 1909, 3.

54   Genn Collection, file 8, O'Meara in Victoria, 5 October 1909, to Stringer in Whitehorse.

55   Ibid., notes by O'Meara on train near Revelstoke, 6 October 1909, for a letter to Stringer.

56   *A Great Question to be Settled,* 2.

57   Ibid.

58   This will is in the Genn Collection, file 2. It names O'Meara's brother Thomas as executor. At the time of O'Meara's death in 1928, Thomas was principal of Wycliffe College, as he had been for many years. It is surprising, therefore, that Mrs. O'Meara had to petition for letters of administration on the grounds that her husband had died intestate. One wonders if she informed her brother-in-law of her husband's death. Perhaps this is an indication of the decline in family relations. The petition is in the probate files for Chilliwack in the Provincial Archives of British Columbia. O'Meara's assets at the time of his death consisted solely of two life-insurance policies, one payable to his wife and a smaller one undesignated, which was divided equally among his wife and two children. It is interesting to note that when the two amounts owing Mrs. O'Meara were added together, a mistake in arithmetic gave her an extra $100.00, resulting in a total of $1,235.05 for Mrs. O'Meara and $241.16 each for Kathleen and Robin. Genn Collection, file 12, contains notes showing that O'Meara took out loans against his insurance policies in 1901 and 1906.

59   Stringer Papers, Series 1-B M 74-3, Box 6.

60   Genn Collection, file 9, Stringer on steamer *Princess May* to Skagway, 5 March 1910, to O'Meara, Victoria.

61   Ibid., Stringer on steamer *Princess May,* 7 March 1910, to O'Meara, Victoria.

62   Ibid. Letters testimonial enabling the transfer were signed and sealed by Stringer and enclosed in a letter to O'Meara in Victoria dated 20 June 1910.

63   "The Indian Land Situation in British Columbia: A lecture delivered in Aberdeen School, Vancouver, under the auspices of the Art Historical and Scientific Association of 22nd April 1910, by Rev. Arthur E. O'Meara, B.A.," 4. The pamphlet (henceforth "The Indian Land Situation") is in the Provincial Archives of British Columbia. O'Meara quotes the Indian Commissioners in his lecture.

64   *A Great Question to be Settled,* 4.

65   Ibid., 5.

66   "The Indian Land Situation," 3.

67   Ibid., 4.

68   Ibid., 5.

69   Ibid., 5-6. O'Meara is quoting Joseph William Trutch. Information from personal communication with Hamar Foster, professor of law, Faculty of Law, University of Victoria.

70   *A Great Question to be Settled,* 6.

71   Quoted by O'Meara in *A Great Question to be Settled,* 7.

72   The full text of the petition that the delegates were to present to His Majesty is printed in the *Victoria Daily Colonist,* 6 July 1906, 8.

73   "The Indian Land Situation," 11.

74   Tennant, *Aboriginal Peoples,* 86.

75   Ibid., 87.

76   Special Committee (1927), *Report,* 52.

77   Ibid., 52-54.

78   Allied Indian Tribes of British Columbia, "Transcript of Conference of Dr. Duncan C. Scott, Deputy Superintendent-General of Indian Affairs of the Dominion of Canada, and W.E. Ditchburn, Chief Inspector of Indian Agencies of British Columbia, with the Executive Committee of the Allied Tribes of British Columbia," 274 pages, 1923, photocopy of a typed transcript, in Provincial Archives of British Columbia. The conference was held in Victoria, 7 August 1923. Mr. Harcourt's letter was quoted by O'Meara, 34 (henceforth Allied Tribes, Scott, Ditchburn Conference).

79 Tennant, *Aboriginal Peoples,* 88.
80 Ibid.
81 Provincial Archives of British Columbia, Microfilm B-317, file 59335-2, vol. 3822, B.C. Indian Land Question, Private Papers, 1913-21.
82 Ibid.
83 Ibid. See letter from O'Meara to Roche, 1 February 1913.
84 This name has been variously spelled "Nishga," "Niska," and currently "Nisga'a." I will use "Nisga'a" except when quoting directly from another work.
85 *The Nishga Petition,* 1. See endnote 42 herein.
86 Ibid., 27. The letter is dated 15 January 1915.
87 Ibid., 37.
88 Ibid., 38-39.
89 Ibid., 56-57.
90 Ibid., 58.
91 The member organizations of the Social Service Council were listed. Most were from the Prairies.
92 *The Nishga Petition,* 60.
93 Ibid., 74.
94 Special Committee (1927), *Report,* 61-64.
95 Patterson, "Arthur E. O'Meara," 94. In December 1999 Patterson told me that he had corresponded with O'Meara, the son, at the time that he was writing the article. O'Meara was at that time living in Australia. Patterson was not sure where the letters were in 1999.
96 Genn Collection, file 5, Letter of 11 March 1909 to Rev. H.A. Cody.
97 For a fascinating discussion of the genesis of this publication, see Tennant, *Aboriginal Peoples,* 47-49.
98 *British Columbia Papers Connected with the Indian Land Question, 1850-1875,* Victoria, Richard Wolfenden, Government Printer, 1875, reprinted by Provincial Archives of British Columbia, 116 (henceforth *Indian Land Question, 1850-1875*).
99 Special Committee (1927), *Report,* 61-64.
100 Ibid.
101 Ibid., 146.
102 *Victoria Daily Times,* 6 February 1919, 7.
103 Provincial Archives of British Columbia, Canada, Dept. of Indian Affairs, Microfilm B1387(1), Royal Commission on Indian Affairs in British Columbia, Miscellaneous Correspondence, 1874-1920, RG 10, vol. 1285, 297-98.
104 See Tennant, Chapter 16, "Aboriginal Title in the Courts," *Aboriginal Peoples,* 213-26, for a discussion of this and other legal precedents concerning Aboriginal title.
105 Special Committee (1927), *Report,* 135 for Kelly, 210 for O'Meara.
106 Allied Tribes, Scott, Ditchburn Conference.
107 Special Committee (1927), *Report,* 56.
108 Ibid., 132. In the copy of *Indian Land Question, 1850-1875* that I have, there is a letter from Carnarvon to Douglas on this date, but it does not contain the words quoted by Paull. Great difficulty was reported by O'Meara, Kelly, and Paull in gaining access to this book, which was missing from the Parliamentary library when O'Meara tried to find it. Although at least two committee members had copies, they did not care to lend them. Prof. Hamar Foster says in his 13 April 2001 e-mail to the author, "Paull goes on in that statement to quote from Fournier's (the minister of justice) 1875 legal opinion on the Crown Lands Act, and the words are his."
109 Special Committee (1927), *Report,* 133.
110 Ibid., 146.
111 Ibid., 149.
112 There were very few references in the copy of the *Report* that I was using.
113 Special Committee (1927), *Report,* vii. Since fifteen years earlier was 1912, this comment does not take into account the trip of Chiefs Capilano, Tsilpaymilt, and Basil David to London in 1906, the formation of the Nisga'a Land Committee in 1907, or the Cowichan Petition, which O'Meara carried to London in 1909, not to mention many earlier

acknowledgements of First Nations' title by both the Imperial government and the government of the settlers.

114   Ibid., viii.
115   Ibid., x.
116   Ibid., xvii.
117   Provincial Archives of British Columbia, Certificate of Registration of Death. Registration #1928-09-405227, BC Archives, Vital Events, Death Registration Index: 1872-1984, Microfilm #B13134.

12
"They Wanted ... Me to Help Them": James A. Teit and the Challenge of Ethnography in the Boasian Era
Wendy Wickwire

> Only those few whites who help us ... uphold the honor of their race.[1]

Large numbers of ethnographers descended on British Columbia during the early decades of the twentieth century, turning the region into one of the most productive social-science laboratories on record.[2] Franz Boas directed much of this work. Concerned that the indigenous cultures of the Northwest were on the brink of extinction, Boas established a rigorous ethnographic research program aimed at salvaging the old ways before they disappeared forever. That his so-called "informants" were several generations removed from what he envisioned as the old ways did not deter him. Over the course of a few decades, he produced thousands of pages of written text framed against the backdrop of a Golden Age Past.[3]

Anthropologist Johannes Fabian was among the first to highlight the problems associated with such temporal distancing. The discourse of anthropology, he argued, had effaced the temporality of its own involvement through the creation of an oppositional timeframe that placed the researcher in the "here and now" and its subjects of study in the "there and then."[4] Social theorists Charles Briggs and Richard Bauman have applied Fabian's argument directly to Boas. "A critical element" in Boas' text-making project, they suggest, "is that the social opposition between the traditional and modern worlds that it sought to construct was sustained by texts whose rootedness in modernist discursive practices and interests was suppressed in favor of producing an aura of authenticity and verisimilitude."[5]

On the surface, Boas' efforts to filter out the modern appear to have worked. His writings are situated squarely in the deep past, with barely a mention of contemporary conditions – for example, that most of his interviewees were horsepackers, cannery workers, construction labourers, or small-scale farmers who had never known life without whites. The irony is that while Boas and his associates were busy writing their subjects of study into an imagined *precontact past* (as hunter-gatherers living in a Golden Age Past), these subjects of study were simultaneously writing themselves into the very tangible political *present* (as targets of one of the most aggressive assimilationist campaigns in Canadian history).

While the anthropological texts moved swiftly into the public sphere, the Aboriginal political statements faded quickly from view. Of the large numbers of ethnographers who built their careers on their Pacific Northwest field research in the early decades of the twentieth century, only one took seriously the contemporary issues confronting his interviewees. He was James A. Teit.

A Shetlander who spent most of his life at Spences Bridge in the south central interior of British Columbia, Teit was employed for many years by Franz Boas of the American Museum of Natural History (and later, Columbia University), New York City. From 1911 on, he was also employed by Edward Sapir of the Anthropology Division, Canadian Geological Survey, Ottawa. Teit's legacy is impressive: 2,200 pages of ethnographic text in forty-two published sources, another 5,000 pages in thirty-four unpublished sources,[6] and an array of artifacts, photographs, sketches, plant specimens, and wax-cylinder recordings deposited in museums across the continent.

While carrying out ethnographic work for Boas and Sapir, Teit found that his Aboriginal "informants" often shifted his interview sessions to more current issues, most notably those related to land title, reserves, hunting and fishing rights, education, and policies of Indian Agents and missionaries on dancing, doctoring, and potlatching. Eventually, the chiefs persuaded him to help them translate their concerns into English. Shortly after agreeing to do so, Teit found himself at the centre of a large political campaign, hosting large meetings at his home to draft petitions and letters, serving on the executive committees of newly formed political organizations, and accompanying Aboriginal delegations to Victoria and Ottawa to lobby provincial and federal politicians. By 1910 this work overshadowed his salvage ethnographic work, and by the time of his death in 1922, it consumed him entirely.

The goal of this chapter is to reassess the scholarly contributions of James Teit in light of his political activism. While his salvage anthropological texts attracted much attention over the years, his political contributions went largely unrecognized.[7] In fact, the general view until recently was that *nothing* survived of Teit's political activities. As Ralph Maud noted, "Who, from reading [Teit's] ethnographic reports would gain an inkling of the depth of his social mission? What Teit really knew about the Indians, their inner life and aspirations and how their politics connected to their tribal past, will never be published. It was never written down. It was not asked for."[8] I argue, in contrast to Maud, that what Teit knew about the

Aboriginal peoples and their politics *can* be retrieved by studying the petitions, memorial statements, and declarations produced by Aboriginal leaders across the province between 1908 and 1922. These documents shed light on his efforts to present his so-called "informants" as fully articulate and functioning members of the British Columbia political community. They also counter the dominant ethnographic myth of cultural demise.

Teit's Salvage Anthropology

The launch of James Teit's anthropological career can be traced to a meeting with Franz Boas on a late September afternoon in 1894 at Spences Bridge, a small village on the Thompson River in the south central interior of British Columbia. Under contract to the British Association for the Advancement of Science (BAAS), Boas was in British Columbia to undertake linguistic and ethnographic work leading to a general "description of the whole region, from north to south, without eliminating any stock."[9] It was an ambitious undertaking, especially given the constant demands of Horatio Hale, the supervisor of the project.[10] (See Chapter 1, this volume.)

The 1894 trip to Spences Bridge was Boas' second visit to British Columbia's southern interior. He was not overly optimistic, as his earlier trip in 1888 had yielded little. At Lytton, a small town at the junction of the Fraser and Thompson Rivers, he was disappointed. "The Indian Village here is not nice," he wrote in his journal. "The people unfortunately have been Christians for a long time, and that stands very much in my way. I hear little about olden times."[11] Moreover, he was surprised to find "horse Indians," who lived on farms and worked as packers along the travel route.[12]

He did not encounter the Nlaka'pamux again until September 1894 during his sixth and second-to-last ethnographic field season for the BAAS. En route to the West Coast from the Okanagan Valley, where his field research had not gone well, Boas decided to spend the night at Spences Bridge, a Canadian Pacific Railway stop just upriver from Lytton. On hearing about a local "Scotsman,"[13] Jimmy Teit, who knew "a great deal about the Indians and was especially kind,"[14] Boas hiked to the latter's Twall Valley ranch to find him.[15] It turned out to be a most productive side trip. Not only was Teit on close terms with the Nlaka'pamux people, but he was married to one of its members, Lucy Antko, and totally immersed in her language and culture. Boas hired him immediately to write "a report" on the Nlaka'pamux.[16] This marked the beginning of a rich collaboration that lasted until Teit's premature death in 1922.

Teit filled an important gap in Boas' research agenda. Despite Hale's request to complete a full ethnographic map of the Aboriginal Northwest, Boas had focused mainly on the West Coast.[17] His few attempts to document the interior peoples had not gone well, thus reinforcing his preference for the coast. "I am not so very much interested in the [Kootenay] tribes," Boas wrote in a letter just prior to arriving at Lytton in 1888, "because they have little relation to all my former work."[18] His fieldwork prior to arriving at Spences Bridge had been particularly disappointing: "My Okanagan trip was a great failure ... I shall be glad when I am back on the coast again!"[19]

After only two days with Teit surveying Nlaka'pamux communities near Spences Bridge, Boas' mood changed dramatically: "The disagreeable feeling I had that I don't get along with the Indians," he wrote to his family, "is slowly wearing off now, and I am hopeful that I will have good results."[20] By the time he left Teit, he wrote to his wife that he was "slowly getting into fieldwork again."[21] He was also excited about the prospect of gaining access to a region of the province that until then was relatively unknown to him.

In December, after completing his coastal work, Boas returned to Spences Bridge, where Teit had organized some special out trips for him. There were many rich ethnographic experiences during this time with Teit, such as one at Stain (Stein), near Lytton, where he took anatomical measurements and listened to chiefs' speeches.[22] Boas was pleased to find that Teit was already well along on a Nlaka'pamux report that he had proposed during his initial September visit.[23] Frustrated with having to shuttle back and forth between his museum job on the East Coast and his field site on the West Coast, Boas welcomed the prospect of an assistant who could help him with his fieldwork.[24] Despite two years among the Inuit of Baffin Island and many months among the Kwakwak'wakw of the central coast of British Columbia, Boas was never fully comfortable with the logistics of fieldwork, particularly when it took him beyond the main rail and water routes. He complained bitterly about the primitive hotel accommodations everywhere.[25] Teit, on the other hand, was a skilled outdoorsman who had spent ten years exploring the most remote regions of southern and central British Columbia. He survived by seasonal wage work that included clerking in his uncle's store, hunting, running the local ferry, and farm work.[26] Having grown up in a middle-class Shetland family that valued education and local history, he welcomed the opportunity to pursue ethnographic work.

In addition to the general ethnographic report on the Nlaka'pamux, Teit pursued four assignments for Boas during the first year of their collaboration. The first was to collect Nlaka'pamux artifacts; the second was to report on the Stuwixamux, an almost extinct Athapascan-speaking group that once resided in the Nicola Valley; the third was to compile a collection of traditional Nlaka'pamux oral narratives; and the fourth was to make a study of local pictograph sites and their meanings. Teit worked on all of these projects simultaneously, mailing his results to Boas as he completed them.[27]

With Teit responding regularly to his questions by mail, Boas had quick access to the Aboriginal cultures of the south central interior of British

Columbia. He was enthusiastic about Teit's Nlaka'pamux report. Teit, on the other hand, felt that even at more than two hundred pages, it was incomplete. "There is no subject," he wrote to Boas, "which I have taken up in the paper, but what I could have treated more fully if I had wanted to, especially as is the case with beliefs and customs, many of which I have never made mention at all in the paper."[28]

Buoyed by the prospect of a new funding opportunity, Boas extended Teit's work on the report. Appointed in 1896 to a curatorial position at the American Museum of Natural History (AMNH), in New York City, Boas was now in charge of his own research project, funded by Morris Jesup, president of the Board of Trustees of the AMNH. This liberated him from the constraints of the BAAS and enabled him to direct his own field project. His ambitious plans for the Jesup Expedition included a range of tasks: to collect linguistic data, gather artifacts, take photographs, measure and make plaster casts of human body features, undertake archaeological digs, and record songs on cylinders.

Boas sought out primary materials of all sorts, most notably accounts of myths, which he considered to be the highest form of ethnography.[29] Since few Aboriginal peoples in the Pacific Northwest understood English, however, such material was relatively inaccessible. Even though he had a fine ear for languages, Boas could not undertake the task of such large-scale ethnographic and linguistic work on his own. He therefore organized his Jesup Expedition around teams of ethnographers. For its first field season in the Pacific Northwest, he appointed Harlan Smith, assistant curator of the archaeology collections at the American Museum of Natural History, to undertake the archaeological component of the project. Boas also brought along Livingston Farrand, a colleague in psychology from Columbia University, to assist with the general ethnographic field research. Unfortunately, however, neither Smith nor Farrand had had any previous field experience in this region. In fact, Farrand had volunteered to join Boas' expedition at his own expense simply to gain some on-the-ground experience under Boas.

To compensate for these limitations, Boas relied heavily on Teit. Not only did he target Spences Bridge as the launch site of the Jesup project in the Pacific Northwest, but he also contracted Teit to prepare everything in advance of his arrival so that work would proceed quickly and efficiently. Teit responded accordingly, noting in a letter that "I have been preparing the Indians here for your taking their pictures. If you bring a camera I think you will have no trouble getting a lot of both men and women."[30] Teit also prepared his friends and neighbours for the plaster-casting process that Boas planned to use to document human facial features. He noted that without such preparation, most people would be reluctant to participate.[31] The research team spent a productive ten days at Spences Bridge prior to heading north by packhorse.[32]

When he returned to New York after his 1897 field season, Boas turned his attention to his "Jesup North Pacific Expedition" monograph series, releasing seven publications between 1898 and 1900.[33] *The Thompson Indians of British Columbia* was among the first to go to print.[34] One of the earliest large-scale efforts to reproduce the reality of a "whole" world in textual form, *The Thompson Indians* was a classic work of early ethnographic realism. Based largely on raw material elicited by Teit at Spences Bridge in response to Boas' questions, the entire manuscript was edited by Boas in New York City. Although he credited Teit as the sole author of this work, he listed himself as the general editor, thereby establishing the text as a collaborative effort.

The goal was to present the full range of precontact Nlaka'pamux life set against as many backdrops as possible – for example, social organization, subsistence, and religious cycles. Boas was pleased with the results, particularly the reviews that praised it for setting new standards in ethnography.[35] As he noted in his "editor's note," the monograph was "remarkably full."[36] Both Boas and Teit, however, knew that *The Thompson Indians* was far from full. For one, the seminomadic hunter-gatherer culture at the centre of the monograph was long gone, replaced by permanent reserve communities administered by the Indian Department and supported by small subsistence farms and wage work. To portray the Nlaka'pamux way of life as it may have existed a century earlier required relying on the fragmentary testimony of the most elderly people, none of whom had directly experienced what Boas envisioned as the "old" way of life. Through a careful process of editing, Boas was able to mask this point.

As Boas' paid assistant, Teit had little choice but to fulfill the latter's research objectives. Following the template established for *The Thompson Indians,* he expanded his fieldwork, publishing within the next nine years two new monographs: *The Lillooet Indians* (1906) and *The Shuswap* (1909).[37] As an established author of these major American Museum of Natural History monographs, a skilled field linguist, and a recognized collector of many of the museum's Northwest artifacts, Teit earned a reputation that could have secured him a permanent post in any number of leading educational or museum institutions. He had little interest, however, in using his anthropological achievements to advance his career. He was by now immersed in a political campaign to fight injustices that were enveloping the lives of his Aboriginal colleagues.

Teit's Activist Anthropology

The first tangible evidence of Teit's response to political issues appears in a letter to Boas in May 1908, in which he described an upcoming meeting of thirty chiefs at Spences Bridge: "I may say that in southern BC there is considerable dissatisfaction & unrest amongst the Indians at present, the settling up of the country & changing of conditions is restricting the Indians more & more to their small reserves, etc. They are also of the opinion that they are very much neglected & kept in an inferior condition. When I return home about 30 Thompson, Shuswap & Okanagan chiefs are to meet at Spences Bridge to hold a big 'talk' preliminary to sending a big 'paper' to Ottawa recounting their grievances."[38]

The outcome of this meeting was a four-page petition entitled "Prayer of Indian Chiefs," dated July 1908. Written in Teit's hand and signed by four Nlaka'pamux chiefs – Peter Poghos, John Tetlenitsa, William Luklusaphen, and John Whistemnitsa – it was addressed to A.W. Vowell, the superintendent general of Indian Affairs. Witnessed by Teit,[39] this petition set out a number of strongly worded demands, such as the need for better schools, resident doctors, care for the elderly and disabled, and compensation for railway rights-of-way through their lands. Its main focus was the land base, which it described as having been "appropriated by the whites without treaty or payment."[40]

Teit's move into politics may have been influenced by his attraction to a growing socialist movement. From 1902 on, he expressed excitement about the ideas that he was gleaning from reading "socialist books by American and German authors."[41] He was also a regular subscriber to newspapers representing the socialist cause, such as the *Canadian Socialist* (later renamed the *Western Socialist*) and the *Western Clarion,* a four-page socialist newspaper based in Vancouver.[42] He was optimistic about the promise of socialism: "Now I understand better what socialism is and what good news it has for people," he wrote to his Shetland friend novelist J.J. Haldane Burgess, noting, "It is wonderful the progress socialism has made in America within the last 12 months or so."[43] He also kept in close touch with a group of Vancouver-based Shetland émigrés who were attracted to socialism. One member of this group, Sam Anderson, for example, recalled after Teit's death that the latter would often drop into the Socialist Party of Canada's (SPC) headquarters in Vancouver to visit his friend Jim Peterson (also a Shetlander), a leader in the SPC who was on close terms with another Shetlander, D. Mackenzie, or 'Mac,' the first editor of the *Western Clarion.*[44]

By 1909, a year after the signing of the Nlaka'pamux petition ("Prayer of Indian Chiefs") at Spences Bridge, Teit was fully immersed in the Aboriginal political lobby, having accepted prominent posts in two organizations formed that year: the Interior Tribes of British Columbia (ITBC) and the Indian Rights Association (IRA). The timing of this shift was ideal. *The Lillooet Indians* had just been published, and *The Shuswap* was in press. As an experienced translator and a seasoned ethnographer, no one was better placed to assist the chiefs with their writing campaign. As he explained it: "I simply could not get out of this work. I was so well known to the Interior tribes and had so much of their confidence, and was so well acquainted with their customs, ideas, languages, and their condition and necessities they kept pressing me to help them and finally simply dragged me into it."[45] The chiefs were desperate for assistance with their *current* concerns: "when engaged among the tribes in ethnological work for Amer. scientific societies and of late for the Can. Gov. the Inds. almost everywhere would bring up questions of their grievances concerning their title, reserves, hunting and fishing rights, policies of Agents and missionaries, dances, potlatches, education, etc. etc. and although I had nothing to do with these matters they invariably wanted to discuss them with me or get me to help them, and to please them and thus to better facilitate my research work I had to listen and give them some advice or information."[46]

Teit, however, had been listening to their concerns well before 1908 and had managed to slip some of these into his early Boasian monographs. For example, in *The Thompson Indians* he highlighted several instances of large-scale deaths from venereal diseases and alcohol and "the great mortality among children."[47] He offered a stiff warning to federal officials: "The actual decrease of the Indians has taken place only since the advent of whites in 1858 and 1859 ... If the Indian Department would provide for resident physicians for the Indians, these conditions might be materially improved."[48] His observations about Nlaka'pamux fears about cultural extinction were particularly poignant indicators that the current scene was not one of perpetual well-being: "The belief that they are doomed to extinction seems to have a depressing effect on some of the Indians. At almost any gathering where chiefs or leading men speak, this sad, haunting belief is sure to be referred to."[49]

Within a year of the 1908 petition, Teit's political activism began to interfere with his output for Boas. Instead of spending endless hours with single individuals recording stories about their mythic past, he took to the road, holding two- and three-day "Indian meetings" with large groups of chiefs to rally support for the IRA's proposal to take the Aboriginal land issue to the Privy Council.[50] His letters to Boas are filled with apologies for failing to make deadlines and lengthy descriptions of the political situation:

> The last two weeks I have done very little ... as I have been busy traveling around, and speaking to the Indians so as to get them united in an effort to fight the BC Government in the Courts over the question of their lands. Owing to more stringency in the laws, increased settlement in the country, and general development of the Capitalist system, the Indians are being crushed, and made poor, and more & more restricted to their small, and inadequate reservations. The BC Government has appropriated all the lands of the country, and claims also to be sole protector of the Ind. Reserves. They refuse to acknowledge the Ind. title, and have taken possession of all without treaty with or consent of the Indians. Having taken the lands

they claim complete ownership of everything in connection therewith such as water, timber, fish, game, etc. They also subject the Indians completely to all the laws of BC without having made any agreement with them to that effect. The Indians demand that treaties be made with them regarding everything the same as has been made with the Indians of all the other provinces of Canada & in the US, that their reservations be enlarged so they have a chance to make a living as easily and as sufficient as among the Whites, and that all the lands not required by them and which they do not wish to retain for purposes of cultivation and grazing, and which are presently appropriated by the BC Government be paid for in cash. The Indians are all uniting and putting up money and have engaged lawyers in Toronto to fight for them, and have the case tried before the Privy Council of England. I came back from Nicola yesterday and am going to Kamloops to address a very large meeting there on Sunday next.[51]

Except for two months of fieldwork for Boas in Puget Sound, Teit spent the better part of 1910 travelling to reserves throughout the southern interior to forge links between the ITBC and the IRA. This work culminated in the production of two important documents by the interior chiefs – a "Declaration," dated 28 July 1910, and a "Memorial to Sir Wilfrid Laurier," dated 4 August 1910[52] – copies of which were presented by representatives of the ITBC to Laurier as he passed through Kamloops by train on 25 August 1910.[53] The "Memorial" articulated the chiefs' view of their historical relations with whites. Laurier responded positively, stressing that he would give their case special consideration.[54]

Teit made his most visible stand in the Aboriginal political campaign on 3 March 1911, when he appeared before Premier Richard McBride in Victoria as part of a delegation of ninety-six chiefs representing most of British Columbia. The purpose of this mission was to request that the issue of land title be placed before the Privy Council. McBride rejected this proposal outright, arguing that there was no proper case for such a submission, as the majority of "Indians" were "well satisfied with their position."[55] Angered by McBride's response, in particular, his accusation that the protest was the work of "white agitators,"[56] sixty-eight Aboriginal chiefs quickly reassembled at Spences Bridge on 10 May, where they decided to send a delegation to Ottawa to meet with Frank Oliver, federal minister of the interior.[57]

This trip materialized quickly. Teit and a nine-member IRA delegation travelled to Ottawa early in January 1912 to meet the newly elected Conservative prime minister, Robert Borden, and his Cabinet. The timing was ideal because it gave Teit an opportunity to meet Edward Sapir, a former student of Boas and newly appointed chief of the Anthropology Division at the Geological Survey of Canada. Sapir had just invited Teit to join the "outside service" of the Anthropology Division.[58] In his role as "ethnologist and translator," Teit and four chiefs – John Chilahitsa (Okanagan), Basil David (Secwepemc), John Tetlenitsa (Nlaka'pamux), and James Raitasket (Sta'atl'imx)[59] – delivered the delegation's written statement, which included an impassioned plea: "Is the B.C. Government right? We say not ... We find ourselves practically landless, and that in our own country, through no fault of ours. We have reached a critical point, and, unless justice comes to our rescue, we must go back and sink out of sight as a race."[60]

When two months passed without a response from Borden, the original delegation reassembled at Kamloops on 15 March 1912, with more than sixty additional chiefs (representing the Tahltan, Okanagan, Shuswap, Lillooet, Kootenays, Arrow Lakes, and Stalo), to intercept Borden's train and deliver a strongly worded statement reiterating their previous demands and reminding the prime minister of his unfulfilled promise: "We demand our rights. And we expect your help, not only because you are men and chiefs, but also because we are called your wards and children."[61] More meetings followed at Spences Bridge, with hundreds of attendees. As Teit explained to Sapir in July 1912: "There was a big meeting here which broke up yesterday. Members of the Carrier, Chilcotin, Shuswap, Kootenay, Okanagan, Ntlakyapamuk, Lillooet, & Stalo tribes were there to the number of about 450. Also several chiefs from the south coast, and one man each from the Spokane and Coeur d'Alene."[62] Borden responded by signing the McKenna-McBride federal agreement on 24 September to initiate a Royal Commission on Indian Affairs that would involve the Province of British Columbia in public hearings on reserves throughout the province to resolve the "Indian Land Question."[63] Teit was in northern British Columbia at Telegraph Creek at the time initiating a large field study of the Tahltan as part of his first major assignment for the Canadian Geological Survey.

Angered by the lack of Aboriginal representation on this commission and its mandate to resolve the reserve question without first settling the issue of title, forty-eight chiefs (representing the Stalo, Chilcotin, Tahltan, Kootenay, Okanagan, Shuswap, Thompson, and Lillooet) met at Spences Bridge on 23 May 1913 to draft a strongly worded letter to Borden rejecting the commission. They stressed that Aboriginal peoples were seeking what they believed to be their natural right: "tribal ownership in all unsurrendered land of the country ... [including] game, fisheries, water, and natural resources."[64]

This was a busy period for Teit. "I am one of some twelve on the executive of the Ind. Rights Association," he explained to Sapir. "The others are all Indians and half-breeds and the executive meetings are held from time to time in Vancouver. The Indians of the Interior have a loose organization for the discussing of their grievances, and the redress of wrongs, etc. and I am secretary for them & treasurer. Some years ago they agreed to affiliate or work together with the Coast Indians (who were organized under the Indian Rights Association) for the settlement of the land question. Therefore delegates from the Interior attend the general meetings of the Indian Rights Association which meets once (sometimes twice) a year."[65]

By this time, Teit had discovered that his new Ottawa-based employer, Edward Sapir, was not only sympathetic to his involvement in the Aboriginal political campaign, but also interested in mounting a petition to protest the potlatch ban. Teit was excited about the prospect, advising Sapir that he would not only support such a petition, but also provide him with the signatures of thirty or forty interior chiefs to add to the list.[66] He reassured Sapir that putting forward such a petition was not a violation of their roles as government anthropologists: "I do not think being Gov. employees will matter. We are not mixing in politics or taking sides openly with any political party. The potlatch whether it should be or should not be is altogether a non political question."[67] Sapir was not convinced, however, because it was not until his superior, the Deputy Superintendent of Indian Affairs, Duncan Campbell Scott, later requested a formal report on the potlatch that he moved on this proposal. And in the end Sapir's potlatch report did not take the form of a petition. It was a compilation of letters that he had solicited from established anthropologists expressing their opposition to the ban. Teit's letter was the most comprehensive of these.

Meanwhile, in July 1914, while the McKenna-McBride Commission was in progress, the federal Cabinet passed Order-in-Council PC 751 in response to the Nisga'a petition. PC 751 stated the terms under which the government would accept referral of the question of Aboriginal title to the Exchequer Court, with the right of appeal to the Privy Council.[68] This new offer carried with it a number of conditions, including acceptance of the McKenna-McBride Commission Report in advance of its publication and an agreement to work with a government-appointed lawyer. Furthermore, it stipulated that if the commission ruled in the Indians' favour, the chiefs would be required to surrender all claims to land title in return for benefits. It also carried with it the possibility of further reductions to reserve lands.

The Nisga'a, not surprisingly, launched a strong attack against this Order-in-Council. Eager to offer their support to the Nisga'a, the ITBC assembled at Spences Bridge for three days in February 1915 to hear two Nisga'a representatives explain the issues to them directly. By the end of the meeting, thirty-eight chiefs (representing the Okanagan, Nlaka'pamux, Lillooet, Shuswap, Chilcotin, Stalo, and Kootenay) drafted and signed in the presence of Teit and William Sanford a letter to Dr. W.J. Roche, federal minister of the interior,[69] declaring support for the Nisga'a and rejecting the terms advanced by the Cabinet. "We consider it is unreasonable," they wrote, "that we should be asked to agree to the findings of the Royal Commission when we have no idea what their findings will be or whether the same will

This photograph was taken by Edward Sapir in Ottawa in 1916. *Left to right, top:* Chief Elie Larue, Chief John Tetlenitsa, James A. Teit, Chief Adolph Thomas, Chief William Pascal; *bottom:* Chief James Raitasket, Chief John Chilahitsa, Chief Paul David, Chief Basil David

be satisfactory to us. We cannot agree to a thing that we know nothing about." They also argued for their right to choose their own lawyer: "We consider that it would only be fair on the part of the Government to allow us the choosing of our own Council [sic] if the question of our claims goes to Court for settlement."[70]

As the Royal Commission approached its conclusion in May 1916, the Aboriginal leadership sent a second Ottawa delegation, composed of Teit and eight chiefs representing the ITBC, to Ottawa to present their views directly to Prime Minister Borden. The outcome was a joint meeting of the ITBC and the IRA immediately following their return in mid-June, which, after three days of discussion, led to the creation of a new Native political body, the "Allied Tribes of British Columbia" (ATBC). The goal of the ATBC was to attract all British Columbia Aboriginal groups who rejected the proposed reference to the Exchequer Court and opposed the work of the Royal Commission.[71]

Teit had been involved in some of the preliminary work leading to this union – for example, a "big inter-tribal mtg. of the Interior Indians [consisting of] people from the Chilcotin, Up. Lillooet, all divisions of the Shuswap, Okanagan, and Ntlak., Kutenai, one Tahltan, and the Stalo from as far down as Chilliwhack held on March 20th."[72] Consequently, it was no surprise when he was asked – along with Shuswap chief Basil David, Okanagan chief John Chilahitsa, Rev. Peter Kelly,[73] and Rev. Arthur O'Meara (see Chapter 11) – to serve on its Executive Committee. Their first order of business was a meeting with Duncan Campbell Scott, who urged them to wait for the findings of the Royal Commission before taking any action.

Preoccupation with the war in Europe, the election of a new Liberal government in September 1916, and the quick succession of two unsympathetic British Columbia premiers, H.C. Brewster and John Oliver, overshadowed discussions about the Aboriginal land question for the following three years. Teit, however, did not lie low during this period. On the contrary, he redirected his energies toward the war and its impact on the Aboriginal community. His correspondence is filled with antiwar rhetoric: "The War probably (under present economic and social conditions) had to come and advancement will probably come out of it and good in the end, but at the same time it is a disgrace for people calling themselves Christian and Civilized. All these nations ... claim to be fighting for democracy. This is quite ridiculous. Who ever heard of any modern capitalist class fighting for democracy?"[74] He saw the growing socialist movements as the only resolution to the situation: "I am quite disgusted. I believe socialism alone is the cure. That is to say S. of the true brand."[75]

When Borden's government appealed to all bachelors and widowers between twenty-four and thirty-four years of age to report for military service under the Military Service Act of 1917, Teit moved quickly to secure an exemption for Aboriginal peoples. Acting under the auspices of the ATBC,[76] he and Peter Kelly sent Borden a telegram on 17 November 1917 opposing forced conscription of Aboriginal men, citing the unresolved land question as key. With Aboriginal peoples denied basic rights and a voice in Canadian affairs, the ATBC, they argued, viewed "enforced military service as enslavement."[77] He also appealed to Duncan Campbell Scott on similar grounds:

I may say that the whole idea of force in the matter of conscription is altogether foreign and repulsive to the Indian mind. In the old military systems of these tribes there was no compulsion of any kind whereby a person could be forced to go to war against his inclination or will. The chiefs and ruling bodies had no powers of this kind. Enlistment for war and other services was altogether voluntary. Men were persuaded to go to war or they saw it in some way to their interests to do so. Physical force in this was unknown. The Indians no where in BC are against the voluntary method although many prefer that none of their people should go to the war.[78]

He urged Scott to amend the Military Service Act to exempt "Indians," many of whom, he noted, would be ineligible anyway due to the difficulty of determining their exact ages. "Very few of those in the Interior, at least," noted Teit, "know their own ages."[79] Teit's position clearly influenced the passage of an Order-in-Council on 17 January 1918 exempting "Indians" from conscription.

The much-awaited "findings" of the Royal Commission, released finally to the public in March 1919, created a huge stir. Although they recommended adding 87,291 acres to existing reserve lands, they advised cutting off 47,058 acres, much of which was rich southern interior and coastal land with high development potential. In response to this and the Liberal government's Indian Affairs Settlement Act authorizing further negotiations and agreements as needed to implement the report,[80] Teit dropped everything to work on the Aboriginal campaign, which he saw as a major class struggle: "The Gov. as a whole and the capitalist class which they represent have no appreciation for anything except [when] dollars are in immediate sight ... The Working Class shows more intelligence, interest, and appreciation of the sciences and of knowledge for the sake of knowledge than any other class."[81]

It was a choice that cost him dearly. Concerned that his ethnographic reports were always late, that his final memoir on the Tahltan had not materialized, and that he was still completing long overdue work for Boas, the Geological Survey terminated its contractual arrangement with Teit in August 1919. Teit expressed his disappointment in strong terms in a letter to Sapir. He questioned the value of government-based anthropology that devalued work with living peoples:

> People in general are more interested in finding out about the dead and their history than investigating the living. It appeals more to their imagination. Of course the two should go as far as possible hand in hand because the one throws light on the other ... It seems there is a tendency among the powers that be in Ottawa to cut out anthropological work altogether or at least pare it down so that it just merely exists. However, what can we expect from the class of people who are in power? They cannot be expected to advance anything except they see dollars in it?[82]

At a meeting of the ATBC at Spences Bridge, Teit and Peter Kelly were appointed to compile a report based on feedback from the province's Aboriginal peoples on the Royal Commission's recommendations.[83] Their

Large delegation of chiefs in front of Parliament buildings, Ottawa, 1920. James Teit is second from the left, centre row

report, which the ATBC Executive Committee adopted formally on 19 November 1919,[84] was published on 19 December in pamphlet form under the title "Statement of the Allied Indian Tribes of British Columbia for the Government of British Columbia." A 6,000-word rejection of the McKenna-McBride Commission Report, its main criticism was the report's failure to address the issue of "Indian" title. Among its proposals were the following: that Indians be granted 160 acres of agricultural land per capita; that there be compensation for lands already occupied by non-Natives; that fishing, hunting, and water rights be fully recognized; and that, in the event that the two governments and the ATBC were unable to reach an agreement regarding land rights, the whole issue be referred to the British secretary of state for the colonies.[85]

Just weeks later, Arthur Meighen, federal minister of Indian Affairs, acting on the advice of Scott, overrode the ATBC response by introducing Bill 13 authorizing the implementation of the McKenna-McBride Commission Report and accordingly that "reductions or cutoffs be effected without surrender of the same by the Indians, notwithstanding any provisions of the Indian Act to the contrary."[86] Members of the ATBC were outraged by this move and immediately sent Teit, Arthur O'Meara, and four chiefs as a protest delegation to Ottawa. They arrived in Ottawa on 17 March, where they prepared a series of press releases and formal statements that attacked Bill 13 as an unjust denial of Indian rights by the federal and provincial governments.[87]

After the bill passed its third reading on 13 April, Teit, O'Meara, and the ATBC moved full force to challenge it.[88] Teit described this effort vividly in a letter to his acquaintance, Walter Baer, who was the provincial secretary of British Columbia at the time:

> We have had a strenuous time opposing the legislation proposed by the Dom. Gov. in Bills 13 and 14 ... I would like you to read over in order all I send you so you may be in a position to realize the seemingly autocratic methods of the Indian Department and Gov. here in dealing with the Indians and their claims, and so that you may also be able to understand fully the work we have been doing here in an attempt to break down the Gov. position and obtain some measure of fair play and justice for the Indians. At first the press was not very responsive, but public opinion is getting interested or worked up to some extent so that lately items furnished by us are taken verbatim even by papers considered to be Gov. sheets. We have managed to get the ear of a considerable number of Members of Commons, especially Liberals and French.[89]

In the middle of this activity, Teit made a quick trip to British Columbia on 16 May to appeal to Premier Oliver for assistance.[90] In Ottawa less than a month later, he and the chiefs presented their views on Bill 13 to the Senate Committee on Banking and Commerce. In addition to translating the chief's speeches, he presented his personal statement as "Special Agent for the Allied Tribes" and a representative "of the leading chief of the Interior Tribes [who] ... for the purpose of proving that I represent him gave me one of his own names at a public meeting and gave me his [King George the Third] medals to wear."[91] Despite their efforts, Bill 13 was signed into law on Dominion Day, 1920, empowering the federal government to implement the McKenna-McBride Commission recommendations without concern for Indian title, treaties, or self-government.

The legislation, however, was not enacted immediately. Just prior to the signing of Bill 13, T. Duff Pattullo, British Columbia's minister of lands, had pressed for a review of some of the report's flaws. In response, Scott met with him in Victoria in September 1920 to discuss the possibilities. The outcome was the appointment of a formal review team, consisting of W.E. Ditchburn for Indian Affairs and Major J.W. Clark for the province, to undertake this work. They in turn invited Teit to be the third member of the team. As Scott explained: "I mentioned to Mr. Teit that this was practically the only opportunity that the Indians will have to represent their reserve claims to the Governments, and that if they fail to take this opportunity I do not see how matters can be reopened as the agreement to be reached will be considered final."[92] Teit responded that he would accept this position only with the approval of the chiefs.[93]

With the chiefs' endorsement, Teit began his work for the Ditchburn-Clark Inquiry in mid-October. He was optimistic about its potential. As he explained to Sapir: "I have now to occupy all my time during the rest of this month and the greater part of next with work for Mr. Scott and the Indians in connection with placing the Indian case before the Board which has been appointed by the two governments to investigate the actual needs of the Indians as regards lands, fishing, hunting, etc. This Board of two officials will later make recommendations to the governments and then an attempt will be made to settle with the Indians and if possible settle this troublesome controversy."[94] Meanwhile, Sapir had successfully convinced his superiors at the Geological Survey to offer Teit lump sums of money for four completed manuscripts on the Tahltan and Kaska. Consequently, while working on the Ditchburn Report, Teit simultaneously worked on these ethnographic reports.

Just weeks into this work, however, Teit was diagnosed with cancer. After a year of treatment, he had recovered sufficiently to resume his work for the inquiry in mid-October 1921: "At present I am doing work for the Indian Department and the Indians in connection with the BC land question."[95] By March he reported that he was approaching the end of his "Indian meetings" and was just beginning to write up the report of his "investigation."[96] Unfortunately, however, he suffered a relapse from which he never recovered.[97] On 30 October 1922, at the age of fifty-eight, Teit died in Merritt, British Columbia.

Teit's death was felt immediately among the Aboriginal leadership. At the ATBC's General Assembly in North Vancouver the following January, Chief Chilahitsa of Douglas Lake and the ITBC threatened to break from the ATBC. Political scientist Paul Tennant attributes the disunity to Teit's death.[98] Kelly, who had worked closely with Teit and the ATBC, was even stronger on this point, noting that "the organization of the Interior Indians fell apart after Teit's death. Not altogether, but it was never the same again."[99] Even Boas noted the loss. Aboriginal peoples, he wrote, "had lost their best friend."[100]

J.A. Teit and the Potential for an Activist Anthropology

That one of Canadian anthropology's pioneers is remembered today primarily as a salvage ethnographer reflects a serious gap in the history of the discipline. Not only was Teit able to draw the timeless Golden Age Past into the present, but he was also able to realize an important social mission.[101] Taking his lead from the Aboriginal leadership, he embarked on a new form of ethnographic text making aimed at mobilizing a united

Aboriginal body against an aggressive assimilationist regime. As a result, he distinguished himself from his peers.

This latter point is particularly evident from 1908 on, when Teit shifted his focus from the heavy demands of Boas' salvage project to the Aboriginal political lobby. Teit came into his own through this work, cultivating sophisticated mediation skills that to this day have rarely been matched.[102] His intimate knowledge of Aboriginal protocols and his self-effacing, quiet manner were key to his success. For example, drawing from his vast experience as a salvage ethnographer, he understood first-hand that among the Aboriginal peoples of the southern interior, leadership was dispersed through the group rather than concentrated in a few individuals at the top. As he explained of the Nlaka'pamux, even the most noted orators "seldom or never acted in matters of public interest without obtaining the consent of all their people."[103] He applied this model to his own role in negotiations: "I seldom advise the Indians at any time (except when asked for advice)," he explained to D.C. Scott. He stated that he preferred instead "to give them information and explain everything as well as I can and then leave them to make their own decisions."[104] His Haida colleague, Peter Kelly, made observations that confirm this: "[Teit] was a clever man, and had a great way with people," he explained. "He did not speak that much but seemed to know what to say to bring them [the Indians] out, and get what information was needed. He had good organizing skills, was a good judge of people, and most people liked him ... The Interior Indians trusted him implicitly and whatever he said was good enough for them. They listened to his every word and believed him. I have never seen anything like it before, or to this day. Teit would patiently explain what they did not understand."[105] The Vancouver newspaper columnist Dr. Snowden Dunn Scott (known by the pen name "Lucian") provides us with one of the only first-hand accounts of his translation style:

> Several years ago there was held in Vancouver a conference of British Columbia Indian chiefs, gathered at the request of Mr. Duncan Campbell Scott, to discuss Indian rights ... On a low chair by the table among the chiefs was a silent white man, who took no part in the proceedings until the chiefs began to address the superintendent-general, each in his own language. Then he began to interpret. As one after another of the natives poured out his complaint or expressed his opinions in various forms of aboriginal eloquence, Mr. Teit, in a low quiet voice, rendered his appeal or argument into clear and cultured English. I was struck with the simplicity, felicity and clearness of his language. Every sentence was ready for the press. And though he must have interpreted from four or five dialects, he showed no doubt or hesitation, though he occasionally asked the speaker a question or made a suggestion evidently in the interest of clearness.[106]

There are many references throughout the political documentation to the importance of orally based knowledge. A 1911 "Memorial," for example, states that Aboriginal peoples had preserved their own oral records of promises and exchanges: "We can tell you all of them if you want to know and prove them through witnesses still living."[107] The documents also highlight the *postcontact* period. "Many of us," they argued, "were driven off our places where we had lived and camped from time immemorial ... even places where we raised food ... It was ... in direct opposition to the promises made to us by the first whites, and Government officials that no white man would be allowed to locate on any place where Indians were settled or which were camping stations and gardens ... Another promise broken, and so on with all."[108]

They characterized whites as the source of their problems. "We know the whites are strong, rich, civilized, and Christian," the chiefs explained to Robert Borden in 1912, "and we expected they would do great things for us ... Instead, they have introduced diseases amongst us of which our forefathers knew nothing; they have killed the best of our people with strong drink."[109] They explained that they could not trust the word of whites, "especially when it is not written word."[110] They depicted the latter as eager to take advantage of weakness and ignorance and quick to mock their chiefs:[111] "They treat us as less than children and allow us no say in anything. They say the Indians know nothing and own nothing, yet their power and wealth has come from our belongings."[112] The 1910 "Memorial to Sir Wilfrid Laurier" acknowledged that some whites were good, while others were inherently bad. The first group of whites to arrive in their territory, they explained, were "real whites," "good" people (also referred to as "guests" and "brothers") who could be trusted; the whites who arrived later (after the Gold Rush of 1858) were "other Whites," greedy, ill-mannered people who were in search of gold and land.[113]

To continue to associate Teit with an anthropological paradigm that stripped Aboriginal peoples of their place in *real* time not only denies what Teit stood for; it defeats the larger purpose of his activism by privileging one set of recollected presentations of a glorified cultural past over a more immediate expression of a struggling cultural present. Ironically, Boas was one of the few who truly understood the depth of Teit's commitment to a political ethnography: "Unceasingly," noted Boas in his obituary of Teit, "he labored for their welfare and subordinated all other interests, scientific as well as personal, to this work, which he came to consider the most important task of his life."[114] By the time of his death in 1922, this "silent white man" who "did not speak that much but [who] seemed to know what to say to bring [the Native voice] out"[115] had helped to mobilize Aboriginal groups in almost every corner of the province. This was perhaps his greatest achievement. It could be argued as well that he laid the groundwork for an activist anthropology that, during this early period, also died with him.[116]

Acknowledgment

This chapter draws heavily on a previous publication by the author: "'We Shall Drink from the Stream and So Shall You': James A. Teit and Native Resistance in British Columbia, 1908-22," *Canadian Historical Review* 79, 2 (1998): 199-236. The main title is taken from a letter from Teit to Duncan Campbell Scott, Library and Archives Canada (henceforth LAC), RG 10, vol. 7781, file 27150-3-3, 2 March 1916.

Notes

1　LAC, RG 10, vol. 7780, file 27150-3-1, "'Memorial' to the Hon. Frank Oliver, Minister of the Interior, from the Chiefs of the Shuswap, Couteau or Thompson, et al.," Spences Bridge, British Columbia, 10 May 1911.

2　Regna Darnell, "The Pivotal Role of the Northwest Coast in the History of Americanist Anthropology," *British Columbia Studies* 125-26 (Spring/Summer 2000): 33-52.

3　George W. Stocking, Jr., ed., *"Volksgeist" as Method and Ethic: Essays on Boasian Ethnography and the German Anthropological Tradition* (Madison: University of Wisconsin Press, 1996); Regna Darnell, *And Along Came Boas: Continuity and Revolution in Americanist Anthropology* (Amsterdam: Benjamins, 1996).

4　Johannes Fabian, *Time and the Other: How Anthropology Makes Its Object* (New York: Columbia University Press, 1983).

5　Charles Briggs and Richard Bauman, "'The Foundations of All Future Researches': Franz Boas, George Hunt, Native American Texts, and the Construction of Modernity," *American Quarterly* 51, 3 (1999): 479-528 at 483.

6　Roderick Sprague, "A Bibliography of James Teit," *Northwest Anthropological Research Notes* 25, 9 (1991): 103-15 at 103.

7　Apart from one essay by me and another by Peter Campbell, there is no systematic study of James Teit's involvement in Aboriginal politics. Wickwire, "We Shall Drink"; Campbell, "Not as a Whiteman, Not as a Sojourner: James A. Teit and the Fight for Native Rights in British Columbia, 1884-1922," *Left History* 2, 2 (1994): 37-57.

8　Ralph Maud, *A Guide to B.C. Indian Myth and Legend* (Vancouver: Talonbooks, 1982), 77. See also David Murray, *Forked Tongues: Speech, Writing and Representation in North American Indian Texts* (Bloomington: Indiana University Press, 1991); and Michael Harkin, "(Dis)pleasures of the Text: Boasian Anthropology on the Central Northwest Coast," in *Gateways: Exploring the Legacy of the Jesup North Pacific Expedition, 1897-1902,* ed. Igor Krupnik and William W. Fitzhugh (Washington: Smithsonian Institution, 2001), 93-105.

9　Quoted in Ronald Rohner, ed., *The Ethnography of Franz Boas* (Chicago: University of Chicago Press, 1969), 139.

10　Douglas Cole, "The Origins of Canadian Anthropology, 1850-1910," *Journal of Canadian Studies* 7, 1 (1973): 33-45.

11　Franz Boas, "Diary," 5 July 1888, in Rohner, ed., *The Ethnography,* 100.

12　Ibid.

13　This was Boas' term. Interestingly, Teit would never have called himself a "Scot" because he was first and foremost a Shetlander.

14　Boas to his parents, 21 September 1894, in Rohner, ed., *The Ethnography,* 140.

15　Ibid.

16　Boas to his wife, 15 December 1894, in Rohner, ed., *The Ethnography,* 196.

17　Wendy Wickwire, "Beyond Boas? Re-assessing the Contribution of 'Informant' and 'Research Assistant' James A. Teit," in *Constructing Cultures Then and Now: The Jesup North Pacific Expedition,* ed. Laurel Kendall and Igor Krupnik (Seattle: University of Washington Press, 2003), 123-33.

18　Boas, "Diary," 18 July 1888, in Rohner, ed., *The Ethnography,* 102.

19 Boas to his wife, 16 September 1894, in ibid., 136.
20 Boas to his wife, 21 September 1894, in ibid., 139.
21 Boas to his wife, 23 September 1894, in ibid., 142.
22 Boas to his wife, 15 December 1894, in ibid., 196.
23 Ibid.
24 Douglas Cole, *Franz Boas: The Early Years, 1858-1906* (Vancouver and Seattle: Douglas and McIntyre and University of Washington Press, 1999).
25 Rohner, ed., *The Ethnography,* 139.
26 Wickwire, "We Shall Drink." Judith Judd Banks was the first to draw attention to Teit's political activism; see "Comparative Biographies of Two British Columbia Anthropologists, Charles Hill-Tout and James A. Teit" (MA thesis, University of British Columbia, 1970).
27 The correspondence between the two men from 1894 to 1922 sheds much light on this. See James Teit Correspondence File, Anthropology Archives, American Museum of Natural History (henceforth TCF); see also the Boas Professional Correspondence, American Philosophical Society, Philadelphia, Pennsylvania (henceforth BPC).
28 TCF, Teit to Boas, 22 February 1995.
29 Judith Berman, "'The Culture as It Appears to the Indian Himself': Boas, George Hunt and the Methods of Ethnography," in *"Volksgeist" as Method and Ethic: Essays on Boasian Ethnography and the German Anthropological Tradition,* ed. George Stocking Jr. (Madison: University of Wisconsin Press, 1996), 215-56 at 220.
30 BPC, Teit to Boas, 10 March 1897.
31 Brian Thom, "Harlan I. Smith's Jesup Fieldwork on the Northwest Coast," in *Gateways: Exploring the Legacy of the Jesup North Pacific Expedition, 1897-1902,* ed. Igor Krupnik and William W. Fitzhugh (Washington: Smithsonian, 2001), 139-80 at 141.
32 See Rohner, ed., *The Ethnography,* 202-5.
33 For a list of these publications, see Maud, *A Guide,* 81-83.
34 James Teit, *The Thompson Indians of British Columbia,* Memoirs of the American Museum of Natural History, vol. 1, part 4 (New York: American Museum of Natural History, 1900).
35 BPC, Boas to Teit, 15 February 1901.
36 Teit, *The Thompson Indians,* 165.
37 James Teit, *The Lillooet Indians,* Memoirs of the American Museum of Natural History, vol. 2, part 5 (New York: American Museum of Natural History, 1906); James Teit, *The Shuswap,* Memoirs of the American Museum of Natural History, vol. 2, part 7 (New York: American Museum of Natural History, 1909).
38 BPC, Teit to Boas, 23 May 1908.
39 LAC, RG 10, vol. 4038, file 329, 350.
40 Ibid.
41 Teit to Haldane Burgess, quoted in Roy Gronneberg, "James Teit: Friend of the Indians," *The New Shetlander* 126 (1978): 28-30 at 28.
42 Banks, "Comparative Biographies," 53-54.
43 Teit to Burgess, quoted in Roy Gronneberg, "James Teit," 28.
44 Shetland Archives, Peter Jamieson Papers, Sam Anderson to Peter Jamieson, 27 November 1930.
45 LAC, RG 10, vol. 7781, file 27150-3-3, Teit to Duncan C. Scott, 2 March 1916.
46 Ibid.
47 Teit, *The Thompson Indians,* 176-77.
48 Ibid., 177.
49 Ibid., 178.
50 In his daily journal of 1910 (henceforth Teit's Journal), Teit mentions attending chiefs' meetings on 8, 22, 23, and 30 January. On 12 February, he travelled to Lytton with some chiefs from Spences Bridge to attend a meeting of sixteen chiefs that started on Sunday, 13 February, and carried on all night. The following Saturday to Monday, he attended more meetings of chiefs at Sulus, a Native community near Merritt. By 26-27 February he was in Kamloops to attend further meetings. He noted on the latter date that "Indian chiefs all favourable." Presumably this refers to Teit's goal to gain the support of the ITBC for the IRA and its efforts to have the Native grievances aired before the Privy Council.

On his return to Spences Bridge, he spent 1-4 March "writing Indian letters." Teit's original 1910 journal is in the possession of Sigurd Teit, Merritt, British Columbia. It is reprinted in full in *Teit Times*, 1 (Summer 1995): 6-12.

51 BPC, Teit to Boas, 23 February 1910.
52 LAC, RG10, vol. 7780, file 27150-3-1, "Declaration of Interior Tribes," 28 July 1910; Reprinted in Teit's Journal, 22. British Columbia Archives, "Memorial to Sir Wilfrid Laurier, Premier of the Dominion of Canada from the Chiefs of Shuswap, Okanagan and Couteau Tribes of British Columbia," 25 August 1910. In a letter to Charles Newcombe on 6 August 1910, Teit notes: "I enclose a copy of the Indian Declaration signed by 24 Shuswap, Okanagan, and Thompson chiefs who attended the meeting here last month." British Columbia Archives (henceforth BCA), Newcombe Papers.
53 *Kamloops Sentinel*, 26 August 1910, reprinted in *Teit Times*, 1 (Summer 1995).
54 Ibid.
55 Robert M. Galois, "The Indian Rights Association, Native Protest Activity and the 'Land Question' in British Columbia, 1903-1916," *Native Studies Review* 8, 2 (1992): 1-34 at 16.
56 McBride's accusation is quoted verbatim in the ITBC memorial statement to the Honourable Frank Oliver, 10 May 1911. LAC, RG10, vol. 7780, file 27150-3-1.
57 Ibid.
58 Archives of Canadian Museum of Civilization, Hull, Quebec (henceforth CMC), Teit to Edward Sapir, 18 December 1913.
59 Note that the spellings of these and other Indian names vary slightly from document to document. "Tedlenitsa," for example, occasionally appears as "Tetlenitsa" and "Tetlanitsa."
60 BCA, "Indian Rights Association of British Columbia to the Honourable R. Borden and Members of the Dominion Cabinet," 6 January 1912.
61 BCA, "Letter of the Indian Rights Association of British Columbia to the Right Honourable R. Borden, Minister of the Dominion of Canada," presented at Kamloops, 15 March 1912.
62 CMC, Teit to Sapir, 2 August 1912.
63 This was undertaken through an Order-in-Council of 24 May 1912.
64 "Statement of Chiefs of the Interior Tribes of British Columbia to the Honourable Mr. Borden, Prime Minister of Canada, and Members of the Dominion Government," 23 May 1913, copy obtained from Sigurd Teit.
65 CMC, Teit to Edward Sapir, 18 December 1913.
66 Ibid.
67 CMC, Teit to Sapir, 4 January 1914.
68 Galois, "The Indian Rights Association," 21.
69 Teit noted in a letter that he had devoted "most of his time for a week on this meeting." CMC, Teit to Sapir, 6 March 1915.
70 BCA, "Indian Rights Association to the Honourable W.J. Roche, Minister of the Interior," 27 February 1915.
71 The Nootka, the Kwakiutl, and the treaty tribes of the Northeast were not part of this organization. The ATBC was also united in its opposition to the IRA lawyer, J.M. Clark, who had erroneously communicated that the IRA was prepared to accept the terms of Order-in-Council PC1422 (19 June 1915). Galois, "The Indian Rights Association," 22. For more on this, see Darcy Mitchell, "The Allied Tribes of British Columbia: A Study in Pressure Group Behaviour" (MA thesis, University of British Columbia, 1977), 38-41.
72 CMC, Teit to Sapir, 20 March 1916.
73 Peter Kelly, a Methodist minister of Haida descent, joined the movement at this time and continued on to become one of its leaders. For more information on Kelly, see Alan Morley, *Roar of the Breakers: A Biography of Peter Kelly* (Toronto: Ryerson Press, 1967).
74 CMC, Teit to Sapir, 12 September 1917.
75 CMC, Teit to Sapir, 29 September 1917.
76 J.A. Teit, "About the Indians," *Victoria Daily Times*, 20 December 1917. Teit wrote this piece as a response to an article entitled "Indians Not against Conscription Plan," *Victoria Daily Times*, 11 December 1917, in which it was reported that some Cowichan Indians were *not* in support of the Teit-Kelly telegram. The Reverend C.M. Tate, general secretary of the IRA, defended Teit: "Mr. Teit never does anything rashly; and as he is a tried and

tested friend of the Indians throughout the province, you may rest assured that whatever he did was perfectly in order," quoted in Campbell, "Not as a Whiteman," 50. For a fuller discussion of Teit's anticonscription lobby, see ibid., 49-51.

77 Telegram, "P.R. Kelly, Chairman, J.A. Teit, Secretary," ATBC to Borden, 17 November 1917, reprinted in *Victoria Daily Colonist*, 20 November 1917.

78 LAC, RG 10, vol. 6768, file 452-20, part 1, Teit to Scott, 20 December 1917.

79 Ibid.

80 Titley, *A Narrow Vision*, 146.

81 CMC, Teit to Sapir, 25 July 1919.

82 CMC, Teit to Sapir, 9 August 1919.

83 Paul Tennant, *Aboriginal Peoples and Politics: The Indian Land Question in British Columbia, 1849-1989* (Vancouver: UBC Press, 1990), 99.

84 Mitchell, "The Allied Tribes," 44.

85 James Teit and Peter R. Kelly, *Statement of the Allied Indian Tribes of British Columbia for the Government of British Columbia* (Vancouver: Cowan and Brookhouse, 1919), 99.

86 Titley, *A Narrow Vision: Duncan Campbell Scott and the Administration of Indian Affairs in Canada* (Vancouver: UBC Press, 1986), 146-48; Tennant, *Aboriginal Peoples*, 99.

87 Mitchell, "The Allied Tribes," 52.

88 *Ottawa Journal*, 15 April 1920; *Ottawa Journal*, 5 May 1920.

89 Teit to Baer, 2 April 1920, copy obtained from Sigurd Teit.

90 As he explained in his statement before the Senate Committee in Ottawa exactly a month later on 16 June, "Whilst in British Columbia about 3 weeks ago I met Premier Oliver and in talking over the matter of reserves he told me that he thought because certain reserves or portions of reserves were not made full use of by the Indians that was not sufficient reason for concluding that these lands should be taken from them." Teit to the Senate Committee, 16 June 1920. Copy obtained from Sigurd Teit.

91 Ibid. It was necessary to explain his role due to accusations that the Native resistance movement was the work of white agitators. See Mitchell, "The Allied Tribes," 54. By this time, a number of "whites" were well known as assisting the Native chiefs. Arthur O'Meara, already mentioned, was one. Another was H.R. Christie, a former Northwest Police Officer, who assisted the Okanagan in some of their dealings with government officials and decisions. For a brief overview of Christie's activities, see Keith Smith, "Surveillance, Measurement, Judgment, and Reform: Indian Reserves in the British Columbia Interior and the Panoptic Mechanism" (MA thesis, University of Victoria, 1996), 89-90.

92 LAC, RG 10, vol. 3820, file 59, 355, part 3, Scott to Sir James Lougheed, 1 October 1920.

93 Ibid. Historian Peter Campbell argues that by taking on this position, Teit was co-opted by Scott. See Campbell, "Not as a Whiteman," 54. All available evidence, however, suggests that this was an important and timely job that offered some promise for the Aboriginal cause. Knowing this, Teit could not easily have turned it down.

94 CMC, Teit to Sapir, 10 November 1920.

95 CMC, Teit to Sapir, 19 October 1921.

96 CMC, Teit to Sapir, 18 March 1922.

97 CMC, Teit to Sapir, 31 July 1922.

98 Tennant, *Aboriginal Peoples*, 102-3.

99 Interview, Sigurd Teit with Peter Kelly, November 1953. Copy of notes from this interview obtained from Sigurd Teit.

100 Franz Boas, "Obituary of James A. Teit," *Journal of American Folklore* 36 (1923): 102-3 at 103.

101 Peter Campbell states, in contrast, that "whatever sense Teit had of his own historical importance was almost entirely tied to his anthropological work, not his political activism." Campbell, "Not as a Whiteman," 45. Unfortunately, however, Campbell provides no evidence for this.

102 Peter Campbell asserts that by 1911 there were many Native people who refused or were hesitant to work with Teit. Campbell, "Not as a Whiteman," 45. The only evidence that I have found suggesting a reluctance to work with Teit is a letter from J.A. McKenna to D.C. Scott in 1916, in which McKenna reports that "When this Commission met Indians

of whose language he [Teit] is a master, the majority view was against his employment. But at one meeting, at least, at which he was present, the Indians insisted on his acting as a sort of checking interpreter, and he may have been paid for that." LAC, RG 10, vol. 3822, file 59, 335-2, 5 February 1916. Without evidence, especially for the 1911 period, Campbell's assertion is questionable.

103   Teit, *The Thompson Indians*, 127.
104   LAC, RG 10, vol. 7781, file 27150-3-3, Teit to Scott, 2 March 1916.
105   Ibid.
106   Scott, Snowden Dunn ("Lucian"), *The Merritt Herald*, 9 and 16 March 1923.
107   "Memorial to the Hon. Frank Oliver, Minister of the Interior, Ottawa," 10 May 1911.
108   Ibid.
109   BCA, "Indian Rights Association," statement, 6 January 1912.
110   "Memorial to the Hon. Frank Oliver, Minister of the Interior, Ottawa," 10 May 1911.
111   Ibid.
112   BCA, "Memorial to Sir Wilfrid Laurier, Premier of the Dominion of Canada, from the Chiefs of the Shuswap, Okanagan and Couteau Tribes of British Columbia," 25 August 1910.
113   Ibid.
114   Boas, "Obituary of James A. Teit," 102-3 at 103. From 1912 until his death, Teit's anthropological production declined significantly. In 1912, for example, Teit was appointed by the Anthropology Division of the Canadian Geological Survey to undertake ethnological research under their auspices. It was an unusual appointment because Teit requested that he remain in Spences Bridge in order to be free to do his guiding for hunters each fall. By 1918, due to his lack of written production, this contract was terminated. See Regna Darnell, "The Sapir Years at the National Museum, Ottawa," *Proceedings of the Canadian Ethnology Society* (1976): 98-121 at 104.
115   See note 107.
116   Diamond Jenness, who replaced Edward Sapir as head of the Anthropology Division in 1925, had no interest in the sort of activist work that Teit pursued. In fact, some scholars have argued that Jenness actively pursued a research program that worked against the Aboriginal political campaign; see Peter Kulchyski, "Anthropology in the Service of the State: Diamond Jenness and Canadian Indian Policy," *Journal of Canadian Studies* 28, 2 (1993): 2-50. Marius Barbeau, a major figure in the Anthropology Division from 1911 until the 1960s, actively supported some of the assimilationist initiatives of the Indian Department under Duncan Campbell Scott; see Andrew Nurse, "'But Now Things Have Changed': Marius Barbeau and the Politics of Amerindian Identity," in *Ethnohistory* 48, 3 (2001): 433-71.

Appendix
The Fair Play Papers – The Future of Our Indians

Paper No. 1
Fair Play
The Canadian Indian
Vol. 1, no. 6, March 1891

This is a problem which has long agitated the minds of thinking people, and one for which the writer of this article is by no means prepared to offer a solution. But it seems that the pages of The CANADIAN INDIAN can scarcely perhaps be put to a better purpose than that of ventilating so important and far-reaching a subject; and he proposes now, in a series of short papers, to throw out a few ideas and suggestions, which, however crude and impracticable they may appear to persons of more profound thought and of riper judgment, may yet perhaps do some good, if only as a means of drawing attention to the subject and inviting criticism on the thoughts suggested. The writer would wish to be understood from the outset that he takes the side of the Indians, and wishes to speak altogether from the Indian's standpoint. There are plenty of persons ready enough to deal with the Indian question from the white man's point of view. All the actions of our Government, of our Indian Department, of our education institutions, even the organizations and carrying on of our Christian missions, are from the white man's stand-point. The Indian is not asked whether he prefers living on an Indian reserve to roaming the country; whether he likes his children to be educated or to lead a wild life; whether he prefers Government beef or buffalo flesh; whether he is to retain the language and the customs of his forefathers, or to give them up; whether in his worship he is to follow the ancient rituals of his ancestors, address the sun as his god, and the rivers, mountains, rocks and other elements of nature as minor deities, or to accept the Christian teaching of the white man and become thereby a Methodist, Episcopalian, a Presbyterian or a Roman Catholic. He is not asked these things. There is no yea or nay about it. They are simply one after another forced upon him. Not only is he expected to accept them without a word, but he is expected also to be grateful, to coin words for which there is no equivalent in his simple, primitive language, to express his gratitude – otherwise he may be dubbed an "ungrateful savage," or even something worse, by his white neighbors.

That the Indians – even the most civilized of them – are not altogether enthusiastic in their desire to accept the white man's methods, to blot out their own nationality, and to wave aloft over their villages either the Stars and Stripes of America or the Union Jack of Canada, has been proved not unfrequently of late on both sides of the line by whispered reports gleaned at their council meetings. The idea of enfranchisement, which in the eyes of white men is esteemed so great a boon, to the Indian appears to have but little charm. And only lately we heard that some of our most civilized Indians were appearing to Government to have their chieftainship made hereditary once more, instead of elective as at present. Then again – across the border, what is this "Messiah craze" that has spread with such wonderful rapidity among the Indians from north to south and from east to west? What a readiness there seems to be on their part to go back to the old ways again, to resume their old customs and their old superstitions, if only the chance were given them. Sometimes it seems to me that all we are doing for them – educating their children, dressing them in white men's clothing, making them talk English, teaching them to pride themselves in being like white people – is a mere veneer; that underneath there is still the love of the wild, roaming life; that hidden beneath outward Christian life are still the remnants of dark heathen superstition. Certain it is, whatever may be said to the contrary, that the Indians, as a people, do not draw towards the white people; and that the white people, as a people, do not draw towards the Indians.

What then, is to be the future of the Indians? Will the day ever come that the Indians as a people will have so utterly and entirely lost their own distinct nationality, their own distinct peculiarities of habit, taste, character, as to mingle freely with the white people, and become one of them? It does not look much like it at present. There are indeed some few isolated cases of Indians who have received a good education, developed talent according to the white man's standard, and taken their position in the midst of us, some as doctors, some as employees in the Indian Department, some as ministers of the Gospel; but there, it must be acknowledged, are exceptional cases; and if they have been received at all into society, it is probably because they have become united in marriage with a "pale face," and have thus identified themselves permanently with the Anglo-Saxon race. The idea has been prevalent of late that the true way to deal with the Indians, and indeed the only method at all likely to be followed with success, is to take their children while young, remove them altogether from their parents, keep them five or six years in a boarding school, teach them entirely in English, let them forget their old barbaric tongue and their old ways and customs; and become, in fact, thoroughly Anglicized. And this idea has been still further improved upon within the last few years; the newest idea of all, and one which is already being acted upon to a considerable extent in the United States, is that when the Indian pupil has been pretty well weaned from his old ways, and well-nigh forgotten his own language, and has learned to read and write and do sums and to follow some trade like a white child, that he should not return to his own home and his own people, but should be placed out among the white people, be apprenticed to some white farmer or mechanic, earn his own living, and prepare to settle down in life – not on an Indian Reserve, but in the midst of the white population.

Now, all this from the white man's point of view, seems to be very plausible and, indeed, desirable. But how is it from the Indian's point of view? Is the Indian himself to have nothing to say about it? How would we white people like it if because we were weak, and another people more powerful than ourselves had possession of our country, we were obliged to give up our little children to go to the schools of this more powerful people – KNOWING that they were taken from us for the *very purpose* of weaning them from the old loves and the old associations – if we found that they were most unwillingly allowed to come back to us for the short summer holidays, and when they came were dressed in the peculiar costumes of our conquerors, and were talking their language instead of the dear old tongue, and then – if, when the time stipulated for their education was drawing to a close, and we were looking forward to welcoming them back to the old home, we were to be coolly told that provision had been made for them to go and live elsewhere, and that we were not very likely to see them again? What would we think of our conquerors if they treated us in this way?

It is said that this Messiah craze, this present disaffection and hostile spirit among the Indians in Dakota and elsewhere, is due to the unjust treatment they have received at the hands of the American Government, and American officials; that their nations have been so cruelly reduced that many of them were on the verge of starvation, – but it seems to me that the real trouble rather is that the Indians, as a people, are not willing to have their own nationality and hereditary laws and customs so entirely effaced and swept away, as it seems to them it is the white man's policy to do. I incline to think that the forcing of their children away to school, the pressing upon them of civilized habits and occupations, the weaning them from the love of home and parents, has perhaps had as much to do with the late disaffection as the limited supply of beef and the poor quality of the flour.

An Indian is a different being to a white man. His history for centuries past has been of a character wholly different to that of the white man. His pleasures, his tastes, his habits, his laws, are all at variance with those accepted by the white man. How, then, can we expect, in the course of two or three decades, to effect such radical changes in his character, habits, thoughts, as it has taken centuries to effect in ourselves? And is it altogether just to treat the Indian in the way we are doing? Is it altogether fair to deprive them of their nationality or to laugh at their old laws and customs and traditions, to force upon them our own laws and customs as though there could be no two questions as to their superiority in every way, and that they must, of course, be just as suitable and applicable to the Indian as they are to ourselves. Is there nothing – nothing whatever – in the past history of this ancient people to merit our esteem, or to call forth our praise? Were their laws in the past all mere childishness? Were there no great minds among their noted chiefs? Do the ruins of their ancient cities show no marks of intelligence, energy or perseverance, in the people that planned and constructed them? While taking steps to preserve their ancient relics in our museums, and while studying their past history and their many and diverse languages, were it not well, as a matter of justice and Christian kindness to them, as well as out of respect for their part and but little-understood history, to allow them to preserve their own nationality, and, under certain restrictions, to enact their own laws? Would it not be pleasanter, and even safer to us, to have living in our midst a contented, well-to-do, self-respecting, thriving community of Indians, rather than a set of dependent, dissatisfied, half-educated and half-Anglicized paupers?

As the writer of this article said at the beginning of this paper, his object in taking up this subject to throw out a few crude ideas; and his hope is that those who are better able than he is to reason out the problem, and whose judgment will have more weight with the public, will take up and thoroughly ventilate the whole question.

Paper No. 2
The Canadian Indian
Vol. 1, no. 7, April 1891

In my last paper I broached the idea that, looking to the future of our young growing country, it might be pleasanter, and perhaps better for us in every way, to have living in our midst a community of self-respecting, contented, well-to-do Indians, rather than the scattered remnants of a people, who against their will, had been forced to give up their old customs, laws and traditions, and to array themselves in the ill-fitting garb of our advanced civilizations. I do not mean by this that I am against the training and educating of our young Indians; far from it. I believe by far the greater number of our semi-civilized Indians are warmly in favor of schools and education. The Cherokees, in Indian Territory, who for many years past have been permitted to manage their own affairs, hold their own public purse, and make their own laws, are, as a people, very far advanced in education; and have large schools and colleges, built out of their own funds, established in their midst. If our civilized Indians in Canada had more management of their own affairs, I believe education and civilization would advance among them, and not retrograde. What I feel so strongly is that the civilized Indians of this country ought to have more voice in their own affairs, that the time has passed for treating them as children, doling out to them their presents and their annuities, and taking their children away from them to be educated, without allowing them to have any voice in the matter. It seems to me that the proper person to deal with the wild blanket Indians of the Northwest Territories and British Columbia are *these civilized Christian Indians* of Ontario and Quebec and some parts of Manitoba. It seems to me that if something of a national spirit were stirred up among them, if more confidence were placed in them as a people, if these presents and annuities were done away with, and the Indian Reserves one by one thrown open, and the white missionaries were one by one withdrawn from their midst – and these Christian civilized Indians had the responsibilities of life thus thrown upon them

– that there would be very soon a great change for the better; and before long we white people would learn to respect the name of Indian instead of despising it. How can any people, however civilized, be expected to advance and to keep pace with the world, when all national sentiment is dried up, and when all spirit of self-dependence is destroyed within them?

Is there nothing in the past history of this people that might lead us to hope that, under wise guidance, and with the object lesson of our own system of government with its beneficial results ever before them, they might in time be permitted to have a constitution of their own, and under certain restrictions, make their own laws and manage their own affairs? Mr. Hale, in his pamphlet on the *Iroquois Confederacy,* says, "The testimony of historians, travellers and missionaries, is that these Indians were, in their own way, acute reasoners, eloquent speakers, and most skilful and far-seeing politicians. For more than a century, though never mustering more than five thousand fighting men, they were able to hold the balance of power on this continent between France and England; and in a long series of negotiations, they proved themselves qualified to cope in council with the best diplomats whom either of those powers could depute to deal with them. Their internal polity was marked by equal wisdom; and had been developed and consolidated into a system of government, embodying many of what are deemed the best principles and methods of political science – representation, federation, self-government through local and general legislatures – all resulting in personal liberty, combined with strict subordination to public law." This is what Mr. Hale, than whom probably no other man in Canada has more thoroughly studied the whole Indian question in all its aspects, says of the Iroquois Indians, or rather of the six nations (Mohawks, Cayugas, Oneidas, Onandagas, Senecas, and Tuscaroras), which form the Iroquois Confederacy. And it should be remembered that representatives of this great Iroquois confederacy are still living in Canada to the number of about 4000, viz., 1000 on the Bay of Quinte, near Deseronto, and upwards of 3000 on the Grand River, near Brantford; and that they are regarded as the most advanced in civilization of all our Indians. Take another tribe, *the Ottawas,* after whom the capital of our Dominion is named. This tribe, closely related to the great Ojebway nation, is now reduced to about 2500, and its remnants are scattered upon our Manitoulin Island and parts of the State of Michigan. An educated Ottawa, now advanced in years, tells how in his young days, before the white men held sway, his people lived under strict laws; they were governed by twenty-one precepts or moral commandments, which they were taught to observe, just as we teach our children the Ten Commandments. The children were taught that the Great Spirit could see them continually both by night and by day, and that they must not do any wicked things to anger him; they were taught, also, that they must not mimic or mock thunder; that they must not mimic or mock the mountains or rivers; they were taught that dishonesty and licentiousness were wrong; that murder ought to be avenged; that they ought to be brave and not fear death. *The Cherokees,* 22,000 in number, living in Indian Territory, U.S., have, as is well known, a regular system of government, framed partly upon the American patterns, partly after their own ideas. They have their own Governor, elected by the popular vote, and their own Parliament; the Legislative Assembly consists of an Upper and Lower House; in the former sit eighteen senators, and in the latter thirty-eight councilors, elected every second year from the nine districts. The Judicial Department consists of a District Court for each of the nine political districts. In cases involving the death penalty, one of the Justices of the Supreme Court presides. The jury and grand jury system is followed the same as in the United States. Their state prison is at Tahlequah, their capital, where also are situated their government offices and Houses of Parliament; also two large, handsomely-built seminaries, one for male and one for female pupils, each with accommodation for 150 scholars. They have very strict prohibitory liquor laws, which are rigidly exacted. And yet, with all this advance in the ways of civilization, these Cherokee Indians do by preference hold their lands in common, and retain several of their other ancient customs. A well-educated Cherokee lawyer has given the following reasons wherefore the Cherokees are opposed to the allotment of land in severalty: (1) By holding it in common they are better able to resist the aggression of the whites; (2) Their present social system has never yet developed a mendicant or a tramp; (3) Although poor, yet they have no paupers, none suffering from the oppression of the rich; (4) They do not believe that the whites have any better condition to offer them, and so they wish to remain as they are.

The Delawares again, of whom there is a remnant still remaining in Canada, have always been regarded as a people of marked intelligence. In the old days they had an ancient art called the "Ola Wampum," which was a sort of chart to assist the memory in recording traditions. When, after being driven from place to place by their white oppressors, they at length settled down in what they hoped would be a permanent colony, in 1866, they framed and adopted a code of laws which provided among other things, for the punishment of horse-stealers; for fining or otherwise punishing those who should take and ride a horse without consent of the owner; for building or keeping up fences to a proper height, for branding cattle; for returning lost articles or strayed cattle; for preventing the sale of liquor; for the making and carrying into effect of a person's will; for paying a man's debts after his death. Their laws dealt also with offences against the person, such as assault, murder and adultery, and defined the punishment of a miscreant who should willfully set fire to a house.

A good deal has been written about the *Zuni* Indians in New Mexico. These people are particularly interesting because they still inhabit the same locality, and are following for the most part the same ancient customs as when first discovered, by Coronado, in the 16th century. Now among these people there exist [sic] a most elaborate religious system. They have priests and high priests. They have thirteen secret religious orders. Of course there is a great deal of what we would call superstition mixed up in all they do; and yet there can be no question but that they are a most religious people; they have the most profound belief in the doctrines handed down to them from their ancestors; nothing is done without prayer; some sort of religious rite or ceremonial seems to be a necessary accompaniment to all their undertakings. Their children, from earliest infancy, are instructed most carefully and constantly in all the religious usages of the tribe, and they have 'god parents' especially deputed to look after them and instruct them.

Much more might yet be said, did space permit to show how the various Indian tribes, in days gone by, have had their own laws and their own religious customs; and how, as a result of being brought into contact with our Eastern civilization, they have in many cases voluntarily adopted, in a great measure, our system, as superior to their own, and have shown themselves, where opportunity has been afforded them, very well capable of self-government; but these records show also, I think, another thing, which it were foolish to hide our eyes from, viz., that the Indians as a people – wherever their location may happen to be – are not prepared to accept our system of government *in toto;* that while gladly accepting the white man's books, and education, and religion, and style of clothing and dwelling, and his various useful inventions and manufactures, they at the same time prefer to take these things and *use them after their own fashion,* and in their own way; they do not want to be forced into giving up all their old customs, which are so dear to them, and transforming themselves into white men; they will not allow that everything the white man makes, or says, or does, is superior to what they can make, or say, or do, themselves. They do not wish to follow the white man in his greediness after earthly gain; they do not believe in one man being very rich and another man very poor; they stick to the old saying of their ancestors, "the earth is our common mother, our mother may not be divided," and again another saying, "earth, air and water, are the Great Spirit's gift to us all, and may not be bought or sold."

Are we to have no respect for these inbred sentiments of our Indians, so deeply rooted in their breasts? Are they not to be allowed to hold and to foster national sentiment as well as ourselves? Is it right, or just, or fair, to deprive them of their tribal intercourse, to deprive them of their language, to blot out all their old associations and traditions, and to force them to be white men against their will? What nation is there upon earth that would submit to this? *We* may believe our ways, our customs, and our laws to be the best, but we cannot force the Indian to believe it. If we desire that he should be brought to accept our laws, and customs, and language, were it not better to lead him gradually to it, instead of forcing so great a change suddenly upon him? People complain of the Indian that he is slow in his movements, and ridicule him because he makes so little progress in comparison with his white brother; but there is this, I think, to be said, that the white man is in the white man's country, in the midst of surroundings that he fully approves and believes in, and he takes a national pride and pleasure in the progress of his country – but with the Indian – why, we know how it is with him. He holds the anomalous position of a stranger in a strange land, even though the soil under his feet be the soil bequeathed to him by his forefathers; he feels strange and bewildered; white men are bustling, hurrying all around him; he understands but very imperfectly either what they are saying or what they are doing; and he is told roughly, by those who take but little trouble to understand his case, that he must either adopt the white man's ways, and become virtually a white man, or else go back out of the way. In this wide country have we no room for an independent Indian community? Can we not place the Indian where he will no longer be hustled and badgered by his impatient white brethren? Or, if the Indian Reserve system must for the present be continued, might we not make the Indian happier, give him more respect for himself, and exact more respect for him from the white people, by placing his own affairs, both temporal and spiritual, more in his own hands, and permit him, with certain restrictions, to make his own laws and carry out his own ideas of government? In time, the two races may become amalgamated, the dividing lines be lost; but surely it is not fair to force the Indian to obliterate himself against his will, neither, do I believe, would it be a good thing for our country.

Paper No. 3
The Canadian Indian
Vol. 1, no. 8, May 1891

Can a people be happy and prosperous, so long as all national feeling is smothered and kept down within them? How is it with ourselves? Is it not the traditions of the past, the history of the by-gone days, that stirs our young men to press on towards the goal of success, and to do honor to their country? You say of the Indian – why can he not give up his own language, and adopt that of the country, as do the Germans, and the Swedes, and the French, and the Italians, that come as settlers to our shores? I wonder how many of these French and Swedes, and others, talk the English language in their own homes! Is it not the tendency with these foreigners to form little settlements and communities of their own people? Are not their songs, when they gather round the hearth-stone at night, all of the Fatherland? Do not they pride themselves on the old home which they have left across the seas? Does not their heart beat quickly at the sound of their old country music, or a sight of the old flag? Why should we expect that Indians alone, of all people, should be ready quietly to give up all old customs and traditions and language, and adopt those of the aggressor upon their soil? The change which we expect the Indian to make, and to make so quickly, is a far greater one than is required of any of those nations above enumerated, who have left the shores of one civilized country to come to those of another. With the Indian, the change is a radical one – a change of dress, a change of dwelling, a change in mode of gaining livelihood, a social change, a religious change, an educational change, a *totum in toto* change. And this – not so much for his own benefit, as for our own convenience. We want the land. We cannot have Indian hunters annoying our farmers and settlers. If the Indian is to remain, he must learn to be a decent neighbor; and to be a decent neighbor, we expect him to accept our religion, our education, our laws, and our customs. We allow him no choice, and we allow him no time. It is very pleasant, no doubt, to pride ourselves on the kindness that we Canadians have always shown to the Indians; it is pleasant to compare ourselves with our neighbors across the border and to congratulate ourselves that while the Americans are killing their Indians off, and are saying that "the only good Indian is a dead Indian," we Canadians are feeding the hungry, teaching the adults to farm, and training the young in our schools. But with all our goodness and kindness, I fear, if the truth were told, it would be found that there is at least one point in which we have failed – and that is – *We have not considered his feelings;* we have not given him sufficient credit for intelligence; we have not sufficiently considered that the love of fatherland, the love of the old traditions of the past, the love of the old language, and the old stories and songs, is as strong in the Indian as in any Englishman or Frenchman or Italian. A highly-educated Mohawk Indian said to me only the other day – and I must confess I was *surprised* to hear him say – "the last thing I would wish to give up is our language."

Now, if it be the case that these patriotic – or whatever name you like to call them – feelings are so strong in the Indian, may not that be the great reason why he seems to be so slow to adopt our civilization, and to make good friends with us; why he seems to prefer – as I have little doubt he does – to live in a community of his own people rather than to intermingle with, and intermarry with the whites? And again, if these patriotic feelings be so strong in him, is it not foolish for us on our part to think that a few years' schooling of his children will knock the ins and outs of our advanced civilization. "You may take your horse to water, but cannot make him drink."

The Indians, I believe, *must have time.* These changes that we think so good for him, must not be forced upon him too suddenly. Surely, if we would be successful in our dealings with these aboriginal people, we must lead them on slowly and kindly to see that these great and radical changes, which civilization necessarily brings in its train, are really for their good. We must give them time to take, taste, try and prove, these various measures which we are taking for their benefit. And if they take them and use them in their way, rather than in our way, what reason can we have for being surprised? They as a people, are so differently constituted to ourselves, that it seems scarcely to be expected that they should accept our laws and customs, and do everything just in the way that we do. If it is our great aim and object to make them self-supporting and self-dependent, then it would seem to be only wise and politic on the part of our rulers, to offer to them a *modus vivendi* that will please them. In order to become an industrious and prosperous people, they must become first a contented people. They can never become prosperous while feeling discontented and aggrieved. How can we expect them to be happy and contented, so long as measure after measure is forced upon them, without any reference to their own desires or their own feelings? Surely it were wiser now that a large proportion of our Indians, especially those living in Ontario, are comparatively civilized and educated, and able to converse in English, to take them into our counsels, and learn from their own lips their own Indian views as to their present position in this country, and their prospects for the future. Do they wish the present Indian Reserve system to be continued? Do they wish to dwell for ever as separate communities? Do they wish to retain for ever their own language?

When trouble arises, when Indians threaten war and put on their war paint, the white man is ready enough to consider the grievances, and listen to their complaints. But why should we wait for war and trouble? Were it not better and nobler now while the poor Indian is at peace with us, to take him into our counsel, and endeavor to devise a way by which he may rise from his present desired and degraded condition, and become a worthy and industrious part of our great and growing nation? I believe if steps were taken to ascertain the real feelings of the Indians, as regards amalgamation with our white population, it would be found that they were almost unanimously against it. My impression is that they do not wish to become Canadians. They wish to adopt our laws and customs up to a certain point; they are ready to throw over their heathenism, with all its dark superstition, and to accept in its stead the light of Christian teaching; they are ready to acknowledge the benefit of education, and wish to have their children educated, – but – they still cling to the old saying of their ancestors, "the earth is our mother, and cannot be divided;" "earth, water and air, are the free gifts of the Great Spirit to his children and cannot be owned by individuals." These and other kindred sentiments, I believe, are strong – very strong; strongly rooted in the Indian breast from Mexico to Hudson Bay, and from the Atlantic to the Pacific. And it is these and other such-like inbred sentiments, that seem to preclude, at any rate for many long years to come, any kind of amalgamation between them and the white race. They prefer, I believe, to live in separate communities, and to hold their land in common, as their forefathers have done before them for ages immemorial.

And does it not seem a little strange, and a little out of place, that we white people should be forcing upon these free children of the forest and prairies the various peculiar religious tenets which we have brought with us across the Atlantic Ocean? Were it not better that these Indians should be free to have their own form and style of worship if they elect to do so? What know these simple people of all our various isms? How are they to judge between the merits of one religious body and another? The Indian agent on the Grand River Reserve, reports that among his 4,000 Six Nations Indians, 1,032 are Church of England, 611 Baptists, 314 Methodists, 72 Salvation Army, 90 Brethren, 25 Roman Catholics, 4 Universalists, 9 Free Church, 9 Presbyterians, 684 Pagans, 534 religion unknown. Does this list comment itself to any read of *The Canadian Indian?* Does it comment itself to any Christian in Canada? It is our object, as Christian people, to perpetrate our religious differences and make us united, and yet we are working to perpetrate these differences among these poor Indians, so recently converted from heathenism. Should it not rather be our aim to promote the establishment of a native church – a self-supporting native church – a church that would have life in itself, and would be the means of extending Christian teaching to distant points among its own heathen. This again is a matter that has, I think, been too much overlooked or lost sight of in our dealings with the Indians – the natural fitness of young Indians to endure the fatigue and the hardships attaching to a missionary's life. They may not perhaps make just the sort of missionaries that young white men would make. Mould them on the white man's pattern, and probably they will turn out failures. But stir up among the young men in an Indian community a true missionary spirit, and encourage them to go out and preach the Gospel in their own way, to their own heathen – supported by their own people – and it seems to me that no better missionaries would be found. An Indian, better than any white man, knows how to bear cold and fasting and shipwreck and peril, and all that long category of suffering which St. Paul underwent patiently and stoically; and surely in this way he is well fitted for the fatigues and trails of missionary work. If only the Indian spirit could be stirred to work and to deny itself for the spread of the true Messiah's kingdom as it was stirred up lately in the States over a false Messiah, we might surely look for Christianity to make great and rapid strides in their midst. The Indians, as I have noted in a former paper, are naturally a religious people, they will give freely even of their poverty to the support of Christian missions. If they were to carry on their own missionary work, there might indeed be some lack of organization, and possibly a lower standard of morals than we white people would require; but on the other hand the feeling of self-dependence, and freedom from the shackles of nineteenth-century churchism, would, I believe, bear its fruits in a wider extension of the truth, and a more universal acceptation, on their part, of Christianity.

Paper No. 4

The Canadian Indian
Vol. 1, no. 9, June 1891

In this fourth and last paper I would like to offer a few suggestions as to what appears to me will be the best way to deal with our Indians in the future. As I said in my first paper on the subject, my ideas may be crude, visionary, impracticable; still I think there can be no harm in offering them, especially as it must surely be universally admitted that the system at present in vogue is but of a temporary character and must sooner or later give place to something of a more permanent form. It can surely never be thought that the Indian Department as it at present exists, with all its expensive machinery, its agents on every reserve, its farm instructors and other servants, is to continue for ever. It cannot be that the wild Indians of the North are for ever to receive the weekly rations of beef and flour, or that the more civilized Indians of Ontario are to be kept penned up on reserves, receive annuities, and be treated as children. Sooner or later this system must either come to an end, or it must at least undergo some great modification. These Indians, who are at present kept under tutelage as the wards of the Government, have either to arrive at maturity and must be recognized as men and women, or else they must be improved off the face of the earth and cease to exist. The latter is not likely, and surely cannot be wished for by any person possessing a grain of humanity in his breast. If, then, they are to become men and women – the great question is: are they to amalgamate with our white population and become one nation with us or are they to be allowed to preserve their own nationality and continue to be Indians? My belief is that the latter alternative is what the Indian desires – and desires *very strongly,* throughout the length and breadth of the land, both in the United States and in Canada – not only the wild Indians of the north, but notably the most civilized and advanced of the tribes; and it is *this* impression, which a wide intercourse with the Indians during many years and over an extended area has produced on my mind, that must be my apology for these four papers on the subject.

The policy of the white man's government, it seems to me, both in Canada and the United States, is to *un-Indianize the Indian,* and make him in every sense a white man. And it is against the policy that the Indian, whether in a wild state, or semi-civilized, or nearly wholly civilized, as it seems to me, is setting up his back. I believe it is this more than anything else that is hindering his progress, for he views everything that the white man does for him with suspicion, believing that this hated policy for the absorption of his race and his nationality is at the back of it. He is willing, ready to adopt the white man's clothing, the white man's language; but he is not willing to give up his nationality or his communism, or his native language in the domestic circle – he wishes to live apart from the white man, in a separate community, and to exercise, so far as is compatible with his position in the country, a control over his own affairs.

And what can be the harm in allowing him to do so? Would it be any menace to the peace of our country if the civilized Indians of Ontario were permitted to have their own center of Government – their own Ottawa, so to speak; their own Lieutenant-Governor, and their own Parliament?

In my former papers, I have shewn that many of the tribes in past days, before the white man came among them, had excellent laws of their own, that there have been many wise heads among them. I have shewn also that the Indian is willing and ready to a certain extent to accept our laws and customs as better than his own, but prefers to take them at our hands and mould them in his own way. I have spoken, too, of the Cherokees in Indian Territory, 22,000 in number, who already have their own Governor, their own Parliament, and make their own laws. What the United States has done for one tribe of 22,000 Indians, I propose our Dominion Government should do for her 17,000 Ontario Indians; hand over to them their funds, which are at present held in trust for them, appoint them a Lieutenant-Governor from among their own people, let them select a spot for their capital, and have their own Parliament and make their own laws. And if this be successful, I think, as time goes on, the whole management of Indian Affairs might be transferred from the Indian Department in Ottawa to the Indian Government at the Indian Capital.

And then the Missionary work. This also, I incline to think, might be far better managed by the Indians themselves. The Christian churches all seem to begrudge the expenditure on Indian Missions, and, as I pointed out in a former paper, it is no credit to us as a Christian nation that the Indians of this country who have accepted our Christianity should already be broken up into so many little sects quarrelling with and abusing one another. If the Indians were united as people, I doubt very much but that they would unite also in the matter of religion. The national sentiment would out-balance the sect sentiment. The lines are not so sharply drawn between the different *isms* where Indians are concerned as they are among the whites. I think the Indians would probably adopt a Christian religion of their own, in which all of them could join. They are a generous, liberal-minded people, thinking more of the general weal than of the individual welfare; and, I believe, would do not less than we have been doing; and perhaps a good deal more for the conversion of their heathen. Neither, I believe, would education be neglected. Among the Cherokees there is not at present a man or woman (except the very aged), or a child of Schoolable age, that cannot read and write. But of their public Treasury they have expended at one time as much as $100,000 in the erection of a college for the training of their youth.

These ideas, in regard to the future of our Indians, will, I daresay, be new altogether to a good many of the readers of *The Canadian Indian*. They are new, the writer admits, and may be, as he has said, crude, visionary, and even impracticable. Still, he believes, they are not unworthy of some thought and consideration. And, above all things, it would seem desirable, as a first step, that the views of the most advanced and intelligent of our Indians should be obtained on the various points enunciated. Nothing probably could be better than this Indian Conference which has already been proposed, and was to have taken place in Toronto in May, but has now, as I understand, been put off until the month of September. I hope the Conference will be held, and that the Indians will come in good numbers and speak for themselves, and then we shall be better able to judge as to the best course to be adopted for our Indians' future.

Editor's note: This conference was never held.

Selected Bibliography

Abler, Thomas S. "Micmacs and Gypsies: Occupation of the Peripatetic Niche." In *Papers of the Twenty-First Algonquian Conference,* ed. William Cowan, 1-11. Ottawa: Carleton University, 1989.

–. "Glooscap Encounters Silas T. Rand: A Baptist Missionary on the Folkloric Fringe." In *Earth, Water, Air and Fire: Studies in Canadian Ethnohistory,* ed. David T. McNab, 127-41. Waterloo: Wilfrid Laurier University Press, 1998.

–. "Protestant Missionaries and Native Culture: Parallel Careers of Asher Wright and Silas T. Rand." *American Indian Quarterly* 16 (1992): 25-37.

Adam, Graeme Mercer. *Prominent Men of Canada: A Collection of Persons Distinguished in Professional and Political Life, and in the Commerce and Industry of Canada.* Toronto: Canadian Biographical Publications, 1892.

Adams, Peter. *Fatal Necessity: British Intervention in New Zealand, 1830-1847.* Auckland: University of Auckland Press, 1977.

Adelman, William. *Haymarket Revisited.* Chicago: Illinois Labor History, 1976.

Alfred, Brother. *Catholic Pioneers in Upper Canada.* Toronto: Macmillan, 1947.

Allen, Robert S. "The British Indian Department and the Frontier in North America, 1755-1830." In *Occasional Papers in Archaeology and History.* Canadian Historical Sites, Research Division, National Historical Parks and Sites Branch, Parks Canada. Ottawa: Information Branch, 1975.

–. *His Majesty's Indian Allies: British Indian Policy in the Defence of Canada, 1774-1815.* Toronto: Dundurn Press, 1993.

Althusser, Louis. *For Marx.* Chicago: University of Chicago Press, 1964.

Armour, David A. "Cadotte, Jean-Baptiste." In *Dictionary of Canadian Biography.* Vol. 5, *1801-1820,* 128-30. Toronto: University of Toronto Press, 1983.

–. "Henry, Alexander." In *Dictionary of Canadian Biography.* Vol. 6, *1821-1835,* 316-18. Toronto: University of Toronto Press, 1987.

Arthur, Elizabeth. "The Frontier Politician." In *Aspects of Nineteenth Century Ontario: Essays Presented to James J. Talman,* ed. F.H. Armstrong, H.A. Stevenson, and J.D. Wilson, 278-96. Toronto: University of Toronto Press, 1974.

–. *Simon J. Dawson, C.E.* Thunder Bay: Thunder Bay Historical Society, 1987.

–. "McKeller, John." In *Dictionary of Canadian Biography.* Vol. 12, *1891-1900,* 645-47. Toronto: University of Toronto Press, 1990.

–. "Dawson, Simon James." In *Dictionary of Canadian Biography.* Vol. 13, *1901-1910,* 261-62. Toronto: University of Toronto Press, 1994.

–, ed. *Thunder Bay District, 1821-1892: A Collection of Documents.* Toronto: Champlain Society, 1973.

Ashbaugh, Carolyn. *Lucy Parsons: American Revolutionary.* Chicago: Charles H. Kerr, 1976.

Assikinack, F. "The Odahwah Language." *Canadian Journal* n.s. 3, 18 (1858): 481-85.

Avery, Donald H. *Reluctant Host: Canada's Response to Immigrant Workers, 1896-1994.* Toronto: McClelland and Stewart, 1995.

Banks, Judith Judd. "Comparative Biographies of Two British Columbia Anthropologists, Charles Hill-Tout and James A. Teit." MA thesis, University of British Columbia, 1970.

Bannister, Robert C. *Social Darwinism: Science and Myth in Anglo-American Social Thought.* Philadelphia: Temple University Press, 1979.

–. *Sociology and Scientism: The American Quest for Objectivity, 1880-1940.* Chapel Hill and London: University of North Carolina Press, 1987.

Barr, Elinor. "Marks, Thomas." In *Dictionary of Canadian Biography.* Vol. 12, *1891-1900,* 698-99. Toronto: University of Toronto Press, 1990.

Baskerville, Peter. "McNab, Sir Allan Napier." In *Dictionary of Canadian Biography.* Vol. 9, *1861-1870,* 519-27. Toronto: University of Toronto Press, 1976.

Battiste, Marie Ann. "An Historical Investigation of the Social and Cultural Consequences of Micmac Literacy." Ed.D. thesis, Stanford University, 1983.

–, and James Youngblood Henderson. *Protecting Indigenous Knowledge and Heritage.* Saskatoon: Purich Publishing, 2000.

Bauman, Zygmunt. *Modernity and the Holocaust.* New York: Cornell University Press. 1991.

Bayliss, Joseph, and Estelle Bayliss. *Historic St. Joseph's Island.* Cedar Rapids: Torch Press, 1937.

Berkhofer, Robert F., Jr. *The White Man's Indian: Images of the American Indian from Columbus to the Present.* New York: Alfred A. Knopf, 1978.

–. "White Conceptions of Indians." In *Handbook of North American Indians.* Vol. 4, *History of Indian-White Relations,* vol. ed. Wilcomb E. Washburn, 522-47. Washington: Smithsonian, 1988.

Berman, Judith. "'The Culture as It Appears to the Indian Himself': Boas, George Hunt and the Methods of Ethnography." In *"Volksgeist" as Method and Ethic: Essays on Boasian Ethnography and the German Anthropological Tradition,* ed. George Stocking Jr., 215-56. Madison: University of Wisconsin Press, 1996.

Berton, Pierre. *The Invasion of Canada, 1812-1813.* Toronto: Penguin Books, 1980.

Bieder, Robert E. *Science Encounters the Indian, 1820-1880: The Early Years of American Ethnology.* Norman: University of Oklahoma Press, 1986.

Bingaman, Sandra Estlin. "The Trials of the 'White Rebels,' 1885." *Saskatchewan History* 25, 2 (Spring 1972): 41-54.

Binnema, Theodore, and Kevin Hutchings. "The Emigrant and the Noble Savage: Sir Francis Bond Head's Romantic Approach to Aboriginal Policy in Upper Canada, 1836-1838." *Journal of Canadian Studies* 39: 115-38.

Birk, Douglas A. "Sayer, John." In *Dictionary of Canadian Biography.* Vol. 5, *1801-1820,* 72-74. Toronto: University of Toronto Press, 1983.

–. "John Sayer and the Fon du Lac Trade: The North West Company in Minnesota and Wisconsin." In *Rendezvous: Selected Papers of the Fourth North American Fur Trade Conference, 1981,* ed. Thomas C. Buckley. St. Paul: North American Fur Trade Conference, 1984.

–, ed. *John Sayer's Snake River Journal, 1804-1805: A Fur Trade Diary from East Central Minnesota.* With commentary by Douglas A. Birk. Minneapolis: Institute for Minnesota Archaeology, 1989.

Blackstock, Michael D. "The Aborigines Report (1837): A Case Study in the Slow Change of Colonial Social Relations." *The Canadian Journal of Native Studies* 20, 1 (2000): 67-94.

–. *Faces in the Forest: First Nations Art Created on Living Trees.* Montreal and Kingston: McGill-Queen's University Press, 2001.

–. "Where Is the Trust?: Using Trust Based Mediation for First Nations Dispute Resolution." *Conflict Resolution Quarterly* 19, 1 (2001): 9-30.

Boas, Franz. "Obituary of James A. Teit." *Journal of American Folklore* 36 (1923): 102-3.

Bodley, John H. *Tribal Peoples and Development Issues: A Global Overview.* Mountain View: Mayfield, 1988.

Bolt, Clarence. *Thomas Crosby and the Tsimshian: Small Shoes for Feet Too Large.* Vancouver: UBC Press, 1992.

Borg, Marcus J. "Reading the Prophets Again." In *Reading the Bible Again for the First Time,* 111-44. San Francisco: Harper Collins, 2001.

Borrows, John. "Listening for a Change." *Osgoode Hall Law Journal* 39, 1 (2001): 1-38.

Bourne, H.R. Fox. *The Aborigines' Protection Society: Chapters in Its History*. London: P.S. King and Son, 1899.

Bowie, Fiona, Deborah Kirkwood, and Shirley Ardener, eds. *Women and Missionaries: Past and Present*. Providence, RI: Berg, 1993.

Braithwaite, Martha, comp. *Memorials of Christine Majolier Alsop*. London: Samuel Harris, 1881.

Bray, Matt. "Lyon, Robert Adam." In *Dictionary of Canadian Biography*. Vol. 13, *1901-1910*, 101-2. Toronto: University of Toronto Press, 1994.

Bray, R. Matthew. "Borron, Edward Barnes." In *Dictionary of Canadian Biography*. Vol. 14, *1910-1920*, DCB website, www.biographi.ca. Toronto: University of Toronto Press, 2001.

Brayshaw, Alfred Neave. *The Quakers: Their Story and Message*. York, England: William Sessions Book Trust, 1982.

Brazer, Marjorie Cahn. *Harps upon the Willows: The Johnston Family of the Old Northwest*. Ann Arbor: The Historical Society of Michigan, 1993.

Bremer, Richard G. *Indian Agent and Wilderness Scholar: Life of Henry Rowe Schoolcraft*. Mount Pleasant: Clarke Historical Library, Central Michigan University Press, 1987.

Briggs, Charles, and Richard Bauman. "'The Foundations of All Future Researches': Franz Boas, George Hunt, Native American Texts, and the Construction of Modernity." *American Quarterly* 51, 3 (1999): 479-528.

Brode, Patrick. "Colonel Rankin's Canadian Lancers in the American Civil War." *Detroit in Perspective* 4 (1980): 170-77.

–. "Rankin, Arthur." In *Dictionary of Canadian Biography*. Vol. 12, *1891-1900*, 884-85. Toronto: University of Toronto Press, 1990.

Brouwer, Ruth Compton. *New Women for God: Canadian Presbyterian Women and India Missions, 1876-1914*. Toronto: University of Toronto Press, 1990.

Brown, Jennifer S.H. *Strangers in Blood: Fur Trade Company Families in Indian Country*. Vancouver: UBC Press, 1980.

Brown, Ron. *Backroads of Ontario*. Erin: Boston Mills Press, 1996.

Bryan, Liz. *The Buffalo People*. Edmonton: University of Alberta Press, 1991.

Buja, J.E. "Arthur Rankin: A Political Biography." MA thesis, University of Windsor, 1982.

Bumsted, J.M. "MacDonell, Alexander (Greenfield)." *Dictionary of Canadian Biography*, Vol. 6, *1821-1835*, 445-46. Toronto: University of Toronto Press, 1987.

–. "McDonell, Alexander (Collachie)." *Dictionary of Canadian Biography*. Vol. 7, *1836-1850*, 554-56. Toronto: University of Toronto Press, 1988.

–. *The Red River Rebellion*. Winnipeg: Watson and Dwyer, 1996.

Campbell, Peter. "Not as a Whiteman, Not as a Sojourner: James A. Teit and the Fight for Native Rights in British Columbia, 1884-1922." *Left History* 2, 2 (1994): 37-57.

Campey, Lucille H. *The Scottish Pioneers of Upper Canada, 1784-1855: Glengarry and Beyond*. Toronto: Natural Heritage, 2005.

Canada. *Indian Treaties and Surrenders from 1680-1890*. 2 vols. Ottawa: Brown, Chamberlin, 1891.

Cannon, Martin J. "Not Simply Social Darwinism: Exploring the Practical and Pedagogical Utility of Social Evolutionism in Contemporary Sociological Theory." Unpublished paper presented to the Congress of Humanities and Social Sciences, University of Western Ontario. 1 June 2005. n.p.

Careless, J.M.S. *Brown of the Globe*. Vol. 1, *The Voice of Upper Canada, 1818-1859*. Toronto: Macmillan, 1959.

–. *The Union of the Canadas: The Growth of Canadian Institutions, 1841-1857*. Toronto: McClelland and Stewart, 1967.

–. *Frontier and Metropolis: Regions, Cities and Identities in Canada before 1914*. Toronto: University of Toronto Press, 1989.

Carey, Hilary M. "Companions in the Wilderness? Missionary Wives in Colonial Australia, 1788-1900." *Journal of Religious History* 19, 2 (1995): 227-48.

Carr, E.H. *What Is History?* London: Penguin Books, 1961.

Carter, Sarah. "The Missionaries' Indian: The Publications of John McDougall, John Maclean and Egerton Ryerson Young." *Prairie Forum* 9, 1 (Spring 1984): 27-44.

–. *Lost Harvests: Prairie Indian Reserve Farmers and Government Policy*. Montreal and Kingston: McGill-Queen's University Press, 1990.

–. "Categories and Terrains of Exclusion: Constructing the 'Indian Woman' in the Early Settlement Era in Western Canada." *Great Plains Quarterly* 13, 3 (Summer 1993): 147-61.

–. *Capturing Women: The Manipulation of Cultural Imagery in Canada's Prairie West*. Montreal and Kingston: McGill-Queen's University Press, 1997.

–. *Aboriginal Peoples and Colonizers of Western Canada to 1900*. Toronto: University of Toronto Press, 1999.

–. "Two Months in Big Bear's Camp, 1885: Narratives of 'Indian Captivity' and the Articulation of 'Race' and Gender Hierarchies in Western Canada." In *Readings in Canadian History: Post-Confederation*, ed. R.D. Francis and Donald Smith, 75-93. Toronto: Nelson Thomson Learning, 2002.

Carter-Edwards, Dennis. "Ironside, George [Sr.]." In *Dictionary of Canadian Biography*. Vol. 6, *1821-1835*, 340-41. Toronto: University of Toronto Press, 1987.

Chamberlin, J. Edward. *If This Is Your Land, Where Are Your Stories: Finding Common Ground*. Toronto: Alfred A. Knopf, 2003.

Champagne, Duane. *Social Order and Political Change: Constitutional Governments among the Cherokee, the Choctaw, the Chickasaw, and the Creek*. Stanford: Stanford University Press, 1992.

Chaput, Donald. "Michipicoten Island: Ghosts, Copper and Bad Luck." *Ontario History* 61, 4 (December 1969): 217-23.

Cherwinski, W.J.C. "Honoré Joseph Jaxon, Agitator, Disturber, Producer of Plans to Make Men Think, and Chronic Objector." *Canadian Historical Review* 46, 2 (June 1965): 122-33.

Chute, Janet E. "Preservation of Ethnic Diversity at Garden River: The Key to Ojibwe Strength." In *Papers of the Twenty-Eighth Algonquian Conference*, ed. David H. Pentland, 44-70. Winnipeg: University of Manitoba, 1997.

–. "A Unifying Vision: Shingwaukonse's Plan for the Future of the Great Lakes Ojibwa." *Journal of the Canadian Historical Association* n.s. 7 (1997): 55-80.

–. *The Legacy of Shingwaukonse: A Century of Native Leadership*. Toronto: University of Toronto Press, 1998.

–. "Mi'kmaq Fishing in the Maritimes: A Historical Overview." In *Earth, Water, Air and Fire: Studies in Canadian Ethnohistory*, ed. David T. McNab, 95-113. Waterloo: Wilfrid Laurier University Press, 1998.

Clark, Jeremiah S. "Editor's Preface." In *Micmac Dictionary from Phonographic Word-Lists*, ed. Jeremiah S. Clark, v-viii. Charlottetown, PEI: Patriot, 1902.

Clarke, John. "McKee, Thomas." In *Dictionary of Canadian Biography*. Vol. 5, *1801-1820*, 535-36. Toronto: University of Toronto Press, 1983.

Clifton, James A. *Being and Becoming Indian*. Chicago: Dorsey Press, 1989.

Coalition for the Advancement of Aboriginal Studies. *Learning About Walking in Beauty: Placing Aboriginal Perspectives in Canadian Classrooms*, http://www.crr.ca.

Cole, Douglas. "The Origins of Canadian Anthropology, 1850-1910." *Journal of Canadian Studies* 8, 1 (1973): 35-45.

–. *Franz Boas: The Early Years, 1858-1906*. Vancouver and Seattle: Douglas and McIntyre and University of Washington Press, 1999.

Coleman, Michael C. *American Indian Children at School, 1850-1930*. Jackson: University Press of Mississippi, 1993.

–. "Representation of American Indians and the Irish in Education Reports, 1850s-1920s." *Irish Historical Studies* 23 (May 2002): 33-51.

Cooper, Virginia J. "A Political History of the Grand River Iroquois, 1784-1880." MA thesis, Carleton University, 1975.

Cormier, Jean-Baptiste. "Jean-Baptiste Perrault." In *Dictionary of Canadian Biography*. Vol. 7, *1836-1850*, 686-97. Toronto: University of Toronto Press, 1988.

Cottam, Barry. "Federal/Provincial Disputes, Natural Resources and the Treaty #3 Ojibwa, 1867-1924." PhD dissertation, University of Ottawa, 1994.

Cowie, Isaac. *The Company of Adventurers: A Narrative of Seven Years in the Service of the Hudson's Bay Company during 1867-1874 on the Great Buffalo Plains*. Toronto: William Briggs, 1913.

Craig, David. *On the Crofter's Trail: In Search of the Clearance Highlanders*. London: Pimlico, 1990.

Crosby, Thomas. *Up and Down the North Pacific Coast by Canoe and Mission Ship*. Toronto: Missionary Society of the Methodist Church, 1914.

Cross, Michael. "Derbishire, Stewart." In *Dictionary of Canadian Biography*. Vol. 9, *1861-1870*, 201-2. Toronto: University of Toronto Press, 1976.

D'Agostino, Peter. "Craniums, Criminals and the 'Cursed Race': Italian Anthropology in American Racial Thought, 1861-1924." *Comparative Studies in Society and History* 44, 2 (2002): 319-43.

Daiches, David. "Scott's *Redgauntlet*." In *From Jane Austen to Joseph Conrad: Essays Collected in Memory of James T. Hillhouse*, ed. Robert C. Rathburn and Martin Steinman, Jr., 46-59. Minneapolis: University of Minnesota Press, 1958.

Darnell, Regna. "The Sapir Years at the National Museum, Ottawa." *Proceedings of the Canadian Ethnology Society* (1976): 98-121.

–. *And Along Came Boas: Continuity and Revolution in Americanist Anthropology*. Amsterdam: Benjamins, 1996.

–. "The Pivotal Role of the Northwest Coast in the History of Americanist Anthropology." *British Columbia Studies* 125-26 (Spring/Summer 2000): 33-52.

Deane, R. Burton. *Mounted Police Life in Canada: A Record of Thirty-One Years' Service*. London: Cassell, 1916.

Delgamuukw: The Supreme Court of Canada Decision on Aboriginal Title. With commentary by Stan Persky. Vancouver: Douglas and McIntyre, 1998.

Dempsey, Hugh A. "Pequis." In *Dictionary of Canadian Biography*. Vol. 9, *1861-1870*, 626-27. Toronto: University of Toronto Press, 1976.

Devereux, Cecily. "'And Let Them Wash Me from this Clanging World': Hugh and Ion, 'The Last Best West' and Purity Discourse in 1885." *Journal of Canadian Studies* 32, 2 (Summer 1997): 100-15.

Dickason, Olive. *Canada's First Nations: A History of Founding Peoples from Earliest Times*. Toronto: Oxford University Press, 1992.

Dion, Susan. "Braiding Histories: Responding to the Problematics of Canadians Hearing First Nations Post-Contact Experiences." PhD dissertation, University of Toronto, 2002.

Donkin, John. *Trooper in the Far North-West*. 1889. Reprint, Saskatoon: Western Producer Prairie Books, 1987.

Dorland, Arthur Garratt. *A History of the Society of Friends (Quakers) in Canada*. Toronto: Macmillan, 1927.

–. *The Quakers in Canada: A History*. Toronto: Ryerson, 1968.

Doughty, A.G., ed. *The Elgin-Grey Papers, 1846-1852*. 4 vols. Ottawa: Patenaude, 1937.

Douglas, R. Alan, ed. *John Prince 1796-1870*. Toronto: The Champlain Society, 1980.

Dragland, Stan. *Floating Voice: Duncan Campbell Scott and the Literature of Treaty 9*. Concord: Anansi, 1994.

Drake, Earl G. *Regina: The Queen City*. Toronto: McClelland and Stewart, 1955.

Duff, Louis Blake. "Amazing Story of the Winghamite Secretary of Louis Riel." *Western Ontario History Nuggets* 22 (1955): 1-37.

Ellis, Elmer. *Mr. Dooley's America: A Life of Finley Peter Dunne*. New York: Alfred A. Knopf, 1941.

Fabian, Johannes. *Time and the Other: How Anthropology Makes Its Object*. New York: Columbia University Press, 1983.

Farrell, David R. "Askin, John." In *Dictionary of Canadian Biography*. Vol. 5, *1801-1820*, 37-39. Toronto: University of Toronto Press, 1983.

Fenton, William N. "Introduction." In Horatio Hale, *The Iroquois Book of Rites*, ed. William N. Fenton, vii-xxvii. Toronto: University of Toronto Press, 1963.

–. "Hale, Horatio Emmons." In *Dictionary of Canadian Biography*. Vol. 12, *1891-1900*, 400-2. Toronto: University of Toronto Press, 1990.

Fingard, Judith. "Rand, Silas Tertius." In *Dictionary of Canadian Biography*. Vol. 11, *1881-1890*, 722-23. Toronto: University of Toronto Press, 1988.

Fisher, Robin. *Contact and Conflict: Indian-European Relations in British Columbia, 1774-1890*. Vancouver: UBC Press, 1986.

Fitz-Gibbon, Mary. *The Diaries of Edmund Montague Morris: Western Journeys, 1907-1910*. Toronto: Royal Ontario Museum, 1985.

Flanagan, Thomas. *Louis 'David' Riel: 'Prophet of the New World.'* Toronto: University of Toronto Press, 1979.

Flemming, Leslie A. *Women's Work for Women: Missionaries and Social Change in Asia*. Boulder: Westview, 1989.

Forman, James D. *Anarchism: Political Innocence or Social Violence?* New York: Dell, 1975.

Foucault, Michel. *Knowledge/Power: Selected Interviews*, ed. C. Campbell. Brighton: Harvester, 1980.

Fowle, Otto. *Sault Ste. Marie and Its Great Waterway*. New York: G.P. Putnam's Sons, 1925.

Francis, Daniel. *The Imaginary Indian: The Image of the Indian in Canadian Culture*. Vancouver: Arsenal Pulp Press, 1992.

Freire, Paulo. *Pedagogy of the Oppressed*. 1970. Reprint, New York: Continuum, 1982.

Frémont, Donatien. "Henry Jackson et l'insurrection du Nord-Ouest." *Memoires de la Société Royale du Canada*, 3rd series, 46 (1952): 19-48.

–. *Les Secretaries de Riel*. Montreal: Les Editions Chantecler, 1953.

Friedrichs, Robert C. *A Sociology of Sociology*. New York: The Free Press, 1970.

Fryer, Harold. *Frog Lake Massacre*. Surrey: Frontier Books, 1984.

Gagan, Rosemary R. *Canadian Methodist Women Missionaries in Canada and the Orient, 1881-1925*. Montreal and Kingston: McGill-Queen's University Press, 1992.

Galois, Robert M. "The Indian Rights Association, Native Protest Activity and the 'Land Question' in British Columbia, 1903-1916." *Native Studies Review* 8, 2 (1992): 1-34.

Giddings, Franklin Henry. *The Principles of Sociology*. 1896. Reprint, New York: Macmillan, 1904.

Gilpin, J. Bernard. "Indians of Nova Scotia." In *The Native Peoples of Atlantic Canada: A History of Ethnic Interaction*, ed. Harold F. McGee, 102-19. Toronto: McClelland and Stewart, 1974.

Ginger, Ray. *Altgeld's America*. Chicago: Quadrangle Books, 1958.

Gmelch, Sharon Bohn. "Groups That Don't Want In: Gypsies and Other Artisan, Trader, and Entertainer Minorities." *Annual Review of Anthropology* 15 (1986): 307-30.

Gonzales, Ellice B. "Changing Economic Roles for Micmac Men and Women: An Ethnohistorical Analysis." National Museum of Man, Mercury Series, Canadian Ethnology Service, Paper 72 (1981).

Goosen, N. Jaye. "Mactavish, William." In *Dictionary of Canadian Biography*. Vol. 9, *1861-1870*, 529-32. Toronto: University of Toronto Press, 1976.

Gough, Barry. *Fighting Sail on Lake Huron and Georgian Bay: The War of 1812 and Its Aftermath*. St. Catharines: Vanwell Publishing, 2002.

Gould, Stephen Jay. *The Mismeasure of Man*. 1981. Reprint, New York: W.W. Norton, 1996.

Govier, Trudy. *Social Trust and Human Communities*. Montreal and Kingston: McGill-Queen's University Press, 1997.

–. *Dilemmas of Trust*. Montreal and Kingston: McGill-Queen's University Press, 1998.

Grant, H. Roger. *Spirit Fruit: A Gentle Utopia*. DeKalb, IL: Northern Illinois University Press, 1988.

Grant, John Webster. *Moon of Wintertime: Missionaries and the Indians of Canada in Encounter since 1534*. Toronto: University of Toronto Press, 1984.

Grant, Neil. *Scottish Clans and Tartans*. London: Hamblyn Publishing: Country Life Books, 1987.

Green, Jesse, ed. *Zuni: Selected Writings of Frank Hamilton Cushing*. Lincoln: University of Nebraska Press, 1979.

Greenhill, Ralph, and Thomas D. Mahoney. *Niagara*. Toronto: University of Toronto Press, 1969.

Greenland, Cyril, and John D. Griffin. "William Henry Jackson (1861-1952) – Riel's Secretary: Another Case of Involuntary Commitment?" *Canadian Psychiatric Association Journal* 23, 7 (November 1978): 469-78.

Griesbach, W.A. *I Remember*. Toronto: Ryerson Press, 1946.

Grimshaw, Patricia. *Paths of Duty: American Missionary Wives in Nineteenth-Century Hawaii*. Honolulu: University of Hawaii Press, 1989.

Gronneberg, Roy. "James Teit: Friend of the Indians." *The New Shetlander* 126 (1978): 28-30.

Gruber, Jacob W. "Horatio Hale and the Development of American Anthropology." *Proceedings of the American Philosophical Society* 111, 1 (1967): 5-37.

Haig-Brown, Celia. *Resistance and Renewal: Surviving the Indian Residential School*. Vancouver: Tillacum Press, 1988.

–. "Contradiction, Power and Control." In *Taking Control: Contradiction and Power in First Nations Adult Education*, 233-54. Vancouver: UBC Press, 1995.

–. "Democratic Research to Inform Citizenship." In *Citizenship in Transformation in Canada*, ed. Yvonne Hébert, 162-74. Toronto: University of Toronto Press, 2002.

Hale, Horatio. *Ethnology and Philology*. Philadelphia: Lea and Blanchard, 1846; reprint, ed. Fred C. Sawyer, Ridgewood, NJ: Gregg Press, 1968.

–. *The Iroquois Book of Rites*. Philadelphia: D.G. Brinton, 1883; reprint, ed. William N. Fenton, Toronto: University of Toronto Press, 1963.

Hamm, Thomas D. *The Transformation of American Quakerism: Orthodox Friends, 1800-1907*. Bloomington: Indiana University Press, 1988.

Harkin, Michael. "(Dis)pleasures of the Text: Boasian Anthropology on the Central Northwest Coast." In *Gateways: Exploring the Legacy of the Jesup North Pacific Expedition, 1897-1902*, ed. Igor Krupnik and William W. Fitzhugh, 93-105. Washington: Smithsonian Institution, 2001.

Harrington, Bernard J. *Life of Sir William Logan*. Montreal: Dawson Brothers, 1883.

Harris, Cole. *The Resettlement of British Columbia: Essays on Colonialism and Geographical Change*. Vancouver: UBC Press, 1991.

–. *Making Native Space: Colonialism, Resistance and Reserves in British Columbia*. Vancouver: UBC Press, 2002.

Hawthorn, H.B., C.S. Belshaw, and S.M. Jamieson, eds. *The Indians of British Columbia: A Study of Contemporary Social Adjustment*. Toronto: University of Toronto Press, 1958.

Hele, Karl. "'By the Rapids': The Anishinabe-Missionary Encounter at Bawating (Sault Ste. Marie), c. 1821-1871." PhD dissertation, McGill University, 2002.

Henderson, Marian. *The McKellar Story*. Thunder Bay: Thunder Bay Historical Society, 1981.

Higham, C.L. "Saviours and Scientists: North American Protestant Missionaries and the Development of Anthropology." *Pacific Historical Review* 72, 4 (2003): 531-59.

Hill, Patricia R. *The World Their Household: The American Woman's Foreign Mission Movement and Cultural Transformation, 1870-1920*. Ann Arbor: University of Michigan Press, 1985.

Hind, H.Y. *Narrative of the Canadian Red River Exploring Expedition of 1858*. Vol. 1. 1860. Reprint, New York: Greenwood Press, 1969.

Hobart, C.W. and C.S. Brant. "Eskimo Education, Danish and Canadian: A Comparison." *Canadian Review of Sociology and Anthropology* 3 (1966): 47-66.

Hodgson-Smith, Kathy L. "Seeking Good and Right Relations: Student Perspectives on the Pedagogy of Joe Duquette High School." MA thesis, University of Saskatchewan, 1997.

Hoebel, E. Adamson. "William Robertson: An 18th Century Anthropologist-Historian." *American Anthropologist* 62 (1960): 648-55.

Hoefel, Roseanne. "'Different by Degree': Ella Cara Deloria, Zora Neale Hurston, and Franz Boas Contend with Race and Ethnicity." *American Indian Quarterly* 25, 2 (2001): 181-202.

Hoig, Stanley W. *The Cherokees and Their Chiefs*. Fayetteville: University of Arkansas Press, 1998.

Holbrook, Stewart H. *The Age of the Moguls*. Garden City, NY: Doubleday, 1953.

Holzkamm, Tim E., and Victor P. Lytwyn. "Rainy River Sturgeon: An Ojibwa Resource in the Fur Trade Economy." *The Canadian Geographer* 32, 3 (Fall 1988): 194-205.

–, and Leo Waisberg. "Agriculture and One 19th Century Ojibwa Band: 'They Hardly Ever Loose [sic] Sight of Their Field.'" In *Papers of the Twenty-Fourth Algonquian Conference*, ed. William Cowan, 407-29. Ottawa: Carleton University, 1993.

Hornick, G. Leigh. *The Call of Copper*. Bruce Mines: North Shore Printing, 1969.

House of Lords, Judicial Committee of the Privy Council and Peerage Cases. *The Law Reports of the Incorporated Council of Law Reporting*. London: William Chowns and Sons, 1903.

Huber, Mary Taylor, and Nancy C. Lutkehaus, eds. *Gendered Missions: Women and Men in Missionary Discourse and Practice*. Ann Arbor: University of Michigan Press, 1999.

Huel, Raymond. "Louis Schmidt: A Forgotten Métis." In *Riel and the Métis*, ed. A.S. Lussier, 93-107. Winnipeg: Manitoba Métis Federation Press, 1979.

Hughes, Katherine. *Father Lacombe, the Black-Robe Voyageur*. Toronto: William Briggs, 1911.

Hughes, Richard David. "Murray, Alexander." *Dictionary of Canadian Biography*. Vol. 11, *1881-1890*, 630-33. Toronto: University of Toronto Press, 1982.

Hulan, Shelly. "Amelia Paget's *The People of the Plains:* Imperialist and Ethnocritical Nostalgia." *Journal of Canadian Studies* 37, 2 (Summer 2002): 47-68.

Hyam, Ronald. *Britain's Imperial Century, 1815-1914: A Study of Empire and Expansion*. Lanham: Barnes and Noble Books, 1993.

–, and Ged Martin. *Reappraisals in British Imperial History*. London: Macmillan, 1975.

Hybels, Robert James. "The Lake Superior Copper Fever, 1841-1847." *Michigan History* 34 (June 1950).

Jacknis, Ira. "The First Boasian: Alfred Kroeber and Franz Boas, 1898-1905." *American Anthropologist* 104, 2 (2002): 520-32.

Jackson, Helen Hunt. *A Century of Dishonor*. New York: Harper and Bros., 1881.

Jacobs, Margaret D. *Engendered Encounters: Feminism and Pueblo Cultures, 1879-1934*. Lincoln and London: University of Nebraska Press, 1999.

Jameson, Anna Brownell. *Winter Studies and Summer Rambles in Canada*. 1838. Reprint, Toronto: McClelland and Stewart, 1990.

Johnston, Barry V. *Pitirim A. Sorokin: An Intellectual Biography*. Lawrence: University Press of Kansas, 1995.

Joyce, Barry Alan. *The Shaping of American Ethnography: The Wilkes Exploring Expedition, 1838-1842*. Lincoln: University of Nebraska Press, 2001.

Judd, Denis. *The Victorian Empire: A Pictorial History*. London: Wiedenfield and Nicholson, 1970.

Kelly, Peter, and J.A. Teit. *Statement of the Allied Indian Tribes of British Columbia for the Government of British Columbia*. Vancouver: Cowan and Brookhouse, 1919.

Knight, Alan. "A Study in Failure: The Anglican Mission at Sault Ste. Marie, 1830-1841." *Journal of the Canadian Church Historical Society* 45, 2 (Fall 2002): 133-224.

Koehn, Daryl. "Should We Trust in Trust?" *American Business Law Journal* 34, 2 (Winter 1996): 183-204.

Krieger, Carlo J. "Ethnogenesis or Cultural Interference? Catholic Missionaries and the Micmac." In *Actes du Vingtième Congrès des Algonquianistes*, ed. William Cowan, 193-200. Ottawa: Carleton University, 1989.

Kuhn, Thomas S. *The Structure of Scientific Revolutions*. 1962. Reprint, Chicago: University of Chicago Press, 1970.

Kulchyski, Peter. "Anthropology in the Service of the State: Diamond Jenness and Canadian Indian Policy." *Journal of Canadian Studies* 28, 2 (1993): 2-50.

Kumar, Satish. *Path without Destination: The Long Walk of a Gentle Hero*. New York: Eagle Brook, 1999.

Lavender, David. *Fist in the Wilderness*. New York: Doubleday, 1964.

Leacock, Eleanor Burke. "Introduction." In Lewis Henry Morgan, *Ancient Society, or Researches in the Lines of Human Progress from Savagery through Barbarism to Civilization*, ed. Eleanor Burke Leacock, i-xx. Cleveland: Meridian Books, 1963.

Leacock, Stephen. *The Dawn of Canadian History: A Chronicle of Aboriginal Canada.* 1915. Reprint, Toronto: Glasgow, Brook, 1920.

Leighton, Douglas. "Ironside, George [Jr.]." In *Dictionary of Canadian Biography.* Vol. 9, *1861-1870,* 407-8. Toronto: University of Toronto Press, 1976.

–. "The Compact Tory as Bureaucrat: Samuel Peters Jarvis and the Indian Department, 1837-1845." *Ontario History* 73 (1981): 40-54.

Lenski, Gerhard E. *Power and Privilege.* New York: McGraw-Hill, 1966.

–. *Human Societies: A Macrolevel Introduction to Sociology.* New York: McGraw-Hill, 1970.

Leslie, John. "The Bagot Commission: Developing a Corporate Memory for the Indian Department." *Canadian Historical Association Papers* (1982): 31-52.

Levine, Donald N. *Visions of the Sociological Tradition.* Chicago: University of Chicago Press, 1995.

Lewis, Reina, and Sara Mills, eds. *Feminist and Postcolonial Theory: A Reader.* New York: Routledge, 2003.

Loomba, Ania. *Colonialism/Postcolonialism.* New York: Routledge, 1999.

Lovesey, Dorothy May. *To Be a Pilgrim: A Biography of Silas Tertius Rand, 1810-1889: Nineteenth Century Protestant Missionary to the Micmac.* Hantsport, NS: Lancelot Press, 1992.

Lovisek, J.A. "Lac des Mille Lacs 'Dammed and Diverted': An Ethnohistorical Study." In *Papers of the Twenty-Fifth Algonquian Conference,* ed. William Cowan, 285-314. Ottawa: Carleton University, 1994.

–. "The Political Evolution of the Boundary Waters Ojibwa." In *Papers of the Twenty-Fourth Algonquian Conference,* ed. William Cowan, 280-305. Ottawa: Carleton University, 1993.

Lynch, Gerald. "An Endless Flow: D.C. Scott's Indian Poems." *Studies in Canadian Literature* 7, 1 (1982).

McDiarmid, Garnet, and David Pratt. *Teaching Prejudice: A Content Analysis of Social Studies Textbooks Authorized for Use in Ontario.* Toronto, Ontario Institute for Studies in Education, 1971.

MacDonald, Allan J. "MacDonell, Angus (Collachie)." In *Dictionary of Canadian Biography.* Vol. 5, *1801-1820,* 518-20. Toronto: University of Toronto Press, 1983.

–. "McDonell, John (Aberchalder)." In *Dictionary of Canadian Biography.* Vol. 5, *1801-1820,* 517-18. Toronto: University of Toronto Press, 1983.

–. "McDonell, Hugh (Aberchalder)." In *Dictionary of Canadian Biography.* Vol. 6, *1821-1835,* 444-45. Toronto: University of Toronto Press, 1987.

McDonald, Donna. *Lord Strathcona: A Biography of Donald Alexander Smith.* Toronto: Dundurn Press, 1996.

MacEwan, Grant. *Frederick Haultain: Frontier Statesman of the Canadian Northwest.* Saskatoon: Western Producer Prairie Books, 1985.

McFeely, Eliza. *Zuni and the American Imagination.* New York: Hill and Wang, 2001.

McGee, Harold F. "Ethnic Boundaries and Strategies of Ethnic Interaction: A History of Micmac-White Relations in Nova Scotia." PhD dissertation, Southern Illinois University, 1973.

–. "White Encroachment on Micmac Reserve Lands in Nova Scotia, 1830-1867." *Man in the Northeast* 8 (1974): 57-64.

McGill, Jean S. *Edmund Morris: Frontier Artist.* Toronto and Charlottetown: Dundurn Press, 1984.

McGrane, Reginald C. "Lyman Judson Gage (1836-1927)." In *Dictionary of American Biography.* Vol. 7, 85-86. New York: Charles Scribner's Sons, 1931.

McIntyre, Clark Martin. "Clark, Alexander." In *Dictionary of Canadian Biography.* Vol. 12, *1891-1900,* 197-98. Toronto: University of Toronto Press, 1990.

McKenzie, N.M.W.J. *The Men of the Hudson's Bay Company.* Fort William: Times-Journal Presses, 1921.

McLean, Duncan, with Eric Wells. "The Last Hostage." In *Frog Lake Massacre,* ed. Harold Fryer, 80-85. Surrey, BC: Frontier Books, 1984.

McLean, Elizabeth M. "The Siege of Fort Pitt." *The Beaver,* outfit 277 (December 1946): 22-25.

Maclean, John. *The Indians of Canada: Their Manners and Customs*. London: Charles H. Kelly, 1892.

McLean, Marianne. "McGillivray, John." In *Dictionary of Canadian Biography*. Vol. 8, *1851-1860*, 546-47. Toronto: University of Toronto Press, 1985.

MacLean, R. "The Highland Tradition in Canada." In *The Scottish Tradition in Canada*, ed. W. Stanford Reid, 93-117. Toronto: McClelland and Stewart, 1977.

McLeod, Ellen Easton. *In Good Hands: The Women of the Canadian Handicraft Guild*. Montreal and Kingston: McGill-Queen's University Press, 1999.

McLoughlin, William G. *After the Trail of Tears: The Cherokees' Struggle for Sovereignty, 1839-1880*. Chapel Hill and London: University of North Carolina Press, 1993.

McLynn, Frank. *Bonnie Prince Charlie: Charles James Stuart*. 1988. Reprint, London: Pimlico, 2003.

McMaster, Gerald R. "Tenuous Lines of Descent: Indian Arts and Crafts of the Reservation Period." *The Canadian Journal of Native Studies* 9, 2 (1989): 205-36.

McMurry, Donald L. *Coxey's Army: A Study of the Industrial Army Movement of 1894*. Seattle: University of Washington Press, 1929.

McNab, David. "Chatelain, Nicolas." In *Dictionary of Canadian Biography*. Vol. 12, *1891-1900*, 187-88. Toronto: University of Toronto Press, 1993.

Mandelbaum, David G. *The Plains Cree: An Ethnographic, Historical and Comparative Study*. 1940. Reprint, Regina: Canadian Plains Research Centre, 1979.

Mardock, Robert W. "Indian Rights Movement until 1887." In *Handbook of North American Indians*. Vol. 4, *History of Indian-White Relations*, vol. ed. Wilcomb E. Washburn, 301-4. Washington: Smithsonian, 1988.

Marshall, M.V. "Silas Tertius Rand and His Micmac Dictionary." *Nova Scotia Historical Quarterly* 5 (1975): 391-410.

Martin, Ged. *Britain and the Origins of Canadian Confederation, 1837-67*. Vancouver: UBC Press, 1995.

Martin, Peggy. "Micmac Indians as Witches in the Newfoundland Tradition." In *Papers of the Tenth Algonquian Conference*, ed. William Cowan, 173-80. Ottawa: Carleton University, 1979.

Martyn, J.P. "Patriot Invasion of Pelee Island 1838." *Ontario History* 56, 3 (September 1964): 153-65.

Maud, Ralph. *A Guide to B.C. Indian Myth and Legend*. Vancouver: Talonbooks, 1982.

Mays, Herbert J. "MacDonell, Miles." In *Dictionary of Canadian Biography*. Vol. 6, *1821-1835*, 440-44. Toronto: University of Toronto Press, 1987.

–. "McDonell, John." In *Dictionary of Canadian Biography*. Vol. 7, *1836-1850*, 552-53. Toronto: University of Toronto Press, 1988.

Meltzer, Milton. *Bread and Roses: The Struggle of American Labor, 1865-1914*. 1967. Reprint, New York: New American Library, 1977.

Mercier, Anne, and Violet Watt. *The Red House by the Rockies: A Tale of Riel's Rebellion*. London: Society for Promoting Christian Knowledge, 1896.

Mercredi, Ovide, and Mary Ellen Turpel. *In the Rapids: Navigating the Future of First Nations*. Toronto: Penguin Books, 1993.

Merivale, Herman. "Policy of Colonial Governments towards Native Tribes, as Regards Their Protection and Their Civilization." 1861. Reprinted in *Tribal Peoples and Development Issues: A Global Overview*, ed. John H. Bodley, 95-104. Mountain View: Mayfield Publishing, 1988.

Miller, J.R. *Skyscrapers Hide the Heavens: A History of Indian-White Relations in Canada*. Revised edition. Toronto: University of Toronto Press, 1991.

Miller, Virginia P. "Silas T. Rand: Nineteenth Century Anthropologist among the Micmac." *Anthropologica* 22 (1980): 235-49.

Milliea, Mildred. "Micmac Catholicism in My Community." In *Actes du Vingtième Congrès des Algonquianistes*, ed. William Cowan, 262-66. Ottawa: Carleton University, 1989.

Millman, Thomas R. "Anderson, Thomas Gummersall." In *Dictionary of Canadian Biography*. Vol. 10, *1871-1880*, 11-13. Toronto: University of Toronto Press, 1972.

Milner, Clyde A., II. *With Good Intentions: Quaker Work among the Pawnees, Otos, and Omahs*. Lincoln: University of Nebraska Press, 1982.

Mitcham, Allison. *Three Remarkable Maritimers*. Hantsport, NS: Lancelot Press, 1985.

Mitchell, Darcy. "The Allied Tribes of British Columbia: A Study in Pressure Group Behaviour." MA thesis, University of British Columbia, 1977.

Momryk, Myron. "Ermatinger, Charles Oakes." In *Dictionary of Canadian Biography*. Vol. 6, *1821-1835*, 236-37. Toronto: University of Toronto Press, 1987.

Monkman, Leslie. *A Native Heritage: Images of the Indian in English-Canadian Literature*. Toronto: University of Toronto Press, 1981.

Morgan, Henry James. *Canadian Men and Women of the Time*. 1898. Reprint, Toronto: Briggs, 1912.

Morgan, Lewis Henry. *Ancient Society, or Researches in the Lines of Human Progress from Savagery through Barbarism to Civilization*. 1877. Reprint, ed. Eleanor Burke Leacock. Cleveland: Meridian Books, 1963.

Morley, Alan. *Roar of the Breakers: A Biography of Peter Kelly*. Toronto: Ryerson Press, 1967.

Morris, Hon. Alexander. *The Treaties of Canada with the Indians of Manitoba and the North West Territories*. Toronto: Bedfords, Clarke, 1880.

Morton, W.L. "VanKoughnet, Philip M.M.K." In *Dictionary of Canadian Biography*. Vol. 9, *1861-1870*, 803-4. Toronto: University of Toronto Press, 1976.

Murphy, James L. *The Reluctant Radicals: Jacob L. Beilhart and The Spirit Fruit Society*. Lanham, MD: University Press of America, 1989.

Murray, David. *Forked Tongues: Speech, Writing and Representation in North American Indian Texts*. Bloomington: Indiana University Press, 1991.

Murray, Ruth. *Under His Wings: A Sketch of the Life of Robert Lindley Murray*. New York: Anson, D.F. Randolph, 1876.

Narayan, Kirin. "'How Native Is a 'Native' Anthropologist?'" In *Feminist and Postcolonial Theory: A Reader*, ed. Reina Lewis and Sara Mills, 285-305. New York: Routledge, 2003.

Nelles, H.V. *The Politics of Development: Forests, Mines and Hydro-Electric Power in Ontario, 1849-1941*. Toronto: Macmillan, 1974.

Neylan, Susan. *The Heavens Are Changing: Nineteenth-Century Protestant Missions and Tsimshian Christianity*. Montreal and Kingston: McGill-Queen's University Press, 2003.

Nichols, Roger L. *Indians in the United States and Canada*. Lincoln and London: University of Nebraska Press, 1998.

Nock, David A. "The Indian Conference That Never Was." *Ontario Indian* 5, 2 (February 1982): 39-45.

–. *A Victorian Missionary and Canadian Indian Policy: Cultural Synthesis vs Cultural Replacement*. Waterloo: Wilfrid Laurier University Press, 1988.

–. "Lessons from Davis: The Sociology of Arthur Kent Davis." *The Canadian Journal of Sociology* 20, 3 (1995): 387-407.

–. "Prophetic versus Priestly Sociology: Arthur K. Davis." *The American Sociologist* 33, 2 (2002): 57-85.

Nurse, Andrew. "'But Now Things Have Changed': Marius Barbeau and the Politics of Amerindian Identity." *Ethnohistory* 48, 3 (2001): 433-71.

Oats, William Nicolle. *A Question of Survival: Quakers in Australia in the Nineteenth Century*. New York: University of Queensland Press, 1985.

Oberschall, Anthony, ed. *The Establishment of Empirical Sociology*. New York: Harper and Row, 1972.

Ofner, Patricia V. *The Indian in Textbooks: A Content Analysis of History Books Authorized for Use in Ontario Schools*. MA thesis, Lakehead University, 1983.

O'Leary, Peter. *Travels and Experiences in Canada, the Red River Territory, and the United States*. London: John B. Day, 1877.

Owram, Doug. *Promise of Eden: The Canadian Expansionist Movement and the Idea of the West, 1856-1900*. Toronto: University of Toronto Press, 1980.

Paget, Amelia McLean. *The People of the Plains*. Toronto: William Briggs, 1909.

Patterson, E. Palmer. "Arthur E. O'Meara: Friend of the Indians." *Pacific Northwest Quarterly* (April 1967): 90-99.

Perdue, Theda. *Cherokee Women: Gender and Culture Change, 1700-1835*. Lincoln and London: University of Nebraska Press, 1998.

Petrone, Penny, ed. *First People, First Voices*. Toronto: University of Toronto Press, 1983.

Pierce, Bessie Louise. *A History of Chicago.* 3 vols. New York: Alfred A. Knopf, 1957.

Pletcher, David M. "Utopian Reformer: Albert Kimsey Owen." In *Rails, Mines, and Progress: Seven American Promoters in Mexico, 1867-1911,* 106-48. Ithaca, NY: Cornell University Press, 1958.

Porterfield, Amanda. *Mary Lyon and the Mount Holyoke Missionaries.* New York: Oxford University Press, 1997.

Prang, Margaret. *A Heart at Leisure from Itself: Caroline Macdonald of Japan.* Vancouver: UBC Press, 1995.

Pratt, Richard Henry. "The Advantages of Mingling Indians with Whites." In *Americanizing the American Indians,* ed. Francis Paul Prucha, 260-71. Lincoln: University of Nebraska Press, 1978.

Prebble, John. *Culloden.* London: Penguin, 1961.

–. *Mutiny: Highland Regiments in Revolt, 1743-1804.* 1975. Reprint, London: Pimlico, 2001.

Priest, Loring Benson. *Uncle Sam's Stepchildren: The Reformation of United States Indian Policy, 1865-1887.* New York: Octagon Books, 1969.

Prins, Harald E.L. *The Mi'kmaq: Resistance, Accommodation, and Cultural Survival.* Fort Worth: Harcourt Brace, 1996.

Prucha, F.P., ed. *Americanizing the American Indians.* Cambridge, MA: Harvard University Press, 1973.

Pullen-Burry, B. *From Halifax to Vancouver.* Toronto: Bell and Cockburn, 1912.

Quaife, Milo, ed. *The John Askin Papers.* Detroit: Detroit Historical Society, 1931.

Ralston, Helen. "Religion, Public Policy, and the Education of Micmac Indians of Nova Scotia, 1605-1872." *Canadian Review of Sociology and Anthropology* 18 (1981): 470-98.

Rand, Silas T. *A Short Statement of Facts Relating to the History, Manners, Customs, Language, and Literature of the Micmac Tribe of Indians, in Nova-Scotia and P.E. Island.* Halifax: James Bowes and Son, 1850.

–. *A Short Account of the Lord's Work among the Micmac Indians with Some Reasons for His Seceding from the Baptist Denomination.* Halifax: William MacNab, 1878.

–. *The Micmac Mission.* Hantsport, NS: n.s., 1882.

–. *Legends of the Micmacs.* Ed. Helen L. Webster. New York: Longmans, Green, 1894.

Rao, Aparna, ed. *The Other Nomads: Peripatetic Minorities in Cross-Cultural Perspective.* Kohn: Bohlau, 1987.

Rawlyk, G.A. "Canada's Immigration Policy, 1945-1962." *The Dalhousie Review* 42 (1962): 287-300.

Ray, Arthur J. *I Have Lived Here since the World Began: An Illustrated History of Canada's Native People.* Toronto: Key Porter Books, 1996.

Rea, J.E. *Bishop Alexander Macdonell and the Politics of Upper Canada.* Ottawa: Ontario Historical Society, Research Paper 4, 1974.

–. "Macdonell, Alexander." In *Dictionary of Canadian Biography.* Vol. 7, *1836-1850,* 544-51. Toronto: University of Toronto Press, 1988.

Redmond, Theresa. "'We Cannot Work Without Food': Nova Scotia Indian Policy and Mi'kmaq Agriculture, 1783-1867." In *Earth, Water, Air and Fire: Studies in Canadian Ethnohistory,* ed. David T. McNab, 115-25. Waterloo: Wilfrid Laurier University Press, 1998.

Richardson, John. *Arctic Searching Expedition.* 1851. Reprint, London: Longman, Brown, Green, and Longman, 1923.

Richeson, David R. "Richardson, James." In *Dictionary of Canadian Biography.* Vol. 11, *1881-1890,* 731-34. Toronto: University of Toronto Press, 1982.

Ring, Dan, ed. *Qu'Appelle: Tale of Two Valleys.* Saskatoon: Mendel Art Gallery, 2002.

Robert, Dana L. *American Women in Mission: A Social History of Their Thought and Practice.* Macon, GA: Mercer University Press, 1996.

Rogers, Edward S. "The Algonquian Farmers of Southern Ontario, 1830-1945." In *Aboriginal Ontario: Historical Perspectives on the First Nations,* ed. Edward S. Rogers and Donald B. Smith, 122-66. Toronto: Dundurn Press, 1994.

–, and Donald B. Smith, eds. *Aboriginal Ontario: Historical Perspectives on the First Nations.* Toronto: Dundurn Press, 1994.

Rohner, Ronald, ed. *The Ethnography of Franz Boas*. Chicago: University of Chicago Press, 1969.

Rowe, Sophie. "Anderson record, from 1699 to 1896," including "Reminiscences of Capt. Thomas Gummersall Anderson." *Ontario History* 6 (1905): 109-35.

Royal Commission on Aboriginal Peoples. *Final Report,* 5 vols. Minister of Supply and Services Canada, 1996.

–. *People to People, Nation to Nation: Highlights from the Report of the Royal Commission on Aboriginal Peoples*. Minister of Supply and Services Canada, 1996.

Rushton, J. Philippe. *Race, Evolution and Behavior.* New Brunswick, NJ: Transaction, 1995.

–. *Race, Evolution, and Behavior: A Life History Perspective*. Port Huron: Charles Darwin Research Institute, 2000.

Rutherdale, Myra. *Women and the White Man's God: Gender and Race in the Canadian Mission Field*. Vancouver: UBC Press, 2002.

Sample, Katherine Ann. "Changes in Agriculture on the Six Nations Reserve." MA thesis, McMaster University, 1968.

Sanderson, Stephen K. *Macrosociology: An Introduction to Human Societies*. New York: Harper and Row, 1988.

Sapolsky, Steven. "The Making of Honore Jaxon." In *Haymarket Scrapbook,* ed. Dave Roediger and Franklin Rosemont, 103-5. Chicago: Charles H. Kerr Publishing Company, 1986.

Saunders, Robert E. "Robinson, John Beverley." In *Dictionary of Canadian Biography.* Vol. 9, *1861-1870,* 668-79. Toronto: University of Toronto Press, 1976.

Schmalz, Peter. *The Ojibwa of Southern Ontario*. Toronto: University of Toronto Press, 1991.

Schneirov, Richard, and Thomas J. Suhrbur. *Union Brotherhood, Union Town: The History of the Carpenters' Union of Chicago, 1863-1987*. Carbondale and Edwardsville: Southern Illinois University Press, 1988.

Schouls, Tim, John Olthuis, and Diane Engelstad. "The Basic Dilemma: Sovereignty or Assimilation." In *Nation to Nation: Aboriginal Sovereignty and the Future of Canada,* ed. Diane Engelstad and John Bird, 12-27. Concord: House of Anansi Press, 1992.

Scollie, F. Brent. "Marks, George Thomas." In *Dictionary of Canadian Biography.* Vol. 13, *1901-1910,* 682-83. Toronto: University of Toronto Press, 1994.

–. "Burk, Daniel Francis." In *Dictionary of Canadian Biography.* Vol. 14, *1911-1920,* 155-56. Toronto: University of Toronto Press, 2001.

–. "Conmee, James." In *Dictionary of Canadian Biography.* Vol. 14, *1911-1920,* 229-31. Toronto: University of Toronto Press, 2001.

Scott, Duncan Campbell. *The Poems of Duncan Campbell Scott*. Toronto: McClelland and Stewart, 1926.

Scott, Walter. *Redgauntlet*. Melrose edition. London: Caxton, n.d.

–. *Rob Roy*. Melrose edition. London: Caxton, n.d.

Senor, Elinor Kyte. "Macdonell, Sir James." In *Dictionary of Canadian Biography.* Vol. 8, *1851-1860,* 538-39. Toronto: University of Toronto Press, 1985.

Shaw, Edward Charles. "Kennedy, William." In *Dictionary of Canadian Biography.* Vol. 11, *1881-1890,* 470-71. Toronto: University of Toronto Press, 1982.

Sheppard, George. "Plummer, William Henry." In *Dictionary of Canadian Biography.* Vol. 14, *1911-1920,* 842-43. Toronto: University of Toronto Press, 2001.

Simmins, Geoffrey, and Michael Parke-Taylor. *Edmund Morris "Kyaiyii," 1871-1913*. Regina: Norman Mackenzie Art Gallery, 1984.

Sioui, Georges E. *For an Amerindian Autohistory: An Essay on the Foundations of a Social Ethic*. Montreal: McGill-Queen's University Press, 1992.

Slonim, Leon. "Notes on Duncan Campbell Scott's 'Lines in Memory of Edmund Morris.'" http://www.uwo.ca/english/canadianpoetry/cpjrn/vol02/slonim.htm.

Smith, Adam. *An Inquiry into the Nature and Causes of the Wealth of Nations*. 1776. Reprint, ed. Kathryn Sutherland. Oxford: Oxford University Press, 1998.

Smith, Donald B. "Nahnebahwequay." In *Dictionary of Canadian Biography.* Vol. 9, *1861-1870,* 590-91. Toronto: University of Toronto Press, 1976.

−. "William Henry Jackson: Riel's Secretary." *The Beaver,* outfit 311, 4 (Spring 1981): 10-19. Footnoted copy in *Pelletier-Lathlin Memorial Lecture Series, Brandon University, 1979-1980,* ed. A.S. Lussier, 47-81. Brandon: Department of Native Studies, 1980.

−. "Honoré Joseph Jaxon: A Man Who Lived for Others." *Saskatchewan History* 34, 3 (Autumn 1981): 81-101.

−. "Rip Van Jaxon: The Return of Riel's Secretary in 1884-1885 to the Canadian West, 1907-1909." In *1885 and After: Native Society in Transition,* ed. F. Laurie Barron and James B. Waldram, 211-23. Regina: Canadian Plains Research Center, 1986.

−. *Sacred Feathers: The Reverend Peter Jones (Kahkewaquonaby) and the Mississauga Indians.* Toronto: University of Toronto Press, 1987.

−. "Nahnebahwequay (1824-1865): 'Upright Woman.'" In *Canadian Methodist Historical Society Papers.* Vol. 13, 74-105. Toronto: Canadian Methodist Historical Society, 2001.

Smith, Keith. "Surveillance, Measurement, Judgment, and Reform: Indian Reserves in the British Columbia Interior and the Panoptic Mechanism." MA thesis, University of Victoria, 1996.

Smith, Nicholas N. "The Economics of the Wabanaki Basket Industry." In *Actes du Vingtième Congrès des Algonquianistes,* ed. William Cowan, 306-16. Ottawa: Carleton University, 1989.

Smith, Sherry L. *Reimagining Indians: Native Americans through Anglo Eyes, 1880-1940.* New York: Oxford University Press, 2000.

Sprague, Roderick. "A Bibliography of James Teit." *Northwest Anthropological Research Notes* 25, 9 (1991): 103-15.

Stacey, C.P., ed. *Records of the Nile Voyageurs, 1884-1889.* Toronto: The Champlain Society, 1959.

Stanley, George F.G. *The Birth of Western Canada.* Toronto: University of Toronto Press, 1961.

−. *Louis Riel.* Toronto: Ryerson, 1963.

Stanton, William. *The Great United States Exploring Expedition of 1838-1842.* Berkeley: University of California Press, 1975.

Starr, Emmet. *History of the Cherokee Indians.* 1921. Reprint, New York: Kraus, 1969.

Statement Respecting the Earl of Selkirk's Settlement upon the Red River, in North America; Its Destruction in 1815 and 1816; and the Massacre of Governor Semple and His Party with Observations. London: John Murray, 1817. Toronto: Coles, 1970, 1974.

Stevenson, Winona. "The Journals and Voices of a Church of England Native Catechist: Askenootow (Charles Pratt), 1851-1884." In *Reading Beyond Words: Contexts for Native History,* ed. Jennifer S. Brown and Elizabeth Vibert, 304-29. Peterborough, ON: Broadview Press, 1996.

Stocking, George W. Jr., ed. *"Volksgeist" as Method and Ethic: Essays on Boasian Ethnography and the German Anthropological Tradition.* Madison: University of Wisconsin Press, 1996.

Stoler, Ann Laura. "Sexual Affronts and Racial Frontiers: European Identities and the Cultural Politics of Exclusion in Colonial Southeast Asia." In *Tensions of Empire: Colonial Cultures in a Bourgeois World,* ed. Frederick Cooper and Ann Laura Stoler, 198-237. Berkeley and Los Angeles: University of California Press, 1997.

−. "Cultivating Bourgeois Bodies and Racial Selves." In *Cultures of Empire: A Reader,* ed. Catherine Hall, 87-119. New York: Routledge, 2000.

Strong-Boag, Veronica, and Carole Gerson. *Paddling Her Own Canoe: The Times and Texts of E. Pauline Johnson (Tekahionwake).* Toronto: University of Toronto Press, 2000.

Sturm, Circe. "Blood Politics, Racial Classification, and Cherokee National Identity: The Trials and Tribulations of the Cherokee Freedmen." *American Indian Quarterly* 22, 1-2 (Winter/Spring 1998): 230-58.

Surtees, Robert J. "The Development of an Indian Reserve Policy in Canada." In *Historical Essays on Upper Canada,* ed. J.K. Johnson, 262-77. Toronto: McClelland and Stewart, 1975.

−. "Land Cessions, 1763-1800." In *Aboriginal Ontario: Historical Perspectives on the First Nations,* ed. Edward S. Rogers and Donald B. Smith, 92-121. Toronto: Dundurn Press, 1994.

Swainson, Donald. "Macdonell, Allan." In *Dictionary of Canadian Biography*. Vol. 11, *1881-1890*, 552-53. Toronto: University of Toronto Press, 1982.

–, ed. *Oliver Mowat's Ontario*. Toronto: Macmillan, 1970.

Szasz, Margaret. *Between Indian and White Worlds: The Cultural Broker*. Norman: University of Oklahoma Press, 1994.

Teit, James. *The Thompson Indians of British Columbia*. Memoirs of the American Museum of Natural History. Vol. 1, part 4. New York: American Museum of Natural History, 1900.

–. *The Lillooet Indians*. Memoirs of the American Museum of Natural History. Vol. 2, part 5. New York: American Museum of Natural History, 1906.

–. *The Shuswap*. Memoirs of the American Museum of Natural History. Vol. 2, part 7. New York: American Museum of Natural History, 1909.

Telford, Rhonda. "The Sound of the Rustling of the Gold Is Under My Feet Where I Stand, We Have a Rich Country: A History of Aboriginal Mineral Resources in Ontario." PhD dissertation, University of Toronto, 1995.

–. "The Nefarious and Far-Ranging Interests of Indian Agent and Surveyor John William Keating, 1837 to 1869." *Papers of the Twenty-Eighth Algonquian Conference*, ed. David Pentland, 372-402. Winnipeg: University of Manitoba, 1997.

Tennant, Paul. *Aboriginal Peoples and Politics: The Indian Land Question in British Columbia, 1849-1989*. Vancouver, UBC Press, 1990.

Thom, Brian. "Harlan I. Smith's Jesup Fieldwork on the Northwest Coast." In *Gateways: Exploring the Legacy of the Jesup North Pacific Expedition, 1897-1902*, ed. Igor Krupnik and William W. Fitzhugh, 139-80. Washington: Smithsonian Institution, 2001.

Thomas, Keith. *Religion and the Decline of Magic: Studies in Popular Beliefs in Sixteenth and Seventeenth-Century England*. Toronto: Penguin Books, 1991.

Thomas, Lewis H. "The Political and Private Life of F.W.G. Haultain." *Saskatchewan History* 23 (1970): 50-58.

Titley, Brian E. *A Narrow Vision: Duncan Campbell Scott and the Administration of Indian Affairs in Canada*. Vancouver: UBC Press, 1986.

Tucker, Gilbert N. "Montreal in 1849, and the Annexation Movement." In *The Canadian Commercial Revolution, 1845-1851*, 129-47. Toronto: McClelland and Stewart, 1964.

Tuhiwai Smith, Linda. *Decolonizing Methodologies: Research and Indigenous Peoples*. London: Zed Books, 1999.

Tulchinsky, Gerald. "Moffatt, George." In *Dictionary of Canadian Biography*. Vol. 9, *1861-1870*, 553-56. Toronto: University of Toronto Press, 1976.

Upton, L.F.S. "Indians and Islanders: The Micmacs in Colonial Prince Edward Island." *Acadiensis* 6, 1 (Autumn 1976): 26-29.

–. *Micmacs and Colonists: Indian-White Relations in the Maritimes, 1713-1867*. Vancouver: UBC Press, 1979.

Valverde, Mariana. *The Age of Light, Soap and Water: Moral Reform in English Canada, 1885-1925*. Toronto: McClelland and Stewart, 1991.

Van Dusen, Conrad (Enemikeese). *The Indian Chief: An Account of the Labours, Losses, Sufferings, and Oppression of Ke-zig-ko-e-ne-ne (David Sawyer), a Chief of the Ojibbeway Indians in Canada West*. London: William Nichols, 1867; reprint, Toronto: Canadiana House, 1969.

Van Kirk, Sylvia. "'What If Mama Is an Indian?': The Cultural Ambivalence of the Alexander Ross Family." In *The Developing West: Essays on Canadian History in Honour of Lewis H. Thomas*, ed. John E. Foster, 123-36. Edmonton: University of Alberta Press, 1983.

Wallace, Anthony F.C. *The Long, Bitter Trail: Andrew Jackson and the Indians*. New York: Hill and Wang, 1993.

Wallace, W. Stewart, ed. *Documents Relating to the North West Company*. Toronto: The Champlain Society, 1934.

Weaver, Sally M. "Six Nations of the Grand River, Ontario." In *Handbook of North American Indians*. Vol. 15, *Northeast*, ed. Bruce G. Trigger, 525-36. Washington: Smithsonian, 1978.

–. "The Iroquois: The Consolidation of the Grand River Reserve in the Mid-Nineteenth Century, 1847-1875." In *Aboriginal Ontario: Historical Perspectives on the First Nations*, ed. Edward S. Rogers and Donald B. Smith, 182-212. Toronto: Dundurn Press for the Government of Ontario, 1994.

–. "The Iroquois: The Grand River Reserve in the Late Nineteenth and Early Twentieth Centuries, 1875-1945." In *Aboriginal Ontario: Historical Perspectives on the First Nations,* ed. Edward S. Rogers and Donald B. Smith, 213-57. Toronto: Dundurn Press for the Government of Ontario, 1994.

Wellcome, Henry S. *The Story of Metlakahtla.* London: Saxon, 1887.

White, Richard. *The Middle Ground: Indians, Empires and Republics in the Great Lakes Region, 1650-1815.* Cambridge: Cambridge University Press, 1991.

Whitehead, Margaret. "Women Were Made for Such Things: Women Missionaries in British Columbia, 1850s-1940s." *Atlantis* 14, 1 (Autumn 1988): 141-50.

–. "'Let the Women Keep Silence': Women Missionary Preaching in British Columbia, 1860s-1940s." In *Changing Roles of Women within the Christian Church in Canada,* ed. Elizabeth Gillan Muir and Marilyn Färdig Whiteley, 117-35. Toronto: University of Toronto Press, 1995.

Whitehead, Ruth Holmes. *Micmac Quillwork: Micmac Indian Techniques of Porcupine Quill Decoration, 1600-1950.* Halifax: Nova Scotia Museum, 1982.

Whitfield, Carol, and Robert Lochiel Fraser. "MacDonell, John (Greenfield)." In *Dictionary of Canadian Biography.* Vol. 5, *1801-1820,* 521-23. Toronto: University of Toronto Press, 1983.

Wickwire, Wendy. "'We Shall Drink from the Stream and So Shall You': James A. Teit and Native Resistance in British Columbia, 1908-22." *Canadian Historical Review* 79, 2 (1998): 199-236.

–. "Beyond Boas? Re-assessing the Contribution of 'Informant' and 'Research Assistant' James A. Teit." In *Constructing Cultures Then and Now: The Jesup North Pacific Expedition,* ed. Laurel Kendall and Igor Krupnik, 123-33. Seattle: University of Washington Press, 2003.

Williams, Glyndwr, ed. *Hudson's Bay Miscellany, 1670-1870.* Winnipeg: Hudson's Bay Record Society, 1975.

Wilson, E.F. *Manual of the Ojebway Language.* Toronto: The Venerable Society for Promoting Christian Knowledge, 1874.

Withrow, W.H. *The Native Races of North America.* Toronto: Methodist Mission Rooms, 1895.

Wolf, Eric R. *Europe and the People without History.* Berkeley and Los Angeles: University of California Press, 1982.

Wolfe, Alexander. *Earth Elder Stories: The Pinayzitt Path.* Saskatoon: Fifth House, 1988.

Woodward, Sir Llewellyn. *The Age of Reform, 1815-1870.* London: Oxford University Press, 1962.

Wright, Richard Thomas. *Overlanders: The Epic Cross-Canada Treks for Gold, 1858-1862.* 1985. Reprint, Williams Lake: Winter Quarters Press, 2000.

Wright, Ronald. *Stolen Continents: The 'New World' through Indian Eyes.* Toronto: Penguin, 1993.

Wylie, William N.T. "MacDonell, Archibald." In *Dictionary of Canadian Biography.* Vol. 7, *1836-1850,* 439-40. Toronto: University of Toronto Press, 1988.

Yellow Bird, Michael. "What We Want to Be Called: Indigenous Peoples' Perspectives on Racial and Ethnic Identity Labels." *American Indian Quarterly* 23, 2 (Spring 1999): 1-21.

Yohn, Susan M. *A Contest of Faiths: Missionary Women and Pluralism in the American Southwest.* Ithaca, NY: Cornell University Press, 1995.

Zaslow, Morris. "Edward Barnes Borron, 1820-1915: Northern Pioneer and Public Servant Extraordinaire." In *Aspects of Nineteenth Century Ontario: Essays Presented to James J. Talman,* ed. F.H. Armstrong et al., 297-311. Toronto: University of Toronto Press, 1974.

–. *Reading the Rocks: The Story of the Geological Survey of Canada, 1842-1972.* Toronto: Macmillan, 1975.

Zeman, Brenda. *To Run with Longboat: Twelve Stories of Indian Athletes in Canada.* Edmonton: GMS2 Ventures, 1988.

Contributors

Thomas S. Abler teaches in the Department of Anthropology at the University of Waterloo. The bulk of his research has dealt with ethnohistorical questions involving the First Nations of eastern North America. He is currently writing the biography of Cornplanter, a Seneca chief prominent during and after the American Revolution.

Jean Barman is Professor Emeritus in the Department of Educational Studies at the University of British Columbia. As well as writing about British Columbia history, she is co-editor, with Yvonne Hébert and Don McCaskill, of *Indian Education in Canada,* and, with Marie Battiste, of *First Nations Education in Canada: The Circle Unfolds.*

Michael D. Blackstock (Ama Goodim Gyet) is an independent scholar who is a member of the Gitxsan Nation in British Columbia. He is a professional forester and mediator with a Master of Arts degree in First Nations Studies. His publications focus on research topics such as First Nations history and art, as well as the First Nations perspective on fresh water; the underlying theme in his discourse is exploring ways to inform the reconciliation process.

Sarah A. Carter is from Saskatoon, Saskatchewan. She obtained her PhD from the University of Manitoba and presently teaches history at the University of Calgary. Her books include *Lost Harvests: Prairie Indian Reserve Farmers and Government Policy; Capturing Women: The Manipulation of Cultural Imagery in Canada's Prairie West;* and *Aboriginal People and Colonizers of Western Canada to 1900.*

Janet Chute, an anthropologist and historian, teaches at Mount Saint Vincent University and also holds a research associateship with the School for Resource and Environmental Studies at Dalhousie University, Halifax. She has worked extensively with Native groups on issues pertaining to Aboriginal lands and resources. Her book, *The Legacy of Shingwaukonse: A Century of Native Leadership,* tells of a major Native campaign to gain resource revenues from mining and logging north of Lakes Huron and Superior.

Celia Haig-Brown is a Professor in the Faculty of Education at York University in Toronto. Originally from British Columbia, she is the author of *Resistance and Renewal: Surviving the Indian Residential School* and *Taking Control: Power and Contradiction in First Nations Adult Education*. Her research focuses on Aboriginal education and the complexities of partnerships between Aboriginal communities and universities.

Mary Haig-Brown is an independent researcher who lives in Saanich, British Columbia. A retired teacher of, among other things, Canadian history, she is currently involved in a variety of environmental initiatives, most of which have an educational component. She has a BA from the University of British Columbia and an MA from the University of Victoria and is married with four children and eight grandchildren.

Jan Hare is an Anishinaabe of the M'Chigeeng First Nation community. Following two years as Assistant Professor in the First Nations Studies Program at the University of British Columbia, she has joined the Department of Languages and Literacy, where she continues to teach about Aboriginal issues in Canada.

Alan Knight is the archivist and priest in the Anglican diocese of Algoma. He started a master's thesis on Allan Macdonell in 1982 for York University before changing his career goals and going into the ministry.

David A. Nock has taught at Lakehead University, Thunder Bay, Ontario, since 1976, where he is a Professor in the Department of Sociology. Nock has written two books and co-edited a third. He has also published more than 40 articles in journals, books, and conference proceedings. Most relevant to this project is his 1988 title, *A Victorian Missionary and Canadian Indian Policy*. A further paper on E.F. Wilson appears in *Star Wars in Canadian Sociology*.

Donald Smith teaches Canadian history at the University of Calgary. His major research interest is in nineteenth- and twentieth-century Native history. He has published three biographies and is one of the three co-authors (with Douglas Francis and Richard Jones) of the Canadian history texts, *Origins* and *Destinies*.

Wendy Wickwire teaches in the Department of History at the University of Victoria. She has published two books with Okanagan elder Harry Robinson (*Write It On Your Heart: The Epic World of an Okanagan Storyteller* and *Native Power: In the Spirit of an Okanagan Storyteller*) and is currently completing a book on James Teit.

Index